THE EPIC OF MAN

THE EPIC

PRENTICE-HALL, INC.   *Englewood Cliffs, New Jersey*

OF MAN

a collection of readings edited by
L. S. STAVRIANOS

THE EPIC OF MAN
A Collection of Readings

EDITED BY L. S. STAVRIANOS

13-283325-5
Library of Congress Catalog Card Number: 77-159452
Printed in the United States of America

Current printing (last digit):

10 9 8 7 6 5 4 3 2 1

PRENTICE-HALL INTERNATIONAL, INC., *London*
PRENTICE-HALL OF AUSTRALIA PTY., LTD., *Sydney*
PRENTICE-HALL OF CANADA LTD., *Toronto*
PRENTICE-HALL OF INDIA PRIVATE LIMITED, *New Delhi*
PRENTICE-HALL OF JAPAN, INC., *Tokyo*

Preface

The distinctive feature of this volume of readings is that it is globally oriented rather than West oriented. It reflects the viewpoint of an observer perched on the moon, surveying our planet as a whole, rather than one who is ensconced in London or Paris, or, for that matter, in Peking or Delhi. The guiding principle has been that no Western movement or institution be treated unless non-Western movements and institutions of similar magnitude or world significance also be treated.

In the ancient, classical and medieval periods, for example, this rationale explains the equal treatment accorded to all the Eurasian civilizations, rather than the usual concentration on Greece and Rome and the medieval West. For the same reason, attention in the early modern period is focussed not only on the European discoveries, but also on the conditions and institutions of the people being "discovered." Likewise there is consideration of the commonly neglected, yet crucial question of why it was the Westerners who took the lead in the fateful overseas expansion rather than some other Eurasians, such as the Chinese who had enjoyed technological superiority during most of the Middle Ages. For the nineteenth century there are readings not only on Western imperialism but also on the manifold effects of that imperialism on the colonial territories. And although the contemporary period's crises, wars, and European alliances cannot be ignored, emphasis is placed on finding out why more than fifty countries have won their independence in the past two decades, and why this is an era of Western decline and triumph.

The criterion for the selection of readings in this book is their effectiveness in illuminating the subject under consideration. Short readings are sometimes more forceful than long ones, and secondary sources often provide more insight than primary ones. Accordingly, the following selections are of varied lengths and from diverse sources. The connective tissue of narrative introductions is designed to provide an integrated account of major trends and to relate the selections to those trends.

L. S. STAVRIANOS

OTHER BOOKS BY L. S. STAVRIANOS:

Contents

Part
IV
MEDIEVAL CIVILIZATIONS OF EURASIA,
500–1500

Part
VIII
WORLD OF WESTERN DECLINE AND TRIUMPH,
1914–

Chapter Forty-two

Decline and triumph of the West 417

PART

I

MAN BEFORE
CIVILIZATION

Chapter One

Introduction:
nature of
world history

WORLD HISTORY: ORIGINS AND NATURE   1

Despite its obvious relevance for our present age, world history remains con-
spicuous by its absence, both in writing and in teaching. In the following selection, a
distinguished British scholar provides the historical background of this situation. He
presents a survey of the history *of world history and analyzes the nature and prospects*
*for this field of study.**

Of all the approaches to history none has been less explored than that which
we usually call world-history or universal or 'oecumenical' history. And yet there
is probably no type of history which is closer to our present preoccupations or
more nearly attuned to the world in which we live. The reasons why the history
most needed today is universal history lie all around us. They are a reflection of
the unification of the world by science and technology and by the revolutionary
advance of mass communications, a consequence of the familiar fact that we can
no longer isolate ourselves from events in any quarter of the globe. Taiwan and
Indo-China today are as near, and what happens there as relevant for us, as
Greece or Portugal a century ago. Furthermore, the processes of industrial society,
which originated in western Europe and North America, are now worldwide, their
impact universal. Because the peoples of the Soviet Union, of China and India, and
the other nations in Asia and Africa and Latin America, are playing an integral
part in the political development of our world, a history which is limited to a more
or less fragmentary account of the evolution of western civilization is inevitably

* Reprinted from Geoffrey Barraclough, "Universal History," in *Approaches to History: A
Symposium,* ed. H. P. R. Finberg (London: Routledge & Kegan Paul Ltd.; Toronto: University of Toronto Press, 1962), pp. 83–87, 102–9.

less than adequate for present needs. The civilizations of China and India and Islam—in interplay, of course, with impulses coming from Europe—are just as much a part of the historical background of our times as is the civilization of the west. The emergence of the greater part of mankind from political subjection to political independence and political influence necessitates a shift in historical perspective. In short, the very forces which have transformed our view of the present compel us to widen our view of the past. It is this new situation which makes the need for universal history—by which we mean a history that looks beyond Europe and the west to humanity in all lands and ages—a matter of immediate practical urgency.

Nevertheless it would be a mistake to suppose that preoccupation with universal history is simply a consequence of the vast political changes which the world has undergone since 1939. In returning to world-history today we are returning to an older tradition which reaches back beyond the nineteenth century to the origins of modern critical historical study and which held its own until the close of the eighteenth century. For the men of the Enlightenment the idea of world-history was particularly congenial. It fitted in with their notion of progress, their view of mankind advancing steadily from primitive barbarism to reason and virtue and civilization. It fitted in also with their secular and rationalist spirit. So long as the authority of the Bible remained unchallenged, and all known historical events had to be fitted into a rigid biblical context, there could be no universal history as we know it; and since the Reformation affirmed rather than weakened the authority of the Bible, the concept of world-history was slow to take shape. Earlier historical interpretation, ever since the time of St. Augustine and Orosius, had followed the pattern of Christian revelation—creation, crucifixion, last judgment—or had divided the past into periods corresponding to the four world-empires presaged in the book of Daniel: the Assyrian, the Persian, the Greek, the Roman. Both schemes gave rise to insoluble difficulties, particularly when the attempt was made to relate them to peoples whose history fell outside the realm of Judaeo-Christian experience. The last great historical work written in the spirit of Christian eschatology was Bossuet's *Discours sur l'histoire universelle* (1681). But Bossuet's position was incompatible with the new spirit of scientific enquiry stirring in the late seventeenth century; and from around 1655 we can perceive how the irreconcilability of biblical tradition with the facts brought to light by the great discoveries was preparing the ground for a new, secular view of world-history. The French Calvinist Isaac de la Peyrère, who was unable to reconcile what he knew of Chinese history with the story of Adam and Eve, and the Dutch historian George Hornius, paved the way for Voltaire, whose *Essai sur les Moeurs et l'Espirit des Nations* (1752) is commonly regarded as "the first real world-history," and for the vast co-operative universal history— the first of its kind—which was published in England in thirty-eight volumes from 1736 onwards. Voltaire expressly accused his predecessor, Bossuet, of doing less than justice to the Arabs and the Babylonians and the Persians, and of ignoring the Chinese and Indians altogether; his history, in short, was unacceptable because his point of view was less than oecumenical.

The first great historical achievement of the eighteenth century was to bring the extra-European world into the field of enquiry and thus to make universal history possible. Its second achievement, associated from about 1760 with the rising Göttingen school led by J. C. Gatterer and A. L. Schlözer, was to ventilate and debate the problems of method and practice involved in the writing of world-history. But this early interest in universal history, so characteristic of the Age of Reason, began to falter at the time of the French Revolution, and from the close of the eighteenth century until the First World War—in many respects, indeed, until the Second World War—it was in eclipse. The causes were many. One was the sense, as historical knowledge deepened and widened, of the insufficiency of the earlier attempts to view the history of the world as a whole. The eighteenth-century approach to world-history was more successful in conception than in execution. It expressed a vision of the general progress of society and culture, instead of a mere calendar of battles and political events; but too often it resulted in a series of facile generalizations or patterns of a philosophical nature imposed on history from outside without criticism or detailed study of the records. And even those, such as Herder and Hegel, who sought to do justice to the oriental peoples, wrote without an adequate foundation of concrete historical knowledge. It was therefore not surprising, as a more scientific attitude to history developed, that the superficiality of eighteenth-century historical writing was more deeply felt, and also that the very feasibility of universal history was called into question. In the first place, it was argued, the foundation of critical knowledge for anything so ambitious was totally insufficient; as Schlözer pointed out, the whole history of the ancient world would require re-writing if the Egyptian and Persian sources ever became as readily available as those of Greece and Rome. In the second place, it seemed that the writing of universal history made demands on human knowledge greater than the human intellect could ever hope to encompass; the field it covered was so immense that inevitably the knowledge which any single individual could bring to bear was too limited to carry the burden. Cooperative histories, on the other hand, amounted to little more than compendia or encyclopaedias; their result was not world-history, which treated mankind as a unity, but an aggregate of national histories with little, if any, cohesion or connection.

These were among the technical reasons why, from the beginning of the nineteenth century, world-history passed into the shadows. But fundamentally more important was a change in the climate of ideas. From the time of the French Revolution cosmopolitan gave way to national thinking; the nation-state asserted its place as the focus of human endeavour, the natural centre of all activity, and increasingly it was doubted whether there was any wider unity than the sovereign nation. But if the nation was the supreme expression of human striving, it followed that national history was the only type of history that ultimately mattered. There were, it is true, a few dissenting voices, such as that of the Swiss historian Jakob Burckhardt; but by the second half of the nineteenth century this was the prevailing view, borne out, it seemed, by the progress of national unification in Germany and Italy. Its victory was aided by the adaptation to historical study of vulgarized Darwinian concepts and by biological analogies, particularly the concepts of the struggle for existence and the survival of the fittest. If, in fact, there were such a thing as universal history in a world in which the ultimate realities were the nation-states, then its subject-matter could only be their rivalries and conflicts, the clash of empires, the attempts of particular powers to establish a position of hegemony and bring the world (or as much of the world as they could encompass) under their rule and influence. But in any case the nation remained the focal point of historical study, for it was here, in the heart of the people and in the minds of its leaders, that the driving forces originated.

It needed the catastrophe of two world wars to shake the foundations of this historical attitude, and even today it is still so engrained that it frequently determines the unconscious assumptions of historians who would not consciously subscribe to such a view. We do not need to consider the problematical character, in the world today, of the concept of sovereignty, which looms so large yet means so little, to realize that the era of the national state, as understood in the nineteenth century, was circumscribed in time and is now in the throes of a process of attrition. Its predominance was a historically conditioned phenomenon which lasted approximately a hundred and fifty years. By every test of national theory—language, racial unity, and the like—the political groups which count in the world of the second half of the twentieth century are supra-national in dimension, and the process of economic and technological change has cast serious doubt on the viability of the national state under modern conditions. If it is to keep pace with these developments history must break through the national framework in which the nineteenth century imprisoned it. . . .

.   .   .

What differences may we expect, in practice, from history conceived and written from a universal point of view? What does the shift in perspective from a parochial or national to a global perspective imply? The question is best answered by practical examples; and it will suffice if we take one from the thirteenth, one from the sixteenth, and one from the nineteenth centuries.

For English historians the dominant feature of the early thirteenth century was the constitutional struggle under John and Henry III; for French historians it was the consolidation of French unity and the strengthening of the monarchy by Philip Augustus and Louis IX; for German historians, it was Frederick II's restoration of imperial fortunes, the conflict of empire and papacy, and the collapse of Germany's position in Europe after Frederick's death in 1250. If, however, we sidestep these national positions, each with its own peculiar emphasis, and try instead to pick out the events which were important from a global point of view, the result is totally different. The most arresting event of the period from the point of view of world-history was undoubtedly the great conquering movement of the Mongol people under Genghis Khan and his son Ogdai, who extended their dominion over China and vast tracts of Asia and swept west across the steppes of Russia into Hungary, Poland, and Silesia. Neither king John nor king Philip nor even the emperor Frederick II was a world-figure (though Frederick came nearer to that rank); Genghis Khan indubitably was. Hence the historian with a global vision will place the great Mongol ruler, whose achievements were far more momentous for mankind than anything which happened in England in his lifetime, at the centre of his picture; and he will redesign the rest to fit the altered perspective. Even European history, looked at from this point of view, will be seen in different proportions: that is to say, the familiar story of the rise of the western national monarchies will loom less large, and the emphasis will shift to Russia and the borderlands of eastern Europe, which felt the brunt of the Mongol incursions, while the historian of the church will be less preoccupied with the quarrels of empire and papacy and more concerned with papal efforts to cope with the situation confronting Christianity in the east.

When we pass to the sixteenth and early seventeenth centuries, the situation is different; but once again a global point of view—or an effort to put those things first which have a more than national or continental bearing—results in a far-reaching change of emphasis. For European historians the main threads in this period are dynastic conflicts—particularly the conflict of France and Spain in Italy, the Netherlands, and Germany—the rise of absolute monarchies, the Protestant revolt and the wars of religion, the Thirty Years' War, the struggle for mastery of the seas, and the beginnings of overseas expansion. From a global point of view much of this is of subordinate interest, if not irrelevant. Nevertheless, this time

Europe remains in the centre of the picture, because even in universal terms there is no doubt that the outstanding development of world-wide significance was the emergence of Europe from a peripheral to a central position. At the close of the fifteenth century Europe was only one of four Eurasian centres of civilization, and by no means the most prominent. By the end of the eighteenth century it had gained control of the ocean routes, organized an immensely profitable worldwide commerce, and conquered vast territories in the Americas and India and Siberia. Thus in the perspective of world-history the period stands out as a period of transition from the regional isolation of the pre-1492 era to the European global hegemony of the nineteenth century; and for this reason, not because of a narrowly 'Europacentric' view of the past, Europe as the main centre of innovation and decision remains prominent. But the aspects of European history which receive emphasis are inevitably different. In terms of their global significance, the battles that stand out will not be those, such as Pavia (1525), which loom so large in the common run of history books, but Mohacs (1526), Lepanto (1571), Itamarca (1640); and it is significant that two of the three were naval battles. The defeat of the Turks at Lepanto, in particular, marked the shift of the axis of European history away from the Mediterranean to the Atlantic seaboard in the west and thus a significant stage in the history of European expansion. This expansion, as the distinguishing feature of the period—in the medieval centuries Europe had been hemmed in by the expanding civilizations of the Near East—is from a universal point of view the central theme. The first question it raises—a question which has not hitherto been systematically studied, though it takes us deep into European history—is what the roots of expansion were, or why it started from Europe and not from one of the other Eurasian centres of civilization. The second question is the manner in which the nature and course of European expansion was affected by the Chinese, Moslem, American, and Eurasian civilizations with which it came into contact. Thirdly, it raises the question of the impact of overseas expansion on European life and culture; and finally it is important to see the fluctuations in Europe's attitude to the non-European world—the rise and decline of respect for the Ottoman Empire, India, and China, the different attitudes of Christian missionaries to the American peoples, and the like. These are some of the questions, largely neglected, which an attempt to review and reinterpret what we call the 'early modern period' from a global point of view brings into new prominence.

When we come to the nineteenth century, we reach a period when the predominance of Europe is as marked in the economic and technological as in the political field, and when the expansion of Europe had carried European ideas and values to every quarter of the globe. Never at any moment in history, it would seem, was there more ample justification for setting Europe at the centre of world affairs; never can we more confidently say that what went on in Europe, the rivalries and conflicts of the European powers, determined the course of events in Asia and Africa and the new world. But here again, if we look at the situation from a global rather than a European standpoint, the familiar dimensions change and new factors come into view. The traditional story, with its concentration on the rise of German and Italian nationalism, the European balance of power, the question of the Straits and of the Narrow Seas, is not wrong, but for a world-wide perspective it is inadequate. Down to 1914, it seemed as though the relations of the European powers would settle the future of the world, and that European expansion was simply carrying the principle of balance of power, on which the relations of the European nations were based, into the other continents. In reality, as the transformation of the war of 1914–18 from a European into a world war was soon to demonstrate, that was only half the story. When the tottering Ottoman Empire was admitted to the concert of European powers in 1856, and when, a generation later, the United States and Japan were recognized as 'great powers', in addition to the six nations which happened at the time to be the strongest in Europe, it was clear that world-leadership was no longer a European prerogative. Hence the detailed studies of European diplomacy and of the conflicts of the European powers to which historians have given so much attention need to be balanced by an analysis of the contacts of the expanding imperialisms of Great Britain and Russia and the United States, on the northwest frontier of India, in Persia, in China, and on the Pacific seaboard of the North American continent, in California and Oregon and Alaska. These contacts, and the conflicts which arose from them, marked the rise, in place of the European balance of power, of the world-wide international system under which we live; they are of fundamental importance because—unlike the international politics of Bismarckian Europe—they were the beginning of a new era in world-history. . . .

.   .   .

It should also be clear from the examples which have been given that there are no insuperable obstacles on a practical level to the study of world-history. It is no more difficult to teach and to learn world-history, at all levels from school to university, than it is to teach and learn European history; indeed, the basic method is exactly the same—that is to say, just as no one in a one-year survey of modern or medieval European history at the university would set out to cover the separate histories of England, France, Germany, Italy, Spain, Russia, the Balkans, and Scandinavia, so no one would attempt to deal, one by one, with all the world's civilizations. But it is no more impossible to convey a basic under-standing of the characteristics and experiences of the major civilizations of the world, and of world-wide movements such as the diffusion of the great religions, the invasions of the central Eurasian nomads, or the expansion of Europe, than it is for the historian of Europe to describe the development of the states which were important at any given period, and European movements such as the Reformation, the Industrial Revolution, or Nationalism. The amount of knowledge to be absorbed is no larger nor is it basically more diversified; it is simply chosen on a different principle. . . . Every present indication is that the central problems with which we shall have to cope in the next generation will not be European problems but the relationship betwen the west and the peoples of Asia and Africa.

.   .   .

In the world as constituted today, not to teach world-history is to court disaster. If history is falling into disrepute, if for many people it seems to be lost in unessentials instead of guiding us to the threshold of the world we know, the reason is not far to seek: what it needs is a larger vision, a breakthrough to new dimensions. It is this breakthrough to new dimensions that world-history offers—and a vision of historical reality which measures up to our experience and to the perspectives opening out before us in the second half of the twentieth century.

Chapter Two

Man the food gatherer

MEN ARE MORE ALIKE   2

*The fundamental basis of world history is the biological unity of mankind. Indeed the two are completely interactive and interdependent. Yet the emphasis customarily is placed on the differences among men rather than on their far more numerous and basic similarities. This common distortion is corrected here by an American historian who draws upon the resources of several disciplines to show that "Men are More Alike." ***

. . . *Homo sapiens* is a species! Within the species varieties occur. But as with the trees and forests the varieties ought not obscure the view. It is upon certain aspects of the common nature and common cultural development of the species that this essay is focused. . . .

The outward likenesses, often overlooked because they are commonplace, are easy to see. All men walk upright, and, unlike most other vertebrates, normally use stairs instead of branches. Nine tenths of the mature members of the species measure four-feet-ten to six-feet-two in height, a relatively small difference if all vertical dimensions are considered. Nearly all men as adults weigh from 90 to 220 pounds, a small range compared to the variations in animal life. All of them require daily, though they may not get them, from 2500 to 4000 calories and a certain variety of vitamins to be gained from meat, grains, green and leafy vegetables, and fruit. With few exceptions all of them have facility for manipulating their thumbs, and for conceptual thought and speech as no other animals do. More than any other living thing they can store up knowledge, establish traditions. They are not forced to start from scratch but can, though this is rare enough, begin with the accumulated ex-

* Reprinted from Boyd C. Shafer, "Men Are More Alike," *American Historical Review*, LVII, No. 3 (April 1952), 593–612, with permission.

9

perience and wisdom of the species. Unlike the dog and the ape, men may use (though they rarely do) the spoken word and books to avoid the mistakes of their ancestors and thus determine the direction of human evolution. Though the opposite seems most often true, man is, to a greater degree than any other form of life, teachable. He is at times, potentially at least, rational and the ranges of his comprehension and adaptability are wider. Men, it also seems, are singular in that they can modify what were once termed their "instincts," and may, without artificial conditioning, acquire neuroses. At the same time only they find escape in laughter and tears. . . .

Men are all vertebrates and mammals. They are all multicellular animals with the same kinds of nervous, blood, respiratory, and reproductive systems. The same approximate percentages of chemical elements make up their bodies. So long as there are males and females reproduction between all varieties is possible, even probable. Their females all carry their young nine months and usually produce only one offspring at a time. Maturation for all offspring is comparatively slow. Unlike all other animals the desire of their adults for sexual activity is continuous: the adult male is normally capable of reproducing at any time and the adult female of about fifteen to forty-five years of age twelve times a year. Probably none of them, Lysenko notwithstanding, can inherit acquired characteristics. All of them, regardless of race or nationality, have the same few O, A, B, and AB blood types. Though learned studies use terms like brachiocephalic and dolichocephalic their head shapes vary little, all being somewhat oblong. While their hair is round or oblong and straight or kinky, it is hair, and all usually have it in slightly varying intensities at the same points on their bodies. Their coloration runs from white to black but all gradations exist, while microscopic examination shows but slight differences in pigmentation and even these differences seem rapidly to be fading.

Where differences occur, little is known of what they signify. On the basis of fact no one can say whether color, hair, head shape, or blood type have any relationship to the quality of a man, to his character, philosophy, and intelligence, or to how he will react in any circumstance. Observable differences like these may be easily classified and the classifications statistically presented in impressive, encyclopedic volumes. That is all. These particular differences occur. Nothing more can be added, no more meaning can be attached to them. . . .

Since Darwin men's differences have been transformed into a sliding scale for moral evaluation, a scale which somehow indicates inferiority and superiority. During the latter half of the nineteenth century men calling themselves scientists, though their interpretation of "survival of the fittest" was certainly erroneous, first erected complex classifications of human characteristics with the clear purpose of showing how much fitter and therefore better were some groups of men than others. Their reasoning (read Houston Stewart Chamberlain or Madison Grant for the popular versions) went something like this: (1) men are naturally different as is proved by their observable physical and mental traits; (2) some are naturally fitter, hence superior; (3) some races and nations are naturally fittest and therefore superior; and (4) nature and evolution made men this way and hence some races and nations should be masters and others servants. With this structure of illogic, differences became the ideological basis of social action. And further to prove superiority, the significance of the obvious differences has been deepened and new distinctions are fanatically sought.

No intelligent man who knows anything of science and methods of scientific research need be told of the absurdity of this unreason. . . .

Who are the "fittest," the little, wiry men who formed the bulk of Rommel's

North African army, the giants who play American football and basketball, the pale, bespectacled, physical scientists in the laboratories, the emaciated saints of the Middle Ages who surely went to Heaven soonest, or that "cream" of contemporary Western nations, the steel-nerved navigators and pilots of the long-range bombing planes? If it be agreed that the last are today's fittest, does it follow that their respective races or nations are? Are races and nations fittest just because they can destroy other races and nations most efficiently? Does, finally, fitness indicate anything about superiority unless certain prejudices are accepted as absolute values? Does, indeed, survival indicate anything but luck? The survivors in the next war, as in those of the past, will very likely be those who survive—nothing more. . . .

Systematic theories of racial differences are of recent origin, dating back for the most part only to the eighteenth century when it was becoming more important to be superior and powerful than to go to Heaven. The theories (they are only that by the grace of inaccurate terminology) have varied widely in time and often with the race or nationality of the investigator. Moreover, racial characters, if they exist, seem to have changed quite unbelievably through the years. Once ("Nordic") England was called "merry" but that was not the England of Attlee and Cripps. Once a Venetian ambassador spoke of the "low morals and excellent cooking" of the English but that was in the sixteenth not the nineteenth century. In praising folly, Erasmus spoke of the martial reputation of the ("Mediterranean") Spaniards, a characteristic few would accuse them of possessing in our times. Once what we call the northern European ("Nordics?") were supposed to be "full of spirit" but unintelligent (Aristotle); the modern version is quite different. None of this proves that theories based upon race are completely untrue. It shows only that there is nothing scientific or God-given about them and that they are for the most part merely *a priori* guesses of men about other men.

The fallacies based upon racial interpretation of human societies may be slowly crumbling. Those pertaining to nationalism still cling as tenaciously as only prejudices can. The human race seems united on a common desire to destroy itself and nationalism happens to be one of the most popular, contemporary methods.

For the present purposes nationalism may be defined as a sentiment of unity held by a social group, a sentiment based upon an apparent common cultural heritage and upon a desire to live separately and independently as a group in the future. This sentiment of unity at the same time is a sentiment of exclusiveness, and members of nations generally feel indifferent or hostile to members of other like nations. Both the unity and the exclusiveness are founded upon real or imagined differences between national groups. If the people of a group has a common past (and historians may give them one if they do not) of language, race, religion, if it has its own historically claimed rocks and rills and "natural" boundaries, in short, if its members have a common culture and a common geographic location, then its language, race, religion, and rocks and rills are held to be different from, and by a long jump in logic better and more beautiful than, those of other like groups. The well-developed nationalist asserts, "My country, right or wrong," or *Deutschland über Alles.* "A true nationalist," declared the *Action française,* which in the French Third Republic was no minor authority, is one who "places the fatherland above everything. . . ."

Of course, there is no more natural basis for the nationalistic interpretation of man and his relationships than there is for prejudices concerning race. . . . Every nationality is a mixture of many peoples, races, tribes, families. The modern French are in origin of the Mediterranean, Alpine, Nordic, and a good many other "races." The modern Italians are compounded of Etruscans, Ligurians, Romans, Iberians,

Greeks, Gauls, Teutons, and in recent times almost every nationality in Europe and some in Africa. Nor are the Germans, Russians, or Americans any purer.

All modern history is a document attesting to national intermixture: migrations, invasions, wars, conquests, marriages. In various degrees every nationality is a conglomeration of the short and tall, the round and the long headed, the dumb and the smart, the virtuous and the sinful. Any one of these characteristics is endlessly duplicated. In fact the attempt to classify nations according to any biological or inherent mental characteristic is only a naive error inherited from early propagandist historians like Tacitus and pseudo-anthropologists like Gobineau. Defoe could have been speaking of any nationality with his

> Thus from a mixture of all kinds began
> That heterogeneous thing, an Englishman.

. . . Men are physiologically, racially, nationally at least as much alike as they are different. That is not surprising. *Homo sapiens* is a species. The individuals of the species are not only much alike but so are their problems and their institutions. This is not so strange either. They have inhabited one globe in a comparatively short period of whatever is universal time. They all have had to provide for sustenance and protection against the elements. They all have had to seek the best circumstances for reproduction and the rearing of their children. They all have had a common desire for some kind of creative activity, for a "noble employment of their leisure" if not an "instinct for workmanship." Now they have the common problem of controlling science so that they may survive. . . .

Schiller sang, "What is the greatest of nations but a fragment?"—A fragment of humanity, one might add, which the Jew Jesus, the Frenchman Montesquieu, the German Goethe held to be above the arbitrary divisions into which petty patriots, narrow scholars, sadistic dictators, cheap journalists, and popular novelists have divided mankind.

3   CULTURE OF THE FOOD GATHERERS

The culture of contemporary food gatherers cannot be assumed to be identical to that of early man in Paleolithic times. Nevertheless the manner of earning a livelihood was the same, and this doubtless determined a basic similarity of cultures in fundamentals if not in details. Hence the significance of the following classic account of the Arunta tribe of Australia for shedding light on the presumed general nature of Paleolithic society. One of the authors of this study was a trained scientist, and the other an Australian official who worked with the aborigines for twenty years. Both men were fully initiated members of the Arunta tribe.*

The native tribes with which we are dealing occupy an area in the centre of the Australian continent which, roughly speaking, is not less than 700 miles in length

---

* Reprinted from B. S. Spencer and F. J. Gillen, *The Native Tribes of Central Australia* (London: Macmillan & Co., Ltd., 1899), pp. 1–54.

from north to south, and stretches out east and west of the transcontinental telegraph line, covering an unknown extent of country in either direction. . . .

Each of the various tribes speaks a distinct dialect, and regards itself as the possessor of the country in which it lives. In the more southern parts, where they have been long in contact with the white man, not only have their numbers diminished rapidly, but the natives who still remain are but poor representatives of their race, having lost all or nearly all of their old customs and traditions. With the spread of the white man it can only be a matter of comparatively a few years before the same fate will befall the remaining tribes, which are as yet fortunately too far removed from white settlements of any size to have become degraded. . . .

Fortunately from this point of view the interior of the continent is not easily accessible, or rather its climate is too dry and the water supply too meagre and untrustworthy, to admit as yet of rapid settlement, and therefore the natives, in many parts, are practically still left to wander over the land which the white man does not venture to inhabit, and amongst them may still be found tribes holding firmly to the beliefs and customs of their ancestors.

If now we take the Arunta tribe as an example, we find that the natives are distributed in a large number of small local groups, each of which occupies, and is supposed to possess, a given area of country, the boundaries of which are well known to the natives. In speaking of themselves, the natives will refer to these local groups by the name of the locality which each of them inhabits. . . .

Still further examination of each local group reveals the fact that it is composed largely, but not entirely, of individuals who describe themselves by the name of some one animal or plant. Thus there will be one area which belongs to a group of men who call themselves kangaroo men, another belonging to emu men, another to Hakea flower men, and so on, almost every animal and plant which is found in the country having its representative amongst the human inhabitants. . . .

As amongst all savage tribes the Australian native is bound hand and foot by custom. What his fathers did before him that he must do. If during the performance of a ceremony his ancestors painted a white line across the forehead, that line he must paint. Any infringement of custom, within certain limitations, is visited with sure and often severe punishment. At the same time, rigidly conservative as the native is, it is yet possible for changes to be introduced. We have already pointed out that there are certain men who are especially respected for their ability, and, after watching large numbers of the tribe, at a time when they were assembled together for months to perform certain of their most sacred ceremonies, we have come to the conclusion that at a time such as this, when the older and more powerful men from various groups are met together, and when day by day and night by night around their camp fires they discuss matters of tribal interest, it is quite possible for changes of custom to be introduced. . . .

Turning again to the group, we find that the members of this wander, perhaps in small parties of one or two families, often, for example, two or more brothers with their wives and children, over the land which they own, camping at favourite spots where the presence of waterholes, with their accompaniment of vegetable and animal food, enables them to supply their wants.

In their ordinary condition the natives are almost completely naked, which is all the more strange as kangaroo and wallaby are not by any means scarce, and one would think that their fur would be of no little use and comfort in the winter time, when, under the perfectly clear sky, which often remains cloudless for weeks together, the radiation is so great that at nighttime the temperature falls several degrees below freezing point. The idea of making any kind of clothing as a pro-

13

tection against cold does not appear to have entered the native mind, though he is keen enough upon securing the Government blanket when he can get one, or, in fact, any stray cast-off clothing of the white man. The latter is however worn as much from motives of vanity as from a desire for warmth; a lubra with nothing on except an ancient straw hat and an old pair of boots is perfectly happy. . . .

If, now, the reader can imagine himself transported to the side of some waterhole in the centre of Australia, he would probably find amongst the scrub and gum-trees surrounding it a small camp of natives. Each family, consisting of a man and one or more wives and children accompanied always by dogs, occupies a *mia-mia,* which is merely a lean-to of shrubs so placed as to shield the occupants from the prevailing wind, which, if it be during the winter months, is sure to be from the south-east. In front of this, or inside if the weather be cold, will be a small fire of twigs, for the black fellow never makes a large fire as the white man does. In this respect he certainly regards the latter as a strange being, who makes a big fire and then finds it so hot that he cannot go anywhere near to it. The black fellow's idea is to make a small fire such that he can lie coiled round it and, during the night, supply it with small twigs so that he can keep it alight without making it so hot that he must go further away.

Early in the morning, if it be summer, and not until the sun be well up if it be winter, the occupants of the camp are astir. Time is no object to them, and, if there be no lack of food, the men and women all lounge about while the children laugh and play. If food be required, then the women will go out accompanied by the children and armed with digging sticks and *pitchis,* and the day will be spent out in the bush in search of small burrowing animals such as lizards and small marsupials. The men will perhaps set off armed with spears, spear-throwers, boomerangs and shields in search of larger game such as emus and kangaroos. The latter are secured by stalking, when the native gradually approaches his prey with perfectly noiseless footsteps. Keeping a sharp watch on the animal, he remains absolutely still, if it should turn its head, until once more it resumes its feeding. Gradually, availing himself of the shelter of any bush or large tussock of grass, he approaches near enough to throw his spear. The end is fixed into the point of the spear thrower, and, aided by the leverage thus gained, he throws it forward with all his strength. Different men vary much in their skill in spear-throwing, but it takes an exceptionally good man to kill or disable at more than twenty yards. . . .

In some parts the leaves of the pituri plant are used to stupefy the emu. The plan adopted is to make a decoction in some small waterhole at which the animal is accustomed to drink. There, hidden by some bush, the native lies quietly in wait. After drinking the water the bird becomes stupefied, and easily falls a prey to the black fellow's spear. Sometimes a bush shelter is made, so as to look as natural as possible, close by a waterhole, and from behind this animals are speared as they come down to drink. It must be remembered that during the long dry seasons of Central Australia waterholes are few and far between, so that in this way the native is aided in his work of killing animals. . . . Smaller birds such as the rock pigeons, which assemble in flocks at any waterhole, are caught by throwing the boomerang amongst them, and larger birds, such as the eagle-hawk, the down of which is much valued for decorating the body during the performance of sacred ceremonies, are procured by the same weapon.

It may be said that with certain restrictions which apply partly to groups of individuals and partly to individuals at certain times of their lives, everything which is edible is used for food. . . .

When a euro or kangaroo is killed, the first thing that is always done is to dislocate the hind-legs so as to make the animal what is called *atnuta* or limp. A small hole is cut with a flint in one side of the abdomen, and after the intestines have been pulled out, it is closed up with a wooden skewer. The intestines are usually cooked by rolling them about in hot sand and ashes, any fat which may be present being carefully removed, as it is esteemed a great delicacy. One of the first things to be done is to extract the tendons from the hind limbs. To do this the skin is cut through close to the foot with the sharp bit of flint which is attached to the end of the spear-thrower. A hitch is next taken round the tendon with a stick, and then, with one foot against the animal's rump, the man pulls until the upper end gives way. Then the loose end is held in the teeth, and, when tightly stretched, the lower end is cut through with the flint and the tendon thus extracted is twisted up and put for safe keeping beneath the waist girdle, or in the hair of the head just behind the ear. These tendons are of great service to the natives in various ways, such as for attaching the barbed points on to the ends of the spears, or for splicing spears or mending broken spear-throwers. Meanwhile a shallow pit, perhaps one or two feet deep, has been dug with sticks, and in this a large fire is made. When this burns up, the body is usually held in the flames to singe off the fur, after which it is scraped with a flint. Sometimes this part of the performance is omitted. The hind legs are cut off at the middle joint and the tail either divided in the middle or cut off close to the stump. When the fire has burnt down the animal is laid in the pit on its back with its legs protruding through the hot ashes, which are heaped up over it. After about an hour it is supposed to be cooked, and is taken off, laid on green boughs so as to prevent it from coming in contact with the earth, and then cut up, the hind legs being usually removed first. In some parts where the fur is not singed off, the first thing that is done after removing the body from the fire is to take off the burnt skin. The carver assists himself, during the process of cutting the body up into joints, to such dainty morsels as the heart and kidneys, while any juice which accumulates in the internal cavities of the body is greedily drunk. . . .

The tracking powers of the native are well-known, but it is difficult to realize the skill which they display unless one has seen them at work. Not only does the native know the track of every beast and bird, but after examining any burrow he will at once, from the direction in which the last track runs, tell you whether the animal is at home or not. From earliest childhood boys and girls alike are trained to take note of every track made by every living thing. . . .

Whilst in matters such as tracking, which are concerned with their everyday life, and upon efficiency in which they actually depend for their livelihood, the natives show conspicuous ability, there are other directions in which they are as conspicuously deficient. This is perhaps shown most clearly in the matter of counting. At Alice Springs they occasionally count, sometimes using their fingers in doing so, up to five, but frequently anything beyond four is indicated by the word *oknira,* meaning much or great. One is *nintha,* two *thrama* or *thera,* three *urapitcha,* four *therankathera,* five *theranka-theranintha.* Time is counted by "sleeps" or "moons," or phases of the moon, for which they have definite terms: longer periods they reckon by means of seasons, having names for summer and winter. . . . In many respects their memory is phenomenal. Their mental powers are simply developed along the lines which are of service to them in their daily life.

. . . If we examine their weapons and implements of various kinds, that is those usually carried about, they will be found to be comparatively few in number and simple. A woman has always a *pitchi,* that is a wooden trough varying in length from one to three feet, which has been hollowed out of the soft wood of the bean tree, or it may be out of hard wood such as mulga or eucalypt. In this she carries food material, either balancing it on her head or holding it slung on to one hip by means of a strand of human hair or ordinary fur string across one shoulder. Not infrequently a small baby will be carried about in a *pitchi*. The only other implement possessed by a woman is what is popularly called a "yam stick," which is simply a digging stick or, to speak more correctly, a pick. The commonest form consists merely of a straight staff of wood with one or both ends bluntly pointed, and of such a size that it can easily be carried in the hand and used for digging in the ground. When at work, a woman will hold the pick in the right hand close to the lower end, and, alternately digging this into the ground with one hand, while with the other she scoops out the loosened earth, will dig down with surprising speed. . . . Of course the children go out with the women, and from the moment that they can toddle about they begin to imitate the actions of their mother. In the scrub a woman will be digging up lizards or honey ants while close by her small child will be at work, with its diminutive pick, taking its first lessons in what, if it be a girl, will be the main employment of her life. . . .

The men's weapons consist of shield, spears, boomerang and spear-thrower, all of which are constantly carried about when on the march. The shields, though they vary in size, are of similar design over practically the whole Central area. They are uniformly made of the light wood of the bean tree, so that their actual manufacture is limited to the more northern parts where this tree grows. . . .

The spear-thrower is perhaps the most useful single thing which the native has. It is in the form of a hollowed out piece of mulga front two feet to two feet six inches in length, with one end tapering gradually to a narrow handle, and the other, more suddenly, to a blunt point, to which is attached, by means of tendon, a short, sharp bit of hard wood which fits into a hole in the end of a spear. At the handle end is a lump of resin into which is usually fixed a piece of sharp-edged flint or quartzite, which forms the most important cutting weapon of the native. . . .

.   .   .

During the day-time the women are sure to be out in search of food, while the men either go out in search of larger game, or else, if lazy and food be abundant, they will simply sleep all day, or perhaps employ their time in making or trimming up their weapons. . . .

As a general rule the natives are kindly disposed to one another, that is of course within the limits of their own tribe, and, where two tribes come into contact with one another on the border land of their respective territories, there the same amicable feelings are maintained between the members of the two. There is no such thing as one tribe being in a constant state of enmity with another so far as these Central tribes are concerned. Now and again of course fights do occur between the members of different local groups who may or may not belong to the same or to different tribes. . . .

.   .   .

When times are favourable the black fellow is as light-hearted as possible. He has not the slightest thought of, or care for, what the morrow may bring forth, and lives entirely in the present. At night time men, women and children gather round the common camp fires talking and singing their monotonous chants hour after hour, until one after the other they drop out of the circle, going off to their different camps, and then at length all will be quiet, except for the occasional cry of a child who, as not seldom happens, rolls over into the fire and has to be comforted or scolded into quietness.

16

. . . Granted always that his food supply is abundant, it may be said that the life of the Australian native is, for the most part, a pleasant one.

In common with all other Australian tribes, those of the Centre have been shut off from contact with other peoples, and have therefore developed for long ages without the stimulus derived from external sources. . . .

Chapter Three

Man the food producer

4   Low Productivity of the Neolithic Tribesman

The agricultural revolution by which man made the fateful transition from food gathering to food producing seems to have occurred first about 7000 B.C. in the Middle East. Despite the technological progress made during Neolithic times, productivity was low compared to that following the advent of civilization. The reason, paradoxically, was the egalitarianism of Neolithic society. Land was available to everyone, and there were no landlords or tax collectors to force production above bare family needs. This is made clear in the following calendar of the work of the Bemba tribe of Northern Rhodesia during the month of September 1933.* Admittedly this is a slack time of the year, and a time when more beer is drunk than normally. Nevertheless it is apparent that the "daily grind," the hallmark of modern society, was conspicuous by its absence under tribal conditions comparable to those of Neolithic times. This is evident also in Reading 6, "Tribesmen and Peasants."

September 1st, 1933. Two gourds of beer ready, one drunk by old men, one by young men. A new baby born. Women gather from other villages to congratulate, and spend two or three days in the village. Women's garden work postponed during this time.

2nd. Old men go out to clear the bush. Young men sit at home finishing the sour dregs of the beer. More visits of neighbouring women to see the new baby. Few women go out to do garden work.

3rd (Sunday). Young men and women go to a church service conducted in a neighbouring village by a visiting Mission doctor. No garden work.

* Reprinted from A. I. Richards, *Land, Labour and Diet in Northern Rhodesia* (London: Oxford Univerity Press and International African Institute, 1939), pp. 162–164.

4th. Visit of the Mission doctor to Kasaka. Protestants and Catholics both attend the services. No garden work.

5th. Old men cut trees. Young men sit at home and shape axe-handles. Some women working again.

6th. Old and young men working by 6:30 a.m. and hard at it till 2 p.m. Two gourds of beer divided between old and young in the evening. Women working in their gardens normally.

7th. A buck shot by observer's party. Young men go out to fetch the meat. Women grind extra flour to eat with it. Two gourds of beer also made ready and drinking begins at 2 p.m. By 4 o'clock young men swaggering around the village, ready to quarrel, which they finally do. Dancing at night. Old women hilarious, and rebuked by their daughters for charging into a rough dance on the village square. Not enough beer for the younger women. They remain sober and express disapproval of the rest. No garden work done, except by old men.

8th. Every one off to their gardens in high spirits at 8 a.m. Back at 12 a.m. Young men sit in shelter and drink beer dregs for two hours, singing Scotch Mission hymns in sol-fa. Young girls go out on a miniature fish-poisoning expedition, but catch nothing.

9th and 10th. Observers away. D10, son of D11 born.* A crowd of relatives from neighbouring villages come to congratulate. No garden work said to have been done.

11th. The baby born on September 1st (daughter of a visiting relative) dies. Mourners arrive from surrounding villages. Eight young women go to do their tribute labour for chief. All garden work postponed.

12th. Mourning party leaves with bereaved mother, accompanied by women of Kasaka wailing up the road. Young women still away at capital. Little garden work done by women. Men tree-cutting half the day.

13th. Heads of A, B, C, D go visiting relatives twenty-two miles away, with their wives, to mourn. Clearing bush by two men. Garden work done by two women. Meat distributed.

14th. A1, B1, C1, D1 and wives still away. One man clears bush. Meat still available. Young women still away doing tribute labour.

15th. Three men begin digging dry-weather gardens by the river. Little boys go bird-snaring. Young women still away at the capital. Nobody to get relish. No proper meal cooked.

16th. Eight men clear bush. One away hunting. Three young men home for week-end from work at Shiwa Dandu. Young women return from doing tribute labour in the evening, greeted by shouts from the whole community. Old women all remain in village.

17th (Sunday). Great heat. Young men sit about in shelter all day, comb each other's hair, shave, and delouse each other. No relish available. Women too tired to cook.

18th. Seven men work again clearing bush. Five women piling branches.

19th. Nine men clear bush. One woman hoeing. Three women piling branches. Young women go fish-poisoning and catch one fish (about 2 lb.).

20th. Six men clear bush. One house-building.

21st. Five men clear bush. Five women pile branches.

22nd. Three men clear bush. One man hoes. Four young men go fishing with three of the wives. Three piling branches.

* Editor's Note: Code numbers and letters refer to persons identified on kinship charts.

19

23rd. Five men clear bush. One goes on digging a dry-weather garden. Five women pile branches. One hoes.

24th (Sunday). Four gourds of beer divided between whole village. Sufficient for women as well as men. Beer-drinking lasts two days off and on.

25th. Two old men only able to tree-cut. Young men afraid to climb trees because of 'beer before the eyes.' They sit in their shelter and make baskets. B4 hunts with his own gun. One woman only does garden work. Young boys snare birds. Remains of beer drunk.

26th. Old men work. Young men 'too cold.' B4 still away hunting.

27th. Five men clear bush. One man and four women carry meat sixteen miles to Shiwa. . . .

28th. Every one (men and women) off at 6 a.m. Work till 2 p.m., declaring they are strong with meat. A little beer in the evening.

29th. Rain at night. First net-hunt possible. All men and children join in. Nothing killed. Six women pile branches.

30th. More beer. Four men clear bush. E3 digs dry-weather garden.

October 1st (Sunday). Young women whitewash houses.

2nd. Headman provides beer for a working bee. All men join to clear bush for him and drink afterwards.

This calendar makes no attempt to give a complete record of the activities of the people, as unfortunately the data are not sufficiently full. It brings out certain interesting points, however. The first is the irregularity of the work done and the greater industry of the old as compared with the young, especially among the men. By noting the chart letters of those two went to clear the bush or to pile branches each day, it will be seen that the only natives who went consecutively to work were the old men of the village, those reckoned by the Government as too feeble to pay tax. . . . This was admittedly a slack time of the year, but it will be noted that the arrival of visitors, such as relatives or the local missionaries, births and deaths in the village or neighbourhood, the absence of the young women doing tribute labour, or beer parties, disrupted the work of the village or brought it to a standstill. On no single day did every man and woman go off to work.

5   ACHIEVEMENTS OF MAN BEFORE CIVILIZATION

*The contemporary world is in large part the product of the great civilizations of Eurasia that followed the agricultural revolution. Yet preliterate man did possess a vast amount of naturalistic knowledge that is taken for granted and thus overlooked, but which nevertheless provided the solid foundation upon which the succeeding civilizations were based. This survey, by an American anthropologist, of the knowledge and techniques attained before civilization makes clear the debt owed by contemporary man to his preliterate ancestors.**

* Reprinted from *The Evolution of Culture: The Development of Civilization to the Fall of Rome*, by L. A. White, pp. 268–72. Copyright © 1959 by McGraw Hill, Inc. Used with permission of McGraw-Hill Book Company.

During the course of cultural evolution up to the Agricultural Revolution a very considerable amount of genuine, matter-of-fact knowledge was acquired and accumulated. Some of this knowledge was very widespread, much of it was locally restricted, depending upon the uniformity or diversity of local circumstances of habitat. The totality of these local knowledges is impressive and forms the foundation for the naturalistic philosophies of more advanced cultures and for the science of our culture. It will be interesting and instructive to pass in review these traditions of genuine knowledge in primitive cultures.

Primitive peoples knew their habitats intimately. They knew what useful resources it contained, where red ocher, clay, or flint might be found. They knew the distribution of flora and fauna and which species were useful or edible and which were useless or injurious. They knew the habits of local birds, animals, fish, and insects and how to take them for food and other uses. Eskimos were able to make topographic sketches of the territory within which they lived and traveled so accurately that they could be used to good advantage by arctic explorers.

Preliterate peoples possessed knowledge concerning the heavenly bodies and temporal and seasonal sequences. Constellations of stars were distinguished and named. Polaris was spotted, and the movements of planets followed. Even such a primitive tribe as the Ona of Tierra del Fuego distinguished Sirius, Procyon, and Betelgeuse. Morning and evening stars received particular attention. They knew that there are twelve to thirteen lunations in a complete solar cycle; these "moons" were frequently named according to the time of the year—"new-leaves moon," or "first-snowflurries moon." Seasons were distinguished according to latitude. Among some tribes systematic observations were made upon the sun. The Pueblo Indians of the Southwest, for example, had a special priest to observe the risings of the sun in order to determine the times of the solstices.

Virtually all kinds of tools were invented and developed by primitive peoples, such as knives, axes, scrapers, hammers, awls, needles, and so on. Machines, i.e., mechanical devices composed of moving and interrelated parts, such as the bow drill and pump drill, were occasionally developed. Tubular drill bits and abrasives were used. In the field of weapons, spears, harpoons, clubs, shields, and armor were developed. The atlatl, or spear thrower, the blowgun, and the bow and arrow are particularly ingenious devices. Hammocks were invented and used by the Indians of the Amazon. All techniques for producing fire known to man prior to the invention of matches in the early nineteenth century were developed by primitive peoples: percussion (flint and iron pyrites), friction (the fire drill and fire saw), and compression (the fire piston). The fire piston is an especially ingenious device. Tinder is placed in the bottom of a cylinder and is ignited by being raised to the kindling temperature by air compression. The principle involved here was later incorporated in the Diesel engine, where fuel is ignited in the cylinder by compression rather than by an electric spark. Rubber was manufactured by the American Indians and used as balls in games in Meso-America and to make enema syringes in Amazonia.

A great many techniques involving considerable knowledge were developed by primitive peoples in one culture or another. The manufacture of good pottery, the proper admixture of tempering material with clay and the subsequent firing, requires a great deal of knowledge and skill. Similarly the art of making buckskin requires an extensive knowledge of materials and techniques. The textile arts—carding, spinning, twinning, twilling, weaving—require knowledge, skill, and apparatus. Bark cloth, made from the inner bark of mulberry or fig trees, beaten to almost paper thinness with corrugated mallets, was made in Polynesia and west Africa. Felt was made by various peoples of central Asia. The nonsubmersible kayak and the sealskin float used to retard the escape of harpooned sea mammals among the Eskimos demonstrate an understanding of physical principles. The snowhouse in the same cultures is also a remarkable exhibition of realistic knowledge and understanding, not to mention the utilization of the thermos-bottle principle in some of these houses. Some Eskimo groups sewed caribou skins together and suspended them from the walls and ceilings of their snowhouses, separating the two by a few inches. A layer of non-heat-conducting air is thus interposed between the skins and the snow wall, which is of course an example of the principle utilized in thermos bottles in our culture. The Eskimos also made and used goggles, with narrow slits instead of lenses, to protect them from the glare of sunlight reflected from the snow. Outrigger canoes are ingenious contrivances which utilize a number of mechanical principles.

In the field of chemistry, primitive peoples by and large amassed a considerable store of knowledge of materials and processes. They knew how to make paints and pigments, some of which had a quality and durability that have never been surpassed. They discovered the use of mordants, substances for fixing colors. One of the most remarkable chemical processes on primitive cultural levels is to be found in northeastern South America. There, some tribes have learned to remove a deadly poison, hydrocyanic acid, from a species of manioc, which then becomes a staple article of diet. They have done this by a complicated process of grinding, drying, and leaching, which incidentally uses a most ingenious mechanical basketry device known as a cassava squeezer. How these primitive Indians ever discovered that they could separate a deadly poison from a plant otherwise nutritious is something to wonder at.

A great many poisons were known and used on preliterate cultural levels. The primitive Semang, and other peoples of Southeast Asia, used the lethal sap of the upas tree (*Antiaris*) to tip darts and arrows. Curare, made from the sap of *Strychnos toxifera,* was widely used in northeastern South America. It paralyzes the respiratory muscles, causing death but leaving the carcass quite edible. Some peoples tipped arrows with a mixture of snake venom and liver. Hemlock and the Calabar bean among other poisons were also used to kill members of one's own society.

Many plant materials have been used to kill or stupefy fish so that they might be easily taken for food. The active, or significant, ingredient of some of these plants is saponin, a soaplike material that smothers the fish. Tannic acid or an alkaloid of some kind is the active agent in others. The aborigines of Australia drugged pools with pituri, an alkaloid, in order to stupefy and catch emu.

Chemical knowledge of many primitive tribes is expressed in other ways also. Tribes of the Northwest Coast of America chewed tobacco with lime, made by burning shells. In the Andean region coca leaves, and in Melanesia and Southeast Asia betel nuts, were chewed with lime in order to produce an effect the nature of which is not too well understood. According to one authority, lime helps to liberate "the arecoline alkaloid from the areca [betel] nut." Also, lime acts as a gastric sedative and is an antidote for mineral and oxalic poisoning.

The Indians of the Andean highlands prepared corn for the manufacture of beer (*chicha*) by chewing it in order to institute a chemical process by the action of saliva upon the grain. Starch must be transformed into sugar before it can be fermented. Saliva contains an enzyme called ptyalin, which breaks down starches, first to simple dextrins, then to maltose, a crystalline sugar. In Polynesia, the kava root was chewed, no doubt for a similar reason, in the preparation of kava, a slightly intoxicating drink.

Agriculture and animal husbandry are the achievements of preliterate peoples. No new plant or animal has been brought under domestication by modern civilized peoples. On the other hand, a number of useful plants, cultivated by primitive peoples, have been virtually ignored by modern civilization: *Chenopodium* (quinoa) and oca, for example. Primitive peoples discovered the most suitable plants to domesticate and cultivate and devised effective techniques for their cultivation. They developed and improved cultivated plants by selective breeding and learned to increase yields by fertilization and irrigation.

All the kinds of foods known to modern civilization—starches, sugars, fats or oils, proteins, "greens," etc.—were known and used on preliterate cultural levels. This does not mean, of course, that the diet of every tribe was varied and well balanced; it merely means that modern civilization uses no kind of food that was not known to some primitive tribe somewhere.

In the preparation and preservation of foods, too, primitive peoples acquired a vast amount of knowledge and skill. Stone boiling and earth ovens exemplify their ingenuity and resourcefulness. Foods were preserved in a variety of ways. In arctic regions they were frozen. In other regions certain foods—fruits, vegetables, and meats—were preserved by drying. Sometimes they were sealed up airtight with tallow. In short, preliterate peoples devised virtually all the techniques known to us today for preserving food except the tin can and the airtight glass jar.

Medical diagnosis and practice among primitive peoples were not wholly magical by any means. They took a rational view of many ailments and attempted to treat them realistically in matter-of-fact ways. In certain cultures, broken bones were set with splints, tourniquets were used, poultices and bandages employed. Steam baths were used and massage practiced by many peoples. Bloodletting was a widespread therapeutic practice, as it was in European culture until quite recent times. Some tribes of South America administered enemas, using a rubber syringe for this purpose. In surgery, the Melanesians and Peruvians developed great skill in cutting out broken bones of the skull to relieve pressure on the brain. "In this delicate operation known as 'trephining,' " says Lowie, "they were more successful than European physicians of the Eighteenth Century." The Peruvian surgeons also amputated feet with success; pictures on pottery bowls show men with an artificial foot, taking part, however, in a ceremony or dance. Doctors among the Ganda are said to have been able "to cure men partially disembowelled from spear wounds by washing the portruding intestines, forcing them gently back into the abdomen, and keeping them in place with a piece of gourd."

The human heads, shrunk by the Jivaro Indians, might be mentioned in this connection, also, since they involve knowledge and skill in anatomical surgery and mummification. The Jivaro remove the bones of the head and reduce it to the size of a fist, retaining at the same time the original facial features. They are preserved by smoking—and perhaps other techniques—and kept as trophies.

Many plant materials were used by primitive peoples in nonmagical or only partially magical, contexts in the treatment of ailments of many kinds. It is now known that many plants used by aborigines for medicinal purposes such as cascara, sweet flag (*Acorus*), *Angelica,* seneca snakeroot, sassafras, licorice, eucalyptus, etc., do have therapeutic value. It is exceedingly difficult, however, to determine what effect certain medicinal plants will have on patients because of the complexity of the chemical content of the plants, on the one hand, and the personal idiosyncrasies of individuals, on the other. In the use of plants for medicinal purposes, however, primitive peoples have discovered and recognized many important drugs, such as tobacco, cocaine, quinine, ipecac, hashish, peyote, datura, and fly agaric.

The roster of beverages among preliterate peoples demonstrates a very considerable knowledge of the properties of materials and of techniques of preparation. Many peoples have brewed leaves of plants to make "teas." The Pueblo Indians made a tasty and nutritious drink of corn which had been soaked and allowed to sprout, then dried, parched, ground, and used as we would use coffee. Coffee is indigenous in Abyssinia, but the origin of coffee drinking is not definitely known. It appears to have been introduced to Western culture by the Arabs about the sixteenth century. Whether coffee drinking was invented by a preliterate people or not is unknown, but it is interesting to note, in this connection, that the Ganda of Uganda did not drink coffee, but carried the beans—boiled, dried, and sometimes roasted—on their persons for occasional chewing. The Aztecs drank chocolate, made from the cacao bean, flavored with vanilla, honey, or pepper. Some tribes drink milk, fresh or fermented, from mares as well as from cows.

The saps of various trees, e.g., maple and palm, are drunk, fresh or fermented. A great variety of "wines," made from sap or fruit juices, are drunk by many peoples. The Hottentots drank an alcoholic beverage made by diluting wild honey with water and adding certain roots to promote fermentation. The Ganda made a mildly intoxicating beer of ripe bananas and millet flour. The Aztecs drank pulque, an alcoholic beverage made from the sap of the agave. We have already spoken of the kava drink of Polynesia and the maize beer, or *chicha,* of Peru. About the only advance made by modern civilization in the art of making liquors is the distillation process.

In the realm of music, primitive peoples have much to their credit. They developed musical systems and styles and advanced the vocal art as far as part singing. Their musical systems were often exceedingly complicated rhythmically —much more so than our own—but were relatively simple harmonically. Virtually all kinds of musical instruments known to the modern world today were invented and developed by primitive peoples: stringed instruments of all kinds, which incidentally may have originated in the musical bow; percussion instruments—drums, clackers, rattles; wind instruments—flutes, trumpets, pan pipes (our great pipe organs today are simply pan pipes enormously magnified).

Primitive peoples have some noteworthy achievements to their credit in ocean travel and navigation. Prior to the voyages of Columbus, the most extensive overseas voyages, as distinguished from coastwise travel, were made by the Polynesians. It is 2,500 miles from Rapa to Easter Island. Regular voyages between Hawaii and Tahiti, a distance of about 2,350 miles, were made. Their seacraft sometimes exceeded 100 feet in length. War canoes of Fiji could accommodate 200 men, warriors, and crew, and some Tahitian canoes are said to have seated as many as 300. Coastwise commercial craft of New Guinea, consisting of as many as seven to fourteen dugouts lashed together side by side, and measuring up to 59 feet long by 51 feet wide, could carry as much as 34 tons of cargo.

The Marshall Islanders devised and used some very ingenious navigational charts. They were frameworks made of the midribs of cocoanut leaves arranged in such a way as to indicate the location of reefs, ocean swells, and currents. The position of islands was indicated by cowrie shells tied to the frame.

The accumulated knowledge, skills, tools, machines, and techniques developed by primitive, preliterate peoples laid the basis for civilization and all the higher cultures. They invented and developed all the basic tools, weapons, and utensils. They developed the major arts and crafts, such as the ceramic and textile arts, and initiated the art of metallurgy. Food and fiber plants were brought under domestication by them, and they developed the techniques for their culture. They originated the domestication of animals.

Thus during the first hundreds of thousands of years of culture history, primitive peoples were acquiring realistic and matter-of-fact knowledge and originating and perfecting rational and effective techniques. This age-old process of accumulation and development culminated in the Agricultural Revolution, which, as we have seen, profoundly transformed the whole cultural tradition. It is indeed remarkable to see how close to the present day primitive peoples have come at many points on the technological level. Western civilization surpassed primitive techniques of making fire by mechanical friction or percussion only within the last 150 years. And the principle underlying artificial illumination—burning fuel with or without a container and with or without a wick—has been outgrown only within the last 75 years. As recently as 1850 in the United States, white frontiersmen as well as Indians were using the bow and arrow in buffalo hunting in preference to the best of firearms then available to them. And Tylor tells us that Russian troops armed with bow and arrow marched down the boulevards of Paris in 1815 in celebration of the defeat of Napoleon. Thus the bow and arrow, a mechanical triumph of preliterate cultures, has been rendered obsolete as a practical device only within recent years—almost within the memory of persons now living.

ANCIENT CIVILIZATIONS

OF EURASIA,

3500–1000 B.C.

Chapter Four

Origins of ancient civilizations

6

From the long-run historical viewpoint, the advent of civilization represented a step forward for mankind. Natural resources were exploited more efficiently, productivity increased, population rose correspondingly, and knowledge accumulated from generation to generation thanks to the new art of writing and to new professions. But from the short-run viewpoint, civilization meant class differentiation and exploitation, which contrasted starkly with the egalitarianism of Neolithic society. The first of the following selections, a description of the Siang tribal rice growers of Central Borneo, brings out the communal spirit that pervades economic and social relationships. This spirit was evident also in Reading 4, "Low Productivity of the Neolithic Tribesman."

The second selection demonstrates how different was the position of a peasant with the rise of civilization in ancient Egypt. This is a typical exhortation to schoolboys, depicting the trials and exploitation of the hapless peasant in contrast to the privileged position of the scribe. The third selection, by a French physician who lived in India for several years in the mid-seventeenth century, is a description of the position of the peasants and urban dwellers under the Mogul dynasty. The final selection, by two American missionaries in India in the 1920's, demonstrates that the position of the Indian peasants has remained basically unchanged and still contrasts strikingly with that of Neolithic tribesmen.

Siang Tribal Rice Growers *

. . . Almost the entire life of these people is concerned with wresting a living from the jungle, hunting the birds and animals, collecting fruits and vegetables, or

---

* Reprinted from J. H. Provine, "Cooperative Ricefield Cultivation among the Siang Dyaks of Central Borneo," *American Anthropologist,* Vol. 39, No. 1 (1937), 80–91, by permission of the American Anthropological Association.

clearing the land to provide space and sunshine for the cultivation of their main crop, rice. The hardest and most important of these activities from the point of view of the effort expended, though not from the amount of time each year devoted to it, is the clearing of the jungle land for cultivation.

The amount of land available for cultivation is practically unlimited, though the people of each village rather definitely regard the land surrounding it as belonging to the men of that village for purposes of cultivation. Individually, however, they do not regard themselves as having anything more than a temporary claim to use the land. As long as a man wishes to use land which is being cleared or has been cleared by him, no one can take it from him. If a man abandons a used plot after its first year, and moves to another without manifesting in some way his intention to retain his use of the first plot, such as by planting *javau*, vegetables, or perhaps rubber, or by simple announcement of his retention of an interest in the plot, someone else may come in and cultivate the old field. There is a well recognized feeling, however, that if an abandoned field is wanted for use by another within one or two or even three years, permission must first be obtained from the user. After two or three years usually anyone may clear and cultivate it.

.   .   .

The site having been chosen, the first work is the clearing of the underbrush, creepers, grass, and small trees. After these have been cut, the debris is allowed to dry out thoroughly—a few days being sufficient—before the larger trees are felled upon it. Then the larger trees are attacked with the small axes, partially cut through until the top or the edge of the clearing is reached, when the peripheral trees are completely felled. . . . Of course, such method of felling does not perfectly nor completely clear a plot, and a good bit of hard work still must be done felling those trees which have withstood the avalanche of the first felling.

After the trees are down many of the larger branches still extend high into the air, and these must be cut off in order to allow for more complete burning. This leveling process, known as *mehera,* is almost as strenuous work as felling the trees originally. After the leveling the trees are allowed to dry out and the plot is burned, on a windy day if possible. A second burning may or may not be necessary. The fields are usually ready for planting by the middle of October.

Each family, that is, a man, his wife, and their unmarried children, has its own ricefield. The fields are not necessarily located in the same general region, nor in the same direction from the village, though in former years when head-hunting and raiding parties had constantly to be taken into consideration, it was usual for all the fields to be very close together if not actually adjoining. At present, two or more families, sometimes as many as ten or twelve, often go together in the preparation of the same area, cooperating through all the different stages of felling the trees, burning, planting, watching, and harvesting. If sufficient good land is available in one location, it is desirable to join together in cultivating it; for though head-hunting and raids no longer give the people much concern, joint cultivation supplies a companionship and economic advantage that is very desirable. During the growing season, when the animal pests are bad, watching of the fields can be done turn and turn about if several families are involved. Further, as one man at Nono Kliwon expressed it, if there are several fields together, it is not likely that the animal pests will ruin any particular crop completely, but rather will injure all partially, whereas if a man is alone the pests may clear out his entire field.

.   .   .

The man is considered as the head of the household, the room in the long house where he and his family reside is referred to as his, and it is expected of him that he will provide to the best of his ability the rice, wild game, and jungle produce, while the women will take care of the children, husk the rice, make mats, and do the cooking. It is unseemly for a woman to do the hardest kinds of work, to fell large trees, to hunt wild pig, or even to bring in a load of firewood; and a man who spends his entire time around the house to the neglect of his jungle work is guilty of a breach of responsibility.

.   .   .

Women who have lost their husbands through death, desertion, or other cause, and who have not been successful in procuring another are oftentimes forced to cultivate their own plots by themselves. Of course, some of them are fortunate enough to have parents or brothers or other relatives to whom they can look for help, but when such is not the case they must engage in the hard work of clearing their own ground, usually confining themselves, however, to those areas which have been previously used and on which the growth has not yet attained any great size. On the whole, the women can swing an axe as effectively as the men. When they do cultivate their own plots, they may enter into *hando* arrangements with their friends and neighbors, and may, if not too poor, which they usually are, secure feast labor. If a woman is left with several small children and has no relatives upon whom she can call, she is usually assisted by the others in the village, through gifts of rice and wild pig or by help in the clearing of her field; at least until such time as the children have become old enough to help her.

With the exception of the children, who until they are married are cared for in their father's house, and the old people who no longer are able to do hard work in the field, everyone must cultivate a field of some sort. The old men and women are cared for by their relatives, or these lacking, by friends and neighbors, and though no definite reciprocal obligations arise from the help extended to them, the old men ordinarily contribute a helpful share to the family existence by gathering and stripping rattan, sharpening tools, carving out boards and troughs, tending the children; the old women by weaving, cooking, tending the children, or such other small duties as devolve upon the stay-at-homes. With these exceptions no one is exempt from the necessity of making a ricefield, not even the medicine man or the chief.

. . . The Siangs, as other Dyaks, are notorious for their hospitality and visitors from other villages are readily accepted and provided for, sometimes for considerable periods of time. But if a man after considerable time makes no attempt or offer to reciprocate in some way for the hospitality afforded him, he is asked to move on. The Siang territory is a small one, communication between the villages is frequent, so that a man's shiftless ways quite soon spread to all the long houses and that man's reception becomes gradually less and less hearty. No really deserving person who through sickness or other misfortune has come to difficulty will be permitted to suffer or starve among the Siangs, but an undeserving person is seldom tolerated longer than is necessary to find out what he is.

Peasants of Ancient Egypt *

I am told, thou dost forsake writing, thou givest thyself up to pleasure; thou settest thy mind on work in the field, and turnest thy back on the God's Words. Dost

* Reprinted from A. Erman, *The Literature of the Ancient Egyptians* (London: Methuen & Co., Ltd., 1927), p. 193.

thou not bethink thee how it fareth with the husbandman, when the harvest is registered? The worm hath taken half of the corn, the hippopotamus hath devoured the rest. The mice abound in the field, and the locust hath descended. The cattle devour, and the sparrows steal. Woe to the husbandman!

The remainder, that lieth upon the threshing floor, the thieves make an end of that. The . . . of copper is destroyed; the pair of horses dieth at the threshing and ploughing.

And now the scribe landeth on the embankment and will register the harvest. The porters carry sticks, and the negroes palm-ribs. They say: "Give corn." "There is none there." He is stretched out and beaten; he is bound and thrown into the canal — — — —. His wife is bound in his presence, his children are put in fetters. His neighbours leave them, they take to flight, and look after their corn.

But the scribe, he directeth the work of all people. For him there are no taxes, for he payeth tribute in writing, and there are no dues for him. Prithee, know that.

Peasants of Seventeenth-Century India *

Of the vast tracts of country constituting the empire of Hindostan, many are little more than sand, or barren mountains, badly cultivated, and thinly peopled; and even a considerable portion of the good land remains untilled from want of labourers; many of whom perish in consequence of the bad treatment they experience from the governors. These poor people, when incapable of discharging the demands of their rapacious lords, are not only often deprived of the means of subsistence, but are bereft of their children, who are carried away as slaves. Thus it happens that many of the peasantry, driven to despair by so execrable a tyranny, abandon the country, and seek a more tolerable mode of existence, either in the towns, or camps; as porters, carriers of water, or cavalry servants. Sometimes they fly to the territories of a rajah, because there they find less oppression, and are allowed a greater degee of comfort.

· · ·

The king [of India], as proprietor of the land, makes over a certain quantity to military men [or timariots], as an equivalent for their pay; and this grant is called jagieer, or, as in Turkey, timar; the word jagieer signifying the spot from which to draw, or the place of salary. Similar grants are made to governors, in lieu of their salary, and also for the support of their troops, on condition that they pay a certain sum annually to the king out of any surplus revenue that the land may yield. The lands not so granted are retained by the king as the peculiar domains of his house and are seldom, if ever, given in the way of jagieer; and upon these domains he keeps farmers, who are also bound to pay him an annual rent.

The persons thus put in possession of the land, whether as timariots, governors or farmers, have an authority almost absolute over the peasantry, and nearly as much over the artisans and merchants of the towns and villages within their district; and nothing can be imagined more cruel and oppressive than the manner in which it is exercised. There is no one before whom the injured peasant, artisan or tradesman, can pour out his just complaints; no great lords, parliaments or judges of presidial courts exist, as in France, to restrain the wickedness of those merciless oppressors, and the cadis, or judges, are not invested with sufficient power to re-

* Reprinted from F. Bernier, *Travels in the Mogul Empire* (London, 1826), pp. 229–30, 252–54, 256–57.

dress the wrongs of these unhappy people. This sad abuse of the royal authority may not be felt in the same degree near capital cities, such as Delhi and Agra, or in the vicinity of large towns and seaports, because in those places acts of gross injustice cannot easily be concealed from the court.

This debasing state of slavery obstructs the progress of trade and influences the manners and mode of life of every individual. There can be little encouragement to engage in commercial pursuits, when the success with which they may be attended, instead of adding to the enjoyments of life, provokes the cupidity of a neighbouring tyrant possessing both power and inclination to deprive any man of the fruits of his industry. When wealth is acquired, as must sometimes be the case, the possessor, so far from living with increased comfort and assuming an air of independence, studies the means by which he may appear indigent: his dress, lodging and furniture, continue to be mean, and he is careful, above all things, never to indulge in the pleasures of the table. In the mean time, his gold and silver remain buried at a great depth in the ground; . . .

. . . The peasant cannot avoid asking himself this question: "Why should I toil for a tyrant who may come tomorrow and lay his rapacious hands upon all I possess and value, without leaving me, if such should be his humour, the means to drag on my miserable existence?"—The timariots, governors and farmers, on their part reason in this manner "Why should the neglected state of this land create uneasiness in our minds? and why should we expend our own money and time to render it fruitful? we may be deprived of it in a single moment, and our exertions would benefit neither ourselves nor our children. Let us draw from the soil all the money we can, though the peasant should starve or abscond, and we should leave it, when commanded to quit, a dreary wilderness."

The facts I have mentioned are sufficient to account for the rapid declension of the Asiatic states. It is owing to this miserable system of government that most towns in Hindostan are made up of earth, mud, and other wretched materials; that there is no city or town which, if it be not already ruined and deserted, does not bear evident marks of approaching decay.

Peasants of Twentieth-Century India *

"To a newcomer we may seem suspicious, obstinate, intolerant, backward— everything that goes with refusal to change. We did not choose these characteristics for ourselves. Experience forced them upon our fathers. And the warnings of our fathers, added to our own experiences, have drilled them into us. Refusal to change is the armor with which we have learned to protect ourselves. If we and our fathers had accepted the new ideas and customs commended to us, we might have made greater progress. But greater progress would have drawn the eyes of a covetous world toward us. And then our lot would have been worse than before. Where are the cities that flouished for a time? In ruins. While they climbed to great heights and fell to the depths of destruction, we kept to the old reliable level. And we have survived. We are not blind to the advantages of the new, but unless we know just where it will lead us, we prefer to let it pass us by.

"At times you cannot hide your impatience with our caution. There was the plow which you urged us to accept. You saw only the advantages it offered in turning

* Reprinted from W. H. and C. V. Wiser, *Behind Mud Walls 1930–1960* (Berkeley and Los Angeles: University of California Press, 1964), pp. 117–20, 122–25, 128. The material in this reading consists entirely of statements by Indian villagers cited by W. H. and C. V. Wiser.

our soil during the months when it has always lain packed and hard. We saw beyond that. We felt the added perspiration of working in the killing sun of June, and saw the risk of exposing our bullocks to the cruelty of heat and sun, especially when they are hardly strong enough to pull such a plow. You know how we dread the sickness or loss of an animal. We knew the weight of the plow and foresaw the difficulties of carrying it on our shoulders from one small plot to another far away. And we saw the eyes of rent collectors, greedily watching the results of our added toil. We were sorry to disappoint you, but we could not risk such an expensive and doubtful experiment, when the benefits would most likely not stay with us. The plow that Bala's brother won at your exhibition last spring is better. It is light, like our plows, and good for ordinary plowing. But Bala's brother has not dared to use it. He is so prosperous that he is afraid of anything that makes a show of still greater prosperity. In that he may seem foolish to you. But we do not blame him for his caution.

.   .   .

"Our walls which conceal all that we treasure, are a necessary part of our defense. Our forefathers hid themselves from a covetous world behind mud walls. We do the same. Barriers are no longer needed as protection against cruel raiders. But they are needed against those ruthless ones who come to extort. For the old purpose, our fathers built their walls strong enough to shut out the enemy, and made them of earth so that they might be inconspicuous. For the present purpose they must remain inconspicuous and yet be high enough to conceal us and our possessions from the greedy ones. But now they are better protection if instead of being kept strong they are allowed to become dilapidated. Dilapidation makes it harder for the covetous vistior to tell who is actually poor and who simulates poverty. When men become so strong that the agents of authority work with them for their mutual benefit, they dare to expose their prosperity in walls of better materials and workmanship. But if the ordinary man suddenly makes his will conspicuous, the extortioner is on his trail. You remember what a short time it was after Puri put up his imposing new veranda with a good grass roof, that the police watchman threatened to bring a false charge against him. He paid well for his show of progress. Old walls tell no tales.

"Neither do old clothes. When we are to deal with strangers we choose our dress to the occasion, not to our means. And most occasions call for poor clothes. You have heard them complain in the hospital that they are at a loss to know who should be charity patients and who should pay. We would be foolish to bring upon ourselves big bills, when the simple matter of dress will give us charity rates.

.   .   .

". . . In the cities they devise ways of exploiting us. We know how to drive bargains when we sell our wheat or our sugar cane. We are at home in the wholesale market. But when we get our money and want to take home some cloth, the shopkeepers get out the pieces which they have been unable to dispose of, and persuade us to buy them at exorbitant prices. We know they are laughing at us. But we want cloth, and the next shopkeeper will cheat us as badly as the last. Wherever we go in the town, sharp eyes are watching to tempt our precious rupees from us. There is no one to advise us honestly or to help us escape from fraudulent men. When we go to town to attend the courts, there are men everywhere waiting to take advantage of our ignorance and fear. Our lawyers charge fees which they know are beyond our means to pay. And then if we win a case they think they deserve an extra large gift. Sometimes there is a sincere helper among them, but we are never sure who is what.

"There are the politicians who come to us and declare themselves champions of the village. They must think us very gullible. Do they suppose we are blind to the fact that it is only during the days before election that they take a passionate interest in us? . . .

"And what of the priests who should be our comforters and guides? Those among us who have priestly duties to perform, go through them punctiliously, just as the ceremonies require. At night our village head sometimes reads aloud from the *Ramayana*. In religion, as in all things, we have learned to depend on whatever we can provide for ourselves, when free from work. The men who devote their lives to priestly duties visit us, to be sure. But they come with a conch or a bell, the sound of which sends our womenfolk scuttling to the grain jar. At our doors they stop just long enough to have the donations poured into their bags. When the bags are full they move on. They tell us that the grain is for the temple on the edge of town, or for one on the Ganges. We do not stop to inquire further. They are priests, and we have always given. Sometimes a priest comes to recite verses. But he does it only in the house where the feast is prepared and his pay is promised. . . .

"There are our landlords, to whom we might look for interest and help, if we dared. But we have learned not to dare. One landlord is on a committee which administers the estate on behalf of a trust fund which is used for various charitable purposes. But the charity evidently limits itself to the city. We see no evidences of it in the men who come to collect rents from us. The other landlord has grown rich from his many villages. But we do not begrudge him his riches, because he proclaims his desire to be just toward his tenants. But he is too busy with his many properties to take time for any one village. We have never seen him. All we know about him are the reports which our headman brings from the big *durbars* to which he is invited once a year. . . ."

Chapter Five

Styles of ancient civilizations

7   MAN'S EARLIEST CIVILIZATION

The first civilization of mankind took form on the arid and forbidding plains of the Tigris-Euphrates Valley. In the lower part of the valley, at the head of the Persian Gulf, were founded the cities of Sumer, the Old Testament's "land of Shinar." In developing these cities the Sumerians made certain technological and institutional innovations that comprise the transition from Neolithic culture to civilization. The following account by a distingushed Sumerologist describes the nature and significance of these innovations.*

The Tigris-Euphrates plain is a hot, arid land. Six thousand years ago it was a wind-swept barren. It had no minerals, almost no stone, no trees, practically no building material of any kind. It has been described as a land with "the hand of God against it." Yet it was in this desolate region that man built what was probably the first high civilization. Here were born the inventions of writing, farming technology, architecture, the first codes of law, the first cities. Perhaps the very poverty of the land provided the stimulus that mothered these inventions. But the main credit must go to the people who created them—a most remarkable people called the Sumerians.

These Sumerians, as now revealed by long archeological research, were a surprisingly modern folk. In many ways they were like the pioneers who built the U. S.—practical, ambitious, enterprising, jealous of their personal rights, technologically inventive. Having no stone or timber, they built with marsh reeds and river mud, invented the brick mold and erected cities of baked clay. They canalled the waters of the Tigris and Euphrates rivers into the arid fields and turned Sumer into a veritable Garden of Eden. To manage their irrigation systems they originated regional government, thus emerging from the petty social order of the family and village to the city-state. They created a written language and committed it to permanent clay tablets. They traded their grain surpluses to distant peoples for metals and other materials they lacked. By the third millennium B.C. the culture and civilization of Sumer, a country about the size of the state of Massachusetts, had spread its influence over the whole Middle East, from India to the Mediterranean. And there is hardly an area of our culture today—in mathematics or philosophy, literature or architecture, finance or education, law or politics, religion or folklore—that does not owe some of its origins to the Sumerians.

One might suppose that the story of the Sumerians and their accomplishments would be one of the most celebrated in history. But the astonishing fact is that until about a century ago the modern world had no idea that Sumer or its people had ever existed. For more than 2,000 years they had simply vanished from the human record. Babylonia and ancient Egypt were known to every history student, but the earlier Sumerians were buried and forgotten. Now, thanks to a century of archaeological labor and to the Sumerians' own cuneiform tablets, we have come to know them intimately—as well as or better than any other people of the early history of mankind. The story of how the lost Sumerian civilization was discovered is itself a remarkable chapter. This article will review briefly how the history of the Sumerians was resurrected and what we have learned about them.

THE CUNEIFORM TABLETS.   Modern archaeologists began to dig in Mesopotamia for its ancient civilizations around a century ago. They were looking for the cities of the Assyrians and Babylonians, who of course were well known from Biblical and Greek literature. As the world knows, the diggers soon came upon incredibly rich finds. At the sites of Nineveh and other ancient Assyrian cities they unearthed many clay tablets inscribed with the wedge-shaped writing called cuneiform. This script was taken to be the invention of the Assyrians. Since the Assyrians were apparently a Semitic people, the language was assumed to be Semitic. But few clues were available for decipherment of the strange cuneiform script.

Then came a development which was to be as important a key to discovery in Mesopotamia as the famous Rosetta Stone in Egypt. In western Persia, notably on the Rock of Behistun, European scholars found some cuneiform inscriptions in three languages. They identified one of the languages as Old Persian, another as Elamite, and the third as the language of the Assyrian tablets. The way was now open to decipher the cuneiform writing—first the Old Persian, then the Assyrian, of which it was apparently a translation.

When scholars finally deciphered the "Assyrian" script, they discovered that the cuneiform writing could not have been originated by the Assyrian Semites. Its symbols, which were not alphabetic but syllabic and ideographic, apparently were derived from non-Semitic rather than Semitic words. And many of the cuneiform tablets turned out to be written in a language without any Semitic characteristics whatever. The archaeologists had to conclude, therefore, that the Assyrians had taken over the cuneiform script from a people who had lived in the region before them.

Who were this people? Jules Oppert, a leading 19th-century investigator of ancient Mesopotamia, found a clue to their name in certain inscriptions which referred to the "King of Sumer and Akkad." He concluded that Akkad was the northern part of the country (indeed, the Assyrians and Babylonians are now called Akkadians), and that Sumer was the southern part, inhabited by the people who spoke the non-Semitic language and had invented cuneiform writing.

So it was that the Sumerians were rediscovered after 2,000 years of oblivion. Oppert resurrected their name in 1869. In the following decades French, American, Anglo-American and German expeditions uncovered the buried Sumerian cities— Lagash, Nippur, Shuruppak, Kish, Ur (Ur of the Chaldees in the Bible), Erech, Asmar and so on. The excavation of ancient Sumer has proceeded almost continuously for three quarters of a century; even during World War II the Iraqi went on digging at a few sites. These historic explorations have recovered hundreds of thousands of Sumerian tablets, great temples, monuments, tombs, sculptures, paintings, tools, irrigation systems and remnants of almost every aspect of the Sumerian culture. As a result we have a fairly complete picture of what life in Sumer was like 5,000 years ago. We know something about how the Sumerians looked (from their statues); we know a good deal about their houses and palaces, their tools and weapons, their art and musical instruments, their jewels and ornaments, their skills and crafts, their industry and commerce, their *belles lettres* and government, their schools and temples, their loves and hates, their kings and history.

THE PEOPLES OF SUMER.   Let us run quickly over the history. The area where the Sumerians lived is lower Mesopotamia, from Baghdad down to the Persian Gulf. It is reasonably certain that the Sumerians themselves were not the first settlers in this region. Just as the Indian names Mississippi, Massachusetts, etc., show that North America was inhabited before the English-speaking settlers came, so we know that the Sumerians were preceded in Mesopotamia by another people because the ancient names of the Tigris and Euphrates rivers (*Indigna* and *Buranum*), and even the names of the Sumerian cities (Nippur, Ur, Kish, etc.), are not Sumerian words. The city names must be derived from villages inhabited by the earlier people.

The same kind of clue—words that turn up in the Sumerian writing but are plainly not Sumerian in origin—tells us something about those first settlers in Sumer. As Benno Landsberger of the University of Chicago, one of the keenest minds in cuneiform research, has shown, among these pre-Sumerian words are those for farmer, herdsman, fishermen, plow, metal smith, carpenter, weaver, potter, mason and perhaps even merchant. It follows that the predecessors of the Sumerians must already have developed a fairly advanced civilization. This is confirmed by excavations of their stone implements and pottery.

The dates of Sumer's early history have always been surrounded with uncertainty, and they have not been satisfactorily settled by tests with the new method of radiocarbon dating. According to the best present estimates, the first settlers occupied the area some time before 4000 B.C.; new geological evidence indicates that the lower Tigris-Euphrates Valley, once covered by the Persian Gulf, became an inhabitable land well before that date. Be that as it may, it seems that the people called Sumerians did not arrive in the region until nearly 3000 B.C. Just where they came from is in doubt, but there is some reason to believe that their original home had been in the neighborhood of a city called Aratta, which may have been near the Caspian Sea: Sumerian epic poets sang glowingly of Aratta, and its people were said to speak the Sumerian language.

Wherever the Sumerians came from, they brought a creative spirit and an extraordinary surge of progress to the land of Sumer. Uniting with the people who already inhabited it, they developed a rich and powerful civilization. Not long after they arrived, a king called Etana became the ruler of all Sumer: he is described in

Sumerian literature as "the man who stabilized all the lands," and he may therefore be the first empire builder in human history. Sumer reached its fullest flowering around 2500 B.C., when its people had developed the cuneiform symbols and thereby originated their finest gift to civilization—the gift of written communication and history. Their own history came to an end some 800 years later: about 1720 B.C. In that year Hammurabi of Babylon won control of the country, and Sumer disappeared in a Babylonian kingdom.

LIFE IN SUMER. The Sumerians' writings and disinterred cities, as I have said, make it possible to reconstruct their life in great detail. Their civilization rested on agriculture and fishing. Among their inventions were the wagon wheel, the plow and the sailboat, but their science and engineering went far beyond these elementary tools. For irrigation the Sumerians built intricate systems of canals, dikes, weirs and reservoirs. They developed measuring and surveying instruments, and a sexagesimal number system (*i.e.,* based on the number 60) with a place notation device not unlike our decimal system. Their farming was highly sophisticated: among their tablets is a veritable farmer's almanac of instructions in agriculture.

In the crafts, the Sumerians' inventions included the potter's wheel, metal casting (of copper and bronze), riveting, soldering, engraving, cloth fulling, bleaching and dyeing. They manufactured paints, leather, cosmetics, perfumes and drugs. Prescriptions recorded on some of their tablets show that the Sumerian physician had command of a large assortment of *materia medica,* prepared from plants, animals and inorganic sources.

Although the Sumerians' economy was primarily agricultural, their life was centered mainly in the cities. Here lived many of the farmers, herdsmen and fishermen, as well as merchants, craftsmen, architects, doctors, scribes, soldiers and priests. Artisans and traveling merchants sold their products in the central town market, and were paid in kind or in money—usually silver coin in the form of a disk or ring. The dozen or so cities in Sumer probably ranged from 10,000 to 50,000 in population. Each was enclosed by a wall and surrounded with suburban villages and hamlets.

The dominant feature of every Sumerian city was a massive temple mounted on a high terrace. It usually had the form of a ziggurat, Sumer's most distinctive contribution to religious architecture. This is a pyramidal tower with a series of ascending terraces winding around the outside. To break the unattractive blankness of the temple's mud-brick walls, the Sumerian architects introduced buttresses and recesses, and they also beautified the building with columns decorated in colored mosaics. Inside the temple were rooms for the priests and a central shrine with a niche for the statue of the god. Each city in Sumer had a different tutelary god, and the Sumerians considered the city the god's property. Thus the city of Nippur, for example, belonged to Enlil, the god of the air. Nippur became Sumer's chief religious and cultural center, and Enlil was elevated to the highest rank as father of all the gods.

Originally the cities were governed by the citizens themselves, presided over by a governor of their selection. On all important decisions the citizens met in an assembly divided into two chambers—the "elders" and the "men." But for military reasons they gradually relinquished this democratic system. Each city acquired a ruler—at first elected, later hereditary—who organized its defense against the other cities and against foreign invaders. In the course of time the king rivaled the city's religious leaders in wealth and influence. The rulers of Sumer's dozen or so city-states also contended with one another for control of the whole country, and the history of Sumer is largely a record of bitter conflicts among its cities, which eventually led to its downfall.

The life of the individual citizen in a Sumerian city was remarkably free and prosperous. The poorest citizen managed to own a farm and cattle or a house and garden. To be sure, slavery was permitted, and a man could sell his children or his entire family to pay off his debts. But even slaves had certain legal rights: they could engage in business, borrow money and buy their freedom. (The average price for an adult slave was 10 shekels—less than the price of an ass.) The great majority of Sumerians were free citizens, going about their business and the pursuit of happiness with a minimum of restrictions. This did not, however, apply to children, who were under the absolute authority of their parents, could be disinherited or sold into slavery, and had to marry mates chosen by the parents. But in the normal course of events Sumerian families cherished their children and were knit closely together by love and mutual obligations. Women had many legal rights, including the right to hold property and engage in business. A man could divorce his wife on comparatively slender grounds, or, if they had no children, he was allowed to take a second wife.

Most Sumerian families lived in a one-story, mud-brick house consisting of several rooms grouped around an open court. The well-to-do had two-story houses of about a dozen rooms, plastered and whitewashed inside and out; these houses boasted servants' rooms and sometimes even a private chapel. Often the house had a mausoleum in the basement where the family buried its dead. The Sumerians believed that the souls of the dead traveled to a nether world where existence continued more or less as on earth. They therefore buried pots, tools, weapons and jewels with the dead. When a king died, the palace sometimes buried with him some of his courtiers and servants and even his chariot and animals.

Sumerian men were often clean-shaven, but many of them wore a long beard and had long hair parted in the middle. In early times their usual dress was a flounced skirt and felt cloak; later these were replaced by a long shirt and a big fringed shawl draped over the left shoulder, leaving the right arm bare. The common dress for women was a long shawl covering the body from head to foot, except for the right shoulder. Women usually braided their hair into a heavy pigtail and wound it around the head, but on important occasions they were elaborate headdresses consisting of ribbons, beads and pendants.

Music apparently occupied a large place in the life of the Sumerians—at home, in school and in the temple. Beautifully constructed harps and lyres were found in the royal tombs at Ur. Research has also turned up references to drums, tambourines, reed and metal pipes, and hymns written on tablets. Some of the important personages in the palaces and temples of the Sumerian cities were musicians.

The Sumerians cannot be said to have produced any great art, but they did show considerable skill in carving and sculpture. Perhaps their most original contribution to the graphic arts was the cylinder seal—a stone cylinder with a carved design which was impressed in clay by rolling the cylinder over it. These designs, or seals, appear on clay tablets, jar covers and so on. They depict scenes such as a king on the battlefield, a shepherd defending his flock from wild beasts, heraldic arrangements of animals. Eventually the Sumerians settled on one favorite seal design which became almost their trademark—a scene showing a worshipper being presented to a god by his personal good angel.

RELIGION. The Sumerians lived by a simple, fatalistic theology. They believed that the universe and their personal lives were ruled by living gods, invisible to mortal eyes. The chief gods were those of water, earth, air and heaven, named respectively Enki, Ki, Enlil and An. From a primeval sea were created the earth, the atmosphere, the gods and sky, the sun, moon, planets and stars, and finally life. There were gods in charge of the sun, moon and planets, of winds and storms, of rivers and mountains, of cities and states, of farms and irrigation ditches, of the pickax, brick mold and plow. The major gods established a set of unchangeable laws which must be obeyed willy-nilly by everything and everybody. Thus the Sumerians were untroubled by any question of free will. Man existed to please and serve the gods, and his life followed their divine orders. Because the great gods were far away in the distant sky and had more important matters to attend to, each person appealed to a particular personal god, a "good angel," through whom he sought salvation. Not that the people neglected regular public devotions to the gods. In the Sumerian temples a court of professionals, including priests, priestesses, musicians and eunuchs, offered daily libations and sacrifices of animal and vegetable fats. There were also periodic feasts and celebrations of which the most important was a royal ceremony ushering in each new year.

This ceremony is traceable to the cycle of nature in Mesopotamia. Every summer, in the hot, parched months, all vegetation died and animal life languished. In the autumn the land began to revive and bloom again. The Sumerian theology explained these events by supposing that the god of vegetation retired to the nether world in the summer and returned to the earth around the time of the new year; his sexual reunion with his wife Inanna, the goddess of love and procreation, then restored fertility to the land. To celebrate this revival and ensure fecundity, the Sumerians each year staged a marriage ceremony between their king, as the risen god, and a priestess representing the goddess Inanna. The marriage was made an occasion of prolonged festival, ritual, music and rejoicing.

The Sumerians considered themselves to be a chosen people, in more intimate contact with the gods than was the rest of mankind. Nevertheless they had a moving vision of all mankind living in peace and security, united by a universal faith and perhaps even by a universal language. Curiously, they projected this vision into the past, into a long-gone golden age, rather than into the future. As a Sumerian poet put it:

> Once upon a time there was no snake, there was no scorpion,
> There was no hyena, there was no lion,
> There was no wild dog, no wolf
> There was no fear, no terror,
> Man had no rival.
>
> Once upon a time . . .
> The whole universe, the people in unison,
> To Enlil in one tongue gave praise.

To students of the ancient religions of the Near East, much of the Sumerian cosmology and theology is easily recognizable. The order of the universe's creation, the Job-like resignation of sinful and mortal man to the will of the gods, the mystic tale of the dying god and his triumphant resurrection, the Aphrodite-like goddess Inanna, the ideals of "humaneness"—these and many other features of the Sumerian creed survive without much change in the later religions of the ancient world. Indeed, the very name of the Sumerian dying god, Dumuzi, endures as Biblical Tammuz, whose descent to the nether regions was still mourned by the women of Jerusalem in the days of the prophet Ezekiel. It is not too much to say that, with the decipherment of the Sumerian tablets, we can now trace many of the roots of man's major religious creeds back to Sumer.

CUNEIFORM. But the Sumerians' chief contribution to civilization was their invention of writing. Their cuneiform script is the earliest known system of writing in man's history. The cuneiform system served as the main tool of written communication throughout western Asia for some 2,000 years—long after the Sumerians themselves had disappeared. Without it, mankind's cultural progress would certainly have been much delayed.

The Sumerian script began as a set of pictographic signs devised by temple administrators and priests to keep track of the temple's resources and activities. They inscribed the signs in clay with a reed stylus, and this accounts for the curious wedge-shaped characters. In the course of the centuries Sumerian scholars developed the signs into purely phonetic symbols representing words or syllables.

More than 90 per cent of the tablets that have been excavated in Sumer are economic, legal and administrative documents, not unlike the commercial and governmental records of our own day. But some 5,000 of the finds are literary works; myths and epic tales, hymns and lamentations, proverbs, fables, essays. They qualify as man's oldest known literature—nearly 1,000 years older than the *Iliad* and the Hebrew Bible. In addition the tablets include a number of Sumerian "textbooks," listing the names of trees, birds, insects, minerals, cities, countries and so forth. There are even commemorative narratives which constitute mankind's first writing of history.

From the Sumerians' invention of writing grew the first formal system of education—another milestone in human intellectual progress. They set up "professional" schools to train scribes, secretaries and administrators; in time these vocational schools became also centers of culture where scholars, scientists and poets devoted their lives to learning and teaching.

The head of the school was called "the school father"; the pupils, "school sons." Among the faculty members were "the man in charge of drawing," "the man in charge of Sumerian," "the man in charge of the whip." There was no sparing of the rod. The curriculum consisted in copying and memorizing the lists of words and names on the textbook tablets, in studying and composing poetic narratives, hymns and essays and in mastering mathematical tables and problems, including tables of square and cube roots.

Teachers in ancient Sumer seem to have been treated not unlike their counterparts in the U. S. today: their salaries were low and they were looked upon with a mixture of respect and contempt. The Sumerians were an aggressive people, prizing wealth, renown and social prestige: As their tablets suggest, they were far more concerned with accounts than with academic learning.

Their restless ambition and aggressive spirit are reflected in the bitter rivalry among their cities and kings. The history of Sumer is a story of wars in which one city after another rose to ascendancy over the country. Although there are many gaps in our information, we can reconstruct the main outlines of that history from references in the tablets. The first recorded ruler of Sumer, as I have mentioned, was Etana, king of Kish. Probably not long afterward a king of Erech by the name of Meskiaggasher founded a dynasty which ruled the whole region from the Mediterranean to the Zagros Mountains northeast of Sumer. The city of Kish then rose to dominance again, only to be supplanted by the city of Ur, whose first king, Mesannepadda, is said to have ruled for 80 years and made Ur the capital of Sumer.

After Mesannepadda's death, Sumer again came under the rule of the city of Erech, under a king named Gilgamesh who became the supreme hero of Sumerian history—a brave, adventurous figure whose deeds were celebrated throughout the ancient world of western Asia. The next great ruler who appears in the record was Lugalannemundu of the city of Adab; he is reported to have ruled 90 years and to have controlled an empire extending far beyond Sumer. But his empire also fell apart, and a king of Kish named Mesilim became the dominant figure in Sumer. Later rule over the country was won by the city of Lagash. The last ruler of the Lagash dynasty, a king named Urukagina, has the distinction of being the first recorded social reformer. He suppressed the city's harsh bureaucracy, reduced taxes, and brought relief to widows, orphans and the poor. One of King Urukagina's inscriptions contains the word "freedom"—the first appearance of this word in man's history. But within less than 10 years a king of the neighboring city of Umma overthrew Urukagina and put the city of Lagash to the torch.

THE FALL OF SUMER.   The cities' incessant struggle for power exhausted Sumer. A Semitic people from the west, under the famous warrior Sargon the Great, marched into the country and established a new dynasty. Sargon founded a capital called Agade (from which came the name Akkadian) and made it the richest and most powerful city in the Middle Eastern world. He conquered almost all of western Asia and perhaps also parts of Egypt and Ethiopia. Sargon's sons held on to the empire, but his grandson, Naramsin, brought Sumer to disaster. For reasons unknown, he destroyed the holy city of Nippur, and soon afterward he was defeated by semibarbaric invaders from the mountains of Iran who overran Sumer and completely wiped out the city of Agade.

It took the Sumerians several generations to recover. But their civilization did come to life again, under a governor of Lagash named Gudea, whose face is the best known to us of all the Sumerians because a score of statues of him have been found in the ancient temples of Lagash. Gudea re-established contacts and trade with the rest of the known world and put Sumer on the path to prosperity. After Gudea, however, the rivalry among its cities broke out again and became Sumer's final undoing. The city of Ur, under a king named Ur-Nammu, defeated Lagash; Ur-Nammu founded a new rule called the Third Dynasty of Ur. It was to be Sumer's last dynasty.

Ur-Nammu was a strong and benevolent ruler. According to inscriptions that have recently come to light, he removed "chiselers" and grafters and established a law code which insured honest weights and measures and took care that the poor should not "fall a prey to the wealthy." Ur-Nammu's code is especially significant for the fact that instead of the barbarous rule of "an eye for an eye and a tooth for a tooth" common among early societies it established a money fine as punishment for assaults.

In spite of Sumers' civilized kings and prosperity, time was running out for the Sumerians. Their internal rivalries and the growing pressure of surrounding peoples soon overwhelmed them. Semitic nomads from the Arabian desert to the west (the Amorites of the Bible) took over the Sumerian cities of Isin, Larsa and Babylon. Ur itself was conquered by the Elamites to the east, who carried off its last king, Ibbi-Sin. In the following two and a half centuries the Semitic rulers of Isin and Larsa, and then Larsa and Babylon, struggled for control of the country. Finally, in about the year 1720 B.C., Hammurabi defeated Rim-Sin, the last king of Larsa, and Babylon emerged as the dominant city of southern Mesopotamia. The Sumerians were submerged by the Semites and lost their identity as a people. In time their name was erased from the memory of man; the Sumerian language disappeared as a living, spoken tongue, though for centuries it continued to be the written language studied in schools.

The Sumerians firmly believed that when man died, his emasculated spirit descended to a dark, dreary world. The spirit and fame of this proud, vigorous people certainly suffered a remarkable eclipse after their empire fell. But what their minds created survives throughout the living corpus of present-day civilization: it appears in the form of a Biblical proverb, a statutory law, a heroic folktale, an Aesopic fable, a zodiacal sign, a Euclidean theorem, the weight of a coin, the degree of an angle. And in the cuneiform tablets which were the Sumerians' pre-eminent gift we have found the earliest intellectual record of man's strivings toward civilization.

8   INDIA'S FORGOTTEN CIVILIZATION

After the appearance of the first civilization in the Tigris-Euphrates valley, others emerged elsewhere in Eurasia, including Egypt, Crete, India and China. Each of these had its distinctive style, as evident in the following description of the Indus Valley civilization. This was contemporary to, though far more extensive than, those of Mesopotamia and Egypt. It flourished in relative isolation for approximately a thousand years (2500–1500 B.C.) before disintegrating under circumstances that are not altogether clear. This civilization was then completely forgotten until the 1920's, when archaeologists began to dig in certain mysterious mounds in a desolate area called by the local people Mohenjo-Daro, or Place of the Dead. The excavations here, and in other localities along the Indus River valley, revealed the existence of this long-dead civilization. Much remains obscure, however, awaiting further excavations and the decipherment of the few remaining examples of the local script. The current state of knowledge is set forth in this account by a well-known British archaeologist.*

When we think of the birthplace of civilization, we are apt to think only of Babylonia and Egypt. It was in the valleys of the Tigris-Euphrates and of the Nile, the archaeologists say, that agriculture began and mankind built the first villages, the first cities and the first kingdoms—Sumer and Egypt. Few people realize that there was a third great kingdom which rose and flourished side by side with them at the same time. This nameless and forgotten empire of antiquity, occupying the Indus Valley in western India, was far larger and more tightly ruled than Sumer or Egypt. It is nameless, and much less known than the other two, only because its language has not yet been deciphered and the remains of its writings cannot be read. Archaeologists hope that the code may some day be broken, as the hieroglyphics of ancient Egypt were deciphered, by discovery of a bilingual inscription— a Rosetta Stone of the Indus Valley. Until that momentous event, the story of this ancient Indian civilization must remain as incomplete as a silent picture. But the

* Reprinted from S. Piggott, "A Forgotten Empire of Antiquity," *Scientific American* (November 1953), pp. 43–48, with permission. Copyright © 1953 by Scientific American, Inc. All rights reserved.

archaeological evidence tells enough to enable us to compare this culture with the more fully documented civilizations of Sumer and Egypt.

The study is a vital and exciting one, for it concerns the history of human ideas. Here in western Asia there rose three parallel but separate civilizations. In all three, technology followed much the same sequence: the invention of writing (that "incidental by-product of a strong sense of private property," as the U. S. archaeologist Ephraim Speiser so pleasantly put it), the development of skill in working bronze and precious metals, the evolution of architecture from mud huts to palaces, the growth of transport and trade and the rise of centralized government. Yet while the technological development of the three empires was nearly identical, their intellectual concepts and forms of society were very different. With respect to the peoples of Sumer and Egypt, we can read their differences of thought in their literature, and in the Indus Valley we can read it in the archaeological record of the people's way of life. For the Indus civilization had a unique individuality of its own, already marked with some of the features of what was to become the characteristic Hindu culture of historic India. The comparative study of these three earliest civilizations shows how varied were the intellectual means whereby mankind found ways to create and maintain a stable society.

Archaeologists have named the Indus kingdom the Harappa Civilization, after a modern village which stands on the site of one of the great ancient towns. The Harappa Civilization had developed from a peasant to an urban culture by about 2500 B.C., and it endured for at least a thousand years before it was destroyed by invaders. It was a nation based on cities, towns and villages, with a Bronze Age technology and a central government strong enough to keep the peace and organize the economy for the common welfare.

Like the other ancient civilizations, it was centered on a river system—that of the Indus and its tributaries. But it was enormously larger, at least seven times bigger in area than the kingdom of Sumer. Two great cities and some 60 to 70 towns, villages and trading posts have already been unearthed, and more are likely to reward diggers in the future. The Harappa empire apparently covered a triangle stretching from a 600-mile seaboard at the base to an apex in the Himalayan foothills nearly 1,000 miles away. Its two cities stood like twin capitals 400 miles apart on the river system; they were at the sites now occupied by Mohenjo-Daro (the Mounds of the Dead) on the Indus and Harappa on the Ravi tributary. The cities were roughly square, and probably each about one square mile in area. We can only guess at their population: probably the cities had some 20,000 inhabitants each and the emipre as a whole a population of at least 70,000 to 100,000.

The cities and towns show every evidence of a culture at least as far advanced as that of the neighboring civilizations to the west. Though they had no stone palaces, their buildings were of brick, which, in response to the climate of monsoon rains, was baked hard in the modern manner, instead of being sundried as elsewhere in the ancient East. The Harappa people did metalwork in copper and bronze, created jewelry of gold and semiprecious stones, wove cotton cloth, made pottery, used wheeled vehicles and were widely literate.

Even a superficial survey of the material culture of the Harappa Civilization shows that we are not dealing with a loose confederacy of city-states, each with its local customs, but with a highly organized kingdom directed by a strong central government according to a carefully planned scheme. The two major cities are very much alike and appear to have spoken with a single voice. Throughout the area there was a remarkable uniformity of products: pottery was mass-produced and the baked bricks were of standard sizes. Indeed, the weights and measures of the

Harappa empire seem to have been regulated to a degree of accuracy unknown elsewhere in the ancient world.

There is little archaeological evidence as to the origins of the Harappa Civilization; we know it only as a fully developed empire. Probably its beginnings stemmed from the region to the northwest some time in the Fourth Millennium B.C. But its development was entirely independent, and even at its height the Harappa kingdom had only sporadic and small-scale trading contacts with Sumer and none at all with the Egyptian empire.

The most remarkable fact about the known history of the Harappa Civilization is its stability and conservatism. For a thousand years, from its arrival at a state of maturity about 2500 B.C., there was almost no significant change, as far as the archaeological record shows. Through all those centuries the culture stood still in an arrested state of development: its script, its pottery, its architecture, its sculpture and seal-engraving, its curiously primitive metal tools—all these remained the same. There are no signs of disturbance by dynastic change or warfare. From time to time the town at Mohenjo-Daro was destroyed by floods, and after each inundation the city was rebuilt exactly as before, even to the same line for the house fronts along the streets. Such immemorial conservatism, such unwavering continuity of tradition, is unparalleled elsewhere in the ancient world, even in Egypt.

When the end did come, it came quickly, and to a people unprepared to defend their long-established civilization against attack from outside. Though the two great cities boasted walled citadels, we find there no sign of weapons such as might equip an army and no evidence of military battles or resistance. Somewhere around 1500 B.C. warrior bands from the west simply overran the kingdom. The urban civilization of the Harappa world ended and was replaced by scattered barbarian farmsteads.

What were the distinctive qualities of this enduring but fragile civilization? For one thing, their writing was unusual for the ancient world. It consisted of a stiff hieroglyphic script with a total of about 400 characters, nearly half of which were variants on a basic 250 or so. This relatively small number of signs in a non-alphabetic language implies an advanced stage in the craft of writing—the earliest writing in Sumer, for instance, had 2,000 signs. The samples of Harappa writing that have been found are mainly engraved stone seals which, as elsewhere in the ancient world, seem to have been used to identify personal property. The Harappa script was pictographic (apparently there was no cursive form), and the longest inscriptions discovered do not exceed 20 characters. Thus even when the Harappa writings are deciphered, they will not give us a lost literature. But to know to what language group they can be assigned will be of great importance.

The Harappa scale of weights was curious and without parallel. The unit was equivalent to 13.64 grams (a little less than half an ounce.) But the scale defining multiples of the unit was calculated in a peculiar way: the unit itself was the ratio 16, and at the lower end of the scale the multiples were binary (doubling each time), while the heavier weights were reckoned in decimal multiples. Thus the weights ran in the ratio 1, 2, 8/3, 4, 8, 16, 32, 64, 160, 200 320, 640 and so on. Fractions of a unit were expressed in thirds. This sequence has been deduced from a number of cubical stone weights found at sites in the Harappa kingdom. Unlike other peoples of antiquity, the Harappans seem to have stuck to their weight system with considerable precision, and the enforcement of the standard over so wide an area suggests careful control and inspection.

The Harappa people also used exact linear measurements. They had two units— a foot of 13.2 inches and a cubit of 20.62 inches. Investigators have found actual

Harappa rules, engraved on shell and on bronze, and by check measurements on buildings have ascertained that the units were accurately followed. The Harappa foot and cubit units were the same as those used in other empires of the ancient Orient, which suggests that they came from a common source.

The centralization of authority which the uniformity of weights and measures and of mass-produced products in the Harappa empire bespeaks is even more insistently expressed in the cities themselves. At Mohenjo-Daro enough has been recovered of the town plan to show that it was conceived and laid out as a conscious civic creation from the start; the city was not the rabbit warren typical of the ancient (and much of the modern) Orient. A grid of streets, some of them 30 feet wide, divided the square city into 12 major blocks. Each measured some 1,200 by 800 feet (roughly six times the size of a typical block in New York City). The houses were set closely together, and on the street side they presented blank walls without any architectural embellishment except their doorways. In back they faced interior courtyards and were separated by lanes and alleyways. The dwellings were extremely well built of fired brick, and their walls seem to have been plastered and painted inside and out. They had bathrooms with paved floors, and drains leading to a main sewer system beneath the streets, where manholes covered by large tiles gave access for cleaning. In the walls were rubbish chutes opening into brick bins. The whole system shows a concern for sanitation and cleanliness, and a civic organization to that end, unique in oriental antiquity.

The houses generally did not vary greatly in size, suggesting no more inequalities in wealth than one would expect to find in a middle-class population of shopkeepers, craftsmen and merchants. But in both major cities there were separate blocks of two-room cottages which apparently were the quarters of manual workers—a supposition which is reinforced by the fact that at Harappa this housing stood hard by a group of circular corn-grinding platforms and a great communal granary.

The dominant feature of each city was its citadel, a massive rectangular platform at least 50 feet high. At Mohenjo-Daro this structure appears to have occupied one of the central blocks on the western side of the grid. The citadel at Harappa seems to have been similarly placed, but its position is less certain because the city is much less well preserved than its twin and has been badly plundered for its brick. The citadel platforms were built of mud brick with walls of burnt brick. Terraced ways led up to their gates, and the citadels were topped by rectangular bastions and angle-towers.

At Mohenjo-Daro the granary was within the citadel walls; there are still remnants of the loading platforms built to handle the grain. Of the buildings that stood on the citadel platform the most remarkable was an open bath about 8 feet deep and 40 feet long by 24 feet wide. The bath was surrounded by a veranda and changing-rooms and had steps leading down into it. Near it was a large building with a cloistered court and a pillared hall some 80 feet square. There was also a building, possibly a temple, which unfortunately is now almost obliterated by a Buddhist monastery later built on the site. And there were buildings similar in plan to the dwellings of the town. But none of the structures in the citadel could be interpreted as a palace.

These citadels, with their monumental walls, gateways, approach ramps and special buildings, must have been the seats of the centralized power of the Harappa Civilization. What was the source of the rulers' extraordinary authority? Clearly it was not primarily the force of arms, for no sign of any distinctively military equipment has been found in the kingdom. One can guess that their authority was spiritual. The conservative uniformity of the culture and the peaceful coexistence of the two major cities suggest that the kingdom was ruled by men who were priests before they were kings. The art and architecture of the Harappa Civilization look very much like precursors of the Hindu culture: nothing could be more characteristic of a Hindu sacred site than the great bath or "tank" at Mohenjo-Daro. On an engraved seal found in the same city is a figure which is easily recognizable as the prototype of Siva, one of the Hindu divinities. There are a hundred similar indications. All the archaeological evidence suggests that the Harappa polity was a theocracy ruled by priest-kings from sacred citadels, as Tibet is ruled today from the Potala at Lhasa and from Shigatse.

With ancient Egypt and Babylonia, the Harappa Civilization in India takes its place as the third area where urban civilization was born in the Old World. Like the others, it was based on a common stock of peasant skills acquired in little corn-growing, cattle-breeding communities, such as had grown up during the fifth and fourth millennia B.C. in many regions between the Nile and the Indus. But the Harappa people, like those of Egypt and Sumer, worked out their own distinctive and arresting variant of an urban civilization.

The very qualities that enabled the Harappa Civilization to endure unchanged for a thousand years apparently were responsible for its quick collapse at the end. Its peaceful, delicately adjusted economy could not survive an invasion. The invaders probably were the Indo-European tribes (the originators of the languages which were to become Sanskrit and Iranian) who began to migrate eastward from the Western rim of Asia soon after 2000 B.C. These horse-driving squires and cattle drovers trampled out the Harappa culture, and a Dark Age of comparative barbarism ensued. But the Harappa Civilization was not completely extinguished, and from the new mixture of peoples and ideas came the traditions which molded historic Hinduism.

Chapter Six

End of ancient civilizations

INDIAN AND GREEK EPICS   **9**

Both Greece and India were invaded in the second millennium B.C. *by Indo-European peoples—the Achaeans and the Dorians in the one case, and the Aryans in the other. These newcomers disrupted the indigenous Minoan and Indus Valley civilizations, substituting new agricultural, tribal, and comparatively primitive societies. These new societies are depicted in their respective epics—Homer's* Iliad *and* Odyssey, *and the* Vedas. *The following comparative study of these epics by a professor of Sanskrit literature at Xavier College, Calcutta, points out their similarities, reflecting their common social background, though it should be noted that differences also existed, arising from contrasting temperaments and perspectives.**

THE GENERAL PATTERN OF HEROIC SOCIETY. All the great heroic traditions owe their existence to tribal culture. The basis on which tribal society rests is the principle of kinship and its social unit is the family group. Whereas the higher culture of the territorial state is founded on the idea of individual citizenship and gives rise to urban civilization, the tribal organization ignores national feeling and finds its social expression in feudalism. Feudalism is essentially an exchange of services between defenseless peasants and the military lord. In return for the protection which the lord gives them, the peasants offer him their land and promise to man his armies. When, to the economic necessity of finding a protector, is added the element of personal devotion to the leader, the cult of the hero is born.

On the other hand, epic poetry is usually retrospective. It develops at a time

* Reprinted from R. Antoine, "Indian and Greek Epics" in *Approaches to the Oriental Classics,* ed. W. T. de Bary (New York: Columbia University Press, 1959), pp. 96–112.

when tribal society enters into contact with a higher civilization and tends to project into the past certain elements of urban culture which give to the old capitals an anachronic aspect of modernity. It is this marginal character of epic poetry which explains how tribal heroes can gradually be transformed into national heroes.

It is interesting to note how epic poetry, in three different historical contexts, blossomed at an intermediary period, a kind of "Middle Ages" between two urban civilizations. In India, after the disappearance of the Indus civilization and before the rise of the Mauriyas; in Greece, after the decline of Aegean culture and before the emergence of Athenian dominance; in Europe, after the fall of the Roman Empire and of the short-lived Carolingian renaissance and before the urban civilization of the fourteenth century.

1. The aristocrats at war. Heroic society is an aristocratic society. In the Greek epic, the heroes are called the *"aristoi,"* i.e., the best among men. Stereotyped adjectives are used, referring probably to some well-known quality of some ancestor, and the name of the father or a patronymic *"taddhitānta"* continually reminds us that nobility is hereditary. The feuds which result in bloody battles have never the character of national wars in which the common people play the prominent part. In fact, the common people do not appear at all except as a necessary background against which the valor and prowess of the heroes stand out in greater splendor. Most of the fights are single fights, extraordinary duels witnessed by a crowd of spellbound soldiers and retainers.

The origin of the great battles is, in all cases, the personal offense of a hero's honor. And it is generally a woman who supplies the occasion. In the *Iliad,* it is self-evident. The Greek tribes, personified in their leaders, agree to avenge the honor of Menelaus whose wanton wife has eloped with the Trojan Paris. There is not the slightest hint of a national campaign, and the leadership of Agamemnon has no other reason than the necessity of a concerted attack. Again, it is the wounded pride of Achilles which proves fatal to the Greek armies and brings the Trojans within an ace of victory. The young lady whom Achilles had received as a prize for his bravery is arbitrarily taken away from him by Agamemnon. Finally, if Achilles decided to enter the fray, it is not out of a sense of solidarity with the routed Greeks, but of the purely personal desire to avenge his friend's death. National feeling, if it exists at all in the *Iliad,* is to be found among the Trojans. For them, everything is at stake, as it will be for the Greeks at the time of Marathon and Salamis. Yet, in spite of the simple solution of returning to her lawful husband the woman who is the cause of their extreme misfortune, they choose to fight because the Greeks have challenged them. It is a question of *panache* and it overrides the security of the city.

The tragedy of the *Rāmāyana* begins with the foolish claim of a vain woman, Kaikeyī. King Dasaratha who knows her claim to be unreasonable considers himself bound by the sacred duty of keeping his word. The welfare of his subjects and their undisguised disapproval count for nothing before his misconceived obligation toward Bharata's mother. And thus Rāma, Sītā, and Lakshmana leave for the forest. Bharata is the only one whose attitude must have made sense to the more enlightened. But his efforts are all in vain. The capture of Sītā by Rāvana constitutes a lesser national problem than Helen's elopement, for the people of Ayodhyā have nothing to do in rescuing her. It is a personal injury to Rāma who, instead of calling on his own people to fight with him for their beloved princess, gets involved in the family dispute of a monkey tribe and gains the allegiance of the winning side. After Rāvana's defeat and recovery of Sītā, it may be argued that Rāma gives up the arbitrary rule of feudal lord and rates very high the feelings and opinions of his subjects. The fire ordeal and the second banishment of Sītā are undeniable proofs of his new policy. Yet, one wonders if that new policy heralds the dawn of a new era. It is so much in keeping with Rāma's submissiveness at the time of his banishment. Rightly has Rāma been given as the ideal of the "shānta" hero and one aspect of his love for peace seems to be that trouble should be avoided at any cost: neither his right to the throne, nor his absolute conviction that Sītā is innocent can arouse in him the passion necessary to resist the trouble-makers.

The destinies of the Pāndavas and the Kauravas are decided in a game of dice. This is typical of a feudal setting where the rulers dispose of their kingdoms as they would of their private fortunes. The overbearing pride of the winners and the spiteful humiliation of the losers reaches its climax in the Draupadī incident. It is around the ill-used Draupadī that the personal antagonism of the feudal lords crystallizes. The terrible imprecation of Bhīma against Duhshāsana, "I shall split his breast and drink his blood" (*Mahābhārata,* Sabhaparva, 90.57), is the real declaration of war and the long exile will be unable to delete its memory. Its gruesome realization can easily bear comparison with the savage profanation of Hector's body at the hands of Achilles.

After the exile, when the Pāndavas delegate Krishna to Duryodhana in order to reach a compromise, it is Draupadī, with her untied hair as a perpetual reminder of her humiliation, who passionately opposes all kinds of peaceful settlement. The way in which Krishna conducts the interview with the leader of the Kauravas is strongly influenced by the bellicose attitude of Pāncālī.

2. The aristocrats in peace time. Success in war being at the same time the condition of survival and the highest glory to which the heroes aspire, it is quite natural to see the young aristocrats apply themselves enthusiastically to their military training. Under the wise guidance of Drona, the young Pāndavas and Kauravas vie with one another in the display of their skill, while the elders and a crowd of simple admirers look on with immense delight. Their loud acclamation fills the air (*Hahābhārata,* Adi-parva, 144.39).

In the *Rāmāyana,* young Rāma receives his training from Vishvāmitra. The expedition against the demons is not just a game but is meant to give Rāma an idea of the evil forces with which he will have to grapple in his maturity. Homer has not depicted the early training of his heroes. Old Phoenix, however, gives us a glimpse of Achilles' education. Pleading with the sulking hero, Phoenix tells him: "My noble Lord Achilles, if you really think of sailing home and are so obsessed by anger that you refuse to save the gallant ships from going up in flames, what is to become of me without you, my dear child? How could I possibly stay there alone? Did not the old charioteer Pelus make me your guardian when he sent you off from Phthia to join Agamemnon? You were a mere lad, with no experience of the hazards of war, nor of debate, where people make their mark. It was to teach you all these things, to make a speaker of you, and a man of action, that he sent me with you; and I could not bring myself to let you go, dear child, and to stay behind, not if God himself undertook to strip me of my years and turn me into the sturdy youngster I was when I first left Hellas, the land of lovely women." (*Iliad,* Rieu trans. [Penguin], Book X, p. 172.)

Skill and strength are the necessary qualities of warriors. But these qualities have also a social importance which cannot be ignored. They are rated so high that a king is ready to give his daughter in marriage to the strongest, irrespective of the caste to which he belongs. Dhrishtadyumna, brother of Draupadī solemnly declares: "Be he a brahmin or a king or a merchant or a shūdra, he who will string this excellent bow will get my sister in marriage." (*Mahābhārata,* Adi-parva, 203.19–20.)

Sītā is won by Rāma because he alone can bend the bow. Draupadī is won by Arjuna for the same reason. Arjuna, to avoid detection, had come in the guise of a brahmin. The amusing scene describing the misgivings of the brahmins as one of them rises to perform a feat which the well-trained princes were unable to accomplish makes us guess the pride and joy they felt when Arjuna defeated the kings at their own game. At the end of the *Odyssey,* Ulysses, having reached Ithaca after his long peregrinations, finds his place occupied by the suitors. Penelope, prompted by Athena, decides to put them to the test: "Listen, my lords, you have fastened on this house in the long absence of its master, as the scene of your perpetual feasts, and you could offer no better pretext for your conduct than your wish to win my hand in marriage. That being the prize, come forward now, my gallant lords; for I challenge you to try your skill on the great bow of King Ulysses. And whichever man among you proves the handiest at stringing the bow and shoots an arrow through everyone of these twelve axes, with that man I will go, bidding goodbye to this house which welcomed me as a bride." The suitors fail. No doubt, they are grieved at the loss of Penelope, but, as Eurymachus puts it, "What does grieve me more is the thought that our failure with his bow proves us such weaklings compared with the godlike Ulysses. The disgrace will stick to our names for ever." Like Arjuna, Ulysses appears unrecognized and humbly asks to be allowed to test the strength of his hands. The suitors are annoyed: "We don't want the common folk to be saying things like this, 'A poor lot, these; not up to the fine gentleman whose wife they want to marry! *They* can't string his bow. But in comes some casual tramp, strings the bow with the greatest ease and shoots through all the marks!' That is the kind of thing they will say; and our reputation might suffer." (*Odyssey,* Rieu trans. [Penguin], Book XXII, pp. 317–18, 324.) We live here in the same world and breathe the same atmosphere as in Drupada's palace and Janaka's capital.

3. *The aristocrats facing the mystery of life.* Life in the Epic Age was essentially active. Games, gambling, conquests, and military campaigns kept the heroes occupied, while the recital by bards of the glorious deeds of their ancestors gave an ever new luster to the flame of chivalry. Before the compilation of the main epic narratives as we have them today, there must have existed a great number of independent lays celebrating different families or dynasties. The *Mahābhārata* contains a great wealth of such stories quoted as examples to the heroes. The *Iliad* and the *Odyssey,* though less rich than the *Mahābhārata,* use the same device and the Greek tragedy testifies to the existence of numerous epic cycles not incorporated in the works of Homer. The teaching which appealed to the knights of old was a concrete teaching which left out abstruse speculations. It may be reasonably surmised that Arjuna and the Krishna of the *Bhagavad Gītā* belong to a later age when speculation had taken precedence over action.

In fact, a life of action has its own problems. Man realizes that his plans are often thwarted and that he is not the sovereign master of his destiny. There are mysterious forces at work which must be reckoned with. Above all, the great mystery of death is ever present in the precarious life of warriors. The heroic mentality acknowledges the presence of the mystery, is deeply impressed by it, but does not attempt to give it an abstract solution.

In the face of the mystery of life with its passions, its failures, its cruelty, the hero, while feeling responsible for his actions, knows that the divine power ordains and guides everything. To our rationalistic minds, his position may seem to be illogical: either one is a fatalist and denies human freedom and responsibility, or one believes in freedom and denies the supreme power of fate. But our argument would not disturb the hero's belief. It is reality which interests him and reality is complex. The human and divine words are not juxtaposed, they intermingle so intimately that to consider one apart from the other destroys the very texture of reality. It is the divine world which gives to human existence its third dimension and makes of it a living and full-blooded tragedy. Who would be so devoid of sensitivity as to affirm that the epic heroes are mere marionettes activated by the mechanical device of a hidden magician?

Naturalism which has cut off human life from its mysterious roots and claims to explain everything by an analysis of superficial psychology would have made our heroes smile. They knew better and the modern tendency to reaffirm the mystery is much closer to the heroic mentality than the so-called realism of the last century. It is not without significance that depth psychology borrows from the epic some of its most important symbolism. The inner mystery it tries to penetrate may not be without connection with the transcendent mystery which the heroes of old acknowledged with awe and trembling.

Death, the lurking and inevitable menace, is a constant reminder of life's precarious stability. Sadly recalling the forebodings of defeat in a long and beautiful threnody, old King Dhritarāshtra, in a crescendo of despair punctuated by the recurring refrain "tadā nashamse vijayāya Sanjaya," concludes by expressing his desire to leave this fruitless existence: "O Sanjaya, since life is such my desire is to die without delay, for I do not see the slightest advantage in keeping alive." (*Mahābhārata*, Adi-parva, i. 245.)

In true epic fashion, Sanjaya replies by quoting the examples of hundreds of kings and warriors, far superior to the Kaurava princes, who have lived, fought, and died. Their death takes nothing away from their fame and valor, and life is worth living as long as fate does not snatch it away. Sanjaya does not speculate about future life or rebirth, he states the mystery of life and death and accepts it as a matter of fact: "There is no reason to lament over what is to be. Who can, through endeavor, change the course of fate? Time is the root of everything, of life and death, of happiness and adversity." (*Mahābhārata*, Adi-parva, i. 271–72.)

In the *Iliad,* the scene between Hector and Andromache has the same message to convey. Andromache is frightened by the bellicose enthusiasm of her husband: "Hector, you are possessed. This bravery of yours will be your end. You do not think of your little boy and of your unhappy wife, whom you will make a widow soon. Some day the Achaeans are bound to kill you in a massed attack. And when I lose you I might as well be dead. There will be no comfort left, when you have met your doom—nothing but grief." Hector is not indifferent to his wife's appeal. He loves his son and his wife dearly. Yet, he is a warrior and fate calls him to battle. "My dear, I beg you not to be too much distressed. No one is going to send me down to Hades before my proper time. But Fate is a thing that no man born of woman, coward or hero, can escape. Go home now, and attend to your own work, the loom and the spindle, and see that the maidservants go on with theirs. War is men's business; and this war is the business of every man in Ilium, myself above all." (*Iliad,* Book VI, pp. 128–29.)

CLASSICAL

CIVILIZATIONS

OF EURASIA,

1000 B.C. – A.D. 500

Chapter Seven

Incipient Eurasian ecumene

Expanding Horizons of the Classical World **10**

One of the fundamental differences between the ancient and classical civilizations was in their range. The ancient civilizations were all confined to their respective river valleys and largely isolated from each other by the surrounding sea of barbarism. The classical civilizations, by contrast, stretched across entire regions and had direct contact with each other. During the first century after Christ, for example, the Roman, Parthian, Kushan and Han empires spanned without any break the entire breadth of Eurasia from the Scottish Highlands to the China Seas. Thus during the Classical Age there existed for the first time a Eurasian entity or ecumene.

This ecumene was still at the incipient stage. The interaction and mutual knowledge of the various regions was rudimentary. The Homeric Greeks, for example, knew only the Middle East; Alexander knew also of India but not of China; the Chinese had heard vaguely of Rome as the place of origin of exotic products such as glass, "stone wool" (asbestos), and "night-shining jewel" (fluorspar). The Classical Age, then, was a period of expanding horizons, but the resulting ecumenism remained at the incipient stage; it did not reach fruition until medieval times.

An example of the expanding horizons of these centuries is to be found in Reading 15, "A Chinese View of India, Seventh Century A.D." The following selection is from the Histories *of Polybius, a Greek writer who, in describing the course of events from 220 to 145 B.C., was impressed by the fact that the Romans had conquered "nearly the whole inhabited world," and hence concluded that "from this time forth History becomes a connected whole: the affairs of Italy and Libya are involved with those of Asia and Greece, and the tendency of all is to unity."* *

* Reprinted from E. S. Shuckburgh, trans., *The Histories of Polybius* (Bloomington: Indiana University Press, 1962), pp. 1–5.

57

Had the praise of History been passed over by former Chroniclers it would perhaps have been incumbent upon me to urge the choice and special study of records of this sort, as the readiest means men can have of correcting their knowledge of the past. But my predecessors have not been sparing in this respect. They have all begun and ended, so to speak, by enlarging on this theme: asserting again and again that the study of History is in the truest sense an education, and a training for political life; and that the most instructive, or rather the only, method of learning to bear with dignity the vicissitudes of fortune is to recall the catastrophes of others. It is evident, therefore, that no one need think it his duty to repeat what has been said by many, and said well. Least of all myself: for the surprising nature of the events which I have undertaken to relate is in itself sufficient to challenge and stimulate the attention of every one, old or young, to the study of my work. Can any one be so indifferent or idle as not to care to know by what means, and under what kind of polity, almost the whole inhabited world was conquered and brought under the dominion of the single city of Rome, and that too within a period of not quite fifty-three years? Or who again can be so completely absorbed in other subjects of contemplation or study, as to think any of them superior in importance to the accurate understanding of an event for which the past affords no precedent.

We shall best show how marvellous and vast our subject is by comparing the most famous Empires which preceded, and which have been the favourite themes of historians, and measuring them with the superior greatness of Rome. There are but three that deserve even to be so compared and measured: and they are these. The Persians for a certain length of time were possessed of a great empire and dominion. But every time they ventured beyond the limits of Asia, they found not only their empire, but their own existence also in danger. The Lacedaemonians, after contending for supremacy in Greece for many generations, when they did get it, held it without dispute for barely twelve years. The Macedonians obtained dominion in Europe from the lands bordering on the Adriatic to the Danube,—which after all is but a small fraction of this continent,—and, by the destruction of the Persian Empire, they afterwards added to that the dominion of Asia. And yet, though they had the credit of having made themselves masters of a larger number of countries and states than any people had ever done, they still left the greater half of the inhabited world in the hands of others. They never so much as thought of attempting Sicily, Sardinia, or Libya: and as to Europe, to speak the plain truth, they never even knew of the most warlike tribes of the West. The Roman conquest, on the other hand, was not partial. Nearly the whole inhabited world was reduced by them to obedience: and they left behind them an empire not to be paralleled in the past or rivalled in the future. Students will gain from my narrative a clearer view of the whole story, and of the numerous and important advantages which such exact record of events offers.

.   .   .

. . . Now up to this time the world's history had been, so to speak, a series of disconnected transactions, as widely separated in their origin and results as in their localities. But from this time forth History becomes a connected whole: the affairs of Italy and Libya are involved with those of Asia and Greece, and the tendency of all is to unity. This is why I have fixed upon this era as the starting-point of my work. For it was their victory over the Carthaginians in this war, and their conviction that thereby the most difficult and most essential step towards universal empire had been taken, which encouraged the Romans for the first time to stretch out their hands upon the rest, and to cross with an army into Greece and Asia.

Now, had the states that were rivals for universal empire been familiarly known to us, no reference perhaps to their previous history would have been necessary, to show the purpose and the forces with which they approached an undertaking of this nature and magnitude. But the fact is that the majority of the Greeks have no knowledge of the previous constitution, power, or achievements either of Rome or Carthage. I therefore concluded that it was necessary to prefix this and the next book to my History. I was anxious that no one, when fairly embarked upon my actual narrative, should feel at a loss, and have to ask what were the designs entertained by the Romans, or the forces and means at their disposal, that they entered upon those undertakings, which did in fact lead to their becoming masters of land and sea everywhere in our part of the world. I wished, on the contrary, that these books of mine, and the prefatory sketch which they contained, might make it clear that the resources they started with justified their original idea, and sufficiently explained their final success in grasping universal empire and dominion.

. . . And combined with this was the fact that no writer of our time has undertaken a general history. Had any one done so my ambition in this direction would have been much diminished. But, in point of fact, I notice that by far the greater number of historians concern themselves with isolated wars and the incidents that accompany them: while as to a general and comprehensive scheme of events, their date, origin, and catastrophe, no one as far as I know has undertaken to examine it. . . . And of this we cannot obtain a comprehensive view from writers of mere episodes. It would be as absurd to expect to do so as for a man to imagine that he has learnt the shape of the whole world, its entire arrangement and order, because he has visited one after the other the most famous cities in it; or perhaps merely examined them in separate pictures. That would be indeed absurd: and it has always seemed to me that men, who are persuaded that they get a competent view of universal from episodical history, are very like persons who should see the limbs of some body, which had once been living and beautiful, scattered and remote; and should imagine that to be quite as good as actually beholding the activity and beauty of the living creature itself. But if some one could there and then reconstruct the animal once more, in the perfection of its beauty and the charm of its vitality, and could display it to the same people, they would beyond doubt confess that they had been far from conceiving the truth, and had been little better than dreamers. For indeed some idea of a whole may be got from a part, but an accurate knowledge and clear comprehension cannot. Wherefore we must conclude that episodical history contributes exceedingly little to the familiar knowledge and secure grasp of universal history. While it is only by the combination and comparison of the separate parts of the whole,—by observing their likeness and their difference,—that a man can attain his object: can obtain a view at once clear and complete; and thus secure both the profit and the delight of History.

Chapter Eight

Greco-Roman civilization

11   VIEWS ON ATHENIAN DEMOCRACY

The classical age of Greece is generally recognized as one of the great golden ages of human history. Fundamental contributions were made in art, literature, philosophy, and science. Also democracy, both in theory and in practice, blossomed for the first time in the Athens of the fifth century B.C. *The classic definition of this democracy was given at the time by its illustrious practitioner Pericles, in the form of his funeral oration commemorating the Athenian soldiers who had fallen in battle against Sparta in 431* B.C. *On the other hand, the following account by a distinguished historian, Professor A. H. M. Jones of Cambridge University, provides a reasoned appraisal of fifth-century* B.C. *Athens in the light of modern scholarship.*

Pericles' Funeral Oration *

Our form of government does not enter into rivalry with the institutions of others. We do not copy our neighbours, but are an example to them. It is true that we are called a democracy, for the administration is in the hands of the many and not of the few. But while the law secures equal justice to all alike in their private disputes, the claim of excellence is also recognized; and when a citizen is in any way distinguished, he is preferred to the public service, not as a matter of privilege, but as the reward of merit. Neither is poverty a bar, but a man may benefit his country whatever be the obscurity of his condition. There is no exclusiveness in our public life, and in our private intercourse we are not suspicious of one another,

* Reprinted from Benjamin Jowett, trans., *The History of Thucydides* (New York: Tandy-Thomas, 1909), Book II, 35–46.

nor angry with our neighbour if he does what he likes; we do not put on sour looks at him which, though harmless, are not pleasant. While we are thus unconstrained in our private intercourse, a spirit of reverence pervades our public acts; we are prevented from doing wrong by respect for the authorities and for the laws, having an especial regard to those which are ordained for the protection of the injured as well as to those unwritten laws which bring upon the transgressor of them the reprobation of the general sentiment.

And we have not forgotten to provide for our weary spirits many relaxations from toil; we have regular games and sacrifices throughout the year; our homes are beautiful and elegant; and the delight which we daily feel in all these things helps to banish melancholy. Because of the greatness of our city the fruits of the whole earth flow in upon us; so that we enjoy the goods of other countries as freely as of our own.

Then, again, our military training is in many respects superior to that of our adversaries. Our city is thrown open to the world, and we never expel a foreigner or prevent him from seeing or learning anything of which the secret if revealed to an enemy might profit him. We rely not upon management or trickery, but upon our own hearts and hands. And in the matter of education, whereas they from early youth are always undergoing laborious exercises which are to make them brave, we live at ease, and yet are equally ready to face the perils which they face. And here is the proof. The Lacedæmonians come into Attica not by themselves, but with their whole confederacy following; we go alone into a neighbour's country; and although our opponents are fighting for their homes and we on a foreign soil, we have seldom any difficulty in overcoming them. Our enemies have never yet felt our united strength; the care of a navy divides our attention, and on land we are obliged to send our own citizens everywhere. But they, if they meet and defeat a part of our army, are as proud as if they had routed us all, and when defeated they pretend to have been vanquished by us all.

If then we prefer to meet danger with a light heart but without laborious training, and with a courage which is gained by habit and not enforced by law, are we not greatly the gainers? Since we do not anticipate the pain, although, when the hour comes, we can be as brave as those who never allow themselves to rest; and thus too our city is equally admirable in peace and in war. For we are lovers of the beautiful, yet simple in our tastes, and we cultivate the mind without loss of manliness. Wealth we employ, not for talk and ostentation, but when there is a real use for it. To avow poverty with us is no disgrace; the true disgrace is in doing nothing to avoid it. An Athenian citizen does not neglect the state because he takes care of his own household; and even those of us who are engaged in business have a very fair idea of politics. We alone regard a man who takes no interest in public affairs, not as a harmless, but as a useless character; and if few of us are originators, we are all sound judges of policy. The great impediment to action is, in our opinion, not discussion, but the want of that knowledge which is gained by discussion preparatory to action. For we have a peculiar power of thinking before we act and of acting too, whereas other men are courageous from ignorance but hesitate upon reflection. And they are surely to be esteemed the bravest spirits who, having the clearest sense both of the pains and pleasures of life, do not on that account shrink from danger. In doing good, again, we are unlike others; we make our friends by conferring, not by receiving favours. Now he who confers a favour is the firmer friend, because he would gain by kindness keep alive the memory of an obligation; but the recipient is colder in his feelings, because he knows that in requiring another's generosity he will not be winning gratitude but only paying a debt. We alone do good to our neighbours, not upon a calculation of interest, but in the confidence of freedom and in a frank and fearless spirit.

To sum up: I say that Athens is the school of Hellas, and that the individual Athenian in his own person seems to have the power of adapting himself to the most varied forms of action with the utmost versatility and grace. . . .

I have dwelt upon the greatness of Athens because I want to show you that we are contending for a higher prize than those who enjoy none of these privileges, and to establish by manifest proof the merit of these men whom I am now commemorating. Their loftiest praise has been already spoken. For in magnifying the city I have magnified them, and men like them whose virtues made her glorious. . . .

. . .

. . . Any one can discourse to you for ever about the advantages of a brave defence, which you know already. But instead of listening to him I would have you day by day fix your eyes upon the greatness of Athens, until you become filled with the love of her; and when you are impressed by the spectacle of her glory, reflect that this empire has been acquired by men who knew their duty and had the courage to do it, who in the hour of conflict had the fear of dishonour always present to them, and who, if ever they failed in an enterprise, would not allow their virtues to be lost to their country, but freely gave their lives to her as the fairest offering which they could present at her feast. The sacrifice which they collectively made was individually repaid to them; for they received again each one for himself a praise which grows not old, and the noblest of all sepulchres—I speak not of that in which their remains are laid, but of that in which their glory survives, and is proclaimed always and on every fitting occasion both in word and deed. For the whole earth is the sepulchre of famous men; not only are they commemorated by columns and inscriptions in their own country, but in foreign lands there dwells also an unwritten memorial of them, graven not on stone but in the hearts of men. Make them your examples, and, esteeming courage to be freedom and freedom to be happiness, do not weigh too nicely the perils of war. The unfortunate who has no hope of a change for the better has less reason to throw away his life than the prosperous who, if he survive, is always liable to a change for the worse, and to whom any accidental fall makes the most serious difference. To a man of spirit, cowardice and disaster coming together are far more bitter than death striking him unperceived at a time when he is full of courage and animated by the general hope.

. . .

To you who are the sons and brothers of the departed, I see that the struggle to emulate them will be an arduous one. For all men praise the dead, and, however pre-eminent your virtue may be, hardly will you be thought, I do not say to equal, but even to approach them. The living have their rivals and detractors, but when a man is out of the way, the honour and good-will which he receives is unalloyed. And, if I am to speak of womanly virtues to those of you who will henceforth be widows, let me sum them up in one short admonition: To a woman not to show more weakness than is natural to her sex is a great glory, and not to be talked about for good or for evil among men.

I have paid the required tribute, in obedience to the law, making use of such fitting words as I had. The tribute of deeds has been paid in part; for the dead have been honourably interred, and it remains only that their children should be maintained at the public charge until they are grown up: this is the solid prize with which, as with a garland, Athens crowns her sons living and dead, after a struggle like theirs. For where the rewards of virtue are greatest, there the noblest citizens are enlisted in the service of the state. And now, when you have duly lamented, every one his own dead, you may depart.

A. H. M. Jones's Appraisal *

Prima facie the Athenian democracy would seem to have been a perfectly designed machine for expressing and putting into effect the will of the people. The majority of the magistrates were annually chosen by lot from all qualified candidates who put in their names, so that every citizen had a chance to take his turn in the administration. In the fifth-century only the military officers, of whom the most important were the ten generals, were elected by the assembly. In the fourth, when finance became a difficult problem, a few high financial officers were also elected. This was an inevitable concession to aristocratic principles: for the Greeks considered popular election to be aristocratic rather than democratic, since the ordinary voter will prefer a known to an unknown name—and in point of fact the generals usually tended to be men of wealth and family, though a professional soldier or two were usually members of the board in the fourth-century. But the assembly, of which all adult male citizens were members, kept a strict control over the generals, who received precise instructions and departed from them at their peril. The assembly was in a very real sense a sovereign body, holding forty regular meetings a year and extraordinary sessions as required, and not merely settling general questions of policy, but making detailed decisions in every sphere of government—foreign affairs, military operations, finance.

The administrative lynch-pin of the constitution was the council of five-hundred, annually chosen by lot from all the demes (wards or parishes) of Athens and Attica in proportion to their size, and thus forming a fair sample of the people as a whole. It had two main functions, to supervise and co-ordinate the activities of the magistrates, and to prepare the agenda of the assembly. No motion might be put to the assembly unless the question had been placed on the order paper by the council and duly advertised; snap divisions were thus precluded. On uncontroversial issues the council usually produced a draft motion, which could however be freely debated and amended in the assembly by any citizen; in this way much formal business was cleared away. On controversial issues the council normally—and naturally in view of its composition—forebore to express an opinion, and merely put the question before the people, leaving it to any citizen to draft the motion during the actual debate. The presidents of the council and the assembly were chosen daily by lot from the council to preclude any undue influence from the chair.

Finally, as ultimate guardians of the constitution, there were the popular law courts. Juries were empanelled by lot for each case from a body of six-thousand citizens annually chosen by lot, and decided not only private cases but political issues. These juries as a regular routine judged any charges of peculation or malfeasance brought against magistrates on laying down their office; they decided the fate of any citizen accused of treason or of "deceiving the people" by his speeches in the assembly; they could quash any motion voted in the assembly as being contrary to the laws, and punish its author. Political trials were frequent in Athens,

* Reprinted from A. H. M. Jones, "The Economic Basis of the Athenian Democracy," *Past & Present,* I (February 1952), 13–25.

and in the fourth-century in particular the indictment for an illegal motion was constantly employed for political purposes, often on very technical grounds. The result was that the popular juries—in such cases sometimes thousands strong—tended to become a Supreme Court.

In general all citizens who were not expressly disqualified for some offence, such as unpaid debt to the treasury, had equal political rights: in particular all could speak and vote in the assembly. For membership of the council and of the juries and probably for all magistracies there was an age qualification of thirty years. For offices, or at any rate some of them, there were also qualifications of property: but these were mostly moderate and, by the late fourth-century, at any rate, and probably by the fifth, were in practice ignored. To make the system work truly democratically it was further necessary that every citizen, however poor, should be able to afford the time for exercising his political rights, and from the time of Pericles pay was provided for this purpose. Magistrates were paid at varying rates according to the nature of their duties; members of the council received five obols a day by the fourth-century—the rate may have been lower in the fifth; and members of the juries were given a subsistence allowance of two obols, raised in 425 B.C. to three. Finally from the beginning of the fourth-century citizens who attended the assembly—or rather the quorum who arrived first, for a limited sum of money was allocated to each assembly—were paid a subsistence allowance of one, then two, then three obols. Later the rate was more liberal, one drachma for ordinary days, one and a half for the ten standing meetings when the agenda was heavier.

Two charges have been brought against the Athenian democracy, one both by ancient and by modern critics, the other in recent times only. The first is that the pay, which was an essential part of the system, was provided by the tribute paid by Athens' allies in the Delian League, and that the democracy was therefore parasitic on the empire: the second, that Athenians only had the leisure to perform their political functions because they were supported by slaves—the democracy was in fact parasitic on slavery.

To the first charge there is a very simple answer, that the democracy continued to function in the fourth-century when Athens had lost her empire; the Second Athenian League, which lasted effectively only from 377 to 357, was never a paying proposition, the contributions of the allies by no means covering the cost of military and naval operations. And not only did the democracy continue to function, but a new and important form of pay, that for attendance in the assembly, was introduced early in the century. This being so it is hardly worth while to go into the financial figures, particularly as there must be many gaps in our calculations. . . .

That Athens profited financially from her empire is of course true. But these profits were not necessary to keep the democracy working. They enabled Athens to be a great power, and to support a much larger citizen population at higher standards of living. One oligarchic critic emphasises the casual profits incidental on Athens' position as an imperial city; the imperial litigation which brought in more court fees, the increased customs revenue, the demand for lodgings, cabs and slaves to hire. Advocates and politicians made money by pleading the legal cases of the allies, and promoting measures in their favour. But these were chicken-feed compared with the solid benefits of empire, the tribute amounting to 400 talents a year and other imperial income raising the annual total to 600 talents, and the acquisition of land overseas, mainly by confiscation from rebellious allied communities or individuals.

The land was utilized either for colonies, which were technically separate states, but being composed of former Athenian citizens were virtually overseas extensions of the Athenian state, or for cleruchies, that is settlements of Athenians who remained full citizens, liable to Athenian taxation and military service, though in practice they naturally would rarely exercise their citizen rights at Athens. Both types of settlement were normally manned from the poorer citizens. Most will have come from the lowest property class, *thetes,* who possessed property rated under 2,000 drachmae and were liable only for naval service or as light-armed troops on land. The allotments were (in the one case where figures are given) of sufficient value to qualify the owner to rank as a *zeugites* liable to military service as a heavy-armed infantryman or hoplite. By her colonies and cleruchies Athens raised more than ten thousand of her citizens from poverty to modest affluence, and at the same time increased her hoplite force by an even larger number, the cleruchs with their adult sons serving in the ranks of the Athenian army and the colonists as allied contingents.

The tribute was partly spent on the upkeep of a standing navy, partly put to reserve. Pericles is stated to have kept sixty triremes in commission for eight months in the year, and he maintained a fleet of three hundred in the dockyards. The dockyards must have given employment to an army of craftsmen, as well as to 500 guards, and the crews of the cruising triremes would have numbered 12,000 men, paid a drachma a day for 240 days in the year. Not all the dockyard workers will have been citizens, nor all the naval ratings, but many thousands of Athenian *thetes* enjoyed regular well-paid employment thanks to the empire. Of the money put to reserve a part, probably 2,000 talents, was spent on public works, notably the Parthenon and the Propylaea, which again, as Plutarch explains, gave employment to the poorer classes. The remainder formed a war fund of 6,000 talents, which was ultimately spent during the Peloponnesian war on pay to hoplites and sailors.

In response to the favourable economic conditions provided by the empire the population of Athens seems to have risen by leaps and bounds during the half-century between the Persian war (480–479) and the opening of the Peloponnesian war (431). . . . .

The Peloponnesian war caused great losses both by battle casualties and by the plague. . . . The loss of the empire and the fall of Athens in 404 must have compelled many thousands of citizens, dispossessed cleruchs and unemployed sailors and dockyard workers, to emigrate or take service as mercenaries abroad. A general decrease in prosperity caused the population to sink to a level well below that of the Persian wars, and in particular reduced the thetic class. Hence the increasingly bourgeois tone of the fourth-century democracy.

The second charge against the Athenian democracy, that it was parasitic on slavery, is more difficult to answer with any certainty. It will be as well first to make plain the elements of the problem. The Athenians, like all Greek peoples, regarded themselves as a kinship group, and citizenship depended strictly on descent (always on the father's side and, by a law passed in 451 and re-enacted in 403, on the mother's side also) and not on residence, however long. The population of Attica therefore consisted not only of citizens, but of free aliens, mainly immigrants who had settled permanently and often lived at Athens for generations, but also including freed slaves and persons of mixed descent; and of slaves, mainly imported but some home-bred. It is unhistorical to condemn the Athenian democracy because it did not give political rights to all residents of Attica; it was the democracy of the Athenian people. It is however relevant to enquire whether the Athenian people was a privileged group depending on the labour of others. Sparta might be called technically a democracy (though the hereditary kings and the council of elders balanced the power of the people) inasmuch as the whole body of Spartiates chose the ephors, in whose hands the government effectively lay, but the Spartiates were a body of *rentiers* supported by ten or twenty times the number of native serfs, the helots. Was the Athenian democracy of this order? The resident aliens (metics) do not concern us here. They made a great contribution to Athenian prosperity, particularly in the fields of industry, commerce and banking—indeed they seem to have dominated the two latter. They were voluntary immigrants and could leave when they wished (except in time of war.) That so many domiciled themselves permanently in Attica—a census taken at the end of the fourth-century showed 10,000 metics as against 21,000 citizens—is a testimony to their liberal treatment. They enjoyed full civil (as opposed to political) rights, except that they could not own land—hence their concentration on industry and commerce—and were subject to all the duties of citizens, including military and naval service and taxation at a slightly higher scale. They were a contented class, and many demonstrated their loyalty to their adoptive city by generous gifts at times of crisis.

What of slaves? Here it will be as well to clear up another misconception. It is often stated, mainly on the authority of Plato and Aristotle, that "the Greeks" considered manual work degrading. Now it is true that gentlemen like Plato and Aristotle despised workers and justified their contempt by asserting that manual work deformed the body and the soul. But that this was the attitude of the average poor Greek there is no evidence. An anecdote recorded by Xenophon probably gives a better insight into his point of view. Eutherus, a dispossessed cleruch, has been reduced to earning his living by manual labour. Socrates asks what he will do when his bodily strength fails and suggests that he find a job as a rich man's bailiff. Eutherus is horrified at the suggestion—"I could not endure to be a slave. . . . I absolutely refuse to be at any man's beck and call." What the Athenian *thes* objected to was not hard work—incidentally his main military duty in the fifth-century was rowing in the galleys, a task in most later civilisations considered fit only for infidel slaves or convicts—but being another man's servant. He would work as an independent craftsman or at a pinch as a casual labourer, but he would not take even a black-coated job as a regular employee; we find that such highly responsible posts as the manager of a bank or the foreman overseer of a mine are filled by slaves or freedmen of the owner.

Is it true, as we are still too often told, that the average Athenian, in the intervals between listening to a play of Sophocles and serving as a magistrate, councillor or juror, lounged in the market place, discussing politics and philosophy, while slaves toiled to support him? Contemporary critics of the democracy did not think so. Plato's Socrates, analysing the people in a democracy, divides them into the drones, that is the active politicians and their cliques of supporters, and the mass of the people "who support themselves by their labour and do not care about politics, owning very little property; this is the largest and most powerful element in a democracy when it is assembled." Xenophon's Socrates, rebuking Charmides for his shyness at addressing the assembly, asks if he is afraid "of the fullers among them or the shoemakers or the carpenters or the smiths or the peasants or the merchants or the shopkeepers: for the assembly is composed of all of them." Aristotle, analysing the people (that is the mass of poor citizens) in different cities, classifies them as craftsmen, shopkeepers, seamen of various kinds —fishermen, ferrymen, sailors on merchantmen or warships—and casual day labourers and those who have little property so that they can enjoy no leisure.

Slaves were employed in many capacities—as domestic servants, as clerks and agents in commerce and banking, in agriculture, and in industry and mining. All well-to-do Athenian families had several servants, and no doubt wealthy men kept large households of a dozen or more—precise figures are lacking—but the domestic servant probably did not go very far down the social scale. A man for whom Lysias wrote a little speech does indeed roundly assert that everyone has slaves; but he is trying to convince the jury that it is contrary to public policy to encourage slaves to inform against their masters. In comedy domestic slaves appear when dramatically convenient, even in the poorest households, but this evidence is suspect: comedy was written after all by well-to-do authors, and slaves provided a variety of stock comic turns. It has been argued that because in the fifth-century every hoplite took with him an attendant to carry nis food and kit, and was allowed a drachma a day by the state on his account (in addition to his own drachma) that every hoplite must have owned an able bodied male slave. Those hoplites who owned suitable slaves certainly used them for this purpose, but there is no evidence that every hoplite's attendant was his own slave. The high rate of the state allowance, on the contrary, is only explicable on the assumption that many hoplites would have to hire a man for the purpose, and Thucydides' inclusion of the baggage carriers with the light armed among the Athenian casualties at Delium implies that they were citizens. More significant than these uncertain inferences is a remark by Demosthenes, who, castigating the harshness with which Androtion and Timocrates collected the arrears of war-tax, pictures them "removing doors and seizing blankets and distraining on a servant girl, if anyone employed one." Now the payers of war tax can be estimated to have numbered only about 6,000 out of a population of 21,000. If not all of them had a domestic servant, one may hazard that under a quarter of the population enjoyed that luxury.

Commerce and banking need not detain us, as the numbers were small. In agriculture, too, we hear little of slaves. The property of large landowners did not normally consist of a single great estate, but of several farms scattered over Attica. Some of these farms were let to free tenants, Athenian or metic; one at least—the home farm—would be worked by a minimum staff of slaves, supplemented by hired labour; for it was uneconomic in a seasonal trade like agriculture to maintain all the year round enough slaves to cope with peak demands. The hired labour was sometimes supplied by slave gangs, leased from a contractor to do a particular job, such as to get in the harvest or the vintage; but it often consisted of free persons—in one of his private speeches Demosthenes remarks that many citizen women were driven by poverty to work in the harvest. Shepherds seem normally to have been slaves, but the politician Phrynichus is alleged to have been one in his poverty-stricken youth. How far down the scale of wealth the use of agricultural slaves went it is difficult to say, but the greater part of Attica was probably occupied by peasant farmers too poor to afford them. Of the six thousand citizens who paid war tax, a large number were, as Demosthenes puts it, "farmers who stinted themselves, but owing to the maintenance of their children and domestic expenses and other public demands fell into arrears with their war tax." These were the men who often could not afford a single domestic servant, and certainly did not maintain a farm hand; they would fall into the class which Aristotle described as using the labour of their wives and children through lack of slaves. Below them were the remaining three thousand of the hoplite class who did not qualify for war tax, and will have owned property to the value of between 25 and 20 minae. These were quite poor men; Demosthenes introducing a poor hoplite witness apologises to the jury—"he is poor, it is true, but not a rascal"— and the wealthy Mantitheus, when his deme mustered for a call-up, found that many of his fellow-demesmen were embarrassed for journey-money, and distributed 30 drachmae to each. A farm worth 20 minae would, on the basis of the single land price recorded, comprise about five acres, and would bring in if let only about 160 drachmae a year in rent, not enough to feed, let alone clothe, a single man; it can only have supported a family if worked by family labour.

In industry, and particularly mining, slaves were employed on a larger scale. The wealthy Nicias in the fifth-century is said to have owned 1,000 slaves, whom he let out to a mining contractor at one obol a day, the contractor feeding and clothing them and replacing casualties; two rich contemporaries are said to have owned 600 and 300 respectively whom they exploited in a similar way. In the fourth-century another mine concessionaire owned 30 slaves, which was probably a more usual number. Well-to-do Athenians also normally invested a small proportion of their wealth in slave craftsmen, who either worked together in a factory, or independently, paying their owner a fixed sum and keeping for themselves whatever they earned beyond it. The largest factory of which we hear, the shield factory of the brothers Lysias and Polemarchus, numbered nearly 120 men; but this is quite exceptional, and is due to the fact that the owners were metics, who could not invest in land, and that the thirty years of the Peloponnesian War had naturally led to a boom in armaments. In the fourth-century Pasion the banker also ran a shield factory as a side-line; it brought in a net revenue of a talent a year, and must have contained over 60 men; Pasion again was a metic, until he was rewarded with the citizenship for his public services, and he was the richest man in Athens of the time—he had before he died acquired land to the value of 20 talents besides his bank and factory. Demosthenes' father was also exceptional in owning two factories, 32 knife makers and 20 bed makers, with a capital value of nearly 6½ talents (4 talents in slaves and 2½ talents in raw materials in stock) out of a total fortune of 14 talents, the rest of which was in cash and investments with the exception of his house and furniture. We hear of some others in the fifth-century whose wealth was entirely invested in slaves; Isocrates' father rose to affluence from the profits of a group of flute-makers, and Xenophon makes Socrates cite five contemporaries, including a miller, a baker and cloakmaker, who lived comfortably on the earnings of their slaves. More usually rich Athenians seem to have distributed their capital between land, house-property, some cash investments and a dozen or so slave craftsmen. Socrates, asking a high-class prostitute where her money came from, suggests (ironically) land, house-property or craftsmen as typical sources of income. Timocrates inherited, besides land and houses, nine or ten shoemakers, who paid two obols a day each as rent: Leostratus owned bronzesmiths to the value of 35 minae (about a dozen, that is): Ciron, besides an estate worth a talent, and two houses, owned a few rent-paying slaves, valued with three domestic slaves and the furniture at 13 minae: Euctaeus possessed a farm, a house, a baths, and a brothel and wineshop and some craftsmen.

These facts and figures concern the well-to-do families who could afford to pay a professional speech-writer to compose a plea in their mutual litigation about their inheritances, and who normally belonged to the 1,200 richest families enrolled on the trierarchic register. How far humbler folk owned industrial slaves it is very difficult to say. Xenophon in one passage speaks of those who could, buying slaves as fellow-workers, which might suggest that a craftsman sometimes bought a man and trained him as an apprentice; and a poor cripple, pleading for his public assistance of 1 obol a day, complains that he is getting old and his children are too young to support him (a rather unlikely conjunction of pleas) and that he is too poor to buy a slave to carry on his work. This may suggest that a craftsman who bought a slave and trained him was looking forward to retiring on his earnings. But, as Aristophanes recognized, the greater part of the work in industry as in agriculture was done by poor citizens. Addressing them Poverty declared in the *Plutus:* "If wealth should gain his sight again and distribute himself equally, no one would practice a craft or skill. And when you have lost both of these, who will work as a smith or a shipwright or a tailor or a wheelwright or a shoemaker or a bricklayer or a launderer or a tanner or plough the land or harvest the crops, if you can live in idleness and neglect all this work?"

We have no reliable evidence for the total number of slaves in Attica at any time. . . . According to Thucydides more than twenty thousand slaves, mainly industrial, escaped during the ten years' occupation of Deceleia by the Spartans; these would probably be in the main miners and agricultural slaves, but would include many city workers, since the seventeen miles of city walls cannot have been so completely patrolled as to prevent escapes. Xenophon declares that the mines could provide employment for many more than ten thousand, as those—if any—who remembered what the slave tax used to fetch before the Deceleian war could testify (he was writing sixty years later). But whatever their numbers their distribution is fairly clear. They were owned in the main by the 1,200 richest families and in decreasing numbers by the next 3,000 or so. It is unlikely that any slaves were owned by two-thirds to three-quarters of the citizen population. The great majority of the citizens earned their living by the work of their hands, as peasant farmers, craftsmen, shopkeepers, seamen and labourers; so contemporary witnesses state, and so the detailed evidence, so far as it goes, suggests. In only one occupation was slave labour predominant, in mining, and even here, contrary to common belief, some citizens worked. Xenophon, advocating that the state acquire a large body of slaves to be leased to the citizens for use in the mines, suggests that not only will existing contractors add to their manpower but that "there are many of those who are themselves in the mines who are growing old, and many others, both Athenians and aliens, who would not or could not work with their hands, but would gladly make their living by supervising." In one of the Demosthenic speeches we meet a man who boasts "In earlier times I made a lot of money from the silver mines, working and toiling myself with my own hands": he had struck lucky and was now one of the three hundred richest men in Athens.

That the poorer citizens lived on state pay for political services is, even for the fourth-century, when the system was most fully developed, demonstrably false. A man could only be a councillor two years in his life, and could hold none of the magistracies chosen by lot for more than one annual tenure. He could by attending the assembly—and getting there in time to qualify for pay—earn a drachma on thirty days and one and a half drachmae on ten days in the year. On some festivals—the number varied according to the state of the exchequer—he could draw his theoric payment of 2 obols. On other days, if lucky enough to be successful in the annual ballot for the 6,000 jurors, he could queue in hopes of being empanelled on a jury and earning 3 obols, just enough to feed himself. At this rate a bachelor without dependants could barely with consistent good luck scrape a living; for a man with a family it was quite impossible.

The majority of the citizens were then workers who earned their own living and whose political pay served only to compensate them in some measure for loss of working time. Agricultural and industrial slaves in the main merely added to the wealth of a relatively small rentier class, whose principal source of income was land; this same class employed most of the domestic slaves. It only remains to ask how far the Athenian state drew its revenue, directly or indirectly, from slaves. The state owned a certain number of slaves. Most famous are the 1,200 Scythian archers who policed the assembly and the law courts and enforced the orders of the magistrates. There were a number of others ranging from the workers in the mint to the city gaoler and the public slave par excellence who had custody of the public records and accounts. Athens thus ran her police force and her rudimentary civil service in part by slave labour—the clerks of the magistrates were mostly salaried citizens. There was apparently a tax on slaves, known only from the mention in Xenophon cited above, but it can hardly have been an important item in the revenue to receive so little notice. . . .

The charge brought by fifth-century oligarchic critics (and thoughtlessly repeated by many modern writers), that the Athenian democracy depended for its political pay on the tribute of the subject allies, was brought to the test of fact when Athens lost her empire in 403 B.C., and was proved to be a calumny when the democracy continued to pay the citizens for their political functions out of domestic revenues. The modern charge that the Athenian democracy was dependent on slave labour was never brought to the test, since the Athenians never freed all their slaves. This is not surprising, for slavery was an established institution, which most people accepted without question as "according to nature," and to abolish it would have meant a wholesale disregard of the rights of property, which the Athenians throughout their history were careful to respect. It is more surprising that on some occasions of crisis motions for a partial or wholesale freeing of slaves were carried. In 406 all male slaves of military age were freed and granted the citizenship to man the ships which won the battle of Arginusae. After the expulsion of the Thirty in 403 Thrasybulus, the left wing leader of the restored democracy, carried a measure, later quashed as illegal by the moderate leader Archinus, to free and enfranchise all slaves who had fought for the democracy. In 338, after the defeat of Chaeronea, the left wing politician Hypereides proposed and carried a motion to free all (able bodied male) slaves to resist the Macedonians; this motion was again quashed as illegal by a conservative politician.

These facts suggest that there was no bitterness between the mass of the citizens and the slaves, but rather a sense of fellow-feeling. This was a point which shocked contemporary Athenian oligarchs. The "old oligarch" speaks bitterly of the insolence of slaves at Athens, and complains that it is illegal to strike them—the reason, he explains, is that the people are indistinguishable in dress and general appearance from slaves, and it would be easy to strike a citizen by mistake. The moderate oligarch Theramenes is careful to assure his colleagues among the Thirty that he is not one of "those who think there would not be a good democracy until slaves and those who through poverty would sell the city for a drachma participate in it." Plato mocks at the excess of freedom in the democracy, in which "men and women who have been sold are no less free than their purchasers."

Though the Athenians treated their slaves with a humanity which was exceptional according to the standards of the time, they never abolished slavery, and the charge that Athenian democracy was dependent on their labour was never brought to the test of fact. But had Hypereides' motion been allowed to stand, and extended to slaves of all ages and both sexes, it would not seem, on the basis of the evidence cited earlier in this article, that its effects would have been catastrophic. All wealthy and well to do citizens (or rather their wives and unmarried daughters) would have been incommoded by having to do their own housework. A very small number of wealthy or comfortably off men who had invested all their money in mining and industrial slaves would have been reduced to penury. And a larger number, but still a small minority, would have lost the proportion of their income which derived from industrial slaves, and would have had to let their farms instead of cultivating them by slave labour. A number of craftsmen would have lost their apprentices and journeymen. But the great majority of Athenians who owned no slaves but cultivated their own little farms or worked on their own as craftsmen, shopkeepers or labourers, would have been unaffected.

FRUITS OF ROMAN IMPERIALISM 12

During the third century B.C. Rome defeated Carthage, its great rival in the western Mediterranean. In the following century Rome expanded eastward, overrunning the Balkans and the eastern Mediterranean, and becoming the ruler of the entire Mediterranean basin. The initial results of this empire building proved disastrous, for Rome as well as for the conquered provinces. The yeomanry of Italy, which had provided the manpower for the triumphant legions, was decimated by the years of overseas service and by the subsequent influx of slaves and cheap grain from the provinces. The peasants were forced to sell their holdings to the new class of ultrarich and to drift to the cities where they became a rootless and restless proletariat. A land reform effort in the second century B.C. by Tiberius Gracchus and his brother Gaius was aborted by the bitter opposition of the Senate. The following description of the social disorders in Italy and the fruitless struggle of the Gracchi brothers is taken from the Roman History *written about* A.D. *150 by a civil servant, Appian of Alexandria.*

As for the conquered provinces, it was said that their governors operated on the following timetable: in the first year they recovered their election expenses; in the second they accumulated funds to appease the judges before whom they would stand trial for extortion; and in the third year they made their personal fortune. What this meant in actual practice is evident in the following indictment by Cicero of the administration of Governor Gaius Verres in Sicily (73–71 B.C.).

The Gracchi *

The Romans, as they subdued the Italian nations successively in war, seized a part of their lands and built towns there, or established their own colonies in those already existing, and used them in place of garrisons. Of the land acquired by war they assigned the cultivated part forthwith to settlers, or leased or sold it. Since they had no leisure as yet to allot the part which then lay desolated by war (this was generally the greater part), they made proclamation that in the meantime those who were willing to work it might do so for a share of the yearly crops—a tenth of the grain and a fifth of the fruit. From those who kept flocks was required a share of the animals, both oxen and small cattle. They did these things in order to multiply the Italian race, which they considered the most laborious of peoples, so that they might have plenty of allies at home. But the very opposite thing happened; for the rich, getting possession of the greater part of the undisturbed lands, and being emboldened by the lapse of time to believe

* Reprinted from Horace White, trans., *The Roman History of Appian of Alexandria* (London: George Bell & Sons, 1899), pp. 5–21.

that they would never be dispossessed, and adding to their holdings the small farms of their poor neighbors, partly by purchase and partly by force, came to cultivate vast tracts instead of single estates, using for this purpose slaves as laborers and herdsmen, lest free laborers should be drawn from agriculture into the army. The ownership of slaves itself brought them great gain from the multitude of their progeny, who increased because they were exempt from military service. Thus the powerful ones became enormously rich and the race of slaves multiplied throughout the country, while the Italian people dwindled in numbers and strength, being oppressed by penury, taxes, and military service. If they had any respite from these evils they passed their time in idleness, because the land was held by the rich, who employed slaves instead of freemen as cultivators.

For these reasons the people became troubled lest they should no longer have sufficient allies of the Italian stock, and lest the government itself should be endangered by such a vast number of slaves. Not perceiving any remedy, as it was not easy, nor exactly just, to deprive men of so many possessions they had held so long, including their own trees, buildings, and fixtures, a law was once passed with difficulty at the instance of the tribunes, that nobody should hold more than 500 jugera of this land, or pasture on it more than 100 cattle or 500 sheep. To ensure the observance of this law it was provided also that there should be a certain number of freemen employed on the farms, whose business it should be to watch and report what was going on. Those who held possession of lands under the law were required to take an oath to obey the law, and penalties were fixed for violating it, and it was supposed that the remaining land would soon be divided among the poor in small parcels. But there was not the smallest consideration shown for the law or the oaths. The few who seemed to pay some respect to them conveyed their lands to their relations fraudulently, but the greater part disregarded it altogether.

At length Tiberius Sempronius Gracchus, an illustrious man, eager for glory, a most powerful speaker, and for these reasons well known to all, delivered an eloquent discourse, while serving as tribune, concerning the Italian race, lamenting that a people so valiant in war, and blood relations to the Romans, were declining little by little in the pauperism and paucity of numbers without any hope of remedy. He inveighed against the multitude of slaves as useless in war and never faithful to their masters, and adduced the recent calamity brought upon the masters by their slaves in Sicily, where the demands of agriculture had greatly increased the number of the latter; recalling also the war waged against them by the Romans, which was neither easy nor short, but long-protracted and full of vicissitudes and dangers. After speaking thus he again brought forward the law, providing that nobody should hold more than 500 jugera of the public domain. But he added a provision to the former law, that the sons of the present occupiers might each hold one-half of that amount, and that the remainder should be divided among the poor by triumvirs, who should be changed annually.

This was extremely disturbing to the rich because, on account of the triumvirs, they could no longer disregard the law as they had done before; nor could they buy the allotments of others, because Gracchus had provided against this by forbidding sales. They collected together in groups, and made lamentation, and accused the poor of appropriating the results of their tillage, their vineyards, and their dwellings. Some said that they had paid the price of the land to their neighbors. Were they to lose the money with the land? Others said that the graves of their ancestors were in the ground, which had been allotted to them in the division of their fathers' estates. Others said that their wives' dowries had been expended

ne to time. On the subject of the murder of Gracchus the city was divided between
orrow and joy. Some mourned for themselves and for him, and deplored the present
condition of things, believing that the commonwealth no longer existed, but had
been supplanted by force and violence. Others considered that everything had turned
out for them exactly as they wished.

Cicero on Verres *

ntlemen of the Court: . . . The character of the man I am prosecuting is
that you may use him to restore the lost good name of these Courts, to
favour at home, and to give satisfaction abroad: he has robbed the Treasury,
ndered Asia and Pamphylia; he has behaved like a pirate in his city praetor-
 d like a destroying pestilence in his province of Sicily.

. . . .

Nowhere did he multiply and magnify the memorials and the proofs of
il qualities so thoroughly as in his governorship of Sicily; which island for
of three years he devastated and ruined so effectually that nothing can
to its former condition, and it hardly seems possible that a long lapse of
a succession of upright governors can in time bring it a partial revival
ity. So long as Verres was governing it, its people were protected neither
vn laws, nor by the decrees of the Roman Senate, nor by the rights that
all nations alike. None of them has anything left to-day, except what
ped the notice of this avaricious and intemperate ruffian, or remained
his greed was glutted. For the space of three years, the law awarded
anybody unless Verres chose to agree; and nothing was so undoubtedly
om a man's father or grandfather that the courts would not cancel his
if Verres bade them do so. Countless sums of money, under a new and
ed regulation, were wrung from the purses of the farmers; our most loyal
treated as if they were national enemies; Roman citizens were tortured
ted like slaves; the guiltiest criminals bought their legal acquittal, while
honourable and honest men would be prosecuted in absence, and con-
and banished unheard; strongly fortified harbours, mighty and well-defended
re left open to the assaults of pirates and buccaneers; Sicilian soldiers and
ur allies and our friends, were starved to death; fine fleets, splendidly
l, were to the great disgrace of our nation destroyed and lost to us. Famous
ient works of art, some of them the gifts of wealthy kings, who intended
adorn the cities where they stood, others the gifts of Roman generals, who
restored them to the communities of Sicily in the hour of victory—this
overnor stripped and despoiled every one of them. Nor was it only the civic
stat es and works of art that he treated thus; he also pillaged the holiest and most
venerated sanctuaries; in fact, he has not left the people of Sicily a single god whose
workmanship he thought at all above the average of antiquity or artistic merit.
As to his adulteries and the like vile offences, a sense of decency makes me
afraid to repeat the tale of his acts of wanton wickedness: and besides, I would
not wish, by repeating it, to add to the calamities of those who have not been

Reprinted by permission of the publishers and The Loeb Classical Library from Cicero, *The
Verrine Orations,* trans. L. H. G. Greenwood (Cambridge, Mass.: Harvard University Press),
cerpts from vols. I and II.

on the estates, or that the land had been given to their own daughters as dowry.
Money-lenders could show loans made on this security. All kinds of wailing and
expressions of indignation were heard at once. On the other side were heard the
lamentations of the poor—that they had been reduced from competence to extreme penury, and from that to childlessness, because they were unable to rear
their offspring. They recounted the military services they had rendered, by which
this very land had been acquired, and were angry that they should be robbed of
their share of the common property. They reproached the rich for employing
slaves, who were always faithless and ill-tempered and for that reason unserviceable in war, instead of freemen, citizens, and soldiers. While these classes were
lamenting and indulging in mutual accusations, a great number of others, composed of colonists, or inhabitants of the free towns, or persons otherwise interested in the lands and who were under like apprehensions, flocked in and took
sides with their respective factions. Emboldened by numbers and exasperated
against each other they attached themselves to turbulent crowds, and waited for
the voting on the new law, some trying to prevent its enactment by all means, and
others supporting it in every possible way. In addition to personal interest the
spirit of rivalry spurred both sides in the preparations they were making against
each other for the day of the comitia.

What Gracchus had in his mind in proposing the measure was not wealth,
but an increase of efficient population. Inspired greatly by the usefulness of the
work, and believing that nothing more advantageous or admirable could ever
happen to Italy, he took no account of the difficulties surrounding it. When the
time for voting came he advanced many other arguments at considerable length
and also asked them whether it was not just to divide among the common people
what belonged to them in common; whether a citizen was not worthy of more
consideration at all times than a slave; whether a man who served in the army
was not more useful than one who did not; and whether one who had a share
in the country was not more likely to be devoted to the public interests. He did
not dwell long on this comparison between freemen and slaves, which he considered degrading, but proceeded at once to a review of their hopes and fears
for the country, saying that the Romans had acquired most of their territory by
conquest, and that they had hopes of occupying the rest of the habitable world,
but now the question of greatest hazard was, whether they should gain the rest
by having plenty of brave men, or whether, through their weakness and mutual
jealousy, their enemies should take away what they already possessed. After
exaggerating the glory and riches on the one side and the danger and fear on
the other, he admonished the rich to take heed, and said that for the realization of
these hopes they ought to bestow this very land as a free gift, if necessary, on
men who would rear children, and not, by contending about small things, overlook
larger ones; especially since they were receiving an ample compensation for labor
expended in the undisputed title to 500 jugera each of free land, in a high state
of cultivation, without cost, and half as much more for each son of those who
had sons. After saying much more to the same purport and exciting the poor, as
well as others who were moved by reason rather than by the desire for gain, he
ordered the scribe to read the proposed law.

Marcus Octavius, another tribune, who had been induced by those in possession
of the lands to interpose his veto (for among the Romans the tribune's veto always prevailed), ordered the scribe to keep silence. Thereupon Gracchus reproached him severely and adjourned the comitia to the following day. Then he
stationed a sufficient guard, as if to force Octavius against his will, and ordered

the scribe with threats to read the proposed law to the multitude. He began to read, but when Octavius again vetoed he stopped. Then the tribunes fell to wrangling with each other, and a considerable tumult arose among the people. The leading citizens besought the tribunes to submit their controversy to the Senate for decision. Gracchus seized on the suggestion, believing that the law was acceptable to all well-disposed persons, and hastened to the senate-house. There, as he had only a few followers and was upbraided by the rich, he ran back to the forum and said that he would take the vote at the comitia of the following day, both on the law and on the magistracy of Octavius, to determine whether a tribune who was acting contrary to the people's interest could continue to hold his office. And so he did, for when Octavius, nothing daunted, again interposed, Gracchus distributed the pebbles to take a vote on him first. When the first tribe voted to abrogate the magistracy of Octavius, Gracchus turned to him and begged him to desist from this veto. As he would not yield, the votes of the other tribes were taken. There were thirty-five tribes at that time. The seventeen that voted first angrily sustained this motion. If the eighteenth should do the same it would make a majority. Again did Gracchus, in the sight of the people, urgently importune Octavius in his present extreme danger not to prevent this most pious work, so useful to all Italy, and not to frustrate the wishes so earnestly entertained by the people, whose desires he ought rather to share in his character of tribune, and not to risk the loss of his office by public condemnation. After speaking thus he called the gods to witness that he did not willingly do any despite to his colleague. As Octavius was still unyielding he went on taking the vote. Octavius was forthwith reduced to the rank of a private citizen and slunk away unobserved.

Quintus Mummius was chosen tribune in his place, and the agrarian law was enacted. The first triumvirs appointed to divide the land were Gracchus himself, the proposer of the law, his brother of the same name, and his father-in-law, Appius Claudius, since the people still feared that the law might fail of execution unless Gracchus should be put in the lead with his whole family. Gracchus became immensely popular by reason of the law and was escorted home by the multitude as though he were the founder, not of a single city or race, but of all the nations of Italy. After this the victorious party returned to the fields from which they had come to attend to this business. The defeated ones remained in the city and talked the matter over, feeling bitterly, and saying that as soon as Gracchus should become a private citizen he would be sorry that he had done despite to the sacred and inviolable office of tribune, and had opened such a fountain of discord in Italy.

At the advent of summer the notices for the election of tribunes were given, and as the day for voting approached it was very evident that the rich were earnestly promoting the election of those most inimical to Gracchus. The latter, fearing that evil would befall if he should not be reelected for the following year, summoned his friends from the fields to attend the comitia, but as they were occupied with their harvest he was obliged, when the day fixed for the voting drew near, to have recourse to the plebeians of the city. So he went around asking each one separately to elect him tribune for the ensuing year, on account of the danger he had incurred for them. When the voting took place the first two tribes pronounced for Gracchus. The rich objected that it was not lawful for the same man to hold the office twice in succession. The tribune Rubrius, who had been chosen by lot to preside over the comitia, was in doubt about it, and Mummius, who had been chosen in place of Octavius, urged him to turn over the comitia to

his charge. This he did, but the remaining tribunes contende[d] [presi]dency should be decided by lot, saying that when Rubrius, who in that way, resigned, the casting of lots ought to be done over ag[ain] there was much strife over this question, Gracchus, who was gett[ing] of it, adjourned the voting to the following day. In utter despair he cl[othed him]self in black, while still in office, and led his son around the forum and in[troduced] him to each man and committed him to their charge, as if he were about to [perish] at the hands of his enemies.

The poor were moved with deep sorrow, and rightly so, both on their ow[n] account (for they believed that they were no longer to live in a free state under equal laws, but were reduced to servitude by the rich), and on account of Gracchus [him]self, who had incurred such danger and suffering in their behalf. So they all ac[com]panied him with tears to his house in the evening, and bade him be of good co[urage] for the morrow. Gracchus cheered up, assembled his partisans before daybre[ak and] communicated to them a signal to be displayed in case of a fight. He the[n took] possession of the temple on the Capitoline hill, where the voting was to take [place,] and occupied the middle of the assembly. As he was obstructed by the other t[ribunes] and by the rich, who would not allow the votes to be taken on this ques[tion, he] gave the signal. There was a sudden shout from those who saw it, and a [resort to] violence in consequence. Some of the partisans of Gracchus took positio[ns about] him like body-guards. Others, having girded themselves, seized the fasces [held] in the hands of the lictors and broke them in pieces. They drove the rich [from the] assembly with such disorder and wounds that the tribunes fled from thei[r places in] terror, and the priests closed the doors of the temple. Many ran away p[ell-mell and] scattered wild rumors. Some said that Gracchus had deposed all the oth[er tribunes,] and this was believed because none of them could be seen. Others said [that he had] declared himself tribune for the ensuing year without an election.

Under these circumstances the Senate assembled at the temple of [Fides. It is] astonishing to me that they never thought of appointing a dictator in this e[mergency,] although they had often been protected by the government of a single ru[ler in] times of peril. Although this resource had been found most useful in fo[rmer times,] few people remembered it, either then or later. After reaching the decisio[n that they] did reach, they marched up to the Capitol, Cornelius Scipio Nasica, th[e pontifex] maximus, leading the way and calling out with a loud voice, "Let those w[ho would] save the country follow me." He wound the border of his toga about his he[ad, either] to induce a greater number to go with him by the singularity of his appea[rance, or] to make for himself, as it were, a helmet as a sign of battle for those wh[o looked] on, or in order to conceal from the gods what he was about to do. When he [arrived] at the temple and advanced against the partisans of Gracchus they yielded [to the] reputation of a foremost citizen, for they saw the Senate following with hi[m. The] latter wrested clubs out of the hands of the Gracchans themselves, or with fra[gments] of broken benches or other apparatus that had been brought for the use [of the] assembly, began beating them, and pursued them, and drove them over the prec[ipice.] In the tumult many of the Gracchans perished, and Gracchus himself wa[s caught] near the temple, and was slain at the door close by the statues of the kin[gs. All the] bodies were thrown by night into the Tiber.

So perished on the Capitol, and while still tribune, Gracchus, [the son of] Gracchus who was twice consul, and of Cornelia, daughter of that [Scipio who sub]jugated Carthage. He lost his life in consequence of a most exce[llent design which,] however, he pursued in too violent a manner. This shocking a[ffair, the first] perpetrated in the public assembly, was seldom without [parallels] on the estates, or that the land had been given to their own daughters as dowry. Money-lenders could show loans made on this security. All kinds of wailing and expressions of indignation were heard at once. On the other side were heard the lamentations of the poor—that they had been reduced from competence to extreme penury, and from that to childlessness, because they were unable to rear their offspring. They recounted the military services they had rendered, by which this very land had been acquired, and were angry that they should be robbed of their share of the common property. They reproached the rich for employing slaves, who were always faithless and ill-tempered and for that reason unserviceable in war, instead of freemen, citizens, and soldiers. While these classes were lamenting and indulging in mutual accusations, a great number of others, composed of colonists, or inhabitants of the free towns, or persons otherwise interested in the lands and who were under like apprehensions, flocked in and took sides with their respective factions. Emboldened by numbers and exasperated against each other they attached themselves to turbulent crowds, and waited for the voting on the new law, some trying to prevent its enactment by all means, and others supporting it in every possible way. In addition to personal interest the spirit of rivalry spurred both sides in the preparations they were making against each other for the day of the comitia.

What Gracchus had in his mind in proposing the measure was not wealth, but an increase of efficient population. Inspired greatly by the usefulness of the work, and believing that nothing more advantageous or admirable could ever happen to Italy, he took no account of the difficulties surrounding it. When the time for voting came he advanced many other arguments at considerable length and also asked them whether it was not just to divide among the common people what belonged to them in common; whether a citizen was not worthy of more consideration at all times than a slave; whether a man who served in the army was not more useful than one who did not; and whether one who had a share in the country was not more likely to be devoted to the public interests. He did not dwell long on this comparison between freemen and slaves, which he considered degrading, but proceeded at once to a review of their hopes and fears for the country, saying that the Romans had acquired most of their territory by conquest, and that they had hopes of occupying the rest of the habitable world, but now the question of greatest hazard was, whether they should gain the rest by having plenty of brave men, or whether, through their weakness and mutual jealousy, their enemies should take away what they already possessed. After exaggerating the glory and riches on the one side and the danger and fear on the other, he admonished the rich to take heed, and said that for the realization of these hopes they ought to bestow this very land as a free gift, if necessary, on men who would rear children, and not, by contending about small things, overlook larger ones; especially since they were receiving an ample compensation for labor expended in the undisputed title to 500 jugera each of free land, in a high state of cultivation, without cost, and half as much more for each son of those who had sons. After saying much more to the same purport and exciting the poor, as well as others who were moved by reason rather than by the desire for gain, he ordered the scribe to read the proposed law.

Marcus Octavius, another tribune, who had been induced by those in possession of the lands to interpose his veto (for among the Romans the tribune's veto always prevailed), ordered the scribe to keep silence. Thereupon Gracchus reproached him severely and adjourned the comitia to the following day. Then he stationed a sufficient guard, as if to force Octavius against his will, and ordered the scribe with threats to read the proposed law to the multitude. He began to read, but when Octavius again vetoed he stopped. Then the tribunes fell to wrangling with each other, and a considerable tumult arose among the people. The leading citizens besought the tribunes to submit their controversy to the Senate for decision. Gracchus seized on the suggestion, believing that the law was acceptable to all well-disposed persons, and hastened to the senate-house. There, as he had only a few followers and was upbraided by the rich, he ran back to the forum and said that he would take the vote at the comitia of the following day, both on the law and on the magistracy of Octavius, to determine whether a tribune who was acting contrary to the people's interest could continue to hold his office. And so he did, for when Octavius, nothing daunted, again interposed, Gracchus distributed the pebbles to take a vote on him first. When the first tribe voted to abrogate the magistracy of Octavius, Gracchus turned to him and begged him to desist from this veto. As he would not yield, the votes of the other tribes were taken. There were thirty-five tribes at that time. The seventeen that voted first angrily sustained this motion. If the eighteenth should do the same it would make a majority. Again did Gracchus, in the sight of the people, urgently importune Octavius in his present extreme danger not to prevent this most pious work, so useful to all Italy, and not to frustrate the wishes so earnestly entertained by the people, whose desires he ought rather to share in his character of tribune, and not to risk the loss of his office by public condemnation. After speaking thus he called the gods to witness that he did not willingly do any despite to his colleague. As Octavius was still unyielding he went on taking the vote. Octavius was forthwith reduced to the rank of a private citizen and slunk away unobserved.

Quintus Mummius was chosen tribune in his place, and the agrarian law was enacted. The first triumvirs appointed to divide the land were Gracchus himself, the proposer of the law, his brother of the same name, and his father-in-law, Appius Claudius, since the people still feared that the law might fail of execution unless Gracchus should be put in the lead with his whole family. Gracchus became immensely popular by reason of the law and was escorted home by the multitude as though he were the founder, not of a single city or race, but of all the nations of Italy. After this the victorious party returned to the fields from which they had come to attend to this business. The defeated ones remained in the city and talked the matter over, feeling bitterly, and saying that as soon as Gracchus should become a private citizen he would be sorry that he had done despite to the sacred and inviolable office of tribune, and had opened such a fountain of discord in Italy.

At the advent of summer the notices for the election of tribunes were given, and as the day for voting approached it was very evident that the rich were earnestly promoting the election of those most inimical to Gracchus. The latter, fearing that evil would befall if he should not be reelected for the following year, summoned his friends from the fields to attend the comitia, but as they were occupied with their harvest he was obliged, when the day fixed for the voting drew near, to have recourse to the plebeians of the city. So he went around asking each one separately to elect him tribune for the ensuing year, on account of the danger he had incurred for them. When the voting took place the first two tribes pronounced for Gracchus. The rich objected that it was not lawful for the same man to hold the office twice in succession. The tribune Rubrius, who had been chosen by lot to preside over the comitia, was in doubt about it, and Mummius, who had been chosen in place of Octavius, urged him to turn over the comitia to his charge. This he did, but the remaining tribunes contended that the presidency should be decided by lot, saying that when Rubrius, who had been chosen in that way, resigned, the casting of lots ought to be done over again for all. As there was much strife over this question, Gracchus, who was getting the worst of it, adjourned the voting to the following day. In utter despair he clothed himself in black, while still in office, and led his son around the forum and introduced him to each man and committed him to their charge, as if he were about to perish at the hands of his enemies.

The poor were moved with deep sorrow, and rightly so, both on their own account (for they believed that they were no longer to live in a free state under equal laws, but were reduced to servitude by the rich), and on account of Gracchus himself, who had incurred such danger and suffering in their behalf. So they all accompanied him with tears to his house in the evening, and bade him be of good cheer for the morrow. Gracchus cheered up, assembled his partisans before daybreak and communicated to them a signal to be displayed in case of a fight. He then took possession of the temple on the Capitoline hill, where the voting was to take place, and occupied the middle of the assembly. As he was obstructed by the other tribunes and by the rich, who would not allow the votes to be taken on this question, he gave the signal. There was a sudden shout from those who saw it, and a resort to violence in consequence. Some of the partisans of Gracchus took position around him like body-guards. Others, having girded themselves, seized the fasces and staves in the hands of the lictors and broke them in pieces. They drove the rich out of the assembly with such disorder and wounds that the tribunes fled from their places in terror, and the priests closed the doors of the temple. Many ran away pell-mell and scattered wild rumors. Some said that Gracchus had deposed all the other tribunes, and this was believed because none of them could be seen. Others said that he had declared himself tribune for the ensuing year without an election.

Under these circumstances the Senate assembled at the temple of Fides. It is astonishing to me that they never thought of appointing a dictator in this emergency, although they had often been protected by the government of a single ruler in such times of peril. Although this resource had been found most useful in former times few people remembered it, either then or later. After reaching the decision that they did reach, they marched up to the Capitol, Cornelius Scipio Nasica, the pontifex maximus, leading the way and calling out with a loud voice, "Let those who would save the country follow me." He wound the border of his toga about his head either to induce a greater number to go with him by the singularity of his appearance, or to make for himself, as it were, a helmet as a sign of battle for those who looked on, or in order to conceal from the gods what he was about to do. When he arrived at the temple and advanced against the partisans of Gracchus they yielded to the reputation of a foremost citizen, for they saw the Senate following with him. The latter wrested clubs out of the hands of the Gracchans themselves, or with fragments of broken benches or other apparatus that had been brought for the use of the assembly, began beating them, and pursued them, and drove them over the precipice. In the tumult many of the Gracchans perished, and Gracchus himself was caught near the temple, and was slain at the door close by the statues of the kings. All the bodies were thrown by night into the Tiber.

So perished on the Capitol, and while still tribune, Gracchus, the son of the Gracchus who was twice consul, and of Cornelia, daughter of that Scipio who subjugated Carthage. He lost his life in consequence of a most excellent design, which, however, he pursued in too violent a manner. This shocking affair, the first that was perpetrated in the public assembly, was seldom without parallels thereafter from time to time. On the subject of the murder of Gracchus the city was divided between sorrow and joy. Some mourned for themselves and for him, and deplored the present condition of things, believing that the commonwealth no longer existed, but had been supplanted by force and violence. Others considered that everything had turned out for them exactly as they wished.

Cicero on Verres *

Gentlemen of the Court: . . . The character of the man I am prosecuting is such, · you may use him to restore the lost good name of these Courts, to regain our at home, and to give satisfaction abroad: he has robbed the Treasury, and plured Asia and Pamphylia; he has behaved like a pirate in his city praetorship, alike a destroying pestilence in his province of Sicily.

.   .   .

. . . where did he multiply and magnify the memorials and the proofs of all his evualities so thoroughly as in his governorship of Sicily; which island for the space three years he devastated and ruined so effectually that nothing can restore it its former condition, and it hardly seems possible that a long lapse of years and succession of upright governors can in time bring it a partial revival of prosper. So long as Verres was governing it, its people were protected neither by their ovlaws, nor by the decrees of the Roman Senate, nor by the rights that belong to i nations alike. None of them has anything left to-day, except what either escap the notice of this avaricious and intemperate ruffian, or remained over when is greed was glutted. For the space of three years, the law awarded nothing to ıybody unless Verres chose to agree; and nothing was so undoubtedly inherited fm a man's father or grandfather that the courts would not cancel his right to it,f Verres bade them do so. Countless sums of money, under a new and unprinciple regulation, were wrung from the purses of the farmers; our most loyal allies were treated as if they were national enemies; Roman citizens were tortured and execud like slaves; the guiltiest criminals bought their legal acquittal, while the mosthonourable and honest men would be prosecuted in absence, and condemned nd banished unheard; strongly fortified harbours, mighty and well-defended cities, wee left open to the assaults of pirates and buccaneers; Sicilian soldiers and sailors, our allies and our friends, were starved to death; fine fleets, splendidly equipped, were to the great disgrace of our nation destroyed and lost to us. Famous and ancient works of art, some of them the gifts of wealthy kings, who intended them to adorn the cities where they stood, others the gifts of Roman generals, who gave or restored them to the communities of Sicily in the hour of victory—this same governor stripped and despoiled every one of them. Nor was it only the civic statues and works of art that he treated thus; he also pillaged the holiest and most venerated sanctuaries; in fact, he has not left the people of Sicily a single god whose workmanship he thought at all above the average of antiquity or artistic merit. As to his adulteries and the like vile offences, a sense of decency makes me afraid to repeat the tale of his acts of wanton wickedness: and besides, I would not wish, by repeating it, to add to the calamities of those who have not been

* Reprinted by permission of the publishers and The Loeb Classical Library from Cicero, *The Verrine Orations,* trans. L. H. G. Greenwood (Cambridge, Mass.: Harvard University Press), excerpts from vols. I and II.

suffered to save their children and their wives from outrage at the hands of this lecherous scoundrel.

. . .

Now I do not suppose that Verres will at this point deny that he has numerous statues, and more pictures than he can count, in his possession. But I understand it to be his habit now and then to assert that these objects, which he has stolen by force or fraud, have really been bought. It would appear that he was sent out to Achaia and Asia and Pamphylia, at the national expense and with the title of assistant governor, in order to engage in the statue and picture trade. . . . You cannot deny that you brought away a large number of beautiful statues and a large number of fine paintings. I only wish you would deny it! Show me the record, either in your own accounts or your father's, of your buying a single one of these things, and I surrender.

. . .

The man of whom I speak, Gavius of Consa, was one of those Roman citizens whom Verres threw into prison. Somehow or other he escaped from the Stone Quarries, and made his way to Messana. Italy was now visible only a few miles away, and the walls of Regium with its population of Roman citizens; he had come forth from the awful shadow of death, revived and strengthened by the light of freedom and the fresh air of justice; and so he began to talk indignantly to people in Messana of how he, a Roman citizen, had been thrown into prison, and how he was going straight to Rome and would be ready for Verres on his arrival there. The poor fellow was not aware that to say such things in Messana was equivalent to saying them to the governor in his own house; for Verres, as I have already explained, had chosen this town to assist him in his crimes, to receive his stolen goods, and to share the secret of all his abominable deeds. The result was that Gavius was at once seized and taken before the chief magistrate of Messana. Verres chanced to arrive there that same day, and it was reported to him that there was a Roman citizen with an angry story about having been in the Stone Quarries at Syracuse, who was already going aboard a ship, uttering unpleasantly savage threats against Verres, when they had dragged him ashore again and kept him in custody for Verres to deal with as he thought best. Verres thanked these people, commending warmly their kind and careful attention to his interests. Then he made for the market-place, on fire with mad and wicked rage, his eyes blazing, and cruelty showing clearly in every feature of his face. Everyone was wondering how far he would go and what he was meaning to do, when he suddenly ordered the man to be flung down, stripped naked and tied up in the open market-place, and rods to be got ready. The unhappy man cried out that he was a Roman citizen, a burgess of Consa; that he had served in the army under the distinguished Roman knight Lucius Raecius, who was in business at Panhormus and could assure Verres of the truth of his story. To this Verres replied that he had discovered that Gavius had been sent to Sicily as a spy by the leaders of the fugitive army, a charge which was brought by no informer, for which there was no evidence, and which nobody saw any reason to believe. He then ordered the man to be flogged severely all over his body. There in the open market-place of Messana a Roman citizen, gentlemen, was beaten with rods; and all the while, amid the crack of the falling blows, no groan was heard from the unhappy man, no words came from his lips in his agony except "I am a Roman citizen." By thus proclaiming his citizenship he had been hoping to avert all those blows and shield his body from torture; yet not only did he fail to secure escape from those cruel rods, but when he persisted in his entreaties and his appeals to his citizen rights, a cross was made ready—yes, a cross, for that hapless and broken sufferer, who had never seen such an accursed thing till then.

. . .

. . . To bind a Roman citizen is a crime, to flog him is an abomination, to slay him is almost an act of murder: to crucify him is—what? There is no fitting word that can possibly describe so horrible a deed. . . . It was not Gavius, not one obscure man, whom you nailed upon that cross of agony: it was the universal principle that Romans are free men. . . .

13   PAX ROMANA

The social ailments and disorders of the late Republican period were finally resolved with the firm but enlightened rule of Julius Caesar and of his adopted son and heir, Octavius, or as he is known in history Augustus (31 B.C.–A.D. 14). It was their strong measures and their sweeping reforms that laid the foundation for the Pax Romana *that was to prevail for two centuries. The following panegyric by Aelius Aristides of Smyrna, delivered in 143, stresses the positive aspects of the Roman Empire at its height. Unlike Tacitus, Aristides reflects the contentment of at least the middle and upper classes with the security and prosperity of imperial rule.**

Some chronicler, speaking of Asia, asserted that one man ruled as much land as the sun passed, and his statement was not true because he placed all Africa and Europe outside the limits where the sun rises in the East and sets in the West. It has now however turned out to be true. Your possession is equal to what the sun can pass, and the sun passes over your land. Neither the Chelidonean nor the Cyanean promontories limit your empire, nor does the distance from which a horseman can reach the sea in one day, nor do you reign within fixed boundaries, nor does another dictate to what point your control reaches; but the sea like a girdle lies extended, at once in the middle of the civilized world and of your hegemony.

Around it lie the great continents greatly sloping, ever offering to you in full measure something of their own. Whatever the seasons make grow and whatever countries and rivers and lakes and arts of Hellenes and non-Hellenes produce are brought from every land and sea, so that if one would look at all these things, he must needs behold them either by visiting the entire civilized world or by coming to this city. For whatever is grown and made among each people cannot fail to be here at all times and in abundance. And here the merchant vessels come carrying these many products from all regions in every season and even at every equinox, so that the city appears a kind of common emporium of the world.

Cargoes from India and, if you will, even from Arabia the Blest one can see in such numbers as to surmise that in those lands the trees will have been stripped

* Reprinted from J. H. Oliver, "The Ruling Power: A Study of the Roman Empire in the Second Century after Christ through the Roman Oration of Aelius Aristides," *Transactions,* American Philosophical Society, Vol. 43 (Philadelphia, 1953), Part 4, pp. 895–99, 901–02, 906–07.

bare and that the inhabitants of these lands, if they need anything, must come here and beg for a share of their own. Again one can see Babylonian garments and ornaments from the barbarian country beyond arriving in greater quantity and with more ease than of shippers from Naxos or from Cythnos, bearing something from those islands, had but to enter the port of Athens. Your farms are Egypt, Sicily and the civilized part of Africa.

Arrivals and departures by sea never cease, so that the wonder is, not that the harbor has insufficient space for merchant vessels, but that even the sea has enough, [if] it really does.

And just as Hesiod said about the ends of the Ocean that there is a common channel where all waters have one source and destination, so there is a common channel to Rome and all meet here, trade, shipping, agriculture, metallurgy, all the arts and crafts that are or ever have been, all the things that are engendered or grow from the earth. And whatever one does not see here neither did nor does exist. And so it is not easy to decide which is greater, the superiority of this city in respect to the cities that now are or the superiority of this empire in respect to the empires that ever were.

.   .   .

For of all who have ever gained empire you alone rule over men who are free. Caria has not been given to Tissaphernes, nor Phrygia to Pharnabazus, nor Egypt to someone else; nor is the country said to be enslaved, as household of so-and-so, to whomsoever it has been turned over, a man himself not free. But just as those in states of one city appoint the magistrates to protect and care for the governed, so you, who conduct public business in the whole civilized world exactly as if it were one city state, appoint the governors, as is natural after elections, to protect and care for the governed, not to be slave masters over them. Therefore governor makes way for governor unobtrusively, when his time is up, and far from staying too long and disputing the land with his successor, he might easily not stay long enough even to meet him.

Appeals to a higher court are made with the ease of an appeal from deme to dicastery, with no greater menace for those who make them than for those who have accepted the local verdict. Therefore one might say that the men of today are ruled by the governors who are sent out, only in so far as they are content to be ruled.

. . . There is an abundant and beautiful equality of the humble with the great and of the obscure with the illustrious, and, above all, of the poor man with the rich and of the commoner with the noble, and the word of Hesiod comes to pass, "For he easily exalts, and the exalted he easily checks," namely this judge and princeps as the justice of the claim may lead, like a breeze in the sails of a ship, favoring and accompanying, not the rich man more, the poor man less, but benefiting equally whomsoever it meets.

.   .   .

But there is that which very decidedly deserves as much attention and admiration now as all the rest together. I mean your magnificent citizenship with its grand conception, because there is nothing like it in the records of all mankind. Dividing into two groups all those in your empire—and with this word I have indicated the entire civilized world—you have everywhere appointed to your citizenship, or even to kinship with you, the better part of the world's talent, courage, and leadership, while the rest you recognized as a league under your hegemony.

Neither sea nor intervening continent are bars to citizenship, nor are Asia and Europe divided in their treatment here. In your empire all paths are open to all. No one worthy of rule or trust remains an alien, but a civil community of the World has been established as a Free Republic under one, the best, ruler and teacher of order; and all come together as into a common civic center, in order to receive each man his due.

. . .

Wars, even if they once occurred, no longer seem to have been real; on the contrary, stories about them are interpreted more as myths by the many who hear them. If anywhere an actual clash occurs along the border, as is only natural in the immensity of a great empire, because of the madness of Getae or the misfortune of Libyans or the wickedness of those around the Red Sea, who are unable to enjoy the blessing they have, then simply like myths they themselves quickly pass and the stories about them.

. . .

Homer said, "Earth common of all," and you have made it come true. You have measured and recorded the land of the entire civilized world; you have spanned the rivers with all kinds of bridges and hewn highways through the mountains and filled the barren stretches with posting stations; you have accustomed all areas to a settled and orderly way of life. Therefore, I see on reflection that what is held to be the life before Triptolemus is really the life before your time,—a hard and boorish life, not far removed from that of the wild mountains. Though the citizens of Athens began the civilized life of today, this life in its turn has been firmly established by you, who came later but who, men say, are better.

Chapter Nine

Indian civilization

*In the perspective of world history, India is the home of one of the most ancient, distinctive, and significant civilizations of mankind. Its roots go back to the original civilization of the Indus Valley (see Reading 8, "India's Forgotten Civilization") and to the innovations introduced by the Aryan invaders (see Reading 9, "Indian and Greek Epics"). The following selection analyzes the basic concepts underlying this traditional civilization, which, to a considerable degree, endures to the present day. The author is a well-known Indian educator who has served as Secretary of the Indian Ministry of Education and Vice-President of the Unesco Executive Board.**

What is culture? I shall not try to define this term. If, however, I was asked this question in India I would reply simply: culture is the soul of a people, the basic beliefs, attitudes and spiritual values of the Indian people which have become their way of life.

The culture of India or the Indian way of life is the product of a long and continuous history, parts of which are unknown and unwritten. From the third millennium before Christ, when a great civilization flourished on the banks of the Indus, to the present day, there has been basically one, unbroken stream of culture which found its course very early, flowing sometimes in rocky country and under rough weather, but always broadening and assimilating. Some time before the Vedic hymns were written, the Indian seers discovered the two great virtues of contemplation and compassion, and passed these on into the making of a civilization; from this all else followed. In the growth of a civilization, material

* Reprinted from P. Kirpal, "Indian Culture Today: I—The Heritage of the Past," *Unesco Features,* June 1969, pp. 6–10.

development precedes and largely determines abstract ideas in the early stages of history. In India it seems that from the earliest times ideas played a dominant rôle in creating a civilized way of life; from the very beginning the poet seer was more important to society than the warlord who led the tribe.

To synthesize different races, languages, creeds, beliefs and customs into a comprehensive whole and to attempt always to create increasing unity out of growing diversity became the main occupation of leaders of thought and action through the long centuries of India's history. We have, therefore, the most diverse racial, social, religious, artistic and cultural elements of the various regions of a vast sub-continent, developed within or received from outside, all welded into an unmistakable cultural pattern. This pattern has different forms and symbols built around the same spirit and essence of things, always attempting to express a broad unity of thought and outlook in the midst of a rich and free diversity of the patterns of living.

What is the essence of Indian culture which is shared by all our people?

There are, I think, three big ideas underlying all the external variety and complex manifestations of Indian culture: (i) an overriding belief in the reality of the life of the spirit and its superiority over temporal phenomena and passing experiences; (ii) conformity to the principle of Ahimsa or non-violence and tolerance as a guide to practical conduct; and (iii) an implicit belief in a sense of order and method governing the life and nature of the individual, of society, of the universe and even of the Divinity.

LIFE OF THE SPIRIT. The most essential feature of Hindu culture is the belief that the essence of man is in reality the same spirit which pervades the whole universe and in which a direct consciousness of God can be experienced. The *Upanishads* proclaim this truth beyond any shadow of doubt: "Thou art that" (Tat Twam asi); "This self is the Absolute Reality" (Ayam Atma Brahma); "The spirit that is in man and the spirit that is in the sun are one and identical" (Sa yascha ayam purusho yasha asan Aditya sa eka). The knowledge of this spiritual reality can be gained by practising various forms of Yoga or discipline. In yoga the processes of introspection, intuition and Samadhi (mystic experience) are refined and perfected, and by these methods incomplete and imperfect man can become aware of the vast unconscious and the limitless conscious strata of being within himself. The Absolute Reality, which is spiritual in essence, cannot be grasped by the mind alone nor can it be described in any language or terms invented by the mind. The seers who have experienced this spiritual Reality say that it is infinite (ananta) awareness (juanam) characterized by bliss (ananda). According to the *Yogavasistha,* "the nature of the Absolute Reality cannot be satisfactorily talked about or discussed; it can only be experienced within the depth of one's own being" (VI b 31.37). "It is neither a being, nor a non-being, nor anything between the two. It is nothing, yet everything. It cannot be grasped by mind and expressed in words. It is empty of all possible contents, yet is the deepest of all enjoyments." (*Yogavasistha,* III, 119–23). The search for the nature of the Absolute or Brahman and the efforts to experience it within ourselves are the main pursuits of Indian philosophy and Religion.

The spiritual identity or interconnectedness of all beings follows from the concept of Brahman. This truth was revealed to Rama by his teacher Vasistha in these words: "How can the thought that some one is one's brother and another is not, hold good when there is one and the same all-pervading self present in all of us? Oh, Ram, beings of all species are your brothers, as there is no being who is unconnected with you." (*Yogavasistha* V 20.4 - V 18.46). The oldest of the *Upanishads*, the *Isha Upanishad*, expressed the same truth in the following words: "Whosoever beholds all beings in the same self and the same self in all beings does not hate anybody. When a man knows that all beings are ultimately the self and realizes this unity in experience, then there remains no delusion or grief for him." Many teachers and seers of ancient India have elaborated this idea and derived from it their ethics of universal brotherhood and benevolence.

Thus the main feature of Hinduism is a deep faith in an unseen reality of which all life is a manifestation, a profound belief in the primacy of spiritual experience which cannot be grasped by the mind alone.

On the authority of Aristoxenus, a writer on musical theory and a pupil of Aristotle, the Greek philosopher Eusebios narrates an interview between Socrates and an Indian philosopher some time in the 5th century B.C. Aristoxenus, the musician, tells the following story about the Indians: one of these men met Socrates at Athens and asked him what was the scope of his philosophy. 'An enquiry into the human phenomena.' Socrates answered. At this the Indian burst out laughing: 'How can a man inquire into human phenomena,' he exclaimed, 'when he is ignorant of divine ones?'

Perhaps this anecdote signifies a profound difference of outlook and approach between East and West. According to the Hindus we cannot understand man, much less plan for his happiness, without being aware of the divine spirit of which he is a part. Only spiritual reality is real; all else is to be transcended and related to this reality in which we experience complete knowledge and absolute truth.

THE PRINCIPLE OF AHIMSA OR NON-VIOLENCE AND TOLERANCE. From this follows the second great principle underlying Indian culture, the principle of Ahimsa or non-violence and tolerance. Mahatma Gandhi once wrote: "Hinduism insists on the brotherhood not only of all mankind but of all that lives. It is a conception which makes one giddy, but we have to work up to it. The moment we have restored real living equality between man and man, we shall be able to establish equality between man and the whole creation. When that day comes we shall have peace on earth and good will to all men." Ahimsa means more than freedom from ill-will against all beings at all times and in all ways, much more than mere non-violence. It is a positive attitude to life, a practical rule of conduct requiring the observance of good will, tolerance and reverence. Mahatma Gandhi used Ahimsa not only as a political weapon in overcoming by moral force the physical force of a mighty empire; he used it equally effectively in awakening the masses of people from sloth and slavery and in rousing their moral fervour and their dormant faith in the greatness of man and his destiny.

SENSE OF ORDER IN THE UNIVERSE. The destiny of man is not governed by blind fate or incomprehensible forces entirely outside our knowledge and control. There is a sense of order in the universe which we can discover—and this brings us to the third great idea permeating the life and thought of the Indians. Most of our religious and philosophical speculation is a search for order and system; all Indian art is the creation and expression of order out of complexity, system out of chaos. Originally the Caste system was a workable ordering of society which was not so irrational in its right observance; later on it degenerated into undeserved privilege and stupid exclusiveness. The life of the individual was regulated by the Ashrama system or the division of life into four distinct periods called the Brahmachavya Ashrama (student life), Grishasta Ashrama (householder's life) Vanaprastha Ashrama (life of social service), and Sanyasa Ashrama (life of meditation). The moral order of society is laid down in the ethical principles and duties according to Dharma.

There is a great emphasis on the performance of duties and on a disciplined way of life in Indian culture. The Indian word for culture is "sanskriti" which comes from a root meaning to purify, to sublimate, to mould and perfect. The concept of "right" is significantly absent from Indian literature. In the *Bhagavadgita,* Lord Krishna teaches his friend Arjuna to perform the duties that are demanded by his station in life, without any expectation of gain or reward from any quarter; the performance of one's duties without any hope of gain or reward is the best worship of God. Duty well done in a spirit of sacrifice is the condition of Rights. In a brief and terse message to Unesco on the subject of Human Rights, Gandhi summed up the Indian view: "I learnt from my illiterate but wise mother that all rights to be deserved and preserved came from duty well done. Thus the very right to live accrues to us only when we do the duty of citizenship of the world. From this one fundamental statement, perhaps it is easy to define the duties of Man and Woman and correlate every right to some corresponding duty to be first performed. Every other right can be shown to be usurpation hardly worth fighting for."

The belief in Reincarnation and the law of Karma is part of the cosmic order. According to the law of Karma everyone must bear the consequences of his deeds. No one can escape Karma. "Even the gods have to undergo the good and evil consequences of their acts" says the author of the *Mahabharata.* It is stated in the *Yogavasistha:* "There is no place in the universe—no mountain, no sky, no ocean, no heaven—where one does not undergo the good or evil consequences of the deeds done by one." (Ill. 95.33) Physical death does not stop the operation of the law of Karma. The soul passes from one body to another and the law of Karma operates relentlessly until enlightenment and good actions lead to Nirvana or emancipation from the cycle of births and deaths.

Spiritual freedom and merit are attained after long discipline and continuous performance of good deeds by the individual. The *Yogavasistha* describes a Jivanmukta or a liberated man who has attained such merit in these words: "Pleasures do not delight him; pains do not distress. Although externally engaged in wordly actions, he has no attachment in his mind to any object whatsoever. His conduct does not annoy anybody; he behaves like an ideal citizen and is a friend of all. Outwardly he is very busy, but at heart very calm and quiet. He is free from the restrictions of Caste, creed, stage of life (Ashrama), custom and scriptures. He rests unagitated in the Supreme Bliss. He does not work to get anything for himself. He is always happy and his face is never without the lustre of cheerfulness. In spite of being occupied with actions appropriate to time, place and circumstance, he is not touched by pleasure or pain arising from them. He never feels despondent, proud, agitated, cast down, troubled or elated. He is full of energy and magnanimity, even when surrounded by enemies. He works without any anxiety, egoistic feeling, pride or impurity of heart. He finds equal pleasure in old age, death, misery, poverty and in ruling over an empire. He keeps his body healthy and does not starve it of its appropriate requirements. The life of a liberated sage is really the noblest and happiest life. From him goodness is scattered all around. Having seem him, having heard about him, having met him and having remembered him, all creatures feel delighted."

Few Indian sources are available for the study of Indian history. Because of the Hindu conviction that human destiny is not to find its fulfillment in this world, history traditionally was regarded as subordinate to philosophy, and of interest only insofar as it could illumine eternal verities. Hence the paucity and amorphousness of Indian historical sources and the need to depend on the accounts left by more secular-minded foreign visitors. This is particularly true of the close to two hundred Chinese Buddhist pilgrims known to have made the long and perilous journey to India to imbibe Buddhist teachings at their source. The most famous was Hsüan-tsang who went to India by way of Central Asia and visited all parts of the country between 635 and 643. Being more observant of secular life than most of his fellow pilgrims, Hsüan-tsang has left an invaluable account, which imparts flesh and blood to the bare bones of dates and dynastic names.*

The countries embraced under this term of India are generally spoken of as the five Indies. In circuit this country is about 90,000 *li;* on three sides it is bordered by the great sea; on the north it is backed by the Snowy Mountains. The north part is broad, the southern part is narrow. Its shape is like the half-moon. The entire land is divided into seventy countries or so. The seasons are particularly hot; the land is well watered and humid. The north is a continuation of mountains and hills, the ground being dry and salt. On the east there are valleys and plains, which being well watered and cultivated, are fruitful and productive. The southern district is wooded and herbaceous; the western parts are stony and barren. Such is the general account of this country.

.　　.　　.

The towns and villages have inner gates; the walls are wide and high; the streets and lanes are tortuous, and the roads winding. The thoroughfares are dirty and the stalls arranged on both sides of the road with appropriate signs. Butchers, fishers, dancers, executioners, and scavengers, and so on, have their abodes without the city. In coming and going these persons are bound to keep on the left side of the road till they arrive at their homes. Their houses are surrounded by low walls, and form the suburbs. The earth being soft and muddy, the walls of the towns are mostly built of brick or tiles. . . . The walls are covered with lime and mud, mixed with cow's dung for purity. At different seasons they scatter flowers about. Such are some of their different customs.

.　　.　　.

Their clothing is not cut or fashioned; they mostly affect fresh-white garments; they esteem little those of mixed colour or ornamented. The men wind their garments round their middle, then gather them under the armpits, and let them fall down across the body, hanging to the right. The robes of the women fall

* From Si-Yu-Ki, *Buddhist Records of the Western World,* trans. Samuel Beal (London: Kegan Paul, 1884), I, 70–89. Reprinted by Paragon Book Reprint Corp. (New York: 1968).

down to the ground; they completely cover their shoulders. They wear a little knot of hair on the crowns, and let the rest of their hair fall loose. Some of the men cut off their moustaches, and have other odd customs. . . .

.   .   .

They are very particular in their personal cleanliness, and allow no remissness in this particular. All wash themselves before eating; they never use that which has been left over (*from a former meal*); they do not pass the dishes. Wooden and stone vessels, when used, must be destroyed; vessels of gold, silver, copper, or iron after each meal must be rubbed and polished. After eating they cleanse their teeth with a willow stick, and wash their hands and mouth.

Until these ablutions are finished they do not touch one another. Every time they perform the functions of nature they wash their bodies and use perfumes of sandal-wood or turmeric.

When the king washes they strike the drums and sing hymns to the sound of musical instruments. Before offering their religious services and petitions, they wash and bathe themselves.

.   .   .

With respect to the division of families, there are four classifications. The first is called the Brâhman (*Po-lo-men*), men of pure conduct. They guard themselves in religion, live purely, and observe the most correct principles. The second is called Kshattriya (*T'sa-ti-li*), the royal caste. For ages they have been the governing class: they apply themselves to virtue (*humanity*) and kindness. The third is called Vaisyas (*feï-she-li*), the merchant class: they engage in commercial exchange, and they follow profit at home and abroad. The fourth is called Sûdra (*Shu-t'o-lo*), the agricultural class: they labour in ploughing and tillage. In these four classes purity or impurity of caste assigns to every one his place. When they marry they rise or fall in position according to their new relationship. They do not allow promiscuous marriages between relations. A woman once married can never take another husband. Besides these there are other classes of many kinds that intermarry according to their several callings. It would be difficult to speak of these in detail.

.   .   .

The chief soldiers of the country are selected from the bravest of the people, and as the sons follow the profession of their fathers, they soon acquire a knowledge of the art of war. These dwell in garrison around the palace (*during peace*), but when on an expedition they march in front as an advanced guard. . . .

The cavalry spread themselves in front to resist an attack, and in case of defeat they carry orders hither and thither. The infantry by their quick movements contribute to the defence. These men are chosen for their courage and strength. They carry a long spear and a great shield; sometimes they hold a sword or sabre, and advance to the front with impetuosity. All their weapons of war are sharp and pointed. Some of them are these—spears, shields, bows, arrows, swords, sabres, battle-axes, lances, halberds, long javelins, and various kinds of slings. All these they have used for ages.

. . . In the investigation of criminal cases there is no use of rod or staff to obtain proofs (*of guilt*). In questioning an accused person, if he replies with frankness the punishment is proportioned accordingly; but if the accused obstinately denies his fault, or in despite of it attempts to excuse himself, then in searching out the truth to the bottom, when it is necessary to pass sentence, there are four kinds of ordeal used—(1) by water, (2) by force, (3) by weighing, (4) by poison.

When the ordeal is by water, then the accused is placed in a sack connected with a stone vessel and thrown into deep water. They then judge of his innocence (*truth*) or guilt in this way—if the man sinks and the stone floats he is guilty; but if the man floats and the stone sinks then he is pronounced innocent.

Secondly, by fire. They heat a plate of iron and make the accused sit on it, and again place his feet on it, and apply it to the palms of his hands; moreover, he is made to pass his tongue over it; if no scars result, he is innocent; if there are scars, his guilt is proved. In case of weak and timid persons who cannot endure such ordeal, they take a flower-bud and cast it towards the fire; if it opens, he is innocent; if the flower is burnt, he is guilty.

Ordeal by weight is this: A man and a stone are placed in a balance evenly, then they judge according to lightness or weight. If the accused is innocent, then the man weighs down the stone, which rises in the balance; if he is guilty, the man rises and the stone falls.

Ordeal by poison is this: They take a ram and make an incision in its right thigh, then mixing all sorts of poison with a portion of the food of the accused men, they place it in the incision made in the thigh (*of the animal*); if the man is guilty, then the poison takes effect and the creature dies; if he is innocent, then the poison has no effect, and he survives.

By these four methods of trial the way of crime is stopped.

.   .   .

As the administration of the government is founded on benign principles, the executive is simple. The families are not entered on registers, and the people are not subject to forced labour (*conscription*). The private demesnes of the crown are divided into four principal parts; the first is for carrying out the affairs of state and providing sacrificial offerings; the second is for providing subsidies for the ministers and chief officers of state; the third is for rewarding men of distinguished ability; and the fourth is for charity to religious bodies, whereby the field of merit is cultivated (*planted*). In this way the taxes on the people are light, and the personal service required of them is moderate. Each one keeps his own worldly goods in peace, and all till the ground for their subsistence. These who cultivate the royal estates pay a sixth part of the produce as tribute. The merchants who engage in commerce come and go in carrying out their transactions. The river-passages and the road-barriers are open on payment of a small toll. When the public works require it, labour is exacted but paid for. The payment is in strict proportion to the work done.

.   .   .

In cultivating the land, those whose duty it is sow and reap, plough and harrow (*weed*), and plant according to the season; and after their labour they rest awhile. Among the products of the ground, rice and corn are most plentiful. With respect to edible herbs and plants, we may name ginger and mustard, melons and pumpkins, the *Heun-to* (*Kandu?*) plant, and others. Onions and garlic are little grown; and a few persons eat them; if any one uses them for food, they are expelled beyond the walls of the town. The most usual food is milk, butter, cream, soft sugar, sugar-candy, the oil of the mustard-seed, and all sorts of cakes made of corn are used as food. Fish, mutton, gazelle, and deer they eat generally fresh, sometimes salted; they are forbidden to eat the flesh of the ox, the ass, the elephant, the horse, the pig, the dog, the fox, the wolf, the lion, the monkey, and all the hairy kind. Those who eat them are despised and scorned, and are universally reprobated; they live outside the walls, and are seldom seen among men.

. . .

. . . There is no lack of suitable things for household use. Although they have saucepans and stewpans, yet they do not know the steamer used for cooking rice. They have many vessels made of dried clay; they seldom use red copper vessels: they eat from one vessel, mixing all sorts of condiments together, which they take up with their fingers. They have no spoons or cups, and in short no sort of chopstick.

Chapter Ten

Chinese civilization

CONFUCIANISM   **16**

The Chinese civilization, like the Indian, is one of the major civilizations of man-kind. But unlike the Indian, its outstanding characterstic is its secularism. It is the only major civilization that did not produce a priestly hierarchy. Its principal thinkers were interested more in man's problems in this world than in his salvation and afterlife. This is quite clear in the teachings of Confucius, China's great culture hero and one of the most influential figures in world history. In contrast to the otherworldly interests of most Indian thinkers, the main concern of Confucius was the formulation of moral principles to guide human relations within a family and between a king and his subjects. The most important of these principles are set forth in the following selections from the Analects, *the record of Confucius' activities and conversations as compiled by his disciples.**

GOVERNMENT AND PUBLIC AFFAIRS.   People despotically governed and kept in order by punishments may avoid infraction of the law, but they will lose their moral sense. People virtuously governed and kept in order by the inner law of self-control will retain their moral sense, and moreover become good.

Ching, Duke of the Ch'i State, questioned Confucius on the art of government. Confucius replied: Let the sovereign do his duty as a sovereign, the subject his duty as a subject, the father his duty as a father, and the son his duty as a son.—A good answer! said the Duke; for unless sovereign and subject, father and son do

---

* Reprinted from Lionel Giles, trans., *The Sayings of Confucius,* Wisdom of the East Series (London: John Murray Publishers Ltd., 1907), pp. 39ff.

89

their respective duties, however much grain there may be in the land, I could obtain none to eat.

The Master said: If the ruler is personally upright, his subjects will do their duty unbidden; if he is not personally upright, they will not obey, whatever his bidding.

The Master said: Government is good when it makes happy those who live under it and attracts those who live far away.

INDIVIDUAL VIRTUE. Tzu Yu put a question on the subject of filial piety. The Master said: The filial piety of today reduces itself to the mere question of maintenance. Yet this is something in which even our dogs and horses have a share. Without the feeling of reverence, what is there to distinguish the two cases?

The nobler sort of man in his progress through the world has neither narrow predilections nor obstinate antipathies. What he follows is the line of duty.

The nobler sort of man is proficient in the knowledge of his duty; the inferior man is proficient only in money-making.

To be able to do to others as we would be done by—this is the true domain of moral virtue.

The Master said: The nobler sort of man emphasises the good qualities in others, and does not accentuate the bad. The inferior sort does the reverse.

The nobler sort of man is dignified but not proud; the inferior man is proud but not dignified.

The higher type of man seeks all that he wants in himself; the inferior man seeks all that he wants from others.

RELIGION. To sacrifice to a spirit with which you have nothing to do, is mere servility.

Chi Lu inquired concerning men's duty to spirits. The Master replied: Before we are able to do our duty by the living, how can we do it by the spirits of the dead?—Chi Lu went on to inquire about death. The Master said: Before we know what life is, how can we know what death is?

17 TAOISM

The chief rival of Confucianism for the allegiance of the Chinese people was Taoism, an escapist and nature-loving creed that opposed any form of interference with the natural course of the universe. In contrast to Confucianism's emphasis on morality and social responsibility, Taoism urged individual freedom and a mystical union with nature.

The ideal society for the Taoists was that which remained the most primitive and least governed, as indicated in the following selections.*

The Sage occupies himself with inaction, and conveys instruction without words.

.   .   .

Purge yourself of your profound intelligence, and you can still be free from blemish. Cherish the people and order the kingdom, and you can still do without meddlesome action.

Who is there that can make muddy water clear? But if allowed to remain still, it will gradually become clear of itself. Who is there that can secure a state of absolute repose? But let time go on, and the state of repose will gradually arise.

Be sparing of speech, and things will come right of themselves.

A violent wind does not outlast the morning; a squall of rain does not outlast the day. Such is the course of Nature. And if Nature herself cannot sustain her efforts long, how much less can man!

Attain complete vacuity, and sedulously preserve a state of repose.

Tao is eternally inactive, and yet it leaves nothing undone. If kings and princes could but hold fast to this principle, all things would work out their own reformation. If, having reformed, they still desired to act, I would have them restrained by the simplicity of the Nameless Tao. The simplicity of the Nameless Tao brings about an absence of desire. The absence of desire gives tranquillity. And thus the Empire will rectify itself.

.   .   .

The Empire has ever been won by letting things take their course. He who must always be doing is unfit to obtain the Empire.

Keep the mouth shut, close the gateways of sense, and as long as you live you will have no trouble. Open your lips and push your affairs, and you will not be safe to the end of your days.

Practice inaction, occupy yourself with doing nothing.

Desire not to desire, and you will not value things difficult to obtain. Learn not to learn, and you will revert to a condition which mankind in general has lost.

Leave all things to take their natural course, and do not interfere.

.   .   .

Were I ruler of a little State with a small population, and only ten or a hundred men available as soldiers, I would not use them. I would have the people look on death as a grievous thing, and they should not travel to distant countries. Though they might possess boats and carriages, they should have no occasion to ride in them. Though they might own weapons and armour, they should have no need to use them. I would make the people return to the use of knotted cords. They should find their plain food sweet, their rough garments fine. They should be content with their homes, and happy in their simple ways. If a neighbouring State was within sight of mine—nay, if we were close enough to hear the crowing of each other's cocks and the barking of each other's dogs— the two peoples should grow old and die without there ever having been any mutual intercourse.

.   .   .

* Reprinted from Lionel Giles, trans., *The Sayings of Lao Tzu,* Wisdom of the East Series (London: John Murray Publishers Ltd., 1905), pp. 30ff.

Those who know do not speak; those who speak do not know.
Abandon learning, and you will be free from trouble and distress.

. . .

There is nothing in the world more soft and weak than water, yet for attacking things that are hard and strong there is nothing that surpasses it, nothing that can take its place.

The soft overcomes the hard; the weak overcomes the strong. There is no one in the world but knows this truth, and no one who can put it into practice.

18   LEGALISM

Very different from both Confucianism and Taoism were the doctrines of Legalism. This was not a philosophy but a set of realistic, Machiavellian tenets designed to strengthen the state for the waging of war. Because China was torn by constant strife amongst rival feudal states during the fourth century B.C. *when Legalism was propounded, the aim of the Legalists was the unification of the country by superior military and economic power. How this power was to be attained is outlined in the following selection from the writings of one of the Legalist theoreticians, Han Fei Tzu.**

When the sage rules the state, he does not count on people doing good of themselves, but employs such measures as will keep them from doing any evil. If he counts on people doing good of themselves, there will not be enough such people to be numbered by the tens in the whole country. But if he employs such measures as will keep them from doing evil, then the entire state can be brought up to a uniform standard. Inasmuch as the administrator has to consider the many but disregard the few, he does not busy himself with morals but with laws.

. . .

Now, when witches and priests pray for people, they say: "May you live as long as one thousand and ten thousand years!" Even as the sounds, "one thousand and ten thousand years," are dinning upon one's ears, there is no sign that even a single day has been added to the age of any man. That is the reason why people despise witches and priests. Likewise, when the Confucianists of the present day counsel the rulers they do not discuss the way to bring about order now, but exalt the achievement of good order in the past. They neither study affairs pertaining to law and government nor observe the realities of vice and wickedness, but all exalt the reputed glories of remote antiquity and the achievements of the ancient kings. Sugar-coating their speech, the Confucianists say: "If you listen to our words, you will be able to become the leader of all feudal lords." Such people are but witches and priests among the itinerant counselors, and are not to be accepted by rulers with principles. Therefore, the intelligent ruler upholds solid facts and discards useless frills. He does not speak about deeds of humanity and righteousness, and he does not listen to the words of learned men.

* Reprinted from W. T. de Bary et al., *Sources of Chinese Tradition* (New York: Columbia University Press, 1960), pp. 141–43, 146–50.

Those who are ignorant about government insistently say: "Win the hearts of the people." If order could be procured by winning the hearts of the people, then even the wise ministers Yi Yin and Kuan Chung would be of no use. For all that the ruler would need to do would be just to listen to the people. Actually, the intelligence of the people is not to be relied upon any more than the mind of a baby. If the baby does not have his head shaved, his sores will recur; if he does not have his boil cut open, his illness will go from bad to worse. However, in order to shave his head or open the boil someone has to hold the baby while the affectionate mother is performing the work, and yet he keeps crying and yelling incessantly. The baby does not understand that suffering a small pain is the way to obtain a great benefit.

Now, the sovereign urges the tillage of land and the cultivation of pastures for the purpose of increasing production for the people, but they think the sovereign is cruel. The sovereign regulates penalties and increases punishments for the purpose of repressing the wicked, but the people think the sovereign is severe. Again, he levies taxes in cash and in grain to fill up the granaries and treasuries in order to relieve famine and provide for the army, but they think the sovereign is greedy. Finally, he insists upon universal military training without personal favoritism, and urges his forces to fight hard in order to take the enemy captive, but the people think the sovereign is violent. These four measures are methods for attaining order and maintaining peace, but the people are too ignorant to appreciate them.

.　　.　　.

The literati by means of letters upset laws; the cavaliers by means of their prowess transgress prohibitions. Yet the ruler treats them both with decorum. This is actually the cause of all the disorder. Every departure fom the law ought to be apprehended, and yet scholars are nevertheless taken into office on account of their literary learning. Again, the transgression of every prohibition ought to be censured, and yet cavaliers are patronized because of their readiness to draw the sword. Thus, those whom the law reproves turn out to be those whom the ruler employs, and those whom the magistrates suppress are those whom the sovereign patronizes. Thus legal standard and personal inclination as well as ruler and ministers are sharply opposed to each other and all fixed standards are lost. Then, even if there were ten Yellow Emperors, they would not be able to establish any order. Therefore, those who practice humanity and righteousness should not be upheld, for if upheld, they would hinder concrete accomplishments. Again, those who specialize in refinement and learning should not be employed, for if employed, they would disturb the laws. There was in Ch'u an upright man named Kung, who, when his father stole a sheep, reported it to the authorities. The magistrate said: "Put him to death," as he thought the man was faithful to the ruler but disloyal to his father. So the man was apprehended and convicted. From this we can see that the faithful subject of the ruler was an outrageous son to his father. Again, there was a man of Lu who followed his ruler to war, fought three battles, and ran away three times. Confucius interrogated him. The man replied: "I have an old father. Should I die, nobody would take care of him." Confucius regarded him as virtuous in filial piety, commended and exalted him. From this we can see that the dutiful son of the father was a rebellious subject to the ruler. Naturally, following the censure of the honest man by the magistrate, no more culprits in Ch'u were reported to the authorities; and following the reward of the runaway by Confucius, the people of Lu were prone to surrender and run away. The interests of superior and subordinate being so different, it would be hopeless for any ruler to try to exalt the deeds of private individuals and, at the same time, to promote the public welfare of the state.

. . .

In the state ruled by an enlightened sovereign, one would find no recorded literature and the law would supply the only instruction; one would find no injunctions from the early kings and the magistrates would serve as the only instructors; one would find no [esteem for] bravery in achieving private vengeance, and killing of the enemy would be regarded as the only courageous deed. As a result, the people in the state would all conform to the law in their discourse, would aim at meritorious achievement in their actions, and would offer their services to the army out of bravery. Therefore, in time of peace the state would be rich; in time of war the army would be strong. These might be called the "kingly resources." When the "kingly resources" were stored up, the sovereign could avail himself of any situation that might arise in the state of the enemy. . . .

This then is the customary experience of a disorderly state: the learned men will exalt the ways of the early kings and make a show of humanity and righteousness. They will adorn their manners and clothes and embroider their arguments and speeches so as to scatter doubts on the law of the age and beguile the mind of the sovereign. The itinerant speakers will advocate deceptive theories and utilize foreign influence to accomplish their selfish purposes, being unmindful of the benefit of the state. The free-lance fighters will gather pupils and followers and set up standards of fidelity and discipline, hoping thereby to spread their reputation, but violating the prohibitions of the Five Ministries in the process. The courtiers will congregate in the powerful houses, use all kinds of bribes, and exploit their contacts with influential men in order to escape the burden of military service. The tradesmen and craftsmen will produce inferior wares and collect cheap articles, and wait for good opportunities to exploit the farmers. These five types of men are the vermin of the state. Should the ruler fail to eliminate such people as the five vermin and should he not uphold men of firm integrity and strong character, then he can hardly be surprised if within the seas there should be states that decline and fall, and dynasties that wane and perish.

Chapter Eleven

End of classical civilizations

THE HAN EMPIRE AND THE HSIUNG-NU   **19**

Between the third and the sixth centuries A.D. *the classical civilizations of Eurasia, weakened by internal dissension and deterioration, succumbed to the onslaught of barbarian invaders. This was true not only of the Roman Empire, whose "fall" has elicited much contemporary and modern commentary, but also of the Han Empire in China and of the Gupta in India. The following selections from the works of Pan Ku, a historian, and Ch'ao Ts'o, a statesman, describe the Hsiung-nu, the nomads who eventually overwhelmed the Han Empire.**

Pan Ku

The Hsiung-nu live in the north and are a nomadic people. They raise a variety of animals, most of which are horses, cattle, and sheep. Other animals such as camels and donkeys are comparatively small in number. They move constantly to seek water and grass; they have no cities, houses, or crop fields. Land, however, is divided among tribal groups.

The Hsiung-nu do not have any written language; consequently all agreements or promises are made in oral form. Small children are taught to ride sheep and shoot birds and squirrels. When they grow older, they begin to shoot foxes and rabbits. Meat, instead of grain, is their staple food. All able-bodied men are expert archers and are members of the cavalry in their respective tribes.

Under normal circumstances when life is comparatively easy, the Hsiung-nu

---

* Reprinted from Pan Ku, "The Hsiung-nu," and Ch'ao Ts'o, "The Defense of Our Northern Frontier." As translated in *The Essence of Chinese Civilization,* by Dun J. Li. Copyright © 1967, by Litton Educational Publishing, Inc., by permission of Van Nostrand Reinhold Company.

earn their livelihood by tending their herds and augment it by hunting. When life becomes difficult, all men are taught the art of warfare, preparing ardently for the launching of attacks. This, you might say, is the nature of the Hsiung-nu. They rely on bows and arrows if the enemy is at a distance and switch to knives and spears in close combat. They attack when they are certain of victory, but are not ashamed to run away from the battlefield if they think that the odds are heavily against them. They go wherever there are profits to be realized; they do not know of such things as righteousness and propriety.

From the king down, all the Hsiung-nu people eat animals' meat, wear their skins, and convert their furs into garments. The young and the strong have priority to the best food; the elderly have to be satisfied with the leftovers. They highly value youth and strength, and look down upon the old and the weak. After the death of his father, a man will marry his step-mother. Likewise he takes his brother's wife as his own when and if his brother dies. . . .

In the first month of each year the khan holds court with all people in his tribe. In the fifth month he gathers all tribal members at Lung where he offers sacrifices to Heaven, Earth, gods, and spirits. Again in the fall when horses are strong and alert, he calls into session another assembly in a forest region, offering sacrifices to gods and spirits and counting the numbers of men and animals.

According to the Hsiung-nu law, he who kills another man will be punished by death. A robber will be condemned to slavery together with all members of his family. Small offenders will be lashed with a stick; serious offenders, on the other hand, will be thrown into jail where they usually die within a period of ten days. Thus throughout the Hsiung-nu empire there are fewer than ten people in jail at any time.

The khan worships the rising sun early in the morning and the moon in the evening. In seating arrangement the person who sits on the left and faces the north is the most honored among the group. The dead are buried in coffins, accompanied with gold, silver, and clothing. But the graves are not marked with trees, nor do the mourners wear mourning clothes. Upon the death of a khan approximately one hundred of his favorite ministers and concubines will be put to death so that their spirits will be able to follow his.

During a military campaign the Hsiung-nu watch closely the size of the moon. They attack when the moon is large and bright and withdraw when it becomes small and dim. A Hsiung-nu soldier who kills an enemy will be awarded one goblet of wine plus whatever material goods he has taken from his victim. If he captures a man or woman alive, the latter becomes his slave. Thus on the battlefield all Hsiung-nu soldiers fight valiantly for their own material ends, upon which they converge like hungry vultures. Upon a setback, however, they disintegrate quickly and disperse like flying clouds. Their favorite strategy is to entice their enemy to a pre-arranged place and then encircle him. After a battle, the warrior who brings home the body of a dead comrade will inherit all of the latter's wordly possessions.

Ch'ao Ts'o

Despite the fact that their territories are barren and unproductive, the northern barbarians have no difficulty in mustering enough strength to invade our border areas repeatedly. Why?

The northern barbarians eat meat, drink milk, and wear animal furs and skins. They have no fields, houses, or cities. Like birds and beasts, they move from place to place and stop only when they find water and good grass. When water or grass is exhausted, they move again until they find the same in some other place. There is no way of telling from where they have come or to which place they will go; nor do we know when they will come or go. This constant migration is the way they make their livelihood, to the same extent as we derive our livelihood from tilling the fields.

During their constant migration they often venture as far as our border provinces. Sometimes they set foot on Yen and Tai, and other times they penetrate as deep as Shangchün. Consequently garrisons have to be maintained throughout the northern frontier and also in the Lunghsi area.

The defense of the frontier by garrison soldiers poses a number of problems. If their number is small, the imperial government will have two choices when encountering a barbarian invasion. It can abstain from sending reinforcements, and in such case the people in the border areas, losing all hope of defending their territories, may decide to surrender themselves to the enemy. Suppose, say, that the imperial government makes the other choice and decides to send reinforcements. If the reinforcements are small, they may not be able to cope with the situation. If they are large, they will have to be dispatched from places far from the border areas; by the time they reach the frontier, the invaders may have already fled. Moreover, once a large force has been gathered on the frontier, the government will have a difficult time to decide what to do with it. If it is not sent back to the districts from where it came, the cost of maintaining it will be exorbitant. If it is, the barbarians will certainly invade again. . . .

THE FALL OF LO-YANG 20

The previous reading reflects the apprehension of Chinese leaders concerning the ever-present sword of Damocles hanging over their heads in the form of the nomads of Central Asia. On many occasions the sword descended, as these nomads overran parts of China, and two of these nomad peoples—the Mongols and the Manchus—conquered the entire country. The following account by a British sinologist describes the capture of Lo-yang, the great capital city in North China, in terms reminiscent of the corresponding fall of Rome in the West a century later.*

In A.D. 311 Lo-yang, the capital of China and the greatest city of the whole eastern world, was captured and sacked by the Huns. For several centuries northern China was under foreign rule, and when at the end of the sixth century the north passed once more into Chinese hands the culture of the great native dynasties that ruled a powerful and united China (such, for example, as that of the T'ang) was in many ways a synthesis of nomad Turkic and traditional Chinese elements. The year 311, then (like the year 410, when the Goths sacked Rome), marks a turning-point in history. Gibbon, before describing the sack of Rome, pauses to give a general account of the city and the people who lived in it. We may well follow his example. What, then, materially and spiritually, was Lo-yang at the beginning of the

* Reprinted from A. Waley, "The Fall of Lo-yang," *History Today,* April, 1951, pp. 7–10.

fourth century? . . . It lies in the north-west corner of the province of Honan, some twenty miles south of the Yellow River. The population at the beginning of the fourth century was about 600,000. That of Rome may have been somewhat larger; otherwise there was probably no city in the world of that size. It measured about two miles from north to south and was about one and a half miles wide. The main streets were divided into three parts. In the middle, the Imperial Road ran between walls about three and a half feet high. Only the Emperor and his family and the highest officials (Presidents of Boards, and the like) could use this central road. Ordinary people used the tracks that ran on each side of it, and these tracks were "One Way"; traffic going from one of the city gates to the centre used the left-hand track; traffic going in the reverse direction used the track on the right. These main roads were flanked by avenues of elm and sophora.

The public buildings were of the utmost magnificence. The Indian monk Jivaka who came to Lo-yang about 305 declared that the great cluster of Palace buildings corresponded exactly with the Thirty-three Palaces of the paramount god Indra, as seen by the religious in ecstatic vision, "allowing (he added) for the fact that they are human work, not divine." The blinds of these Palace buildings were of mother-of-pearl, and at sunset flashed with a dazzling radiance. The great boulevard that led up to the Palace buildings was called Bronze Camel Street, after the huge bronze figure of a camel that stood at its head, in the square outside the Palace gates. The Government offices were in the Palace precincts; the city offices of the provincial administrations lay near the eastern city gates. There were three markets: the Metal Market in the centre of the town, the Horse Market in the east and a general market outside the southern walls. It would be possible to give a much more detailed picture of Lo-yang at other periods, both earlier and later. For Lo-yang c. 311 our sources are limited.

When we turn from the city to the people that lived in it we naturally find ourselves provided with ample information about the educated, governing class, but are left completely in the dark about the lives and thoughts of the ordinary people who formed the bulk of the population. This is inevitable; for all the records come from members of the ruling class (which was at this period almost completely hereditary), and this class was interested in the common people mainly in regard to their corporate utility as soldiers and tax-payers, though always with an eye to the menace that they constituted as possible insurgents.

The prevailing faction in this ruling class was strongly Taoist. They justified conservative *laissez-faire* of a familiar kind by the argument that Being must have sprung from Non-being. Thus Everything is the product of Nothing, and this Nothing (which had the power to produce a whole universe) must be a prodigious force. They identified this force with Tao, the Absolute of the early Taoists, and believed that by conforming to it one can share in its magic; that one has only to do nothing, and everything gets done. This led to (or was the excuse for) a contempt for administrative duties and social obligations. . . .

As representative of these aristocratic Nihilists let us take Wang Yen (A.D. 266–311), Prime Minister at the time of the fall of Lo-yang. He belonged to one of the most distinguished families in China, the Wangs of Lang-yeh, and was descended from a long line of high officials. He was famous for his great beauty and in particular for the jade-like whiteness of his hands. . . . He did his best to take a negative line towards everything, merely to drift with the tide of events; and as he belonged to the privileged class, had great ability, and, despite his principles, a considerable capacity for decisive action, he "drifted" into high post after high post, until (as we have seen) he became Prime Minister, though still protesting that he had "never had any such ambition" and had only reached his present eminence "by a series of routine promotions".

The favourite distraction of Wang Yen and his friends was "pure conversation", that is to say, talk for talk's sake, as opposed to talking with a view to action. "Mysteries" (*hsüan*), such as how the universe came into existence, were discussed, and problems about the relation of words to facts. For example, is a white horse a horse? And interwoven with these high themes were endless discussions about the characters of absent friends. The conversation, in fact, was very like that of clever undergraduates at our own Universities. . . .

.   .   .

Now let us turn to the Huns. They were remote cousins of the Western Huns who invaded Europe in the fifth century. Hard-pressed by another Turkic people, the Hsien-pi, they had been given permission by the Chinese at various times in the third century to settle in north-eastern China, where they were intended to act as a buffer against attacks by other nomads. Shih Lo, whom I am taking as the representative of the Hun side, was born in 274. His father was leader of one of the Hun tribes that had been settled by the Chinese on the north-east frontier. About A.D. 302 the Governor of this part of China who, like most provincial governors at that period, was a member of the Chinese Imperial family, found himself short of funds for military expenses and raised the necessary amount by kidnapping a number of Huns and selling them as slaves. Among those that were marched off "chained in pairs" was Shih Lo. He was purchased by a man who lived at P'ing-yüan, in north-western Shantung, close to the Imperial horse-breeding pastures. Here he got into touch with one of the grooms, and with money obtained by petty brigandage bribed him to join a band of adventurers who Shih Lo had collected, and mount them on horses from the Imperial paddocks. They were joined by a number of Chinese malcontents, and under the leadership of the groom, who had now become their General with Shih Lo as his second-in-command, they began to plunder north-eastern China. In 307 they sacked the great city of Yeh, about 115 miles north-east of Lo-yang, and slaughtered its commander who was, in fact, the Governor who had sold Shih Lo into slavery. Shortly after this the groom General was heavily defeated by Government troops and Shih Lo, retiring to the north, put himself at the disposition of the main Hun ruler. He had by that time made himself a reputation as a soldier and at once became one of the most important Hun generals. The Huns had now determined to get even with the Chinese, who for so long had treated them as chattels. In 308 they reached the gates of Lo-yang, but were driven off under the energetic leadership of our Nihilist philosopher Wang Yen, who apparently had only a limited faith in the magic of Inactivity. There were more Hun reverses in 309. These were thought by the Huns to be due to the fact that the spirit of Mt. Sung, the guardian mountain of Lo-yang, had not been properly placated. After sacrifice to the spirit the Hun leaders were anxious to continue the attack; but their astrologer discovered that 311 not 309 would be the propitious year, and the Hun armies withdrew. In 310 the Hun chief died and there was a brief war of succession, which gave Lo-yang a breathing-space. In the winter of that year, however, the attack was renewed. Much of the country round Lo-yang was occupied by the Huns; food-supplies in the city ran out and a terrible famine began. In the early summer of 311 the main Chinese armies, under the command of Wang Yen, were completely routed at Hu-hsien, about 150 miles to the east of

Lo-yang. Hu-hsien, strangely enough, was the place where Lao Tzu, the legendary founder of Taoism, was supposed to have been born and where sacrifices were made to his spirit. Did Wang Yen, one wonders, pause at his shrine?

A number of high-ranking prisoners were brought to Shih Lo's tent and questioned about the state of affairs in Lo-yang. Among the prisoners was Wang Yen himself. He gave "a full account of the reasons for the defeat." What he considered these to be we are not told. He mentioned, presumably, the chaos produced by a long period of dissension between the various royal princes, and the refusal of the provinces to come to the aid of the Capital. Shih Lo was much interested and sent for him again next day. In the course of the conversation Wang Yen spoke of his own career and once more protested, as he had done when he was made Prime Minister, that he was not interested in politics. It was Wang Yen's maxim (as we have seen above) that whereas the full-fledged Taoist saint can perform miracles by his detachment from concrete realities, the most that the common man can do is to "save his own skin", undeterred by conventional non-Taoist ideas of dignity and morality. True to this principle and hoping (or so we are told) to curry favour with Shih Lo, he suggested that the Hun should proclaim himself Emperor of China. "You took office when you were quite young," said Shih Lo, ignoring Wang Yen's suggestion, "made a name for yourself everywhere within the Four Seas, and now hold the highest office. How can you say that you have never had political ambitions? If any one man is responsible for the ruin of the Empire it is you." And he ordered him to be removed. Then turning to his lieutenant, K'ung Ch'ang, he said, "I have travelled about a good deal in my time, but nowhere have I met such a man as this. Oughtn't we to make use of him?" "He is one of the Three Grandees of the Chinese Empire," said K'ung Ch'ang. "He would never work whole-heartedly in the interest of the Huns. Moreover, he has certainly done nothing on this occasion to make us respect him." "We can at least not put him to the sword," said Shih Lo, and that night he sent men to push over the wall of the room in which Wang Yen was sleeping and suffocate him. Death by suffocation was more honourable than decapitation.

The Hun armies entered Lo-yang from the south and east. The destruction of the city began with the burning of the offices of the provincial administrations which lay, as we have seen, just inside the eastern gates. Fierce street-fighting ensued and it was not till a fortnight later that the Palace, in the northern part of the city, was reached. It was ransacked by the Huns who carried off everything of value, including the ladies of the Emperor's harem. The Emperor himself had made a previous attempt to escape by river to the east; but the Huns burnt his boats before the expedition was ready to start. He now slipped out by a back gate and attempted to escape westwards, in the direction of Ch'ang-an; but he was overtaken and captured. After being held captive for a short time he was sent to the Hun Capital in the north-east where, stripped of all his grandeurs, he was made to carry round the wine at Hun banquets. After sacking the Palace the Huns pillaged and burned the Imperial Tombs, the Ancestral Shrines and the various Ministries. There had been at one moment a plan to spare Lo-yang and make it the Hun Capital. But it was still almost surrounded by unsubdued Chinese territory and the leaders decided that it might prove difficult to hold. The whole city was therefore burnt to the ground and no considerable town stood there till the Wei Tartars made Lo-yang their Capital in 493.

News of the fall of Lo-yang, which was the terminus of a great Asiatic trade route, must have spread far beyond China. The one non-Chinese comment upon it that has come down to us occurs in a fragmentary letter (written probably in the summer of 313) by the Sogdian merchant Nanai-vandak to his colleague Nanaidvār in Samarkand. It was found in the ruins of a watch-tower to the west of Tun-huang, on the western frontiers of China. The letter which is in Sogdian, an eastern dialect of early Persian, expresses astonishment that "those Huns who yesterday were the Emperor's vassals" should now have overthrown the empire. "And, Sir," Nanai-vandak writes, "the last Emperor—so they say—fled from Saragh (i.e., Lo-yang) because of the famine, and his Palace and walled city were set on fire . . . So Saragh is no more, Ngap (i.e., Yeh) no more!"

THE ROMAN EMPIRE AND THE GERMANS 21

*The German barbarians that were encamped on the eastern frontiers of the Roman Empire were the counterpart of the Hsiung-nu on the northwestern frontiers of the Han Empire. The historian Tacitus spent some time among the Germans, apparently as an official of the imperial government. In the following account, written about A.D. 100, he describes the customs and manners of the Germans, stressing their virtues as an example for his luxury-loving fellow countrymen.**

I myself subscribe to the opinion of those who hold that the German tribes have never been contaminated by intermarriage with other nations, but have remained peculiar and unmixed and wholly unlike other people. Hence the bodily type is the same among them all, notwithstanding the extent of their population. They all have fierce blue eyes, reddish hair and large bodies fit only for sudden exertion; they do not submit patiently to work and effort and cannot endure thirst and heat at all, though cold and hunger they are accustomed to because of their climate.

In general the country, though varying here and there in appearance, is covered over with wild forests or filthy swamps, . . . It is suitable enough for grain but does not permit the cultivation of fruit trees; and, though rich in flocks and herds, these are for the most part small, the cattle not even possessing their natural beauty nor spreading horns. The people take pride in possessing a large number of animals, these being their sole and most cherished wealth. Whether it was in mercy or wrath that the gods denied them silver and gold, I know not. Yet I would not affirm that no vein of German soil produces silver or gold; for who has examined? They do not care for their possession and use as much as might be expected. There are to be seen among them vessels of silver that have been presented as gifts to their ambassadors and chiefs, but they are held in no more esteem than vessels of earthenware; however, those nearest to us prize gold and silver because of its use in trade, and they recognize certain of our coins as valuable and choose those. The people of the interior practice barter and exchange of commodities in accordance with the simple and ancient custom. They like the old and well-known coins, those with milled edges bearing the stamp of a two-horse chariot. They are more anxious also for silver coins than for gold, not because of any special liking, but because a number of silver coins is more convenient in purchasing cheap and common articles.

Not even iron is abundant, as is shown by the character of their weapons. Some

* Reprinted from A. C. Howland, *Translations and Reprints from the Original Sources of European History*, VI, No. 3, "The Early Germans" (Philadelphia: University of Pennsylvania Press, n.d.), pp. 4–16.

few use swords or long spears, but usually they carry javelins, called in their language *framea,* tipped with a short narrow piece of iron but so sharp and so easy to handle that as occasion demands they employ the same weapon for fighting at close range or at a distance. A horseman is content with a shield or a javelin, but the footmen, either nude or lightly clad in a small cloak, rain missiles, each man having many and hurling them to a great distance. There is no particular adornment to their weapons except that their shields are distinguished by the most carefully chosen colors. A few wear cuirasses, but hardly any have helmets of metal or leather. Their horses are noted neither for their beauty nor their speed, nor are they trained to perform evolutions, as with us. They move straight ahead or make a single turn to the right, the wheel being executed with such perfect alignment that no man drops behind the one next to him. One would say that on the whole their chief strength lies in their infantry. A picked body of these are chosen from among all the youth and placed in advance of the line where they fight mixed with the horsemen, since their swiftness makes them fully equal to engaging in a cavalry contest. Their number is fixed; there are a hundred from each canton, and from this circumstance they take their name among their own people, so that what was at first a number is now become an appellation of honor. The main body of troops is drawn up in wedge-shaped formation. To yield ground, provided you press forward subsequently, is considered a mark of prudence rather than a sign of cowardice. They carry off the bodies of the fallen even where they are not victorious. It is the greatest ignominy to have left one's shield on the field, and it is unlawful for a man so disgraced to be present at the sacred rites or to enter the assembly; so that many after escaping from battle have ended their shame with the halter.

They choose their kings on account of their ancestry, their generals for their valor. The kings do not have free and unlimited power and the generals lead by example rather than command, winning great admiration if they are energetic and fight in plain sight in front of the line.

. . .

Concerning minor matters the chiefs deliberate, but in important affairs all the people are consulted, although the subjects referred to the common people for judgment are discussed beforehand by the chiefs. Unless some sudden and unexpected event calls them together, they assemble on fixed days either at the new moon or the full moon, for they think these the most auspicious times to begin their undertakings. They do not reckon time by the number of days, as we do, but by the number of nights. So run their appointments, their contracts; the night introduces the day, so to speak. A disadvantage arises from their regard for liberty in that they do not come together at once as if commanded to attend, but two or three days are wasted by their delay in assembling. When the crowd is sufficient they take their places fully armed. Silence is proclaimed by the priests, who have on these occasions the right to keep order. Then the king or a chief addresses them, each being heard according to his age, noble blood, reputation in warfare and eloquence, though more because he has the power to persuade than the right to command. If an opinion is displeasing they reject it by shouting; if they agree to it they clash with their spears. The most complimentary form of assent is that which is expressed by means of their weapons.

. . .

In the intervals of peace they spend little time in hunting, but much in idleness, given over to sleep and eating; all the bravest and most warlike doing nothing, while the hearth and home and the care of the fields is given over to the women, the old men, and the various infirm members of the family. . . .

It is well known that none of the German tribes live in cities, nor even permit their dwellings to be closely joined to each other. They live separated and in various places, as a spring or a meadow or a grove strikes their fancy. They lay out their villages, not as with us in connected or closely-joined houses, but each one surrounds his dwelling with an open space, either as a protection against conflagration or because of their ignorance of the art of building. They do not even make use of rough stones or tiles. They use for all purposes undressed timber, giving no beauty or comfort. Some parts they plaster carefully with earth of such purity and brilliancy as to form a substitute for painting and designs in color. They are accustomed also to dig out subterranean caves which they cover over with great heaps of manure as a refuge against the cold and a place for storing grain, for retreats of this sort render the extreme cold of their winters bearable and, whenever an enemy has come upon them, though he lays waste the open country, he is either ignorant of what is hidden underground or else it escapes him for the very reason that it has to be searched for.

Generally their only clothing is a cloak fastened with a clasp, or if they haven't that, with a thorn; this being their only garment, they pass whole days about the hearth or near a fire. . . . The women wear the same sort of dress as the men except that they wrap themselves in linen garments which they adorn with purple stripes and do not lengthen out the upper part of the tunic into sleeves, but leave the arms bare the whole length. The upper part of their breasts is also exposed. However, their marriage code is strict, and in no other part of their manners are they to be praised more than in this. For almost alone among barbarian peoples they are content with one wife each, excepting those few who because of their high position rather than out of lust enter into more than one marriage engagement.

.   .   .

No other race indulges more freely in entertainments and hospitality. It is considered a crime to turn any mortal man away from one's door. According to his means, each one receives those who come with a well-furnished table. When his food has been all eaten up, he who had lately been the host becomes the guide and companion of his guest to the next house, which they enter uninvited. There is no distinction between guests; they are all received with like consideration. No one makes any difference between friend and stranger so far as concerns the rights of hospitality. If the guest on going away asks for any gift, it is customary to grant it to him, and the host on his side feels the same freedom from constraint in making a request. They take great pleasure in presents, but they do not reckon them as favors nor do they put themselves under obligations in accepting them.

.   .   .

But they do not employ slaves as we do with distinct functions prescribed throughout the establishment. Each has his own domicile and rules his own house. The Lord exacts a certain amount of grain or cloth or a certain number of cattle as in the case of a tenant and this is the extent of his servitude. Other duties, those of the household, are performed by the lord's wife and children. To beat a slave or to punish him with chains and task work is rare. They occasionally kill one, not in the severity of discipline, but impetuously and in sudden wrath as they would kill an enemy, except that the deed goes without punishment. Freedmen do not rank much above slaves; they are not of much account in the household and never in the state, except only in those tribes that are ruled by kings. For there they are elevated above the free born and the nobles. The inferior position of the freedman elsewhere is the mark of the free state.

To trade with capital and to let it out at interest is unknown, and so it is ignorance rather than legal prohibition that protects them. Land is held by the villages as communities according to the number of the cultivators, and is then divided among the freedmen according to their rank. The extent of their territories renders this partition easy. They cultivate fresh fields every year and there is still land to spare. They do not plant orchards nor lay off meadow-lands nor irrigate gardens so as to require of the soil more than it would naturally bring forth of its own richness and extent. Grain is the only tribute exacted from their land, whence they do not divide the year into as many seasons as we do. The terms winter, spring and summer have a meaning with them, but the name and blessings of autumn are unknown.

.   .   .

Such are the facts I have obtained in general concerning the origin and customs of the Germans as a whole. . . .

22 ST. JEROME ON THE FALL OF ROME

By the fifth century A.D. *the Germans, whom Tacitus had depicted as a model to emulate, had become conquerors to fear. This is evident in the following selection from the letters of St. Jerome, one of the great doctors of the Church. He was in Jerusalem when Rome was sacked in 410, and his observations on that disaster reflect the shock that it caused throughout the empire.**

For twenty years and more the blood of Romans has every day been shed between Constantinople and the Julian Alps. Scythia, Thrace, Macedonia, Thessaly, Dardania, Dacia, Epirus, Dalmatia, and all the provinces of Pannonia, have been sacked, pillaged and plundered by Goths and Sarmatians, Quadians and Alans, Huns and Vandals and Marcomanni. How many matrons, how many of God's virgins, ladies of gentle birth and high position, have been made the sport of these beasts! Bishops have been taken prisoners, presbyters and other clergymen of different orders murdered. Churches have been overthrown, horses stabled at Christ's altar, the relics of martyrs dug up.

> Sorrow and grief on every side we see
> And death in many a shape.

The Roman world is falling, ... The East seemed to be immune from these dangers and was only dismayed by the news that reached her. But lo! last year the wolves—not of Arabia, but from the far north—were let loose upon us from the distant crags of Caucasus, and in a short time overran whole provinces. How many

* Reprinted by permission of the publishers and The Loeb Classical Library from St. Jerome, *Select Letters,* trans. F. A. Wright (Cambridge, Mass.: Harvard University Press), pp. 301–5, 463.

monasteries did they capture, how many rivers were reddened with men's blood! They besieged Antioch and all the other cities on the Halys, Cydnus, Orontes, and Euphrates. They carried off troops of captives. Arabia, Phoenicia, Palestine and Egypt in their terror felt themselves already enslaved.

> Had I a hundred tongues, a hundred mouths,
> A voice of brass, I could not tell the names
> Of all those punishments.

. . . The soldiers of Rome, who once subdued and ruled the world, now tremble and shrink in fear. . . .

. . . A dreadful rumour reached us from the West. We heard that Rome was besieged, that the citizens were buying their safety with gold, and that when they had been thus despoiled they were again beleaguered, so as to lose not only their substance but their lives. The city which had taken the whole world was itself taken; nay, it fell by famine before it fell by the sword, and there were but a few found to be made prisoners. The rage of hunger had recourse to impious food; men tore one another's limbs, and the mother did not spare the baby at her breast, taking again within her body that which her body had just brought forth. "In the night was Moab taken, in the night did her wall fall down." "O God, the heathen have come into thine inheritance; thy holy temple have they defiled; they have made Jerusalem an orchard. The dead bodies of thy servants have they given to be meat unto the fowls of the heaven, the flesh of thy saints unto the beasts of the earth. Their blood have they shed like water round about Jerusalem; and there was none to bury them."

MEDIEVAL CIVILIZATIONS OF EURASIA,

500–1500

Chapter Twelve

Eurasian ecumene

Expanding Horizons of the Medieval World 23

The Classical Age, as noted in Reading 10, "Expanding Horizons of the Classical World," was characterized by the emergence for the first time of an incipient Eurasian ecumene. During the Medieval Age the unifying process developed a step further with the evolution of a full-fledged Eurasian ecumene. This was partly the result of continued technological advance, especially in shipbuilding and navigation, and partly of the establishment of great empires such as the Islamic and the Mongol, which spanned not merely entire regions but a large part of all Eurasia. The classic manifestation of the new ecumene is the career of the Venetian merchant Marco Polo, who entered the service of Kublai Khan and travelled back and forth across the breadth of Eurasia. The following selections from Marco Polo's great travel account make clear how spectacularly the horizons of the medieval world were opening up, thanks to the existence of the Mongol Empire and to the advances in naval technology that made possible the far-flung voyages of Chinese as well as Western navigators. Marco Polo's concluding remarks point up the upsurge of maritime activity that was bringing together to an unprecedented degree the various parts of the Eurasian landmass.*

Great Princes, Emperors, and Kings, Dukes and Marquises, Counts, Knights, and Burgesses! and People of all degrees who desire to get knowledge of the various races of mankind and of the diversities of the sundry regions of the World, take this Book and cause it to be read to you. For ye shall find therein all kinds of

* Reprinted from Sir Henry Yule, ed. and trans., *The Book of Ser Marco Polo,* 3rd ed. (New York: Charles Scribner's Sons, 1903), I, 1, 2, 27, 30, 31, 374, 375, 423–26, II, 249–50, 253–54, 272, 331, 338, 341, 343, 411, 500.

wonderful things, and the divers histories of the Great Hermenia, and of Persia, and of the Land of the Tartars, and of India, and of many another country of which our Book doth speak, particularly and in regular succession, according to the description of Messer Marco Polo, a wise and noble citizen of Venice, as he saw them with his own eyes. Some things indeed there be therein which he beheld not; but these he heard from men of credit and veracity. And we shall set down things seen as seen, and things heard as heard only, so that no jot of falsehood may mar the truth of our Book, and that all who shall read it or hear it read may put full faith in the truth of all its contents.

For let me tell you that since our Lord God did mould with his hands our first Father Adam, even until this day, never hath there been Christian, or Pagan, or Tartar, or Indian, or any man of any nation, who in his own person hath had so much knowledge and experience of the divers parts of the World and its Wonders as hath had this Messer Marco!

. . .

Now it came to pass that Marco, the son of Messer Nicolo, sped wondrously in learning the customs of the Tartars, as well as their language, their manner of writing, and their practice of war; in fact he came in brief space to know several languages, and four sundry written characters. And he was discreet and prudent in every way, insomuch that the Emperor held him in great esteem. And so when he discerned Mark to have so much sense, and to conduct himself so well and beseemingly, he sent him on an ambassage of his, to a country which was a good six months' journey distant. The young gallant executed his commission well and with discretion.

. . .

When Mark returned from his ambassage he presented himself before the Emperor, and after making his report of the business with which he was charged, and its successful accomplishment, he went on to give an account in a pleasant and intelligent manner of all the novelties and strange things that he had seen and heard; . . .

Thereafter Messer Marco abode in the Kaan's employment some seventeen years, continually going and coming, hither and thither, on the missions that were entrusted to him by the Lord [and sometimes, with the permission and authority of the Great Kaan, on his own private affairs.] . . . And thus it came about that Messer Marco Polo had knowledge of, or had actually visited, a greater number of the different countries of the World than any other man; the more that he was always giving his mind to get knowledge, and to spy out and enquire into everything in order to have matter to relate to the Lord.

. . .

Now there was on that spot in old times a great and noble city called Cambaluc, which is as much as to say in our tongue "The city of the Emperor." But the Great Kaan was informed by his Astrologers that this city would prove rebellious, and raise great disorders against his imperial authority. So he caused the present city to be built close beside the old one, with only a river between them. . . .

As regards the size of this (new) city you must know that it has a compass of 24 miles, for each side of it hath a length of 6 miles, and it is four-square. And it is all walled round with walls of earth which have a thickness of full ten paces at bottom, and a height of more than 10 paces; but they are not so thick at top, for they diminish in thickness as they rise, so that at top they are only about 3 paces thick. And they are provided throughout with loop-holed battlements, which are all whitewashed.

There are 12 gates, and over each gate there is a great and handsome palace, so that there are on each side of the square three gates and five palaces; for (I ought to mention) there is at each angle also a great and handsome palace. In those palaces are vast halls in which are kept the arms of the city garrison.

The streets are so straight and wide that you can see right along them from end to end and from one gate to the other. And up and down the city there are beautiful palaces, and many great and fine hostelries, and fine houses in great numbers. [All the plots of ground on which the houses of the city are built are four-square, and laid out with straight lines; all the plots being occupied by great and spacious palaces, with courts and gardens of proportionate size. All these plots were assigned to different heads of families. Each square plot is encompassed by handsome streets for traffic; and thus the whole city is arranged in squares just like a chess-board, and disposed in a manner so perfect and masterly that it is impossible to give a description that should do it justice.]

.   .   .

Now that I have told you in detail of the splendour of this City of the Emperor's, I shall proceed to tell you of the Mint which he hath in the same city. . . .

. . . And the way it is wrought is such that you might say he hath the Secret of Alchemy in perfection, and you would be right! For he makes his money after this fashion.

He makes them take of the bark of a certain tree, in fact of the Mulberry Tree, the leaves of which are the food of the silkworms,—these trees being so numerous that whole districts are full of them. What they take is a certain fine white bast or skin which lies between the wood of the tree and the thick outer bark, and this they make into something resembling sheets of paper, but black. . . .

With these pieces of paper, made as I have described, he causes all payments on his own account to be made; and he makes them to pass current universally over all his kingdoms and provinces and territories, and whithersoever his power and sovereignty extends. And nobody, however important he may think himself, dares to refuse them on pain of death. . . .

Furthermore all merchants arriving from India or other countries, and bringing with them gold or silver or gems and pearls, are prohibited from selling to any one but the Emperor. . . .

When any of those pieces of paper are spoilt—not that they are so very flimsy neither—the owner carries them to the Mint, and by paying three per cent. on the value he gets new pieces in exchange. . . .

Now you have heard the ways and means whereby the Great Kaan may have, and in fact *has,* more treasure than all the Kings in the World; and you know all about it and the reason why.

.   .   .

Having finished our discourse concerning those countries wherewith our Book hath been occupied thus far, we are now about to enter on the subject of India, and to tell you of all the wonders thereof.

And first let us speak of the [Chinese] ships in which merchants go to and fro amongst the Isles of India.

These ships, you must know, are of fir timber. They have but one deck, though each of them contains some 50 or 60 cabins, wherein the merchants abide greatly at their ease, every man having one to himself. The ship hath but one rudder, but it hath four masts; and sometimes they have two additional masts, which they ship and unship at pleasure.

. . .

The fastenings are all of good iron nails and the sides are double, one plank laid over the other, and caulked outside and in. The planks are not pitched, for those people do not have any pitch, but they daub the sides with another matter, deemed by them far better than pitch; it is this. You see they take some lime and some chopped hemp, and these they knead together with a certain wood-oil; and when the three are thoroughly amalgamated, they hold like any glue. And with this mixture they do paint their ships.

Each of their great ships requires at least 200 mariners [some of them 300]. They are indeed of great size, for one ship shall carry 5000 or 6000 baskets of pepper [and they used formerly to be larger than they are now].

. . .

Chipangu [Japan] is an Island towards the east in the high seas, 1500 miles distant from the Continent; and a very great Island it is.

The people are white, civilized, and well-favoured. They are Idolaters, and are dependent on nobody. And I can tell you the quantity of gold they have is endless; for they find it in their own Islands, [and the King does not allow it to be exported. Moreover] few merchants visit the country because it is so far from the main land, and thus it comes to pass that their gold is abundant beyond all measure.

. . .

When you sail from Chamba [Indochina], 1500 miles in a course between south and south-east, you come to a great Island called Java. And the experienced mariners of those Islands who know the matter well, say that it is the greatest Island in the world, and has a compass of more than 3000 miles. It is subject to a great King and tributary to no one else in the world. The people are Idolaters. The Island is of surpassing wealth, producing black pepper, nutmegs, spikenard, galingale, cubebs, cloves, and all other kinds of spices.

This Island is also frequented by a vast amount of shipping, and by merchants who buy and sell costly goods from which they reap great profit. Indeed the treasure of this Island is so great as to be past telling.

. . .

When you leave the Island of Seilan [Ceylon] and sail westward about 60 miles, you come to the great province of Maabar which is styled India the Greater; it is best of all the Indies and is on the mainland.

. . .

You must know that in all this Province of Maabar there is never a Tailor to cut a coat or stitch it, seeing that everybody goes naked! For decency only do they wear a scrap of cloth; and so 'tis with men and women, with rich and poor. . . .

. . .

The people are Idolaters, and many of them worship the ox, because (say they) it is a creature of such excellence. They would not eat beef for anything in the world, nor would they on any account kill an ox.

.   .   .

You must know that the heat here is sometimes so great that 'tis something wonderful. And rain falls only for three months in the year, viz. in June, July, and August. Indeed but for the rain that falls in these three months, refreshing the earth and cooling the air, the drought would be so great that no one could exist.

.   .   .

Madeigascar is an Island towards the south, about a thousand miles from Scotra. The people are all Saracens, adoring Mahommet. They have four *Esheks, i.e.* four Elders, who are said to govern the whole Island. And you must know that it is a most noble and beautiful Island, and one of the greatest in the world, for it is about 4000 miles in compass. The people live by trade and handicrafts.

In this Island, and in another beyond it called Zanghibar, about which we shall tell you afterwards, there are more elephants than in any country in the world. The amount of traffic in elephants' teeth in these two Islands is something astonishing.

In this Island they eat no flesh but that of camels; and of these they kill an incredible number daily. They say it is the best and wholesomest of all flesh; and so they eat of it all the year round.

.   .   .

And now ye have heard all that we can tell you about the Tartars and the Saracens and their customs, and likewise about the other countries of the world as far as our researches and information extend. Only we have said nothing whatever about the Greater Sea and the provinces that lie around it, although we know it thoroughly. But it seems to me a needless and useless task to speak about places which are visited by people every day. For there are so many who sail all about that sea constantly, Venetians, and Genoese, and Pisans, and many others, that everybody knows all about it, and that is the reason that I pass it over and say nothing of it.

Chapter Thirteen

Rise of Islam

24   THE KORAN

The Koran, or "recitation," is the Sacred Book of Islam, regarded by Moslems as the word of Allah. Its 114 suras, or chapters, were revealed to Mohammed and written down after his death by his followers. Except for the opening prayer, the chapters were arranged in order of length, with the longest first, so that many of Mohammed's earliest statements appear towards the end of the book. Consequently it cannot be read with any expectation of logical exposition, though it is universally agreed that it is written with utmost elegance and purity of style in the original Arabic. The following passages from the Koran elucidate some of its more basic doctrines.*

The Koran

    Chapter II., Verse 1.   In the name of the Merciful and Compassionate God.
    That is the Book! there is no doubt therein; a guide to the pious, who believe in the unseen, and are steadfast in prayer, and of what we have given them expend in alms; who believe in what is revealed to thee, and what was revealed before thee, and of the hereafter they are sure. These are in guidance from their Lord, and these are the prosperous.

.   .   .

    Chapter XLI., Verse 1.   In the name of the Merciful and Compassionate God.
    A revelation from the Merciful, the Compassionate; a book whose signs are

* Reprinted from Arthur N. Wollaston, *The Religion of the Koran* (London: John Murray Publishers Ltd., 1908), pp. 27–68, excerpts.

detailed; an arabic Koran for a people who do know; a herald of glad tidings and a warning.

Unity of God

Chapter II., Verse 256. God, there is no god but He, the living, the self-subsistent. Slumber takes Him not, nor sleep. His is what is in the heavens and what is in the earth. Who is it that intercedes with Him save by His permission? He knows what is before them and what behind them, and they comprehend not aught of His knowledge but of what He pleases. His throne extends over the heavens and the earth, and it tires Him not to guard them both, for He is high and grand.

Chapter CXII., Verse 1. In the name of the Merciful and Compassionate God. Say, "He is God alone!
"God the Eternal!
"He begets not and is not begotten!
"Nor is there like unto Him any one!"

Muhammad the Apostle of God

Chapter III., Verse 136. Muhammad is but an apostle; apostles have passed away before his time; what if he die or is killed, will ye retreat upon your heels? He who retreats upon his heels does no harm to God at all; but God will recompense the thankful. It is not for any soul to die, save by God's permission written down for an appointed time; but he who wishes for the reward of this world we will give him of it, and he who wishes for the reward of the future we will give him of it, and we will recompense the grateful.

Chapter XXXIII., Verse 40. Muhammad is not the father of any of your men, but the Apostle of God, and the Seal of the Prophets; for God all things doth know!

Resurrection

Chapter III., Verse 182. Every soul must taste of death; and ye shall only be paid your hire upon the resurrection day.

Chapter IV., Verse 89. God, there is no God but He! He will surely assemble you on the resurrection day, there is no doubt therein; who is truer than God in His discourse?

Chapter XVII., Verse 52. They say, "What! when we have become bones and rubbish are we to be raised up a new creature?" Say, "Be ye stones or iron, or a creature, the greatest your breasts can conceive!" Then they shall say, "Who is to restore us?" Say, "He who originated you at first;" and they will wag their heads and say, "When will that be?" Say, "It may perhaps be nigh."

Hell

Chapter IV., Verse 18. But whoso rebels against God and His Apostle, and transgresses His bounds, He will make him enter into fire, and dwell therein for aye; and for him is shameful woe.

Chapter IX., Verse 69. God has promised unto the hypocrites, men and women, and unto the misbelievers, hell-fire, to dwell therein for aye; it is enough for them! God shall curse them, and theirs shall be enduring woe.

Chapter LXXVIII., Verse 24. Verily, Hell is an ambuscade, a reward for the outrageous, to tarry therein for ages. They shall not taste therein cool nor drink, (25) but only boiling water and pus—a fit reward!

Paradise

Chapter III., Verse 14. Say, "But shall we tell you of a better thing than this?" For those who fear are gardens with their Lord, beneath which rivers flow; they shall dwell therein for aye, and pure wives and grace from God.

Chapter IV., Verse 123. But he who doeth good works—be it male or female—and believes, they shall enter into Paradise, and they shall not be wronged a jot.

Chapter LXXVIII., Verse 31. Verily, for the pious is a blissful place—gardens and vineyards, and girls with swelling breasts of the same age as themselves, and a brimming cup; (35) they shall hear therein no folly and no lie—a reward from thy Lord, a sufficient gift!

Almsgiving

Chapter II., Verse 211. They will ask thee what they are to expend in alms: say, "Whatsoever good ye expend it should be for parents and kinsmen, and the orphan and the poor, and the son of the road; and whatsoever good ye do, verily, of it God knows!"

. . . Verse 263. The likeness of those who expend their wealth in God's way is as the likeness of a grain that grows to seven ears, in every ear a hundred grains; for God will double unto whom he pleases; for God both embraces and knows.

Wine, Gaming, Foods and Usury, Infanticide, Ill-Treatment of Orphans

Chapter II., Verse 216. They will ask thee about wine and games of chance; say, "In them both is sin and profit to men; but the sin of both is greater than the profit of the same."

Chapter V., Verse 92. O ye who believe! verily, wine, and games of chance, and statues, and divining (arrows) are only an abomination of Satan's work; avoid them then that haply ye may prosper. Satan only desires to place enmity and hatred between you by wine and games of chance, and to turn you from the remembrance of God and from prayer; but will ye not desist, and obey God, and obey the Apostles, and beware, for if ye turn back, then know that our Apostle has only his message to preach.

Chapter V., Verse 4. Forbidden to you is that which dies of itself, and blood, and the flesh of swine, and that which is devoted to other than God, and the strangled, and the knocked down, and that which falls down, and the gored, and what wild beasts have eaten—except what ye slaughter in time—and what is sacrificed to idols and dividing carcases by arrows.

Chapter II., Verse 276. Those who devour usury shall not rise again, save as he riseth whom Satan hath paralysed with a touch; and that is because they say, "Selling is only like usury," but God has made selling lawful and usury unlawful;

and he to whom the admonition from his Lord has come, if he desists, what has gone before is his; his matter is in God's hands. But whosoever returns (to usury) these are the Fellows of the Fire, and they shall dwell therein for aye. God shall blot out our usury, but shall make almsgiving profitable, for God loves not any sinful misbeliever.

Chapter VI., Verse 142. Losers are they who kill their children foolishly, without knowledge, and who prohibit what God has bestowed upon them, forging a lie against God, they have erred and are not guided.

Chapter XVII., Verse 33. And slay not your children for fear of poverty; we will provide for them; beware! for to slay them is ever a great sin!

Chapter IV., Verse 10. Verily, those who devour the property of orphans unjustly, only devour into their bellies fire, and they shall broil in flames.

MOSLEMS AND CRUSADERS 25

Following Mohammed's death in A.D. 632, Islam expanded rapidly over North Africa and the Middle East, so that within little more than a century its sway extended from Morocco and the Pyrenees to India and Central Asia. By the eleventh century the West had become sufficiently strong to counterattack in a series of campaigns known as the Crusades. For two hundred years Christianity and Islam were engaged in the Holy Land in warfare interspersed with precarious truces. This was a clash of cultures as well as of religions, each side regarding the other as outlandish and uncivilized. This is apparent in the memoirs of Usāmah, Arab warrior, gentleman, and man of letters. Born in Syria in 1095, he was brought up in the tradition of Syrian chivalry, fighting constantly against the Crusaders. In his old age he wrote numerous books, the most outstanding being his memoirs. In addition to rich detail on methods of warfare and on the day to day battles, the reminiscences reflect the Moslem reaction to the Western intruders and their culture. The following selections deal with Western medical practice, sexual customs, and judicial procedures as seen through Moslem eyes.*

The lord of al-Munaytirah wrote to my uncle asking him to dispatch a physician to treat certain sick persons among his people. My uncle sent him a Christian physician named Thābit. Thābit was absent but ten days when he returned. So we said to him, "How quickly hast thou healed thy patients!" He said:

> They brought before me a knight in whose leg an abscess had grown; and a woman afflicted with imbecility. To the knight I applied a small poultice until the abscess opened and became well; and the woman I put on diet and made her humor wet. Then a Frankish physician came to them and said, "This man knows nothing about treating them." He then said to the knight, "Which wouldst thou prefer, living with one leg or dying with two?" The latter replied, "Living with one leg." The physician said, "Bring me a strong knight

---

* Reprinted from Philip K. Hitti, trans., *An Arab-Syrian Gentleman and Warrior in the Period of the Crusades: Memoirs of Usāmah ibn-Munquidh* (Beirut: Khayats, 1964), pp. 162–63, 164–66, 167–69.

and a sharp ax." A knight came with the ax. And I was standing by. Then the physician laid the leg of the patient on a block of wood and bade the knight strike his leg with the ax and chop it off at one blow. Accordingly he struck it—while I was looking on—one blow, but the leg was not severed. He dealt another blow, upon which the marrow of the leg flowed out and the patient died on the spot. He then examined the woman and said, "This is a woman in whose head there is a devil which has possessed her. Shave off her hair." Accordingly they shaved it off and the woman began once more to eat their ordinary diet—garlic and mustard. Her imbecility took a turn for the worse. The physician then said, "The devil has penetrated through her head." He therefore took a razor, made a deep cruciform incision on it, peeled off the skin at the middle of the incision until the bone of the skull was exposed and rubbed it with salt. The woman also expired instantly. Thereupon I asked them whether my services were needed any longer, and when they replied in the negative I returned home, having learned of their medicine what I knew not before.

I have, however, witnessed a case of their medicine which was quite different from that.

The king of the Franks had for treasurer a knight named Bernard [*barnād*], who (may Allah's curse be upon him!) was one of the most accursed and wicked among the Franks. A horse kicked him in the leg, which was subsequently infected and which opened in fourteen different places. Every time one of these cuts would close in one place, another would open in another place. All this happened while I was praying for his perdition. Then came to him a Frankish physician and removed from the leg all the ointments which were on it and began to wash it with very strong vinegar. By this treatment all the cuts were healed and the man became well again. He was up again like a devil.

Another case illustrating their curious medicine is the following:

In Shayzar we had an artisan named abu-al-Fath, who had a boy whose neck was afflicted with scrofula. Every time a part of it would close, another part would open. This man happened to go to Antioch on business of his, accompanied by his son. A Frank noticed the boy and asked his father about him. Abu-al-Fath replied, "This is my son." The Frank said to him, "Wilt thou swear by thy religion that if I prescribe to thee a medicine which will cure thy boy, thou wilt charge nobody fees for prescribing it thyself? In that case, I shall prescribe to thee a medicine which will cure the boy." The man took the oath and the Frank said:

> Take uncrushed leaves of glasswort, burn them, then soak the ashes in olive oil and sharp vinegar. Treat the scrofula with them until the spot on which it is growing is eaten up. Then take burnt lead, soak it in ghee butter [*samn*] and treat him with it. That will cure him.

The father treated the boy accordingly, and the boy was cured. The sores closed and the boy returned to his normal condition of health.

I have myself treated with this medicine many who were afflicted with such disease, and the treatment was successful in removing the cause of the complaint.

·   ·   ·

Franks lack jealousy in sex affairs.   The Franks are void of all zeal and jealousy. One of them may be walking along with his wife. He meets another man who takes the wife by the hand and steps aside to converse with her while the husband is standing on one side waiting for his wife to conclude the conversation. If she lingers too long for him, he leaves her alone with the conversant and goes away.

Here is an illustration which I myself witnessed:

When I used to visit Nāblus, I always took lodging with a man named Mu'izz, whose home was a lodging house for the Moslems. The house had windows which opened to the road, and there stood opposite to it on the other side of the road a house belonging to a Frank who sold wine for the merchants. He would take some wine in a bottle and go around announcing it by shouting, "So and so, the merchant, has just opened a cask full of this wine. He who wants to buy some of it will find it in such and such a place." The Frank's pay for the announcement made would be the wine in that bottle. One day this Frank went home and found a man with his wife in the same bed. He asked him, "What could have made thee enter into my wife's room?" The man replied, "I was tired, so I went in to rest." "But how," asked he, "didst thou get into my bed?" The other replied, "I found a bed that was spread, so I slept in it." "But," said he, "my wife was sleeping together with thee!" The other replied, "Well, the bed is hers. How could I therefore have prevented her from using her own bed?" "By the truth of my religion," said the husband, "if thou shouldst do it again, thou and I would have a quarrel." Such was for the Frank the entire expression of his disapproval and the limit of his jealousy.

Another illustration:

We had with us a bath-keeper named Sālim, originally an inhabitant of al-Ma'arrah, who had charge of the bath of my father (may Allah's mercy rest upon his soul!). This man related the following story:

> I once opened a bath in al-Ma'arrah in order to earn my living. To this bath there came a Frankish knight. The Franks disapprove of girding a cover around one's waist while in the bath. So this Frank stretched out his arm and pulled off my cover from my waist and threw it away. He looked and saw that I had recently shaved off my pubes. So he shouted, "Sālim!" As I drew near him he stretched his hand over my pubes and said, "Sālim, good! By the truth of my religion, do the same for me." Saying this, he lay on his back and I found that in that place the hair was like his beard. So I shaved it off. Then he passed his hand over the place and, finding it smooth, he said, "Sālim, by the truth of my religion, do the same to madame [al-dāma]" (al-dāma in their language means the lady), referring to his wife. He then said to a servant of his, "Tell madame to come here." Accordingly the servant went and brought her and made her enter the bath. She also lay on her back. The knight repeated, "Do what thou hast done to me." So I shaved all that hair while her husband was sitting looking at me. At last he thanked me and handed me the pay for my service.

Consider now this great contradiction! They have neither jealousy nor zeal but they have great courage, although courage is nothing but the product of zeal and of ambition to be above ill repute.

·　　·　　·

Their judicial trials: A duel.   I attended one day a duel in Nāblus between two Franks. The reason for this was that certain Moslem thieves took by surprise one of the villages of Nāblus. One of the peasants of that village was charged with having acted as guide for the thieves when they fell upon the village. So he fled away. The king sent and arrested his children. The peasant thereupon came back to the king and said, "Let justice be done in my case. I challenge to a duel the man who claimed that I guided the thieves to the village." The king then said to the tenant who held the village in fief, "Bring forth someone to fight the duel with him."

The tenant went to his village, where a blacksmith lived, took hold of him and ordered him to fight the duel. The tenant became thus sure of the safety of his own peasants, none of whom would be killed and his estate ruined.

I saw this blacksmith. He was a physically strong young man, but his heart failed him. He would walk a few steps and then sit down and ask for a drink. The one who had made the challenge was an old man, but he was strong in spirit and he would rub the nail of his thumb against that of the forefinger in defiance, as if he was not worrying over the duel. Then came the viscount [al-biskund], i.e., the seignior of the town, and gave each one of the two contestants a cudgel and a shield and arranged the people in a circle around them.

The two met. The old man would press the blacksmith backward until he would get him as far as the circle, then he would come back to the middle of the arena. They went on exchanging blows until they looked like pillars smeared with blood. The contest was prolonged and the viscount began to urge them to hurry, saying, "Hurry on." The fact that the smith was given to the use of the hammer proved now of great advantage to him. The old man was worn out and the smith gave him a blow which made him fall. His cudgel fell under his back. The smith knelt down over him and tried to stick his fingers into the eyes of his adversary, but could not do it because of the great quantity of blood flowing out. Then he rose up and hit his head with the cudgel until he killed him. They then fastened a rope around the neck of the dead person, dragged him away and hanged him. The lord who brought the smith now came, gave the smith his own mantle, made him mount the horse behind him and rode off with him. This case illustrates the kind of jurisprudence and legal decisions the Franks have—may Allah's curse be upon them!

Ordeal by water. I once went in the company of al-Amīr Mu'īn-al-Dīn (may Allah's mercy rest upon his soul!) to Jerusalem. We stopped at Nāblus. There a blind man, a Moslem, who was still young and was well dressed, presented himself before al-amīr carrying fruits for him and asked permission to be admitted into his service in Damascus. The amīr consented. I inquired about this man and was informed that his mother had been married to a Frank whom she had killed. Her son used to practice ruses against the Frankish pilgrims and coöperate with his mother in assassinating them. They finally brought charges against him and tried his case according to the Frankish way of procedure.

They installed a huge cask and filled it with water. Across it they set a board of wood. They then bound the arms of the man charged with the act, tied a rope around his shoulders and dropped him into the cask, their idea being that in case he was innocent, he would sink in the water and they would then lift him up with the rope so that he might not die in the water; and in case he was guilty, he would not sink in the water. This man did his best to sink when they dropped him into the water, but he could not do it. So he had to submit to their sentence against him— may Allah's curse be upon them! They pierced his eyeballs with red-hot awls.

AVICENNA   26

The far-flung conquests of the Arabs brought them under the influence of Greek thought, particularly the science and philosophy of Aristotle. This is evident in the case of one of the greatest and most original thinkers of Islam, Abu Ali al-Husain ibn

Abd Allah, called Ibn Sina, and known to the West as Avicenna. Born in Bukhara in A.D. *980, he describes in his* Autobiography *how he early mastered all fields of knowledge, and especially the writings of Aristotle.**

Autobiography

My father was a man of Balkh, and he moved from there to Bukhara during the days of Nūh ibn Mansūr; in his reign he was employed in the administration, being governor of a village-centre in the outlying district of Bukhara called Kharmaithan. Near by is a village named Afshana, and there my father married my mother and took up his residence; I was also born there, and after me my brother. Later we moved to Bukhara, where I was put under teachers of the Koran and of letters. By the time I was ten I had mastered the Koran and a great deal of literature, so that I was marvelled at for my aptitude.

Now my father was one of those who had responded to the Egyptian propagandist (who was an Ismaili); he, and my brother too, had listened to what they had to say about the Spirit and the Intellect, after the fashion in which they preach and understand the matter. They would therefore discuss these things together, while I listened and comprehended all that they said; but my spirit would not assent to their argument. Presently they began to invite me to join the movement, rolling on their tongues talk about philosophy, geometry, Indian arithmetic; and my father sent me to a certain vegetable-seller who used the Indian arithmetic, so that I might learn it from him. Then there came to Bukhara a man called Abū 'Abd Allāh al-Nātilī who claimed to be a philosopher; my father invited him to stay in our house, hoping that I would learn from him also. Before his advent I had already occupied myself with Muslim jurisprudence, attending Ismā'īl the Ascetic; so I was an excellent enquirer, having become familiar with the methods of postulation and the techniques of rebuttal according to the usages of the canon lawyers. I now commenced reading the *Isagoge* (of Porphyry) with al-Nātilī: when he mentioned to me the definition of *genus* as a term applied to a number of things of different species in answer to the question "What is it?" I set about verifying this definition in a manner such as he had never heard. He marvelled at me exceedingly, and warned my father that I should not engage in any other occupation but learning; whatever problem he stated to me, I showed a better mental conception of it than he. So I continued until I had read all the straightforward parts of Logic with him; as for the subtler points, he had no acquaintance with them.

From then onward I took to reading texts by myself; I studied the commentaries, until I had completely mastered the science of Logic. Similarly with Euclid I read the first five or six figures with him, and thereafter undertook on my own account to solve the entire remainder of the book. Next I moved on to the *Almagest* (of Ptolemy); when I had finished the prolegomena and reached the geometrical figures, al-Nātilī told me to go on reading and to solve the problems by myself; I should merely revise what I read with him, so that he might indicate to me what was right and what was wrong. The truth is that he did not really teach this book; I began to solve the work, and many were the complicated figures of which he had no knowledge until I presented them to him, and made him understand them. Then al-Nātilī took leave of me, setting out for Gurganj.

I now occupied myself with mastering the various texts and commentaries on

* Reprinted from A. J. Arberry, trans., *Avicenna on Theology*, Wisdom of the East Series (London: John Murray Publishers Ltd., 1951), pp. 9–13.

natural science and metaphysics, until all the gates of knowledge were open to me. Next I desired to study medicine, and proceeded to read all the books that have been written on this subject. Medicine is not a difficult science, and naturally I excelled in it in a very short time, so that qualified physicians began to read medicine with me. I also undertook to treat the sick, and methods of treatment derived from practical experience revealed themselves to me such as baffle description. At the same time I continued between whiles to study and dispute on law, being now sixteen years of age.

The next eighteen months I devoted entirely to reading; I studied Logic once again, and all the parts of philosophy. During all this time I did not sleep one night through, nor devoted my attention to any other matter by day. I prepared a set of files; with each proof I examined, I set down the syllogistic premisses and put them in order in the files, then I examined what deductions might be drawn from them. I observed methodically the conditions of the premisses, and proceeded until the truth of each particular problem was confirmed for me. Whenever I found myself perplexed by a problem, or could not find the middle term in any syllogism, I would repair to the mosque and pray, adoring the All-Creator, until my puzzle was resolved and my difficulty made easy. At night I would return home, set the lamp before me, and busy myself with reading and writing; whenever sleep overcame me or I was conscious of some weakness, I turned aside to drink a glass of wine until my strength returned to me; then I went back to my reading. If ever the least slumber overtook me, I would dream of the precise problem which I was considering as I fell asleep; in that way many problems revealed themselves to me while sleeping. So I continued until I had made myself master of all the sciences; I now comprehended them to the limits of human possibility. All that I learned during that time is exactly as I know it now; I have added nothing more to my knowledge to this day.

I was now a master of Logic, natural sciences and mathematics. I therefore returned to metaphysics; I read the *Metaphysica* (of Aristotle), but did not understand its contents and was baffled by the author's intention; I read it over forty times, until I had the text by heart. Even then I did not understand it or what the author meant, and I despaired within myself, saying, "This is a book which there is no way of understanding." But one day at noon I chanced to be in the booksellers' quarter, and a broker was there with a volume in his hand which he was calling for sale. He offered it to me, but I returned it to him impatiently, believing that there was no use in this particular science. However he said to me, "Buy this book from me: it is cheap, and I will sell it to you for four dirhams. The owner is in need of the money." So I bought it, and found that it was a book by Abū Nasr al-Fārābī *On the Objects of the Metaphysica.* I returned home and hastened to read it; and at once the objects of that book became clear to me, for I had it all by heart. I rejoiced at this, and upon the next day distributed much in alms to the poor in gratitude to Almighty God.

Now the Sultan of Bukhara at that time was Nūh ibn Mansūr, and it happened that he fell sick of a malady which baffled all the physicians. My name was famous among them because of the breadth of my reading; they therefore mentioned me in his presence, and begged him to summon me. I attended the sick-room, and collaborated with them in treating the royal patient. So I came to be enrolled in his service. One day I asked his leave to enter their library, to examine the contents and read the books on medicine; he granted my request, and I entered a mansion with many chambers, each chamber having chests of books piled one upon another. In one apartment were books on language and poetry, in another law, and so on; each apartment was set aside for books on a single science. I glanced through the catalogue of the works of the ancient Greeks, and asked for those which I required; and I saw books whose very names are as yet unknown to many—works which I had never seen before and have not seen since. I read these books, taking notes of their contents; I came to realize the place each man occupied in his particular science.

So by the time I reached my eighteenth year I had exhausted all these sciences. My memory for learning was at that period of my life better than it is now, but to-day I am more mature; apart from this my knowledge is exactly the same, nothing further having been added to my store since then.

IBN KHALDUN   27

Although philosophy was frowned upon by orthodox Islam, other fields were cultivated by Moslem scholars, including history, in which the outstanding figure was Ibn Khaldun (1332–1406). Born in Tunis, he held various offices in Fez, Granada, Algeria, and Cairo. In his great work Kitab al-Ibar *(Universal History) he was far in advance of his age in treating history as a science and anticipating modern principles of sociology. In the following selection he emphasizes the need for accurate scholarship and analyzes the historical role of Bedouins and the dynamics of empires.**

164

Prolegomena showing the excellence of the science of History, establishing the methods proper to it, and glancing at the errors into which Historians fall, together with some account of their causes.

Know that the science of History is noble in its conception, abounding in instruction, and exalted in its aim. It acquaints us with the characteristics of the ancient peoples, the ways of life followed by the prophets, and the dynasties and government of kings, so that those who wish may draw valuable lessons for their guidance in religious and wordly affairs. The student of History, however, requires numerous sources of information and a great variety of knowledge; he must consider well and examine carefully in order to arrive at the truth and avoid errors and pitfalls. If he rely on bare tradition, without having thoroughly grasped the principles of common experience, the institutes of government, the nature of civilisation, and the circumstances of human society, and without judging what is past and invisible by the light of what is present before his eyes, then he will often be in danger of stumbling and slipping and losing the right road. Many errors committed by historians, commentators, and leading traditionists in their narrative of events have been caused by their reliance on mere tradition, which they have accepted without regard to its (intrinsic) worth, neglecting to refer it to its general principles, judge it by its analogies, and test it by the standard of wisdom, knowledge of the natures of things, and exact historical criticism. Thus they have gone astray from the truth and wandered in the desert of imagination and error. Especially is this the case in computing sums of money and numbers of troops, when such matters occur in their narratives; for here falsehood and

* Reprinted from Reynold A. Nicholson, *Translations of Eastern Poetry and Prose* (Cambridge University Press, 1922), pp. 176–85.

exaggeration are to be expected, and one must always refer to general principles and submit to the rules (of probability). For example, Mas'údí and many other historians relate that Moses—on whom be peace!—numbered the armies of the Israelites in the wilderness, after he had reviewed all the men capable of bearing arms who were twenty years old or above that age, and that they amounted to 600,000 or more. Now, in making this statement he forgot to consider whether Egypt and Syria are large enough to support armies of that size, for it is a fact attested by well-known custom and familiar experience that every kingdom keeps for its defence only such a force as it can maintain and furnish with rations and pay. Moreover, it would be impossible for armies so huge to march against each other or fight, because the territory is too limited in extent to allow of it, and because, when drawn up in ranks, they would cover a space twice or three times as far as the eye can reach, if not more. How should these two hosts engage in battle, or one of them gain the victory, when neither wing knows anything of what is happening on the other? The present time bears witness to the truth of my observations: water is not so like to water as the future to the past.

The Persian Empire was much greater than the kingdom of the Israelites, as appears from the conquest of the latter by Nebuchadnezzar, who attacked their country, made himself master of their dominions, and laid waste Jerusalem, the chief seat of their religion and power, although he was only the governor of a Persian province: it is said that he was the satrap of the western frontiers. The Persians ruled over the two 'Iráks, Khurásán, Transoxania, and the lands opening on the Caspian Sea—an empire far more extensive than that of the Israelites; yet their armies never equalled or even approached the number mentioned above. Their army at Kádisíya, the greatest they ever mustered, was 120,000 strong, and each of these was accompanied by a retainer. Saif, by whom this is related, adds that the whole force exceeded 200,000. According to 'Á'isha and Zuhrí, the troops under Rustam who were opposed to Sa'd at Kádisíya were only 60,000 strong, each man having a follower.

Again, if the Israelites had reached this total, vast would have been the extent of their kingdom and wide the range of their power. Provinces and kingdoms are small or great in proportion to the numbers of their soldiery and population, as we shall explain in the chapter concerning empires in the First Book. Now, it is well-known that the territories of the Israelites did not extend, in Syria, beyond al-Urdunn and Palestine, and in the Hijáz, beyond the districts of Yathrib (Medina) and Khaibar.

Furthermore, according to the trustworthy authorities, there were only four fathers (generations) between Moses and Israel. Moses was the son of 'Imrán the son of Yas-hur the son of Káhat or Káhit the son of Láwí or Láwá the son of Jacob or Isrá'ílu 'llah (Israel of God). This is his genealogy as given in the Pentateuch. The length of time separating them is recorded by Mas'údí, who says that when Israel entered Egypt and came to Joseph with his sons, the (twelve) Patriarchs and their children, seventy persons in all, they abode in Egypt under the dominion of the Pharaohs, the kings of the Copts, two hundred and twenty years until they went forth into the wilderness with Moses, on whom be peace. It is incredible that in the course of four generations their offspring should have multiplied so enormously.

165

That being so, the rule for distinguishing the true from the false in history is based on possibility or impossibility; that is to say, we must examine human society, by which I mean civilisation, and discriminate between the characteristics essential to it and inherent in its nature and those which are accidental and unimportant, recognizing further those which cannot possibly belong to it. If we do that, we shall have a canon for separating historical fact and truth from error and falsehood by a method of proof that admits of no doubt; and then, if we hear an account of any of the things that happen in civilised society, we shall know how to distinguish what we judge to be worthy of acceptance from what we judge to be spurious, having in our hands an infallible criterion which enables historians to verify whatever they relate.

Such is the purpose of the First Book of the present work. And it would seem that this is an independent science. For it has a subject, namely, human civilisation and society; and problems, namely, to explain in succession the accidental features and essential characters of civilisation. This is the case with every science, the intellectual as well as those founded on authority.

The matter of the following discourse is novel, original, and instructive. I have discovered it by dint of deep thought and research. It appertains not to the science of oratory, which is only concerned with such language as will convince the multitude and be useful for winning them over to an opinion or persuading them to reject the same. Nor, again, does it form part of the science of civil government, i.e. the proper regulation of a household or city in accordance with moral and philosophical laws, in order that the people may be led to live in a way that tends to preserve and perpetuate the species. These two sciences may resemble it, but its subject differs from theirs. It appears to be a new invention; and indeed I have not met with a discourse upon it by any one in the world. I do not know whether this is due to their neglect of the topic—and we need not think the worse of them for that—or whether, perhaps, they may have treated it exhaustively in books that have not come down to us. Amongst the races of mankind the sciences are many and the savants numerous, and the knowledge we have lost is greater in amount than all that has reached us. What has become of the sciences of the Persians, whose writings were destroyed by 'Umar (may God be well-pleased with him!) at the time of the conquest? Where are those of Chaldaea, Assyria, and Babylonia, with all that they produced and left behind them? Where are those of the Copts and of peoples yet more ancient? We have received the sciences of but one nation, the Greeks, and that only because Ma'mún took pains to have their books translated from the language in which they were composed. He was enabled to do this by finding plenty of translators and expending large sums on the work. Of the sciences of other peoples we know nothing.

· · ·

Now we shall set forth in this Book the various features of civilisation as they appear in human society: kingship, acquisition of wealth, the sciences, and the arts. We shall employ demonstrative methods to verify and elucidate the knowledge spread amongst all classes, to refute false opinions, and to remove uncertainties.

Man is distinguished from the other animals by attributes peculiar to himself. Amongst these are

(1) The sciences and arts produced by the faculty of reflection, which distinguishes men from the animals and exalts him above the rest of created beings.

(2) The need for an authority to restrain and a government to coerce him. Of the animals he is the only one that cannot exist without this. As for what is said concerning bees and locusts, even if they have something of the sort, they have it by instinct, not from reflection and consideration.

(3) The labour and industry which supply him with diverse ways and means of obtaining a livelihood, inasmuch as God has made nourishment necessary to him for the maintenance of his life and has directed him to seek it and search after it. *"He gave unto all things their nature: then He directed."*

(4) Civilisation, *i.e.* settling down and dwelling together in a city or in tents for the sake of social intercourse and for the satisfaction of their needs, because men are naturally disposed to help each other to subsist, as we shall explain presently. This civilisation is either nomadic (*badawí*) or residential (*hadarí*). The former is found in steppes and mountains, among the pastoral tribes of the desert and the inhabitants of remote sands; the latter in towns, villages, cities, and cultivated tracts, whither men resort for safety and in order to be protected by walls. In all these circumstances it exhibits the phenomena characteristic of a social state. Accordingly, the matter of this Book must be comprised in six chapters:

 I. Human society in general, its various divisions, and the part of the earth which it occupies.
 II. Nomadic civilisation, with an account of the wild tribes and peoples.
 III. Dynasties, the Caliphate, kingship, and the high offices of government.
 IV. The settled civilisation of countries and cities.
 V. Crafts, means of livelihood, and the various ways of making money.
 VI. The sciences, and how they are acquired and learned.

166

The tribes of the desert are kept off from each other by the authority of their chiefs and elders, whom they respect greatly. For the defence of their encampments against a foreign enemy, each tribe has a troop of warriors and knights famous for their prowess; but they would not make a firm resistance and defence unless they were united by kinship and a feeling of solidarity (*'asabíya*). That is what renders them so strong and formidable. . . . In those who are not drawn together by the bonds of kinship this feeling towards their comrades is seldom aroused: when dark warclouds threaten disaster, every man will slip away in alarm to look after his own safety, because he fears to be forsaken by his allies. Such a people cannot live in the desert: they would fall an easy prey to any race that attacked them. Now, if this is clear with regard to those dwelling together, who must needs defend and protect themselves, similarly you will see that it holds good in the case of any enterprise that excites hostility, such as the mission of a prophet or the founding of a kingdom or the propaganda of a sect. An object of this kind is only attained by fighting for it, since opposition is natural to man; and in order to fight with success, there must be a feeling of solidarity as we said just now. Let this principle be your guide in perusing the observations which we are about to make. God aids us to arrive at the truth.

167

On the inability of the Arabs to establish an empire unless they are imbued with religion by a prophet or a saint, or generally inspired by religious enthusiasm.

The reason of this is that, being naturally wild, they are of all peoples the most reluctant to submit to one another owing to the rudeness of their manners, their arrogance, their high spirit, and their jealousy of authority. Seldom, therefore, are they unanimous. But when they follow a prophet or a saint, they are restrained by something within themselves; their pride and jealousy depart from them, submission and concord are no longer difficult. Religion brings them together: it takes away their rudeness and insolence, it removes envy and jealousy from their hearts. If there be among them the prophet or saint who urges them to fulfil the command of God, and requires that they shall abandon their evil ways and cleave to the good, and bids them be of one voice to make the truth prevail, they will become completely united and gain victory and empire. Moreover, no people is so quick to receive the truth and the right. Their natures are uncorrupted by vicious habits and free from base qualities; and as for their savagery, it is conformable and adaptable to good in consequence of its having preserved the original constitution of man (which renders him capable of accepting the true religion), and because it is remote from the bad habits and dispositions which stamp themselves on men's souls. For, according to the Apostolic Tradition already quoted, "Every one is born with a capacity for receiving the truth."

168

Showing that empires, like individuals, have their natural term of life.

You must know that physicians and astrologers declare the natural life of man to be a hundred and twenty years of the kind which astrologers call "the greatest years of the moon"; but it varies in every race according to the conjunctions of the planets, so that sometimes it is more than this and sometimes less. Those born under certain planetary conjunctions live a full century, others fifty years or seventy or eighty; and stargazers believe that all this is indicated by the position of the heavenly bodies. In the Moslem community, as is recorded in Traditions of the Prophet, life runs to sixty or seventy years. The natural life, *i.e.* 120 years, is rarely exceeded: such cases as that of Noah (on whom be peace!), and a few of the people of 'Ád and Thamúd, depend on extraordinary positions in the celestial sphere. The lives of empires, too, vary according to the conjunctions of the planets; but as a rule an empire does not last more than three generations— reckoning a generation as the middle life of an individual, *i.e.* 40 years, a period which marks the end of the body's growth and development. . . . That indicates that forty years, which is the (middle) life on an individual, is the length of a generation.

An empire, as we remarked, seldom outlives three generations. The first maintains its nomadic character, its rude and savage ways of life; inured to hardships, brave, fierce, and sharing renown with each other, the tribesmen preserve their solidarity in full vigour: their swords are kept sharp, their attack is feared, and their neighbours vanquished. With the second generation comes a change. Possessing dominion and affluence, they turn from nomadic to settled life, and from hardship to ease and plenty. The authority, instead of being shared by all, is appropriated by one, while the rest, too spiritless to make an effort to regain it, abandon the glory of ambition for the shame of subjection. Their solidarity is weakened in some degree; yet one may notice that notwithstanding the indignity to which they submit, they retain much of what they have known and witnessed in the former generation—the feelings of fierceness and pride, the desire for honour, and the resolution to defend themselves and repulse their foes. These qualities they cannot lose entirely, though a part be gone. They hope to become again such men as their fathers were, or they fancy that the old virtues still survive amongst them.

In the third generation the wandering life and rough manners of the desert are forgotten, as though they had never been. At this stage men no longer take delight in glory and patriotism, since all have learned to bow under the might of a sovereign and are so addicted to luxurious pleasures that they have become a burden on the state; for they require protection like the women and young boys. Their national spirit is wholly extinguished; they have no stomach for resistance, defence, or attack. Nevertheless they impose on the people by their (military) appearance and uniform, their horsemanship, and the address with which they manœuvre. It is but a false show: they are in general greater cowards than the most helpless women, and will give way at the first assault. The monarch in those days must needs rely on the bravery of others, enrol many of the clients (freed-men), and recruit soldiers capable, to some extent, of guarding the empire, until God proclaims the hour of its destruction and it falls with everything that it upholds. Thus do empires age and decay in the course of three generations.

Chapter Fourteen

Turco-Mongol invasions

CIVILIZATION AND NOMADISM $\qquad$ 28

The great river valley civilizations on the periphery of the Eurasian landmass have from the beginning been subject to periodic invasions by the nomadic peoples of the interior. These invasions played a vital role in Eurasian history, being responsible not only for the rise and fall of empires but also for the diffusian of new techniques and ideas. This analysis by a distinguished American authority on Central Eurasian history emphasizes the interaction between nomadism and civilization and interprets the invasions as a response to the dynamism of civilization.*

Inner Asia, in the past as in the present, has always been a region whose history has been shaped by the spread up to its edges, and intermittently the penetration into it, of the military activities and economic and cultural influences of the great civilized regions to the west, south and east of it. The order of development was as follows:

The improvement of agriculture in the regions of the great river-valley civilizations and the Mediterranean basin, providing enough surplus to feed large cities, created civilizations which had urban superstructures on agrarian bases. When the best farming land was taken up, there was an overflow into secondary land, where the populations had lagged behind the rate of specialization in the more productive areas. In part, these lagging populations were now caught up in the continuing progress of the advanced peoples, but many retreated from their already less favorable land into land which, agriculturally estimated, was even less favorable, and by so doing committed themselves to a new process of speciali-

* Reprinted from O. Lattimore, *Studies in Frontier History: Collected Papers 1928–1958* (New York: Oxford University Press, 1962), pp. 503–5.

zation of their own, with less reliance on agriculture and increasing reliance on livestock. This process was one of the origins, though not the sole origin, of pastoral nomadism.

This dual process of the expansion of large, agriculturally supported states, with high urban development, and the formation around their fringes of differently specialized "frontier barbarians" could not go on indefinitely in the same form. The civilized and civilizing peoples encountered problems of magnitude which could not be solved by their pre-industrial technology—the distance to which troops could move and supplies be brought up to them or gathered locally; the speed with which administrative orders could be executed, without dilution or evasion along the chain of command; the costs of moving grain from the provinces to feed cities and fill state granaries. These problems can be summarized in the form of a double question: How high a social, political, and institutional pyramid could be built on how broad a territorial base?

In their search—unconscious of course—for the answers to these questions— the experience of the ancient civilizations can be analyzed under two classifications. Under the first, they either subdivided, or annexed from each other, or conquered each other. This part of the historical experience does not concern us here.

Under the second classification, which concerns Inner Asia, they learned by experiment to discriminate between those territories, resources, and peoples which could be profitably included within their imperial expansion and those which it was better to exclude because military action, administration, and the collection of revenue cost more than they were worth. Inner Asia forms the eastern half of a northern frontier along which all the ancient civilizations found it better to halt, to limit their expansion, and from time to time to fortify—in order not only to "keep out the barbarians" but to keep their own population and responsibilities from spreading beyond control. The western half of this northern frontier is marked by the Greek settlements on the northern shore of the Black Sea and by the Roman fortified *limes* along the Danube and Rhine and between England and Scotland. South of this frontier, from the Atlantic to the Pacific were to be found cities, supported by relatively intensive agriculture (including irrigated agriculture) and the growing of special crops like grapes and olives. In forested Europe there was a mixture of limited, low-yield agriculture, livestock-breeding (especially horned cattle), and forest hunting; north of the Greek wheat-growing colonies on the Black Sea shore there was grazing, giving way still farther north to forest-clearing agriculture and other forest activities; north of the Middle Eastern and Chinese civilizations were the steppes and deserts of Inner Asia, with their northern forest fringes.

This long preamble leads up to the true starting point for analysis of the societies of Inner Asia and their history: not only the frontier between civilization and barbarism, but the barbarian societies themselves, were in large measure created by the growth and the geographical spread of the great ancient civilizations. It is proper to speak of the barbarians as "primitive" only in that remote time when no civilization yet existed, and when the forbears of the civilized peoples were also primitive. From the moment that civilization began to evolve it began also to spread, seeking more land in which to establish the practices of civilization; in taking up more land, it recruited into civilization some of the people who had held that land, and displaced others, and the effect on those who were displaced was that they had diverged from whatever had been their own line of evolution out of the primitive state; they modified their economic practices and experimented with new kinds of specialization, and they also evolved new kinds of social cohesion and political organization, and new ways of fighting. Civilization itself created its own barbarian plague; the barbarian terror that harried the northern frontiers of civilization did not erupt from a distant, dark and bloody ground that had nothing to do with civilization; it was an activity of peoples who were the kind of people they were because their whole evolution had been in contact with, and had been molded by, the advance of civilization.

From archaeology, before written history, from what remains of Greek accounts of the Scyths on the Black Sea, and from the Chinese accounts, which enable us to follow the change from wars in which the Chinese, in chariots, fought against barbarians who were on foot, in the eighth and sixth centuries B.C., to the wars along the line of the future Great Wall at the end of the fourth century B.C. when the Chinese first encountered the mounted archers of a society of true steppe nomads, and, in order to fight them, adopted their costume and imitated their tactics, the record is unbroken, though far from complete. It leads us down through the centuries to 1453, when the Turks took Constantinople; to the end of the Old World's isolation and the eve of the great navigations which discovered the New World and ushered in new modes of history.

By the end of these long centuries of symbiotic development the Inner Asian societies were permeated with Chinese, Indian, Iranian, and Near Eastern influences. All of their practices of production, trade, and war have been evolved through interaction with the fringes of civilization. Nowhere in history can we identify a tribe or a people who appeared abruptly at the gates of civilization in a state of pristine barbarism; a people, that is to say, whose economic, social, and military characteristics had up to that moment never been modified by the influences of civilization.

MARCO POLO ON THE MONGOLS   29

By all odds the most formidable onslaught of the Eurasian nomads upon the centers of civilization was that of the Mongols in the thirteenth century. Within a few decades they conquered the greatest empire in Eurasian history, an empire extending from the Adriatic to the China Seas, and from Muscovy to Indonesia. Soon after the founding of this empire, the famous Venetian merchant Marco Polo visited in 1275 the Mongol capital Cambuluc (Peking), where he entered the service of Kublai Khan. For seventeen years Polo functioned in various capacities, thereby gaining an unequalled firsthand knowledge of the Mongols, or Tartars as he calls them, and of their empire. The following selection presents some of his observations, including his revealing and significant comment concerning the rapid assimilation of the Mongols by their subject peoples—a process foreshadowing the early dissolution that the Mongol empire was to suffer.

Now that we have begun to speak of the Tartars, I have plenty to tell you on that subject. The Tartar custom is to spend the winter in warm plains, where they find good pasture for their cattle, whilst in summer they betake themselves to

* Reprinted from Sir Henry Yule, ed. and trans., *The Book of Ser Marco Polo,* 3rd ed. (New York: Charles Scribner's Sons, 1903), I, 251–52, 256–57, 260–63, 331, 356–58.

a cool climate among the mountains and valleys, where water is to be found as well as woods and pastures.

Their houses are circular, and are made of wands covered with felts. These are carried along with them whithersoever they go; for the wands are so strongly bound together, and likewise so well combined, that the frame can be made very light. Whenever they erect these huts the door is always to the south. They also have waggons covered with black felt so efficaciously that no rain can get in. These are drawn by oxen and camels, and the women and children travel in them. The women do the buying and selling, and whatever is necessary to provide for the husband and household; for the men all lead the life of gentlemen, troubling themselves about nothing but hunting and hawking, and looking after their goshawks and falcons, unless it be the practice of warlike exercises.

They live on the milk and meat which their herds supply, and on the produce of the chase; and they eat all kinds of flesh, including that of horses and dogs, and Pharaoh's rats, of which last there are great numbers in burrows on those plains. Their drink is mare's milk.

They are very careful not to meddle with each other's wives, and will not do so on any account, holding that to be an evil and abominable thing. The women too are very good and loyal to their husbands, and notable housewives withal. [Ten or twenty of them will dwell together in charming peace and unity, nor shall you ever hear an ill word among them.]

.　　.　　.

This is the fashion of their religion. [They say there is a Most High God of Heaven, whom they worship daily with thurible and incense, but they pray to Him only for health of mind and body. But] they have [also] a certain [other] god of theirs called Natigay, and they say he is the god of the Earth, who watches over their children, cattle, and crops. They show him great worship and honour, and every man hath a figure of him in his house, made of felt and cloth; and they also make in the same manner images of his wife and children. The wife they put on the left hand, and the children in front. And when they eat, they take the fat of the meat and grease the god's mouth withal, as well as the mouths of his wife and children. Then they take of the broth and sprinkle it before the door of the house; and that done, they deem that their god and his family have had their share of the dinner.

.　　.　　.

All their harshness of war is excellent and costly. Their arms are bows and arrows, sword and mace; but above all the bow, for they are capital archers, indeed the best that are known. On their backs they wear armour of cuirbouly, prepared from buffalo and other hides, which is very strong. They are excellent soldiers, and passing valiant in battle. They are also more capable of hardships than other nations; for many a time, if need be, they will go for a month without any supply of food, living only on the milk of their mares and on such game as their bows may win them. Their horses also will subsist entirely on the grass of the plains, so that there is no need to carry store of barley or straw or oats; and they are very docile to their riders. These, in case of need, will abide on horseback the livelong night, armed at all points, while the horse will be continually grazing.

Of all troops in the world these are they which endure the greatest hardship and fatigue, and which cost the least; and they are the best of all for making wide conquests of country. And this you will perceive from what you have heard and shall hear in this book; and (as a fact) there can be no manner of doubt that now they are the masters of the biggest half of the world. Their troops are admirably ordered in the manner that I shall now relate.

You see, when a Tartar prince goes forth to war, he takes with him, say, 100,000 horse. Well, he appoints an officer to every ten men, one to every hundred, one to every thousand, and one to every ten thousand, so that his own orders have to be given to ten persons only, and each of these ten persons has to pass the orders only to other ten, and so on; no one having to give orders to more than ten. And every one in turn is responsible only to the officer immediately over him; and the discipline and order that comes of this method is marvellous, for they are a people very obedient to their chiefs. Further, they call the corps of 100,000 men a *Tuc;* that of 10,000 they call a *Toman;* the thousand they call . . . ; the hundred *Guz;* the ten. . . . And when the army is on the march they have always 200 horsemen, very well mounted, who are sent a distance of two marches in advance to reconnoitre, and these always keep ahead. They have a similar party detached in the rear, and on either flank, so that there is a good look-out kept on all sides against a surprise. When they are going on a distant expedition they take no gear with them except two leather bottles for milk; a little earthenware pot to cook their meat in, and a little tent to shelter them from rain. And in case of great urgency they will ride ten days on end without lighting a fire or taking a meal. On such an occasion they will sustain themselves on the blood of their horses, opening a vein and letting the blood jet into their mouths, drinking till they have had enough, and then staunching it.

They also have milk dried into a kind of paste to carry with them; and when they need food they put this in water, and beat it up till it dissolves, and then drink it. [It is prepared in this way; they boil the milk, and when the rich part floats on the top they skim it into another vessel, and of that they make butter; for the milk will not become solid till this is removed. Then they put the milk in the sun to dry. And when they go on an expedition, every man takes some ten pounds of this dried milk with him. And of a morning he will take a half pound of it and put it in his leather bottle, with as much water as he pleases. So, as he rides along, the milk-paste and the water in the bottle get well churned together into a kind of pap, and that makes his dinner.]

When they come to an engagement with the enemy, they will gain the victory in this fashion. [They never let themselves get into a regular medley, but keep perpetually riding round and shooting into the enemy. And] as they do not count it any shame to run away in battle, they will [sometimes pretend to] do so, and in running away they turn in the saddle and shoot hard and strong at the foe, and in this way make great havoc. Their horses are trained so perfectly that they will double hither and thither, just like a dog, in a way that is quite astonishing. Thus they fight to as good purpose in running away as if they stood and faced the enemy, because of the vast volleys of arrows that they shoot in this way, turning round upon their pursuers, who are fancying that they have won the battle. But when the Tartars see that they have killed and wounded a good many horses and men, they wheel round bodily, and return to the charge in perfect order and with loud cries; and in a very short time the enemy are routed. In truth they are stout and valiant soldiers, and inured to war. And you perceive that it is just when the enemy sees them run, and images that he has gained the battle, that he has in reality lost it; for the Tartars wheel round in a moment when they judge the right time has come. And after this fashion they have won many a fight.

All this that I have been telling you is true of the manners and customs of the genuine Tartars. But I must add also that in these days they are greatly degenerated; for those who are settled in Cathay have taken up the practices of the Idolaters of the country, and have abandoned their own institutions; whilst those who have settled in the Levant have adopted the customs of the Saracens.

Chapter Fifteen

Traditional Byzantine civilization

Constantinople 30

With the fall of Rome, the West Roman Empire gave way to a collection of barbarian states. The East Roman Empire, by contrast, survived for another millennium and is generally known as the Byzantine Empire. This empire, unlike the West, which declined to agrarian manorialism, was dotted with small towns and boasted a capital, Constantinople, that was the envy of all visitors, who marvelled at its large populaton, magnificent buildings, dazzling wealth, and commanding location on the Straits separating Europe and Asia. Typical were the reports of the following two visitors: the monk Odo of Deuil, who in 1147 accompanied Louis VII of France on the Second Crusade, and the Jewish traveller Benjamin of Tudela, who was in the capital in 1160.

Odo of Deuil *

Constantinople, the glory of the Greeks, rich in renown and richer still in possessions, is laid out in a triangle shaped like a ship's sail. In its inner angle stand Santa Sophia and Constantine's Palace, in which there is a chapel that is revered for its exceedingly holy relics. Moreover, Constantinople is girt on two sides by the sea; when approaching the city we had the Arm of St. George on the right and on the left a certain estuary, which, after branching from the Arm, flows on for about four miles. In that place the Palace of Blachernae, although having foundations laid on low ground, achieves eminence through excellent construction and elegance and, because of its surroundings on three sides, affords its inhabitants the triple pleasure of looking out upon sea, fields, and city. Its exterior

---

* Reprinted from Odo of Deuil, *De Profectione Ludovici VII in Orientem*, trans. Virginia G. Berry, No. XLII of the Records of Civilization: Sources and Studies (New York: Columbia University Press, 1948), pp. 63–67.

135

is of almost matchless beauty, but its interior surpasses anything that I can say about it. Throughout it is decorated elaborately with gold and a great variety of colors, and the floor is marble, paved with cunning workmanship; and I do not know whether the exquisite art or the exceedingly valuable stuffs endows it with the more beauty or value. The third side of the city's triangle includes fields, but it is fortified by towers and a double wall which extends for about two miles from the sea to the palace. This wall is not very strong, and it possesses no lofty towers; but the city puts its trust, I think, in the size of its population and the long period of peace which it has enjoyed. Below the walls lies open land, cultivated by plough and hoe, which contains gardens that furnish the citizens all kinds of vegetables. From the outside underground conduits flow in, bringing the city an abundance of sweet water.

The city itself is squalid and fetid and in many places harmed by permanent darkness, for the wealthy overshadow the streets with buildings and leave these dirty, dark places to the poor and to travelers; there murders and robberies and other crimes which love the darkness are committed. Moreover, since people live lawlessly in this city, which has as many lords as rich men and almost as many thieves as poor men, a criminal knows neither fear nor shame, because crime is not punished by law and never entirely comes to light. In every respect she exceeds moderation; for, just as she surpasses other cities in wealth, so, too, does she surpass them in vice. Also, she possesses many churches unequal to Santa Sophia in size but equal to it in beauty, which are to be marveled at for their beauty and their many saintly relics. Those who had the opportunity entered these places, some to see the sights and others to worship faithfully.

Conducted by the emperor, the king also visited the shrines and, after returning, when won over by the urgency of his host's requests, dined with him. That banquet afforded pleasure to ear, mouth, and eye with pomp as marvelous, viands as delicate, and pastimes as pleasant as the guests were illustrious.

Benjamin of Tudela *

. . . [O]ne comes to Constantinople, an exceeding great city, and the head of the kingdom of Javanites, or those called Greeks. This is the principal seat of the Emperor Emanuel, whose command twelve Kings obey; for every one whereof there are several palaces at Constantinople, and they have also fortresses and governments, and unto these the whole land is subject. The principal and chiefest is called Apripus, the second Mega Domestikutz, the third Dominot, the fourth Mackducus, the fifth Iknomus Megli, and the rest have names like unto these. The compass of the city of Constantinople containeth eighteen miles, one half of it standeth upon the sea, but the other half on the continent, and it is seated upon two arms of the sea, into one of which the sea flows out of Russia, but into the other from Spain, and it is frequented by many traders from the provinces and countries of Babylon, Senaar, Media, Persia, and all the kingdom of Egypt and land of Canaan, and the kingdoms of Russia, Hungary, and Psanki, Buria, Lombardy, and Spain.

The city itself is excessively populous, unto which merchants resort out of all countries, travelling thither both by sea and land. It hath none to compare with it in the world, except Bagdat, that mighty city of the Ismaelites. Here is the most famous temple of St. Sophia, and the Patriarch of the Grecians dwelleth here, nor do they agree in doctrine with the Pope of Rome. There are in it also as many

* Reprinted from J. Pinkerton, *Voyages and Travels* (London: Longman, Hurst, 1811), pp. 4–6.

altars in number as days in the year; but it hath an exceeding great treasure, almost beyond all estimation, by the offerings and riches, yearly brought from divers countries, islands, castles, forts, and palaces, so that the wealth of no temple in the world can be compared with the riches thereof; and in the midst of the temple there are pillars of gold and silver, huge candlesticks, lanthorns, lamps, and other ornaments of these precious metals, more than any man is able to reckon. Next adjoining to the walls of the temple, there is a place built for the Emperor's diversion, called Hippodromus, where yearly, upon the birthday of Jesus of Nazareth, great spectacles are publicly presented, and there all sorts of men in all manner of habits of the whole world appear before the King and Queen. Lions also, and bears, leopards, and wild asses, are brought forth into the place where these spectacles are to be seen, that they may fight together, and birds also after the same manner: and my opinion is that in no country of the world such princely sports are to be seen.

But this King Emanuel, besides that palace left him by his ancestors, hath built him another upon the sea-shore, which they call Bilbernæ, the pillars and walls whereof he hath overlaid with beaten gold and silver, whereon he hath engraved all the wars made by him and his ancestors; and he hath prepared a throne there for himself of gold and precious stones, and hath adorned it with a golden crown hanging on high by gold chains; the composure whereof is equal with the throne itself, so enriched with precious stones and pearls, that the price thereof no man is able to value; of so great a lustre, that without the assistance of light they shine, and may be seen in the night.

Moreover there are such valuable things in the same place as were incredible if told; and tributes are yearly brought into that palace, wherewith the towers are filled with scarlet and purple garments, and gold; so that the like example of building and riches can no where else be found in the world. And it is affirmed, that the revenue only of this city itself, gathered from the markets, haven, and tribute of merchants, amounted to 20,000 crowns a day. Furthermore, the Grecians themselves, inhabitants of the country, are exceeding rich in gold, and have abundance of precious stones, and are dressed in most sumptuous apparel, their garments being made of crimson intermingled with gold, or embroidered with needle-work, and are all carried upon horses, as if they were the children of Kings. The country itself being very large, abounds with all sorts of fruits, and hath great plenty of corn, flesh, and wine; nor is there a finer spot in the whole world to be found. They are also learned and skilful in the discipline of the Grecians; but giving themselves wholly to pleasure, they eat and drink every one under his own vine and under his own fig-tree. Of all the nations which they call barbarians, they have soldiers to fight with the Soldan, King of the children of Thogarna, who are commonly called Turks, because they themselves, through idleness and luxury, are become quite unfit for the wars, and seem to me more like women than men, through their excessive love of pleasure.

Economic Decline   31

The thousand years of Byzantine history were marked by recurring periods of glory and greatness, as well as of weakness and decline. Yet the fact remains that Byzantium did disappear in the fifteenth century when Constantinople fell to the ad-

vancing Turks. And this was a time when the West was bursting with energy and beginning the overseas expansion that was to lead to global domination. The question naturally arises, then, why the end result in Byzantium was extinction, when in the West it was world hegemony. Many factors were involved, one of the most important being economic, as set forth in the following article by a distinguished American Byzantinist.*

It is now five hundred years since the Byzantine empire was brought to an end by the Ottoman Turks. Scholars today quite justly reject Gibbon's assumption that the Byzantine empire was, throughout its entire existence, in a state of decline. They have come to rank it, instead, as one of the great empires in history. And this for good reasons. It endured for over a thousand years. Down to about the middle of the eleventh century it was the center of civilization in Christendom. It preserved the thought and literature of antiquity; it developed new forms of art; it held back the barbarians. It produced great statesmen, soldiers, and diplomats as well as reformers and renowned scholars. Its missionaries, aided by its diplomats and sometimes by its armies, spread the gospel among the pagan tribes, especially the Slavs, which dwelt along its frontiers and beyond. As a Czech historian has put it, Byzantium "molded the undisciplined tribes of Serbs, Bulgars, Russians, Croats even, and made nations out of them; it gave to them its religion and institutions, taught their princes how to govern, transmitted to them the very principles of civilization— writing and literature." Byzantium was a great power and a great civilizing force.

Yet in a sense Gibbon was right. For the Byzantine empire did not come to an end as the result of a single blow as, for instance the battle of Nineveh of 612 B.C. is said to have brought to an end the mighty Assyrian empire. The empire which Mohammed II destroyed on May 29, 1453, had been wasting away for over three hundred years, although part of this time, notably during the period of the Comneni, it was not an insignificant force. By the time of the fall of Constantinople, however, the Morea, one or two islands in the Aegean, and Constantinople were all that had been left of its once widely extensive territories. Constantinople itself, which in the tenth century had a population of perhaps one million people, had been reduced to probably not more than 75,000 inhabitants. As a center of commerce it had long been eclipsed by Galata, the Genoese colony on the opposite side of the Golden Horn. The Byzantine emperors became puppets in the hands of the Italian commercial republics, notably Genoa and Venice, served the Ottoman sultans as vassals, or miserably toured the West begging for help in return for which they were ready to sacrifice the religious traditions of their people. What a far cry from the august position of their predecessors of the tenth century who challenged East and West and challenged them not without success! "I shall conquer your lands," wrote Nicephorus Phocas to the Caliph of Bagdad, "and I shall go as far as Mecca. . . . I shall conquer all the Orient and the Occident and I shall spread everywhere the religion of the cross." The same emperor declared to the ambassador of the German emperor, Otto I: "Do you want a greater scandal than that [Otto] should call himself emperor and claim for himself provinces belonging to our empire? Both these things are intolerable; and if both are unsupportable, that especially is not to be borne, nay, not to be heard of that he calls himself emperor." What brought the empire from this pinnacle of power down to the abject position in which we find it in

---

* Reprinted from Peter Charanis, "Economic Factors in the Decline of the Byzantine Empire," *Journal of Economic History*, XIII (Fall 1953), 412–24.

the fourteenth and fifteenth centuries is one of the most interesting problems in history.

In the history of the Byzantine empire, war and religion were the two principal factors that molded the society of the empire and determined its external position. War was the normal state of things throughout its long existence. The external crisis, however, that particularly affected the evolution of its society was that of the seventh century.

The advances of the Saracens and the incursions of the Slavs and Bulgars reduced virtually the whole empire to a frontier province. To cope with this situation the emperors of the seventh century reorganized the provincial administration of the empire, introducing what is known as the *theme* system, the essence of which was the subordination of civil to military authority exercised in each province by the commander of the army corps stationed there. But with the establishment of the *theme* system is connected the establishment of another institution, the system of military estates. These military estates, small in size and granted to individuals in return for military service, became the opening wedge in the formation of a new class of free peasant proprietors. The soldiers themselves constituted the nucleus of this class, but others gradually were added. For while the eldest son of a soldier inherited his father's plot together with the obligation of military service, the rest of the family were free to reclaim and cultivate the land that was vacant. The free peasants, cultivating their own land, paying the taxes, and, if necessary, serving in the army, came to constitute the dominant element in the agrarian society of Byzantium. They became a bulwark of the state, lent to it new vigor, and enabled it eventually to recover its position in the Orient. By the end of the tenth century, Byzantium had become the most powerful state throughout the Christian-Moslem world.

The situation changed in the eleventh century. During the second half of that century the empire suffered a series of military reverses from which it never fully recovered. The most serious of these was the disastrous defeat at Manzikert (1071). The battle of Manzikert decided the fate of Asia Minor and conditioned the subsequent history of the Byzantine empire. But Manzikert was only a battle, and battles had been lost before without the serious consequences that followed Manzikert. What explains the decline that set in after it and that would lead eventually to the disappearance of the empire were the conditions which came to prevail in the social and economic life of the empire in the eleventh century and later. Manzikert itself was the result of these conditions.

The dominant fact in the social and economic life of the empire in the eleventh century is the triumph of the landed military aristocracy and the decline of the soldiery-peasantry which had for centuries served as the bulwark of the state.

From the very beginning of its history the large estate had been a feature of Byzantine society. The complicated and burdensome fiscal administration affected by the reorganization of the empire following the political and economic crisis of the third century worked in such a way as to give impetus to the growth of the large estates. The society revealed by the papyri and the great legislative monuments of the fifth and the sixth centuries is a society dominated by these estates. *Coloni,* reduced to serfs, composed the vast majority of the agrarian population, although the free peasant proprietors did not disappear completely. The development of the soldiery-peasantry in the seventh century lessened the extent of the large estates, but did not eliminate them. By the end of the ninth century they had become larger and more numerous. Those who possessed them occupied important positions in the administration and used these positions to increase their holdings. This they did by absorbing, often through dubious means, the properties of the small peasants. Thus the small, free peasant proprietors began to disappear.

The great emperors of the tenth century realized the dangerous social and political implications of this development and tried to check it. Every major emperor from Romanus Lecapenus to and including Basil II, with the exception of John Tzimeskes, issued more than one novel for this purpose. These emperors sought to preserve the free peasantry because they considered it an essential element for the health of the state. As Romanus Lecapenus put it in one of his novels:

> It is not through hatred and envy of the rich that we take these measures, but for the protection of the small and the safety of the empire as a whole. . . . The extension of the power of the strong . . . will bring about the irreparable loss of the public good, if the present law does not bring a check to it. For it is the many, settled on the land, who provide for the general needs, who pay the taxes and furnish the army with its recruits. Everything falls when the many are wanting.

The strictest among the measures taken for the protection of the free peasantry was that issued by Basil II concerning the *allelengyon,* a measure which required the landed aristocracy to pay the tax arrears of peasants too poor to meet their own obligations. But with the death of Basil (1025) the effort to stop the growth of the large estates came to an end. His law concerning the *allelengyon* was repealed and the other measures, although kept in the books, were not enforced. The fate of the free peasantry was definitely decided.

Meanwhile, a similar fate befell the class of the enrolled soldiers, holders of the military estates. For the aristocracy, which, by one means or another, absorbed the estates of the small peasants, absorbed also those of the soldiers. The protection of the interests of these soldiers had been one of the deepest concerns of the emperors of the tenth century. Wrote Constantine Porphyrogenitus in the novel that he issued for the protection of the estates of the soldiers: "The army is to the state what the head is to the body. . . . He who neglects it neglects the safety of the state. . . . Therefore in promulgating our Constitution [on the military estates], we feel we are working for the welfare of all." But in this as in the case of the small peasants the measures taken by the emperors of the tenth century were of no avail. It proved impossible to stop the aristocracy from absorbing the properties of the small, whether the latter were soldiers or not.

What consummated the depression of the enrolled soldiers, however, was the anti-military policy which some of the emperors of the eleventh century followed in order to reduce the power of the military magnates in the administration of the empire. Those who occupied the high military posts in the empire were also great landholders. Their wealth, plus the powers which they exercised as military commanders, made them extremely dangerous to the central government. This danger, indeed, was one of the principal reasons why Basil II issued the novel concerning the *allelengyon* to which reference has already been made. He had faced two formidable revolts, both headed by members of the powerful aristocracy, and it was only with difficulty that he survived. When, after 987, Basil was reconciled with Bardas Skleros, one of the powerful rebels, the latter advised him that, if he wished to preserve the imperial authority, he should permit no one of the aristocracy to prosper and should exhaust their means by heavy taxes. Hence, the various measures he took, including that of the *allelengyon,* were designed not only to protect the poor peasants but also to crush the aristocracy. But on both the question of land and that of taxation the aristocracy triumphed.

One of the important reasons for the triumph of the artistocracy was the very strong hold that it had upon the military organization of the empire. If it could be shaken from this hold, it would lose in power and influence and would become more amenable to the wishes of the imperial government. And this is precisely what certain emperors of the eleventh century, notably Constantine IX Monomachos (1042–1055), Michael VI (1056–1057), and Constantine X Dukas (1059–1067), tried to do. The means of attack which they employed was to weaken the military organization by reducing the size of the army, thus depriving the aristocracy of its military commands. The great military triumphs of the tenth century, the crushing of the Saracens and the Bulgarians and the pushing of the frontiers to the Euphrates and the Tigris in the east and to the Danube in the Balkans, created a sense of security and the feeling that the maintenance of a powerful army was no longer necessary. With Constantine IX, peace became the keynote of the imperial foreign policy, and there began a systematic elimination of the aristocracy from the army while at the same time the development of a civil bureaucracy was promoted. But the aristocracy fought back, and a new struggle ensued, this time between the aristocracy as a military class and a new party of civil officials who came to dominate the imperial court.

The struggle plunged the empire into a series of civil wars that squandered its resources and manpower at a time when new and formidable enemies were making their appearance, both in the East and in the West. But the most serious result of the imperial policy was the deterioration of the army and the depression of the enrolled soldiers. By the time of Constantine X Dukas the profession of the soldier had lost much of its attraction and so, as a Byzantine historian puts it, "the soldiers put aside their arms and became lawyers or jurists." The same author, writing of the army that took the field in one of the expeditions against the Seljuks, states:

> The army was composed of Macedonians and Bulgarians and Varangians and other barbarians who happened to be about. There were gathered also those who were in Phrygia [the *theme* Anatolikon]. And what one saw in them [the enrolled soldiers of the *theme* Anatolikon] was something incredible. The renowned champions of the Romans who had reduced into subjection all of the east and the west now numbered only a few and these were bowed down by poverty and ill treatment. They lacked in weapons, swords, and other arms, such as javelins and scythes. . . . They lacked also in cavalry and other equipment, for the emperor had not taken the field for a long time. For this reason they were regarded as useless and unnecessary and their wages and maintenance were reduced.

The enrolled soldiers, depressed and forgotten, became more and more a minor element in the Byzantine army. The bulk of this army, in the eleventh century and later, came to be composed almost entirely of foreign mercenaries—Russians, Turks, Alans, English, Normans, Germans, Patzinaks, Bulgarians, and others. These mercenaries were swayed more by their own interests than by those of the empire.

Meanwhile, the development of two institutions, the *pronoia* and the *exkuseia*, added further to the wealth and power of the landed aristocracy, both lay and ecclesiastic. The *pronoia* was the principal means that the emperors of the second half of the eleventh century, but especially later, adopted to recuperate much of the deserted land, to reconstitute the class of soldiers with landed interests, and to reward many of their partisans. A *pronoia* was granted to an individual for a specific period of years, usually his lifetime, in return for military or other services rendered or to be rendered. It was never hereditary, unless it was specifically declared so by a special measure. It consisted usually of land, but it could be a river or a fishery. Some of the *pronoiae* were very extensive, others less so, but the general effect of all was to increase the power and influence of the aristocracy and to lessen the hold of the central government over the agrarian population. For the holder of a *pronoia* exercised over those who inhabited it important financial and judicial powers which were granted to him along with the land. He was expected to serve in the army and also to furnish troops according to the size of his *pronoia*. But when we first meet with the *pronoia* in the second half of the eleventh century, it was not primarily a military grant; it became so during the reign of Alexius Comnenus and those of his successors. The *pronoia* differed from the old military estate in that it was held by persons high in the social order, whereas the recipients of the latter were peasant soldiers. In a study which I devoted to the aristocracy of Byzantium in the thirteenth century I showed that many of the holders of *pronoiae* belonged to the great families of the empire, families that were related to each other and to the ruling dynasty. The extensive use of the *pronoia* contributed not only to the increase, relatively speaking, of the power and wealth of the aristocracy but also to the development of the appanage system and thus weakened the central administration.

The central administration was weakened also by the development of the *exkuseia*. The term, which derives no doubt from the Latin *excusatio* (*excusare*), refers to the fiscal and judicial immunities that the imperial government often granted, especially to monasteries. It was formerly thought that the *exkuseia* first appeared in the eleventh century, but it is now known to be older than that, and may have developed out of the various privileges granted to the Christian clergy in the fourth century. Its use on a wide scale, however, is associated with the eleventh century and later. As the monastic properties during this period were very extensive, the revenue that the imperial government lost by the grant of *exkuseiae* must have been considerable. At the same time the *exkuseia* contributed to increasing the wealth of members of the lay aristocracy, for the emperors of the second half of the eleventh century and later often rewarded their partisans by granting to them the revenues of monasteries, such grants being then known as *kharistikia*. And monasteries whose revenues were thus granted often enjoyed the privilege of *exkuseia*.

Thus the failure to enforce the measures that had been issued for the protection of the soldiery-peasantry and the various grants of privileges made to the aristocracy had made the large estates, by the eleventh century, the dominant features of the agrarian landscape of Byzantium. These estates were worked by tenant peasants, the *paroikoi* of the Byzantine texts, people who were personally free, but who were tied to certain obligations and corvées that curtailed their movement. Some free peasant proprietors continued to exist, but they had become hardly distinguishable from the *paroikoi*. Besides working for the lord, the *paroikoi* had allotments of their own for which they paid rent and performed various obligations and from which, after the passage of a number of years, they could not be evicted. These allotments were transmissible from father to son. These tenant peasants, weighed down by the heavy burden of taxation and numerous corvées, lost all feeling for the welfare of the state as a whole. It is well known that the peasantry of the interior of Asia Minor offered no resistance to the Seljuk Turks, whose establishment in Asia Minor after Manzikert started the empire on the road to general decline. In the twelfth century the Comneni, by utilizing every resource at their disposal, succeeded in bringing about a partial recovery of the political power of the state, but neither they nor their successors tried to check the economic decay of the agrarian population. In the fourteenth century the deplorable economic conditions of the population were a big factor in the social and political strife that shook the empire and opened the way for the rise of the Ottoman Turks. In the tenth century, as we have pointed out above, Romanus Lecapenus had declared in one of his novels designed to protect the free peasantry that the extension of the power of the strong and the depression of the many would "bring about the irreparable loss of the public good." His prediction had come true. The disappearance of the free peasantry, the increase in the wealth, privileges, and power of the aristocracy, and the consequent depression of the agrarian population constitute, I think, some of the principal factors in the decline of the Byzantine empire.

But the society of the Byzantine empire was not purely agrarian. Included in the empire were a number of cities—Constantinople and Thessalonica immediately come to mind—whose role in the economic life of the empire was by no means insignificant. The penury of the sources makes impossible a detailed analysis of the urban economy of Byzantium, but that it was comparatively highly developed there can be no doubt.

What characterized the urban economy of Byzantium during the great days of the empire was its strict regulation by the state. This regulation consisted of two elements: the strict control over foreign commerce and the organization of the domestic trades and professions into private and public guilds supervised by the government. The object of this regulation was both political and economic: political in that the government sought to assure for itself arms and an ample supply of manufactured goods—in the main, luxuries—not only for the imperial household but also for the use of its diplomacy in the form of presents to barbarian chieftains and other princes; economic in that the government sought to keep the great cities well provisioned with the necessities of life, assure the quality of goods, and prevent exorbitant prices. The urban economy was also an important source of revenue. All imports and exports were subject to a 10 per cent duty, and the professions and trades, besides being liable for certain taxes, also performed various liturgies. The precise amount of this revenue, because of the fragmentary nature of the sources, cannot be determined, but it must have been considerable.

The regulation of urban economy was relaxed beginning with the last quarter of the eleventh century. The significant step in this development was taken in 1082 when Alexius Comnenus granted to the Venetians, in return for their alliance against the Normans of Sicily, various privileges among which the most important was that of trading freely, wihout the payment of any duty, in virtually all the cities of the empire, including the capital. These privileges, renewed by the emperors of the twelfth century, although not without reluctance, rendered the Venetians virtual masters of the commercial life of the empire. In the thirteenth century, in an effort to lessen the influence of the Venetians, similar privileges were granted to the Genoese (the treaty of Nymphaeum, 1261), but that was the substitution of one exploiter for another. The Italian merchants, whether Genoese or Venetians, became so entrenched in Constantinople that they controlled the economy of that city and determined the price of even the daily necessities. According to the patriarch Athanasius (end of the thirteenth century), the fate of the Romans had completely passed into the hands of the Latins, "who," he complained bitterly to the emperor Andronicus II, "make fun of us and scorn us to the point that, full of overweening conceit, they take the wives of our compatriots as security for the wheat which they deliver to us."

Meanwhile, the guild organization which was such a strong feature of the urban organization of the tenth century had virtually ceased to exist by the end of the thirteenth century. This at least is the impression created by the letters of the patriarch Athanasius which, although not yet published, have been analyzed by two different scholars. The patriarch complained to the emperor that false weights were used, that the wheat was hoarded, was often mixed with chaff or wheat that had rotted, and was sold at exorbitant prices. He urged the emperor to appoint a commissioner to supervise everything that concerned the provisioning of the capital. The emperor (Andronicus II) took cognizance of the complaints and ordered an investigation. He was especially anxious to determine who were those who exercised the trade of baker, how many of them there were, and under what conditions were the ships, which brought the food supplies to Constantinople, sold and bought. Thus, at the end of the thirteenth century it was not officially known who were the bakers in Constantinople and how many of them there were. Nor were they supervised with the view of assuring the quality of and a fair price for their produce. Contract this with what the *Book of the Prefect* says about the bakers as they functioned in the tenth century:

> The bakers shall make their profits according to the amount of grain purchased at the order of the Prefect. They shall purchase the proper amount of grain by the nomisma from their assessor. When they have ground it and leavened it, they shall calculate their profit at a keration and two miliarisia on the nomisma. The keration will be pure profit, while the two miliarisia will go for the support of their workmen, the food of their mill animals, the fuel for the ovens, and the lighting. . . .
>
> Whenever there is an increase or decrease in the supply of grain, the bakers shall go to the Prefect to have the weights of their loaves fixed by the assessor in accordance with the purchase price of grain.

Obviously by the end of the thirteenth century the bakers' guild had completely broken down; there was not even a semblance of governmental control over the baker's trade. And what was true of this trade was probably also true of the others. The only indication of a trade organization in the fourteenth century was that of the mariners of Thessalonica. It has been suggested that this guild was organized by the mariners themselves in order to protect their interests, but more probably it was a continuation of an older organization which became more or less autonomous as the power of the central government declined in the fourteenth century. The guild of the mariners took the leadership in the terrible social upheaval that shook Thessalonica in 1345 and resulted in the slaughter of about one hundred members of the aristocracy.

It has been said that "Byzantium's weakness, which led to her fatal decline in the course of the eleventh century" was "her rigid, defensive attitude toward the outside world . . . embodied in the cultural and economic barriers she raised against all outsiders." The economic barriers spoken of in this statement refer no doubt to the strict controls that Byzantium had exercised over commerce and industry. It is extremely doubtful if this indeed was Byzantium's weakness. The simple observation that the period during which these controls were most rigidly enforced is the period of the greatness of the empire suggests the opposite, and this suggestion is reinforced by the further observation that the period of decline coincides with the breakdown of these controls. The power of a state and as a consequence its ability to maintain its position in the world is commensurate with its financial resources, the principal source of which is taxation. In Byzantium this source, seriously compromised by the disappearance of the free peasantry and the increase in the wealth, privileges, and power of the aristocracy was reduced almost to the vanishing point by the commercial privileges granted to the Italian republics and the consequent loss by Byzantium of control over its urban economy. This was Byzantium's weakness that brought about its decline and final fall.

Economic decline, together with various other factors, including religious dissension, social cleavage, and bitter conflict with the Latins, culminated finally in the downfall of Byzantium. This occurred in two stages, the first being in 1204 when the leaders of the Fourth Crusade captured Constantinople and established a number of feudal states. These never took root, and in 1261 Constantinople was retaken by the Byzantines, but the restored empire was a small and unviable fragment. The final end came in 1453 with the Turkish conquest, which proved durable, Constantinople becoming the capital of the Ottoman Empire until its demise after World War I. The following selection is a Byzantine view of the Latin sack of Constantinople, the author being the contemporary Greek historian Nicetas Choniates.*

. . . How shall I begin to tell of the deeds wrought by these nefarious men! Alas, the images, which ought to have been adored, were trodden under foot! Alas, the relics of the holy martyrs were thrown into unclean places! Then was seen what one shudders to hear, namely, the divine body and blood of Christ was spilled upon the ground or thrown about. They snatched the precious reliquaries, thrust into their bosoms the ornaments which these contained, and used the broken remnants for pans and drinking cups,—precursors of Anti-christ, authors and heralds of his nefarious deeds which we momentarily expect. Manifestly, indeed, by that race then, just as formerly, Christ was robbed and insulted and His garments were divided by lot; only one thing was lacking, that His side, pierced by a spear, should pour rivers of divine blood on the ground.

Nor can the violation of the Great Church [Santa Sophia] be listened to with equanimity. For the sacred altar, formed of all kinds of precious materials and admired by the whole world, was broken into bits and distributed among the soldiers, as was all the other sacred wealth of so great and infinite splendor.

When the sacred vases and utensils of unsurpassable art and grace and rare material, and the fine silver, wrought with gold, which encircled the screen of the tribunal and the ambo, of admirable workmanship, and the door and many other ornaments, were to be borne away as booty, mules and saddled horses were led to the very sanctuary of the temple. Some of these which were unable to keep their footing on the splendid and slippery pavement, were stabbed when they fell, so that the sacred pavement was polluted with blood and filth.

Nay more, a certain harlot, a sharer in their guilt, a minister of the furies, a servant of the demons, a worker of incantations and poisonings, insulting Christ, sat in the patriarch's seat, singing an obscene song and dancing frequently. Nor, indeed, were these crimes committed and others left undone, on the ground that these were of lesser guilt, the others of greater. But with one consent all the most heinous sins and crimes were committed by all with equal zeal. Could those, who showed so great madness against God Himself, have spared the honorable matrons and maidens or the virgins consecrated to God?

---

* Reprinted from D. C. Munro, trans., *Translations and Reprints from the Original Sources of European History*, Series I, Vol. III, No. 1, rev. ed. (Philadelphia: University of Pennsylvania Press, 1912), pp. 15–16.

Nothing was more difficult and laborious than to soften by prayers, to render benevolent, these wrathful barbarians, vomiting forth bile at every unpleasing word, so that nothing failed to inflame their fury. Whoever attempted it was derided as insane and a man of intemperate language. Often they drew their daggers against any one who opposed them at all or hindered their demands.

No one was without a share in the grief. In the alleys, in the streets, in the temples, complaints, weeping, lamentations, grief, the groaning of men, the shrieks of women, wounds, rape, captivity, the separation of those most closely united. Nobles wandered about ignominiously, those of venerable age in tears, the rich in poverty. Thus it was in the streets, on the corners, in the temple, in the dens, for no place remained unassailed or defended the suppliants. All places every-where were filled full of all kinds of crime. Oh, immortal God, how great the afflictions of the men, how great the distress!

33   BYZANTINE CHRISTIANITY IN RUSSIA

Historians no longer accept Edward Gibbon's verdict on the thousand years of Byzantium's existence as "a uniform tale of weakness and misery." Rather, they now stress the vital historical contributions of Byzantium in shielding the West against east-ern invasions, in serving as an economic dynamo for the entire Mediterranean basin, in salvaging and transmitting the intellectual and artistic treasures of antiquity, and in introducing the arts of civilization to the Slavs of Eastern Europe as Rome had done earlier for the Germans to the West. This last contribution is the subject of the follow-ing selection from a contemporary source, the Russian Primary Chronicle, *compiled by Kievan monks in the eleventh and twelfth centuries. This reading describes the circum-stances in which Prince Vladimir of Kiev, after considering the teachings and practices of Catholicism, Islam, and Judaism, opted for the Christian faith of the Byzantines. His decision was binding also on all his subjects, so the* Chronicle *depicts the mass Baptism that followed in the waters of the Dnieper River. After conversion came the building of churches, the organization of an ecclesiastical hierarchy, and the spread of "book learning." The Russians had acquired a new civilization along with their new religion.**

Vladimir summoned together his boyars and the city-elders, and said to them, "Behold, the Bulgars came before me urging me to accept their religion. Then came the Germans and praised their own faith; and after them came the Jews. Finally the Greeks appeared, criticizing all other faiths but commending their own, and they spoke at length, telling the history of the whole world from its beginning. Their words were artful, and it was wondrous to listen and pleasant to hear them. They preach the existence of another world. 'Whoever adopts our religion and then dies shall arise and live forever. But whosoever embraces another faith, shall be consumed with fire in the next world.' What is your opinion on this

---

* Reprinted from S. H. Cross and O. P. Sherbowitz-Wetzor, trans. and eds., *The Russian Primary Chronicle: Laurentian Text* (Cambridge, Mass.: Mediaeval Academy of America, 1953), pp. 96ff.

subject, and what do you answer?" The boyars and the elders replied, "You know, oh Prince, that no man condemns his own possessions, but praises them instead. If you desire to make certain, you have servants at your disposal. Send them to inquire about the ritual of each and how he worships God."

Their counsel pleased the prince and all the people, so that they chose good and wise men to the number of ten, and directed them to go first among the Bulgars and inspect their faith. The emissaries went their way, and when they arrived at their destination they beheld the disgraceful actions of the Bulgars and their worship in the mosque; then they returned to their country. Vladimir then instructed them to go likewise among the Germans, and examine their faith, and finally to visit the Greeks. They thus went into Germany, and after viewing the German ceremonial, they proceeded to Tsar'grad, where they appeared before the Emperor. He inquired on what mission they had come, and they reported to him all that had occurred. When the Emperor heard their words, he rejoiced, and did them great honor on that very day.

On the morrow, the Emperor sent a message to the Patriarch to inform him that a Russian delegation had arrived to examine the Greek faith, and directed him to prepare the church and the clergy, and to array himself in his sacerdotal robes, so that the Russes might behold the glory of the God of the Greeks. When the Patriarch received these commands, he bade the clergy assemble, and they performed the customary rites. They burned incense, and the choirs sang hymns. The Emperor accompanied the Russes to the church, and placed them in a wide space, calling their attention to the beauty of the edifice, the chanting, and the pontifical services and the ministry of the deacons, while he explained to them the worship of his God. The Russes were astonished, and in their wonder praised the Greek ceremonial. Then the Emperors Basil and Constantine invited the envoys to their presence, and said, "Go hence to your native country," and dismissed them with valuable presents and great honor.

Thus they returned to their own country, and the Prince called together his boyars and the elders. Vladimir then announced the return of the envoys who had been sent out, and suggested that their report be heard. He thus commanded them to speak out before his retinue. The envoys reported, "When we journeyed among the Bulgars, we beheld how they worship in their temple, called a mosque, while they stand ungirt. The Bulgar bows, sits down, looks hither and thither like one possessed, and there is no happiness among them, but instead only sorrow and a dreadful stench. Their religion is not good. Then we went among the Germans, and saw them performing many ceremonies in their temples; but we beheld no glory there. Then we went to Greece, and the Greeks led us to the edifices where they worship their God, and we knew not whether we were in heaven or on earth. For on earth there is no such splendor or such beauty, and we are at a loss how to describe it. We only know that God dwells there among men, and their service is fairer than the ceremonies of other nations. For we cannot forget that beauty. Every man, after tasting something sweet, is afterward unwilling to accept that which is bitter, and therefore we cannot dwell longer here." Then the boyars spoke and said, "If the Greek faith were evil, it would not have been adopted by your grandmother Olga who was wiser than all other men."

. . .

When the Prince arrived at this capital, he directed that the idols should be overthrown, and that some should be cut to pieces and others burned with fire.

He thus ordered that Perun should be bound to a horse's tail and dragged down Borichev to the stream. He appointed twelve men to beat the idol with sticks, not because he thought the wood was sensitive, but to affront the demon who had deceived man in this guise, that he might receive chastisement at the hands of men. Great art thou, oh Lord, and marvelous are thy works! Yesterday he was honored of men, but today held in derision. While the idol was being dragged along the stream to the Dnieper, the unbelievers wept over it, for they had not yet received holy baptism. After they had thus dragged the idol along, they cast it into the Dnieper. But Vladimir had given this injunction "If it halts anywhere, then push it out from the bank, until it goes over the falls. Then let it loose." His command was duly obeyed. When the men let the idol go, and it passed through the rapids, the wind cast it out on the bank, which since that time has been called Perun's sandbank, a name that it bears to this very day.

Thereafter Vladimir sent heralds throughout the whole city to proclaim that if any inhabitant, rich or poor, did not betake himself to the river, he would risk the Prince's displeasure. When the people heard these words, they wept for joy, and exclaimed in their enthusiasm, "If this were not good, the Prince and his boyars would not have accepted it." On the morrow, the Prince went forth to the Dnieper with the priests of the Princess and those from Kherson, and a countless multitude assembled. They all went into the water: some stood up to their necks, others to their breasts, and the younger near the bank, some of them holding children in their arms, while the adults waded farther out. The priests stood by and offered prayers. There was joy in heaven and upon earth to behold so many souls saved. But the devil groaned, lamenting, "Woe is me! how am I driven out hence! For I thought to have my dwelling-place here, since the apostolic teachings do not abide in this land. Nor did this people know God, but I rejoiced in the service they rendered unto me. But now I am vanquished by the ignorant, not by apostles and martyrs, and my reign in these regions is at an end."

When the people were baptized, they returned each to his own abode. Vladimir, rejoicing that he and his subjects now knew God himself, looked up to heaven and said, "Oh God, who has created heaven and earth, look down, I beseech thee, on this thy new people, and grant them, oh Lord, to know thee as the true God, even as the other Christian nations have known thee. Confirm in them the true and inalterable faith, and aid me, oh Lord, against the hostile adversary, so that, hoping in thee and in thy might, I may overcome his malice." Having spoken thus, he ordained that wooden churches should be built and established where pagan idols had previously stood. He thus founded the Church of St. Basil on the hill where the idol of Perun and the other images had been set, and where the Prince and the people had offered their sacrifices. He began to found churches and to assign priests throughout the cities, and to invite the people to accept baptism in all the cities and towns.

He took the children of the best families, and sent them for instruction in book-learning. The mothers of these children wept bitterly over them, for they were not yet strong in faith, but mourned as for the dead. When these children were assigned for study, there was fulfilled in the land of Rus' the prophecy which says, "In those days, the deaf shall hear words of Scripture, and the voice of the stammerers shall be made plain" (*Is.,* xxix, 18). . . . .

Chapter Sixteen

Traditional Confucian civilization

<small>CHANGE WITHIN TRADITION</small>   **34**

The millennium between the sixth century, when the Sui dynasty restored imperial unity, and the sixteenth, when the Westerners began their intrusion by sea, was for China an era of unparalleled stability. It was during those centuries that China, after having caught up with the other Eurasian civilizations during the Han period, now forged ahead to become the most populous and wealthiest country in the world. Despite the common belief that Chinese civilization remained inflexible during this period, the fact remains that change was occurring gradually but constantly and decisively. The following selection by an American authority analyzes the precise nature of this "change within tradition" during the Sung period.*

When we speak of social change in China we most often have in mind one or the other of two pictures. The first is the change that we see today, when radically new ideas, techniques and forces from foreign countries have shaken the traditional social order, altering the old patterns rapidly and sometimes violently. The second picture is that of the dynastic cycle, a concept that we have inherited from the traditional Chinese historian, sometimes adding a few embellishments of our own. The political fortunes of a ruling house are often reflected (and perhaps affected) by a characteristic cycle in the whole political and economic order of the nation: from successful adjustment and control to maladjustment and chaos. The end of each cycle, if we focus our attention only on these factors, leaves Chinese society much as it was at the end of the cycle before. But this perspective tends to omit qualitative changes that occur in Chinese society on a different plane.

* Reprinted from E. A. Kracke, Jr., "Sung Society: Change Within Tradition," *Journal of Asian Studies*, XIV (August 1955), 478–88. Copyright by the Association for Asian Studies, Inc., reprinted with permission.

The kind of social change to be considered now differs from both of these. It is the long and continuous process of social development that in China as in our own civilization has accompanied the interplay between the traditional ideas and ways of life and the new concepts, techniques, and patterns of activity that evolve at home or enter from abroad. While at times this process of development moved slowly, and at times even retrogressed in some respects, the Chinese way of life nevertheless underwent through the centuries a cumulative alteration that was essentially irreversible. At times the forces of change so interacted that their gathered momentum was almost revolutionary in its social impact. An outstanding example of such rapid and far-reaching change is supplied by the Sung period, from the tenth century to the thirteenth.

The beginnings of the movement that attained so dramatic a tempo in the Sung period can be traced back, in some respects, through several centuries. Perhaps the first clearly perceptible aspect of the movement is the striking shift in the mass of China's population, from the northern plain country to the valleys of the mountainous south and the southeast coast. This migration had begun in the early centuries of our era, impelled both by economic difficulties and by foreign invaders of the old homeland; but as late as the middle of the eighth century the Yangtse valley and the areas further south still held only some forty to forty-five percent of China's people. By the end of the thirteenth century this area reported no less than eighty-five to ninety percent of the nation's population, and no less than twenty percent were established in the valleys of Fukien and eastern Chekiang along the southeast coast.

The rich new delta lands of the South became the chief suppliers of China's granaries. Some of the economic consequences of this are already well known, and need only be recapitulated here. To feed the armies guarding the northern border, and to provision the capital in the North, the central administration undertook to expand the canal system and subsidiary land communications from the South on a mammoth scale. Aided by the new facilities, private commerce grew rapidly. The Chinese now living along the remote southern coast no doubt found it necessary to import tools and other goods from the older settlements, and exchanged for these the new products native to the semi-tropical land in which they found themselves, as well as products from the South Seas and the countries of the Indian Ocean. Easier contacts by sea with Persia and Arabia encouraged the growth of foreign commerce, soon bringing to the growing coastal cities settlements of Hindu and Arab merchants. The Chinese also, as Mr. Lo points out in the following article in this issue, turned to the sea and assumed a leading place among maritime peoples. Internal commerce among the regions of China, at first confined for the most part to luxury items for the few, now expanded in variety and in its significance for larger groups of the nation.

With the growth of inter-regional trade, money came into its own, for many purposes rapidly superseding the old transactions in kind. By the eleventh century, a system of regulated paper currency was in operation, and the coinage of copper money reached proportions never again approached in Chinese dynastic history. Facilities for the transfer of funds and the provision of credit also developed. The various regions of China were no longer self-sufficient economically, but increasingly specialized in their produce—foods or goods or services—and therefore interdependent. These developments brought into being, by the eleventh century, a Chinese economy apparently far more complex than any of earlier times.

Of the social change that accompanied this economic development we have as yet only a very incomplete picture. But certain of its aspects stand out strikingly in the records. One aspect—perhaps of key significance—is the changing role of the great city. In earlier periods the few outstanding cities had achieved their greatness and economic importance only after designation as national capitals. Their symmetrical and regular plan, centered on the principal imperial palace, gave visible evidence of their origin and purpose. From the tenth century to the thirteenth this was not so. In this later period the cities chosen as capitals had already achieved importance as trade centers at strategic points on the lines of communication.

K'ai-feng, the first Sung capital, exemplified this particularly well. Originally a regional administrative seat at a main transfer point on the arterial canal from the South, its access to southern rice supplies recommended it during the troubled years succeeding the T'ang. The city had grown with its commercial importance, as successive new walls inclosed the suburbs that grew spontaneously beyond the older city gates. Within the sixteen-mile circuit of the outer walls, space was at a premium. The second Sung emperor renounced the planned expansion of his palace because it would have forced the demolition of private dwelling quarters. As a result of this history, although the city lay in the level valley of the Yellow River, it lacked the symmetry that had marked earlier national capitals and would later distinguish Peking (also primarily political in its character).

The later Sung capital of Hang-chou was also an important trade center at the time of its political elevation in 1135. Its population was huge; the numbers within its walls during the later years of the dynasty have been estimated as 900,0000, and those in its suburbs as some 600,000 more.

While the capitals of the eleventh to thirteenth centuries had thus grown strongly commercial in character, their supremacy among Chinese cities was challenged by other urban centers still more reliant on business activity. By the year 1100 at least four urban areas far surpassed the capital area in population. We have no exact data on the numbers living within the walls of these cities or in their immediate suburbs, but census reports suggest that each of the urban areas held a million or more people within the borders of its prefecture—a space very roughly comparable to the greater metropolitan areas of London or New York. Such population concentrations would seem to outdistance by far the largest urban agglomerations of that time in Europe, even by the largest estimates of the latter.

During the next two centuries the urban growth continued, and in several instances the prefectural populations apparently doubled, tripled, or quadrupled by 1290. Among the most dramatic increases, three were on the southeast coast (Hang-chou, Su-chou, and Fu-chou), and one (Jao-chou) near the inland trade route from the Yangtse to Canton. The prefecture of Fu-chou in 1290 reported approximately 3,875,000 people, suggesting an urban concentration of impressive proportions.

It was just around this time, soon after the Sung downfall, that Marco Polo visited these places, as an agent of the Mongol conqueror Kubilai. His descriptions of the magnificience of Hang-chou, the capital, and of the trade metropolis Ch'üan-chou, are well known. But he also observed another phenomenon that is suggested by contemporary census figures—the growth and multiplication of smaller cities and towns. In describing the journey from Hang-chou to Fu-chou (less than three hundred miles as the crow flies), he tells of no less than six "large, noble, and beautiful" or "noble and great" cities, and in the stages of his journey between these he notes no less than seven times "always finding cities and villages enough, very beautiful and very great"; on one two-day ride he remarks that these are "so frequent and continuous that you seem as you ride to go through the middle of a single city." Allowing for the colorful exaggerations we must permit to this oldest of China-hands, the regions that Polo saw along the southeast coast must certainly have been advanced in urban development compared with his native Italy—the most urbanized part of Europe in that day. While most of the terrain was mountainous and poorly adapted to farming, the few lands available had been fully exploited. A Sung writer notes that intensive cultivation had transformed once worthless acres to the most fertile in the empire, and while Marco Polo refers occasionally to the livestock he saw (oxen, buffalo, cows, goats, swine, and fowl) and to certain special plant products, he speaks not of fields but of "fine gardens."

But rich as the fields were, they were still too few. The coastal regions still depended for their prosperity on the income from their mines, commerce, manufactures, tea, and sea produce, and beyond the narrow valley floors must have preserved some of the air of an unsettled borderland. On four stages of his journey Polo mentions the "hunting and chase enough of beasts and birds" and refers as many times to the great and fierce "lions" (tigers?) that molest travellers, to such an extent that in one part of the route at least "it is very dangerous to pass through those regions unless people go in great numbers." In an area seeming thus sparsely settled over much of its extent, and developing rapidly in industry and trade, typifying the new trend, it is difficult not to suspect analogies with the frontier of opportunity that played a vital role in the development of our own civilization.

Who were the people that lived in the growing cities of this area? We have no clear picture of them, but there are at least some clues to their character. As in earlier times, there must have been a considerable number of civil and military officials, stationed there for limited terms by the central government, along with a more or less permanent corps of clerks and official underlings. There were the army garrisons usually stationed in all large places. There were no doubt well-to-do scholars without official employment, and poorer scholars who lived on their earnings as teachers, or from such miscellaneous employments as public letter-writing or story-telling. And there were the merchants and artisans, great and small, blending at the lowest economic level with the unskilled laborers. Considering the indicated sizes of the cities, the last three occupations must have constituted the preponderant group of inhabitants in most cases. The composition of the Sung populations cannot have differed too greatly from that observed by Marco Polo only around a decade after the dynasty's fall: in all his comments on the six larger cities he saw between Hang-chou and Fu-chou, and in four of his comments on the places between, he notes that the inhabitants "live by trade and by crafts," and implies mercantile activities indirectly by repeated references to the "abundance of all things for life," which he notes were very cheap. (To other activities he makes very little reference.)

What was true of this area was probably true also, to a more limited degree, of the great cities more widely scattered in other parts of China at this time. All were joined by the same commercial links, and often frequented by the same far-travelling merchants.

Surviving records tell us of the merchants' activities and mode of life chiefly at the capitals, but in these respects too different regions may have presented a rather similar picture.

The merchants, artisans, and providers of services were organized in guilds, which had powers of discipline over their own members, although these organizations had no apparent role in the general administration of the cities. The guild members had to some extent emancipated themselves from the close official supervision that existed during the T'ang. Their business activities were no longer confined within the great walled markets, or limited to the hours in which the government permitted the opening of the market portals. Commerce and manufacture were now carried on in shops scattered throughout the city or beyond the city gates, though establishments of the same trade tended to group together.

Long and persistent governmental efforts to regulate trade and control prices were matched by equally persistent and largely successful evasion on the part of the merchants. Attempts of the state to monopolize certain profitable industries had been costly and only partly successful. But in the Sung the state had learned to apply its taxes more flexibly and to restrict its monopolies to certain key operations of an industry; through such policies the state diverted what was perhaps the lion's share of the profits to its treasuries.

Such state controls may well have retarded significantly the growth of commercial activity and power. At the time, however, there must have been little evidence of this. The more successful merchants accumulated great wealth, and their style of living vied with that of the imperial princes. Sumptuary laws had always, before this, restricted the colors that should be used by each class of society. By 995, however, sumptuary laws were unenforceable, and all were repealed but the ban on a certain shade of deep purple reserved for the imperial house and the highest officials. There is evidence that even this color was taken over by commoners within a few years. We read that the families of great merchants wore pearls and jade. Their carriages thronged the roads, and in the words of a contemporary "rubbed hubs with those of distinguished families." In the T'ang, we are told, even a servant who had served in an aristocratic family scorned a master who haggled in person with a merchant. By the eleventh century, even important officials had discovered the attractions of commerce, and many augmented their income by combining business operations with their official journeys. Merchants were socially accepted in elite circles. Through such connections, or through their wealth, some of them secured government office, and served in positions of some importance.

But the professional trader still found certain barriers to his social advancement. He still lacked the approval of more conservative scholars. His indulgence in luxuries elicited complaints very much like those that had been evoked by a more modest commercial expansion a millennium earlier. His pursuit of money was felt to be unworthy. The officials criticized his disposition to make profits by cornering the market; because this was at the expense of the poor—and no doubt because the official preferred that the state monopolies should garner such profits. The grumbling of the conservatives, however, may have been in itself another indication that power of commerce was recognized as a potential threat to the supremacy of the bureaucrat; in fact, specific complaints of the growing influence that merchants exercised over officials are not lacking.

The new social environment created by the cities surely had its impact on the evolution of Chinese culture. The operation of any but the simplest business naturally required at least a certain minimum of literacy, and the city environment gave better opportunities for even the poorest to gain a smattering of the written character. The successful and ambitious tradesman would naturally hope that education would win for his sons an entree into the bureaucracy. When the new urban reader competed with the older scholar for written texts, a new demand for books was created. In the century after 950 the technique of wood engraving, long used to multiply Buddhist charms and texts, suddenly found new uses, and in a short time the art of printing was applied to practically all the existing varieties of literature.

For the relatively unlettered, a multiplicity of entertainments was also devised, ranging from troops of acrobats and displays of fireworks to puppet shows, shadow plays, and simple theatrical presentations. Through the stories that served as themes for such public performances, some parts of the sophisticated culture could reach the illiterate, and facilitate a sharing of the great tradition with larger groups. Particularly important in this respect was the role of the story-teller: unemployed scholars frequently made their living by recounting some of the dramatic episodes of history to audiences in the market place. Through the prompting-books some of them wrote to aid their confreres, they created the prototypes of the later great fictional themes. At the same time the old themes were presented in the language of the people and transmuted to appeal to a more popular audience, until the content itself reflected their viewpoint and their tastes. It could scarcely be accidental that the Chinese popular novel traces back to this period.

The influence of the new city life also had its impact on society beyond the city walls. The growing importance of a money economy must surely have contributed a significant share to the increasing complications of the farm problem. The crops of different regions were becoming more specialized, leaving the farmer often less self-sufficient, and more vulnerable in years of crop failure. While the farmer probably relied little on the cities for his basic necessities, it seems that travelling merchants from the cities already came to the country fairs to sell such things as salt, and buy for the city market. The glamor of the city had its weakening effect on the old rural patterns of life in other ways, The wealthy peasant, we are told, tended to emulate the merchant's style of living, and we hear repeatedly that the rewards of commerce tempted the poor farmer to abandon the hard and often unrewarding work on his lands, sell his farm implements, and engage in trade.

Finally, we must note the change that came about in the bureaucratic class itself. It was also in this period that new recruitment procedures opened a governmental career to far wider numbers than before. Competitive recruitment examinations were regularly used from the beginning of the eleventh century on a scale far greater than ever before. Improved through the development of elaborate techniques to make the examinations more objective, the new system helped to break the power monopoly once held by a small group of northern aristocratic families. The social origin of the newcomers who replaced them is not entirely clear. The broader distribution of opportunity was certainly made possible by the increase in literacy and the wider availability of books that we have already noted. Several hundred candidates commonly passed the final stage of the triennial examinations, and we are told that for each of these some hundred candidates had attempted the local preliminary tests. The competition was wide indeed. But the fiercest rivalry and the most numerous successful candidates during most of the dynasty came from the southeast coast, where we have seen the rapid pace of urbanization at this time.

How many of these men came from the great cities? How many traced their educational opportunity to families of ultimately mercantile origin? It is still impossible to say. But data from two lists of graduates that have come down to us from the twelfth and thirteenth centuries show that the regions with more and larger urban concentrations tended to supply not only more graduates in proportion to their area, but also more graduates per 'family, so that they clearly dominated the field. Moreover the largest proportion of apparently new blood tended to appear in the circuits of most rapid population growth, if we may judge from the numbers of graduates counting no officials among their direct paternal forebears. Conspicuous among these regions of growing population were again those containing the great coastal cities and those on the main inland trade routes. We have here, then, a seeming link between the broadening social base of the bureaucracy and the social mobility that probably characterized the great cities in their period of most rapid expansion.

The political importance of this changing character of the bureaucracy is obvious. Its cultural effect, while less tangible and less calculable, was perhaps none the less real. For while the Sung was a time of beginnings for the more popular literary forms, it was also a time of great vigor, and in some ways a time of culmination, in the intellectual activities practiced or patronized by the bureaucrat: the fine arts, the more sophisticated literary forms, and critical scholarship. In government, it was a time of imaginative reform schemes and experiments. It saw great advances in several fields of technology. In all of these realms the contribution made by men of the Southeast was outstanding.

Thus we have evidence that a genuine alteration of Chinese social patterns accompanied the rise of the great city. The influence of the city extended beyond the bourgeois to the farmer and the bureaucrat. Despite the inhibiting pressures of official conservatism, and at times in disregard of laws and decrees, the merchant had expanded his influence and breached many of the barriers that surrounded him when the period of change began.

The limits of his rise are also apparent. If he achieved a place in government, it was by transforming himself into a bureaucrat; as a merchant he still enjoyed no active political role. The professional official remained supreme, and steadfastly unsympathetic toward the development of private economic interests.

The history of Chinese urbanization after the thirteenth century, and the reasons why the movement failed to go further than it did, are beyond the scope of the present topic. As we contemplate the situation of the thirteenth century bourgeois, however, it is difficult to discern any single insuperable barrier to his further social rise. Most of his disadvantages were also faced by some at least of his European confreres during the later Middle Ages or the Renaissance. In the thirteenth century, the Chinese bourgeois had demonstrated by his will and his resourcefulness that under favorable conditions, the traditional Chinese social patterns could be significantly modified through the operation of internal forces.

BUDDHISM IN CHINA 35

During the medieval period, religion and thought in China were profoundly affected by the impact of Buddhism from India. The diffusion of Buddhism was on a scale comparable to, and as significant as, the diffusion of Christianity from the Middle East through the whole of Europe. Buddhism flourished in China, and, through China, in Korea and Japan, long after it had disappeared in India where it had originated. In this selection, a Chinese scholar analyzes the circumstances of the diffusion of Buddhism, its far reaching repercussions on all aspects of Chinese civilization, and its eventual sinicization and absorption.*

* Reprinted from Hu Shih, "The Indianization of China: A Case Study in Cultural Borrowing," by permission of the publishers from *Harvard Tercentenary Conference of Arts & Sciences,* Childe *et al.*, eds., *Independence, Convergence, and Borrowing,* pp. 223–46. Cambridge, Mass.: Harvard University Press, Copyright 1937, 1965, by the President and Fellows of Harvard College.

It is my purpose to trace this long process of Indianization through its various stages. Broadly speaking, these stages are:—

1. Mass Borrowing
2. Resistance and Persecution
3. Domestication
4. Appropriation

By mass borrowing I mean not only the simple process of China's taking from India all those things which were either totally absent or weak in the indigenous civilization, but also that mass movement of religious enthusiasm which blindly embraced everything that accompanied the new faith. By resistance and persecution I mean to include those periods of history when the invading culture was openly opposed by Chinese thinkers and persecuted by governmental action. By domestication I mean to include all those tendencies consciously or unconsciously to make the Indian religion, art, thought, and institutions take up more and more Chinese colors, to make them more "at home" in China in order that the Chinese people might feel more at home in them. By appropriation I mean the culminating stage of successful borrowing when the essence, if not the bodily totality, of the borrowed culture was unconsciously "appropriated," recognized by the native population as their own.

In order to appreciate the vast scope of Chinese borrowings from India, it is necessary first to understand the truly striking contrast between the ancient cultures of the two peoples, especially in their religious beliefs and practices. The ancient Chinese people, who built up their civilization in the north temperate zone where the struggle against the forces of nature was severe, had worked out only a very simple and plain religion, consisting of the worship of ancestors, of the natural forces, and of a supreme God or Heaven; the belief in divination; and a vague conception of retribution of good and evil. There was neither Heaven in the sense of a Paradise, nor Hell in the sense of the place of Last Day Judgment. There were practically no mythologies, nor elaborate rituals. It was the religion of a hard-working and plain-thinking people.

But, as the race became more mature and more sophisticated, it began to yearn for something more satisfying or at least more tantalizing than the too simple religion of its ancient fathers. Throughout the third and second centuries B.C., there were numerous ambitious quests for strange innovations in religious belief and practice, grandiose imperial quests for the great unknown mystery which the too pragmatic and rational mentality of indigenous China could not possibly satisfy.

Then there came the great religion of the Buddha, together with all the Mahāyāna trimmings of the pre-Buddhist and non-Buddhist religions of India. Never before had China seen a religion so rich in imagery, so beautiful and captivating in ritualism, and so bold in cosmological and metaphysical speculations. Like a poor beggar suddenly halting before a magnificent storehouse of precious stones of dazzling brilliancy and splendor, China was overwhelmed, baffled, and overjoyed. She begged and borrowed freely from this munificent giver. The first borrowings were chiefly from the religious life of India, in which China's indebtedness to India can never be fully told. India gave China, for example, not only one Paradise, but tens of paradises, not only one Hell, but many hells, each varying in severity and horror from the other. The old simple idea of retribution of good and evil was replaced by the idea of transmigration of the soul and the iron law of *karma* which runs through all past, present, and future existences.

156

These and thousands of other items of belief and practice have poured from India by land and by sea into China, and have been accepted and gradually made into parts of the cultural life of China. The ideas of the world as unreal, of life as painful and empty, of sex as unclean, of the family as an impediment to spiritual attainment, of celibacy and mendicancy as necessary to the Buddhist order, of alms-giving as a supreme form of merit, of love extended to all sentient beings, of vegetarianism, of rigid forms of asceticism, of words and spells as having miraculous power—these are only a few drops in that vast flux of Indian religious and cultural invasion.

The general aspects of the story of the spread of Buddhism in China are comparatively well known. Suffice it to say that, according to our present knowledge, Buddhism had probably come to China long before the year 68 A.D. commonly assigned as the date of its introduction; that probably it had come to China, not as religion officially introduced by an emperor, but only as a form of popular worship and belief gradually taking root among the people—probably among the poorest and the most lowly, to whom the Buddhist missionaries, traders, and travelers had brought the good tidings of mercy and delivery from pain. In all probability, it was from the populace that the prince Liu Ying (died 70), younger brother of the emperor, caught the contagion and was converted to Buddhism. It was also from the popular worship that the Emperor Huan-ti (147–167) elevated the Buddha and made him an object of worship in his palace. The apparently rapid progress made by Buddhism in the Yangtse Valley and on the southern coast towards the end of the second century A.D. seems to indicate that it had had a long period of slow but steady permeation among the people. By the third century, when the men of letters began to admire and defend it, Buddhism had already become a powerful religion, not because of governmental patronage, of which there was very little, but because of its powerful following among the people.

It was as a popular religion of the poor and the lowly that Buddhism first came to stay in China. As such, Mahāyāna Buddhism came *in toto,* and was accepted by the Chinese believers almost *in toto.* It was not for the masses to choose and reject. A great religion of powerful popular appeal came and was accepted. That was all.

Indeed, in their religious enthusiasm, the Chinese people soon came to look to India as "the Land of the Buddha," and even as "the Western Heaven" from which nothing but the great truths could come. Everything that came from the "Western Heaven" must have a reason and commanded acceptance. Buddhism, or that whole movement of cultural invasion which went by the name of Buddhism, was bodily taken over by China on the high waves of religious fervor and fanaticism.

But the Indianization of a country with an established civilization like China could not long be smooth sailing. Gradually grave doubts began to crop up. Chinese thinkers began to realize that this Indian or Buddhist culture was in many fundamental aspects directly opposed to the best tradition of China. They began to resent the conquest of their ancient civilization by a "barbarian country." Of the truly fundamental differences, a few may be mentioned here.

First, the Buddhist negation of life was contrary to Chinese, especially to Confucianist, ideas. To the Confucianist, the individual life is a sacred inheritance and it is the duty of the individual to make the best of that life—at least not to degrade it or destroy it. One of the most popular texts of Confucianism, "The Book of Filial Piety," says: "The human body, even every hair and every skin of it, is inherited from the parents, and must not be annihilated or degraded." Ancient Chinese thinkers of the fourth century B.C. taught that life is of the highest value. The Buddhist doctrines that life is an illusion and that to live is pain, led to practices which the

Chinese in their moments of calmer judgment could not but regard as revolting and inhuman. Throughout the history of Buddhist China, it was common practice for a monk to burn his thumb, his fingers, or even his whole body, as a form of merit in emulation of the supreme sacrifice of the Bodhisattva Bhaishajyarāja, the King of Medicine, one of the deities of Mahāyāna Buddhism. Each of the two great Buddhist Biographical Series devoted one section to biographies of Chinese monks who had burned themselves to death, or otherwise committed suicide, as supreme sacrifices. This section is under the heading "Those who gave up their lives." It contains detailed stories of hundreds of such suicides. A monk would announce his date of self-destruction and, on that day, would tie his whole body in oiled cloth, light the fagot pyre and his own body with a torch in his own hand, and go on mumbling the sacred titles of the Buddhas until he was completely overpowered by the flames. Very often such human sacrifices were witnessed by thousands of pious Buddhists whose plaintive wailings would accompany the slow burning of the pious monk. China seems to have gone completely mad in one of her strange periods of religious fanaticism.

Secondly, the Buddhist monk and nun must renounce all their family relations and must practice celibacy. This was also contrary to Chinese traditions. The whole Confucianist ethics had been one of relationships, of which the family ties, being the most universal and most intimate, were regarded as the most important. Indeed, Mencius once said that of all acts against filial piety the failure to have children was the worst. Celibacy was directly opposed to this traditional emphasis on posterity. The seriousness of this practice became all the more apparent when the number of monks and nuns grew to millions.

Thirdly, the mendicancy of the whole Buddhist order was condemned by Chinese moral and economic thinkers as "parasitic" and as responsible for the poverty and disorder in the country. All the orthodox economic thought of pre-Buddhist China had taught that labor alone was essential to production and that the merchant class were to be discouraged because they were parasites who "were fed without cultivating the fields, and were clothed without their women working in sericulture." And now came the vast host of monks and nuns who not only would not work, but often accumulated immense wealth for their monastic orders through the extravagant almsgiving of the lay patrons. The economic consequences became quite alarming in those times when almost every eighth person in the Empire was a monk, a nun, or a dependent of a monastery.

Fourthly, the whole outlook of Buddhism on life was "other-wordly," pointing to an escape from this world and this life. That too was quite opposed to the moral teachings of Classical China. The Buddhist practices all forms of mental control and meditation, and accumulates "merit" by all forms of sutra reading and spell reciting —but for what purpose? The only answer was: For the salvation of the practitioner. Which, of course, was a petty and selfish motive in the eyes of the Chinese thinker. As a Chinese critic of the twelfth century put it: "What we should attend to is precisely that span of life from birth to death. Buddhism completely ignores this life and devotes itself to speculating about what goes before birth and after death. But the earth, the mountains and rivers, which the Buddhists consider as empty and unreal, nevertheless stand out as concrete realities that cannot be conjured away by magic or philosophy."

Fifthly, the whole Indian imaginative power, which knows neither limitation nor discipline, was indeed too much for the Chinese mind. Indigenous China was always factual and rarely bold in imagination. "Extend your knowledge, but leave out those things about which you are in doubt." "Say you know when you really know, and say you don't know when you really don't know—that is knowledge." Such were the wise instructions of Confucius on knowledge. This emphasis on veracity and certainty was one of the most marked traits of ancient Chinese literature, which is strikingly free from mythological and supernatural elements. Confucius once said: "I have devoted whole days without food and whole nights without sleep, to thinking. But it was of no use. It is better to learn [than to think in abstract]." This self-analysis on the part of one of China's greatest sages is of peculiar significance in showing the suspicion with which Chinese thinkers regarded the unbridled exercise of thought and imagination. It must have been very difficult for Chinese readers to swallow down all that huge amount of sacred literature of sheer fancy and imagination. It was probably this native detestation of the unbridled imagination which led the first Chinese leaders of anti-Buddhist persecution in the fifth century to declare that the entire Buddhist tradition was a myth and a lie.

These and many other fundamental differences between indigenous China and the Indianized China were largely responsible for the numerous religious controversies and for the four major anti-Buddhist persecutions of 446, 574, 845, and 955. It is significant to note that all edicts for the persecution of Buddhism emphasized the fact that Buddhism was an alien religion introduced from a foreign barbarian country, and that it was a national disaster and humiliation for the Middle Kingdom to be thus "barbarized." Han Yü (768–824), probably the intellectual father of the great persecution of 845, coined these concise slogans: "Restore their people to humanity! Burn their books! And convert their buildings to human residences!" The first slogan literally reads "Man their men!" meaning that all those who embraced this alien religion were not to be considered as "men." Thus in the edict of persecution of 845, after enumerating the temples and monasteries demolished, the millions of acres of monastic land confiscated, and the vast numbers of monks and nuns forced to return to lay life, the Emperor said: "Henceforth all affairs of monks and nuns shall be dealt with by the Bureau of Foreign Affairs." That is to say, all who are converted by a foreign religion are no longer considered as Chinese subjects.

These were expressions of a nationalistic consciousness behind which was the only partially articulate recognition that this great religion introduced from the "Western Heaven" contained many ideas and practices which had undermined the moral, social, and economic traditions of the Chinese nation.

But none of these nation-wide persecutions ever lasted more than a few years and none succeeded in eradicating or even diminishing the tremendous influence of the Indian religion in the country. When a persecuting Emperor died, his successor invariably adopted a more lenient policy, and in the course of the years the once persecuted religion flourished again in all its former splendor and grandeur.

It is a significant historical fact, however, that while no more governmental persecution of Buddhism was undertaken after the tenth century, the religion of Buddhism gradually weakened, withered, dwindled in its power and influence, and finally died a slow but natural death. Why? Where drastic persecution had failed, the more subtle processes of domestication and appropriation were meeting with greater and greater successes. Buddhism in its domesticated form was gradually and unconsciously "appropriated" by the Chinese people.

Domestication is a common phenomenon in all cultural borrowings. A folksong or a folk story introduced from a distant province is soon revised by nobody knows whom, and, while the main theme—the motif—is always retained, most of the details (names, scenery, fashion, dress, footwear, hair-dress, et cetera) are re-touched with "local color." And, after a period of successive domestications, it becomes quite difficult to recognize its distant or even alien origin.

Almost every phase or element of Buddhism has undergone some degree of domestication during these twenty-odd centuries. Look at the faces of the deities in a Buddhist temple in China today and trace each to its earliest Indian originals, and you will realize how the process of domestication has worked. The most striking examples are the various stages of transformation of the god Avalokiteśvara, who was long ago "unsexed" and became the Goddess of Mercy, often represented as a beautiful woman with tiny bound feet. Maitreya has now become the big-bellied, good-natured, heartily laughing Chinese monk that greets you as you enter any Buddhist monastery in China. Indeed, all faces of the Buddhist deities have been Sinicized—through a long but unconscious process of domestication. Even in those cases, as in the case of the sixteen or 500 Arhats, where the sculptor or molder consciously tries to create "foreign" types, the resultant creations are invariably more Chinese than Indian.

Music, painting, architecture, and the other fine arts which came from India together with the Buddhist religion were also subject to processes of domestication. The reciting and sing-songing of Sanskrit texts have become entirely Sinicized; and Indian melodies have been made vehicles of Chinese songs in which their Indian origins are often forgotten. In painting, as in sculpture, the domestication went so far that later Buddhist paintings are essentially Chinese and differ radically from the early Buddhist art and also from the later artistic development in India herself.

The most difficult phase of domestication, naturally, lay in the sphere of the religious, moral, and philosophical teachings of Buddhism. Being in most cases basically opposed to ancient Chinese tradition and contrary to the intellectual habits of the Chinese people, these teachings could not be easily digested. Sufficiently abstruse in themselves, they became unintelligible in the translations, of which, as we know, very few were made by really competent scholars well versed in the languages and in the subject matter.

The most natural step in early attempts to understand this alien religion was to interpret it in terms of concepts which came nearest to the foreign ideas and which were most familiar to the native mind. Buddhism came to China at a time when the philosophical ideas of Lao-Tze and Chuang-Tze were being revived and having a general vogue among the intellectuals who had tired of the Neo-Confucianists of the Han Dynasty. The philosophical naturalism and nihilism of this Taoist school had certain affinities with a number of ideas of philosophical Buddhism, and it soon became a fashion to translate Buddhist terminology into words bodily taken from the sayings of these Taoist thinkers. Such borrowed terms are never exact; *Nirvāna,* for example was not *wu-wei,* and an *arhat* was not a *shien jen.* But that was the best that could be done in the early stages of intellectual and philosophical borrowings. These Taoistic interpretations furnished the bridge of cultural trans-mission and made the new ideas of India more easily acceptable to the Chinese intelligentsia. It was the first stage of domestication.

As the work of translation proceeded in later centuries, the Buddhists insisted on the importance of not using existing philosophical terms of the historic schools of ancient Chinese thought. They preferred the method of exact transcription of the original sound, such as *bodhi* (wisdom), *prajñā-pāramitā* (the path of attainment through philosophic understanding), *nirvāna, yoga, dhyāna, samādhi* and so forth. But the Chinese readers continued to "interpret" and understand them in the light of what had been most familiar and intelligible to them. And it was the naturalistic and nihilistic background of ancient Taoistic philosophy that made it possible for the philosophical thought of such Mahāyāna schools as the Madhymaka to be understood by the Chinese intellectuals.

Wherever such a favorable background was lacking, understanding and acceptance became well-nigh impossible, despite great native leadership and imperial patronage. Hsüan Chuang (596–664), the great Chinese pilgrim, went to India at the height of Vijñānavāda thought, and, after spending fifteen years studying it, brought back a vast amount of Vijñānavāda literature and devoted the remainder of his life to translating it into Chinese. This school had developed a most abstruse system of what may be termed introspective psychology which analyzed consciousness into over 500 states of mind and their corresponding faculties and objects. Such hairsplitting differentiation simply could not be done in the Chinese language. In spite of the great personal leadership of Hsüan Chuang and some of his immediate disciples, the vast amount of Vijñānavāda literature remained a sealed book and exerted practically no influence on the intellectual life of China. The study of the psychological and logical treatises of this school was revived during the recent decades in Japan and later in China because the introduction of modern European psychology and logic had furnished new materials and a new set of terms for comparison and for interpretation. This is another illustration of the fact that borrowing in the field of speculative thought can only be done under such favorable conditions as to make it possible to interpret the unfamiliar in terms of the familiar.

The failure of the Vijñānavāda system in China also shows the negative phase of cultural domestication. What we cannot digest, we discard. Discarding means the elimination of all those elements which the native culture cannot assimilate or which the native population regard as non-essential. The never-ending importation of new sutras and treatises from Buddhist India throughout many centuries began to trouble the Chinese intellectuals. As early as the fourth century, Chinese Buddhists began to ask the question: What after all is the essence of this great system of the Buddha? Gradually they formulated their answer: The essence of Buddhism is Meditation and Insight. All else can be discarded. Gradually it was recognized that these two phases might be conveniently combined in the one term *yoga* or *dhyāna,* which means meditation but which also implies and relies on philosophical insight. From 400 on, there was a clear tendency among Chinese Buddhists to grasp the idea and practice of *dhyāna* or *yoga* as the essence and consummation of Buddhism.

Simultaneously, there arose the movement to give special prominence to the Amitābha or Pure Land Sect. This sect laid special stress on Faith. Faith in the existence of the Pure Land presided over by the Amita Buddha of infinite longevity and infinite enlightenment, and constant reminding oneself of his faith by daily repeating the formula "Nama Amitābha!"—these alone are sufficient to insure final attainment and salvation. This form of Buddhism, because of its extreme simplicity, has had the greatest appeal to all classes, and has survived all other more sophisticated sects.

All these tendencies were towards simplification or filtration. But a more radical voice arose in the fifth century in the person of the learned monk Tao Sheng, who taught the revolutionary idea of "Sudden Enlightenment" as against all forms of "gradual attainment." He had been trained in the nihilistic philosophy of Lao-tze and Chuang-tze and, paraphrasing the latter, he declared: "The word is the symbol for the idea; and when the idea is grasped, the symbol may be discarded." In these words we hear the first declaration of Chinese Zennism revolting against the terrible burden of the hairsplitting verbalism and pedantry of Indian scholasticism. And "sudden enlightenment" was to be the weapon of this revolt. Grasp the idea and throw away the wordy symbols!

For even *dhyāna* or *yoga* includes a tediously long series of arduous and minute practices of gradual attainment, beginning with the simple form of breath control, passing through all intermediate stages of rigid mental and emotional control, and finally ending in the attainment of perfect tranquillity and ease together with the acquisition of magical powers. Even this was too scholastic for the Chinese mind.

From the seventh century on, there arose the Southern Schools of Chinese Zennism, which was built on the central idea of Sudden Enlightenment and discarded all the scholastic verbalism, the slavish ritualism, and even the minute practices of meditation. "Buddhahood is within you. Worship not the Buddha, for the Buddha means the Enlightened One, and Enlightenment is within you. Abide not by the Law, for the Law simply means Righteousness, and Righteousness is within you. And abide not by the *Sangha* (the brotherhood of monks), for the brotherhood simply means purity in life, and purity is within you." Thus spoke Hui-neng (died 713), the founder of Southern Zennism.

By the eighth and ninth centuries, the Zennists were becoming truly iconoclastic. They frankly said: "There is neither Buddhahood to attain, nor the Truth to obtain." "Wherefore do ye busy yourselves without cease? Go home and take a rest. Try to be an *ordinary man,* who eats, drinks, sleeps, and moves his bowels. What more do you seek?"

And they developed a pedagogic technique of their own, the essence of which consisted of urging the novice to seek his own awakening or enlightenment through his own thinking and living. No other salvation was possible.

The whole Zen movement from 700 to 1100 was a revolt against Buddhist verbalism and scholasticism, but it was also a movement to Sinicize Buddhism by sweeping away all its scholastic verbiage and giving special prominence to the idea of salvation through one's own intellectual liberation and insight.

True, this process of discarding and expurgation left very little of Buddhism in the net outcome. But we must admit as a historical truth that 400 years of Zennist expurgation had really domesticated the Buddhist religion and made it intelligible and attractive to the Chinese mind. By the eleventh century, Zennist Buddhism was more a philosophy than a religion. But that was exactly what it should be. For was not original Buddhism more a philosophy than a religion? Unconsciously and unwittingly the Chinese Buddhists, throughout a long period of a thousand years, had succeeded in shearing Mahāyāna Buddhism of all its extraneous verbiage and in remaking it into a philosophy, a method, and a technique. Unconsciously, they had made their Buddhism nearer to primitive Buddhism than any Hīnayāna or Mahāyāna sects had ever been. And incidentally, they had thereby so domesticated Buddhism as to make it easily understood and appreciated by the Chinese intelligentsia.

By the eleventh century, this process of domestication was complete, and it remained for the Chinese intelligentsia to appropriate this domesticated Buddhism as an integral part of Chinese cultural life.

No cultural borrowing is permanent until the borrowed culture is "appropriated" by the native people as their own and its alien origin is completely forgotten. In the case of Buddhism, all those elements which have not been so appropriated by the Chinese people remain to this day as the unassimilated elements of a foreign culture. The work of Indianization of Chinese thought and institutions has come about through those phases of Buddhism and Indian culture in general which have been so thoroughly domesticated and assimilated as to be unconsciously regarded by the Chinese people as their own.

Chinese borrowings from the culture of India were made in two main instalments. The first portion of the borrowings came as a result of the period of mass conversion to Buddhism. The religion of Mahāyāna Buddhism which contains numerous elements of the pre-Buddhist Hindu religions, became firmly established as a great popular religion in China. Many of the cultural elements that came with the Buddhist faith, as I have pointed out, were things which the traditional culture of ancient China never possessed. They filled what may be called a cultural (at least religious) vacuum and were eagerly accepted by the believing masses. It was this portion of the borrowed culture that was the first to be appropriated by the Chinese.

The second portion consisted of more subtle elements of the Indian culture—the philosophy of the world and of life, the moral and social standards, the intellectual habits—things to which the believing masses were indifferent, and which had much resistance to encounter from the age-long cultural make-up of the Chinese people. It was these elements which had required much intermediate work of shifting, discarding, distilling, and reinterpreting, before some of them were sufficiently domesticated to be unconsciously appropriated into the Chinese culture.

Historically, the first period of appropriation coincided with the rise of the religion of Taoism, and the second appropriation coincided with the revival of the secular Confucianist philosophy.

Taoism as a popular religion (as distinct from Taoism as a philosophy) rose in the centuries following the gradual spread of Buddhism in China. "Tao" means "a way." There were many "ways" toward the end of the second century A.D. After the third century, one form of Taoism, with its charity organizations, its practices of healing by praying and of confession of sins, and its polytheistic worships, gradually acquired a large following, not only among the people, but also among the upper classes. Beginning as a consolidated form of the earlier "Sinitic" religion of the Chinese people, Taoism received a great impetus from its impact with the imported religious system of Buddhism. There seemed to be a strong desire on the part of the Taoists to supersede and kill this foreign rival by imitating every feature of it. They accepted the heavens and hells from the Indian religion, gave them Chinese names, and assigned to them Chinese gods to preside over them. A Taoist canon was consciously forged after the model of the Buddhist sutras. Buddhist rituals were freely adopted into the Taoist worship. Orders of priests and priestesses were established after the fashion of the Buddhist orders of monks and nuns. The Taoists had also a form of meditation which was undoubtedly a modification of the Yoga practice of India. The ideas of *karma* and transmigration of the soul throughout the existences were also appropriated by the Taoists and made the central idea in their conception of retribution of good and evil. The idea of transmigration was only modified by the Taoist belief that the individual could attain personal and physical immortality, and thereby escape transmigration, by contemplation, medical aid, and accumulation of merit.

Since the fifth century, there had been many attempts of the Taoists to oust Buddhism as an alien religion and to establish Taoism as its sole native substitute. Taoist influence was behind practically all the governmental persecutions of Buddhism.

While Taoism was intended to be a rival and substitute for Buddhism, it was too much an imitation—indeed a crude imitation—of that foreign religion to differentiate itself from it and to command real respect and adherence from the intellectual class. Moreover, its whole outlook on life was just as other-wordly as the

163

Buddhist's. The Taoist ideal was also to flee from this life and this world and seek individual salvation. It was as selfish and anti-social as the Buddhist. It was for this reason that, in the Confucianist attacks on the medieval religions, Taoism and Buddhism were always mentioned together as the joint object of attack. By too much appropriation of an ill-digested alien religion, Taoism had alienated the sympathy of the more nationalistic critics in the country.

The revival of the secular Confucianist philosophy in the eleventh and twelfth centuries was professedly anti-Buddhistic. Its object was to revive and re-interpret the moral and political philosophy of the school of Confucius and Mencius as a substitute for the individualistic, anti-social, and other-wordly philosophies of the Buddhist and Zennist schools which had prevailed throughout the medieval period. The object was to revive a purely secular Chinese philosophy to take the place of the religious and non-Chinese thought of the previous age.

A statesman of the eleventh century had pointed out that, during the whole Buddhist period of about a thousand years, the best minds of the nation flocked to Buddhist schools of thought and belief merely because the Confucianist teachings were too simple and insipid to attract them. The problem in the revival of Confucianist thought, therefore, was how to re-interpret the Confucianist classics so as to make them sufficiently interesting and attractive to the best minds of the nation.

As if by a miracle, the Confucianist philosophers of the eleventh century suddenly discovered that the old classical writings of Confucius and his school could be made as interesting and attractive as the Buddhist and Zennist teachings. They discovered, to their great delight, that all the philosophical problems of the universe, of life, of the mind, of knowledge, and of religious reverence, which had engaged the speculative philosophers of Buddhism for centuries, were to be found in the ancient classical writings and only required a little re-interpretation to bring forth the hidden meanings of those long-neglected works of the ancient sages. So they set themselves to work at this re-interpretation.

These philosophers succeeded in working out a "rational philosophy of Neo-Confucianism" which had a cosmology, a theory or theories of the nature and method of knowledge, and a moral and political philosophy. This new secular philosophy also laid great stress on the perfection of the individual which was to be achieved through extension of knowledge, purification of the will, and rectification of the mind. The extension of knowledge was to be achieved by going to the things and investigating the reasons thereof. And the rectification of the mind and purification of the will depended upon the cultivation of the attitude of reverence.

But, these Confucianists proudly pointed out, the perfection of the individual was not the end in itself, as it was with the medieval religions. The perfection of the individual was only a step leading to the social ends of successfully ordering the affairs of the family, the state, and the world. All intellectual and moral training leads to the rectification of the individual life from which shall radiate all its social and political activities. It was this social end which differentiated the secular Confucianism from the other-wordly religious system of old.

And all this new philosophy was found in the old neglected writings of Classical Confucianism. The new interpretation seemed so natural, so reasonable, and so satisfactory, that it was really inconceivable how such precious teachings could have been allowed to lie unnoticed for all those centuries.

The historical fact was that all this re-interpretation had been the result of one thousand years of Buddhistic philosophizing and training. Especially the four hundred years of Zennist Buddhism had given the Chinese philosopher a new insight, a new set of intellectual habits, and a new source of reference material. It was as if the naked eye had been aided by a new eyeglass which enabled him to see things which he had been unable to see before. And the eyeglass was, unfortunately, colored. He now saw things through this eyeglass colored by centuries of Buddhist and Zennist training. He now re-interpreted all he saw in that new light. He was unconsciously appropriating what he had honestly disowned and revolted against.

The Rationalist philosophers made a great success of their Confucianist revival and of their re-interpretation of the Confucianist philosophy, which had now become sufficiently interesting to attract the best minds of the nation, who from that time on no longer flocked to the doors of the Zennist monasteries. And when the first-rate minds of the nation ceased to be recruited into Buddhism, that great Indian religion gradually faded into nonentity and died almost an unmourned death.

But what was the real nature of this secular substitute for the Indian religion? Was it a real repudiation of the Buddhist religion, as it claimed to be?

In reality, the Confucianist revival since the eleventh century has been only a *secularization* of the Indian religion. By secularizing it, the Chinese philosophers had actually *universalized* it, so that what had once ruled the life of the members of the Buddhist order was now extending its control over the whole non-Buddhist population through the teachings of the philosophers.

Prior to the Rational philosophers, Indianization was more or less confined to those who actually fled the world; but after the secularization of Buddhist ideals by the Rational philosophers, the rules of life of an other-wordly religion were seriously applied to secular life. The age of Rational Philosophy presents to us, not the human and common-sense atmosphere which one finds in the writings of Confucius and Mencius, but an austere and icy atmosphere of the medieval monastery. Indianization was universalized by being unconsciously appropriated by the philosophers and extended by them to regions never before seriously invaded by the Indian religion.

Let us first examine into this philosophy itself to see how much it differs from the medieval religions. This new philosophy has been formulated as consisting of two main paths: "To increase learning, one must extend one's knowledge to the utmost. For moral cultivation, one must resort to the attitude of reverence." (Cheng Yi, 1033–1107.) The first road is intellectualistic; the second, moral and religious. "Reverence" to the ancients simply meant taking things seriously. But to the Rational philosophers it has acquired a religious connotation. To be reverent now means to act in accordance with the Divine Reason. Now, what is this Divine Reason? The answer is: It is the opposite of human desire. And how can one know the Divine Reason? The answer is: The best way is through sitting in quiet meditation.

Even the other path, that of extension of knowledge, was not free from the religious impress of medieval China. To Chu Hsi (1130–1200), extension of knowledge was to be achieved through piecemeal investigation into the reasons of things—which was a strictly intellectualistic and scientific attitude. But, in the absence of the necessary equipment and of the experimental procedure, this was a difficult path, too difficult for the soft-minded majority of the philosophers, who soon gave it up in despair and declared that true knowledge must come from within one's own mind and the approach must be through quiet meditation and introspection.

But it is in the peculiar exaltation of Divine Reason and suppression of human desire that we see the best evidence of the deepening of the influence of the Indian religion through its secularization. When asked whether a widow of a very destitute family might not be justified in remarrying, Cheng Yi, the philosopher, calmly replied: "No. Death by starvation is a very small matter. But violation of chastity is a very important thing." This famous saying was included by Chu Hsi in his "Text Book for Elementary Schools" which became the standard reading in all China for seven hundred years.

Now, this prohibition of the remarriage of widows had never been the practice of pre-Buddhist China. In the first century A.D., when the sister of the first Emperor of the Eastern Han Dynasty became a widow, the Emperor offered to make a new match for her and asked her to choose her ideal husband from among his ministers. She expressed her preference for Minister Sung Hung. The Emperor invited the Minister for a chat and approached the subject by saying: "What do you think of the proverb that 'Wealth changes friends and high position changes wives'?" The Minister answered: "That proverb is not so good as the other one which says, 'A friend of poverty should never be forgotten, and the wife who has shared the coarsest meals with me should never be deserted.'" Upon hearing this, the Emperor shouted across the screen which shielded his widowed sister, "Sister, I am afraid my match-making has failed." What a human tale this was! And how different it was from the austere puritanism of the philosopher of a thousand years afterwards who cold-bloodedly laid down the principle that death by starvation was preferable to the remarriage of a destitute widow!

What had happened during these thousand years to bring about such a tremendous difference in the Chinese outlook on life? Nothing but the gradual deepening and intensifying of the Indianization of Chinese thought, life, and institutions. Buddhism was fading away, but its cultural content had been domesticated and appropriated by the secular thinkers and had penetrated into Chinese life and institutions far beyond the confines of the monasteries and nunneries of Buddhism. . . .

Chapter Seventeen

Revolutionary Western civilization

TECHNOLOGY IN THE MEDIEVAL WEST $\qquad$ **36**

In most of medieval Eurasia, traditional civilizations flourished that carried on many of the basic institutions and practises of the preceding classical civilizations. China, for example, did undergo "change within tradition," as noted in Reading 34, yet its civilization remained fundamentally Confucian within an agrarian-based bureaucratic imperial structure. In the sprawling Moslem world, the indigenous Greco-Roman, Iranian, Semitic, and Egyptian traditions were not obliterated, but rather fused into the syncretic civilization of Islam. Likewise the East Roman Empire continued without interruption for a full millennium as the Byzantine Empire, so that its inhabitants referred to themselves until modern times as Romaioi, *or Romans. The one exception to this general pattern was in the West where the classical civilization was disrupted to an unprecedented degree by prolonged invasions and turmoil. Only in the West, therefore, was the ground sufficiently cleared for the emergence of a revolutionary new civilization. One of the features of this new civilization was a unique labor-saving power technology and productive new agricultural methods, as described in the following account by a noted American medievalist.**

The Dark Ages doubtless deserve their name: political disintegration, economic depression, the debasement of religion and the collapse of literature surely made the barbarian kingdoms in some ways unimaginably dismal. Yet because many aspects of civilization were in decay we should not assume too quickly that everything was back-sliding. Even an apparent coarsening may indicate merely a shift of interest: in modern painting we recognize that Van Gogh's technical methods were not those

---

* Reprinted from L. White, Jr., "Technology and Invention in the Middle Ages," *Speculum*, XV (April 1940), 149–56.

167

of David; so, when we contrast a Hellenistic carved gem with a Merovingian enamel, our judgment should be cautious. Few will dispute that the Irish illumination and the Scandinavian jewelry of the seventh and eighth centuries stand among the supreme arts of all time; yet they are far from classical canons of taste, being rooted in an ancient, and quite separate, tradition of Northern art. So in the history of technology we must be discriminating. Changing tastes and conditions may lead to the degeneration of one technique while the technology of the age as a whole is advancing. The technology of torture, for example, which achieved such hair-raising perfection during the Renaissance, is now happily in eclipse: viewed historically, our modern American 'third degree' is barbaric only in its simplicity.

Indeed, a dark age may stimulate rather than hinder technology. Economic catastrophe in the United States during the past decade has done nothing to halt invention—quite the contrary; and it is a commonplace that war encourages technological advance. Confusion and depression, which bring havoc in so many areas of life, may have just the opposite effect on technics. And the chances of this are particularly good in a period of general migration, when peoples of diverse backgrounds and inheritances are mixing.

There is, in fact, no proof that any important skills of the Graeco-Roman world were lost during the Dark Ages even in the unenlightened West, much less in the flourishing Byzantine and Saracenic Orient. To be sure, the diminished wealth and power of the Germanic kings made engineering on the old Roman scale infrequent; yet the full technology of antiquity was available when required: the 276-ton monolith which crowns the tomb of Theodoric the Ostrogoth was brought to Ravenna from Istria; while more than two centuries later Charlemagne transported not only sizable columns but even a great equestrian statue of Zeno from Ravenna across the Alps to Aachen. Incidentally, we should do well to remember that the northern peoples from remote times were capable of managing great weights, as witness Stonehenge and the dolmens.

In military machines especially we might expect the barbarians to fall below the ancient standard; but at the siege of Paris in 886 we discover the Vikings, who presumably would be as untouched by Roman methods as any western people, using elaborate and powerful artillery; while the city itself was defended with catapults. However, the Dark Ages do not seem to have improved on ancient artillery: the Roman level was not surpassed until the twelfth century when the trebuchet, worked by counterweights, began to drive the less efficient tension and torsion engines from the field.

If the political and economic decay of the Dark Ages affected any technique adversely, it was that of road-building. Yet even here the case is not clear. For northern climates at least, the technical excellence of Roman roads has been exaggerated. They had massive foundations, which sometimes survive to the present day; but the surface, consisting of slabs of masonry cemented together, made no provision for contraction or expansion. Heat made the slabs buckle and crack; water seeped under them and froze, separating them from the foundation. Repairs were difficult and expensive: no modern road-builder would consider imitating Roman methods. It was the Middle Ages which developed the cheaper and more efficient method of laying cubes of stone in a loose bed of earth or sand which permitted expansion and made repairs easy: a type of paving still common.

Indeed, the technical skill of classical times was not simply maintained: it was considerably improved. Our view of history has been too top-lofty. We have been dazzled by aspects of civilization which are in every age the property of an élite, and in which the common man, with rare exceptions, has had little part. The so-called 'higher' realms of culture might decay, government might fall into anarchy, and trade be reduced to a trickle, but through it all, in the face of turmoil and hard times, the peasant and artisan carried on, and even improved their lot. In technology, at least, the Dark Ages mark a steady and uninterrupted advance over the Roman Empire. Evidence is accumulating to show that a serf in the turbulent and insecure tenth century enjoyed a standard of living considerably higher than that of a proletarian in the reign of Augustus.

The basic occupation was, of course, agriculture. We have passed through at least two agricultural revolutions: that which began with 'Turnip' Townshend and Jethro Tull in the early eighteenth century, and another, equally important, in the Dark Ages.

The problem of the development and diffusion of the northern wheeled plow, equipped with colter, horizontal share and moldboard, is too thorny to be discussed here. Experts seem generally agreed: (1) that the new plow greatly increased production by making possible the tillage of rich, heavy, badly-drained river-bottom soils; (2) that it saved labor by making cross-plowing superfluous, and thus produced the typical northern strip-system of land division, as distinct from the older block-system dictated by the cross-plowing necessary with the lighter Mediterranean plow; (3) most important of all, that the heavy plow needed such power that peasants pooled their oxen and plowed together, thus laying the basis for the medieval coöperative agricultural community, the manor. But whatever may be the date and origin of the fully developed heavy plow, its effects were supplemented and greatly enhanced in the later eighth century by the invention of the three-field system, an improved rotation of crops and fallow which greatly increased the efficiency of agricultural labor. For example, by switching 600 acres from the two-field to the three-field system, a community of peasants could plant 100 acres more in crops each year with 100 acres less of plowing. Since fallow land was plowed twice to keep down the weeds, the old plan required three acres of plowing for every acre in crops, whereas the new plan required only two acres of plowing for every productive acre.

In a society overwhelmingly agrarian, the result of such an innovation could be nothing less than revolutionary. Pirenne is only the most recent of many historians to speculate as to why the reign of Charlemagne witnessed the shift of the center of European civilization, the change of the focus of history, from the Mediterranean to the plains of Northern Europe. The findings of agricultural history, it seems, have never been applied to this central problem in the study of the growth of the northern races. Since the spring sowing, which was the chief novelty of the three-field system, was unprofitable in the south because of the scarcity of summer rains, the three-field system did not spread below the Alps and the Loire. For obvious reasons of climate the agricultural revolution of the eighth century was confined to Northern Europe. It would appear, therefore, that it was this more efficient and productive use of land and labor which gave to the northern plains an economic advantage over the Mediterranean shores, and which, from Charlemagne's time onward, enabled the Northern Europeans in short order to surpass both in prosperity and in culture the peoples of an older inheritance.

In ways less immediately significant the Dark Ages likewise made ingenuous improvements. One of the most important of these was a contribution to practical mechanics. There are two basic forms of motion: reciprocal and rotary. The normal device for connecting these—a device without which our machine civilization is inconceivable—is the crank. The crank is an invention second in importance only to the wheel itself; yet the crank was unknown to the Greeks and the Romans. It appears, even in rudimentary form, only after the Invasions: first, perhaps, in hand-querns, then on rotary grindstones. The later Middle Ages developed its application to all sorts of machinery.

Clearly there are nuggets in this stream for anyone to find. Perhaps the most successful amateur student of early medieval technology was the Commandant Lefebvre des Noëttes, who after his retirement from active service in the French cavalry, devoted himself to his hobby, the history of horses. He died in 1936 having made discoveries which must greatly modify our judgment of the Carolingian period. From his investigations Lefebvre des Noëttes concluded that the use of animal power in antiquity was unbelievably inefficient. The ancients did not use nailed shoes on their animals, and broken hooves often rendered beasts useless. Besides, they knew only the yoke-system of harness. While this was adequate for oxen, it was most unsatisfactory for the more rapid horse. The yoke rested on the withers of a team. From each end of the yoke ran two flexible straps: one a girth behind the forelegs, the other circling the horse's neck. As soon as the horse began to pull, the flexible front strap pressed on his windpipe, and the harder he pulled the closer he came to strangulation. Moreover the ancient harness was mechanically defective: the yoke was too high to permit the horse to exert his full force in pulling by flinging his body-weight into the task. Finally, the ancients were unable to harness one animal in front of another. Thus all great weights had to be drawn by gangs of slaves; since animal power was not technically available in sufficient quantities.

According to Lefebvre des Noëttes this condition remained unchanged until the later ninth or early tenth century when, almost simultaneously, three major inventions appear: the modern horse-collar, the tandem harness, and the horse-shoe. The modern harness, consisting of a rigid horse-collar resting on the shoulders of the beast, permitted him to breathe freely. This was connected to the load by lateral traces which enabled the horse to throw his whole body into pulling. It has been shown experimentally that this new apparatus so greatly increased the effective animal power that a team which can pull only about one thousand pounds with the antique yoke can pull three or four times that weight when equipped with the new harness. Equally important was the extension of the traces so that tandem harnessing was possible, thus providing an indefinite amount of animal power for the transport of great weights. Finally, the introduction of the nailed horseshoe improved traction and greatly increased the endurance of the newly available animal power. Taken together these three inventions suddenly gave Europe a new supply of non-human power, at no increase of expense or labor. They did for the eleventh and twelfth centuries what the steam-engine did for the nineteenth. Lefebvre des Noëttes has therefore offered an unexpected and plausible solution for the most puzzling problem of the Middle Ages: the sudden upswing of European vitality after the year 1000.

However, Lefebvre des Noëttes failed to point out the relation between this access of energy and the contemporary agricultural revolution. He noted that the new harness made the horse available for agricultural labor: the first picture of a horse so engaged is found in the Bayeux Tapestry. But while the horse is a rapid and efficient power-engine, it burns an expensive fuel—grain—as compared with the slower, but cheaper, hay-burning ox. Under the two-field system the peasant's margin of production was insufficient to support a work-horse; under the three-field system the horse gradually displaced the ox as the normal plow and draft animal of the northern plains. By the later Middle Ages there is a clear correlation on the one hand between the horse and the three-field system and on the other between the ox and the two-field system. The contrast is essentially one between the standards of living and of labor-productivity of the northern and the southern peasantry: the ox saves food; the horse saves man-hours. The new agriculture, therefore, enabled the north to exploit the new power more effectively than the Mediterranean regions could, and thereby the northerners increased their prosperity still further.

Naturally Lefebvre des Noëttes made mistakes: only when his work receives the recognition it deserves will these be rectified. His use of the monuments is not impeccable; his almost exclusive concern with pictures led him to neglect the texts, particularly Pliny's assertion that at times Italian peasants (presumably in the Po valley) plowed with several yokes of oxen; and he overlooks the complex question of the eight-ox plow-team as a basis for land division in pre-Carolingian times. Moreover an etymologist has recently shown that the word for 'horse-collar' in the Teutonic and Slavic tongues (English: hames) is derived from Central-Asiatic sources, implying a diffusion of the modern harness westward from the nomadic steppe-culture. Doubtless criticism will eventually show that Lefebvre des Noëttes' three inventions developed rather more slowly than he thought. But that they grew and spread during the Dark Ages, and that they profoundly affected European society, seems already proved.

These discoveries regarding the utilization of animal power illustrate the novel results which may be expected from the study of medieval technology. No less profitable is Marc Blocks' brilliant and thoroughly documented investigation of the origin and spread of the water-driven mill. His conclusion that, while it was invented in the first century before Christ, it did not become common until after the collapse of the Empire, confirms Lefebvre des Noëttes' contention that the technological position of the Dark Ages has been misunderstood.

The development of the windmill has not been so carefully sought out. Windmills are found in tenth-century Persia, but rotating on a vertical rather than on a horizontal axis. The first authenticated windmill in Europe turns up in Normandy *ca* 1180. Twelve years later Jocelin of Brakelond mentions one near St. Edmundsbury and gives no indication that he considers it unusual. Within a generation this power-engine had become a typical part of the landscape on the plains of northwestern Europe. In such a region it was a great boon; for the fall of rivers was so gradual that expensive dams and mill-ponds often had to be constructed to run water-driven mills; likewise these mill-ponds must often have flooded good agricultural land which the windmill freed for production. The spread of the windmill into the more mountainous southern regions, which were better equipped with rapid streams, was slow. The first Italian reference to a windmill seems to be Dante's description (*ante* 1321) of Satan threshing his arms like 'un molin che il vento gira' (*Inferno*, XXXIV, 6). This southward and eastward diffusion, together with the horizontal axis of the western mill, probably indicates that the windmill was not an importation from Islam.

The cumulative effect of the newly available animal, water, and wind power upon the culture of Europe has not been carefully studied. But from the twelfth and even from the eleventh, century there was a rapid replacement of human by non-human energy wherever great quantities of power were needed or where the required motion was so simple and monotonous that a man could be replaced by a mechanism. The chief glory of the later Middle Ages was not its cathedrals or its epics or its scholasticism: it was the building for the first time in history of a complex civilization which rested not on the backs of sweating slaves or coolies but primarily on non-human power.

The study of mediaeval technology is therefore far more than an aspect of economic history: it reveals a chapter in the conquest of freedom. More than that, it is a part of the history of religion. The humanitarian technology which our modern world has inherited from the Middle Ages was not rooted in economic necessity; for this 'necessity' is inherent in every society, yet has found inventive expression only in the Occident, nurtured in the activist or voluntarist tradition of Western theology. It is ideas which make necessity conscious. The labor-saving power-machines of the later Middle Ages were produced by the implicit theological assumption of the infinite worth of even the most degraded human personality, by an instinctive repugnance towards subjecting any man to a monotonous drudgery which seems less than human in that it requires the exercise neither of intelligence nor of choice. It has often been remarked that the Latin Middle Ages first discovered the dignity and spiritual value of labor—that to labor is to pray. But the Middle Ages went further: they gradually and very slowly began to explore the practical implications of an essentially Christian paradox: that just as the Heavenly Jerusalem contains no temple, so the goal of labor is to end labor.

37   ROLE OF WESTERN CITIES

Technological progress meant increased productivity, a growing surplus for trading purposes, and hence the rise of commerce and of commercial centers. This, of course, was not peculiar to the West. Commerce and cities were to be found also in the other Eurasian civilizations, and often on a larger scale, as noted by Marco Polo in thirteenth-century China. Yet commerce and cities and merchants played a revolutionary role in transforming Western society, in contrast to China where they were encapsulated and immobilized within the bureaucratic imperial structure. The nature and historical significance of this fundamental difference is analyzed in the following selection.*

Every sedentary society has built cities, for even in a subsistence economy essential functions of exchange and of organization (both functions dealing with minds and ideas as much as with goods or with institutions) are most conveniently performed in a central location on behalf of a wider countryside. The industrial revolution has emphasized the economic advantages of concentration and centrality. But is it true to say that change, revolutionary change, has found an advantage in urbanization; in concentration and in numbers? The city has instigated or led most of the great changes in Western society, and has been the center of its violent and non-violent revolutions. In western Europe the city has been the base of an independent entrepreneur group which has successfully challenged and broken the authority of the traditional order. In China, while cities with the same universal economic functions arose, they tended until recently to have the opposite effect on the pattern of change. China has consistently reasserted itself as a single political unit, but it is otherwise the appropriate qualitative and quantitative counterpart of Europe, and provides a reasonable basis for comparison. China and Europe have

---

* Reprinted from R. Murphey, "The City as a Center of Change: Western Europe and China," pp. 349–62. Reproduced by permission from the *Annals* of the Association of American Geographers, Volume 44, 1954.

been the two great poles of world civilization, and an examination of the different roles which their cities played may help to elucidate other differences between them.

.   .   .

The cities of western Europe have been, at least since the high middle ages, centers of intellectual ferment; of economic change; and thus, in time, of opposition to the central authority. They became rebels in nearly every aspect of their institutional life. It was trade (and to a somewhat lesser extent specialized manufacturing) which made them strong enough to maintain their challenge to the established order. Their spirit of ferment was the spirit of a new group, urban merchant-manufacturers, which could operate from a base large and rich enough to establish increasingly its own rules. This setting tended to ensure that the universities, which grew up in cities originally for convenience and centrality, would frequently nourish skepticism, heresy, and freedom of enquiry. Even where they did not overtly do so, the concentration of literacy and learning in the cities was a stimulus to dissent.

Most of the cities which rose out of the cultural and social chaos following the destruction of Roman unity and preceding the development of a new national unity grew in answer to new conditions, for northwest Europe was ideally situated for trade. Most of them were in their origins much older than this, and had begun as administrative, military, or ecclesiastical centers. But a score of major rivers, navigable and free from floods, silting, or ice throughout the year in this mild maritime climate, led across the great European plain to the open sea; the peninsular, indented nature of the coast critically heightened mobility. The invitation which this presented to inter-European trade furthered the ascendancy of the commercial function. The shift of commerce and associated urbanism from the Mediterranean to northwest Europe seems to have begun before the Age of the Discoveries, notably in the Hansa towns and in Flanders. This may be in part a reflection of the mobility inherent in the lands around the Baltic and North Seas, once they had learned from the Mediterranean the lessons of commerce and absorbed the civilizing influences of this earlier developed area. In any case, these northern cities came to be dominated by trader-manufacturers. Trade was a heady diet, and enabled urban merchants to command cities which had originally been administrative creations. While the cities did not alone destroy feudalism, they owed much of their prosperity and independence to its decline: freer trade, wider exchange, and failing power of the landed mobility. And their very growth as rival power bases accelerated the collapse of the old feudal order.

As the growth of national unity progressed, under the institutional and emotional leadership of monarchy, an alliance of convenience between king and city arose which met the crown's demands for funds and the city's demand for representation. Urban merchants had the money to support the king in his foreign wars and in his struggle with the divisive domestic ambitions of the nobility and the church. In return the city received an increasing voice in the affairs of state, through representation in parliaments, and indirectly through the making of policy in which the throne was obliged to follow. But while this alliance of revenue in exchange for concessions was one of mutual interest, its ultimate result was the strengthening of the urban commercial sector until it overthrew or emasculated the monarchy, and with it the traditional order as a whole. Having helped the king to power over the nobility, the city achieved a *modus vivendi* with him which left it in control of the affairs vital to it. As a current reminder of the development of urban independence, "the city" of London retains its originally hard-won privilege of excluding the reigning monarch, who is also excluded from the House of Commons, in part the city's creation and in part its weapon. To a certain extent the king, and even the nobility, were willing to go along with the process of economic change instigated by the city since they profited from it as the principal source of wealth in which they were often investors as well as tax collectors. But the new values which the city emphasized, and their institutional expression, were in direct conflict with the traditional society based on land; the city repeatedly bred overt revolutionary movements designed to establish its new order as the national way of life.

As centers of trade, the cities were free of the land and of its social and political limitations embodied in the institutions of post-Roman society. They developed their own law which was in differing degrees independent of the traditional, rural law. Their institutions were self-made, and they were not beholden to the traditional system which they challenged. The companies and corporations which the merchants organized went far beyond the scope of guilds in their successful attempt to order most of the social and economic fabric (instead of being limited to a trade-union function, as the guilds of China predominantly were). Traditional guilds were overlaid with new merchant organizations, or were clothed with new functions and powers, although some of the older guilds remained as conservative or retarding influences. The economic institutions which arose concurrently were also new-made sources of strength: banking, letters of credit, private property, interest, speculation and investment, representing needs and ideas which were almost wholly foreign to the traditional society of the countryside, and which were the accompaniment of an ever-widening trade. For the invitation to commercial expansion overseas was as strong in Europe's geography as the earlier invitation to trade among the lands surrounding the Baltic, Mediterranean, and North Seas. A leading agent of this process was necessarily the city, where trade flowed through break-in-bulk points such as the mouths of the Rhine or the English ports facing the Channel. Merchant corporations for overseas trade became the strongest and most progressive, or revolutionary, of the city's agents. Interestingly, the original charter of the British East India Company stated that "gentlemen" (by which was meant the landed gentry) "shall be excluded" from membership.

The city was the natural center of political change as it had been of economic change. The growth of modern Europe may be regarded as the steady progress of a new class of urban traders and manufacturers toward a position of control in a society and economy which their own enterprise had largely created. It was they who had realized the potential of Europe's location for world trade, and they who had developed and applied the technological and economic tools which made Europe the center of the world. The destruction of the old pattern was implicit in this process, and also implicit was the revolutionary expression, by the cities, of their claim to political power. . . .

. . . The first great modern revolution, in seventeenth century England, was the work of a city-country alliance, but London was mainly Puritan, and the outcome might be regarded as the victory of urban merchants and their country confreres over the traditional authoritarian alliance of cavalier and peasant based on the land. Two centuries later Manchester and Birmingham had joined London in the final stages of the contest between urban "radicalism" and country "conservatism," epitomized in the struggle over the Corn Laws, the Reform Bills, free trade, and the Manchester School. By this time cotton textiles had well supplanted woolen textiles as the chief manufacturing industry; since it came relatively late it was not greatly hampered by guild restrictions, as wool had been; it established itself in Manchester, which as a then unincorporated town lacked formalized controls. It may irritate many readers as a loose generalization, but still seems worth stating for argument, that representative government and the industrial revolution, perhaps modern Europe's two most significant products, were created by the city. The Low Countries provide as good an illustration of this as does England.

In France the picture was less clear since urban merchant-manufacturers were less prominent in the national economy. Even so, it was Paris which created and carried the revolution. Paris used peasant distress and rebellion, but was never dethroned by it. One may say that Paris later destroyed Charles X and Louis Philippe. . . . In eastern Europe it is difficult to draw distinctions between city and country, or to find an independent urban-based group living on trade and challenging the existing order. Nevertheless even in twentieth century Russia, while the Soviet revolution was in part carried by peasant groups, leadership remained in the urban intellectual group which had instigated the change.

.   .   .

In China, while the peasant and the countryside were in some respects like the West, the city's role was fundamentally different. Chinese cities were administrative centers. With few exceptions this function dominated their lives whatever their other bases in trade or manufacturing. Their remarkably consistent, uniform plan, square or rectangular walls surrounding a great cross with gates at each of the four arms, suggests their common administrative creation and their continued expression of this function.

.   .   .

. . . In China, most cities or towns of 5,000 or more had well-defined commercial or manufacturing districts, and special areas for each important enterprise: banking, metal goods, food markets, textiles, woodwork, and so on. This pattern remains in most contemporary Chinese cities. But the cities were not decisive centers of change in a commercialized economy. They served as imperial or provincial capitals, seats for garrison troops, and residences for governors, viceroys, and the ubiquitous cloud of officials and quasi-officials with their "service-providers." Their business was administration, and exploitation, of the countryside. Marco Polo, in describing the magnificence of Peking, accounts for it as follows:

> . . . and this happens because everyone from everywhere brings there for the lord who lives there and for his court and for the city which is so great and for the ladies and barons and knights of whom there are so many and for the great abundance of the multitude of the people of the armies of the lord, which stay round about as well for the court as for the city, and of other people who come there by reason of the court which the great lord holds there, and for one and for another . . . and because the city is in too good a position and in the middle of many provinces.

Here is a clear picture of a city based on administration from a central location, where trade flows in largely in response to the existing structure of officials, troops, court, hangers-on, and the host of people necessary to support them, from secretaries and servants to bakers and dancers. Six hundred years later at the end of the nineteenth century European travellers in China reported the same phenomenon, on a smaller regional scale: large cities whose sole function appeared to be administration, or important trading cities at key locations which were nevertheless dominated by officials and the magistrates' *yamen* (office). . . .

The trade process appears to have lacked the dynamic quality by means of which Europe's cities rose to power. Pre-eighteenth century China had a trade as great as or greater than pre-eighteenth century Europe, but Europe's subsequent commercial expansion left China far behind. Why this happened, and why China never produced the revolutionary economic and political changes which remade Europe into an arbiter for the rest of the world is a vital question. An analysis of the city's role may help to suggest some relevant factors. Why was the Chinese city not a European-style center of change?

China is geographically isolated by a formidable assemblage of barriers. To landward lies the greatest mountain mass in the world, with its extensions from the Pamir Knot, reinforced on the south by rainforests and spectacular river gorges, on the north by the barren wastes of Siberia, and on the west and northwest by a vast sweep of desert. Seaward a coast deficient in harbours faces a huge and until recently commercially underdeveloped ocean, by European standards. Chinese trade with Japan was at several periods considerable, and with southeast Asia even larger, but it did not approach eighteenth or nineteenth century European levels. It tended to be characterized by luxury goods, strategic goods (such as copper for coinage), or specialties such as Chinese porcelain. With these exceptions, especially the highly developed and diversified trade between southeast coastal China, and southeast Asia, China did not greatly extend herself commercially, and was for the most part content to send specialized goods, like silk, to the rest of the world through middlemen intermediaries: the Arabs by sea and the Turkish peoples of central Asia by land. Significantly, the largest concerted Chinese attempt in foreign trade was an imperial government project (the famous Ming expeditions of the fifteenth century), which lasted only some 30 years and apparently found no solid base in the Chinese economy or in its merchant group.

Internally, trade moved largely on the great river systems, running fortunately east and west, but there was no such close interconnection between these river basins as in Europe, by sea or across plains. Physically China is built on a grander scale, but the landscape presents no such invitation to exchange as has sparked the development of Europe. Europe is multi-peninsular, each peninsula tending toward economic distinctiveness and political independence, but joined by cheap sea and river routes. This plethora of complementary areas and their transport links magnified the basis and the means of exchange. Although its early trade development was not larger than China's, by the middle of the eighteenth century commercial expansion overseas had joined and accelerated commercialization at home, and Europe stood in a class by itself. The cities of western Europe were both the creators and inheritors of this development. But in China the cities remained centers of the unitary national state and of the traditional order rather than its attackers, epitomes of the status quo. As direct links in the official hierarchy, they were the props of the empire. The universities were urban, for convenience as in Europe, but they stimulated no dissent. Their accepted function was to train scholars who could staff the imperial civil service, and they fed their graduates into the imperial examination system. This, and the better economic and social position of scholars generally in China than in Europe, encouraged the universities and the literati to support the status quo; European intellectuals may have taken a vow of poverty, but they remained a dissident or discontented group.

Physically, China lacked Europe's outstanding advantages for trade, and on the other hand presented a base for highly productive agriculture, through irrigation. Wittvogel's revealing work on the organic connection between the need for mass organized water control and the growth of a monolithic bureaucratic state in China lends insight into the origins and pattern of the institutional structure. With China's environmental advantages, water control made agriculture the massive core of the economy, and at the same time left the bureaucracy in a position of ramified command. It was not possible for urban merchants to win independence from this system. They had less economic leverage than the rising European merchants because, with the preponderant position of agriculture, they never occupied proportionately as large a place in the economy.

The state of course did its part to prevent the development of a rival group, and by taxation, requisition, and monopoly ensured that the merchants would be kept relatively impotent. This was a job which European states and monarchs, though equally determined, failed to accomplish; their merchants were in a stronger position, and the state was weaker: it was merely *primus inter pares*. Land hunger in China, as a reflection of a population too large for the available arable land (increasingly serious during the past 200 years, but even in Han times worse than in most other parts of the world, including Europe), also acted to restrict commercial development, since it meant high land rents. Capital could almost always be invested with greater profit and safety in land, or in rural loans, than in productive or capital-generating enterprises outside the agrarian sphere.

Where extra-agricultural opportunities for investment did exist, the individual entrepreneur was at the mercy of the bureaucratic state. Many of the major trade goods were government monopolies. Elsewhere the essentially Western concepts of private property and due process of law, in a word, of the entrepreneur, were lacking in a society dominated by agriculture and officials. Extortion, forced levies, confiscation, and simple financial failure as the result of arbitrary government policies were the daily risk of the merchant. Some individuals did indeed become very rich, for example the famous *hong* merchants of Canton, but their wealth came necessarily through official connection: by possession of gentry status, by office holding or official favour, or by trading as part of a government monopoly (such as foreign trade under the Canton system and at most other periods was). Even so their gains were never secure. The greatest and richest of the *hong* merchants died in poverty, having lost official favour. While this also happened to many of the pre-eighteenth century European capitalists, it did not prevent the survival and growth of individual capitalist families or firms or of a moneyed group. The famous Ch'ing dynasty billionaire Ho Shen, said to have been worth the equivalent of nearly a billion and a half U. S. dollars, was not a merchant at all, but a favourite minister of the emperor Ch'ien Lung, which demonstrates the real source of wealth in traditional China. Yet he too died in poverty and disgrace (by suicide in place of a suspended death sentence in 1799) at the hands of Ch'ien Lung's successor.

In China merchant-capitalists did not use their money to establish their independence, as did the merchants of London or Antwerp, or to stimulate the growth of a new economic pattern. Unfortunately for the Chinese merchants, the imperial revenue was at most periods derived largely from the land tax and from the government trade monopolies. Agriculture was proportionately more productive than in Europe, and revenue from trade less necessary. Peking thus did not need the merchants as the king had needed them in Europe to finance the ascendancy of the national state, to pay for its wars with rival states, or to meet its normal bills. No concessions were necessary; the merchants could be squeezed dry, and were, with no harm to the state. The commanding position of the bureaucracy, and the fact of the bureaucratic state, are perhaps explainable by a similar process of default. Merchants were necessary or useful to perform essential (and, to the state, profitable) commercial functions; they were tolerated, but kept under strict control, and this was simpler and cheaper than for the state to manage all commercial dealings itself.

But the merchants were also identified with the state as well as being stifled by it. Their numbers were recruited largely from the gentry class, who had the capital and the official connections essential to commercial success. Gentry merchants worked willingly with gentry officials in the management of the state monopolies, including foreign trade. Outside the monopolies, the same partnership operated, as a matter of mutual interest. In addition, most gentry members, whether or not they were engaged in trade, also performed other semi-official functions, comparable in some degree to the British landed gentry. These "services" represented a considerable part of their income; they were not likely to attack the system which nourished them. In a more general sense, the tradition of revolt in this hierarchical society did not include the re-ordering of social or economic groups, but concentrated on the removal of bad government. Individual or group improvement was not to be won by destroying the fabric, but my making optimum use of one's position within it.

Finally, China had maintained since Han times and with few breaks a remarkable degree of unity and a central power which no single European state achieved until quite late in its modern development. In China even towns of the *chen* (market town) rank (population c. 3000–5000) were seats of garrison troops, whatever their prominence in trade. In Europe in the course of the crown's contest with the nobles, and of the international rivalries which also developed among the plethora of separate national states, urban merchants found an opportunity which contrasted sharply with the rooted monolithic nature of the Chinese state.

The cities of China were consequently microcosms of the empire, not deviants. . . .

. . . The city has been a center of change in western Europe, while it has been the reverse in traditional China, despite the broad similarity in urban economic functions in both areas. Urban character and urban roles may be useful indicators of the nature and dynamics of the diverse entities of society.

38   RELIGION AND THE EXPANSION OF EUROPE

The new civilization taking form in Western Europe was unique also because of the militancy of its Christian religion, which asserted itself as a universal faith. Thus, missionary effort has characterized the church from the days of the apostles to modern times. When the technological and economic development described in the preceding readings led to an increase in the number and power of the Western Europeans, they promptly took the offensive against the enemies of the faith. One manifestation was the series of crusades to reconquer the Holy Land. These were precipitated by the famous speech delivered by Pope Urban II in 1095, one of several versions of which is given below. Another manifestation of the aggressive dynamism of Western Christendom was the drive of the German crusading orders into northeast Europe at the expense of the heathen Slavs. The following account by the monk Helmold (born ca. 1125) describes the manner in which Count Adolph of Holstein conquered the pagan lands, built fortresses, and planted colonies. This crusading tradition of the Western Europeans is of particular significance for world history because their later expansion overseas was in part a continuation of their earlier crusades, as suggested by the red crosses on the sails of Columbus' ships.

Pope Urban II *

. . . Since, oh sons of God, you have promised the Lord more earnestly than heretofore to maintain peace in your midst and faithfully to sustain the laws of the church, there remains for you, newly fortified by the correction of the Lord, to show the strength of your integrity in a certain other duty, which is not less your concern than the Lord's. For you must carry succor to your brethren dwelling in the East, and needing your aid, which they have so often demanded. For the Turks, a Persian people, have attacked them, as many of you know, and have advanced into the territory of Romania as far as that part of the Mediterranean which is called the Arm of St. George; and occupying more and more the lands of those Christians, have already seven times conquered them in battle, have killed and captured many, have destroyed the churches and devastated the kingdom of God. If you permit them to remain for a time unmolested, they will extend their sway more widely over many faithful servants of the Lord.

Wherefore, I pray and exhort, nay not I, but the Lord prays and exhorts you, as heralds of Christ, by frequent exhortation, to urge men of all ranks, knights and foot-soldiers, rich and poor, to hasten to exterminate this vile race from the lands of our brethren, and to bear timely aid to the worshippers of Christ. I speak to those who are present, I proclaim it to the absent, but Christ commands. Moreover, the sins of those who set out thither, if they lose their lives on the journey, by land or sea, or in fighting against the heathen, shall be remitted in that hour; this I grant to all who go, through the power of God vested in me.

Oh, what a disgrace if a race so despised, degenerate, and slave of the demons, should thus conquer a people fortified with faith in omnipotent God and resplendent with the name of Christ! Oh, how many reproaches will be heaped upon you by the Lord Himself if you do not aid those who like yourselves are counted of the Christian faith! Let those who have formerly been accustomed to contend wickedly in private warfare against the faithful, fight against the infidel and bring to a victorious end the war which ought long since to have been begun. Let those who have hitherto been robbers now become soldiers of Christ. Let those who have formerly contended against their brothers and relatives now fight as they ought against the barbarians. Let those who have formerly been mercenaries at low wages, now gain eternal rewards. Let those who have been striving to the detriment both of body and soul, now labor for a two-fold reward. What shall I add? On this side will be the sorrowful and poor, on the other the joyful and the rich; here the enemies of the Lord, there His friends. Let not those who are going delay their journey, but having arranged their affairs and collected the money necessary for their expenses, when the winter ends and the spring comes, let them with alacrity start on their journey under the guidance of the Lord.

* Reprinted from D. C. Munro, trans., *Translations and Reprints from the Original Sources of European History,* Series I, Vol. I, No. 2, rev. ed. (Philadelphia: University of Pennsylvania Press, 1902), pp. 2–3.

. . . In those days a variety of idolatrous cults and superstitious aberrations grew strong again throughout all Slavia.

Besides the groves and the household gods in which the country and towns abound, the first and foremost deities are Prove, the god of the land of Oldenburg; Siva, the goddess of the Polabi; Redigast, the god of the land of the Abodrites. To these gods are dedicated priests, sacrificial libations, and a variety of religious rites. When the priest declares, according to the decision of the lot, what solemnities are to be celebrated in honor of the gods, the men, women, and children come together and offer to their deities sacrifices of oxen and sheep, often, also, of Christians with whose blood they say their gods are delighted. . . .

. . . Besides, there has been inborn in the Slavic race a cruelty that knows no satiety, a restlessness that harries the countries lying about them by land and sea. It is hard to tell how many kinds of death they have inflicted on the followers of Christ. They have even torn out the bowels of some and wound them about a stake and have affixed others to crosses in ridicule of the sign of our redemption. . . .

Since the illustrious Caesar Lothar and his very worthy consort Richenza were most devoutly solicitous for the divine service, the priest of Christ, Vicelin, went to him while he was tarrying at Bardowiek and suggested to him that he should provide for the Slavic race some means of salvation in keeping with the power that had been bestowed on him by Heaven. Vicelin, moreover, made known to him that there is in the province of Wagria a mountain adapted for the erection of a royal castle for the protection of the land. . . . The emperor attended to the prudent counsel of the priest and sent competent men to determine the fitness of the mountain. On being assured by the reports of the messengers, he crossed the river and went into the land of the Slavs to the place appointed. He ordered all the Nordalbingian people to come together for the building of the castle. In obedience to the emperor, the princes of the Slavs also were present, taking part in the business, but with great sadness, for they discerned that the structure was being erected for their oppression. One prince of the Slavs, therefore, said to another:

> Do you see this strong and commanding structure? Behold, I foretell to you that this castle will prove a yoke for the whole land; for going out hence, they will first break upon Plön and afterward Oldenburg and Lübeck; then they will cross the River Trave and subdue Ratzeburg and all the land of the Polabi. And the country of the Abodrites will not escape their hands.

The castle was finished and secured with a numerous soldiery and called Segeberg. In charge of the castle the Caesar put Hermann, one of his henchmen. Not content with these arrangements, he ordered the establishmnt of a new church at the foot of the mountain and set aside, for the maintenance of divine worship and for the support of the brethren to be congregated there, six or more villages, confirming the grant by charters according to usage. Furthermore, he committed the stewardship of that basilica to the lord Vicelin, that he might be the more disposed to push forward the erection of dwellings and bring together clerics. He also made a like arrangement about the church of Lübeck, warning Pribislav, if

* Reprinted from Helmold, *The Chronicle of the Slavs,* trans. F. J. Tschan (New York: Columbia University Press, 1935), pp. 158–61, 168–69.

he would hold his favor, to be with all diligence mindful of the priest there, or whomsoever acted in his stead. His purpose was, as he himself publicly declared, to subject the whole Slavic race to the divine religion and to make a great bishop of the minister of Christ.

.   .   .

. . . As the land was without inhabitants, he sent messengers into all parts, namely, to Flanders and Holland, to Utrecht, Westphalia, and Frisia, proclaiming that whosoever were in straits for lack of fields should come with their families and receive a very good land,—a spacious land, rich in crops, abounding in fish and flesh and exceeding good pasturage. To the Holzatians and Sturmarians he said:

> Have you not subjugated the land of the Slavs and bought it with the blood of your brothers and fathers? Why, then, are you the last to enter into posses-sion of it? Be the first to go over into a delectable land and inhabit it and partake of its delights, for the best of it is due you who have wrested it from the hands of the enemy.

An innumerable multitude of different peoples rose up at this call and they came with their families and their goods into the land of Wagria to Count Adolph that they might possess the country which he had promised them. First of all the Hol-zatians received abodes in the safest places to the west in the region of Segeberg along the River Trave, also the Bornhöved open and everything extending from the River Schwale as far as Agrimesov and the Plöner-See. The Westphalians settled in the region of Dargune, the Hollanders around Eutin, and the Frisians around Süssel. The country about Plön, however, was still uninhabited. Oldenburg and Lütjenburg and the rest of the lands bordering on the sea he gave to the Slavs to live in, and they became tributary to him.

NON-EURASIAN
WORLD TO 1500

Chapter Eighteen

Africa

THE NATURE OF AFRICAN HISTORY $\quad$ 39

Archaeologists and research scholars are now uncovering the errors in widely-held assumptions that the African Negro is incapable of progress and that his history is one of stagnation and savagery before the advent of the white man in the fifteenth century. Findings clearly demonstrate that the African Negro had reached a high level of political and cultural development before the appearance of the Europeans, and even of the Arabs before them. In fact, the more advanced indigenous Negro cultures were in many respects comparable to those of Europe until the past few centuries when the Europeans bounded ahead with their scientific, technological, and economic revolutions. "Allowing for the difference between the Moslem and the Christian intellectual climates," writes an English scholar, "a citizen of 14th century Timbuktu would have found himself reasonably at home in 14th century Oxford. In the 16th century he still would have found many points in common between the two university cities. By the 19th century the gulf had grown very deep." * The important point here is that the gulf had grown deep not only between the Europeans and the Africans, but also between the Europeans and all the other people of the world. For the Europeans were the mavericks—the deviants—while the Africans, together with the rest of humanity, represented the norm in continuing along the traditional channels. In the following selection, this new approach to African history is expounded, and its implications are analyzed. †

. . . Just because various African peoples have known nothing of the industrial revolution in its later, urban, phases; have remembered orally and not literally;

---

* T. Hodgkin, "Islam in West Africa," *Africa South,* II (April-June, 1958), 98.
† Reprinted from Basil Davidson, "The Fact of African History: An Introduction," *Africa South,* II (January–March, 1958), 44–49 by permission of Curtis Brown, Ltd.

185

fought without chariots; and refrained from sailing across the seas that lapped their shores, there is no ground for saying that they are not inherently as capable as anyone else. . . . But the fact remains that these African peculiarities are often used to buttress the general European belief that all was savage chaos before the Europeans came, and to suggest that the reason for this savage chaos lay not in a certain set of objective circumstances, but in African incapacity to emerge from them. "Their thinking," a South African publicist wrote lately, "was not concerned with objective validity and was pre-occupied by the mystic powers of persons and things. This centuries-long stagnation cannot be attributed to their isolation from the main stream of civilization"; the implication, of course, being that it must be attributed to an African inability to evolve and progress.

So it is a matter of quite unusual interest and importance that the last few years should have raised the whole subject of African history—pre-European history—to a new and academically respectable status. Many scholars are producing many new facts about it. Far from being unconcerned with "objective validity" or hypnotized by the "mystic powers of persons and things," Africans, it would appear, were engaged in a great many "civilized activities," of one kind and another, for many centuries before European settlement, or even before European discovery. At a time when European mariners had yet to reach the Indian Ocean, or even the Bight of Benin, the kings and counsellors of Central Africa were eating from Chinese porcelain, and when Mr. Strijdom's forebears drove their ox carts into the old Transvaal, they encountered men and women who were not at the beginning of a long period of civilized development, but, through times of painful dissolution, were perilously near the end of one. In this tide of new information, and of reassessment of old information, the study of humanity in Tropical and Southern Africa has really begun: even if it is still in its infancy, its findings are a long way beyond the point where any but the obsessively bigoted will care to ignore them. . . .

Africans south of the Sahara were in fact evolving and progressing towards destinations recognizably the same as Europeans (or Asians)—at a time long before Europeans first came across them.

A gap in social and technical development may always have existed, no doubt, between those who lived close to the cradles of ancient civilization and those who lived far from them. There is no more sense in sentimentalizing about the misery and barbarism of much of the African past than there is in pretending that European history does not tell the same kind of story. The important point is the width of the gap at any one time. If, as people are fond of saying, the gap was *always* immensely wide, then something might well be missing from the African make-up. But if the gap, though wide to-day, had once been relatively narrow, then history will draw quite other conclusions. Now the main consequence of a good deal of recent research into Southern and Central and East African history—over the past thousand years or so—is precisely to suggest that the gap was once a relatively narrow one, and not always to Europe's advantage either.

Writing in 1067, the mediaevel Arab scholar El Bekri described the court of the king of Ghana such as the Arabs knew it from their penetration and eventual conquest of that country. "When he gives audience to his people," wrote El Bekri, "to listen to their complaints and set them to rights, he sits in a pavillion around which stand his horses caparisoned in cloth of gold; behind him stand ten pages holding shields and gold-mounted swords; on his right hand are the sons of the princes of his empire, splendidly clad and with gold plaited into their hair. . . ." A barbaric king and a barbaric kingdom? But were they more barbaric or less civilized than the king and kingdom that William of Normandy had conquered the year before? Were they not, conceivably, less barbaric and more civilized?

When the Portuguese adventurers first rounded the Cape of Good Hope they were certainly as much concerned with "the mystic powers of persons and things" as the most superstitious native of any part of Africa. Their ignorance of the Eastern world was no smaller than East Africa's ignorance of Europe and was quite possibly greater. They were astonished to find the harbours of the East Coast—of what are now Mozambique and Tanganyika and Kenya—the goal and shelter of long-range ocean shipping; and when they sailed for India it was with pilots whose navigational equipment was, in some ways, better than their own. The superiority of the society of Lisbon over the society of Kilwa and Mombasa was not, in those days, by any means obvious. The one certain superiority of those Europeans was in cruelty and aggressiveness.

Yet three hundred and fifty years later, in the hey-day of Victorian rediscovery, the gap had grown immensely wide—so wide, indeed, that it became easy for Europeans to wonder (as many still do) whether Negroes did not after all belong to an inferior species. There is little mystery about the reasons for this widening of the gap: while Europe, freeing itself from mediaeval limits, plunged into commercialism and industrialism and won its great technical superiority over the rest of the world, much of Africa lay fettered in the oversea slave trade. The one went forward, the other went back, and the gap, narrow enough in 1500, grew into a gulf.

Historians and archaeologists are now building new bridges of explanation across that gulf. . . .

What appears to emerge from the present state of knowledge is nothing like a state of savage chaos, but, on the contrary, the long-enduring growth and development of an African Metal Age—beginning over two thousand years ago and producing, for example, the Monomotapa culture of what were Rhodesia and Mozambique in the 15th century—that went through many phases and vicissitudes, but showed remarkable flexibility of invention and resource. It is certain that there developed down the East Coast, sometime after the discovery of the trading use of the monsoon winds in the first century A.D., a flourishing and stable African trade with Arabia, Persia, India, Indonesia and China. It is probable that while the Arabs became the intermediaries and chief carriers in this trade, they were no more the originators of it in Africa than they were in India or China. They established trading posts as far south as Sofala, at points where African kingdoms already existed or subsequently grew. Behind these coastal kingdoms, in the hinterland of Africa, there was meanwhile developing a network of Metal Age polities whose growth was increasingly stimulated by the coastal and oversea demand for gold, ivory and iron. These African goods were exchanged by Africans —through Arab and Indian intermediaries—for Indian textiles, Indonesian beads, and Chinese porcelain. Only when the Portuguese arrived to monopolize this trade, and rapidly destroy it, did these coastal and inland civilizations enter their decline. The hand of the European guided, as it came about, not away from chaos, but towards it.

And what continually surprises, in reviewing the evidence so far available, is the *coherence* of these African cultures. Already it is possible to glimpse connexions, whether by cultural drift, migration, or trade, between the early kingdoms of Uganda, for example, and those of Rhodesia; between Zimbabwe and the coastal cities as far north as Gedi, sixty miles beyond Mombasa; between the wooden cities of West Africa and the stone cities of Monomotapa. All these links between

African societies of the past, whether immediate or remote, have the same kind of coherence and suggestions of common origin, native origin, as those which gave the Indo-European tribes their historical affinity as they spread across the northern world. We are clearly in the presence of a large segment of the human story: of another contribution to the proof of that unity-in-diversity which scientists otherwise ascribed to all branches of *homo sapiens*.

40   MALI EMPIRE IN THE SUDAN

Westerners commonly refer to their appearance in Africa as the "Opening of Africa." But the fact is that Africa had been "opened" to the outside world many centuries earlier. This was particularly true after the conversion of large regions of Africa to Islam, which drew those regions into the far-flung Moslem world. Thus in 1324 Mansa Kankan Musa, the famous ruler of the great Sudanese Mali empire, left his capital on the Upper Nile for a pilgrimage to Mecca. His camel trains, servants, and wives, and the vast supplies of gold that he distributed lavishly, all created such an impression that the event was long remembered, as indicated in the following account by Allah al Omari, a Cairo resident. Omari also provides illuminating information concerning Mali, making clear the high level of development of that empire.*

TRAVELING THROUGH CAIRO.   During my first journey to Cairo and sojourn there I heard talk of the arrival of the Sultan Musa [*Mansa* Musa, emperor of Mali] and I found the Cairenes very glad to talk of the large expenditures of those people. I questioned the Emir Abu'l 'Abbas Ahmed ben Abi'l Haki, el Mehmendar, who spoke of the sultan's noble appearance, dignity and trustworthiness. "When I went out to greet him in the name of the glorious Sultan el Malik en Nasir [of Egypt]," he told me, "he gave me the warmest of welcomes and treated me with the most careful politeness. But he would talk to me only through an interpreter [that is, his spokesman or linguist] although he could speak perfect Arabic. He carried his imperial treasure in many pieces of gold, worked or otherwise.

"I suggested that he should go up to the palace and meet the Sultan [of Egypt]. But he refused, saying 'I came for the pilgrimage, and for nothing else, and I do not wish to mix up my pilgrimage with anything else.' He argued about this. However, I well understood that the meeting was repugnant to him because he was loath to kiss the ground [before the Sultan] or to kiss his hand. I went on insisting and he went on making excuses. But imperial protocol obliged me to present him, and I did not leave him until he had agreed. When he came into the Sultan's presence we asked him to kiss the ground. But he refused and continued to refuse, saying: 'However can this be?' Then a wise man of his suite whispered several words to him that I could not understand. 'Very well,' he thereupon declared, 'I will prostrate myself before Allah who created me and brought me into the world.' Having done so he moved toward the Sultan. The

* Reprinted from *The African Past*, ed. Basil Davidson, pp. 75–79, by permission of Atlantic-Little, Brown and Co. Copyright © 1964 by Basil Davidson.

latter rose for a moment to welcome him and asked him to sit beside him: then they had a long conversation. After Sultan Musa had left the palace the Sultan of Cairo sent him gifts of clothing for himself, his courtiers and all those who were with him; saddled and bridled horses for himself and his chief officers. . . .

"When the time of pilgrimage arrived, [the Sultan of Egypt] sent him a large quantity of drachmas, baggage camels and choice riding camels with saddles and harness. [The Sultan of Egypt] caused abundant quantities of foodstuffs to be bought for his suite and his followers, established posting-stations for the feeding of the animals, and gave to the emirs of the pilgrimage a written order to look after and respect [the Emperor of Mali]. When the latter returned it was I who went to greet him and settle him into his quarters. . . .

"This man, el Mehmendar also told me, spread upon Cairo the flood of his generosity: there was no person, officer of the [Cairo] court or holder of any office of the [Cairo] sultanate who did not receive a sum in gold from him. The people of Cairo earned incalculable sums from him, whether by buying and selling or by gifts. So much gold was current in Cairo that it ruined the value of money." . . .

Let me add [continues Omari] that gold in Egypt had enjoyed a high rate of exchange up to the moment of their arrival. The gold *mitqal* that year had not fallen below twenty-five drachmas. But from that day [of their arrival] onward, its value dwindled; the exchange was ruined, and even now it has not recovered. The *mitqal* scarcely touches twenty-two drachmas. That is how it has been for twelve years from that time, because of the great amounts of gold they brought to Egypt and spent there.

THE EMPIRE OF MALI. The king of this country is known to the people of Egypt as the king of Tekrur [roughly, inland Senegal]; but he himself becomes indignant when he is called thus, since Tekrur is only one of the countries of his empire. The title he prefers is that of lord of Mali, the largest of his states; it is the name by which he is most known. He is the most important of the Muslim Negro kings; his land is the largest, his army the most numerous; he is the king who is the most powerful, the richest, the most fortunate, the most feared by his enemies and the most able to do good to those around him.

His kingdom consists of the lands of Gana, Zagun, Tirakka, Tekrur, Bambugu, Zarquatabana, Darmura, Zaga, Kabora, Baraguri, Gao-gao. The inhabitants of Gao-gao are of the tribes of Yarten. The region of Mali is that where the residence of the king is situated [in] the town of Niane, and all the other regions are dependent on it; it has the official name of Mali because it is the capital of this kingdom which also includes towns, villages and centers of population to the number of fourteen.

The honorable and truthful Sheikh Abu Sa'id Otman ed Dukkali, who has lived in the town of Niane for thirty-five years and traveled throughout the kingdom, has told me that this is square in shape, being four months [of travel] in length and at least as much in breadth. . . .

The sultan of this country has sway over the land of the "desert of native gold," whence they bring him gold every year. The inhabitants of that land are savage pagans whom the sultan would subject to him if he wished. But the sovereigns of this kingdom have learned by experience that whenever one of them has conquered one of these gold towns, established Islam there and sounded the call to prayer, the harvest of gold dwindles and falls to nothing, meanwhile it grows and expands in neighboring pagan countries. When experience had confirmed them in this observation, they left the gold country in the hands of its pagan in-habitants and contented themselves with assuring their obedience and paying tribute.

RECEPTION AT COURT.   The sultan of this kingdom presides in his palace on a great balcony called *bembe* where he has a great seat of ebony that is like a throne fit for a large and tall person: on either side it is flanked by elephant tusks turned towards each other. His arms stand near him, being all of gold, saber, lance, quiver, bow and arrows. He wears wide trousers made of about twenty pieces [of stuff] of a kind which he alone may wear. Behind him there stand about a score of Turkish or other pages which are bought for him in Cairo: one of them, at his left, holds a silk umbrella surmounted by a dome and a bird of gold: the bird has the figure of a falcon. His officers are seated in a circle about him, in two rows, one to the right and one to the left; beyond them sit the chief commanders of his cavalry. In front of him there is a person who never leaves him and who is his executioner; also another who serves as intermediary [that is, official spokesman] between the sovereign and his subjects, and who is named the herald. In front of them again, there are drummers. Others dance before their sovereign, who enjoys this, and make him laugh. Two banners are spread behind him. Before him they keep two saddled and bridled horses in case he should wish to ride.

THE IMPORTANCE OF HORSES.   Arab horses are brought for sale to the kings of this country, who spend considerable sums in this way. Their army numbers one hundred thousand men of whom there are about ten thousand horse-mounted cavalry: the others are infantry having neither horses nor any other mounts. They have camels in this country but do not know the art of riding them with a saddle. . . .

The officers of this king, his soldiers and his guard receive gifts of land and presents. Some among the greatest of them receive as much as fifty thousand *mitqals* of gold a year, besides which the king provides them with horses and clothing. He is much concerned with giving them fine garments and making his cities into capitals.

ROYAL BUREAUCRACY.   It is one of their customs that whenever someone charged with a certain task of important affair reports to the king, the latter ques-tions him on everything that has happened from the time of his departure to the time of his return, and in great detail. Legal cases and appeals also go up to the sovereign who examines them himself. Generally he writes nothing; but gives his orders, most of the time, orally. He has *qadis,* secretaries, offices.

41   PYGMIES OF THE CONGO

Very different from the advanced culture of the Mali Empire is the Paleolithic culture of the Pygmies of the Ituri forest in the Congo. These are a people who are exclusively food gatherers, who do not know how to make fire, and who have no rulers, courts, *armies, or bureaucrats as in the case of Mali. Their retardation may be explained in part by the difficult rain-forest environment. But at least equally important is their isolation from the centers of civilization in Eurasia. Whereas the culture of Mali had been much stimulated by contact with the Islamic world, the Pygmies by contrast were completely isolated except for their relations with their Negro neighbors who provided them with plantains and tools in return for the honey and meat that the Pygmies collected in the forests. With Patrick Putnam, who lived with the Pygmies for nearly two decades, we catch a glimpse of their way of life.**

The Ituri forest is rolling country, so densely covered with trees that the relief of the landscape is invisible except from the air. It is a primary rain forest; that is, in most of the region it rains every day or every other day, averaging about one half of the days, from four to six in the afternoon—some 180 days a year. . . .

This forest is inhabited by two kinds of people. Negroes and pygmies, who maintain an almost symbiotic relationship, based on trade. A Negro village may own approximately 100 square miles of forest territory. In this territory are the Negro village and the pygmy village. The former is permanent, in a clearing; the latter is temporary, under the forest trees. In maintaining their relationship, it is the pygmies' job to take in honey and meat, while the Negroes' obligation is to give them plantains. In addition, the pygmies may bring in a certain amount of wild baselli fruit in season, or roofing leaves, or rattan and fibers for net making; in return they may acquire ax blades, knives, and arrowheads from the Negroes.

There is no strict process of barter involved, and no accounting kept, other than through general observation. If the pygmies are stingy, their Negroes will hold back their bananas. If the Negroes are stingy, the pygmies will leave the territory and go to live with other pygmies serving other Negro hosts.

This relationship is interfamilial, between a pygmy family and a Negro family. It is a matter of close personal relations, inherited, on both sides, from father to son. These alliances may change from time to time, but when they do there are usually hard feelings; if a man's pygmy leaves him to serve another host it is a kind of divorce. In the old days, a frequent cause of inter-village warfare among the Negroes was the luring away of each other's pygmies.

Before the Belgians stopped inter-village and intertribal warfare, the most important single duty of the pygmy was to act as scout and intelligence agent in the forest. As soon as he became aware of a raiding party crossing the boundary of his host's territory he would hotfoot it to the village to give warning. This eternal vigilance on the part of the pygmy was probably of more value to his hosts than the meat that he brought in. Now that the need of this has ceased he is fulfilling only half of his contract; the Negro, who still provides plantains and manufactured objects, is still fulfilling all of his. Still both are satisfied. . . .

BASIC TOOLS. The keynote to the simple and specialized pygmy technology is the fact that they do not have to make any of their basic tools, but instead obtain effective iron cutting tools from their Negro hosts. This eliminates much work and the need for much skills in toolmaking, and provides them with more efficient

* Reprinted from "The Pygmies of the Ituri Forest," in *A Reader in General Anthropology*, ed. Carleton S. Coon, pp. 322–34. Copyright 1948 by Holt, Rinehart & Winston, Inc. Reprinted by permission of Holt, Rinehart & Winston, Inc.

instruments than they could possibly make for themselves at a food-gathering level of technology.

When a pygmy needs an ax he will beg one from his Negro host. Perhaps the Negro will give him a whole ax, haft and all. The blade is a triangular piece of iron, made locally by Negro smiths, and set in a solid wooden handle, adzed out of a larger piece of wood. The handle has a hole which has been burned through it from side to side with a hot iron. Through this hole goes the narrow end of the ax. This is essentially a Neolithic type of hafting.

Perhaps the Negro will give him only the ax head, without a haft. In this case the pygmy will cut down a thin sapling, or a tree branch, just the right thickness, and use it bark and all. He splits this with his knife, at one end. Then he wraps the split and the blade which he has thrust through it with twine or rattan. The pygmy will use the Negro-hafted ax on the ground, but if he is climbing a tree and needs an ax while up there, he will take along one of his own hafting by preference, because it is lighter. . . .

FIRE. The pygmies do not know how to make fire, nor do many of the Negroes with whom they are associated. Throughout all this countryside people keep fires going, and when one fire dies out the people will borrow it from each other. While on the march the pygmies carry glowing embers with them; they can keep a brand lighted for ten miles during a rainstorm. They do this by wrapping the burning ends in green leaves, and swinging it up and down; every two or three minutes they uncover it a bit and blow on it. At night these brands serve as torches. The Negroes have special wood which they use for torches but the pygmies do not. Their firewood is always fallen wood, and therefore always somewhat rotten and punky. . . .

Hunting is the principal occupation of the pygmies; it is their principal reason for being able to maintain their relationship with their Negro hosts. Although between themselves the pygmies have little division of labor, in another sense they are all specialists in hunting, and the division of labor is between them and the Negroes. In this sense the pygmies form an ethnic caste, a genetically and occupationally segregated segment of a larger economic entity.

This does not mean that the Negro does no hunting. However, the pygmy spends all of his time hunting, the Negro only a portion of his. The pygmy depends largely on his ability to move noiselessly and swiftly about the forest, and to climb trees. The Negro depends on his greater patience and mechanical ingenuity, for he hunts largely by means of elaborate traps, deadfalls, pits, weighted spears dangled over elephant paths, and other deadly devices. The pygmy could never be induced to dig a pit; it is too much work, takes too long, and takes too much concentration and persistence. Nor do they ever use traps. . . .

BOW AND ARROW HUNTING. In bow and arrow hunting, the pygmy relies not on his endurance but on his ability to move through the forest silently; that is his greatest skill and greatest asset. He can track an antelope to a thicket where it has lain down to sleep, and shoot it from five yards' distance before it wakes up. He shoots machine-gun style; he will pump five arrows in rapid sequence in the antelope's direction, and probably but one will hit him. The pygmy can do just as well by leaping on the animal barehanded, and either strangle it or kill it with a knife, and he often does this.

In his quiver the pygmy usually carries two kinds of arrows, the first with iron tips, which he generally uses on the larger, antelope-size, animals, and wooden-tipped ones which are poisoned, and which he uses for monkeys. He rarely shoots a monkey with an iron-tipped arrow, through fear of losing it. Each man makes his own poison as well as his own darts. The plants from which the poison is made are well known, and there is neither ritual nor mystery attached to the process. The vital plant is a strophanthus; they will mix other plants with it, but they know which one does the trick.

The strophanthus poison is a heart stimulant. Its action is not immediate. The monkey runs along a bit, grows weaker, and urinates. The pygmies watch for this, for the moment of urinating is the fatal one. If the monkey is out on a limb where there are no other branches, he will fall off; if he is within reach of a lateral branch or one rising upward, he will clutch it, and the hunter will be obliged to climb the tree if he wants the monkey. . . .

GOVERNMENT. There are no chiefs, councils, or any other formal governing bodies in a pygmy camp. In making any decisions concerning the whole camp, two factors are involved. The first of these is respect for older people.

A pygmy will always, in addressing a man of an older age group in any formal situation, call him "senior"; he will listen respectfully to an older man and will always obey any reasonable orders he may give. If a younger man shows disrespect, the other members of the camp will gang up on him and berate him. This respect for age, and for the opinions of wise old men, is the basis of pygmy government.

Secondly, while the opinions of most of the old men are respected, every man in the camp is entitled to state his own views on any subject. Thus, during the evening talking time, the pygmies will discuss whether to move camp, where to move it, and why; or whether to go nut hunting, and where to hunt. The discussion has no leader and may go on for several evenings. Finally the men who are shouting out different opinions will come to an agreement and the decision will be acted upon.

In general it is the older and more experienced men who make the decision, but as some of the old men are considered eccentrics and freaks, little attention is paid to them. Rather, it is an oligarchy of the more respected among the old men, a body with no formal membership or specific composition. In their decisions the pungent remarks of the women also have a considerable influence.

Chapter Nineteen

Americas and Australia

42   AZTEC CIVILIZATION OF MEXICO

In Australia, all the aborigines were still at the food-gathering stage when the Europeans arrived in the late eighteenth century. This is a prime example of the effect of complete and prolonged geographic isolation, this island continent being the home of archaic plants such as the eucalyptus, archaic animals such as the monotremes and marsupials, and archaic humans—the aborigines. The paleolithic culture of these aborigines is described in Reading 3, "Culture of the Food Gatherers."

In the Americas, by contrast, there was great diversity in the levels of development attained by the various Indian peoples. Most advanced were the Aztecs and Mayas of Mesoamerica and the Incas of Peru. The nature of the Aztec civilization is described below by Bernal Díaz, a conquistador who accompanied Cortez in the conquest of Mexico. Bernal Díaz was a gifted and objective observer, describing with color and accuracy the religion and institutions of the Aztecs, their palaces, temples, and markets, and the character of their leader Montezuma.*

When it was announced to Cortes that Motecusuma himself was approaching, he alighted from his horse and advanced to meet him. Many compliments were now passed on both sides. Motecusuma bid Cortes welcome, who, through Marina, said, in return, he hoped his majesty was in good health. If I still remember rightly, Cortes, who had Marina next to him, wished to concede the place of honor to the monarch, who, however, would not accept of it, but conceded it to Cortes, who now brought forth a necklace of precious stones, of the most beautiful colours and shapes, strung upon gold wire, and perfumed with musk, which

* Reprinted from J. I. Lockhart, trans., *The Memoirs of the Conquistador Bernal Díaz de Castillo* (London: J. Hatchard, 1844), I, 220–23, 228–41.

he hung about the neck of Motecusuma. Our commander was then going to embrace him, but the grandees by whom he was surrounded held back his arms, as they considered it improper. Our general then desired Marina to tell the monarch how exceedingly he congratulated himself upon his good fortune of having seen such a powerful monarch face to face, and of the honour he had done us by coming out to meet us himself. To all this Motecusuma answered in very appropriate terms, and ordered his two nephews, the princes of Tetzuco and Cohohuacan, to conduct us to our quarters. He himself returned to the city, accompanied by his two other relatives, the princes of Cuitlahuac and Tlacupa, with the other grandees of his numerous suite. As they passed by, we perceived how all those who composed his majesty's retinue held their heads bent forward, no one daring to lift up his eyes in his presence; and altogether what deep veneration was paid him.

The road before us now became less crowded, and yet who would have been able to count the vast numbers of men, women, and children who filled the streets, crowded the balconies, and the canoes in the canals, merely to gaze upon us? . . .

We were quartered in a large building where there was room enough for us all, and which had been occupied by Axayacatl, father of Motecusuma, during his life-time. Here the latter had likewise a secret room full of treasures, and where the gold he had inherited from his father was hid, which he had never touched up to this moment. Near this building there were temples and Mexican idols, and this place had been purposely selected for us because we were termed teules, or were thought to be such, and that we might dwell among the latter as among our equals. The apartments and halls were very spacious, and those set apart for our general were furnished with carpets. There were separate beds for each of us, which could not have been better fitted up for a gentleman of the first rank. Every place was swept clean, and the walls had been newly plastered and decorated.

When we had arrived in the great court-yard adjoining this palace, Motecusuma came up to Cortes, and, taking him by the hand, conducted him himself into the apartments where he was to lodge, which had been beautifully decorated after the fashion of the country. He then hung about his neck a chaste necklace of gold, most curiously worked with figures all representing crabs. The Mexican grandees were greatly astonished at all these uncommon favours which their monarch bestowed upon our general.

Cortes returned the monarch many thanks for so much kindness, and the latter took leave of him with these words: "Malinche, you and your brothers must now do as if you were at home, and take some rest after the fatigues of the journey," then returned to his own palace, which was close at hand.

We allotted the apartments according to the several companies, placed our cannon in an advantageous position, and made such arrangements that our cavalry, as well as the infantry, might be ready at a moment's notice. We then sat down to a plentiful repast, which had been previously spread out for us, and made a sumptuous meal.

This our bold and memorable entry into the large city of Temixtitlan, Mexico took place on the 8th of November, 1519. Praise be to the Lord Jesus Christ for all this. . . .

The mighty Motecusuma may have been about this time in the fortieth year of his age. He was tall of stature, of slender make, and rather thin, but the symmetry of his body was beautiful. His complexion was not very brown, merely approaching to that of the inhabitants in general. The hair of his head was not very long, excepting where it hung thickly down over his ears, which were quite hidden by it. His black beard, though thin, looked handsome. His countenance was rather of an elongated form, but cheerful; and his fine eyes had the expression of love or severity, at the proper moments. He was particularly clean in his person, and took a bath every evening. Besides a number of concubines, who were all daughters of persons of rank and quality, he had two lawful wives of royal extraction, whom, however, he visited secretly without any one daring to observe it, save his most confidential servants. He was perfectly innocent of any unnatural crimes. The dress he had on one day was not worn again until four days had elapsed. In the halls adjoining his own private apartments there was always a guard of 2000 men of quality, in waiting: with whom, however, he never held any conversation unless to give them orders or to receive some intelligence from them. Whenever for this purpose they entered his apartment, they had first to take off their rich costumes and put on meaner garments, though these were always neat and clean; and were only allowed to enter into his presence barefooted, with eyes cast down. No person durst look at him full in the face, and during the three prostrations which they were obliged to make before they could approach him, they pronounced these words: "Lord! my Lord! sublime Lord!"

. . .

Above 300 kinds of dishes were served up for Motecusuma's dinner from his kitchen, underneath which were placed pans of porcelain filled with fire, to keep them warm. Three hundred dishes of various kinds were served up for him alone, and above 1000 for the persons in waiting. He sometimes, but very seldom, accompanied by the chief officers of his household, ordered the dinner himself, and desired that the best dishes and various kinds of birds should be called over to him. We were told that the flesh of young children as a very dainty bit, were also set before him sometimes by way of a relish. Whether there was any truth in this we could not possibly discover; on account of the great variety of dishes, consisting in fowls, turkeys, pheasants, partridges, quails, tame and wild geese, venison, musk swine, pigeons, hares, rabbits, and of numerous other birds and beasts; besides which there were various other kinds of provisions, indeed it would have been no easy task to call them all over by name.

. . .

I had almost forgotten to mention, that during dinner-time, two other young women of great beauty brought the monarch small cakes, as white as snow, made of eggs and other very nourishing ingredients, on plates covered with clean napkins; also a kind of long-shaped bread, likewise made of very substantial things, and some pachol, which is a kind of water-cake. They then presented him with three beautifully painted and gilt tubes, which were filled with liquid amber, and a herb called by the Indians tabaco. After the dinner had been cleared away and the singing and dancing done, one of these tubes was lighted, and the monarch took the smoke into his mouth, and after he had done this a short time, he fell asleep.

About this time a celebrated cazique, whom we called Tapia, was Motecusuma's chief steward: he kept an account of the whole of Motecusuma's revenue, in large books of paper which the Mexicans call *Amatl*. A whole house was filled with such large books of accounts.

Motecusuma had also two arsenals filled with arms of every description, of which many were ornamented with gold and precious stones. These arms consisted in shields of different sizes, sabres, and a species of broadsword, which is wielded with both hands, the edge furnished with flint stones, so extremely sharp that they cut much better than our Spanish swords: further, lances of greater length than ours, with spikes at their end, full one fathom in length, likewise furnished with several sharp flint stones. The pikes are so very sharp and hard that they will pierce the strongest shield, and cut like a razor; so that the Mexicans even shave themselves with these stones. Then there were excellent bows and arrows, pikes with single and double points, and the proper thongs to throw them with; slings with round stones purposely made for them; also a species of large shield, so ingeniously constructed that it could be rolled up when not wanted: they are only unrolled on the field of battle, and completely cover the whole body from the head to the feet. Further, we saw here a great variety of cuirasses made of quilted cotton, which were outwardly adorned with soft feathers of different colours, and looked like uniforms. . . .

I will now, however, turn to another subject, and rather acquaint my readers with the skilful arts practised among the Mexicans: among which I will first mention the sculptors, and the gold and silversmiths, who were clever in working and smelting gold, and would have astonished the most celebrated of our Spanish goldsmiths: the number of these was very great, and the most skilful lived at a place called Ezcapuzalco, about four miles from Mexico. After these came the very skilful masters in cutting and polishing precious stones, and the calchihuis, which resemble the emerald. Then follow the great masters in painting, and decorators in feathers, and the wonderful sculptors. Even at this day there are living in Mexico three Indian artists, named Marcos de Aguino, Juan de la Cruz, and El Crespello, who have severally reached to such great proficiency in the art of painting and sculpture, that they may be compared to an Apelles, or our contemporaries Michael Angelo and Berruguete. . . .

The powerful Motecusuma had also a number of dancers and clowns: some danced in stilts, tumbled, and performed a variety of other antics for the monarch's entertainment: a whole quarter of the city was inhabited by these performers, and their only occupation consisted in such like performances. Last, Motecusuma had in his service great numbers of stone-cutters, masons, and carpenters, who were solely employed in the royal palaces. Above all, I must not forget to mention here his gardens for the culture of flowers, trees, and vegetables, of which there were various kinds. In these gardens were also numerous baths, wells, basins, and ponds full of limpid water, which regularly ebbed and flowed. All this was enlivened by endless varieties of small birds, which sang among the trees. Also the plantations of medical plants and vegetables are well worthy of our notice: these were kept in proper order by a large body of gardeners. All the baths, wells, ponds, and buildings were substantially constructed of stonework, as also the theatres where the singers and dancers performed. There were upon the whole so many remarkable things for my observation in these gardens and throughout the whole town, that I can scarcely find words to express the astonishment I felt at the pomp and splendour of the Mexican monarch. . . .

We had already been four days in the city of Mexico, and neither our commander nor any of us had, during that time, left our quarters, excepting to visit the gardens and buildings adjoining the palace. Cortes now, therefore, determined to view the city, and visit the great market, and the chief temple of Huitzilopochtli. . . . The moment we arrived in this immense market, we were perfectly astonished at the vast numbers of people, the profusion of merchandise which was there exposed for sale, and at the good police and order that reigned throughout. The grandees who accompanied us drew our attention to the smallest circumstance, and gave us full explanation of all we saw. Every species of merchandise had a separate spot for its sale. We first of all visited those divisions of the market appropriated for the sale of gold and silver wares, of jewels, of cloths interwoven with feathers, and of other manufactured goods; besides slaves of both sexes. This slave market was upon as great a scale as the Portuguese market for negro slaves at Guinea. To prevent these from running away, they were fastened with halters about their neck, though some were allowed to walk at large. Next to these came the dealers in coarser wares—cotton, twisted, thread, and cacao. In short, every species of goods which New Spain produces were here to be found; and everything put me in mind of my native town Medino del Campo during fair time, where every merchandise has a separate street assigned for its sale. In one place were sold the stuffs manufactured of nequen; ropes, and sandals; in another place, the sweet maguey root, ready cooked, and various other things made from this plant. In another division of the market were exposed the skins of tigers, lions, jackals, otters, red deer, wild cats, and of other beasts of prey, some of which were tanned. In another place were sold beans and sage, with other herbs and vegetables. A particular market was assigned for the merchants in fowls, turkeys, ducks, rabbits, hares, deer, and dogs; also for fruit-sellers, pastry-cooks, and tripe-sellers. Not far from these were exposed all manner of earthenware, from the large earthen cauldron to the smallest pitchers. Then came the dealers in honey and honey-cakes, and other sweetmeats. Next to these, the timber-merchants, furniture-dealers, with their stores of tables, benches, cradles, and all sorts of wooden implements, all separately arranged. What can I further add? If I am to note everything down, I must also mention human excrements, which were exposed for sale in canoes lying in the canals near this square, and is used for the tanning of leather; for, according to the assurances of the Mexicans, it it impossible to tan well without it. I can easily imagine that many of my readers will laugh at this; however, what I have stated is a fact, and, as further proof of this, I must acquaint the reader that along every road accommodations were built of reeds, straw, or grass, by which those who made use of them were hidden from the view of the passers-by, so that great care was taken that none of the last mentioned treasures should be lost. But why should I so minutely detail every article exposed for sale in this great market? If I had to enumerate everything singly, I should not so easily get to the end. . . .

.   .   .

Before we mounted the steps of the great temple, Motecusuma, who was sacrificing on the top to his idols, sent six papas and two of his principal officers to conduct Cortes up the steps. There were 114 steps to the summit. . . . Indeed, this infernal temple, from its great height, commanded a view of the whole surrounding neighbourhood. From this place we could likewise see the three causeways which led into Mexico,—that from Iztapalapan, by which we had entered the city four days ago; that from Tlacupa, along which we took our flight eight months after, when we were beaten out of the city by the new monarch Cuitlahuatzin; the third was that of Tepeaquilla. We also observed the aqueduct which ran from Chapultepec, and provided the whole town with sweet water. We could also distinctly see the bridges across the openings, by which these causeways were intersected, and through which the waters of the lake ebbed and flowed. The lake itself was crowded with canoes, which were bringing provisions, manufactures, and other merchandize to the city. From here we also discovered that the only communication of the houses in this city, and of all the other towns built in the lake, was by means of drawbridges or canoes. In all these towns the beautiful white plastered temples rose above the smaller ones, like so many towers and castles in our Spanish towns, and this, it may be imagined, was a splendid sight.

.   .   .

On this occasion Cortes said to father Olmedo, who had accompanied us: "I have just been thinking that we should take this opportunity, and apply to Motecusuma for permission to build a church here."

To which father Olmedo replied, that it would, no doubt, be an excellent thing if the monarch would grant this; but that it would be acting overhasty to make a proposition of that nature to him now, whose consent would not easily be gained at any time.

Cortes then turned to Motecusuma, and said to him, by means of our interpretress, Doña Marina: "Your majesty is, indeed, a great monarch, and you merit to be still greater! It has been a real delight to us to view all your cities. I have now one favour to beg of you, that you would allow us to see your gods and teules."

To which Motecusuma answered, that he must first consult the chief papas, to whom he then addressed a few words. Upon this, we were led into a kind of small tower, with one room, in which we saw two basements resembling alters, decked with coverings of extreme beauty. On each of these basements stood a gigantic, fat-looking figure, of which the one on the right hand represented the god of war Huitzilopochtli. This idol had a very broad face, with distorted and furious-looking eyes, and was covered all over with jewels, gold, and pearls, which were stuck to it by means of a species of paste, which, in this country, is prepared from a certain root. Large serpents, likewise, covered with gold and precious stones, wound round the body of this monster, which held in one hand a bow, and in the other a bunch of arrows. Another small idol which stood by its side, representing its page, carried this monster's short spear, and its golden shield studded with precious stones. Around Huitzilopochtli's neck were figures representing human faces and hearts made of gold and silver, and decorated with blue stones. In front of him stood several perfuming pans with copal, the incense of the country; also the hearts of three Indians, who had that day been slaughtered, were now consuming before him as a burnt-offering. Every wall of this chapel and the whole floor had become almost black with human blood, and the stench was abominable.

.   .   .

Respecting the abominable human sacrifices of these people, the following was communicated to us: The breast of the unhappy victim destined to be sacrificed was ripped open with a knife made of sharp flint; the throbbing heart was then torn out, and immediately offered to the idol-god in whose honour the sacrifice had been instituted. After this, the head, arms, and legs were cut off and eaten at their banquets, with the exception of the head, which was saved, and hung to a beam appropriated for that purpose. No other part of the body was eaten, but the remainder was thrown to the beasts which were kept in those abominable dens, in which there were also vipers and other poisonous serpents, and, among the latter in particular, a species at the end of whose tail there was a kind of rattle. This last mentioned serpent, which is the most dangerous, was kept in a cabin of a diversified form, in which a quantity of feathers had been strewed: here it laid its eggs, and it was fed with the flesh of dogs and of human beings who had been sacrificed. We were positively told that, after we had been beaten out of the city of Mexico, and had lost 850 of our men, these horrible beasts were fed for many successive days with the bodies of our unfortunate countrymen. Indeed, when all the tigers and lions roared together, with the howlings of the jackals and foxes, and hissing of the serpents, it was quite fearful, and you could not suppose otherwise than that you were in hell.

.   .   .

Our commander here said smilingly, to Motecusuma: "I cannot imagine that such a powerful and wise monarch as you are, should not have yourself discovered by this time that these idols are not divinities, but evil spirits, called devils. In order that you may be convinced of this, and that your papas may satisfy themselves of this truth, allow me to erect a cross on the summit of this temple; and, in the chapel, where stand your Huitzilopochtli and Tetzcatlipuca, give us a small space that I may place there the image of the holy Virgin; then you will see what terror will seize these idols by which you have been so long deluded."

Motecusuma knew what the image of the Virgin Mary was, yet he was very much displeased with Cortes' offer, and replied, in presence of two papas, whose anger was not less conspicuous, "Malinche, could I have conjectured that you would have used such reviling language as you have just done, I would certainly not have shown you my gods. In our eyes these are good divinities: they preserve our lives, give us nourishment, water, and good harvests, healthy and growing weather, and victory whenever we pray to them for it. Therefore we offer up our prayers to them, and make them sacrifices. I earnestly beg of you not to say another word to insult the profound veneration in which we hold these gods."

As soon as Cortes heard these words and perceived the great excitement under which they were pronounced, he said nothing in return, but merely remarked to the monarch with a cheerful smile: "It is time for us both to depart hence." To which Motecusuma answered, that he would not detain him any longer, but he himself was now obliged to stay some time to atone to his gods by prayer and sacrifice for having committed *gratlatlacol,* by allowing us to ascend the great temple, and thereby occasioning the affronts which we had offered them.

43   INDIAN AGRICULTURISTS OF VIRGINIA

At the next level below that of the great civilizations of Mesoamerica and Peru were the farming cultures of the eastern United States and most of South America, except for the Argentine plains. Typical of this group were the Indians of Virginia, described below by Captain John Smith, founder of Jamestown in 1607.* In an entirely different category were the third general type of American Indians—the food gatherers of Canada, the western United States, and the Argentine plains. No description of their mode of life is provided here because it was essentially the same type of nomadic existence as that of the Australian aborigines and the Congo Pygmies depicted above in Readings 3 and 41.

* Reprinted from Captain John Smith, "The General History of Virginia, New England, and the Summer Isles," in J. Pinkerton, *Voyages and Travels* (London, 1812), XIII, 32–43.

OF THEIR PLANTED FRUITS IN VIRGINIA, AND HOW THEY USE THEM. . . . The greatest labour they take is in planting their corn, for the country naturally is overgrown with wood. To prepare the ground, they bruise the bark of the trees near the root, then do they scorch the roots with fire that they grow no more. The next year with a crooked piece of wood they beat up the weeds by the roots, and in that mould they plant their corn. Their manner is this. They make a hole in the earth with a stick, and into it they put four grains of wheat and two of beans. These holes they make four feet one from another. Their women and children do continually keep it weeding, and when it is grown middle high, they hill it about like a hop-yard.

In April they begin to plant, but their chief plantation is in May, and so they continue till the midst of June. What they plant in April they reap in August, for May in September, for June in October. Every stalk of their corn commonly beareth two ears, some three, seldom any four, many but one, and some none. Every ear ordinarily hath between two hundred and five hundred grains. The stalk being green hath a sweet juice in it, somewhat like a sugar cane, which is the cause that when they gather their corn green, they suck the stalks: for as we gather green peas, so do they their corn being green, which excelleth their old. They plant also peas they call assentamens, which are the same they call in Italy fagioli. Their beans are the same the Turks call garnanses; but these they much esteem for dainties.

Their corn they roast in the ear green, and bruising it in a mortar of wood with a polt, lap it in rolls in the leaves of their corn, and so boil it for a dainty. They also reserve that corn late planted that will not ripe, by roasting it in hot ashes, the heat thereof drying it. In winter they esteem it being boiled with beans for a rare dish, they call pausarowmena. . . .

In May also amongst their corn they plant pumpions, and a fruit like unto a muskmelon, but less and worse, which they call macocks. These increase exceedingly, and ripen in the beginning of July, and continue until September. They plant also maracocks, a wild fruit like a lemon, which also increase infinitely. They begin to ripen in September, and continue till the end of October. When all their fruits be gathered, little else they plant, and this is done by their women and children; neither doth this long suffice them, for near three parts of the year they only observe times and seasons, and live of what the country naturally affordeth from hand to mouth, &c. . . .

OF THE NATURAL INHABITANTS OF VIRGINIA. The land is not populous, for the men be few; their far greater number is of women and children. Within sixty miles of James Town, there are about some five thousand people, but of able men fit for their wars scarce fifteen hundred. To nourish so many together they have yet no means, because they make so small a benefit of their land, be it never so fertile. . . . Each household knoweth their own lands and gardens, and most live of their own labour. For their apparel, they are sometime covered with the skins of wild beasts, which in winter are dressed with the hair, but in summer without. . . .

Their buildings and habitations are for the most part by the rivers, or not far distant from some fresh spring; their houses are built like our arbours, of small young springs bowed and tied, and so close covered with mats, or the barks of trees very handsomely, that notwithstanding either wind, rain, or weather, they are as warm as stoves, but very smoky, yet at the top of the house there is a hole made for the smoke to go into right over the fire.

Against the fire they lie on little hurdles of reeds covered with a mat, borne from the ground a foot and more by a hurdle of wood, on these round about the house they lie heads and points one by the other against the fire, some covered with mats, some with skins, and some stark naked lie on the ground, from six to twenty in a house. Their houses are in the midst of their fields or gardens, which are small plots of ground, some twenty acres, some forty, some one hundred, some two hundred, some more, some less. In some places from two to fifty of those houses together, or but a little separated by groves of trees. Near their habitations is little small wood or old trees on the ground by reason of their burning of them for fire, so that a man may gallop a horse amongst these woods any way, but where the creeks or rivers shall hinder. . . .

Their fire they kindle presently by chafing a dry pointed stick in a hole of a little square piece of wood, that firing itself, will to fire moss, leaves, or any such like dry thing that will quickly burn. In March and April they live much upon their fishing wires, and feed on fish, turkies, and squirrels. In May and June they plant their fields, and live most of acorns, walnuts, and fish. But to amend their diet, some disperse themselves in small companies, and live upon fish, beasts, crabs, oysters, land-tortoises, strawberries, mulberries, and such like. In June, July, and August, they feed upon the roots of tocknough berries, fish, and green wheat. It is strange to see how their bodies alter with their diet, even as the deer and wild beasts they seem fat and lean, strong and weak. . . .

In their hunting and fishing they take extreme pains, yet in being their ordinary exercise from their infancy, they esteem it a pleasure, and are very proud to be expert therein; and by their continual ranging and travel, they know all the advantages and places most frequented with deer, beasts, fish, fowl, roots, and berries. At their huntings they leave their habitations, and reduce themselves into companies, as the Tartars do, and go to the most desert places with their families, where they spend their time in hunting and fowling up towards the mountains, by the heads of their rivers, where there is plenty of game; . . .

OF THEIR RELIGION.   There is yet in Virginia no place discovered to be so savage in which they have not a religion, deer, and bow and arrows. All things that are able to do them hurt beyond their prevention, they adore with their kind of divine worship; as the fire, water, lightning, thunder, our ordnance, pieces, horses, &c. But their chief god they worship is the devil. Him they call Okee, and serve him more of fear than love. They say they have conference with him, and fashion themselves as near to his shape as they can imagine. In their temples they have his image evil favouredly carved, and then painted and adorned with chains of copper, and beads, and covered with a skin in such manner as the deformities may well suit with such a god. By him is commonly the sepulchre of their kings. Their bodies are first bowelled, then dried upon hurdles till they be very dry, and so about the most of their joints and neck they hang bracelets, or chains of copper, pearl, and such like, as they use to wear, their inwards they stuff with copper beads, hatchets, and such trash. Then lap they them very carefully in white skins, and so roll them in mats for their winding sheets. And in the tomb which is an arch made of mats, they lay them orderly. What remaineth of this kind of wealth their kings have, they set at their feet in baskets. These temples and bodies are kept by their priests.

For their ordinary burials they dig a deep hole in the earth with sharp stakes, and the corpse being lapped in skins and mats with their jewels, they lay them upon sticks in the ground, and so cover them with earth. The burial ended, the women, being painted all their faces with black coal and oil, do sit twenty-four hours in the houses mourning and lamenting by turns, with such yelling and howling, as many express their great passions. . . .

Upon the top of certain red sandy hills in the woods, there are three great houses filled with images of their kings and devils, and tombs of their predecessors. Those houses are near sixty feet in length, built harbour-wise, after their building. This place they count so holy as that but the priests and kings dare come into them; nor the savages dare not go up the river in boats by it, but they solemnly cast some piece of copper, white beads, or pocones into the river, for fear their Okee should be offended and revenged of them.

.   .   .

OF THE MANNER OF THE VIRGINIANS' GOVERNMENT.   Although the country people be very barbarous, yet have they amongst them such government as that their magistrates for good commanding, and their people for due subjection and obeying, excel many places that would be counted very civil. The form of their commonwealth is a monarchical government, one as emperor, ruleth over many kings or governors. Their chief ruler is called Powhatan; but his proper name is Wahunsonacock. Some countries he hath which have been his ancestors, and came unto him by inheritance, as the country called Powhatan, Arrohateck, Appamatuck, Pamaunkee, Youghtanund, and Mattapanient. All the rest of his territories expressed in the map, they report, have been his several conquests. In all his ancient inheritances he hath houses built after their manner, like arbours, some thirty, some forty yards long, and at every house provision for his entertainment, according to the time. At Werowcomoco, on the north side of the river Pamaunkee, was his residence, when I was delivered him prisoner, some fourteen miles from James Town, where, for the most part, he was resident; but at last he took so little pleasure in our near neighbourhood, that he retired himself to Orapakes, in the desert betwixt Chickahamanta and Youghtanund. He is of personage a tall-well-proportion man, with a sour look, his head somewhat grey, his beard so thin that it seemeth none at all, his age near sixty, of a very able and hardy body to endure any labour; about his person ordinarily attendeth a guard of forty or fifty of the tallest men his country doth afford. . . .

A mile from Orapakes, in a thicket of wood, he hath a house, in which he keepeth his kind of treasure, as skins, copper, pearl, and beads, which he storeth up against the time of his death and burial. Here also is his store of red paint, for ointment, bows and arrows, targets and clubs. This house is fifty or sixty yards in length, frequented only by priests. At the four corners of this house stand four images as sentinels, one of a dragon, another a bear, the third like a leopard, and the fourth like a giant-like man, all made evil favouredly, according to their best workmanship.

.   .   .

He nor any of his people understand any letters, whereby to write or read, only the laws whereby he ruleth is custom. Yet, when he listeth, his will is a law, and must be obeyed; not only as a king, but as half a god, they esteem him.

WORLD OF
THE EMERGING WEST,
1500–1763

Chapter Twenty

West European expansion:
Iberian phase, 1500–1600

CHINESE AND PORTUGUESE EXPANSIONISM: **44**
A CONTRAST

Both China and Portugal undertook major overseas enterprises during the fifteenth century. But the motives and methods of their overseas activities were fundamentally different, and it is precisely this difference that has determined to a large degree the course of world history in modern times. The following analysis by a British authority makes clear the passiveness and tolerance of Chinese enterprise, in contrast to the aggressiveness and ruthless acquisitiveness of the Portuguese.*

. . . Indeed it is an extraordinary historical coincidence that Chinese long-distance navigation from the Far East reached its high-water mark just as the tide of Portuguese exploration from the Far West was beginning its spectacular flow. These two great currents almost met, but not quite, and in a single region, the coasts of the African continent. Their wind-angels, their inspirers, were two equally extraordinary men active in maritime affairs, on the one side a royal patron of navigators, on the other an imperial eunuch, ambassador and admiral. The contrast is inescapable, for this was the apogee of Chinese maritime enterprise. All the time that the Portuguese were exploring slowly southwards down the west coast of Africa, the Chinese were trading and visiting all up and down the east coast, with larger ships and larger fleets; but by the time that the Portuguese rounded the Cape and made their way to India, a fundamental change of national policy within China had withdrawn the Chinese fleets from the Indian Ocean so that the Portuguese found nothing but recent memories of their presence. Such was the confrontation that failed to occur; it is extremely interesting to speculate what would have

* Reprinted from J. Needham, *Clerks and Craftsmen in China and the West* (Cambridge, Eng.: Cambridge University Press, 1970), pp. 48–58.

happened if the smaller flotillas full of ambitious, even blood-thirsty, occidental adventurers had met the larger, peaceful fleets of great junks, the vessels of a philosophical people which had never had any part in the crusading strife between Christian and Moor.

It is not necessary to say much about Prince Henry the Navigator (+ 1394 to + 1460), a figure so well known to European historians. It is a commonplace to say that it was under his influence that the west coasts of Africa were first explored. By + 1444 Nuño Tristão had reached the mouth of the Senegal River, and two years later Alvaro Fernandes was on the Guinea coast. The year + 1453 was marked by two events, one colossal blow and one seemingly minor affair: Byzantium fell to the Turks, as if to show the Portuguese they were none too soon in their endeavours, while along the African coasts sailed Cid da Sousa, leading the first expedition to Guinea with the primary object of trade. Just after this Prince Henry died. By + 1486 Diogo Cão was on the Angola coast and then Bartolomeu Dias rounded the Cape of Good Hope in + 1488. Thus the way was open for the culminating cruise, that of Vasco da Gama, who left Lisbon in + 1497 and was off the mouth of the Zambezi early in the following year; then, entering the 'Chinese' area, touched at Malindi in April, just about fifty years after the Ming navy had ceased to frequent those shores. This was the place where he was fortunate enough to get the services of one of the leading Arab pilots of the age, Ahmad ibn Mājid, already mentioned, who brought the Portuguese admiral to Calicut in India the following month. The die was now cast, the Europeans were in the Indian Ocean for good or evil—and of the latter much.

The complementary figure to Prince Henry the Navigator on the Chinese side was Chêng Ho, known in his lifetime and afterwards as San Pao Thai Chien (The Admiral of the Triple Treasure), fl. + 1385 to + 1440. This celebrated eunuch, ambassador, admiral and explorer, 'the Vasco da Gama of China', as Debenham has called him, was born of a Yunnanese Muslim family, the son of a father who had made the pilgrimage to Mecca. Between + 1405 and + 1433 he accomplished seven diplomatic expeditions with large fleets of great junks, the biggest vessels afloat at that time, called 'Treasure-ships' . . . ; ranging from Borneo to the Zanguebar coast of East Africa and greatly stimulating Chinese interest in foreign countries. The three voyages between + 1405 and + 1411 went to Champa, Java, Palembang, Siam, Ceylon, Calicut, Cochin, etc. Between + 1413 and + 1415 elaborate visits were paid to Ormuz and the Persian Gulf, as also the Maldive Islands. Then three expeditions between + 1417 and + 1433 covered the whole of the east coast of Africa, including Mogadishiu, Mozambique, etc., as far south as the Straits of Madagascar. The motives of these great voyages, comparable with the Portuguese discoveries and closely parallel with them in time, were (a) to search for the dethroned Chien-Wên Emperor, who was suspected of having fled beyond the seas; (b) to demonstrate the power and glory of China as the leading political and cultural nation in Asia to the kings and sultans of Southern and Western Asian regions; (c) to induce them to acknowledge the nominal suzerainty of the Chinese Emperor and to send tribute missions to the Chinese court; (d) to encourage maritime trade; (e) to collect natural curiosities of all kinds for the imperial cabinets, including strange animals and hitherto unknown drugs; (f) to survey the sea routes and coastal defences; (g) to make reconnaissance of the strength and capacities of neighbouring countries, especially in the South Seas. We may discuss some of these aspects in turn. The half-century of the voyages gave rise to a large literature in Chinese which is only now being fully translated. They certainly led to a great increase in the Chinese knowledge of the rest of the world.

It must not be supposed that Chinese knowledge of Africa began at this time. Already in the middle of the + 9th century a book like the *Yu-Yang Tsa Tsu* contains an interesting account of Berbera on the south coast of the Gulf of Aden. The *Hsin Thang Shu,* written in + 1060, has an account of the country of Malindi on the coast of Kenya. Chao Ju-Kua, in the book already mentioned, has a whole section on Tshêng-Pa, the whole Zanguebar coast between the Juba River in Somaliland and the Mozambique Channel, while in the *Ling Wai Tai Ta* (Information on what is beyond the Passes), written in + 1178, Chou Chhü-Fei describes Madagascar at some length. By the + 14th century all these regions were well known. Wang Ta-Yuan, who travelled widely between + 1330 and + 1349, deals with most of them in his *Tao I Chih Lüeh* (Records of the Barbarian Islands), including such places not mentioned before as the Comoro Islands in the Mozambique Channel.

Among the things which the Chinese wanted from Africa were elephant tusks, rhinoceros horns, strings of pearls, aromatic substances, incense gums and the like. Al-Idrīsī, on the other hand, tells us that Aden (and hence the coast) received from China and India iron, damascened sabres, musk and porcelain, saddles, rich textiles, cotton goods, aloes, pepper and South Sea spices. Much of this hardware has actually survived until today. "I have never seen," wrote Wheeler in 1955, "so much broken china as in the past fortnight between Dar-es-Salaam and the Kilwa Islands, literally fragments of Chinese porcelain by the shovelful. I think it is fair to say that as far as the Middle Ages is concerned from the + 10th century onwards the buried history of Tanganyika is written in Chinese porcelain." Another kind of Chinese hardware on the East African coast is monetary, coins and coin hoards, the earliest dating from about + 620. Early Chinese knowledge of Africa is evinced by considerations of quite a different kind. Rockhill was impressed nearly a century ago by the fact that in Chinese maps of the + 16th century South Africa was shown in its right shape, i.e. with its tip pointing to the south. As he well knew, the European cartographical tradition before the Portuguese discoveries was to have it pointing to the east. In the magnificent Korean world map due to the cartographer Yi Hoe and the astronomer Kwŏn Kŭn in + 1402, before the first Portuguese caravel had sighted Cape Nun, Africa was made to point south, with a roughly correct triangular shape, and some thirty-five European and African place-names, including Alexandria, were marked upon it. It is interesting that a pagoda-like object represents the Pharos. This map is greatly superior to the Catalan atlas of + 1475, and even to the map of Fra Mauro (+ 1459), presumably because the knowledge of Europe and Africa which the Chinese scholars obtained from their Arab informants was much better and more abundant than all that Marco Polo and the other Western travellers could bring home about East Asia. In fact the Chinese were a good century ahead.

Fascinating comparisons can be made between the Chinese and the Portuguese activities. First let us take the purely maritime point of view and the nautical technology. It would seem on the whole that the Chinese achievement of the + 15th century involved no revolutionary technical break with the past while that of the Portuguese was more original. The Chinese had had their fore-and-aft lug-sails since the + 3rd century at least, and already in the time of Marco Polo and Chao Ju-Kua their ships were many-masted. If they used their mariner's compasses in the Mozambique Channel, they were only doing what their predecessors had done in the Straits of Thaiwan right back to the foundation of the Sung navy at the beginning of the + 12th century. Although their stern-post rudders were attached in weaker fashion to the hulls than those of the Westerners with pintle and gudgeon, they were highly efficient in more ways than one and descended from inventions of the + 1st century. The most obvious difference which would have struck everyone if the vessels of da Gama had met those of Chêng Ho lay in the much greater size of the Treasure-ships of the Grand Fleet, for many of these were of 1,500 tons, if not considerably more, while those of Vasco's were of 300 tons and some were much less; but while the Chinese craft were the culmination of a long evolutionary development, those of the Portuguese were relatively new in type. As is well known, the Portuguese had thrown overboard the square-sail rig and had adopted for their famous caravels a fore-and-aft one in the form of the lateen sail, taken from their enemies the Arabs. By + 1436 these ships carried triangular lateen sails on as many as three masts. Then as the century went on, the superior advantages of the square-sail for running before the wind reasserted themselves and ships began to be built which combined both rigs. The originality of the Portuguese, however, seems somewhat qualified when we remember that of the basic inventions they assembled, the mariner's compass and the stern-post rudder were transmissions from much earlier Chinese practice, the principle of multiple masts was characteristically Asian, and the lateen sail was taken directly from the Arabs.

There was another matter, however, in which the Portuguese showed seemingly more originality than the Chinese, namely, the understanding and use of the régime of winds and currents. It might be truer to say that the problems set for them by Nature were much more difficult and that they rose gallantly to the occasion. In the East Asian and South Asian waters monsoon sailing had been and remained traditional. But the more inhospitable Atlantic had never encouraged sailors by the same regularity, and though there had been a number of attempts to sail to the West, that ocean had never been systematically explored. Thus what is called the Sargasso Arc, and later the Brazilian or Cape San Roque Arc, were brilliant applications of what was fundamentally new meteorological and hydrographic knowledge.

In matters of war and conflict the contrast is truly extraordinary. The entire Chinese operations were those of a navy paying friendly visits to foreign ports, while on the other hand the Portuguese East of Suez engaged themselves almost at once in total war. Indeed, the term navy is hardly applicable to the Chinese fleets, which were more like the assemblies of merchant ships of a nationalised trading authority. As long as the Portuguese were working down the West African coast their aggressive activities (apart from slaving) were relatively restrained, and it was only after + 1500, when they were in a position to carry on terrorist warfare against the East African Arabs and then against the Indians and other Asians, that European naval power showed what it could do in earnest. The Portuguese in fact perpetuated the Crusader mentality and applied it in an attempted naval conquest of all South Asia.

The Chinese fleets were certainly armed, and with gunpowder weapons. As a famous Chinese text says: "They bestowed gifts upon the kings and rulers and those who refused submission they overawed by the show of armed might." But in fact if the historical records are carefully examined, it is found that the Chinese only got into trouble on three occasions. The first was in + 1406, when they had to repel a surprise attack by a tribal chief of Palembang, who was defeated and sent to Peking. Another small fracas happened in north-western Sumatra, seven or eight years afterwards. The most famous occasion was when in + 1410 the king of Ceylon, Alagakkonara (probably but not certainly Bhuvaneka Bahu V), enticed Chêng Ho's expeditionary guard into the interior and then demanded excessive presents of gold and silk, meanwhile sending troops to burn and sink his ships, which lay in all probability in Galle harbour. But Chêng Ho pushed on to the capital, most probably Kotte, took the king and his court by surprise and then fought his way back to the coast, routing the Sinhalese army on the journey. The prisoners were taken to Peking, where they were kindly treated and sent home again after an arrangement had been made to choose a relative of the king as his successor. Naval armed might thus meant something very different indeed in the Chinese and the Portuguese interpretations. The Chinese set up no forts or strongholds anywhere and founded no colonies of any kind.

As regards trade, we still know relatively little about it, but it was only natural that what was done both by the Chinese and the Portuguese was done under the aegis of their respective economic systems, and these were very different. It seems clear that from the start the Portuguese activities were concerned more with private enterprise than the Chinese. The search for an 'El Dorado' which would make one's personal fortune was after all an integral part of the Conquistador mentality. By contrast, the Chinese expeditions were the well-disciplined operations of an enormous feudal-bureaucratic state, the like of which was not known in Europe. Their impetus was primarily governmental, their trade, though large, was incidental, and the "irregular" merchant mariners whose trafficking was to be encouraged were mostly men of small means. The slave trade was a particular case. The Chinese and other Asian nations had been using negro slaves for many centuries but the fact that their slavery was basically domestic kept the practice within bounds. Not so the use of African agricultural plantation labourers in the New World, which brought it about that between + 1486 and + 1641 no less than 1,389,000 slaves were taken by the Portuguese from Angola alone. In general we have the paradox that while the feudal state of Portugal, hardly emerged from the Middle Ages, founded an empire of mercantile capital, on the other hand bureaucratic feudalism, though certainly not the economy of the future, gave to China in the + 15th century the lineaments of an empire without imperialism.

But it is important to notice a further difference. The Chinese probably never had to face an adverse balance of trade, for silk, lacquer, porcelain, etc., were everywhere esteemed and quite good in exchange for anything the Chinese ever wanted. On the other hand, the Portuguese were caught in an intractable economic necessity, for Western Europe did not at that time produce anything that Asians wanted to buy. When da Gama first visited Calicut in + 1498, a highly significant event occurred. When the Portuguese presented the goods which they had brought, consisting of striped cloths, scarlet hoods, hats, strings of coral, hand washbasins, sugar, oil and honey, the king laughed at them and advised the Admiral rather to offer gold. At the same time the Muslim merchants already on the spot affirmed to the Indians that the Portuguese were essentially pirates, possessed of nothing that the Indians could ever want, and prepared to take what the Indians had by force if they could not get it otherwise. There is something very familiar about this scene; in fact it symbolised perfectly the fundamental pattern of trade imbalance which had been characteristic of relations between Europe and East Asia from the beginning and was destined to continue so until the industrial age of the late 19th century. Broadly speaking, Europeans always wanted Asian products far more than the Easterners wanted Western ones, and the only means of paying for them was in precious metals. This process occurred at many places along the East-West trade routes, but finally, of course, in medieval times at the Levantine borders between Christendom and Islam. Even during the Roman Empire there was a great drain of gold and silver to the East. Nearly two thousand years later the opium traffic with the Manchu dynasty, and hence the Opium Wars, arose because the East

India Company, alarmed at the drain of silver from Europe to pay for its silk, tea and lacquer, sought for some substitute commodity. The Portuguese, of course, in the + 15th century were after spices. They wanted to break the Muslim monopoly. It was fortunate for them that during the exploration of the West African coast they were able to tap the gold of the Sudan successfully about + 1445 and thus in time gained the precious metal necessary for the Eastern trade. It does not seem that the Portuguese defrauded the Africans greatly in this exchange, for, unlike Asians, they were pleased to get horses, wheat, wine and cheese, copperware and other metals, blankets and strong cloth. Unfortunately the gold of Africa was never anything like enough for the ambitions of the Portuguese in the Eastern Seas, and out of the need for bases there arose naturally the temptation to accumulate further treasure by appropriating at sword-point the wealth of coastal port cities such as Malacca. The real criticism of their operations is that they were not content with a reasonable share of Asian trade; what they wanted before long was the complete domination of the trade and the traders. This it was given only to others to achieve and then but for a time. The Chinese, on the other hand, carried on for half a century what was essentially government trading with the emirs and sultans of the western parts of the Indian Ocean. They obtained, as nominal "tribute," all the strange commodities that they sought for, never having any difficulty in "paying" for them by means of imperial "gifts" of silk, lacquer, porcelain, etc.

Equally profound differences between the Chinese and the Portuguese behaviour appear in matters of religion. Missionary activity, well intended no doubt, accompanied the Portuguese explorations from an early time, but before the end of the century the war against all Muslims was being extended to all Hindus and Buddhists too, save those with whom the Portuguese might find it expedient to arrange a temporary alliance. In + 1560 the Holy Inquisition was established at Goa, where it soon acquired a reputation even more unsavoury than that which it had in Europe. It subjected the non-Christian as well as the Christian subjects of the Empire to all those forms of secret police terror which have disfigured our own century, yet more abominable here perhaps because enlisted in the interests of higher religion. On board the Chinese ships what a contrast! Without forsaking the basic teaching of the sages Khung and Lao, Chêng Ho and his commanders were "all things to all men." In Arabia they conversed in the tongue of the Prophet and recalled the mosques of Yunnan; in India they presented offerings to Hindu temples and venerated the traces of the Buddha in Ceylon. Ceylon indeed provided the occasion for a particularly interesting example of this almost excessive urbanity. In 1911 a stele with an inscription in three languages (Chinese, Tamil and Persian) was unearthed by road engineers within the town of Galle. This act commemorated, as was soon clear, one of the visits of the Ming navy under Chêng Ho, and took the form of an address accompanying religious gifts. Owing to differential weathering, the Chinese version was the first to be deciphered. It says that the Chinese emperor, having heard of the fame of the Buddhist temples of Ceylon, such as the Temple of the Tooth relic, sent envoys to present a number of rich gifts—its date was + 1409. When the Tamil version was deciphered and translated later on, it turned out to say that the Chinese emperor, having heard of the fame of the god Devundara Deviyo, caused the stone to be set up in his praise. Still more remarkable, the Persian version, the most damaged of the three, was found to say that the presentation was to the glory of Allah and some of his (Muslim) saints. But while the texts are thus different, they all agree in one thing—the list of the presents is almost exactly identical. There is thus hardly any escape from the conclusion that three parallel sets of gifts were brought out by sea and handed over to the representatives of the three most important religions practised on the island. Such humanistic catholicity contrasts indeed with the *autos-da fé* of Goa later on.

We have already mentioned some of the stated motives of the Chinese expeditions, but there may have been others. Purely geographical exploration as such was probably never one of them. What the Chinese sought rather was cultural contacts with foreign peoples, even if quite uncivilised. The Chinese voyages were essentially an urbane but systematic tour of inspection of the known world. The Portuguese motive was not primarily geographical exploration either; their discoveries were really secondary achievements in the great attempt of a nation which believed itself to be the champion of Christendom in an unceasing war to find a way round to the Indies and so to take the Islamic world in the rear. On the Chinese side, probably the search for the dethroned emperor was never more than a pretext, the main motive was surely the demonstration of Chinese prestige by obtaining the nominal allegiance and exchange tribute of far-away princes. If one compares the Chinese and the Portuguese ventures over the whole range of our knowledge of them, it does seem as if the proto-scientific function of collecting natural rarities, strange gems and animals, was more marked in the former. For example the Chinese were extremely interested in giraffes. Undoubtedly one of the departments that concerned Chêng Ho's men was materia medica; the search for new drugs may have been a much more important motive than has usually been thought. There is a great deal of evidence that new drug-plants, and even crop-plants, were sought for intensively by the Chinese and recorded in their biological literature at the time.

The decline and fall of the Chinese navy (or national merchant navy) in the middle of the + 15th century was a rather dramatic process.[1] The great Treasure-ships had always been strongly criticised by the Confucian bureaucrats, whose minds were traditionally agrarian in interest, and to some extent the naval expansion was suspect as being an enterprise of the eunuchs—always in conflict with the Confucian bureaucracy. Military events also intervened, the serious deterioration of the position on the north-western frontiers diverting all attention from the sea, and in + 1450 at the disastrous battle of Thu-mu, that Chinese emperor who had suppressed the Treasure-ship fleets was himself taken into captivity by the Mongol and Tartar armies. At the same time there was a significant shift of population from the south-eastern seaboard provinces, reversing the trend which had been so strong at the beginning of the Southern Sung. The navy simply fell to pieces. By + 1474 only 140 warships of the main fleet of 400 were left. By + 1503 the Têngchow squadron had dropped from 100 vessels to 10. China had to pay heavily for this in the + 16th century when the time came to repel the concerted attacks of Japanese pirates. Gradually Chinese shipping recovered and most of the traditional types of build were preserved, but what a difference it would have made to Lin Tsê-Hsü and his friends at the time of the Opium Wars in the '40s of the 19th century if the short-sighted landsmen of the Ming court had not won the day.

So this was the confrontation. On the one hand there were the voyagers from the East, the Chinese, calm and pacific, unencumbered by a heritage of enmities, generous (up to a point), menacing no man's livelihood, tolerant, if a shade patronising, in panoply of arms yet conquering no colonies and setting up no strong points. On the other hand there were the voyagers from the West, the Portuguese Crusader traders out to take hereditary enemies in the rear, wrest a mercantile foothold from unsympathetic soil, hostile to other faiths yet relatively

[1] See Lo Jung-Pang, *Oriens Extremus,* **5** (1958):149.

free from racial prejudice, hot in the pursuit of economic power and heralds of the Renaissance. In all the maritime contacts between Europe and Asia in that dramatic age, our forefathers were quite sure who the "heathen" were; today we suspect that these were not the less civilised of the two.

45   SPAIN IN THE NEW WORLD

Aggressiveness and acquisitiveness were characteristic also of Spanish enterprise in the New World. This is evident in the following report by Columbus concerning his fateful discovery, in which he emphasized the possibilities for enslaving the peaceful native Indians and of exploiting the natural wealth of their country.* It is evident also in Pizarro's ruthless and treacherous conquest of the Inca Empire, described below by the nineteenth-century American historian, William H. Prescott.†

Columbus Discovers the New World

As I know that it will afford you pleasure that I have brought my undertaking to a successful result, I have determined to write you this letter to inform you of everything that has been done and discovered in this voyage of mine.

On the thirty-third day after leaving Cadiz I came into the Indian Sea, where I discovered many islands inhabited by numerous people. I took possession of all of them for our most fortunate King by making public proclamation and unfurling his standard, no one making any resistance. To the first of them I have given the name of our blessed Saviour, trusting in whose aid I had reached this and all the rest; but the Indians call it Guanahani. To each of the others also I gave a new name, ordering one to be called Sancta Maria de Concepcion, another Fernandina, another Hysabella, another Johana; and so with all the rest. . . . From there I saw another island to the eastwards, distant 54 miles from this Johana, which I named Hispana, and proceeded to it. . . .

In the island, which I have said before was called Hispana, there are very lofty and beautiful mountains, great farms, groves and fields, most fertile both for cultivation and for pasturage, and well adapted for constructing buildings. The convenience of the harbors in this island, and the excellence of the rivers, in volume and salubrity, surpass human belief, unless one should see them. In it the trees, pasture-lands, and fruits differ much from those of Johana. Besides, this Hispana abounds in various kinds of spices, gold, and metals. The inhabitants of both sexes of this and of all the other islands I have seen, or of which I have any knowledge, always go as naked as they came into the world, except that some of the women cover parts of their bodies with leaves or branches, or a veil of cotton, which they prepare themselves for this purpose. They are all, as I said before, unprovided with any sort of iron, and they are destitute of arms, which are entirely unknown to them, and for which they are not adapted; not on account of any bodily deformity,

---

* Reprinted from *Old South Leaflets,* Vol. II, No. 33 (Boston: Directors of the Old South Work, 1897).

† Reprinted from W. H. Prescott, *History of the Conquest of Peru* (Philadelphia: J. B. Lippincott Co., 1874), I, 402–413, 420–423, 428, 450–451, 453–455.

for they are well made, but because they are timid and full of terror. They carry, however, canes dried in the sun in place of weapons, upon whose roots they fix a wooden shaft, dried and sharpened to a point. But they never dare to make use of these, for it has often happened, when I have sent two or three of my men to some of their villages to speak with the inhabitants, that a crowd of Indians has sallied forth; but, when they saw our men approaching, they speedily took to flight, parents abandoning their children, and children their parents. This happened not because any loss or injury had been inflicted upon any of them. On the contrary, I gave whatever I had, cloth and many other things, to whomsoever I approached, or with whom I could get speech, without any return being made to me; but they are by nature fearful and timid. But, when they see that they are safe, and all fear is banished, they are very guileless and honest, and very liberal of all they have. No one refuses the asker anything that he possesses; on the contrary, they themselves invite us to ask for it. They manifest the greatest affection toward all of us, exchanging valuable things for trifles, content with the very least thing or nothing at all. But I forbade giving them a very trifling thing and of no value, such as bits of plates, dishes, or glass, also nails and straps; although it seemed to them, if they could get such, that they had acquired the most beautiful jewels in the world. . . .

They do not practise idolatry; on the contrary, they believe that all strength, all power, in short, all blessings, are from Heaven, and that I have come down from there with these ships and sailors; and in this spirit was I received everywhere, after they had got over their fear. They are neither lazy nor awkward, but, on the contrary, are of an excellent and acute understanding. Those who have sailed these seas give excellent accounts of everything; but they have never seen men wearing clothes, or ships like ours.

.   .   .

In all these islands, as I understand, every man is satisfied with only one wife, except the princes or kings, who are permitted to have 20. The women appear to work more than the men, but I could not well understand whether they have private property or not; for I saw that what every one had was shared with the others, especially meals, provisions, and such things. I found among them no monsters, as very many expected, but men of great deference and kind; nor are they black like Ethiopians, but they have long, straight hair. . . .

I was informed that there is another island larger than the aforesaid Hispana, whose inhabitants have no hair; and that there is a greater abundance of gold in it than in any of the others. Some of the inhabitants of these islands and of the others I have seen I am bringing over with me to bear testimony to what I have reported. Finally, to sum up in a few words the chief results and advantages of our departure and speedy return, I make this promise to our most invincible Sovereigns, that, if I am supported by some little assistance from them, I will give them as much gold as they have need of, and in addition spices, cotton, and mastic, which is found only in Chios, and as much aloes-wood, and as many heathen slaves as their Majesties may choose to demand. . . .

.   .   .

Therefore let King and Queen and Princes, and their most fortunate realms, and all other Christian provinces, let us all return thanks to our Lord and Saviour Jesus Christ, who has bestowed so great a victory and reward upon us; let there be processions and solemn sacrifices prepared; let the churches be decked with festal boughs; let Christ rejoice upon earth as he rejoices in heaven, as he foresees that so many souls of so many people heretofore lost are to be saved; and let us be glad not only for the exaltation of our faith, but also for the increase of temporal prosperity, in which not only Spain, but all Christendom is about to share.

As these things have been accomplished, so have they been briefly narrated. Farewell.

CHRISTOPHER COLOM,
Admiral of the Ocean Fleet.

Lisbon, March 14th.

Spanish Conquest of the Inca Empire

Elevated high above his vassals came the Inca Atahuallpa, borne on a sedan or open litter, on which was a sort of throne made of massive gold of inestimable value. The palanquin was lined with the richly-colored plumes of tropical birds and studded with shining plates of gold and silver. The monarch's attire was much richer than on the preceding evening. Round his neck was suspended a collar of emeralds of uncommon size and brilliancy. His short hair was decorated with golden ornaments, and the imperial *borla* [silk diadem] encircled his temples. The bearing of the Inca was sedate and dignified; and from his lofty station he looked down on the multitudes below with an air of composure, like one accustomed to command.

As the leading files of the procession entered the great square, larger says an old chronicler, than any square in Spain, they opened to the right and left for the royal retinue to pass. Every thing was conducted with admirable order. The monarch was permitted to traverse the *plaza* in silence, and not a Spaniard was to be seen. When some five or six thousand of his people had entered the place, Atahuallpa halted, and, turning round with an inquiring look, demanded, "Where are the strangers?"

At this moment Fray Vicente de Valverde, a Dominican friar, Pizarro's chaplain, and afterwards Bishop of Cuzco, came forward with his breviary, or, as other accounts say, a Bible, in one hand, and a crucifix in the other, and, approaching the Inca, told him that he came by order of his commander to expound to him the doctrines of the true faith, for which purpose the Spaniards had come from a great distance to his country. . . . The friar concluded with beseeching the Peruvian monarch to receive him kindly, to abjure the errors of his own faith, and embrace that of the Christians now proffered to him, the only one by which he could hope for salvation, and, furthermore, to acknowledge himself a tributary of the Emperor Charles the Fifth, who, in that event, would aid and protect him as his loyal vassal.

. . .

The eyes of the Indian monarch flashed fire, and his dark brow grew darker, as he replied, "I will be no man's tributary. I am greater than any prince upon earth. Your emperor may be a great prince; I do not doubt it, when I see that he has sent his subjects so far across the waters; and I am willing to hold him as a brother. As for the Pope of whom you speak, he must be crazy to talk of giving away countries which do not belong to him. For my faith," he continued, "I will not change it. Your own God, as you say, was put to death by the very men whom he created. But mine," he concluded, pointing to his Deity,—then, alas! sinking in glory behind the mountains,—"my God still lives in the heavens and looks down on his children."

216

He then demanded of Valverde by what authority he had said these things. The friar pointed to the book which he held, as his authority. Atahuallpa, taking it, turned over the pages a moment, then, as the insult he had received probably flashed across his mind, he threw it down with vehemence, and exclaimed, "Tell your comrades that they shall give me an account of their doing in my land. I will not go from here till they have made me full satisfaction for all the wrongs they have committed."

The friar, greatly scandalized by the indignity offered to the sacred volume, stayed only to pick it up, and, hastening to Pizarro, informed him of what had been done, exclaiming, at the same time, "Do you not see that while we stand here wasting our breath in talking with this dog, full of pride as he is, the fields are filling with Indians? Set on, at once; I absolve you." Pizarro saw that the hour had come. He waved a white scarf in the air, the appointed signal. The fatal gun was fired from the fortress. Then, springing into the square, the Spanish captain and his followers shouted the old war-cry of "St. Jago and at them." It was answered by the battle-cry of every Spaniard in the city, as, rushing from the avenues of the great halls in which they were concealed, they poured into the *plaza*, horse and foot, each in his own dark column, and threw themselves into the midst of the Indian crowd. The latter, taken by surprise, stunned by the report of artillery and muskets, the echoes of which reverberated like thunder from the surrounding buildings, and blinded by the smoke which rolled in sulphurous volumes along the square, were seized with a panic. They knew not whither to fly for refuge from the coming ruin. Nobles and commoners,—all were trampled down under the fierce charge of the cavalry, who dealt their blows, right and left, without sparing; while their swords, flashing through the thick gloom, carried dismay into the hearts of the wretched natives, who now for the first time saw the horse and his rider in all their terrors. They made no resistance,—as, indeed, they had no weapons with which to make it. Every avenue to escape was closed, for the entrance to the square was choked up with the dead bodies of men who had perished in vain efforts to fly. . . .

.   .   .

The Indian monarch, stunned and bewildered, saw his faithful subjects falling around him without fully comprehending his situation. The litter on which he rode heaved to and fro, as the mighty press swayed backwards and forwards; and he gazed on the overwhelming ruin, like some forlorn mariner, who, tossed about in his bark by the furious elements, sees the lightning's flash and hears the thunder bursting around him with the consciousness that he can do nothing to avert his fate. At length, weary with the work of destruction, the Spaniards, as the shades of evening grew deeper, felt afraid that the royal prize might, after all, elude them; and some of the cavaliers made a desperate attempt to end the affray at once by taking Atahuallpa's life. But Pizarro, who was nearest his person, called out, with stentorian voice, "Let no one who values his life strike at the Inca"; and, stretching out his arm to shield him, received a wound on the hand from one of his own men,—the only wound received by a Spaniard in the action.

The struggle now became fiercer than ever round the royal litter. It reeled more and more, and at length, several of the nobles who supported it having been slain, it was overturned, and the Indian prince would have come with violence to the ground, had not his fall been broken by the efforts of Pizarro and some other of the cavaliers, who caught him in their arms. The imperial *borla* was instantly snatched from his temples by a soldier named Estete, and the unhappy monarch, strongly secured, was removed to a neighboring building, where he was carefully guarded.

All attempt at resistance now ceased. The fate of the Inca soon spread over town and country. The charm which might have held the Peruvians together was dissolved. Every man thought only of his own safety. Even the soldiery encamped on the adjacent fields took the alarm, and, learning the fatal tidings, were seen flying in every direction before their pursuers, who in the heat of triumph showed no touch of mercy. At length night, more pitiful than man, threw her friendly mantle over the fugitives, and the scattered troops of Pizarro rallied once more at the sound of the trumpet in the bloody square of Caxamalca.

.   .   .

It was not long before Atahuallpa discovered, amidst all the show of religious zeal in his Conquerors, a lurking appetite more potent in most of their bosoms than either religion or ambition. This was the love of gold. He determined to avail himself of it to procure his own freedom. . . .

In the hope, therefore, to effect his purpose by appealing to the avarice of his keepers, he one day told Pizarro that if he would set him free he would engage to cover the floor of the apartment on which they stood with gold. Those present listened with an incredulous smile; and, as the Inca received no answer, he said, with some emphasis, that "he would not merely cover the floor, but would fill the room with gold as high as he could reach"; and, standing on tiptoe, he stretched out his hand against the wall. All stared with amazement; while they regarded it as the insane boast of a man too eager to procure his liberty to weigh the meaning of his words. Yet Pizarro was sorely perplexed. As he had advanced into the country, much that he had seen, and all that he had heard, had confirmed the dazzling reports first received of the riches of Peru. Atahuallpa himself had given him the most glowing picture of the wealth of the capital, where the roofs of the temples were plated with gold, while the walls were hung with tapestry and the floors inlaid with tiles of the same precious metal. There must be some foundation for all this. At all events, it was safe to accede to the Inca's proposition; since by so doing he could collect at once all the gold at his disposal, and thus prevent its being purloined or secreted by the natives. He therefore acquiesced in Atahuallpa's offer, and, drawing a red line along the wall at the height which the Inca had indicated, he caused the terms of the proposal to be duly recorded by the notary. The apartment was about seventeen feet broad, by twenty-two feet long, and the line round the walls was nine feet from the floor. This space was to be filled with gold; but it was understood that the gold was not to be melted down into ingots, but to retain the original form of the articles into which it was manufactured, that the Inca might have the benefit of the space which they occupied. He further agreed to fill an adjoining room of smaller dimensions twice full with silver, in like manner; and he demanded two months to accomplish all this.

No sooner was this arrangement made than the Inca despatched couriers to Cuzco and the other principal places in the kingdom, with orders that the gold ornaments and utensils should be removed from the royal palaces, and from the temples and other public buildings, and transported without loss of time to Caxamalca. . . .

But the distances were great, and the returns came in slowly. They consisted, for the most part, of massive pieces of plate, some of which weighed two or three *arrobas*,—a Spanish weight of twenty-five pounds. On some days, articles of the value of thirty or forty thousand *pesos de oro* were brought in, and, occasionally, of the value of fifty or even sixty thousand *pesos*. The greedy eyes of the Conquerors gloated on the shining heaps of treasure, which were transported on the shoulders of the Indian porters, and, after being carefully registered, were placed in safe deposit under a strong guard.

. . . . .

. . . Without further delay, the division of the treasure was agreed upon. Yet, before making this, it was necessary to reduce the whole to ingots of a uniform standard, for the spoil was composed of an infinite variety of articles, in which the gold was of very different degrees of purity. These articles consisted of goblets, ewers, salvers, vases of every shape and size, ornaments and utensils for the temples and the royal palaces, tiles and plates for the decoration of the public edifices, curious imitations of different plants and animals. Among the plants, the most beautiful was the Indian corn, in which the golden ear was sheathed in its broad leaves of silver, from which hung a rich tassel of threads of the same precious metal. A fountain was also much admired, which sent up a sparkling jet of gold, while birds and animals of the same material played in the waters at its base. . . .

The business of melting down the plate was intrusted to the Indian goldsmiths, who were thus required to undo the work of their own hands. They toiled day and night, but such was the quantity to be recast that it consumed a full month. When the whole was reduced to bars of a uniform standard, they were nicely weighed, under the superintendence of the royal inspectors. The total amount of the gold was found to be one million three hundred and twenty-six thousand five hundred and thirty-nine *pesos de oro,* which, allowing for the greater value of money in the sixteenth century, would be equivalent, probably, at the present time, to near *three millions and a half of pounds sterling,* or somewhat less than *fifteen millions and a half of dollars* [worth approximately 40 million dollars in 1960]. The quantity of silver was estimated at fifty-one thousand six hundred and ten marks. History affords no parallel of such a booty—and that, too, in the most convertible form, in ready money, as it were—having fallen to the lot of a little band of military adventurers, like the Conquerors of Peru.

Chapter Twenty-one

West European expansion:
Dutch, French, British phase,
1600–1763

46   AMERICAN TREASURE AND THE
                           RISE OF NORTHWESTERN EUROPE

The sixteenth was the Iberian century. Spain and Portugal dominated overseas enterprise and received vast profits from the spice trade with the East and from the silver mines of the New World. But Iberian predominance did not endure. Spain and Portugal gave way to Holland, France, and Britain. Why northwestern Europe rose to a position of leadership is an intriguing, basic question, answered in part by Professor Hamilton's study * of the effects of American bullion on Europe's economy. The influx of treasure is shown to be a stimulant to capital accumulation in northwestern Europe and a financial basis for economic growth.

The present paper purposes to examine the effects of the discovery of an all-water route to the East Indies, the opening of extensive markets in the New World, and above all the heavy European imports of Mexican and Peruvian treasure upon the rise of modern capitalism. For two reasons the study is confined to the sixteenth and seventeenth centuries. First, during this period American gold and silver and the markets of the East and West Indies exerted their greatest influence upon the progress of capitalism. Second, there was a significant development of capitalism in England, France, and the Low Countries. In fact, the progress of capitalism during the sixteenth and seventeenth centuries prepared the way for the Industrial Revolution. Significant experiments with the factory system were carried out in England in the sixteenth century and in France during the seventeenth. There is abundant evidence of a groping toward the factory system before the great inventions of the eighteenth century made such a course inevitable. . . .

* Reprinted from E. J. Hamilton, "American Treasure and the Rise of Capitalism (1500–1700)," *Economica* (November 1929), 338–356, by permission of the author and the London School of Economics and Political Science.

220

Capitalism did not develop out of a void during the early modern period. There were traces of it in the great nations of antiquity, and near the end of the Middle Ages it played an important role in the economy of Flanders, the Italian city states, and certain French cities. In these oases, especially in the great industrial, commercial, and financial centres of Italy—Amalfi, Pisa, Genoa, Florence, and Venice —many of the characteristic features of modern capitalism evolved. Arabic notation, destined to supersede cumbersome Roman numerals in accounting, was introduced. Double-entry bookkeeping, an indispensable instrument for the rational conduct of business, was developed. The mariner's compass, invaluable to ocean shipping, was introduced into the Western World. Portolan charts, later to be combined with the resuscitated theoretical geography of Ptolemy and Strabo to give birth to modern geography, arose to meet the needs of navigation in the Mediterranean. Important advances were achieved in naval architecture and in the art of navigation. Oriental arts and products were diffused through the trading centres of Italy. In the great seaports and in the fairs arose the law merchant—flexible, expeditious, and fashioned to meet the needs of trade. As a concomitant development, negotiable instruments originated or were popularised. Perhaps the development of organised dealings in foreign exchange and advances in the technique of banking by houses located in Genoa, Venice, and Florence—with agents scattered to the utmost confines of Europe—represented the greatest contribution of the Middle Ages to the rise of modern capitalism. These great banking houses aided materially in the perfection of banking and in the spread of the institution into countries where a fully developed species of capitalism was destined to emerge.

Although, as has been shown, many other forces contributed to the rise of modern capitalism, the phenomena associated with the discoveries of America and of the passage around the Cape of Good Hope to the East Indies were the principal factors in this development. Long distance voyages led to increases in the size of vessels and improvements in the instruments and technique of navigation analogous to the recent advances in aviation stimulated by transatlantic flying. As Adam Smith pointed out, the widening of the market facilitated division of labour and led to technological improvements. The introduction of new agricultural commodities from America and of new agricultural and manufactured goods, especially luxury products, from the East stimulated greater industrial activity to provide the wherewithal to pay for them. Emigration to colonies in the New World and to settlements in the East lessened the pressure of population upon the soil of the mother countries and thus enhanced the surplus—the excess of national production over national subsistence—from which savings could be drawn. The opening of distant markets and sources of supply for raw materials was a significant factor in the transfer of the control of industry and commerce from the guilds to capitalist employers. The old guild organisation—unable to cope with the new problems in purchasing, production, and marketing—commenced to disintegrate and finally gave way to the capitalist employer, a more efficient medium of control.

Let us turn to the greatest influence that the discovery of America had upon the progress of capitalism, to the vast influx of gold and silver from American mines. . . .

All the great colonising powers of the early modern period sought gold and silver. Greed for treasure was one of the greatest stimuli to colonisation, but Spain alone was successful in her quest. As early as 1503 Spain commenced to receive gold from Hispaniola with surprising regularity and shortly afterwards from Cuba and Porto Rico as well. Bating the driblets of gold from the region around Panama after 1513, no treasure came from the American continent before November 5th, 1519, when the first Aztec spoils reached Spain. Some fifteen years later the motherland began to enjoy Incan booty sent by Pizarro. Though the conquests of Mexico and Peru, with the resultant robbery, are among the most dramatic episodes in human history, the treasure obtained in this way was—contrary to general opinion—a mere bagatelle in comparison with the receipts from mining at a later date, especially after the discoveries of the renowned silver mines at Potosí, Guanajuato, and Zacatecas and the perfection of the amalgamation process for extracting silver, all of which occurred between 1545 and 1560. From the middle of the sixteenth century to the 'thirties of the seventeenth the treasure of the Indies poured into the motherland at a rate that exceeded the most fantastic dreams of the *conquistadores*. Thereafter the stream of gold and silver lessened considerably, but did not cease entirely. . . .

Undoubtedly the discovery of the Good Hope passage to the fabled Spice Islands would have stimulated trade in any event, but the physical barriers to transportation and the political throttling of trade along former routes by the Ottoman Turk were not the only obstacles to be overcome. For some inexplicable reason Orientals have always had a penchant for hoarding treasure. Hence, even in response to a protracted inflow of specie, Oriental prices, unlike those of the Western World, did not rise sufficiently to induce a counter flow. For more than two thousand years the East has proved a necropolis for European gold and silver. The seventeenth-century pamphleteers who in tract after tract denounced the English East India Company for draining away the country's treasure were not mistaken as to the facts. European products were carried to the East, but silver was the commodity that could be exchanged for Oriental goods on the most advantageous terms. So treasure flowed from Portugal, Holland, England, and France to the Orient in exchange for the eagerly sought spices and luxury goods of that region. Notwithstanding the enormous profits obtained in the East India trade, the passage around the Cape of Good Hope might have been rendered nugatory by a dearth of specie but for the vast streams of Mexican and Peruvian silver flowing into Europe. The voyage of Columbus was an imperative supplement to that of da Gama.

For about two thousand years monopoly of the East India trade—a trade that has always enriched the nations able to control it—has been an object of policy and a prize of diplomacy. But in the first two and a half centuries after the voyages of da Gama and Columbus the struggle for hegemony in the East Indies was intensified manyfold. Not only did statesmen precipitate or sanction sanguinary wars, but writers counselled aggression as a means of achieving political and economic ascendancy. Did the profits of the trade justify this rivalry?

From the very beginning of the modern era trade with the East Indies by the Cape route was almost incredibly lucrative. It is difficult to find in the annals of business either greater profits than those obtained on some of the early voyages to the Spice Islands or records of sustained earnings that surpass those of the English and Dutch East India Companies during the seventeenth century. "Da Gama returned to Lisbon in 1499 with a cargo which repaid sixty times the cost of the expedition," affording a profit of about 6,000 per cent. The Victoria, sole survivor of the memorable fleet of Magellan, brought back to Spain 556.72 quintals of spice of which 501.35 were sold in Seville at 42 ducats per quintal. If we assume that the remaining 55.37 quintals were saleable—and at the same price—, the cargo was worth 23,382.24 ducats, a sum comparable to the value of the specie borne by the average treasure ship at that time. I know of no satisfactory account of the profits Portugal obtained from commerce with the East in the sixteenth century, during most of which she was in the ascendency; but such figures are not wanting for Holland—

the nation upon which the Portuguese mantle fell in the seventeenth century. The Dutch East India Company, organised in 1602, was a highly successful enterprise until the close of the seventeenth century. "For nearly two hundred years it declared dividends ranging from 12½ per cent. to 20, 40, or even 50 per cent.; the average dividend from 1602 to 1796 was over 18 per cent." The earnings of the English East India Company were stupendous. On some of the early voyages profits of 195, 221, 311, 318, and 334 per cent. were realised. During the seventeenth century dividends averaged about 100:21 per cent. . . .

The enormous profits obtained from the East India trade doubtless contributed powerfully to capital formation and thus to the rise of modern capitalism. The bulk of savings at the present time come directly or indirectly from individuals with high incomes, and presumably this has always been true. Therefore the profits of the Dutch and English East India Companies, not to mention those of interlopers engaged in the same trade, must have afforded considerable stimulus to saving. Bating loans to Governments and ecclesiastical organisations, most of the savings were invested in commercial, industrial, or financial enterprises. . . .

The price revolution set in motion by American gold and silver contributed directly to the progress of capitalism. . . .

In England and France the vast discrepancy between prices and wages, born of the price revolution, deprived labourers of a large part of the incomes they had hitherto enjoyed, and diverted this wealth to the recipients of other distributive shares. As has been shown, rents, as well as wages, lagged behind prices, so landlords gained nothing from labour's loss. For a period of almost two hundred years English and French capitalists—and presumably those of other economically advanced countries—must have enjoyed incomes analogous to those American profiteers reaped from a similar divergence between prices and wages from 1916 to 1919. . . .

The windfalls thus received, along with gains from the East India trade, furnished the means to build up capital equipment, and the stupendous profits obtainable supplied an incentive for the feverish pursuit of capitalistic enterprise. We find, as might be expected, that during the seventeenth and latter part of the sixteenth centuries England, France, and the Low Countries were seething with such genuinely capitalistic phenomena as systematic mechanical invention, company formation, and speculation in the shares of financial and trading concerns. The developments of this period, accelerated and fructified by the important series of mechanical inventions in the last half of the eighteenth century, were a significant step in the direction of the modern factory system, with the concomitant developments in commerce and finance.

Chapter Twenty-two

Russian expansion in Asia

47   RUSSIAN CONQUEST AND EXPLOITATION OF SIBERIA

At the same time that the Western European peoples were discovering and occupying new continents overseas, the Russian peoples were expanding overland and winning equally extensive territories in Siberia. The Russian eastward expansion to the Pacific is an epic story comparable to the American westward expansion to the same ocean. Its long-range implications were equally significant: Just as the Western European overseas enterprise ensured that the New World would become primarily Caucasoid in ethnic composition and European in culture, so the Russian conquest of Siberia made certain a similar outcome in that vast area. The policies of the Russians in conquering and exploiting Siberia are analyzed in the following account by an American authority on this topic.*

OSTROGS. The conquest of the khanate of Sibir during the latter part of the sixteenth century, first undertaken by the Volga pirate, Ermak, and completed by the tsar's voevodas, laid the foundation for the Russian Empire in Asia. After defeating the khan Kuchum, the Russians continued their eastward advance until the whole of Siberia became the possession of the Muscovite sovereign.

The Siberian natives, politically disunited, backward, and unfamiliar with firearms, were invariably defeated whenever they dared offer open resistance to the military organization and superior military equipment of the Russians. The latter, however, were handicapped by inferiority in numbers and by the fact that they had

* Reprinted from G. V. Lantzeff, *Siberia in the Seventeenth Century: A Study of the Colonial Administration,* Univ. of California Publications in History, XXX (Berkeley: University of California Press, 1940), pp. 87–115, by permission of The Regents of the University of California. Originally published by the University of California Press.

to scatter their forces over such a vast territory. These unfavorable circumstances the Russians overcame by building a well-planned system of forts and blockhouses, generally referred to as *ostrogs*.

To control the chief means of communication and transportation, the Russians chose the sites for ostrogs along important waterways. By virtue of their location, ostrogs prevented any organized hostile action on the part of the natives in whose territory they were erected. In time of peace the ostrogs were administrative centers; in time of war they became bases for military operations.

The main feature of an ostrog was a stockade made of large timber; the tops of the stocks were sharpened, and along the stockade at certain intervals there were embrasures for marksmen. On the corners of the stockade and above the gates towers equipped with artillery were erected. The largest ostrogs were built in western Siberia. The towns there were fenced off by one or two lines of the stockade which protected the town population; within the stockade stood a wooden citadel, which contained the government buildings and storehouses. The walls of the citadel were surmounted by towers, twenty to thirty feet high, parapets and *gorodni* (places for marksmen). Sometimes a moat was dug along the walls of the citadel and stockade. Special care was taken to safeguard the landing place on the river with two or three rows of *nadolby* (palisades), so that during a siege communication with other towns would not be interrupted. . . .

Application of "Divide et empera." Once an ostrog was established, the immediate problem of providing for the safety of the Russian expeditionary force was solved, and the local voevodas could proceed with subduing the natives within the vicinity of the ostrog and imposing upon them delivery of the *iasak* (fur tribute). For such purposes military prowess alone was not sufficient; the voevodas had to be diplomats as well as warriors. I. M. Trotskii, in his preface to the recently published collection of Siberian documents, remarks with surprise that

> . . . it is curious to note that the hostility among the natives themselves, apparently, increased with the advent of the conquerors: the iasak-paying natives helped to impose iasak on their neighbors, while the hostile natives chose as their victims those who accepted the domination.

As a matter of fact, it seems to have been a deliberate policy of the Russians to isolate the tribes by building ostrogs and fomenting intertribal hostility in the Russian interest. There are abundant proofs that such a policy bore fruit. . . .

In eastern Siberia there was continuous hostility between the Tungus and the Iukagirs, both sides appealing to the Russians for help. The Iukagirs were also having trouble with the Chukchis, and the Russian expeditionary force against the latter in 1659 consisted largely of Iukagirs, who in 1678–1679 again asked Russian protection against the Chukchis. The Tungus chief, Mozheul, offered his services in leading the Russians against his enemies, the Buriats, who had not as yet paid the iasak. . . .

RUSSIAN TREATMENT OF THE NATIVE UPPER CLASS. As soon as the natives in the newly acquired territory became more or less reconciled to Russian domination, the Russian administration, in order to establish regular and uninterrupted delivery of the iasak, tried to introduce peace and order among them.

The government sought especially to win the favor of the wealthy and influential natives. This policy was pursued from the very beginning of the Siberian occupation. Captured members of the native nobility were treated with consideration and sometimes released in the hope that they would bring their relatives and supporters to the Russian side. Mametkul, a relative of Kuchum, was taken prisoner by Ermak's cossacks and sent to Moscow, where he was well received and later given a military rank in the Russian service. As a voevoda he participated in the Swedish war of 1590 and in the Crimean expedition of 1598. Other members of Kuchum's family were treated in Moscow with the courtesy due their rank. . . .

The good will and support of the native chiefs was a weighty factor in the country, where the natives greatly outnumbered their conquerors. To win them over to the Russian side, special methods were used. Whenever a new voevoda was appointed, one of the first things he had to do was to invite the native chiefs and the "best men" from the surrounding territory to the ostrog, and to meet them in an impressive fashion, appealing to the natives' psychology. A solemn "reception" was held, with the voevoda and the serving men garbed in gala "colored dress." The chiefs passed between the ranks of serving men standing in military formation, while cannon and muskets were discharged in salute. The voevoda delivered a speech, emphasizing the power and benevolence of the governmnt, enumerating the injustices from which the natives suffered, and promising, in the future, new favors and the elimination of evil practices. The procedure ended with a feast, where the natives were given an opportunity to gorge themselves with food and drink. Strong drinks were especially popular, and a petition has been preserved in which the natives complained that they were served beer instead of strong liquor. Similar feasts were held on the occasions when the chiefs arrived in town with the iasak from their volosts and were rewarded with various gifts in the form of cloth, metal tools, and brightly colored beads.

Some of the native chiefs, however, did not respond to the inducements offered by the Russians and remained stubborn in their resistance to the invaders. Toward them the government used ruthless and unscrupulous methods, quite in keeping with the times. There was no room for sentimentality, and treachery as a political weapon was lauded. . . .

GOVERNMENT POLICIES TOWARD THE NATIVES IN GENERAL. Once the government felt confident that the loyalty of the natives was reasonably assured, it prescribed that local officials use kindness and consideration in their treatment of them. The general tendency was to regard the natives as special wards of the state who needed supervision and protection. It was considered necessary to keep arms from reaching the natives, who might be tempted into some mischief, and to prevent, as far as possible, their demoralization by vices imported by the Russians, because it would affect their economic welfare and their ability to deliver the iasak. Therefore, in spite of protests from the natives, the merchants were forbidden to sell them axes, knives, or any arms or objects which could be converted into arms, as well as wine, tobacco, or any gambling devices. . . .

The government had shown considerable leniency toward the natives even in the matter of fur collection, which was its chief concern. In 1599 the natives of Siberia were informed with all due pomp and ceremony that the tsar, Boris Godunov, on account of his ascension to the throne, had released them from the delivery of iasak for one year. In general the voevodas were instructed not to require the delivery of iasak from poor, old, sick, or crippled natives. If, for some good reason, the iasak men could not deliver furs on time, the voevodas were to extend the date of delivery. Collection of the iasak had to be made with "kindness and not by cruelty and flogging . . . corporal punishment was not to be used . . . so as not to insult the natives and drive them away. . . ."

In accordance with its policy of preserving native tribal organization and native customs, the Muscovite government did not interfere with the religious beliefs of the natives. However, the conversion of the natives to Christianity had certain advantages. The baptized men, alienated by the change of religion from their kinsmen and former associates, were enlisted into Russian service and thus strengthened the garrisons. The baptized women solved the problem of the shortage of women in Siberia because they might marry serving men, as well as baptized natives. Therefore the government had reason to encourage somewhat the spread of Christianity and it did so by making gifts to those who embraced the new faith. As the Russians had no race prejudice and regarded religion as the only barrier separating them from the natives, the newly baptized were treated on equal terms with the Russians.

Nevertheless, in spite of the proselyting zeal of the churchmen, the government was not at all eager to baptize large numbers of natives. The advantages gained by their conversion were more than overbalanced by the financial losses, as the baptized natives, in effect, received Russian citizenship and ceased to pay iasak. Consequently, both the clergy and the local officials were repeatedly and explicitly forbidden to use any coercion in converting the natives. Christianity, if introduced at all, should prevail by "love and not by cruelty." For each baptism it became necessary to ask special permission from the administration. . . .

OBLIGATIONS AND GRIEVANCES OF THE NATIVES. The delivery of the iasak was the most important obligation the natives had toward the government. In addition to this the natives were called upon to perform other duties in connection with the various problems which confronted the colonial administration. . . .

The shortage of food supplies was one of the greatest difficulties which the Russians had to face in Siberia. At the beginning of the conquest, the grain had to be brought at considerable expense from European Russia. Therefore, one of the first tasks of the Siberian administration was to develop the local cultivation of land, and in an attempt to do this the voevodas of several uezds (Pelym, Verkhoturi, Turinsk, Tiumen, and later Eniseisk) tried to organize state farms operated by native labor. For the most part such enterprises were unsuccessful; the natives made poor farmers and repeatedly complained that they were not accustomed to agriculture. Fortunately, the gradual arrival of Russian colonists made further encouragement of farming among the natives unnecessary.

The natives were also used for other purposes. Shortage of guides and interpreters among the serving men necessitated the employment of natives in these roles, and the shortage of labor led to the use of them in the building and repairing of town fortifications and roads. For transportation, the Russians had to use natives as rowers of boats and drivers of carts. This caused a great deal of dissatisfaction among the natives, who were forced to provide horses, oxen, dogs, and even reindeer to carry men, supplies, and furs. They disliked the transportation service so much that in exchange for release from it some of them offered to pay triple the required amount of iasak. Frequently, the natives, besides their iasak obligation, had to catch fish, gather berries, bring wood for fuel or for building purposes, furnish hunting hawks, and, in general, "to serve the sovereign's service at the orders of the voevodas." Some of the voevodas interpreted this as justification for using natives for all kinds of personal service as well.

Imposition of the iasak delivery and of other forms of service constituted a heavy burden for the natives, who, because of their cultural backwardness and their inability to cope with the severe climate, already led a wretched and precarious existence. They needed all the "clemency and kindness" which were mentioned so often in the government instructions. The same instructions, however, demanded that the voevodas "seek profit for the sovereign with zeal." It is hardly surprising that the local officials, eager to win a reputation for financial efficiency (which might lead to another lucrative appointment) and more than anxious to fill their own pockets, were likely to forget all about "clemency" and to concentrate on "profit"—especially to themselves. . . .

The natives suffered from the Russian rule in many other ways. The government imported a number of colonists from Russia and a great many other Russian colonists came on their own initiative. In order to give room to these settlers, the natives often had to abandon their hunting grounds and fishing places, although some were able to recover at least a part of their land through appeals to Moscow. On several occasions, because of the lack of Russian women in Siberia, both colonists and serving men abducted native women, especially when their fathers and husbands were away hunting. In general, the conduct of the Russian settlers, as well as of numerous promyshlenniks [private Russian traders and hunters], was frequently such that, . . . the government had to issue special instructions to the local officers demanding protection for the natives. Instead of following the government instructions, the local administrators themselves often mistreated the natives. The voevoda of Narym kidnapped a son of the local chief and kept him until a ransom of one hundred rubles was paid. An official of Okhotsk gathered together all the children of the local tribe of Tungus and required the natives to bring a sable in return for each child. The officials of Tomsk, traveling in 1606 along the Ob' River, "tortured the natives and extorted exorbitant gifts." The voevoda of Tobolsk reported that in Pelym the local voevoda had flogged many Ostiaks to death. Golovin, the notorious voevoda of Iakutsk, "hanged 23 of the best men" and "flogged many Iakuts to death, used torture, and starved others to death in a dungeon." The boiar son Pushkin, in charge of the ostrog of Olekminsk, in order "to satisfy his greed, flogged the natives with rods and kept them in irons." The stolnik Bibikov in Okhotsk, repeating the methods of his predecessor, Krizhanovskii, hanged a number of Tungus, flogged others with a knout or mutilated them by cutting off their ears and noses. The golova Poiarkov, who was sent on an expedition to subdue a hostile chief, Kamuk, not only drove away the cattle belonging to the natives and appropriated all their possessions, but also burned the native town with its three hundred inhabitants, including the chief and his family. . . .

In response to oppression, the natives tried to protest to Moscow, to refuse the delivery of the iasak, to move to other lands, and, finally, to oppose the Russians with arms. Continual murders of the iasak collectors and attacks upon shipments of furs and food seriously hampered the collection of furs, and required constant military viligance, while some of the largest uprisings even threatened the towns and centers of the administration.

Chapter Twenty-three

Significance
of the period
for world history

DAWN OF A NEW WORLD ERA   48

The overseas expansion of the Western Europeans marked the beginning of a new era in world history. Hitherto, this history had been essentially, though not exclusively, regional in scope. It is true that a Eurasian ecumene had gradually evolved, incipient during classical times and full-fledged during the medieval period. Yet relations between Eurasia and Africa remained restricted and tenuous because of formidable geographic barriers, both within Africa and between Africa and the outside world. And as for Australia and the Americas, their isolation had been complete since the distant period when immigrants had been able to cross over to these regions from Eurasia because of the lowered sea levels during the Ice Ages.

*This traditional regional pattern of world relationships changed suddenly and dramatically when the Europeans expanded overseas in all directions, establishing for the first time direct contact among all continents. The nature and significance of this transition from regional to global history is the subject of this interpretative essay by the well-known historian Arnold J. Toynbee.**

. . . Since about A.D. 1500 (to reckon in terms of our Western parochial era), mankind has been gathered into a single world-wide society. From the dawn of history to about that date, the earthly home of man had been divided into many isolated mansions; since about A.D. 1500, the human race has been brought under one roof. This has been accomplished, under God, by human action, and here we come to the really sensational point. The agent of this revolutionary change in the affairs of men might have been any one of the divers parochial societies that were

* Reprinted from A. J. Toynbee, *Civilization on Trial*, pp. 64–71, by permission. Copyright 1948 by Oxford University Press, Inc.

229

on the map when the revolution was put in hand, but the particular parochial society that has actually done the deed is the one that, of all of them, was the most unlikely candidate.

In an effort to jump clear of my native Western standing-ground and to look at this question from a less eccentric point of view, I have asked myself who was the most centrally placed and most intelligent observer that I could think of among notable non-Westerners who were alive at the moment when a few ships' companies of Western mariners embarked on the enterprise of unifying the world, and I have found my man in the Emperor Babur. Babur was a descendant, in the fifth generation, of Tamerlane, the Transoxanian conqueror who made the last attempt to unify the world by land operations from a continental centre. Within Babur's lifetime—A.D. 1483–1530—Columbus reached America by sea from Spain and da Gama India from Portugal. Babur started his career as prince of Farghana in the upper valley of the Jaxartes: a small country which had been the centre of the [ecumene] since the second century B.C. Babur invaded India overland twenty-one years after da Gama had arrived there by sea. Last but not least, Babur was a man-of-letters whose brilliant autobiography in his Turkish mother-tongue reveals a spirit of outstanding intelligence and perceptiveness.

What was Babur's horizon? To the east of Farghana it included both India and China, and to the west it extended to Babur's own distant kinsmen, the Ottoman Turks. Babur took lessons from the 'Osmanlis in military technique, and he admired them for their piety and prowess in extending the bounds of Islam. He refers to them as the Ghāzis of Rum': the happy warriors who had succeeded, where the primitive Muslim Arabs had signally failed, in conquering for Islam the homeland of Eastern Orthodox Christendom. I could not recollect any mention of Western Christendom in Babur's memoirs, and I have found none in the exhaustive geographical index of Mrs. Beveridge's magnificent English translation. Of course Babur was aware of the existence of the Franks, for he was a cultivated man and he knew his Islamic history. If he had had occasion to allude to them, he would probably have described them as ferocious but frustrated infidels living in a remote corner of the world at the extreme western tip of one of the many peninsulas of the Continent of Asia. About four hundred years before his time, he would have gone on to relate, these barbarians had made a demonic attempt to break out of their cramped and uninviting corner into the broader and richer domains of Rum and Dar-al-Islam. It had been a critical moment for the destinies of civilization, but the uncouth aggressors had been foiled by the genius of Saladin, and their military reverses had been capped by a crushing moral defeat when the Christians of Rum, faced with a choice between two alternative future masters, chose the side of the angels by opting for 'the Prophet's turban' in preference to 'the Pope's tiara,' and accepted the boon of an Ottoman Peace.

The arrival of Frankish ships in India in A.D. 1498, twenty-one years before Babur's own first descent upon India in A.D. 1519, seems to have escaped Babur's attention—unless his silence is to be explained not by ignorance of the event, but by a feeling that the wandering of these water-gypsies were unworthy of a historian's notice. So this allegedly intelligent Transoxanian man-of-letters and man-of-action was blind to the portent of the Portuguese circumnavigation of Africa? He failed to perceive that these ocean-faring Franks had turned the flank of Islam and taken her in the rear? Yes, I believe Babur would have been utterly astonished if he had been told that the empire which he was founding in India was soon to pass from his descendants to Frankish successors. He had no inkling of the change that was to come over the face of the world between his generation and ours. But this,

I submit, is not a reflection on Babur's intelligence; it is one more indication of the queerness of the major event in the history of the world in our time.

Since A.D. 1500 the map of the [ecumene] has indeed been transformed out of all recognition. Down to that date it was composed of a belt of civilizations girdling the Old World from the Japanese Isles on the north-east to the British Isles on the north-west: Japan, China, Indo-China, Indonesia, India, Dar-al-Islam, the Orthodox Christendom of Rum, and another Christendom in the West. Though this belt sagged down, in the middle, from the North Temperate Zone to the Equator and thus ran through a fairly wide range of climates and physical environments, the social structure and cultural character of these societies was singularly uniform. Each of them consisted of a mass of peasants, living and working under much the same conditions as their forefathers on the morrow of the invention of agriculture some six to eight thousand years back, and a small minority of rulers enjoying a monopoly of power, surplus wealth, leisure, knowledge, and skill which in turn enhanced their power. There had been one or two earlier generations of civilizations of the same type in the Old World. In A.D. 1500 some of these were still remembered, while others (since brought to light by modern Western archaeologists) had been forgotten. There were two of the same type in existence at this date in the New World, unknown to those of the Old World and barely known even to each other. The living civilizations of the Old World were in touch with each other, though not so closely as to be, or feel themselves to be, members of a single society.

Their contact, such as it was, down to A.D. 1500, had been established and maintained along two different lines of communication. There was a maritime line which will be familiar to latter-day Westerners as the Peninsular and Oriental Steamship Company's route to Kobe from Tibury. In A.D. 1500, and indeed as recently as the time of a great-uncle of mine (a vivid memory of my childhood) who commanded one of the Honorable East India Company's passenger sailing ships and retired from the sea before the cutting of the Suez Canal without ever having served on board a steamer, this waterway through a chain of inland seas was broken by a portage between the Mediterranean and the Red Sea, with an alternative portage between the Mediterranean and the Persian Gulf. In the Mediterranean and Japanese sections of this maritime route, traffic had frequently been lively, and, from about 120 B.C. onwards, an infectious wave of maritime enterprise, set in motion by Greek mariners from Alexandria who found their way to Ceylon, had travelled on eastwards through Indonesia till it had carried Polynesian canoes to Easter Island. Yet, adventurous and romantic as these pre-Western seafarers were, the water-route that they opened up never came to be of more than secondary importance as a line of communication between the civilizations. The main line was provided by the chain of steppes and deserts that cut across the belt of civilizations from the Sahara to Mongolia.

For human purposes, the Steppe was an inland sea which, in virtue of happening to be dry, was of higher conductivity for human intercourse than the salt-water sea ever was before the close of the fifteenth century of the Christian era. This waterless sea had its dry-shod ships and its quayless ports. The steppe-galleons were camels, the steppe-galleys horses, and the steppe-ports 'caravan cities'—ports of call on oasis-islands and termini on the coasts where the sand-waves of 'the Desert' broke upon 'the Sown': Petra and Palmyra, Damascus and Ur, Tamerlane's Samarkand and the Chinese emporia at the gates of the Great Wall. Steppe-traversing horses, not ocean-traversing sailing ships, were the sovereign means of locomotion by which the separate civilizations of the world as it was before A.D. 1500 were linked together—to the slight extent to which they did maintain contact with each other.

In that world, as you see, Babur's Farghana was the central point, and the Turks were, in Babur's day, the central family of nations. A Turco-centric history of the world has been published in our lifetime by the latest in the series of the great Ottoman Turkish Westernizers, President Mustafa Kemal Atatürk. It was a brilliant device for restoring the *morale* of his fellow-countrymen, but it was a still more brilliant feat of genuine historical intuition; for, from the fourth century of the Christian era, when they pushed the last of their Indo-European-speaking predecessors off the Steppe, down to the seventh century, which witnessed the collapse of the Ottoman, the Safawai, and the Timurid Turkish dynasties in their respective domains of Rum, Iran, and India, the Turkish-speaking peoples really were the keystone of the Asiatic arch from which the pre-da Gaman belt of civilizations hung suspended. During those twelve hundred years, the overland link between the separate civilizations was commanded by Turkish steppe-power, and, from their central position in this pre-da Gaman world, the Turks rode out, conquering and to conquer, east and west and south and north: to Manchuria and Algeria, to the Ukraine and the Deccan.

But now we come to the great revolution: a technological revolution by which the West made its fortune, got the better of all the other living civilizations, and forcibly united them into a single society of literally world-wide range. The revolutionary Western invention was the substitution of the Ocean for the Steppe as the principal medium of world-communication. This use of the Ocean, first by sailing ships and then by steamships, enabled the West to unify the whole inhabited and habitable world, including the Americas. Babur's Farghana had been the central point of a world united by horse-traffic over the Steppe; but in Babur's lifetime the centre of the world made a sudden big jump. From the heart of the Continent it jumped to its extreme western verge, and, after hovering round Seville and Lisbon, it settled for a time in Elizabeth's England. In our own lifetime we have seen this volatile world-centre flit again from London to New York, but this shift to a still more eccentric position on the far side of the 'herring pond' is a local movement, not comparable in magnitude to the jump, in Babur's day, from the steppe-ports of Central Asia to the ocean-ports of the Atlantic. That huge jump was caused by a sudden revolution in the means of locomotion. The steppe-ports were put out of action when the ocean-going sailing-ship superseded the camel and the horse; and now that, under our eyes, the ocean-going steamship is being superseded by the aeroplane we may ask ourselves whether the centre of the world is not likely to jump again—and this time as sensationally as in the sixteenth century—under the impetus of a technological revolution that is at least as radical as the sixteenth-century substitution of da Gama's caravel for Babur's *tipuchaq*. . . .

WORLD OF
WESTERN DOMINANCE,
1763–1914

Chapter Twenty-four

*Basis of dominance:
the scientific revolution*

49

*The distinguished British scholar, Joseph Needham, speculates in the following se-
lection on the roots of the scientific revolution which is the hallmark of Western civilization. His analysis, of which only a fragment is here reproduced, emphasizes the social
dynamism and general aggressiveness of Western mercantile society, and their absence in
China's agrarian bureaucratic civilization. This is similar to his analysis of the contrast
between Portuguese and Chinese overseas enterprise (see above Reading Number 44).**

No question is more difficult than that of historical causation. Yet the development of modern science in Europe in the + 16th and + 17th centuries has either
to be taken as miraculous or to be explained, even if but provisionally and tenta-
tively. This development was not an isolated phenomenon; it occurred *pari passu*
with the Renaissance, the Reformation, and the rise of mercantile capitalism followed by industrial manufacture. It may well be that concurrent social and economic changes supervening only in Europe formed the milieu in which natural
science could rise at last above the level of the higher aritsanate, the semi-
mathematical technicians. The reduction of all quality to quantities, the affirmation
of a mathematical reality behind all appearances, the proclaiming of a space and
time uniform throughout all the universe; was it not analogous to the merchant's
standard of value? No goods or commodities, no jewels or monies there were, but
such as could be computed and exchanged in number, quantity and measure.

Of this there are abundant traces among our mathematicians. The first literary
exposition of the technique of double-entry book-keeping is contained in the best

* Reprinted from J. Needham, "Mathematics and Science in China and the West," *Science
and Society*, XX (Fall 1956), 341–43.

mathematical text-book available at the beginning of the + 16th century, the *Summa de Arithmetica* (+ 1494) of Luca Pacioli. The first application of double-entry book-keeping to the problems of public finance and administration was made in the works of the engineer-mathematician Simon Stevin (+ 1608). Even Copernicus wrote on monetary reform (in his *Monetae Cudendae Ratio* of + 1552). The book of Robert Recorde, in which the equality symbol was first used (*Whetstone of Witte,* + 1557), was dedicated to "The Governors and the reste of the Companie of Venturers into Moscovia," with the wish for "continuall increase of commodities by their travell." Stevin's *Disme* opens with the words "To all astronomers, surveyors, measurers of tapestry, barrels and other things, to all mintmasters and merchants, good luck!" Such examples could be indefinitely multiplied. Commerce and industry were "in the air" as never before.

The problem of the exact relations between modern science and technology and the socio-economic circumstances of its birth constitutes, perhaps, the Great Debate of the history of science in Europe. I believe that in due course the study of parallel civilizations such as that of agrarian-bureaucratic China will throw some light on the events which took place in the West. For example, Koyré, in criticizing the socio-economic theory of the causation of post-Renaissance science, urges, with Cassirer, that there was a purely theoretical current stimulated by the rediscovery of Greek mathematics, and under recognizably Platonic and Pythagorean inspiration. This is doubtless part of the truth. He also urges that the supporters of the socio-economic theory insufficiently allow for what he calls the autonomous evolution of astronomy. But here is the kind of point where it is profitable to compare parallel events in China. The Chinese should have been interested in mechanics for ships, in hydrostatics for their vast canal system (like the Dutch), in ballistics for guns (after all, they had possessed gunpowder three or four centuries before Europe), and in pumps for mines. If they were not, could not the answer be sought in the fact that little or no private profit was to be gained from any of these things in Chinese society, dominated by its imperial bureaucracy? Their techniques and industries . . . were all essentially "traditional," the product of many centuries of slow growth under bureaucratic oppression or at best tutelage, not the creations of enterprising merchant-venturers with big profits in sight. As for astronomy, no organization stood more in need of it than the Chinese imperial court, which by immemorial custom gave forth the calendar to be accepted by all under heaven. And . . . Chinese astronomy was far from negligible. If an "autonomous evolution" of astronomy was ever going to give rise to the mathematization of natural science, it is hard to see why this did not occur, or had not already occurred, in China. If the need had been sufficiently great, there would surely not have been wanting those who could have burst the bonds of the old mathematical notation, and made the discoveries which in fact were only made in Europe. But this was evidently not the force from which modern science could spring, and indigenous Chinese mathematics went down into a kind of tomb, from which the filial care of Mei Ku-Chhêng and his successors only later succeeded in resurrecting it.

Put in another way, there came no vivifying demand from the side of natural science. Interest in Nature was not enough, controlled experimentation was not enough, empirical induction was not enough, eclipse-prediction and calendar-calculation were not enough—all of these the Chinese had. Apparently a mercantile culture alone was able to do what agrarian bureaucratic civilization could not—bring to fusion point the formerly separated disciplines of mathematics and nature-knowledge.

One reason why non-Western peoples found Western civilization so fascinating and impressive was its scientific and technological achievements. This is made strikingly clear in the following passage from the autobiography of a Christian Arab, Edward Atiyah, who was born in Lebanon and spent his childhood in Lebanon, Egypt, and the Sudan. Educated in an English school in Alexandria and later at Oxford University, he had roots in two very different societies; this, together with his sensitive perceptiveness and his writing talents, makes his autobiography an unusually revealing document.*

The mechanical inventions of the West were beginning to invade the Near East about that time [the early twentieth century]. The telegraph and the railway had been there for some time. They were familiar to my generation, but not to the extent that breeds contempt. Now new wonders were appearing. The electric tram, electric light, motor-cars and gramophones. Miracle after miracle, and all invented by Europeans. When you first heard of these strange things you perhaps doubted, but then the miracles arrived and you saw and heard them. There were, too, rumours of stranger, more incredible miracles, of motor-cars that could fly, ships that went under the sea, and telegraphy without wire; and all, all invented by the extremely clever Europeans. Surely the cleverest people in the world, much cleverer than the Orientals who had never invented anything.

Among the factors that wrought for the apotheosis of the West in Eastern minds, the mechanical aspect of European civilization—inventions and scientific appliances —was beyond doubt the most potent. For there was not and never had been anything corresponding to it in the East. Oriental genius had produced great religions, achieved great triumphs in art and literature, constructed colossal empires, but it had never tamed and canned the elements, packed scientific principles into little mechanical parcels. And it happened that while the intellect of awaking Europe was ferreting out and applying the secrets of nature, the East was passing through a phase of decline and somnolence. When therefore this flood of mechanical inventions burst in upon the Near East towards the end of the 19th and the beginning of the 20th century, Easterners were completely dazzled and fascinated by these undreamt-of-wonders and the mysterious power that lay behind them.

I was eleven when I saw the first aeroplane. It was 1914 (just before the war) and we were living at Omdurman. Early in the winter rumours began to go round that a French aviator was coming to Khartoum. No aeroplane had yet visited the Sudan, and so everybody was tremendously excited about it, especially the natives, most of whom at first would not believe that there were such things as aeroplanes. Then the rumours became more and more definite; the name of the aviator was given, the route he was following, the approximate date of his arrival, the place of landing. It was becoming real, imminent. At last the day and the hour were announced; and the whole population of Khartoum, from the Governor-General to

* Reprinted from E. Atiyah, *An Arab Tells His Story* (London: J. Murray, 1946), pp. 29–32, by permission of the publisher.

street boys, assembled to see the miracle. The landing-place was in a stretch of sand some way outside the town, and we went there by cab. I was consumed with excitement. A good many of the natives were still sceptical, thought that there must be some trick afoot, some huge jest. Impossible that a man, a real man, should come in a machine flying like a bird. Impossible.

2 o'clock . . . 2.15 . . . 2.30 . . . Excitement, impatience, doubt. And then a low distant drone, and a black speck in the sky, there, coming from the north. A hush for a second . . . exclamations, jabberings, strained necks, stretched arms. There he is, there he is! Yes . . . No . . . yes . . . no . . . yes, yes, yes. The noise is louder, the speck is bigger. "What? that thing," said a doubting Sudanese standing next to us. "Why it is a vulture, and the noise is coming from the Power Station." But soon all doubt, all argument ceased. The vulture was above our heads, huge as ten eagles, filling the air with its deafening drone, and as it circled down, a human arm stretched out of it and waved to the crowd. The miracle had come off. Several Sudanese falling on their knees with upstretched arms exclaimed: "There is no god but Allah; the Resurrection Day has come."

Before the machine reached the ground, the seething crowd, beyond itself with excitement, had broken through the police cordon, and rushed towards the landing spot. The Governor-General, who according to plan was to advance with becoming dignity towards the machine, and welcome the distinguished aviator, while the watching crowd watched from a respectful distance, had to forget his dignity and advance with hurried steps to be able to get there at all, while the crowd pushed and jostled in its mad eagerness to see this huge artificial bird, and especially the man in it. Was it really a man, this weird-looking creature with its leather head and huge protruding oval eyes, stepping down on to the ground? See, see, he's waving his arm again, he is shaking hands with the Governor-General. *Wallahi zol, zol sahih.* (By God it's a man, a real man!) But even after this, our old Sudanese woman-servant had still some lingering doubts. "Really, Ya Sitt," she asked my mother when we had gone back home, "is it a real man, a *zol* like us, who eats and drinks and gets married?"

The cinema in its early days produced some curious reactions in the more primitive parts of the Sudan. An English friend of mine took with him a film-projector and some films to an out-station in Kordofan. One day he gathered several hundred tribesmen, and treated them to a performance. They squatted out on the sand before the screen, and shouted in great excitement at every picture. One of the films was an animated-drawings story, in which a man attacks a dog with an axe and splits him into two, after which the severed hind part runs along its legs until it catches up the front part, and the dog is thus reintegrated. "By the living God," said one of the spectators of this miracle, "if I hadn't seen it with my own eyes, I should never have believed it." This, of course, was an extreme case of unquestioning credulity in a primitive African. But even in Syria and Egypt, on sophisticated minds with a great civilization in their cultural background, these inventions made a profound impression.

Here was something uncanny, apparently supernatural, and it was entirely the product of Western minds. No conjurer producing rabbits from a hat could have more impressed an assembly of unsophisticated children. The children had yet to learn that the conjurer was no god, and that they too when they grew up, could, if they took the trouble, learn to produce rabbits from a hat. . . .

True, the older and more fanatical Moslems disapproved of these inventions. They looked upon them with aversion and suspicion, as the diabolical contrivances of the Kuffar [Unbelievers], as something alien to Islam and the Koran, since they did not exist when the Prophet of God walked the earth. They scented in them half consciously the coming of a new world, mysterious, pregnant with alarming possibilities, hostile to them because incompatible with their old world, in which they and their ancestors have lived, secure in their faith, untroubled in their beliefs and prejudices. They saw this new world coming, and had the first premonition that their old world, which they had hitherto thought eternal, would soon begin to slip away from under their feet.

Chapter Twenty-five

Basis of dominance:
the Industrial Revolution

51

THE INDUSTRIAL REVOLUTION RECONSIDERED

Europe was transformed by the Industrial Revolution as well as by the scientific. Although the term "Industrial Revolution" has been popular since the late nineteenth century, economic historians increasingly feel that it is a misnomer for what actually occurred. The reasons for their misgivings are set forth in the following article by a distinguished scholar in this field.*

The editor's letter asked for an article on the industrial revolution, "with the view to bringing teachers up to date on newer scholarship and interpretations." So I spent the morning of Thanksgiving Day examining several recent high school or university history or social science texts to see how they handled economic developments. I soon found I had a new reason for being thankful. One *History of Europe* gives 102 pages out of 845 to economic conditions and trends, and another gives 136 pages out of 1024. This is a mighty advance since the 'eighties, when Fyffe wrote over a thousand pages and never mentioned a machine or a railroad. It is even better than conditions were thirty years ago, when the *Cambridge Modern History* included only three economic chapters in its fourteen volumes. The "Manor," the "Commercial Revolution," "Mercantilism," and the "Industrial Revolution" have definitely been admitted to the texts. My daughter tells me she has heard the manor described in five different lecture courses, and I notice that in her prescribed books the famous plan of a "typical manor" has been improved: a stork stands forlornly in the swamp, and the landlord is hunting a deer and a boar— simultaneously—in the Woodland.

* Reprinted from Herbert Heaton, "The Industrial Revolution," *Social Education,* II (March 1938), 159–165, by permission of the author and the National Council for the Social Studies.

This flush of gratitude for the many crumbs that are now falling from the general historian's table is, however, tempered a little by the staleness of some of the crumbs. Even the best of the university texts have provoked me to make several query marks in the margin; and some of the high school books ought to have whole paragraphs or even pages torn out.

.   .   .

Of the "Industrial Revolution," the sharp lines and strong colors—chiefly rose and black—of the old picture have become so blurred that some of us now put the title in quotation marks or avoid using it.

That old picture, painted about 1880 by Arnold Toynbee, is a triptych, or a melodrama in three acts. First there is "The Eve," still, placid, quiet, at the end of a long day that reaches back to the Normans, Nero, or even Noah. The methods of agriculture, industry, and transportation have changed little in a thousand years. Production is carried on by small manufacturers or farmers. The former, like the latter, live in the country, combine industry and agriculture, and supplement the family labor supply by training an apprentice and perhaps employing a journeyman or two. The wage earner usually works, aided by his family, in his own home on materials put out to him by his employer; but he may work under his master's roof. Between master and man is a "warm attachment"; they call each other by their Christian nicknames. The class of capitalist employers is still "in its infancy"; some merchant-employers put out material to be processed in the homes of their employees or of small masters, and a few factories or central workshops exist. But in general the family firm and the family farm prevail. Division of class and of labor is slight. The worker can express his personality in his work, though what happens if it is crooked is not clear. Production is for local markets or for the producer's larder and wardrobe, since defective means of transportation and mercantilistic policies shut off distant consumers. No one earns great rewards, but the domestic system insures on the whole a sound and healthy life under conditions favorable to the development of mind, body, and personal dignity. Contentment spins at the cottage door; there is plenty of honeysuckle, ivy, and good ale in this "quiet world" of "scarcely perceptible movement." A comprehensive code of state regulation of production and trade combines with technical inertia to prevent anything from changing.

Then, with a rapidity known in the tropics, "The Night" falls, a night full of noise and action. Seven men—four Lancashire men (Kay, Hargreaves, Arkwright, and Crompton), two Scots, (Adam Smith and James Watt), and one Episcopalian parson (Cartwright)—invent some textile machines, improve the steam engine, or write *The Wealth of Nations*. Meanwhile other men revolutionize agriculture and redraw the village map, while others improve roads and rivers or cut canals. But it is the seven men who get their names on the record, for their actions or thoughts "destroyed the old world and built a new one." And what they did was crowded into a brief night that lasted from about 1760 to 1780.

Act Three is "The Murky Dawn," in which the effects become visible. It is a period of "economic revolution and anarchy," as machinery and steam overrun industry, and Smith's plea for laissez faire sweeps the statute book clear of the mercantilistic devil. Population is "torn up by the roots" and dragged "from cottages in distant valleys into factories and cities"; independent farmers, expelled from their lands and impoverished by the extension of sheep raising and the inclosure movement, join the small manufacturing master or journeymen in this rural exodus. In the towns a landless propertyless proletariat is the victim of the seven deadly sins of unrestrained inhuman industrial capitalists. The sins are the factory system, long hours, child labor, the exploitation of women, low wages, periodical or chronic unemployment, and slums. If the victims dislike the contrast between their deplorable lot and the fortunes made by fat factory owners; if they object, riot, join labor unions, or become chartists or socialists, they are shot down, put in jail, or sent to Botany Bay. Their economic masters become their political lords by displacing the landowners in the seats of government, and then legislate—or refuse to do so— with one eye on the cashbox and the other on some page of Smith, Ricardo, or Malthus. A dreary, tragic, selfish, sordid dawn! But by lunch time the weather is improving. The exploited grow class-conscious and organized, some employers grow softhearted, laws are passed to permit unions, to regulate child labor, or to provide a better water supply. Mass production makes goods cheaper the corn laws are repealed, Victoria becomes queen, Albert the Good builds the Crystal Palace, and by the time it is opened in 1851 the grim tragedy is promising to turn into whatever the urban counterpart of a pastoral should be called.

This story has got into the general books, and the title for it has become so widely accepted that some wit has said all college courses now begin with the amoeba, Aristotle, or the industrial revolution. That is—all courses except those given by the economic historian, for he is getting more and more suspicious of the name and of the crisp dramatic conception. In the great university schools of economic history, Manchester admits that the name was useful when first adopted but thinks it has now served its turn and can scarcely be applied aptly to a movement which was in preparation for two centuries and then occupied at least one more. Oxford finds there is "no hiatus in economic development, but always a constant tide of progress and change, in which the old is blended almost imperceptibly with the new." Edinburgh chimes in with the remark that "sudden catastrophic change is inconsistent with the slow gradual process of human evolution." Harvard insists that the technological changes of the eighteenth century were "only the completion of tendencies which had been significantly evident since Leonardo da Vinci." Birmingham reinforces this by asserting that the developments between 1760 and 1830 "did but carry further, though on a far greater scale and with far greater rapidity, changes which had been proceeding long before." Cambridge finds the period presents a study in slow motion, and in London they tell the pass students there was an industrial revolution, but tell the honors students there never was any such thing.

These quotations give a composite picture of the revised view of the industrial revolution. Let me put it in three generalizations. (1) Steam and the textile machines did not break in on an almost unchanging world of smallscale slightly capitalistic enterprise. (2) The rate of technical change was *lento* rather than *allegro* for a long time; it took decades or even generations to transform old industries and build up new ones. (3) The social and economic "evils" were not new; they were not as black or as widespread as is usually asserted; their causes were often due to special or non-economic factors; and they were in no small measure offset by a substantial improvement in the real wages and living standards of a large part of the wage-earning population. Sentimental unhistorical hysteria is not a good approach to a problem, whether present or past, but it dominated much of the discussion a hundred years ago and the description of a hundred years ago.

Let me elaborate these three contentions. In Toynbee's day little was known of sixteenth-century economic life, and little of any eighteenth-century industry except textiles. Now we know that during this period there were important changes in methods of production, and a quickening spirit of scientific inquiry and of inventive curiosity. New methods of extracting and refining metals were discovered;

the preparation of silk yarn, the knitting of hose, the weaving of ribbons, the making of clocks, the finishing of cloth, all obtained new or improved equipment, as did shipbuilding, brewing, mining, sugar refining, and the manufacture of chemicals. The harnessing of wind, water, and animal power was made more efficient, and coal was used in increasing quantities by industries which needed heat. Professor Nef has shown that England had an industrial revolution between 1540 and 1640, and that the rate of technical change was possibly as striking during the age of Shakespeare as during that of Wordsworth or Byron. Holland, Sweden, France, and England alike contributed to technical progress, and by 1700 scientists, especially physicists, had learned enough to be able to answer some questions asked by industrialists. True, some industries or processes stood still, and spinning and weaving did not change much; but many were on the march.

At the same time the organization of production was changing. Small craftsmen did not have the capital necessary for some of the new equipment, or for bridging the long gap between buying raw material and getting paid for the finished article by a dilatory or distant customer. Hence where materials were costly or came from afar, where equipment was expensive, where the market was large or distant, the initiative had to be taken by merchants or large producers. Some of them bought the raw materials and put them out to be processed by small masters or by wage earners. Sometimes they supplied the equipment as well and paid the master only for his labor, just as he in turn might pay wages to his journeymen. Some of them gathered workers in, because the material could not be put out. You could not put out coal mining, smelting, sugar refining, building, cloth finishing, shipbuilding, calico printing, or the making of glass, bricks, paper, leather, or gunpowder. As these industries grew, so did the number of persons working for wages in their employer's plant; and the combined expansion of putting out and gathering in had created a large propertyless proletariat long before 1760. It may be true that in 1640 the great majority of industrial workers 'laboured in their homes, in town cellars or garrets, or in village cottages. But that majority was by no means so overwhelming as has been supposed" (Nef) and was declining rapidly before a flying shuttle flew or a spinning jenny was devised, even in Lancashire cotton production. Wherever men worked, many of them were wage earners.

If they were, their wages tended to be low; but so were all returns in an age of low productivity. Their hours were long—twelve or more a day—but so were those of their employers and of independent workers, since the rate of production was so slow. Their children and their wives had to work, for every scrap of labor was needed; but so did all children and wives, except those of the rich. Unemployment was frequent and severe, industrial diseases and accidents were common, living and working conditions were often dank, unhealthy, and malodorous, whether in town or village. Labor unions were formed, class conflicts occurred, and the state usually took the employers' side.

This sketch of the period before 1760 takes much of the melodrama out of the next seventy years. Some of the remainder disappears, when we examine the pace at which the textile machines and the improved steam engines were adopted. The cotton industry, which was the scene of the famous inventions, has been used as a sample case. But it was not typical; various factors, such as the newness of the industry, the suitability of the cotton fiber for mechanical treatment, and the great market existing for cheap cotton cloth, prevent the story of cotton from being typical of the changes in industry at large. The transfer from domestic hand spinning of cotton to factory machine spinning was rapid—a matter of about twenty years. By 1815 "the power loom was entering into effective rivalry with the hand loom in the cotton industry, though another generation was to elapse before the battle was finally decided." . . . But cotton was a lonely hare in an industrial world of tortoises. It loomed far less large in that world than it has done in the textbooks, for even in the 1830's the number of its employees was only two-thirds that of the number of female domestic servants.

When we get our eyes off this exception, we find the pace of change in the rest of industry much more sedate. Wool spinning, on hand jennies instead of on wheels, was still being done in Yorkshire homes in 1850. Power looms had not seriously threatened the woolen hand weaver at that date; the transfer from hand to power weaving came quietly during the next twenty-five years, but even in 1877 I find one manufacturer contending that the old method was as cheap as the new. As for steam power, Watt had only 320 of his engines at work in England in 1800, and in 1830 a quarter of the power used by cotton mills was still drawn from water-wheels. Mining had no great technical change, but a series of little ones. Building remained a manual industry until the concrete mixer came. The pottery industry relied less on machinery than on other factors. Clothes making, glass blowing, and printing were late in getting mechanical equipment, while mechanical engineering only slowly developed the tools it needed for shaping metal parts cheaply and accurately. In 1850 everything was not over except the shouting. Cheap steel, cheap lubricants, industrial chemistry, and cheap electricity were still to come. The railroad had won its battle, but the steamship was still fighting its sailing rival, even on the North Atlantic. Away from Lancashire and the railroad tracks, technical change between 1760 and 1850 had been gradual, slow, and unspectacular.

What then of the social and economic consequences and of the seven deadly sins? In the first place, if we leave out one or two exceptional industries or areas, people were not torn loose from a rural life of pleasant and virtually independent enterprise and plunged almost overnight into the horrible existence of an urban factory slum-dwelling proletariat. Many of them were already proletarian; many of them already lived in industrial towns which now grew large or in villages which grew into towns; and some of them already worked under the employer's roof. For them there was not much shift of habitat or of economic class. There was little mass migration, and little long distance movement, except by the Irish, who swarmed into England before they swarmed into North America, and who made many labor and urban problems much more acute than they would otherwise have been.

In the second place, before we beat our anger to white heat in describing the slums, the foul streets, the smoke-laden atmosphere, the lack of water or sanitation, the ravages of disease, etc., let us remember three controlling considerations. (a) Technical. Cheap bricks, cheap sewer or water pipes, and cheap house fixtures were not available till at least 1840, and knowledge concerning public health was still scanty. Compare conditions in the industrial towns with those of non-industrial communities or with rural housing facilities; then it is evident that the housing and sanitary short-comings of the manufacturing districts were not wholly due to the new machinery and the factory system. (b) Constitutional. Until 1835 no town government had adequate powers to cope with the new urban problems. (c) Economic. The provision of houses was never, until recent years, regarded as a public duty. It was left to private enterprise and the stimulus of investment or speculation. The potential builder considered whether his capital would yield a better return in houses than in the many other fields that were thirsty for capital; and the amount he put into a dwelling was limited by what the tenant could afford to pay. In one English town 76 per cent of the houses were rented at a dollar a week or less in 1839; the total capital outlay for one house could not be more than six hundred dollars. In view of the western world's housing impasse since 1914, we must speak more kindly of the builder who a century ago put a roof over the head of the poor, without the aid of mass-produced materials, machinery, or government subsidies.

In the third place, few of the factory working conditions were new. Not even the discipline of fixed hours of work was new to industries which had been conducted in central workshops. Night work may have been new, but long and late hours were not. The cruel treatment of some children by foremen was a personal matter; parents had not been free from it in the domestic workshop, and it was part of that streak of cruelty common in prisons, the army and navy, schools, and homes. The thing that was new and revolutionary was not the "evils," but the discovery that they were evils. For that we have to thank those employers who were heartless. We have to thank the factory for making noticeable in the mass what had been ignored in scattered small instances. We can thank onlookers, whether lay or ecclesiastic, and even Tory politicians who saw in factory conditions a new whip with which to flog their Whig industrial opponents. Finally, much credit must go to those employers—and they were many—who treated their workers decently. These men belonged to that growing army of humanitarians who cleaned up slavery, made the penal code less fierce, welcomed the attack on excessive drinking, pushed the cause of education, built hospitals, dispensaries, and charitable institutions, organized the relief of the unemployed in depressed days, established good working conditions, and fought for better factory laws and better town government.

One final comment may help us to understand better the years between 1760 and 1830. Twenty-six of those years (1789–1815) were dominated by the emotions and strain of the French Revolution and the Napoleonic war, and sixteen of them (1815–1830) were filled with the task of readjustment after a generation of war. The first period was torn by the fear of Jacobinism and the stress of war and famine. There could be little tolerance of mutterings of social discontent or of organized protest during those years; and there was little time to think of domestic problems. The second period we understand better because we have lived through a similar one. The legacies of war were high prices which collapsed, high interest rates and taxes which did not, a scarcity of houses, wide agrarian distress, a disarranged currency, a chaotic credit system, economic nationalism, choked trade channels, prohibitive tariffs, demobilized soldiers without jobs, and so forth. Much that has been blamed on the economic transition was not new, and much of the rest has to be put on the shoulders of the war. The remarkable thing is that by 1830 British opinion had got rid of most of its war phobias and was tackling its problems realistically and constructively by a combination of voluntary organization and state action. If anything was rapid and revolutionary in this whole period it was the change in outlook that between 1824 and 1835 removed the ban on labor organization, passed an effective factory act, reformed the poor law, lowered the tariff wall, made a hole in the navigation laws, remodelled urban government, reformed the House of Commons, liberated the slaves, emancipated Roman Catholics, fashioned a good banking system, and sowed the seeds of national education, trade unionism, and the cooperative movement.

Behind all this was the intense energy of manufacturers and merchants who, either with old equipment or new, enterprised and adventured. This energy is denounced by some as "an orgy of soulless cupidity," and praised by others as "a triumph of the spirit of enterprise." In general it was a bit of both. Cupidity, yes, as in all ages and occupations. Enterprise, yes, but not always triumphant, for the field was strewn with the wreckage of men who failed. When the classical economists said profit was the reward of risk and interest the reward of abstinence, they meant it. Not the abstinence that today would lead a man to pick a Buick for his twelfth car instead of a Rolls Royce, but one which meant meager living and the ploughing back of every spare penny into the business. As for risk, some day somebody will study the industrial revolution through the bankruptcy records; but we know enough to realize on what a treacherous sea the entrepreneur launched his tiny bark.

How does all this affect the teacher's presentation of economic aspects of modern Europe? It takes out some of the heroics—and the villainics, if I can coin a word—it cuts down the pace, and leaves the tale that of a trend rather than of a tumult. But there is enough left, and space has been made available for more that is of first class importance. Any survey of the making of modern Europe should have something to say about the gradual industrialization of parts of the continent, including the effect of hydro-electricity, industrial chemistry, and post-Bessemer metallurgical developments; the emergence of intensive agriculture; the effect of good roads, canals, railroads, steamships, and refrigeration; the end of serfdom in other countries than Russia and the evolution of an efficient peasant proprietor economy; the growing need for more capital and better banking; the unprecedented growth of population and the mass migration of 50,000,000 Europeans to other continents in a century; the steady advance of voluntary association and the influence of the social conscience in producing the social service state; the instability of a complex capitalistic system in a world economy; the twentyfold increase in the value of world trade; the impact of the new world on the old; and the ability of Europe to raise greatly the standard of living of an expanding population, thanks to better technique, better organization, and freedom for a hundred years from Armageddon. And if textbooks must have illustrations, I would dispense with pictures of the spinning jenny, Louis Blanc, and even Karl Marx, if thereby I had room for two graphs, one of the movement of general prices and one of the business cycle. These two would explain a lot of social, political, and even diplomatic history.

52   ENGLAND'S LEADERSHIP IN INDUSTRIALIZATION

The fact that England led the world in industrialization is of first-rate historical significance. It explains in large part England's primacy in world affairs in the nineteenth century. Contemporary observers were aware of the importance of the industrialization process and a few of them speculated as to why it occurred first in England. One of the soundest analyses is contained in the following selection, found in a history of the British cotton industry published in 1835.* This analysis does not deal with all the factors that we are aware of today with the advantage of historical insight. Yet it is a sound interpretation which reveals a thorough understanding of current developments in England and on the continent.

The history of civilization consists greatly in the history of the USEFUL ARTS. These arts form the basis of social improvement. By their means men are raised above abject want, become possessed of comforts and luxuries, and acquire the

* Reprinted from Edward Baines, *History of the Cotton Manufacturers in Great Britain* (London, 1835), pp. 5–7, 85–89.

246

leisure necessary to cultivate the higher departments of knowledge. There is also an intimate connexion between the arts and natural science. Mutually aiding each other, they go hand in hand in the course of improvement. The manufactory, the laboratory, and the study of the natural philosopher, are in close practical conjunction. Without the aid of science, the arts would be contemptible: without practical application, science would consist only of barren theories, which men would have no motive to pursue.

These remarks apply with peculiar force to the arts by which clothing is produced, and, above all, to the Cotton Manufacture of England, which is the very creature of mechanical invention and chemical discovery, and which has, in its turn, rendered the most important service to science, as well as increased the wealth and power of the country.

The subject of this volume may therefore claim attention from the man of science and the political philosopher, as well as from the manufacturer and merchant. To trace the origin and progress of so great a manufacture, with the causes of that progress, is more worthy the pains of the student, than to make himself acquainted with the annals of wars and dynasties, or with nineteen-twentieths of the matters which fill the pages of history.

The Cotton Manufacture of England presents a spectacle unparalleled in the annals of industry, whether we regard the suddenness of its growth, the magnitude which it has attained, or the wonderful inventions to which its progress is to be ascribed. Within the memory of many now living, those machines have been brought into use, which have made as great a revolution in manufactures as the art of printing effected in literature. Within the same period, the Cotton Manufacture of this country has sprung up from insignificance, and has attained a greater extent than the manufactures of wool and linen combined, though these have existed for centuries.

Sixty years since, our manufacturers consumed little more than THREE millions lbs. of raw cotton annually; the annual consumption is now TWO HUNDRED AND EIGHTY million lbs. In 1750 the county of Lancaster, the chief seat of the trade, had a population of only 297,400; in 1831, the number of its inhabitants had swelled to 1,336,854. A similar increase has taken place in Lanarkshire, the principal seat of the manufacture in Scotland. The families supported by this branch of industry are estimated to comprise A MILLION AND A HALF of individuals; and the goods produced not only furnish a large part of the clothing consumed in this kingdom, but supply nearly one-half of the immense export trade of Britain, find their way into all the markets of the world, and are even destroying in the Indian market the competition of the ancient manufacture of India itself, the native country of the raw material, and the earliest seat of the art.

The causes of this unexampled extension of manufacturing industry are to be found in a series of splendid inventions and discoveries, by the combined effect of which a spinner now produces as much yarn in a day, as by the old processes he could have produced in a year; and cloth, which formerly required six or eight months to bleach, is now bleached in a few hours.

It is the object of this volume to record the rise, progress, and present state of this great manufacture;—briefly to notice its ancient history in the East, and its sluggish and feeble progress in other countries, until the era of invention in England. . . .

·   ·   ·

The natural and physical advantages of England for manufacturing industry are probably superior to those of every other country on the globe. The district where those advantages are found in the most favourable combination, is the southern part of Lancashire, and the south-western part of Yorkshire, the former of which has become the principal seat of the manufacture of cotton. In the counties of Cheshire, Derbyshire, and Nottinghamshire, and in Renfrewshire and Lanarkshire, in Scotland, all of which districts are likewise seats of this branch of industry, advantages of a similar nature are found, though not in such close concentration as in Lancashire.

Three things may be regarded as of primary importance for the successful prosecution of manufactures, namely, water-power, fuel, and iron. Wherever these exist in combination, and where they are abundant and cheap, machinery may be manufactured and put in motion at small cost; and most of the processes of making and finishing cloth, whether chemical or mechanical, depending, as they do, mainly on the two great agents of water and heat, may likewise be performed with advantage.

The tract lying between the Ribble and the Mersey is surrounded on the east and north by high ranges of hills, and has also hills of some magnitude in the hundreds of Blackburn and Salford; owing to which cause the district is intersected by a great number of streams, which descend rapidly from their sources towards the level tract in the west. In the early part of their course, these streams and streamlets furnish water-power adequate to turn many hundred mills: they afford the element of water, indispensable for scouring, bleaching, printing, dyeing, and other processes of manufacture: and when collected in their larger channels, or employed to feed canals, they supply a superior inland navigation, so important for the transit of raw materials and merchandise.

Not less important for manufactures than the copious supply of good water, is the great abundance of coal found in the very same district. Beds of this invaluable mineral lie beneath almost the whole surface of Blackburn and Salford hundreds, and run into West Derby to within a few miles of Liverpool; and being near the surface, so as to yield their treasures easily, they are incomparably more fertile sources of wealth than mines of silver and gold. It is superfluous to remark that this mineral fuel animates the thousand arms of the steam-engine, and furnishes the most powerful agent in all chemical and mechanical operations.

Of the equally indispensable metal, iron, the southern part of Lancashire is nearly destitute; but being at no great distance from the iron districts of Staffordshire, Warwickshire, Yorkshire, Furness, and Wales, with all of which it has ready communication by inland or coasting navigation, it is as abundantly and almost as cheaply supplied with this material, as if the iron was got within its own boundaries.

In mentioning the advantages which Lancashire possesses as a seat of manufactures, we must not omit its ready communication with the sea by means of its well-situated port, Liverpool, through the medium of which it receives, from Ireland, a large proportion of the food that supports its population, and whose commerce brings from distant shores the raw materials of its manufactures, and again distributes them, converted into useful and elegant clothing, amongst all the nations of the earth. Through the same means a plentiful supply of timber is obtained, so needful for building purposes.

To the above natural advantage of a canal communication, which ramifies itself through all the populous parts of this county, and connects it with the inland counties, the seats of other flourishing manufactures, and the sources whence iron, lime, salt, stone, and other articles in which Lancashire is deficient, are obtained. By this means Lancashire, being already possessed of the primary requisites for manufactures, is enabled, at a very small expense, to command things of secondary importance, and to appropriate to its use the natural advantages of the whole kingdom. The canals, having been accomplished by individual enterprise, not by national funds, were constructed to supply a want already existing: they were not, therefore, original sources of the manufactures, but have extended together with them, and are to be considered as having essentially aided and accelerated that prosperity from whose beginnings they themselves arose. The recent introduction of railways will have a great effect in making the operations of trade more intensely active, and perfecting the division of labour, already carried to so high a point. By the railway and the locomotive engine, the extremities of the land will, for every beneficial purpose, be united.

In comparing the advantages of England for manufactures with those of other countries, we can by no means overlook the excellent commercial position of the country—intermediate between the north and south of Europe; and its insular situation, which, combined with the command of the seas, secures our territory from invasion or annoyance. The German ocean, the Baltic, and the Mediterranean are the regular highways for our ships; and our western ports command an unobstructed passage to the Atlantic, and to every quarter of the world.

A temperate climate, and a hardy race of men, have also greatly contributed to promote the manufacturing industry of England.

The political and moral advantages of this country, as a seat of manufactures, are not less remarkable than its physical advantages. The arts are the daughters of peace and liberty. In no country have these blessings been enjoyed in so high a degree, or for so long a continuance, as in England. Under the reign of just laws, personal liberty and property have been secure; mercantile enterprise has been allowed to reap its reward; capital has accumulated in safety; the workman has "gone forth to his work and to his labour until the evening"; and, thus protected and favoured, the manufacturing prosperity of the country has struck its roots deep, and spread forth its branches to the ends of the earth.

England has also gained by the calamities of other countries, and the intolerance of other governments. At different periods, the Flemish and French protestants, expelled from their native lands, have taken refuge in England, and have repaid the protection given them by practising and teaching branches of industry, in which the English were then less expert than their neighbours. The wars which have at different times desolated the rest of Europe, and especially those which followed the French revolution, (when mechanical invention was producing the most wonderful effects in England,) checked the progress of manufacturing improvement on the continent, and left England for many years without a competitor. At the same time, the English navy held the sovereignty of the ocean, and under its protection the commerce of this country extended beyond all former bounds, and established a firm connexion between the manufacturers of Lancashire and their customers in the most distant lands.

When the natural, political, and adventitious causes, thus enumerated, are viewed together, it cannot be matter of surprise that England has obtained a preeminence over the rest of the world in manufactures.

Chapter Twenty-six

Basis of dominance:
the political revolution

53   SIGNIFICANCE OF THE ENGLISH REVOLUTION

In addition to the scientific and industrial revolutions, Europe was transformed in modern times by the political revolution. By this is meant the ending of the assumption of a divinely ordained division of mankind into rulers and ruled. Instead, the masses of the people gradually awakened and increasingly participated in governmental processes. One of the earliest manifestations of this political revolution was the English Revolution of the seventeenth century.

The significance of the English Revolution is that it defined and implemented the principles of liberalism, which were, at that time, primarily freedom of religion and security of person and of property. But the English Revolution, like the French, witnessed a split between moderate and radical elements. The latter, known as the Levellers, wished to democratize liberalism by basing it on the principle of the inherently equal rights of all individuals, regardless of birth or property, and they prepared the document An Agreement of the People *(1647) which represents the first systematic exposition of democratic liberalism. This type of liberalism was resolutely opposed by Cromwell and his followers, who were willing to accept equality before the law but not before the ballot box. What lay behind this conflict is apparent in the following selections, the first being the text of* An Agreement of the People, *and the second, a sampling of the debate over the* Agreement.**

---

* Reprinted from A. S. P. Woodhouse, *Puritanism and Liberty* (London: J. M. Dent & Sons Ltd., 1938), pp. 53–59, 63, 69–70, 443–445, by permission of The University of Chicago Press and J. M. Dent & Sons Ltd.

I. That the people of England, being at this day very unequally distributed by counties, cities, and boroughs, for the election of their deputies in Parliament, ought to be more indifferently proportioned, according to the number of the inhabitants; the circumstances whereof, for number, place, and manner, are to be set down before the end of this present Parliament.

II. That to prevent the many inconveniences apparently arising from the long continuance of the same persons in authority, this present Parliament be dissolved upon the last day of September, which shall be in the year of our Lord 1648.

III. That the people do of course choose themselves a Parliament once in two years, *viz.,* upon the first Thursday in every second March, after the manner as shall be prescribed before the end of this Parliament, to begin to sit upon the first Thursday in April following, at Westminster (or such other place as shall be appointed from time to time by the preceding representatives), and to continue till the last day of September then next ensuing, and no longer.

IV. That the power of this, and all future Representatives of this nation is inferior only to theirs who choose them, and doth extend, without the consent or concurrence of any other person or persons, to the enacting, altering, and repealing of laws; to the erecting and abolishing of offices and courts; to the appointing, removing, and calling to account magistrates and officers of all degrees; to the making war and peace; to the treating with foreign states; and generally to whatsoever is not expressly or impliedly served by the represented to themselves.

Which are as followeth:

1. That matters of religion, and the ways of God's worship, are not at all entrusted by us to any human power, because therein we cannot remit or exceed a title of what our consciences dictate to be the mind of God, without wilful sin; nevertheless the public way of instructing the nation (so it be not compulsive) is referred to their discretion.

2. That the matter of impressing and constraining any of us to serve in the wars is against our freedom, and therefore we do not allow it in our representatives; the rather because money (the sinews of war) being always at their disposal, they can never want numbers of men apt enough to engage in any just cause.

3. That after the dissolution of this present Parliament, no person be at any time questioned for anything said or done in reference to the late public differences, otherwise than in execution of the judgments of the present representatives, or House of Commons.

4. That in all laws made, or to be made, every person may be bound alike, and that no tenure, estate, charter, degree, birth, or place, do confer any exemption from the ordinary course of legal proceedings, whereunto others are subjected.

5. That as the laws ought to be equal, so they must be good, and not evidently destructive to the safety and well-being of the people.

These things we declare to be our native rights, and therefore are agreed and resolved to maintain them with our utmost possibilities against all opposition whatsoever, being compelled thereunto not only by the examples of our ancestors, whose blood was often spent in vain for the recovery of their freedoms, suffering themselves, through fraudulent accommodations, to be still deluded of the fruit of their victories, but also by our own woeful experience, who, having long expected, and dearly earned, the establishment of these certain rules of government, are yet made to depend for the settlement of our peace and freedom upon him that intended our bondage and brought a cruel war upon us.

Debates

MAJOR RAINBOROUGH (Leveller). . . . I think that the poorest he that is in England hath a life to live, as the greatest he; and therefore truly, sir, I think it's clear, that every man that is to live under a government ought first by his own consent to put himself under that government; and I do think that the poorest man in England is not at all bound in a strict sense to that government that he hath not had a voice to put himself under; and I am confident that, when I have heard the reasons against it, something will be said to answer those reasons, insomuch that I should doubt whether he was an Englishman or no, that should doubt of these things.

GENERAL HENRY IRETON (Cromwell's son-in-law). . . . Give me leave to tell you, that if you make this the rule I think you must fly for refuge to an absolute natural right, and you must deny all civil right; and I am sure it will come to that in the consequence. This, I perceive, is pressed as that which is so essential and due: the right of the people of this kingdom, and as they are the people of this kingdom, distinct and divided from other people, and that we must for this right lay aside all other considerations; this is so just, this is so due, this is so right to them. . . . For my part, I think it is no right at all. I think that no person hath a right to an interest or share in the disposing of the affairs of the kingdom, and in determining or choosing those that shall determine what laws we shall be ruled by here —no person hath a right to this, that hath not a permanent fixed interest in this kingdom, and those persons together are properly the represented of this kingdom, and consequently are [also] to make up the representers of this kingdom, who taken together do comprehend whatsoever is of real or permanent interest in the kingdom. And I am sure otherwise I cannot tell what any man can say why a foreigner coming in amongst us—or as many as will coming in amongst us, or by force or otherwise settling themselves here, or at least by our permission having a being here—why they should not as well lay claim to it as any other. We talk of birthright. Truly [by] birthright there is thus much claim. Men may justly have by birthright, by their very being born in England, that we should not seclude them out of England, that we should not refuse to give them air and place and ground, and the freedom of the highways and other things, to live amongst us—not any man that is born here, though by his birth there come nothing at all (that is part of the permanent interest of this kingdom) to him. That I think is due to a man by birth. But that by a man's being born here he shall have a share in that power that shall dispose of the lands here, and of all things here, I do not think it a sufficient ground. I am sure if we look upon that which is the utmost (within [any] man's view) of what was originally the constitution of this kingdom, upon that which is most radical and fundamental, and which if you take away, there is no man hath any land, any goods, [or] any civil interest, that is this: that those that choose the representers for the making of laws by which this state and kingdom are to be governed, are the persons who, taken together, do comprehend the local interest of this kingdom; that is, the persons in whom all land lies, and those in corporations in whom all trading lies. This is the most fundamental constitution of this kingdom and [that] which if you do not allow, you allow none at all. . . .

RAINBOROUGH. . . . I do hear nothing at all that can convince me, why any man that is born in England ought not to have his voice in election of burgesses. It is said that if a man have not a permanent interest, he can have no claim; and [that] we must be no freer than the laws will let us be, and that there is no [law in any] chronicle will let us be freer than that we [now] enjoy. Something was said to this yesterday. I do think that the main cause why Almighty God gave men reason, it was that they should make use of that reason, and that they should improve it for that end and purpose that God gave it them. And truly, I think that half a loaf is better than none if a man be an hungry: [this gift of reason without other property may seem a small thing], yet I think there is nothing that God hath given a man that any [one] else can take from him. And therefore I say, that either it must be the Law of God or the law of man that must prohibit the meanest man in the kingdom to have this benefit as well as the greatest. I do not find anything in the Law of God, that a lord shall choose twenty burgesses, and a gentleman but two, or a poor man shall choose none: I find no such thing in the Law of Nature, nor in the Law of Nations. But I do find that all Englishmen must be subject to English laws, and I do verily believe that there is no man but will say that the foundation of all law lies in the people. . . .

IRETON.   . . . Now I wish we may all consider of what right you will challenge that all the people should have right to elections. Is it by the right of nature? If you will hold forth that as your ground, then I think you must deny all property too, and this is my reason. For thus: by that same right of nature (whatever it be) that you pretend, by which you can say, one man hath an equal right with another to the choosing of him that shall govern him—by the same right of nature, he hath the same [equal] right in any goods he sees—meat, drink, clothes—to take and use them for his sustenance. He hath a freedom to the land, [to take] the ground, to exercise it, till it; he hath the [same] freedom to anything that any one doth account himself to have any propriety in. Why now I say then, if you, against the most fundamental part of [the] civil constitution (which I have now declared), will plead the Law of Nature, that a man should (paramount [to] this, and contrary to this) have a power of choosing those men that shall determine what shall be law in this state, though he himself have no permanent interest in the state, [but] whatever interest he hath he may carry about with him—if this be allowed, [because by the right of nature] we are free, we are equal, one man must have as much voice as another, then show me what step or difference [there is], why [I may not] by the same right [take your property, though not] of necessity to sustain nature. . . .

RAINBOROUGH.   . . . For my part, as I think, *you* forgot something that was in *my* speech, and you do not only yourselves believe that [some] men are inclining to anarchy, but you would make all men believe that. And, sir, to say because a man pleads that every man hath a voice [by right of nature], that therefore it destroys [by] the same [argument all property—this is to forget the Law of God]. That there's a property, the Law of God says it; else why [hath] God made that law, *Thou shalt not steal?* . . . And therefore I think that to that it is fully answered: God hath set down that thing as to propriety with this law of his, *Thou shalt not steal.* And for my part I am against any such thought, and, as for yourselves, I wish you would not make the world believe that we are for anarchy.

CROMWELL.   I know nothing but this, that they that are the most yielding have the greatest wisdom; but really, sir, this is not right as it should be. No man says that you have a mind to anarchy, but [that] the consequence of this rule tends to anarchy, must end in anarchy; for where is there any bound or limit set if you take away this [limit], that men that have no interest but the interest of breathing [shall have no voice in elections]? Therefore I am confident on't, we should not be so hot one with another.

RAINBOROUGH. I know that some particular men we debate with [believe we] are for anarchy.

COLONEL NATHANIEL RICH. I confess [there is weight in] that objection that the Commissary-General last insisted upon; for you have five to one in this kingdom that have no permanent interest. Some men [have] ten, some twenty servants, some more, some less. If the master and servant shall be equal electors, then clearly those that have no interest in the kingdom will make it their interest to choose those that have no interest. It may happen, that the majority may by law, not in a confusion, destroy property; there may be a law enacted, that there shall be an equality of goods and estate. . . .

SEXBY (Leveller). I see that though liberty were our end, there is a degeneration from it. We have engaged in this kingdom and ventured our lives, and it was all for this: to recover our birthrights and privileges as Englishmen; and by the arguments urged there is none. There are many thousands of us soldiers that have ventured our lives; we have had little propriety in the kingdom as to our estates, yet we have had a birthright. But it seems now, except a man hath a fixed estate in this kingdom, he hath no right in this kingdom. I wonder we were so much deceived. If we had not a right to the kingdom, we were mere mercenary soldiers. There are many in my condition, that have as good a condition [as I have]; it may be little estate they have at present, and yet they have as much a [birth] right as those two who are their lawgivers, as any in this place. I shall tell you in a word my resolution. I am resolved to give my birthright to none. Whatsover may come in the way, and [whatsoever may] be thought, I will give it to none. If this thing [be denied the poor], that with so much pressing after [they have sought, it will be the greatest scandal]. There was one thing spoken to this effect; that if the poor and those in low condition [were given their birthright it would be the destruction of this kingdom]. I think this was but a distrust of Providence. I do think the poor and meaner of this kingdom—I speak as in relation [to the condition of soldiers], in which we are—have been the means of the preservation of this kingdom. I say, in their stations, and really I think to their utmost possibility; and their lives have not been [held] dear for purchasing the good of the kingdom. [And now they demand the birthright for which they fought.] Those that act to this end are as free from anarchy or confusion as those that oppose it, and they have the Law of God and the law of their conscience [with them]. . . .

54   SIGNIFICANCE OF THE AMERICAN REVOLUTION

A stirring appraisal of the American Revolution is found in Thomas Paine's Rights of Man *(1791), written in reply to Edmund Burke's denunciatory* Reflections on the French Revolution. *Paine's work was immediately accepted as a veritable declaration* *of the rights of man rather than as a mere rejoinder to Burke. The English political philosopher William Godwin, who had secured an early copy, exclaimed enthusiastically: "I have got it! It this do not cure my cough, it is a damned perverse mule of a cough." Paine had had similar success with his earlier work,* Common Sense, *which had contributed appreciably to the outbreak of the American Revolution. His extraordinary effectiveness as a polemicist stemmed from the fact that he made preaching democracy democratic. He shunned the sonorous language of Parliament and affected no refinements of scholarship, as is evident in the following passages from his* Rights of Man.**

What Archimedes said of the mechanical powers, may be applied to Reason and Liberty: "Had we," said he, "a place to stand upon, we might raise the world."

The revolution of America presented in politics what was only theory in mechanics. So deeply rooted were all the governments of the old world, and so effectually had the tyranny and the antiquity of habit established itself over the mind, that no beginning could be made in Asia, Africa, or Europe, to reform the political condition of man. Freedom had been hunted round the globe; reason was considered as rebellion; and the slavery of fear had made men afraid to think.

But such is the irresistible nature of truth, that all it asks, and all its wants, is the liberty of appearing. The sun needs no inscription to distinguish him from darkness; and no sooner did the American governments display themselves to the world, than despotism felt a shock, and man begin to contemplate redress.

The independence of America, considered merely as a separation from England, would have been a matter but of little importance, had it not been accompanied by a revolution in the principles and practice of governments. She made a stand, not for herself only, but for the world, and looked beyond the advantages herself could receive. Even the Hessian, though hired to fight against her, may live to bless his defeat; and England, condemning the viciousness of its government, rejoice in its miscarriage.

As America was the only spot in the political world, where the principles of universal reformation could begin, so also was it the best in the natural world. An assemblage of circumstances conspired, not only to give birth, but to add gigantic maturity to its principles. The scene which that country presents to the eye of a spectator, has something in it which generates and encourages great ideas. Nature appears to him in magnitude. The mighty objects he beholds, act upon his mind by enlarging it, and he partakes of the greatness he contemplates.—Its first settlers were emigrants from different European nations, and of diversified professions of religion, retiring from the governmental persecutions of the old world, and meeting in the new, not as enemies, but as brothers. The wants which necessarily accompany the cultivation of a wilderness produced among them a state of society, which countries, long harassed by the quarrels and intrigues of governments, had neglected to cherish. In such a situation man becomes what he ought. He sees his species, not with the inhuman idea of a natural enemy, but as kindred; and the example shews to the artificial world, that man must go back to Nature for information.

From the rapid progress which America makes in every species of improvement,

* Reprinted from Thomas Paine, *Rights of Man, Part the Second Combining Principle and Practice* (London, 1792), pp. 1–5.

it is rational to conclude, that if the governments of Asia, Africa, and Europe, had begun on a principle similar to that of America, or had not been very early corrupted therefrom, that those countries must, by this time, have been in a far superior condition to what they are. Age after age has passed away, for no other purpose than to behold their wretchedness.—Could we suppose a spectator who knew nothing of the world, and who was put into it merely to make his observations, he would take a great part of the old world to be new, just struggling with the difficulties and hardships of an infant settlement. He could not suppose that the hordes of miserable poor, with which old countries abound, could be any other than those who had not yet had time to provide for themselves. Little would he think they were the consequence of what in such countries is called government.

If from the more wretched parts of the old world, we look at those which are in an advanced stage of improvement, we still find the greedy hand of government thrusting itself into every corner and crevice of industry, and grasping the spoil of the multitude. Invention is continually exercised, to furnish new pretences for revenue and taxation. It watches prosperity as its prey, and permit none to escape without a tribute.

As revolutions have begun, (and as the probability is always greater against a thing beginning, than of proceeding after it has begun), it is natural to expect that other revolutions will follow. The amazing and still increasing expences with which old governments are conducted, the numerous wars they engage in or provoke, the embarrassments they throw in the way of universal civilization and commerce, and the oppression and usurpation they practice at home, have wearied out the patience, and exhausted the property of the world. In such a situation, and with the examples already existing, revolutions are to be looked for. They are become subjects of universal conversation, and may be considered as the Order of the day.

If systems of government can be introduced, less expensive, and more productive of general happiness, than those which have existed, all attempts to oppose their progress will in the end be fruitless. Reason, like time, will make its own way, and prejudice will fall in a combat with interest. If universal peace, civilization, and commerce, are ever to be the happy lot of man, it cannot be accomplished but by a revolution in the system of governments. All the monarchical governments are military. War is their trade, plunder and revenue their objects. While such governments continue, peace has not the absolute security of a day. What is the history of all monarchical governments, but a disgustful picture of human wretchedness, and the accidental respite of a few years repose? Wearied with war, and tired with human butchery, they sat down to rest, and called it peace. This certainly is not the condition that Heaven intended for man; and if *this be monarchy,* well might monarchy be reckoned among the sins of the Jews.

The revolutions which formerly took place in the world, had nothing in them that interested the bulk of mankind. They extended only to a change of persons and measures, but not of principles, and rose or fell among the common transactions of the moment. What we now behold, may not improperly be called a *"counter revolution."* Conquest and tyranny, at some early period, dispossessed man of his rights, and he is now recovering them. And as the tide of all human affairs has its ebb and flow in directions contrary to each other, so also is it in this. Government founded in a *moral theory, on a system of universal peace, on the indefeasible hereditary Rights of Man,* is now revolving from west to east, by a stronger impulse than the government of the sword revolved from east to west. It interests not particular individuals, but nations, in its progress, and promises a new era to the human race.

256

The essence of the French Revoluton is summarized in the Declaration of the Rights of Man and the Citizen,* *a statement of principles, or a bill of rights, adopted on August 26, 1789, as a preamble to a new constitution that was being drawn up by the National Assembly. The* Declaration, *with its ringing proclamation of the rights of the individual, reflects the influence of the English and the American revolutions, but it also reflects the dominant role of the bourgeoisie in its explicit enunciation of the rights of property. Robespierre, the Jacobin leader, observed, "You have . . . afford[ed] the largest possible latitude to the right to use one's property, and yet you have not added a word in limitation of this right, with the result that your* Declaration of the Rights of Man *might make the impression of having been created not for the poor, but for the rich, the speculators, for the stock exchange jobbers." Nevertheless, the* Declaration *was, in the words of a French historian, "the death certificate of the old regime." It was even more than this, for the document was translated into dozens of languages and it propagated the principles of the French Revolution throughout Europe, and eventually throughout the world.*

The Representatives of the people of France, formed into a National Assembly, considering that ignorance, neglect, or contempt of human rights, are the sole causes of public misfortunes and corruptions of Government, have resolved to set forth, in a solemn declaration, these natural, imprescriptible, and unalienable rights: that this declaration being constantly present to the minds of the members of the body social, they may be ever kept attentive to their rights and their duties: that the acts of the legislative and executive powers of Government, being capable of being every moment compared with the end of political institutions, may be more respected: and also, that the future claims of the citizens, being directed by simple and incontestible principles, may always tend to the maintenance of the Constitution, and the general happiness.

For these reasons, the National Assembly doth recognize and declare, in the presence of the Supreme Being, and with the hope of his blessing and favour, the following sacred rights of men and of citizens:

I. Men are born, and always continue, free, and equal in respect of their rights. Civil distinctions, therefore, can be founded only on public utility.

II. The end of all political associations is the preservation of the natural and imprescriptible rights of man; and these rights are liberty, property, security, and resistance of oppression.

III. The nation is essentially the source of all sovereignty; nor can any Individual, or Any Body of Men, be entitled to any authority which is not expressly derived from it.

IV. Political Liberty consists in the power of doing whatever does not injure another. The exercise of the natural rights of every man, has no other limits than those which are necessary to secure to every other man the free exercise of the same rights; and these limits are determinable only by the law.

V. The law ought to prohibit only actions hurtful to society. What is not

---

* Cited in Thomas Paine, *Rights of Man: Being an Answer to Mr. Burke's Attack on the French Revolution* (London, 1791), pp. 116–119.

prohibited by the law, should not be hindered; nor should any one be compelled to that which the law does not require.

VI. The law is an expression of the will of the community. All citizens have a right to concur, either personally, or by their representatives, in its formation. It should be the same to all, whether it protects or punishes; and all being equal in its sight, are equally eligible to all honours, places, and employments, according to their different abilities, without any other distinction than that created by their virtues and talents.

VII. No man should be accused, arrested, or held in confinement, except in cases determined by the law, and according to the forms which it has prescribed. All who promote, solicit, execute, or cause to be executed, arbitrary orders, ought to be punished, and every citizen called upon, or apprehended by virtue of the law, ought immediately to obey, and renders himself culpable by resistance.

VIII. The law ought to impose no other penalties but such as are absolutely and evidently necessary: and no one ought to be punished, but in virtue of a law promulgated before the offence, and legally applied.

IX. Every man being presumed innocent till he has been convicted, whenever his detention becomes indispensable, all rigour to him, more than is necessary to secure his person, ought to be provided against by the law.

X. No man ought to be molested on account of his opinions, not even on account of his religious opinions, provided his avowal of them does not disturb the public order established by the law.

XI. The unrestained communication of thoughts and opinions being one of the most precious rights of man, every citizen may speak, write, and publish freely, provided he is responsible for the abuse of this liberty in cases determined by the law.

XII. A public force being necessary to give security to the rights of men and of citizens, that force is instituted for the benefit of the community, and not for the particular benefit of the persons with whom it is entrusted.

XIII. A common contribution being necessary for the support of the public force, and for defraying the other expenses of government, it ought to be divided equally among the members of the community, according to their abilities.

XIV. Every citizen has a right, either by himself or his representative, to a free voice in determining the necessity of public contributions, the appropriation of them, and their amount, mode of assessment, and duration.

XV. Every community has a right to demand of all its agents, an account of their conduct.

XVI. Every community in which a separation of powers and a security of rights is not provided for, wants a constitution.

XVII. The right to property being inviolable and sacred, no one ought to be deprived of it, except in cases of evident public necessity, legally ascertained, and on condition of a previous just indemnity.

Chapter Twenty-seven

Impact of dominance: Russia

TRADITIONAL RUSSIA   56

Because of her geographic location and historic ties, Russia was the first country to experience the impact of the dynamic West. To appreciate the significance of this impact it is necessary to understand the nature of traditional Russia—the Russia of the peasants in the countless villages that dotted the immense Eurasian plain. Dr. John Rickman has left a remarkable picture of these peasants on the basis of his experiences as a country doctor with the Friends Relief in southern Russia between 1916 and 1918.*

Iron

The peasants were desperately poor and their standard of living was low. When the crops were bad they starved, when good they filled out again; but even a succession of good seasons did not raise them out of their sunken condition of endless struggle for the barest living. Four factors in about equal degree united to keep them down. Their religion told them that suffering was acceptable in God's sight, and their Church, which fattened on their offerings, made return by an education better in Old Church Slavonic than in modern Russian and arithmetic. Their Temporal Rulers, even more rapacious than their Spiritual, taxed the poor almost to starving-point while allowing the rich to go almost duty-free—a business error which the Church never makes. In addition the Czarist régime opposed initiative on the ground that it was conducive to revolution, so that an enterprising villager who went about picking up ideas, even though only on farming, was suspect.

A third factor was their ill health. Undernourishment and lack of drugs, ignorance of hygiene and the belief that illness was from God, kept them more inert

---

* Reprinted from G. Gorer and J. Rickman, *The People of Great Russia: A Psychological Study* (New York: W. W. Norton, 1962), pp. 23–25, 44–51, by permission of W. W. Norton & Company, Inc. Copyright 1949 by the Cresset Press, Ltd.; 1962 by Geoffrey Gorer.

259

than they should have been. At times they rose like giants to great feats of toil, but like sick people the world over, they had not the capacity for a sustained activity which at the same time called for initiative. They were not lazy, but their grasp of new ideas, a new technique, was slow and feeble; the external world did not seem to them to be theirs to master.

A fourth factor lay in the unwillingness of the villagers to allow competition among themselves; as members of a community they must all think alike and act alike. The sharing of almost every task encouraged a certain handiness at many crafts but discouraged the development of outstanding skill in any one. It was against the village spirit to compel respect for any achievement that all could not in fairly close degree emulate. Peasants in other parts of Russia had village industries, here there were none. Those who felt an itch to be doing more or better than their neighbors found their way to the towns, returning for the harvests, and going thier ways when country duties were over.

. . .

Here follows a small piece of amateurish 'field work', as anthropologists might call it which though not strictly medical, nevertheless could not easily have been carried out except by a doctor (or a priest) since no other persons had the privilege, accorded only to "one of us," to enter the houses without knocking, and whose presence did not create a class-consciousness or sense of being Visited.

I set out to make a survey of the consumption of iron, and I will give at once my estimate of it in the poorest village that I visited, viz. about five pounds per head per generation! When I added the ounces up and divided by the number surviving in the village during the previous thirty years as near as one could estimate, that was the astonishing result. With this small consumption that community kept even in its struggle with nature. Through constant wear, loss by rust and burning away by heat, renewals of this (to them) most precious metal are needed from time to time. But iron is hard and elastic, it gives under strain and does not often snap, breakages were not common and such was the care lavished on the metal that very little was lost through carelessness and the consumption was due almost wholly to wear. When I add that on a rougher estimate but on the same basis, rather more than six hundred pounds of wood was used it will be seen how near the raw earth these people lived.

. . .

Placenta Praevia

A note came one day from a nurse who was working in an outlying village to say that a patient under her care who was before long expecting a child had begun to bleed; the case looked serious and would I come at once.

An examination showed that her urgent summons was justified but that if we took immediate steps the woman could probably be delivered of a living child.

There was the usual crowd of old women in the room observing everything. When not murmuring of comparisons between this terrible event and the score of others they had witnessed, they consoled themselves with short exclamations of piety or with deep sighs which surpassing the physical emptied their souls to the very fundament of woe. These noises are not in themselves disturbing, on the contrary I find in them an echo of my own mood when engaged on obstetric business of unusual difficulty; the worry lay not in their interruptions but in the fact that they might in their ignorance imitate what they thought I had done. In this case all that they would notice was a plunge of the hand nearly to the elbow into the womb, some rummaging about there, then the withdrawal, legs first, of a child. What they would not notice was the careful cleansing of my hands and of the patient and further, what they could not even guess, was why just this particular time is chosen for the work. To their dull eyes and fidgety brains the important thing, the new piece of cunning which they might learn from watching me, would be that dramatic plunge into the interior. It was the master stroke which they would try out when opportunity came, and if they hadn't my magical formula to mumble while doing the trick they would substitute, despite endless failures, one of their own, till they too without harm could thus wrench new life from the bowels of the living.

· · ·

So the old women were coaxed out of the room with the promise that they would be the first to have the news and that they should have a description of what transpired. To make the place private, as it had fallen dark, I put clouts over some besoms which I found in an outhouse and propped them against the window panes.

This done I turned to the nurse with some satisfaction and said that with those old biddies out of the way and having the place to ourselves (us two and the patient) it made quite a cosy hospital atmosphere even in a peasant's hut. Nothing irrelevant to intrude, nothing we did would start false ideas going in these greedily curious people—the relief was prodigious.

From my first arrival with the nurse to the exclusion of the old women was perhaps the matter of a quarter of an hour. We now set to work busily; arranged tables, sterilizers, instruments and chloroform all neatly to hand, had lamps hanging in just the right place and everything ready.

The nurse and I worked together swiftly and in silence. The patient needed a whiff of chloroform, which acted I think more by suggestion than by its anaesthetic property, for she needed only a few drops, and its administration by the nurse was skilfully done. The delivery—after that plunge of the arm—was straightforward, and was followed by the afterbirth with very small delay. At this dramatic moment I heard a gentle but long-drawn-out 'k-k-oo-oo'. "What are you saying, nurse?" "Nothing, I didn't speak." I was puzzled, for I could have sworn someone spoke, and that it wasn't the patient; it was an articulated sound, not the relaxed puffing or stertorous gargling noise of a person under an anaesthetic, and I did not think the mother was then fully under.

It was a finely shaped child, with no moles or other devil's marks upon which malice could fasten, and in a trice she was breathing. The mother was soon round and comfortable. I was sweating with the nervous strain, for it's a touch and go matter at the best of times, and it seemed to me a good day's work. I flung myself on a stool, leaned back against the wall and looked up at the ceiling while I wiped my forehead—and there only five feet above the bed in full view of it was a row of boys' and girl's faces. Half a dozen of them.

When clearing the hut of all but the nurse and the patient I had forgotten to look for the shelf which hangs about two feet from the ceiling and runs about five or six feet out from the wall. It is used for stowage, but often enough the members of the family old enough to climb and young enough to be wanted out of the way house themselves there for the night and lie chattering and wriggling, listening to their elders and watching all that goes on till sleep overtakes them.

I was mightily annoyed, at them without reason and at myself with some cause, for having overlooked the common hiding-place; so I hauled them out and gave them a smack on the bottom apiece, telling them not to watch such doing again, and be off!

The nurse and I had a good laugh when they were gone and then ushered in the old women, but it was no longer possible for them to be the first to have details of the birth. They were not, however, angry at the children having been there, because they were only children, they did not matter, their turn had not yet come for the rub of birth and death.

Then in came the proud grandmother, chewing a rag in which was pocketed bacon rind and baked flour; this she was about to pop into the child's mouth to be the first intruding touch from the outside world when I stopped her, and asked her to consider whether it was as nice and clean a comforter as the mother's breast; and, besides, had she not got pyorrhoea (her gums were awash with pus) —in fact, the usual hygienic pleas. It was an ill-judged if not unkind interruption, because in any case the cosy rag would be thrust in the moment our backs were turned and by giving the babe something she had herself chewed she was in an animal sort of way binding her love to it as best she knew how.

There was no need to be worried over the nurse's status in the villages. The half-dozen young witnesses gave a full version of how she had killed the woman with a rag wet from a bottle while I had gouged the brat out with my arm, and then between us we had pulled both round to life again. With them the exciting spectacle would only give colour to their dreams; they were too young to crave for the details as a means of holding in their jealous grip the destinies of a younger generation.

57   Russia and the West

Because of her location, Russia has been deeply affected by both European and Asian influences. Consequently, Russian thinkers for long have debated the relations of their country with Europe: Is Russia European? Are the differences between Russia and Europe to be deplored as an indication of Russian backwardness or to be hailed as signs of a distinctive and superior civilization?

Tsar Peter the Great (1689–1725) contributed greatly to this debate by using his imperial authority and Herculean energy to Westernize Russia as rapidly as possible. He reorganized his army and bureaucracy, founded industries, established schools, and forced his subjects to shave their beards, wear Western clothes, drink coffee, and smoke tobacco. His violent measures of enforcement left an indelible imprint on the country, and also left it divided between the Westerners and the Slavophils—between those who hailed Peter as the great innovator and regenerator, and those who denounced him as the corruptor of Russia's Slavic spirit and culture. The conflicting views of these two groups are set forth in the following selections. The first * is from a book review written in 1841 by the famous literary critic and spokesman for the Westerners, V. G. Belinsky. Especially revealing is his low opinion of the Chinese and Japanese societies because

* Reprinted from V. G. Belinsky, *Selected Philosophical Works* (Moscow: Foreign Languages Publishing House, 1948), pp. 107, 114–115, 128–129, 133–140.

they had not yet been galvanized by Europe's dynamism, and also his reference to the subject status of India. The second selection * is from a speech delivered by the Slavophil poet Ivan Aksakov on the occasion of the assassination of Alexander II in 1881. The third selection, by Maurice Baring, an informed British observer in Russia, demonstrates that the issue of Russia's relations with the West remained unresolved on the eve of World War I.†

Belinsky

> *Russia was covered in darkness for many years:*
> *God said: let there be Peter—and there was light in Russia!*

Russia, . . . before Peter the Great was only a people and became a nation as a result of the *motion* given to it by the reformer.

From nothing, nothing is made, and a great man does not create of his own, but merely gives actual being to what existed in potentiality before him. That all Peter's efforts were aimed against ancient Russian usage is as clear as daylight, but the idea that he endeavoured to destroy our substantial spirit, our nationality, is more than ungrounded: it is simply absurd! . . .

In pre-Petrine Russia there was no trade, no industry, no police, no civil security, no diversity of wants and demands, no military organization, for this was all poor and insignificant, since it was not law but custom. And morals?—What a sad spectacle! How much there was that was Asiatic, barbaric, Tataric! How many rites degrading to human dignity there were, e.g., in marriage, and not only practised by the common people, but by the highest personages in the realm! How much was there that was vulgar and coarse in feasting! Compare those heavy repasts, those incredible beverages, those gross kissings, those frequent knockings of the forehead on the floor, those grovellings on the ground, those Chinese ceremonies—compare them with the tournaments of the Middle Ages, the European fetes of the seventeenth century. . . . Remember what our long-bearded knights and chevaliers were like! Think of our gay ladies lapping up vodka! Men married they knew not whom! Deluded, they beat and tormented their wives in order to raise them by brute force to angelic status—and if that did not work, poisoned them with philters; they ate Homerically, drank almost in tubfuls, kept their wives out of sight, and only when flushed after having eaten several score peppery dishes and drunk several buckets of wine and mead would they call them out for a kiss. . . . All this is as *moral* as it is aesthetic. . . . But, for all that, this has not the slightest bearing on a nation's degradation either morally or philosophically: for it was all the result of isolated historical growth and Tatar influence. No sooner did Peter open his nation's door to the light of the world than the darkness of ignorance was gradually dispersed—the nation did not degenerate, did not yield its native soil to another tribe, but it became something it had not been before. . . . Yes, gentlemen, defenders of ancient custom, say what you will, but the horse statue to Peter the Great on St. Isaac's Square is not enough: altars should be put up to him in all the squares and streets of the great kingdom of Russia! . . .

If Russia was to learn the military art of Europe of the seventeenth century she had to study mathematics, fortification, the artillery and engineering arts and navi-

* Reprinted from O. Novikov, *Skobelleff and the Slavonic Cause* (London: Longman Group Ltd., 1883), pp. 354–362.

† Reprinted from M. Baring, *A Year in Russia*, rev. ed. (New York: E. P. Dutton & Co., Inc., 1917), pp. 281–284, by permission of E. P. Dutton & Co., Inc., and A. P. Watt and Son.

gation, and she could not, consequently, take up geometry before she had thoroughly mastered arithmetic and algebra, the study of which would have had to make complete and equal progress among all estates of the nation. Uniformity of soldiers' clothes is not a whim but a necessity. Russian costume was not suited for soldiers' uniforms; consequently the European uniform had to be adopted; and how could that be done with the soldiers, alone, unless the repugnance to foreign clothes was overcome in the whole nation? And what sort of separate nation within a nation would the soldiery have presented if all the rest of menfolk went about in beards, long and flowing *balakhons* and huge ugly boots? To clothe the soldiers, mills were needed (and, thanks to patriarchal crudities there weren't any); was one to wait for the free and natural development of industry? Soldiers must have officers (is that not so, Messieurs Old Believers and Anti-Europeans?), and the officers had to be from a higher stratum of society than those from which the soldiers were recruited, and their uniforms had to be of finer cloth than those of the soldiers: was that cloth then to be purchased from foreigners with Russian money, or was the country to bide its time until (in perhaps 50 years) the soldiers' cloth mills were brought to perfection and evolved into fine-cloth mills? It is preposterous! No, everything had to be begun in Russia at a leap. . . . Whatever you may say about the poverty of our literature and the paucity of our book trade, we do have books that enjoy a ready sale, and bookdealers who have made an annual turnover of a quarter of a million rubles on periodical publications alone! How is that? Because our great Empress, our Little Mother Catherine II, was solicitous about creating a literature and a reading public, compelled her court to read, and from them the appetite passed on through the higher nobility to the lower and thence to officialdom, and now it is beginning to pass to the merchantry. . . .

True, Russia would probably have linked herself with Europe and adopted its civilization without the reforms of Peter, but in the same fashion as India did with England. . . .

Some people impute to Peter the Great's reforms the mischievous effect of having placed the nation in a singular position by divorcing it from its native sphere and throwing it off its ground of innate horse sense without having inoculated real Europeanism. Despite the fallacy of this view, it possesses a foundation and is at least worthy of being refuted. . . . Naturally, the old boyars, . . . looked with profound contempt on those new-fledged and home-bred Europeans who, through lack of practice, got their legs entangled in their sword, dropped their cocked hat from under their arm, trod on the ladies' toes when coming up to kiss their hand, needlessly, parrot-fashion, employed foreign words, substituted for courtesy rude and impudent gallantry and, as sometimes happened, put their clothes on the wrong way. Even today, though in another shape, vestiges of this sham, distorted Europeanism still survive: these forms sans ideas, that courtesy sans respect to self and others, that urbanity sans aesthetics, that foppery and *lionhood* sans elegance. . . . Yes, that is all true, but it would be as absurd to blame Peter for it as it would be to blame the physician who, in order to cure a sick man of the fever, first weakens and utterly debilitates him by bloodletting and plagues him when convalescent by a strict diet. The point is not whether Peter made us half-Europeans and half-Russians, consequently neither Europeans nor Russians: the point is are we always to remain in this characterless condition? If not, if we are destined to become European Russians and Russian Europeans, we should not reproach Peter, but rather wonder how he could have accomplished such a gigantic, such an unprecedented task! And so the crux of the matter consists in the words, "shall we"—and we can answer firmly and explicitly that we not only *shall be,* but are already *becoming*

European Russians and Russian Europeans, that we have been becoming so since the reign of Catherine II, and are making progress therein day by day. We are today the pupils and no longer the zealots of Europeanism, we no longer wish to be either Frenchmen, or Englishmen or Germans, we want to be Russians in the European spirit. . . .

The building of St. Petersburg is also placed by many to the discredit of its great founder. It is said: on the margin of a vast realm, on swamps, in a terrible climate, with the sacrifice of many workmen's lives, many were forced against their wishes to build their homes there and so on and so forth; but the question is, was it necessary, and was it avoidable? Peter had to abandon Moscow—the beards hissed at him there; he had to secure a safe haven for Europeanism, make the visitor welcome in the bosom of the family, so that he may quietly and unobtrusively influence Russia and act as the lightning conductor for ignorance and bigotry. For such a haven he required an entirely new and traditionless soil, where his Russians would find themselves in an utterly new environment in which they could not help but recast their customs and habits of their own accord. . . .

There are only two tranquil states in the world—China and Japan; but the best the former produces is tea, and the latter, I believe, lacquer: nothing else can be said of them.

Aksakov

Gentlemen,—I came from Moscow to take part in your assembly, and to join my Moscow voice to yours. I should greatly like to convey to you what is said and thought at Moscow, but it is beyond expression by spoken word. How, indeed, are we to define the impressions which fill our souls at this moment? . . .

The Emperor is murdered; the same Emperor who was the greatest benefactor to his country, who emancipated, bestowing upon them human and civil rights, tens of millions of Russian peasants. He is murdered; not from personal vengeance, not for booty, but precisely because he is the Emperor, the crowned head, the representative, the first man of his country, that vital, single man, who personified the very essence, the whole image, the whole strength and power, of Russia. From time immemorial that power constituted the strength of the country. The attempt directed against the person of the Tzar is always directed against the whole people; but in this case the whole historical principle of the national life has been attacked, the autocratic power bestowed upon the Emperor by the country itself. Who are those who dared to bring that awful shame upon the people, and, as if by mockery, in the name of the people? Who are they? Is it merely a handful of criminals, blood-thirsty blockheads, enslaved by the demon of destruction? Where did they come from? Let us address that question sternly to ourselves. Is it not the product of our moral treason, of which is guilty almost all the so-called liberal press? Can it be anything else but the logical, extreme expression of that Westernism which, since the time of Peter the Great, demoralised both our government and our society, and has already marred all the spiritual manifestations of our national life? Not content to profit by all the riches of European thought and knowledge, we borrowed her spirit, developed by a foreign history and foreign religion. We began idolising Europe, worshipping her gods and her idols! Who is to be blamed? Some forty years ago has not Khomiakoff warned us, threatening us with Divine punishment for "deserting all that is sacred to our hearts"? But really, what are these "Anarchists," "Social Democrats," and Revolutionists, as they call themselves?

Have they the smallest particle of Russian spirit in all their aspirations and aims? Is there the slightest shade in their teachings of a protest against the real shortcomings of which Russia is suffering? Just the opposite; what they despise most is precisely the Russian people. In their servile imitation of foreign teaching and foreign idols, they only borrow what can easily be explained, if not excused, in Western Europe by historical and social conditions. There, results of that kind are the natural protest caused by unequal partition of land, the unjust reign of the *bourgeoisie* over the fourth class—deprived of all civil organisation and political rights —a protest, therefore, against the present constitutional forms.

But that injustice is exactly what we do not possess. Thank God, and thanks to that very martyr-Emperor so brutally murdered, our "fourth class," or our peasantry, forming almost eighty per cent, of the whole realm, now possess land, organisation, and the most complete self-government. To this very day, that fourth class is the keeper of our historical instinct, of our religion, and of the whole element of our political organism. They, and not the so-called "Intelligencia," are the real supporters of our country. . . .

. . .

The time is come for us to bethink ourselves. The time is come to fix our mobile heart, our mobile thoughts, on the rock of Divine and national truth. I am happy to have been able to express aloud, in the name of the Slavonic society, the civil and moral aims and ideals of the Russian people. But that is not sufficient. It is necessary—it is absolutely necessary—for us to implore our Emperor to allow us, the whole country, the whole nation, to surround his throne and to express fearlessly, openly to the whole world, our horror and indignation to all who dare to make any attempt against what is most sacred to our national feeling, the historical principle of the autocracy, which constitutes the very foundation of our political life. Yes; let us implore that the old union between the Emperor and the country shall be revived, based upon reciprocal, sincere confidence, love, and union of souls.

Baring

. . . In Russia the two classes are the defenders and the opponents of the Government, or rather of the autocracy. The former base their arguments on the affirmation that Russia is an Oriental country and that Western institutions are unsuited to the Russian people. Parenthetically, I must mention that I am not alluding to the extreme reactionaries—to those people who wish to go back to institutions which existed before the time of Peter the Great. I am referring to intelligent people who, while belonging to no political parties, simply disbelieve in the Liberal movement in Russia, consider it to be the hysterical cackling of an unimportant minority, and think that the whole matter is mere stuff and nonsense. The opinion of these people is certainly worth considering, not because they are more impartial than others who belong to parties, since their ideas are equally based upon prejudice, but because they may be right. These people say that all talk of a Constitution is beside the mark. They argue thus:

"We must have a Constitution, just as we have an Army and a Navy, because the idea soothes the revolution-haunted breasts of foreign financiers, but we shall never have a real Constitution because we don't want one. Reforms? Oh, yes, as many as you please, on paper, signed and countersigned, but they will remain a dead letter, because they are not adapted to the character and the spirit of the nation. You cannot force Russian peasants to own land in the way Western peasants do. You can make laws telling them to do so, but if you force them you will only drive them to rebellion. Russia is like China; you can draw up a Constitution for Russia, but when it is carried out you will find that the only practical difference between the old state of affairs and the new is that the writing-table of the Minister of Foreign Affairs is to be oblong instead of round. People say that the Russian people is good and that its Government is bad, but the faults of the people are not the result of the inherent vices of the Government; the vices of the Government are the logical result of the faults, which in their turn are the inevitable complement of the good qualities, of the people. The desire for Liberal reforms based on Western examples is merely a fictitious agitation of a minority, namely, the 'Intelligentsia' or middle class, who have forgotten and lost their native traditions and instincts and have adopted and not properly assimilated the traditions and instincts of Western Europe. They have ceased to be Russian, and they have not become European. They have taken the European banner of ideals, but they do not know what to do with it; they cannot hold it up in their weak Slav hands. The result is words, words. This chatter will continue for a time, and when people get tired of listening, it will cease. As for the people, the real people, they will settle their affairs with those immediately connected with them, with their landlords, etc. The Government will make plenty of reforms on paper and have a Duma; but everything will go on exactly as it was before. Because you cannot change the character of a people, and the form of government they enjoy is the result and the expression of their qualities and of their defects."

Such are the arguments I have often heard advanced by these people, and I say once more that they may be right. Three years ago I was firmly convinced that they were right, and even now I have an open mind on the subject, although two years of close contact with Russians of all classes have led me to change my own opinion, and to agree with the other equally impartial people, who are just as Russian and have just as much knowledge of the country and experience of their fellow-countrymen, and who flatly deny the whole thing. According to this school, . . . the present *régime* in Russia is not the natural expression of national characteristics, but a fortuitous disease which has been allowed to spread without ever having been radically treated. Neither Autocracy nor Bureaucracy is a thing which has grown out of the immemorial traditions and habits of the Russian people; Autocracy was the product of a comparatively recent change in Russian history, and Bureaucracy the accidental result of the further changes introduced by a man of genius. The Government made certain things impossible: such as education for the peasants, laws for the peasants, justice, etc.; then, when the results of these prohibitions began to make themselves felt, turned round and said: "You see what these men are like; it is no use giving them anything because they are hopeless; they are like niggers and must be treated as such." This has been the proceeding of the Government: to prevent, prevent, and prevent again; and then, when the explosion resulting from the prevention occurred, to observe how right they had been in preventing, and how necessary it was to prevent more and more, because it was the only thing the people understood. In this blindness and obstinacy, year after year deferring the payment of their debt, they have let the interest accumulate; and when they eventually have to pay, far more will be required of them than they need originally have surrendered.

The people who represent these two schools of thought both say that they are Russia. . . . Which really represents Russia, we shall know perhaps in ten years' time.

Chapter Twenty-eight

Impact of dominance:
the Middle East

58

DIMITRIJE OBRADOVIĆ:
BALKAN DISCIPLE OF THE WEST'S ENLIGHTENMENT

The next area after Russia to feel the impact of the West was the Middle East, a region with a great variety of peoples, religions, and cultures. Furthermore, it was a loosely organized region, since the Ottoman Empire was a ramshackle imperial structure. Accordingly, the response to Western intrusion varied greatly from one part of the Middle East to the other. The following readings will deal, therefore, with the response of Balkan Christians, Moslem Turks, Arabs.

An outstanding example of the West's influence on the Balkans is found in the work of Serbian leader Dimitrije Obradović. He was born in 1743 at a time when the Serbians had no literature of any sort in their spoken language — other than ecclesiastical literature in the artificial Church Slavonic. Obradović became a monk, but being restless, he set forth in 1760 on travels that were to take him to Germany, England, France, and Russia. His observations and experiences transformed him from a monk with an intellectual outlook that was essentially Byzantine into an enthusiastic champion of the current rationalism and enlightenment. He now found it intolerable that his people should have no literature in their own language. So he proceeded to write about his adventures and his new secular ideas in the unaffected spoken language of his countrymen. The following passages reflect his militant rationalism, his critical attitude toward superstition and traditional religious practices, and his nationalistic objectives in writing in "our common Serbian language." *

* Reprinted from G. R. Noyes, *The Life and Adventures of Dimitrije Obradović* (Berkeley: University of California Press, 1953), pp. 99–100, 107, 133–135, by permission of The Regents of the University of California. Originally published by the University of California Press.

I have learned to think and to pass judgment in a better and more rational manner on my religious beliefs and my faith. The books of learned men have given me the means to distinguish orthodoxy from superstition and the pure teaching of the Gospels from all manner of human traditions and additions. . . . I am no longer deceived by any gay colors, by gilding and by external glitter: I recognize what is necessary and fundamental and what is accidental and superfluous; what is true and internal reverence and piety and what are external customs, ritual, and ceremonies. . . .

You ask me why I have rebelled against fasts, long prayers, and the great number of holidays; and wherein they offend me and make me take up arms against them. Read the Holy Gospel and you will see that the same things offended our Savior, so that he cried out against them and on that account rebuked the Pharisees, saying: "Woe unto you, scribes and Pharisees, hypocrites, who by fasting make pale and sad your faces and pray in the streets and byways, that men may see you." The abuses that were committed in those times by those acts are committed also today; and whoever receives, recognizes, and loves the teaching of Christ must hate all that Christ hated and against which he cried out. I have spent twenty-five years with various peoples of our faith in Greece, Albania, Bosnia, Herzegovina, Moldavia, and other regions: practically the entire population are conscious of being Christians of the Eastern Church only through its fasts and its holidays. And how do they fast? Ah, my brethren, God sees and hears all things; we must tell the truth! No one fasts except such as are extremely poor, people who live on sterile soil and who during several months of the year would think that they sat at royal tables if they merely had bread of wheat or of maize. These poor people fast the greater part of their lives, but by grim necessity. But those who have various fasting foods, as we term them, including olive oil and wine, never fast at any time whatever. (You should know that I do not regard it as fasting when a man has no dinner but at supper eats enough for both dinner and supper, nor when a man eats no meat but stuffs himself with beans and sauerkraut till his belly rumbles and sweat comes out on his brow.) But you will say: "The custom is old, let it be kept up! If it does no good, neither does it do harm!" Ha, I too want to speak about that! That it does no good, sensible men recognized long, long ago, but here is the trouble: it does much harm! You know well that an Albanian or a Montenegrin will kill a man like a wild goat and then atone for his act by fasting. Theft, lying, and every sort of injury and injustice he is confident of blowing away by peppered beans and of scattering it as if by a thunderbolt. There is no stench or impurity that he is not confident of washing away with sorrel and vinegar, of driving off with leeks and onions. If people only fasted as the divine Apostle Paul bids them, as a restraint on themselves, of their own free will, and not by compulsion, then who would be foolish enough to cry out against fasting? "Let not him that fasteth not blame him that fasteth; and let not him which fasteth condemn him that fasteth not." . . .

You ask me who I am and who gave me authority to assume the tone of a teacher. Among so large a multitude of Serbs God willed that I be born; being a rational man, I have a God-given and natural authority to communicate my thoughts to my fellow men and to tell them whatever good and sensible things I have heard and learned from others. In every nation and society there must be men of all sorts of callings and occupations, and among them there should be firm cooperation and harmony: it is not right for one man to say to another, "You are not needed." . . . Man is not only carnal but also rational. Therefore, as many trades and inventions are required for our bodily needs, it is just and proper that there be some trade which will serve our rational qualities; and this is the more needful since man surpasses all other animals solely through his superiority in intellect and reason. Consequently, since so many men work and strive in behalf of various needs of mine—some bear arms in order to defend my peace and security; others till the soil that they may give me bread to eat; some men clothe me and provide me with footwear; others bring me from distant provinces all manner of necessary things,—therefore it is right that I by my trade do something in their behalf: that I compose and write something that will be necessary and useful for their more noble parts; that is to say, for the heart, intellect, and reason. That is my trade! . . .

Here [in Leipzig] I purpose to remain for at least a year, and with the help of God and of some kind Serbian I intend to publish in our common Serbian language a book printed in the civil alphabet that shall be called *Counsels of Sound Reason,* for the benefit of my nation, that my toil and my long wanderings may not be all in vain. My book will be written in pure Serbian, just as is this letter, that all Serbian sons and daughters may understand it, from Montenegro to Smederevo and the Banat. So for all the Serbian race I shall translate the thoughts and counsels of famous and wise men, desiring that all of us may profit by them. My book will be intended for every person who understands our language and who with a pure and honest heart desires to enlighten his mind and to improve his character. I shall pay no heed whatever to what religion and faith any man belongs, nor is that a matter for consideration in the present enlightened age. . . .

Let us cast a brief glance at the enlightened nations of all Europe. At the present time every one of those nations is striving to perfect its own dialect. This is a very useful object, seeing that when learned men write their thoughts in the general language of the whole nation, then the enlightenment of the intellect and the light of learning are not confined to persons who understand the old literary language, but are spread abroad and reach even the villagers, being taught to the humblest peasants and to the shepherds, provided only that they know how to read. And how easy it is to teach a child how to read his own language! . . . I am aware that someone may reply to me that if we begin to write in the common dialect the old language will be neglected and will gradually disappear. I answer: "What profit have we from a language which, taking our nation as a whole, not one person in ten thousand understands properly and which is foreign to my mother and my sisters?". . . "Then let them learn it!" you may object. That is easier said than done. How many people have the time and means to learn the old literary language? Very few! But everybody knows the general, common dialect; and in it all who can read may enlighten their minds, improve their hearts, and adorn their manners. A language derives its value from the good that it does. And what language can do more good than the general language of the whole nation? The French and the Italians had no fears that the Latin language would perish if they began to write their own languages, and indeed learned men of our nation will always know it.

*For various reasons—including their geographic location, their religion, and their social organization and values—the Turks were influenced later than the Balkan Christians by the West. But eventually they also felt the impact, as reflected in the following account analyzing the nature and extent of Western influence in the field of education.**

Into Muslim Turkish society came Western educational influences, beginning in a trickle in the later eighteenth century, and growing into a flood by the early twentieth. All parts of the Ottoman Empire were affected, Egypt and the Balkan areas in some ways more profoundly than the rest. Our concern here, however, is with the Turkish portions of the empire in particular. Turks were affected by Western educational influences which came through six channels. The most important of these is too broad to deal with in brief compass, and will have to be dismissed with only a mention of its significance. This channel is education in its truest sense —the totality of life-long individual experience, gained on the job, in travel, through private reading, and in discussions with others, often in the salons and coteries of learning that congregated about one or another of the leading statesmen, poets or writers of Istanbul. Suffice it to note here that those nineteenth-century Turks who were best educated and who best absorbed Western learning were essentially autodidacts, whatever their formal schooling—Ahmed Vefik Paşa, a voracious reader, who was nicknamed an "upset library" by his contemporaries; Ali Paşa, who learned his French under a tree in the Ottoman embassy garden in Vienna; Münif Paşa, whose private studies far eclipsed his three years at the University of Berlin; Ziya Gökalp, who studied French philosophy and sociology by himself in nine years of Anatolian exile. Each took from the Islamic past and from the West what suited his intellectual needs. Each was a decided individual, yet all realized the advantages of borrowing from Western education. These men and others like them were the first real leaders for the Westernization of education in the empire.

The other five channels through which Western educational influences flowed into the empire were those of formal schools or school systems. The most obvious channel was the large group of schools in the Ottoman Empire which were supported and operated by Westerners. Almost all were mission schools. Although some foreign Catholic schools, in particular French, had existed for many years in the empire, the rapid growth of mission schools came in the nineteenth and earlier twentieth centuries. These were the years of the great flowering of Protestant oversea missions, of Catholic reaction in kind, and of the new imperialism which led governments and peoples of several European powers to support in the Near East schools purveying their own brand of culture. By the eve of World War I an unofficial count put French Catholic schools in the Ottoman Empire at 500, American schools at 675, British at 178. The French schools enrolled 59,414 students, the American schools 34,317, and the British 12,800. There were also German, Italian, Austro-Hungarian and Russian schools in lesser numbers. Most of these schools were elementary, though there were among them some excellent secondary schools and a few collegiate level. It looks as if, in the century before 1914, the

* Reprinted from R. H. Davison, "Westernized Education in Ottoman Turkey," *The Middle East Journal* (Summer 1961), 290–291, 294–299, by permission of the Middle East Institute.

Ottoman Empire had received a massive infusion of Western education. What impact had this on the Turks?

To the extent that the impact is measurable, it was slim. This is in part because the figures for schools are deceptive. Many of the foreign schools were located in the Arab portions of the empire, where few Turks lived; and the Arabs who attended such schools were largely Christians, of whatever communion. Many of the schools were in fact run by native Christians, with a bit of foreign support and supervision. But the major reason for the lack of influence on the Turks was that, even in the Turkish-populated areas, very few of them attended such schools. In part this was owing to suspicion of things foreign, but even more the suspicion of things Christian, coupled with the tradition that each millet, or religious community, should provide its own schools for its own communicants. . . .

Far more important in total impact on Turks were the specialized higher schools set up by the Ottoman government itself. These provided what was probably the major educational channel for the introduction of Western ideas into the empire. The need for such schools was felt when defeat in eighteenth-century wars brought home the lesson of Ottoman military backwardness in relation to Europe. Army and navy schools for mathematics and engineering were created in the later eighteenth century, with the aid of European renegades and translated textbooks. More such special higher schools were established in the nineteenth century, including a school of military medicine and a military academy. Civil schools of public affairs, of medicine, of languages, of law, and others were added. Though designated "higher" schools, most began at quite an elementary level, or confounded in themselves all grades from primary years to technical college. In the naval academy in the 1830's, for instance, half of the 200 students were just learning to read and write; only 30 were advanced enough to study navigation.

Until past mid-century these schools provided little of the leadership needed for modernizing the Ottoman Empire. Such leadership still came largely from the self-taught. Graduates of the military schools did, however, sometimes become teachers and so exercised influence in the secular lower and middle schools which the government began to institute in the 1860's. And from about 1875 on the higher schools were producing a significant portion of the leadership of the empire. The great advantage of these schools was to teach French, which opened up a new world of ideas, and to bring Western concepts of mathematics, science, geography, history, politics. . . .

Another method by which Westernized schooling was introduced into the Ottoman Empire was the creation of a whole system of elementary and secondary education and of a university, all under government auspices. A proclamation made in the mosques by Sultan Abdülmecid on March 7, 1845, started this development off with the assertion that "the Will of the Padishah is that ignorance, the source of much evil, should vanish from among the people." A commission of able men was appointed to work out educational reform, and shortly a ministry of education was created. Kemal Efendi, inspector-general of schools, was sent to study the systems of England, France and Germany. The very fact of government initiative, of governmental assumption of responsiblity for education, was a step toward Westernization. Sultans and officials had long supported educational institutions with their personal gifts, but the government as such had not heretofore planned or financed a school system. Except for the higher special schools, state-supported because they were directly training officials, education had been left to private charity and religious foundations.

While governmental responsibility for education was an accepted fact after the

1840's, the start toward creating the new system was fitful, and characteristic of the reform from the top down that has so often taken place in the Near East. A university was thrice still-born—in 1846, 1870 and 1879—and did not become firmly established until 1900. . . . Some progress in reforming the primary schools was achieved after 1870, but it was painfully slow. Until the end of the Ottoman Empire there remained many examples of the traditional primary school in which "the main duty of the teacher was to see that each child shouted, and that the accent and enunciation were passable." Ömer Seyfeddin, a writer who had his primary education in the 1890's, describes his experience in "Falaka," one of his popular short stories: "We were forty youngsters in the school. . . . We had no division into grades. In chorus we learned the alphabet and texts from the Koran, in chorus we learned the multiplication table by repetition, in chorus we chanted the prayers. So all our lessons went along in an endless learning by rote of things, the meaning of which we never were able to comprehend." But Westernized education had at least added the chant of the multiplication table to the chorus of Quranic passages. . . .

The other two educational channels which brought Western influence to the Turks may be mentioned briefly. One was the schooling of Turks abroad. From 1834 on the government sent, at irregular intervals, groups of young Turks to Western Europe for study. At the start, most of these were graduates of the military schools. Later more civilians went, and more Turks went to Europe as individuals to study. Some returned home quite well educated, and fairly Westernized; others did not. Some on return became leaders in reform efforts; others became cynical or disillusioned when they compared conditions at home to those they had known in Europe. The wife of one of the empire's grand viziers said her husband got in Europe a veneer of knowledge over a mass of ignorance, like "the greater number of those who have been sent to Europe to be educated." Mehmed Said Paşa, educated in Britain at Edinburgh and at Woolwich, said in 1877, "I had lived abroad till I fancied I had made myself a man, and when I came back to my country I saw about me merely brutes. . . ." Some acquired only expensive Western tastes and vices: in the acid jest of an Ottoman statesman, they were "syphilized, not civilized." But by the early twentieth century those Turks who had studied abroad probably exercised, as a group, considerable influence on Ottoman development. . . .

The final channel of Westernized educational influence was indirect. This influence came from the non-Turkish minorities—principally Greeks, Armenians and Jews—who in some cases were getting education abroad, but in most cases were getting a more modernized education in the schools maintained within the empire by each of these millets. Such schools grew rapidly in the later nineteenth century, and often had some significant foreign financial and educational support—from the *Alliance Israélite* for Jewish schools, from Greeks abroad and the University of Athens for Greek schools, and a little Armenian support from Russia for Armenian schools. Turks did not attend these schools, but the progress in non-Muslim education was a spur to the Turks. . . . Ziya Bey complained bitterly that the Turks were far behind in promoting literacy: ten-year-old boys in a Greek or Armenian school could read newspapers in their own languages, while it was rare that a Turkish boy of fifteen could do so, or could write a short letter. The conservative Istanbul newspaper *Basiret* in the 1870's demanded as a remedy that the government severely control the Greek and Armenian schools. But the actual result of improved Westernized schools among the non-Muslim millets seems to have been to prod the Turks to greater efforts.

The most influential of the early Westernizers amongst the Arabs were both non-Arabs: Napoleon and Mehemet Ali. When Napoleon invaded Egypt in 1798 he distributed widely a proclamation in Arabic. The excerpts given below* informed Egyptians about such novel concepts and institutions as "republic, . . . liberty and equality," and the right of anyone to advancement on the basis of ability and performance. Napoleon was forced to leave Egypt after 14 months because of the destruction of his fleet by Lord Nelson, yet he overthrew the ruling Mamluk class and thus paved the way for the rise to power of an Albanian adventurer, Mehemet Ali. Although he recognized the nominal suzerainty of the Sultan in Constantinople, Mehemet Ali became the de facto ruler of Egypt and proceeded with an unprecedented program for its modernization. The following analysis of his policies and his final failure † reveals the obstacles that prevented the Middle East and other non-Western regions from keeping pace with Europe in economic development.

Napoleon

. . . In the name of God, the Merciful and Compassionate; there is no God but God;

In the name of the French Republic, based upon the foundations of Liberty and Equality, Bonaparte, the Commander-in-Chief of the French Forces, informs all the population of Egypt:

For a long time, those in power in Egypt have insulted the French Nation and unfairly treated her merchants by various deceitful and aggressive tactics. Now, the hour of their punishment has arrived.

For many decades, these Mamluks, who were brought in from the Caucasus and Georgia, have been corrupting the best region of the whole world. But God, the Omnipotent, the Master of the Universe, has now made the destruction of their state imperative.

People of Egypt, some may say to you that I did not come except to obliterate your religion. That is an outright lie; do not believe it. Tell those fabricators that I came only to rescue your rights from the oppressors. And that I worship Almighty God, and respect his Prophet Muhammad and the glorious *Qur'an* more than the Mamluks do. Tell them also that all people are equal before God.

The only grounds for distinctions among them are reason, virtue and knowledge. [But] what virtue, reason and knowledge distinguish the Mamluks from others which would give them exclusive rights over everything that makes life sweet? Wherever there is fertile land, it belongs to the Mamluks; so also do they exclusively possess the most beautiful maids, horses and houses.

If the Egyptian land has been bestowed on them, let them produce the Title which God wrote for them. But God, the Master of the Universe, is compassionate and just with his people. With God's help, from now on, no Egyptian will be barred

---

* Reprinted from Ibrahim A. Abu-Lughod, *Arab Rediscovery of Europe: A Study in Cultural Encounters* (Princeton: Princeton University Press, 1963), pp. 13–15, by permission of the publisher. Copyright © 1963 by Princeton University Press.
† Reprinted from A. Bonné, *State and Economics in the Middle East* (New York: Humanities Press, Inc., 1948; London: Routledge & Kegan Paul Ltd., 1955), pp. 238–239, 241–246, by permission of the publishers.

from entering the highest positions [of the State] and from acquiring the most elevated status. The intelligent, virtuous and learned men will take charge of affairs and thus the plight of the entire nation will improve.

Formerly, there were great cities, wide canals, and thriving commerce in Egypt, all of which have disappeared as a result of the Mamluks' greed and oppression.

Judges, Shaykhs, Imams, officers and notables of the country, inform your people that the French are also faithful Muslims. As proof of this, they attacked Great Rome, where they destroyed the Papal Throne, which was always urging the Christians to fight the Muslims. Then they went to Malta from which they expelled the Knights who allege that Almighty God asked them to fight the Muslims. In addition, the French at every time have been the most faithful friend of the Ottoman Sultan and the enemy of his enemies, may God preserve his reign, and destroy the Mamluks who refused to obey him and heed his orders. They [Mamluks] only obeyed him originally to advance their personal greed.

Blessings and happiness to the Egyptian people who agree with us promptly, thus improving their own condition and elevating their status. Happiness also to those who remain at home, taking no side in the fighting; they will hasten to our side when they know us better.

But woe to those who join the Mamluks and aid them in the war against us; they will find no way to escape and no trace of them will be left.

Mehemet Ali

Conditions of industrial production in the Middle East at the turn of the eighteenth and during the first third of the nineteenth century were determined by

1. The predominantly agrarian character of the population in general.
2. The widespread custom amongst the agricultural and, to a certain extent, the urban population also, of providing itself with consumer goods of its own.
3. The gradual shrinking of local handicrafts in line with the general economic decline of the Middle East as a result of
   (a) the diversion of traffic routes (new sea route to India, growing importance of the Western Hemisphere).
   (b) the increasing competition from European production.
4. The stagnation and alienation of production technique and loss of initiative in trade and handicrafts.
5. The decay of vocational organisations (guilds and the like).

It is only when this background is clearly visualised that the approach and achievement of Mohammed Ali can be duly appreciated. . . .

In view of the general stagnation and the improbability that the Egyptians would of their own accord make profitable use of the ideas infiltrating from Europe, the conviction grew in Mohammed Ali that active intervention on the part of Government in the sphere of industry and education was imperative. The mentality of the Oriental at that time did not hold out much hope that he would be able to overcome all the difficulties confronting the revival of industrial initiative, let alone the introduction of European production methods on his own account. This could be achieved only by some dominant body invested with extensive powers. Thus, the State itself, i.e. its ruler, embarked in grand style on an ambitious programme of economic and political activities and took on a number of national-economic functions direct.

As the principal instrument in this policy Mohammed Ali turned to the establishment of trade monopolies and State industries. The problem of securing the necessary experts was solved by engaging foreigners. Thus, he did not hesitate, for instance, to summon hundreds of foreign workers to Cairo and to take into his service at high salaries a vast number of European experts and officers as managers of factories, schools and institutes. Their gradual replacement by native personnel was envisaged, and several hundred young Egyptians were despatched to European schools and institutions. . . .

In keeping with Mohammed Ali's general policy aimed at making the Egyptian State as far as possible independent of external factors, even as regards the supply of important war materials, was his interest in the development of iron and metal works, quite unusual at that time. In 1820, in the Bulaq quarter of Cairo, a foundry was erected after the plans of an Englishman where practically every class of foundry goods could be executed. The works contained eight furnaces and could turn out 50 cwt. of castings per day, including machinery, looms, spinning machines, and even repairs to steam engines and essential parts of the arsenal. . . .

In order to convey some idea of the extent of Mohammed Ali's work, it will suffice to mention that the number of workers engaged in Egyptian factories during the years 1830–1840 amounted to over 30,000, the workers in the arsenals to 5,000, and that the capital invested in machinery and plant is estimated at no less than £12 million. In 1836, 95 per cent. of total exports came out of the Government's stores, whilst 40 per cent. of the total imports came into the country on the Government's account. . . .

In appraising this first large-scale plan for the inauguration of the industrial revolution in the Orient, our interest centres not merely in the fact that the originator was sorely disappointed in his expectations, but at least to an equal extent in the reasons for this lack of success. . . .

First, there is the problem of the bureaucratic management of such enterprises by officials of the State, and, allied thereto, comes the general question how to procure the entrepreneur personalities, to say nothing of the lower personnel who must possess the necessary qualifications for the modern production process. Egypt had neither the factory managers nor the skilled workers. Both categories were at that time lacking. The European experts often came too late to save a badly-run undertaking, or were inadequate in numbers to meet the demands on them. . . .

. . . Whatever these deficiencies were, they could have been overcome in the course of time, had not a political factor interfered in a decisive fashion with the industrial plans. This was the inevitable clash between foreign and local interests; for Mohammed Ali, who had already appropriated the whole of the agricultural land and its returns, was about to make himself the owner of non-agricultural production, and thus the sole regulator of the country's total circulation of goods. In this, however, he was encroaching on the sphere of interests of foreign powers who were interested in the sale of their goods and the purchase of certain raw materials from Egypt. Egypt represented an important market for the products of the new English and continental factories, and this position was seriously threatened by the Pasha's bold experiments. . . .

The result of this [British] intervention was the treaty of 1838, based on the Capitulations which guaranteed the foreign subject freedom of industry and shipping. It led to the abolition of most of the monopolies: in Turkey in 1839, in Egypt in 1840. [This meant the end of Egyptian industry since it was all a government "monopoly."] . . .

British intervention broke the Pasha's spirit of initiative in the industrial field once and for all. Even as early as 1840, two years before the final ratification of the treaty, a number of factories which could not show a profit were closed. When the treaty came into force, nearly all the other factories followed suit. A few years later the ruins of factories and rusted machinery were the sole indication of what was left of the first industrial revolution in Egypt.

The reasons for the collapse of the Pasha's programme of industrialisations are to be found in various fields. They may be summed up as follows:

1. Shortcomings in the internal management, faulty economic calculation in the majority of undertakings, inadequate qualifications on the part of the personnel; lack of engineers and masters, lack of technical experience as regards the industrial production process in Egypt.
2. Difficulties of marketing and commercial policy; competition of cheap European goods. Political intervention on the part of export countries in favour of competition goods.
3. Sociological shortcomings: Absence of entrepreneur qualities in the Egyptians of that period. Arbitrary treatment of private trade interests by the State (inadequate protection of rights and property), clash between the liberal tendencies in industrial practice in Europe and the State-capitalistic planned economy of Mohammed Ali.

As long as these causes and deficiencies were effective, a development such as that witnessed in Europe was not possible. Mohammed Ali's attempt in itself proves that the more important prerequisites for a successful industrialisation must be present simultaneously in order to achieve the desired result. As matters stood the most essential conditions were lacking. The only chance of success, in these circumstances, lay in an attempt by the head of the State himself to solve problems of industrialisation by a planning policy pursued along almost modern lines, and for this purpose to employ all material and personal means at his disposal.

Chapter Twenty-nine

Impact of dominance: India

61   INDIA'S TRADITIONAL SOCIETY

The basic feature of the pre-British traditional Indian society was the self-contained and self-perpetuating village, virtually a little world unto itself. Customary patterns and conventions of immemorial antiquity governed the social and economic relations of such a community. The following account, by an American authority on India, analyzes the nature and functioning of the typical village.*

When the Europeans arrived in India, they found an ancient civilization ruled by recent invaders from the North—the Moghuls. The Moghul Empire was an agrarian-based, semi-feudal society. Its Government was staffed by a bureaucracy, its revenues were primarily from the land, and its form of feudalism was that of rights to land revenues granted to nobles of the military or administrative hierarchy in return for their services in maintaining the Empire.

Underneath the Moghul state-system lay the myriad of ancient Indian villages. India lived in its villages, as it had from time immemorial, and the economic, political, social and religious life of the vast majority of the Indian people revolved around the individual village.

While generalizations are unsafe, one can say that most of the villages of India were organized on a self-sufficient and localistic basis. Usually the village land was held in common by members of the village, being divided among the cultivating households at intervals by the traditional village *panchayat*—Council of Elders. Generally, the village paid its land tax to the Government in kind, as a percentage of its total crop. This percentage of the annual harvest passed into the hands of

---

* Reprinted from R. I. Crane, "India: A Study of the Impact of Western Civilization," *Social Education,* XV (December 1951), 365–366, by permission of the author and the National Council for the Social Sciences.

the Moghul administrators and moved up the line to support the various levels of the Moghul State. The basic contact of the village with the outside world was in the payment of a portion of its crop to the officials and in the irregular demands made on it for forced labor.

Within the tiny, self-sufficient village, economic life was generally of a non-commercial character. The residents of the village farmed their share of the village land, raised families, and died with almost no reference to commercial affairs or to matters outside the village.

In each village there were, in addition to the cultivating households, several families of secondary producers. These included the blacksmith, silversmith, carpenter, leather worker, scavenger, priest and astrologer. They served the rest of the village community on something akin to a barter basis. The carpenter or blacksmith produced for a known demand and was paid for his services by receiving grain from the cultivating households for whom he had performed such services, or by receiving a small portion of the village land for his own cultivation.

This intimate society, based on a face-to-face economy, was closely bound together by ancient tradition and by religious practice. The caste system usually indicated the hereditary occupation of each villager and fixed the relations between castes. The economic relations of exchange of goods and services were defined by the caste system and, at least in parts of India, by the closely-allied *jajmani* system.

The *jajmani* system provided that each caste family in the village had a fixed relationship in terms of duties, services and responsibilities with the other families of the village. Thus the shoemaker owed so many pairs of shoes a year to the other members of the village in terms of their status in the caste hierarchy and was paid or otherwise rewarded for the shoes as prescribed by the traditional regulations of the *jajmani* system. In this way the life of each of the villagers was intimately bound up with the life of the others.

In addition, the villager was supported and, in turn, controlled, by his caste council which supervised the social and religious life of the members of the caste residing in the village. The caste council also played what may be described as a legal role by representing its members in altercations with members of a different caste. The villager was also supported and controlled by the *joint-family* system. In the joint-family system, the family remains a social and economic unit, dwelling together under the paternalistic rule of the father or eldest male. As the sons marry they bring their wives home to the joint-family and continue as members of it, subject to its rulings. In economic affairs the joint-family takes precedence over its individual members and each is responsible for the welfare of the whole family while the family, in turn, shares what it has among all of its members.

The primary associations of joint-family, caste council, and village council thus provided control and direction over the activities of the villagers as well as support and integration for the individual. This close integration made for intellectual and emotional stability and for economic security. True enough, the economic security was generally at a very low level of subsistence. The village seldom produced much of a surplus and officialdom sometimes siphoned off most of the surplus to support the State. But, within the limits of a subsistence economy, each member of the village had an unquestioned right to some share in the total net produce of the family and of its village. Nor was this right conditioned in any significant way by non-local economic factors.

These hundreds of thousands of localistic, self-sufficient and non-commercial villages—virtually static as they were—comprised the base and bulk of Indian society. Kings might come and go, dynastic wars might rage and local bureaucrats might revolt, but the self-sufficient village held tenaciously to its piece of land, to its binding social interrelationships and to its traditional mores, beliefs and practices.

62   British Impact: Economic and Social

The British Empire in India, begun after 1750, lasted almost two hundred years, thus enduring as long as the Mogul Empire which preceded it. But British rule had an incomparably greater impact on traditional Indian society than did the Mogul. Since the British originally arrived in India with economic objectives in mind, their control of that country had far-reaching repercussions on its economic and social structure. These are analyzed in the following selections, the first by Professor R. I. Crane, author of the preceding reading,* and the second by E. Baines, an early nineteenth-century English writer, who shows how India's initial superiority over England in textiles was gradually overcome and reversed with the assistance of discriminatory imports.†

R. I. Crane

Into this rather static scene came the energetic entrepreneurs of Western commercial and trading organizations. Concerned, at first, with trade and profits, these roving merchants were anxious to obtain a monopoly of the rich trade with the Orient.

The representatives of the Great Trading Companies chartered by Britain, Holland, or France, confirmed believers in mercantilist theory, were anxious to exclude their rivals from the Orient trade and were similarly anxious to eliminate competition from the indigenous merchants of India or Southeast Asia. The key to their commercial thinking was monopoly, and the key to monopoly was power. The ultimate result was the consolidation of European political rule over non-European peoples of India and the East.

In India, between 1600 and 1763, the English East India Company contested with rivals from Portugal, Holland, and France, and finally emerged triumphant. In the process the Company became a political power in Bengal and, subsequently, in other parts of India. In becoming a political power, the Company added to its normal commercial activities the right to collect taxes in those areas given over to it by the Moghul Emperor or by his deputies. With the power to collect taxes went other forms of political control: judicial authority, the right to regulate trade, and so forth. Between 1763 and 1858 the Company extended its military and political power over ever larger areas of India.

The primary interest of the Company was in profitable trade and in the revenues

---

* Reprinted from R. I. Crane, "India: A Study of the Impact of Western Civilization," *Social Education*, XV (December 1951), 367–369, by permission of the author and the National Council for the Social Sciences.

† Reprinted from E. Baines, *History of the Cotton Manufactures in Great Britain* (London, 1835), pp. 56, 76–79, 81–82.

to be gained from collecting the land tax. As a result it rapidly became involved in activities that struck at the core of the self-sufficient Indian village. The first great change was the introduction of a new land-tenure system based on English concepts of private ownership that differed from general Indian practice. Whereas formerly the tax-collectors, or *zamindars,* had been State officials charged with securing the State's portion of the crop from a number of villages assigned to them, the Permanent Settlement, established in 1793 by Lord Cornwallis, transformed the tax-collectors into English-style landlords, while most of the villagers, who had formerly held the land in common, were reduced to the status of tenants-at-will.

Accompanying this unprecedented change was the spread and dominance of other English legal concepts: individual ownership, contract law, mortgage, distraint, and forced sale. These legal concepts were mostly unknown or even repugnant to the traditional law of Indian society. Enforced as they were, in good part, by English judges in the English or Latin tongue, they disturbed the traditional economic and social polity of the Indian villager and caused him to suffer under a distinct disadvantage. Taken together, these new elements, introduced from outside, were the beginning of a fundamental "revolution" in Indian society. This revolution shook it at its very base—the village.

Moreover, the English revenue system was applied whereby each plot of land was assessed for value and paid a land-tax in cash to the Government.

In the *zamindari* areas the landlord paid the cash assessment and secured rent in cash or kind from his tenants. In other parts of India the arrangement was made by the Company directly with each separate peasant proprietor and in this instance the peasant proprietor had to pay the assessment in cash. The creation of a fixed cash land-tax payment struck directly at the old, localistic, non-commercial life of the village. The village land now belonged to a landlord or, in parts of India, to individual proprietors. Land could now be bought, sold, mortgaged, and lost. Communal rights in land had largely been wiped out and the land-tax had, in most instances, to be paid in cash rather than in kind.

Even worse, the land-tax was a fixed sum (though in many parts of India it could be revised periodically by English magistrates) and had to be paid on a certain day or the property would be put up for tax sale. In previous times the land-tax had been a percentage of the crop and if the crop failed the tax was not paid. Under the new system, until late nineteenth century reforms, the rigidity of the new cash was firmly maintained. The result, as the decades passed, was an increased loss of land.

Finally, all of this came to be administered by an alien bureaucracy, speaking an alien tongue and, generally, but poorly acquainted with local exigencies or ancient customs. These men were hardly conscious of the profound change they were working in the heart of Indian society and could not foresee its long-range, deleterious results. The process, however, continued.

Since the village members now had to pay taxes in cash they had to operate in terms of the cash-nexus. They had to sell their crop or their services to raise money with which to pay the tax. And, as time passed, English machine-made goods entered the Indian market, ousting the more costly handicraft products of the old society. When this process had extended its range throughout the countryside, the peasant had to find cash in order to purchase the simple necessities of life. Moreover, the establishment of a Government Salt Tax put an added monetary burden on the villager. The end result was, of course, that the Indian peasant was tied ever more firmly into a cash economy and into the world market with all of its fluctuations and uncertainties.

With this development much of the old security and stability passed away. The peasant no longer had a firm claim on a share of the village land; the *jajmani* system tended to become commercialized; the secondary producer lost his craft and turned to the land for a living; the binding integration of the old village society was increasingly disrupted by the new commercial and legal systems erected by the foreign rulers. The peasant now stood as a luckless tenant working for a grasping landlord, or tried to eke out an existence in an unfamiliar economic and legal world as a peasant proprietor selling in the world market and subject to world economic conditions of which he had little understanding.

When the village economy was thus transformed, the old social institutions tended to wither away, or at least to lose much of their *raison d'être*. As they moved toward loss of social utility, these institutions tended to lose their ability to support the individual and to define his value system for him. This involved a serious psychological disruption of which Landon says: "It is inevitable that the break-up of the traditional isolated social group, the decay of the usual ethical forms, should exert an influence on the psyche of the people . . . it tends to cause a feeling of distress, a notion of unfair suppression. . . ."

True, the joint-family system remained in force, but with its base in communal land eliminated, its power to give economic support to its members diminished and, as a matter of fact, under the new economic conditions the joint-family became in certain ways an economic hindrance to its members in a new setting of individual enterprise. True, the caste system remained as a religious and ritual institution but its support of the member tended to become minimal as the new world outside the village cast its shadow over his daily life.

The process, begun with a new land law and a new revenue system, was hastened by developments during the nineteenth century. These included the effective opening of India as a market for British goods, the development of a railway and road network which tied the village more firmly into the world market, and the rise of urban centers in which a way of life radically different from that of rural India soon developed.

The old stability, the old security, the old supports were losing their vitality. Forced into commercial agriculture, deprived of communal supports, the peasant strove to keep his head above water. Statistics on land ownership, rural debt, expropriation, and famine, however, indicate that he fought a losing battle. A significant portion became landless agricultural laborers while an even larger number were reduced to the rank of sharecropper.

Another instance of European impact which has had deleterious results, would seem to be the rise of a parasitic entrepreneurial class in India. The character of the new land system, described above, created landlords and landlordism and caused Indians with wealth or with hopes of wealth to flock to the land, buying it up or securing it on mortgage-sale and making a handsome living by rack-renting their tenants.

As the East India Company strengthened its own monopoly on the India trade, a large number of the indigenous merchants found it impossible to compete. Abandoning an unprofitable business career they turned to land ownership and to living off rents. For a variety of reasons the easiest way to make an excellent return on investment was to push the level of rents up and live as absentee landlords whose position was reinforced and guaranteed by British law.

Moreover, as the full impact of commercialism broke upon the peasantry, the latter tended to sink ever deeper in debt. Under these circumstances it was apparent that rural money-lending would prove a profitable form of enterprise. Thus there arose a number of local money-lenders, almost unknown to India in pre-British days who advanced credit to the agriculturists at ruinous rates of interest. The landlord-money-lender, as time passed, tended to become the local grain and produce merchant, buying from the peasantry, transporting the crop to the seaports, and there selling to the European businessman who shipped goods to the West. In each case the Indian entrepreneur was to be found occupying the role of non-productive middleman, making a profit by buying and selling or by lending, mortgaging and rack-renting. These activities consisted in making money out of money and not in adding to the total net productive capacity.

Since it was in these essentially non-productive fields of activity that the Indian well-to-do found greatest scope for their energy, it was probably inevitable that an attitude toward capital would develop which has proven inimical to modern India. Today India needs large amounts of investment capital in order to modernize and expand her productive plant, but Indian businessmen, by and large, prefer to make their profits by speculation, rack-renting, money-lending and intermediary trade.

E. Baines

The Indians have in all ages maintained an unapproached and almost incredible perfection in their fabrics of cotton. Some of their muslins might be thought the work of fairies, or of insects, rather than of men; but these are produced in small quantities, and have seldom been exported. In the same province from which the ancient Greeks obtained the finest muslins then known, namely, the province of Bengal, these astonishing fabrics are manufactured to the present day.

We learn from two Arabian travellers of the ninth century, that "in this country (India) they make garments of such extraordinary perfection, that no where else are the like to be seen. These garments are for the most part round, and wove to that degree of fineness that they may be drawn through a ring of moderate size." Marco Polo, in the thirteenth century, mentions the coast of Coromandel, and especially Masulipatam, as producing "the finest and most beautiful cottons that are to be found in any part of the world"; and this is still the case as to the flowered and glazed cottons, called chintzes. . . .

The commerce of the Indians in these fabrics has been extensive, from the Christian era to the end of the last century. For many hundred years, Persia, Arabia, Syria, Egypt, Abyssinia, and all the eastern parts of Africa, were supplied with a considerable portion of their cottons and muslins, and with all which they consumed of the finest qualities, from the marts of India. . . .

Owing to the beauty and cheapness of Indian muslins, chintzes, and calicoes, there was a period when the manufacturers of all the countries of Europe were apprehensive of being ruined by their competition. In the seventeenth century, the Dutch and English East India Companies imported these goods in large quantities; they became highly fashionable for ladies' and children's dresses, as well as for drapery and furniture, and the coarse calicoes were used to line garments. To such an extent did this proceed, that as early as 1678 a loud outcry was made in England against the admission of Indian goods, which, it was maintained, were ruining our ancient woollen manufacture,—a branch of industry which for centuries was regarded with an almost superstitious veneration, as a kind of palladium of the national prosperity, and which was incomparably the most extensive branch of manufactures till the close of the eighteenth century. . . .

So sagacious and far-sighted an author as Daniel De Foe did not escape the general notion, that it was not merely injurious to our woollen and silk manufactures, but also a national evil, to have clothing cheap from abroad rather than to manufacture it dear at home. In his *Weekly Review,* [January 31, 1708] which contains so many opinions on trade, credit, and currency far beyond the age, he thus laments the large importations of Indian goods:—

> The general fansie of the people runs upon East India goods to that degree, that the *chints* and *painted callicoes,* which before were only made use of for carpets, quilts, &c., and to clothe children and ordinary people, become now the dress of our ladies; and such is the power of a mode as we saw our persons of quality dressed in Indian carpets, which but a few years before their chambermaids would have thought too ordinary for them: the chints was advanced from lying upon their floors to their backs, from the foot-cloth to the petticoat; and even the queen herself at this time was pleased to appear in China and Japan, I mean China silks and callico. Nor was this all, but it crept into our houses, our closets, and bed-chambers; curtains, cushions, chairs, and at last beds themselves, were nothing but callicoes or Indian stuffs; and in short, almost every thing that used to be made of wool or silk, relating either to the dress of the women or the furniture of our houses, was supplied by the Indian trade.
>
> Above half of the (woollen) manufacture was entirely lost, half of the people scattered and ruined, and all this by the intercourse of the East India trade.

. . . It appears, then, that not more than a century ago, the cotton fabrics of India were so beautiful and cheap, that nearly all the governments of Europe thought it necessary to prohibit them, or to load them with heavy duties, in order to protect their own manufactures. How surprising a revolution has since taken place! The Indians have not lost their former skill; but a power has arisen in England, which has robbed them of their ancient ascendancy, turned back the tide of commerce, and made it run more rapidly against the Oriental than it ever ran against the English. Not to dwell upon a point which will afterwards be illustrated, the following document furnishes superabundant proof how a manufacture which has existed without a rival for thousands of years, is withering under the competition of a power which is but of yesterday: it would be well if it did not also illustrate the very different measure of protection and justice which governments usually afford to their subjects at home, and to those of their remote dependencies:—

PETITION OF NATIVES OF BENGAL, RELATIVE TO DUTIES ON COTTON AND SILK.

Calcutta, 1st. Sept. 1831.

To The Right Honourable the Lords of His Majesty's Privy Council for Trade, &c.

The humble Petition of the undersigned Manufacturers and Dealers in Cotton and Silk Piece Goods, the fabrics of Bengal;

Sheweth—That of late years your Petitioners have found their business nearly superseded by the introduction of the fabrics of Great Britain into Bengal, the importation of which augments every year, to the great prejudice of the native manufactures.

That the fabrics of Great Britain are consumed in Bengal, without any duties being levied thereon to protect the native fabrics.

That the fabrics of Bengal are charged with the following duties when they are used in Great Britain—

On manufactured cottons, 10 per cent.

On manufactured silks, 24 per cent.

Your Petitioners most humbly implore your Lordships' consideration of these circumstances, and they feel confident that no disposition exists in England to shut the door against the industry of any part of the inhabitants of this great empire.

They therefore pray to be admitted to the privilege of British subjects, and humbly entreat your Lordships to allow the cotton and silk fabrics of Bengal to be used in Great Britain 'free of duty,' or at the same rate which may be charged on British fabrics consumed in Bengal.

Your Lordships must be aware of the immense advantages the British manufacturers derive from their skill in constructing and using machinery, which enables them to undersell the unscientific manufacturers of Bengal in their own country: and, although your Petitioners are not sanguine in expecting to derive any great advantage from having their prayer granted, their minds would feel gratified by such a manifestation of your Lordships' good will towards them; and such an instance of justice to the natives of India would not fail to endear the British government to them.

They therefore confidently trust, that your Lordships' righteous consideration will be extended to them as British subjects, without exception of sect, country, or colour.

And your Petitioners, as in duty bound, will ever pray.

[Signed by 117 natives of high respectability.]

BRITISH IMPACT: INTELLECTUAL   63

British rule in India affected the intellectual as much as the economic development of that country, mainly because of the fateful British decision in 1835 to use government funds to support an educational system based on the English language and English type of curriculum. The effect of this decision was to greatly accelerate the diffusion of Western ideas among Indian intellectuals, which, in turn, led to the development of an anti-British nationalist movement. The person most responsible for the decision was Thomas Babington Macaulay, whose famous "Minute on Education," given below, presented the reasoning behind his policy.* Macaulay grossly underestimated Indian literature when he stated that "a single shelf of a good European library was worth the whole native literature of India and Arabia." But he was proven fully justified in anticipating that his program would lead to the regeneration of Indian thought and learning.

How stands the case? We have to educate a people who can not at present be educated by means of their mother tongue. We must teach them some foreign language. The claims of our own language it is hardly necessary to recapitulate. It stands pre-eminent even among the languages of the West. It abounds with works of imagination not inferior to the noblest which Greece has bequeathed to us; with models of every species of eloquence; with historical compositions, which, con-

* Reprinted from G. O. Trevelyan, *Life and Letters of Lord Macaulay* (New York: Harper, 1875), I, 353–355.

sidered merely as narratives, have seldom been surpassed, and which, considered as vehicles of ethical and political instruction, have never been equaled; with just and lively representations of human life and human nature; with the most profound speculations on metaphysics, morals, government, jurisprudence, and trade; with full and correct information respecting every experimental science which tends to preserve the health, to increase the comfort, or to expand the intellect of man. Whoever knows that language has ready access to all the vast intellectual wealth which all the wisest nations of the earth have created and hoarded in the course of ninety generations. It may safely be said that the literature now extant in that language is of far greater value than all the literature which three hundred years ago was extant in all the languages of the world together. Nor is this all. In India, English is the language spoken by the ruling class. It is spoken by the higher class of natives at the seats of government. It is likely to become the language of commerce throughout the seas of the East. It is the language of two great European communities which are rising, the one in the south of Africa, the other in Australasia; communities which are every year becoming more important, and more closely connected with our Indian empire. Whether we look at the intrinsic value of our literature, or at the particular situation of this country, we shall see the strongest reason to think that, of all foreign tongues, the English tongue is that which would be the most useful to our native subjects.

The question now before us is simply whether, when it is in our power to teach this language, we shall teach languages in which, by universal confession, there are no books on any subject which deserve to be compared to our own; whether, when we can teach European science, we shall teach systems which, by universal confession, whenever they differ from those of Europe, differ for the worse; and whether, when we can patronize sound philosophy and true history, we shall countenance, at the public expense, medical doctrines which would disgrace an English farrier—astronomy, which would move laughter in the girls at an English boarding-school—history, abounding with kings thirty feet high, and reigns thirty thousand years long—and geography, made up of seas of treacle and seas of butter.

We are not without experience to guide us. History furnishes several analogous cases, and they all teach the same lesson. There are in modern times, to go no further, two memorable instances of a great impulse given to the mind of a whole society—of prejudice overthrown—of knowledge diffused—of taste purified—of arts and sciences planted in countries which had recently been ignorant and barbarous.

The first instance to which I refer is the great revival of letters among the Western nations at the close of the fifteenth and the beginning of the sixteenth century. At that time almost every thing that was worth reading was contained in the writings of the ancient Greeks and Romans. Had our ancestors acted as the Committee of Public Instruction has hitherto acted; had they neglected the language of Cicero and Tacitus; had they confined their attention to the old dialects of our own island; had they printed nothing and taught nothing at the universities but chronicles in Anglo-Saxon and romances in Norman-French, would England have been what she now is? What the Greek and Latin were to the contemporaries of More and Ascham, our tongue is to the people of India. The literature of England is now more valuable than that of classical antiquity. I doubt whether the Sanscrit literature be as valuable as that of our Saxon and Norman progenitors. In some departments—in history, for example—I am certain that it is much less so.

Another instance may be said to be still before our eyes. Within the last hundred and twenty years, a nation which had previously been in a state as barbarous as that in which our ancestors were before the Crusades, has gradually emerged from the ignorance in which it was sunk, and has taken its place among civilized communities. I speak of Russia. There is now in that country a large educated class, abounding with persons fit to serve the state in the highest functions, and in no wise inferior to the most accomplished men who adorn the best circles of Paris and London. There is reason to hope that this vast empire, which in the time of our grandfathers was probably behind the Punjab, may, in the time of our grandchildren, be pressing close on France and Britain in the career of improvement. And how was this change effected? Not by flattering national prejudices; not by feeding the mind of the young Muscovite with the old woman's stories which his rude fathers had believed; not by filling his head with lying legends about St. Nicholas; not by encouraging him to study the great question, whether the world was or was not created on the 13th of September; not by calling him "a learned native" when he has mastered all these points of knowledge; but by teaching him those foreign languages in which the greatest mass of information had been laid up, and thus putting all that information within his reach. The languages of Western Europe civilized Russia. I can not doubt that they will do for the Hindoo what they have done for the Tartar.

RISE OF INDIAN NATIONALISM   64

When Macaulay recommended that the Indians be educated along English lines, he foresaw that "they may in some future age demand European institutions," a premonition that proved completely justified. At first, most Indian intellectuals who had contact with British schools and learning were greatly impressed and usually became champions of British rule, as was the case with Dadabhai Naoroji who, though criticizing the British on grounds of economic exploitation, considered their rule to be generally beneficial and therefore accepted it. This attitude is illustrated in the following excerpts from Naoroji's presidential address before the Second Congress in 1886.* But later Indian leaders, referred to as the "Extremists" in contrast to the earlier "Moderates," were more impressed by the exactions than the benefactions of British rule, and demanded self-government. A prominent leader of this group was B. G. Tilak, whose views are presented in the following selections from speeches he delivered in 1906 and 1907.†

Naoroji

The assemblage of such a Congress is *an event of the utmost importance in Indian History*. I ask whether in the most glorious days of Hindu rule, in the days of Rajahs like the great Vikram, you could imagine the possibility of a meeting of this kind, whether even Hindus of all different provinces of the kingdom could have

---

* Reprinted from *Speeches and Writings of Dadabhai Naoroji,* 2nd ed. (Madras: G. Nateson, n.d.), pp. 2–4.
† Reprinted from B. G. Tilak, *His Writings and Speeches,* 3rd ed. (Madras: Ganesh, 1923), pp. 42–45, 55–56, 65, by permission of the publisher.

collected and spoken as one nation. Coming down to the later Empire of our friends, the Mahomedans, who probably ruled over a larger territory at one time than any Hindu monarch, would it have been, even in the days of the great Akbar himself, possible for a meeting like this to assemble composed of all classes and communities, all speaking one language, and all having uniform and high aspirations of their own.

. . . Well, then, what is it for which we are now met on this occasion? We have assembled to consider questions upon which depend our future, whether glorious or inglorious. It is our good fortune that we are under a rule which makes it possible for us to meet in this manner. (*Cheers.*)

It is under the civilizing rule of the Queen and people of England that we meet here together, hindered by none, and are freely allowed to speak our minds without the least fear and without the least hesitation. Such a thing is possible under British rule and British rule only. (*Loud Cheers.*) Then I put the *question* plainly: Is this Congress a nursery for sedition and rebellion against the British Government (*cries of "No, no"*); or is it another stone in the foundation of the stability of that government? (*Cries of "Yes, yes."*) There could be but one answer, and that you have already given, because we are thoroughly sensible of the numberless blessings conferred upon us, of which the very existence of this Congress is a proof in a nutshell. (*Cheers.*) Were it not for these blessings of British rule, I could not have come here, as I have done, without the least hesitation and without the least fear that my children might be robbed and killed in my absence; nor could you have come from every corner of the land, having performed, within a few days, journeys, which in former days would have occupied as many months. (*Cheers.*) These simple facts bring home to all of us at once some of those great and numberless blessings which British rule has conferred upon us. But there remain even greater blessings for which we have to be grateful. It is to British rule that we owe the education we possess; the people of England were sincere in the declarations made more than half a century ago that India was a sacred charge entrusted to their care by Providence, and that they were bound to administer it for the good of India, to the glory of their own name, and the satisfaction of God. (*Prolonged cheering.*) When we have to acknowledge so many blessings as flowing from British rule,—and I could descant on them for hours, because it would simply be recounting to you the history of the British Empire in India—is it possible that an assembly like this, every one of whose members is fully impressed with the knowledge of these blessings, could meet for any purpose inimical to that rule to which we owe so much? (*Cheers.*)

The thing is absurd. Let us speak out like men and proclaim that we are loyal to the backbone (*cheers*); that we understand the benefits English rule has conferred upon us; that we thoroughly appreciate the education that has been given to us, the new light which has been poured upon us, turning us from darkness into light and teaching us the new lesson that kings are made for the people, not peoples for their kings; and this new lesson we have learned amidst the darkness of Asiatic despotism only by the light of free English civilization. . . .

Tilak

. . . India is under a foreign rule and Indians welcomed the change at one time. Then many races were the masters and they had no sympathy and hence the change was welcomed and that was the cause why the English succeeded in establishing an empire in India. Men then thought that the change was for their good. The confusion which characterised native rule was in striking contrast with the constitutional laws of the British Government. The people had much hope in the British Government, but they were much disappointed in their anticipations. They hoped that their arts and industries would be fostered under British rule and they would gain much from their new rulers. But all those hopes had been falsified. The people were now compelled to adopt a new line, namely, to fight against the bureaucracy.

Hundred years ago it was said, and believed by the people, that they were socially inferior to their rulers and as soon as they were socially improved they would obtain liberties and privileges. But subsequent events have shown that this was not based on sound logic. Fifty years ago Mr. Dadabhai Naoroji, the greatest statesman of India, thought that Government would grant them rights and privileges when they were properly educated, but that hope is gone. Now it might be said that they were not fitted to take part in the administration of the country owing to their defective education. But, I ask, whose fault it is. The Government has been imparting education to the people and hence the fault is not theirs but of the Government. The Government is imparting an education to make the people fit for some subordinate appointments. . . .

Protests are of no avail. Mere protest, not backed by self-reliance, will not help the people. Days of protests and prayers have gone. . . . Three P's—pray, please and protest—will not do unless backed by solid force. Look to the examples of Ireland, Japan and Russia and follow their methods. . . .

Two new words have recently come into existence with regard to our politics, and they are *Moderates* and *Extremists*. These words have a specific relation to time, and they, therefore, will change with time. The Extremists of to-day will be Moderates to-morrow, just as the Moderates of to-day were Extremists yesterday. When the National Congress was first started and Mr. Dadabhai's views, which now go for Moderates, were given to the public, he was styled an Extremist, so that you will see that the term Extremist is an expression of progress. We are Extremists to-day and our sons will call themselves Extremists and us Moderates. Every new party begins as Extremists and ends as Moderates. The sphere of practical politics is not unlimited. We cannot say what will or will not happen 1,000 years hence— perhaps during that long period, the whole of the white race will be swept away in another glacial period. We must, therefore, study the present and work out a programme to meet the present condition.

It is impossible to go into details within the time at my disposal. One thing is granted, *viz.,* that this Government does not suit us. As has been said by an eminent statesman—the government of one country by another can never be a successful, and therefore, a permanent Government. There is no difference of opinion about this fundamental proposition between the Old and New schools. One fact is that this alien Government has ruined the country. In the beginning, all of us were taken by surprise. We were almost dazed. We thought that everything that the rulers did was for our good and that this English Government has descended from the clouds to save us from the invasions of Tamerlane and Chengis Khan, and, as they say, not only from foreign invasions but from internecine warfare, or the internal or external invasions, as they call it. We felt happy for a time, but it soon came to light that the peace which was established in this country did this, as Mr. Dadabhai has said in one place—that we were prevented from going at each other's throats, so that a foreigner might go at the throat of us all. Pax Britannica has been established in this country in order that a foreign Government may exploit the country. That this is the effect of this Pax Britannica is being gradually realised in these days. . . .

Every Englishman knows that they are a mere handful in this country and it is the business of every one of them to befool you in believing that you are weak and they are strong. This is politics. We have been deceived by such policy so long. What the New Party wants you to do is to realise the fact that your future rests entirely in your own hands. If you mean to be free, you can be free; if you do not mean to be free, you will fall and be for ever fallen. So many of you need not like arms; but if you have not the power of active resistance, have you not the power of self-denial and self-abstinence in such a way as not to assist this foreign Government to rule over you? This is boycott and this is what is meant when we say, boycott is a political weapon. We shall not give them assistance to collect revenue and keep peace. We shall not assist them in fighting beyond the frontiers or outside India with Indian blood and money. We shall not assist them in carrying on the administration of justice. We shall have our own courts, and when time comes we shall not pay taxes. Can you do that by your united efforts? If you can, you are free from to-morrow.

Chapter Thirty

Impact of dominance:
China and Japan

CHINA'S RESPONSE TO THE WEST: **65**
TECHNOLOGICAL PHASE

China's development during four millennia led that country to have the world's most populous and, in certain respects, most cultivated society. This achievement, in turn, led to self-sufficiency and self-centeredness—to the feeling that China was indeed the Middle Kingdom, and the rest of the world was essentially subsidiary and inferior. Consequently, China's defeat by the West in the second half of the nineteenth century was a traumatic experience. It prompted soul-searching and eventually generated an intellectual revolution that has continued to the present day. At first the scholar bureaucracy that traditionally had ruled the country tried to cope with the barbarian intruders by making as few adjustments as possible. Typical was a certain Wei Yuan who published in 1842 a work entitled Record of the Imperial Military Exploits, *from which the following selection is taken.* Wei Yuan proposed to check the Westerners by discovering and imitating their "superior techniques." At this stage, the Chinese were not questioning the fundamentals of their civilization; they were merely trying out a few tricks to put the barbarians in their place.*

The Japanese barbarians (who raided China in the sixteenth century) were strong in land fighting and weak in water warfare, because the pirates who came were all desperadoes from poor islands, who had no means to build large ships and big guns, but relied upon sheer courage to cross the ocean, and depended upon their swords and spears to invade China. Therefore, whenever they went ashore it was

* Reprinted from Ssu-yu Teng and J. K. Fairbank, *China's Response to the West: A Documentary Survey 1839–1923* (Cambridge: Harvard University Press, 1954), pp. 31, 33–35, by permission of the publisher. Copyright 1954 by the President and Fellows of Harvard College.

impossible to resist them. But when the Japanese ships met the junks of Fukien and Kwangtung, then they were like rice on a grindstone. If the Japanese ships met big cannons and firearms, they would be like goats chased by wolves. . . . In general, the strength of the Japanese was on the land. To attack them on the open ocean was to assail their weak point. The strength of the British barbarians is on the ocean. Wait for them in the inland rivers. Wait for them on the shore and they will lose their strength. Unfortunately, the Ming people, in warding off the Japanese, did not know how to oppose them on the ocean, and nowadays those who are guarding against the British do not lay ambushes in the interior.

The situation today is this: if there is a discussion about getting and using Western warships, then someone is sure to say that he fears borrowing aid from the outer barbarians would show our weaknesses. Yet when suddenly our weakness has been several times more fully exposed than this would have involved, they have been glad to do it without shrinking. If there is a discussion about building ships, making weapons, and learning the superior techniques of the barbarians, they say it is too expensive. But when suddenly the cost is ten times more than this, they say it is a matter of exigency to meet an emergency and is not regrettable. If there is a discussion about the translation of barbarian books and prying into barbarian affairs, they are sure to say it would cause trouble. (Note: during the reign of Chiach'ing there was someone in Kwangtung who intended to publish a book giving transliterations of Chinese and barbarian characters, which would be very convenient for Chinese translating their characters. Yet it was forbidden by the Kwangtung authorities.) When suddenly something has happened, they ask, "What is the distance between the English capital and the Russian capital?" Or, "Via what route can the English barbarians communicate with the Mohammedan tribes? . . ."

It is proper for us to learn the barbarians' superior techniques in order to control them. The superior techniques of the barbarians are three: (1) warships, (2) firearms, and (3) methods of maintaining and training soldiers. . . .

The materials in their shipyards are piled up like hills and craftsmen congregate there like a cloud. Within twenty or thirty days a large warship can be completed. They can instantly spread the sails and adjust the tiller with a few shouted orders. Their craftsmen compete with each other in their talents and abilities. In construction they compete for speed and in navigation also. Construction goes on all year long, the fire illuminates the sky, and the noise shakes the earth. Thus, while the British ships and guns are regarded in China as due to extraordinary skill, in the various countries of Europe they are considered as quite ordinary. In Canton international trade has been carried on for two hundred years. At first the products of their strange skills and clever craftsmanship were received, and then their heterodox religions and poisonous opium. But in regard to their conduct of war and the effectiveness of their weapons, we are learning not a single one of their superior skills. That is, we are only willing to receive the harm and not . . . the benefit of foreign intercourse.

Let us establish a shipyard and an arsenal at two spots, Chuenpi and Taikoktow outside of the Bogue in Kwangtung, and select one or two persons from among the foreign headmen who have come from France and America, respectively, to bring Western craftsmen to Canton to take charge of building ships and making arms. In addition, we should invite Western helmsmen to take charge of teaching the methods of navigating ships and of using cannon, following the precedent of the barbarian officials in the Imperial Board of Astronomy. We should select clever artisans and good soldiers from Fukien and Kwangtung to learn from them, the craftsmen to learn the casting of cannon and building of ships, and the good soldiers to learn their methods of navigation and attack. . . . In Kwangtung there should be ten thousand soldiers; in Fukien, ten thousand; in Chekiang, six thousand; and in Kiangsu, four thousand. In assigning soldiers to the ships we must rely on selection and training. Eight out of ten should be taken from among the fishermen and smugglers along the sea coast. Two out of ten should be taken from the old encampments of the water forces. All the padded rations and extra rations of the water force should be . . . used for the recruiting and maintenance of good soldiers. We must make the water forces of China able to navigate large ships overseas, and able to fight against foreign barbarians on the high seas.

CHINA'S RESPONSE TO THE WEST: INSTITUTIONAL PHASE 66

Repeated defeats at the hands of the West forced China's leaders to reconsider their traditional values and policies. They were compelled to go beyond military technology and to consider institutional change. Outstanding in this respect was a gifted journalist, Wang T'ao, who wrote under the protection of British rule in Hong Kong, and boldly urged sweeping reforms. The following excerpts from a letter that he wrote between 1858 and 1860 * advocate reorganization of education, administration, and the armed forces, and also describe favorably and perceptively the nature of Britain's government.

Formerly it was said, "The Europeans who have trade relations with China are more than one country; it is better to use them to attack each other, or to use them so that they make compromises with each other, or use them so as to separate them from each other." These three statements all seem to be calculations based on profound deliberation and far-reaching thought. And yet nowadays I am afraid that they are impracticable. Why? Because all European countries have the intention of keeping China on the outside. How can they be utilized by us? Even though there were one country which was willing to be utilized by us, all the other nations would undoubtedly ridicule her. As for two countries which engage in a prolonged struggle against each other, with the issue not yet decided, the practice in Western countries is to persuade them to make peace. If the advice is not taken, then assistance is given the weak party to attack the strong, just as England and France helped Turkey to attack Russia in recent years. . . . But the practice in the West is, after all, not a sufficient rule to be applied to China. The most tractable Western country is the United States of America. Nevertheless she still takes the victory or failure of England as her own glory or disgrace. . . . Thus there has been occasions for her to assist England, but there has never been an occasion for her to assist us and attack England. As to her relations with us, though she has never made unreasonable demands on us, she has shared all the benefits gained by England and France. . . . If she sincerely wants to give us support, how could she act in this way? . . .

* Reprinted from Ssu-yu Teng and J. K. Fairbank, *China's Response to the West: A Documentary Survey 1839–1923* (Cambridge: Harvard University Press, 1954), pp. 137–140, by permission of the publisher. Copyright 1954 by the President and Fellows of Harvard College.

If, suddenly, the Westerners seized an opportunity to attack us, how could we resist them? Our soldiers are inferior to theirs, our finances are inferior to theirs, our weapons are inferior to theirs, and our military strategies are also inferior to theirs. They already thoroughly understand the hostile actions which we on our side may take, whereas we are as yet incapable of knowing what hostilities they may commit. We excuse ourselves by saying that it is because they are too far away from us. Yet with all the publication of daily newspapers and the spread of postal communications, can we not make some inquiries and obtain some information?

If Confucius were born today we may be certain that he would not stubbornly believe in antiquity and oppose making changes. . . . First, the method of selecting civil servants should be reformed. The examination essays up to the present day have gone from bad to worse. . . . And yet we are still using them to select scholars.

Secondly, the method of training soldiers should be reformed. Now our army camps and water forces have only names registered on books, but no actual persons. The authorities consider our troops unreliable, and then they recruit militia, who can be assembled but cannot be disbanded. . . . This is called "using the untrained people to fight," which is no different from driving them to their deaths.

Thirdly, the empty show of our schools should be reformed. Now district directors of schools and sub-directors of schools are installed, one person for a small city, and two for a larger city. It is a sheer waste. . . . Such people are usually degenerate, incompetent, and senile and have little sense of shame. They are unfit to set the example for scholars. . . .

He who rules the empire should establish the foundation and not merely mend the superstructure. . . . Formerly we thought that the foundation of our wealth and strength would be established if only Western methods were respected or adopted and that the result would be achieved immediately. . . . Now in all the coastal provinces there have been established special factories to make guns, bullets, and ships. Young men have been selected and sent to study abroad. Seen from the outside, the effort is really great and fine. Unfortunately, however, we are still copying the superficialities of their methods, getting the terminology (of Western civilization) but little actual substance. The ships which were formerly built at Foochow were entirely based on old methods of Western countries, beneath contempt, to those who know. As to things made in other places, for the trick of moving a machine or valve we must rely on the instruction of Westerners. Yet, if we watch the bearing of the Chinese manufacturers, they already feel noisily pleased with themselves. They usually believe that their thinking and wisdom are sufficient to match those of the Westerners, or that they have even surpassed them.

In general [the advantage of] guns lies in the fine technique of discharging them, that of ships in the ability to navigate them. . . . The handling of effective weapons depends upon the people. . . . But the so-called able minds of our people are not necessarily able, and the so-called competent ones are not necessarily competent. They are merely mediocrities who accomplish something through the aid of others.

Therefore, the urgent problem of our nation today lies primarily in the governance of the people; next in the training of soldiers; and in these two matters the crucial thing to aim at is the accumulation of men of ability. Indeed, superficial imitation in practical matters is certainly not as effective as arousing genuine intellectual curiosity. The polishing and pounding in factories is definitely not as important as the machining of peoples' minds. . . .

Let us now talk about the conventional examination subjects. The themes on classics in the second examination ought to be replaced by some practical knowledge . . . so that the candidates can understand the body politic and can transfer their knowledge into actual practice.

England is in a remote spot overseas, three islands which stand like mountains off the northwest of Europe. . . . In view of the fine quality and strength of her armament and soldiers, the richness of her revenue and the abundance of her natural resources on European country dares to be stiff-necked with her. . . . In recent years she has maintained her prosperity and preserved her state of peace and has been so cautious in resorting to arms that unless there is no other way out she never carelessly starts a military expedition. . . .

The real strength of England, however, lies in the fact that there is a sympathetic understanding between the governing and the governed, a close relationship between the ruler and the people. . . . My observation is that the daily domestic political life of England actually embodies the traditional ideals of our ancient Golden Age.

CHINA'S RESPONSE TO THE WEST: 67
REVOLUTIONARY PHASE

By the end of the nineteenth century, some reformers in China were demanding not only institutional change but also outright revolution, a shift brought about by China's humiliating defeat at the hands of the Japanese in 1894–1895, and by the growth of a Chinese merchant class (within China and abroad) which felt little loyalty to the reigning Manchu dynasty. The leader of the revolutionists, Dr. Sun Yat-sen, who received a Western education in Honolulu and Hong Kong, founded in Tokyo in 1905 the T'ung-meng hui, or League of Common Alliance. Its program, from which the following selection is taken,* called not only for the overthrow of the Manchus, but also for the establishment of a republic and the distribution of land amongst the peasants.

We proclaim to the world in utmost sincerity the outline of the present revolution and the fundamental plan for the future administration of the nation.

1. DRIVE OUT THE TARTARS.   The Manchus of today were originally the eastern barbarians beyond the Great Wall. They frequently caused border troubles during the Ming dynasty; then when China was in a disturbed state they came inside Shan-haikuan, conquered China, and enslaved our Chinese people. Those who opposed them were killed by the hundreds of thousands, and our Chinese have been a people without a nation for two hundred and sixty years. The extreme cruelties and tyrannies of the Manchu government have now reached their limit. With the righteous army poised against them, we will overthrow the government, and restore our sovereign rights. Those Manchu and Chinese military men who have a change of heart and come over to us will be granted amnesty, while those who dare to resist

---

* Reprinted from Ssu-yu Teng and J. K. Fairbank, *China's Response to the West: A Documentary Survey 1839–1923* (Cambridge: Harvard University Press, 1954), pp. 227–229, by permission of the publisher. Copyright 1954 by the President and Fellows of Harvard College.

will be slaughtered without mercy. Chinese who act as Chinese traitors in the cause of the Manchus will be treated in the same way.

2. RESTORE CHINA. China is the China of the Chinese. The government of China should be in the hands of the Chinese. After driving out the Tartars we must restore our national state. Those who dare to act like Shih Ching-t'ang or Wu San-kuei will be attacked by the whole country.

3. ESTABLISH THE REPUBLIC. Now our revolution is based on equality, in order to establish a republican government. All our people are equal and all enjoy political rights. The president will be publicly chosen by the people of the country. The parliament will be made up of members publicly chosen by the people of the country. A constitution of the Chinese Republic will be enacted, and every person must abide by it. Whoever dares to make himself a monarch shall be attacked by the whole country.

4. EQUALIZE LAND OWNERSHIP. The good fortune of civilization is to be shared equally by all the people of the nation. We should improve our social and economic organization, and assess the value of all the land in the country. Its present price shall be received by the owner, but all increases in value resulting from reform and social improvements after the revolution shall belong to the state, to be shared by all the people, in order to create a socialist state, where each family within the empire can be well supported, each person satisfied, and no one fail to secure employment. Those who dare to control the livelihood of the people through monopoly shall be ostracized.

The above four points will be carried out in three steps in due order. The first period is government by military law. When the righteous army has arisen, various places will join the cause. The common people of each locality will escape from the Manchu fetters. Those who come upon the enemy must unite in hatred of him, must join harmoniously with the compatriots within their ranks and suppress the enemy bandits. Both the armies and the people will be under the rule of military law. The armies will do their best in defeating the enemy on behalf of the people, and the people will supply the needs of the armies, and not do harm to their security. The local administration, in areas where the enemy has been either already defeated or not yet defeated, will be controlled in general by the Military Government, so that step by step the accumulated evils can be swept away. Evils like the oppression of the government, the greed and graft of officials, the squeeze of government clerks and runners, the cruelty of tortures and penalties, the tyranny of tax collections, the humiliation of the queue—shall all be exterminated together with the Manchu rule. Evils in social customs, such as the keeping of slaves, the cruelty of footbinding, the spread of the poison of opium, the obstructions of geomancy (feng-shui), should also all be prohibited. The time limit for each district (hsien) is three years. In those hsien where real results are achieved before the end of three years, the military law shall be lifted and a provisional constitution shall be enacted.

The second period is that of government by a provisional constitution. When military law is lifted in each hsien, the Military Government shall return the right of self-government to the local people. The members of the local council and local officials shall all be elected by the people. All rights and duties of the Military Government toward the people and those of the people toward the Government shall be regulated by the provisional constitution, which shall be observed by the Military Government, the local councils, and the people. Those who violate the law shall be held responsible. Six years after the securing of peace in the nation the provisional constitution shall be annulled and the constitution shall be promulgated.

The third period will be government under the constitution. Six years after the provisional constitution has been enforced, a constitution shall be made. The administrative and military powers of the Military Government shall be annulled; the people shall elect the president, and elect the members of parliament to organize the parliament.

PIONEER JAPANESE ADVOCATE OF WESTERNIZATION   68

Japan led all other Asian countries in the nineteenth century in the speed and thoroughness of her modernization. Yukichi Fukuzawa (1834–1901), a pioneer in this modernization, learned Dutch and English, and traveled widely in the United States and Europe. On his return to Japan, he wrote books in which he enthusiastically described the advantages of certain aspects of Western civilization. Millions of copies were sold, making it possible for Fukuzawa to establish a newspaper through which he continued his campaign for change. In 1898, shortly before his death, Fukuzawa dictated his autobiography, from which the following passages have been selected.* They reveal his opposition to the traditional Chinese learning, his keen interest in Western science, his reactions and difficulties while traveling in Europe, and his reflections on his life's work.

The true reason of my opposing the Chinese teaching with such vigor is my belief that in this age of transition, if this retrogressive doctrine remains at all in our young men's minds, the new civilization cannot give its full benefit to this country. In my determination to save our coming generation, I was prepared even to face, single-handed the Chinese scholars of the country as a whole.

Gradually the new education was showing its results among the younger generation; yet men of middle age or past, who held responsible positions, were for the most part uninformed as to the true spirit of Western culture, and whenever they had to make decisions, they turned invariably to their Chinese sources for guidance. And so, again and again I had to rise up and denounce the all-important Chinese influence before this weighty opposition. It was not altogether a very safe road for my reckless spirit to follow.

.   .   .

Of course at that time there were no examples of industrial machinery. A steam engine could not be seen anywhere in the whole of Japan. Nor was there any kind of apparatus for chemical experiments. However, learning something of the theories of chemistry and machinery in our books, we of the Ogata household spent much effort in trying out what we had learned, or trying to make a thing that was illustrated in the books.

I had known since my residence in Nagasaki that iron could be tin-plated if we

---

* Reprinted from *The Autobiography of Yukichi Fukuzawa,* trans. Eiichi. Kiyooka (New York: Columbia University Press, 1966), pp. 216–217, 84–86, 126–129, 333, 334–335, by permission of the translator and publisher.

had zinc chloride. In Japan the art of plating copper with tin by the use of pine pitch had been known, for all the copper or bronze cooking vessels were tin-plated. We students decided that we would plate iron by the modern method. There was no standard chloric acid to be purchased in a store, so we had to find out a way of preparing it ourselves. After laboring over it from the description in the text, we finally made the acid, and melting some zinc in it, we succeeded in plating iron with tin— a feat beyond the practice of any tin craftsman in the land. Such was the irresistible fascination of our new knowledge.

.　　.　　.

Then we tried ammonium chloride. The first requisite for this experiment was bone, but we learned that horse-hoof would serve as well. So we went to a store where they sold tortoise-shell ware to get some fragments of horse-hoofs. It was quite cheap; we could have it for the asking. I had heard that horse-hoof was used for fertilizing, but that was of no concern to us. We took a large quantity of the hoofs and covered it in an earthenware jar with a layer of clay; then placed it on a charcoal fire in a large bowl. As we fanned the fire vigorously, a smelly vapor came out; this we condensed in an earthenware pipe.

Our experiment was going very well, and the condensed vapor was dripping freely from the pipe, but the disadvantage proved to be the awful stench of the vapor. It can easily be imagined what the result of heating bones and horse-hoofs would be, especially in the small back yard of the dormitory. Our clothing became so saturated with the gas that when we went to the bath house in the evening, the street dogs howled at us. Then we tried the experiment naked; our skins absorbed the smell. The young men were so keen on their experiment that they stood the smelly ordeal without complaint. But all the neighbors objected and the servants in the Ogata household wailed that they could not eat their dinner on account of the sickening gas.

After all our hardships and the complaints and apologies, a strange powdery thing was the result—not very pure, nor the correct crystals of ammonium chloride. At this stage most of the young men, including myself, decided they had had enough. But others, more stouthearted, would not give up the search; they insisted that to give up a work unfinished was a disgrace to their profession. And so ammonium chloride was pursued.

They hired a cheap boat on the Yodo River, and placing their brazier and utensils on board, continued the odorous experiment in midstream. Still the vapor penetrated the nearby shores, and the people would come out and yell to them to get out of the way. Then the young men would have the boat rowed upstream, keeping on with the experiment until they were urged to move again downstream. So up and down from Tenjin Bridge to Tamae Bridge they went on for many days. The chief of these determined students was Nakamura Kyōan from Kompira in Sanuki province.

Besides such experiments in chemistry, the Ogata students were interested in dissecting animals, stray dogs and cats, and sometimes even the corpses of decapitated criminals. They were a hardened, reckless crowd, these aspirants for Western learning, . . .

.　　.　　.

There were about forty men in the party [travelling in Europe]. . . . We all wore our Japanese dress with a pair of swords in our girdles, and appeared on the streets of London and Paris in such attire. A sight indeed it must have been!

.　　.　　.

When we reached Paris and had been formally received by the welcoming French officials, the first request we had to make was that as many of our party as possible be quartered near the chief envoy's hotel because of our number and the amount of our baggage. The heads of the mission were evidently anxious, because if different members of the party were scattered in remote hotels, it might be inconvenient and unsafe in the strange land. The host of the welcoming committee understood, nodded his approval and asked the number of our party. When he was told it was forty, he replied, "If you are only forty, why, one of our hotels could accommodate ten or twenty of such parties." We did not comprehend what he meant, but on reaching the hotel assigned to us, we found that he was not jesting.

Our headquarters were the Hotel du Louvre, opposite the entrance to the imperial palace. It was really a huge edifice of five stories with six hundred rooms and over five hundred employees. More than a thousand guests could be accommodated at one time. So the large party of our Japanese envoys was lost in it. Instead of our anxiety lest the party might have to be separated in distant hostelries, our real anxiety became the possibility of losing our way in the maze of halls and corridors in the one hotel.

No stove or steam radiators were necessary in our rooms, for heated air circulated through them. Numerous gaslights served to illuminate the rooms and halls so that we could not tell the coming of darkness outside. In the dining hall there was such a spread of food, delicacies of "both the woods and the sea," that even those in the mission who professed their dislike of "foreign objects" could not maintain this aversion in the choice of food. The joke was in the stock of Japanese supplies brought along in our baggage. We could not cook our rice in the kitchen of the hotel; nor was it possible within reason to use the oil-wick lamps in the halls. Finally, disgusted with all this useless impedimenta, we piled them up in an apartment and offered the entire store of rice, oil-lamps, and all to one of the lesser members of the welcoming committee, M. Lambert (?), and asked him to take it gratis.

As we were unfamiliar with Western life and customs, there was naturally no end of farcical situations occurring among our party. A servant brought *sugar* when ordered to go for *cigars*. Our doctor of Chinese medicine had intended to buy some powdered carrot, but instead he had come away with *ginger,* as he found later.

When one of the lord-envoys had occasion to use the toilet, he was followed to the doorway by one of his personal attendants carrying a lighted paper lantern. The attendant in his most formal dress was to be seen squatting patiently outside the open door, holding his master's removed sword. This happened to be in the bustling corridor of the hotel where people were passing constantly, and the gas was burning as bright as day. But unperturbed sat the faithful guardian. I happened to come along and see the incident which I ended by shutting the doors. Then turning to the man, I told him quietly of the etiquette of Europeans on such occasions, but my heart was fluttering with consternation.

         •   •   •

Sixty odd years is the length of life I have now come through. It is often the part of an old man to say that life on looking back seems like a dream. But for me it has been a very merry dream full of changes and surprises.

         •   •   •

Were I to dwell on difficulties and hardships, I might easily describe this life of mine as a pretty hard one. The old proverb reminds us, "Once past the throat, the burn [of the food] is forgotten." Of course poverty and other hardships were hard to bear. But as I look backward now, they seem dear among the old glowing memories which remain.

When I first began my studies, all that I hoped for was to acquire some knowledge of the Western culture and then so manage my living that I should not become a burden upon other men. That was my first ambition. Unexpectedly came the Restoration, and to my delight Japan was opened to the world.

Seiyō Jijō (Things Western) and other books of mine published during the old shogunate régime were written with no real expectation that they would interest the public at all. Even if they were to win some attention, I had no idea that the contents of the books would ever be applied to our own social conditions. In short, I was writing my books simply as stories of the West or as curious tales of a dream-land. Then contrary to all my expectations these books were read widely and were even taken for guidance by the people of the day. Moreover, the government of the new age proved itself most courageous in applying the new thoughts. It went far beyond what was advocated in my Seiyō Jijō, and began to surprise even the author of the book himself.

In this unexpected turn of events I found that I could not be satisfied with my former ambition. I must take advantage of the moment to bring in more of Western civilization and revolutionize our people's ideas from the roots. Then perhaps it would not be impossible to form a great nation in this far Orient, which would stand counter to Great Britain of the West and take an active part in the progress of the whole world. So I was led on to form my second and greater ambition.

Consequently I renewed activities with "tongue and brush," my two cherished instruments. On one side I was teaching in my school and making occasional public speeches, while on the other I was constantly writing on all subjects. And these comprise my books subsequent to Seiyō Jijō. It was a pretty busy life but no more than doing my bit or "doing the ten thousandth part" as we put it.

As I consider things today, while there are still many things to be regretted, on the whole I see the country well on the road to advancement. One of the tangible results was to be seen a few years ago in our victorious war with China, which was the result of perfect cooperation between the government and people.

Chapter Thirty-one

Impact of dominance:
Africa

EUROPE'S IMPACT: ECONOMIC   # 69

The partitioning of Africa brought with it far-reaching economic consequences. Mines were opened, roads and railways constructed; white settlers moved into the fertile and healthy uplands, and Africans everywhere were compelled by various means to work on plantations and in mines. For the first time, the African was involved in the world-wide money economy, and subordinated, directly or indirectly, to the white man who was everywhere the boss. Precisely what these changes meant is evident in the following reply of an Anang (Nigerian) chief when asked which were better, the "old days" or modern times.*

Things have changed very much during the last few years. The beginning of Native ["indirect"] Administration and taxation has not all been good. The old men and chiefs are much poorer than the young men today. Children were more obedient to their parents than at present. Strong-headed sons and daughters were mercilessly punished. The young men lived in their fathers' compounds and worked for them. They might work for others and have some money but they could not make use of it without the knowledge and consent of the old men. The Father of the House had to protect them and provide food and clothing. He would marry wives for his sons and give them some yams to add with their own to maintain themselves with their wives. They had to continue helping the old men and the people of the compound. Now, they look after their own interests. Sometimes they will give assistance if there is any big trouble. But at present, it is very hard for

---

* Reprinted from "The Story of Udo Akpabio of the Anang Tribe, Southern Nigeria," recorded by the Rev. W. Groves, in M. F. Perham, ed., *Ten Africans* (London: Faber & Faber Ltd., 1936), pp. 57–59, by permission of Northwestern University Press.

some people to get a helping hand if they have no money, for every small piece of work needs payment.

Before taxation we were informed that the price of palm produce would be raised, but now, oil and palm kernels are very little valued by the Europeans. As palm produce is the chief means of living, I do not know what the life of the people will be in a few years' time as regards the payment of tax and the buying of food. It is a struggle to work out ways and means of maintenance and taxation.

Taxation has also increased the number of thieves. There are many whose names have been recorded as taxpayers, but they have no means of fulfilling this condition. They have no proper work and neither can they get any in these days. Men come to me for help, asking for work to save them from stealing. I do my best for them. When the time comes to pay the tax there seems to be a plague of thieving. Sometimes the young men run away to different parts of the country and do not return to their homes for a long time. Some will stay away for one and two years. During this long absence the Father of the Family has to find the money to pay the full assessment of the tax. He has to pay for the absent ones and can get no relief unless he can prove that they are dead.

The paying of tax has done another evil thing. Young men apply to the District Officer [British colonial official] for work as clerks, messengers or labourers. The officers refer them to the chiefs. If the applicants are disappointed in their request they put the blame on the chiefs. For this they find ways and means of killing their chiefs.

In the native courts there are many more disturbances than there used to be years ago. In judging cases many people stand up and give their own decision even though they are not the elected chiefs. The District Officers of this time differ very much from those we had formerly; whenever they go to some courts they tell the non-members [those who are not chiefs] that they all have right in everything just because they have paid the tax. . . .

On the other hand there are many advantages derived from this new fashion of government. There are many new and better roads throughout the district. We are not now compelled to make and look after them. There are special labourers who work every day to keep them in good condition. They are paid from taxation funds. We have no trouble about carrying loads. This is all done by motors bought from the tax money. When we are called to build any house or do any kind of work we are paid for it. Many bridges have been built. In some places where the people have to walk many miles for their water, deep wells have been made in their towns.

The establishment of many courts has done good in keeping all the villages in closer touch with the Government. At the same time it is bad in some ways. It brings a separation, jealousy and enmity between one clan and another. At present, when a man from one clan sues a man of another clan and the case is tried in the defendant's area, the chiefs of that court may sometimes be partial and spoil the case. This was not so when we had the central court. . . . The people would deal with one another as brothers.

This new system has also done good in the way it is encouraging education. Several schools have been built for different clans. There is also a Training College where our best young men can become teachers. These are all paid for and supported by our tax.

Europe affected Africa's culture as well as its economy. The key role in this field was played by the missionary, the only European who came with the deliberate intention of changing the African's way of life. At the onset the missionaries had much difficulty in altering the traditional customs and beliefs, especially in the early days when the African villages were virtually unaffected by the white man. But gradually, and in various ways, the missionaries left their mark. How one of them did so is described in the following account from the autobiography of Prince Modupe, an African who came to the United States in 1922 and decided to remain here. The incident he describes occurred during his boyhood when he was living amongst his people, the So-So tribe, in the village of Dubricka in present-day Guinea.*

Everyone was abuzz about the expected arrival of the white man with the powerful juju. If his magic was more powerful than ours, then we must have it. That was Grandfather's decree. Grandfather wanted our people to have the best of everything. I doubt now that he had the slightest notion of the sweeping changes the new juju would bring with it. He probably thought of it as similar to the juju with which we were familiar, only more potent.

We believed in the existence of a demon who was said to be white in color. But of course this man we were expecting could not be an ogre or Grandfather would not receive him. There were a few other white, or nearly white things in our lives —cotton, white chickens, white cola, grubs in rotten stumps, white ants. These seemed natural and everyday enough but a white human was beyond simple imagining.

As I listened to the wild speculation among the villagers, the image which formed in my mind was that of a white ant or termite queen. After she has been fertilized, she is sealed in a clay cyst in the castellated termite mound and her abdomen becomes hugely distended, several inches long. If this cyst is dug out and cracked open, the amazing abdomen, egg-swollen, can be seen softly palpitating. I wondered whether white human skin was soft as a swollen termite belly and whether the coursing of blood and the processes of digestion could be seen through a milky transparent outer covering, unpleasantly soft to the touch.

·   ·   ·

Finally, the white man arrived. My first sight of him was a delightful relief. He did not appear to have demon quality and although his belly was large, it was not out of proportion to his head like the termite queen's. The only part of him that was much out of scale was his feet which were encased in leather. For some reason, I had believed from childhood that to be a real man one had to have a large belly and big feet. This fellow had both and he looked human besides. Furthermore, he was not really white as milk is white, not the portion of him which showed, at least; he was more the color of leather. Most of him was covered; the black coat hung down past his knees, and the short stocky neck was bound with a band of cloth which was really white. His lips seemed like nothing more than a faintly red

* Reprinted from Prince Modupe, *I Was a Savage* (New York: Harcourt Brace Jovanovich, Inc., 1957), pp. 62–72, by permission of Harcourt Brace Jovanovich and Paul R. Reynolds. Copyright © 1957 by Harcourt Brace Jovanovich, Inc.

slit in his face and his nose seemed bird-beakish long and thin. His wife and a little girl-child were with him, and they, too, were encased in clothing. The child had hair which hung to her shoulders and was the color of gold. It was in ringlets like shavings from the chisels of our wood carvers, not springy and crisp like mine. The three were led across the clearing to the royal stool where my grandfather sat waiting for them. The elders, the witch doctors, and the head warriors moved forward with them as they advanced to stand before the chief. The rest of us, out of custom, remained in the background, not pressing too close. . . . Grandfather sat his stool with grave dignity. There was a waiting-to-see in his posture as the missionary placed gifts at his feet. . . .

Finally, stools were brought for the man and his family. If the stools had not been fetched, it would have meant lack of approval of the missionary's manners and lack of further interest on Grandfather's part. The interview would have been over. . . . All that interested me at the moment was getting closer to the heap of gifts at Grandfather's feet.

When I had wormed my way into view of them, the objects seemed to be new things and there was glitter among them. They did not have the earth quality of our own artifacts. I later came to know these things as a Bible, a camera, a mirror, a kaleidoscope, shoes, a high hat, cigarettes, matches, canned goods, shiny trinkets, and yard goods. There was something else which may need a bit of explanation to an American reader—a keg of whiskey. We had palm wine to drink, a mild fermented brew of palm sap, but we had never heard of distilled liquor. In time I was to learn that the particular missionary who visited us belonged to a denomination which makes a distinction between temperance and abstinence. Their ministers are allowed to drink and to smoke but not to excess. I suppose our visitor thought that mellowing our minds toward his words was a worthy use of whiskey.

The photographs which the man brought showing bridges and cities, trains, boats, big buildings, were not impressive to us even when we were allowed to view them at close range. Having had no experience with the diminished scale of things in a photograph, we gained no concept of magnitude. But there were other pictures which disturbed me deeply. They were bright depictions of heaven and hell, which I later learned were made expressly for mission use. In them all the bright angels hovering over the golden streets had white faces. The tortured creatures in hell with the orange-red flames licking over agonized contorted bodies all had black faces! . . .

The missionary spoke to us through his interpreter. He denounced our old ceremonious life, the rituals, especially sacrifice. He said that we worshipped wood and stone and graven images. This was not accurate but no one was impolite enough to contradict him. Anyway, it would have been too difficult to make a stranger understand. For a moment there was a deep silence. Some one coughed. An old man shuffled his feet. An elder next to me rumbled in his throat. I turned my head and saw that it was Granduncle D'gba. I gave my attention back to the missionary, wondering why Grandfather allowed him to go on insulting everything we held sacred and valuable. I could see that Grandfather was trying his best to follow the spirited ranting of the white man. His expression was puzzled and he was trying his best to understand. Perhaps the juju would be clearer to us than the speech.

The crowd became restless. All this talk-talk! Their politeness held up but they shifted their weight on their feet, squirmed a little, rustled quietly. Finally, the harangue ended.

The missionary picked up the mirror, made a few twists of his wrist as though gathering up the invisible power in the vicinity of it, and gazed into the glass.

Grandfather leaned forward watching closely. The white man proffered the shiny handle to Grandfather. My grandfather, who had always been considered a brave man by his people, jerked back away from it. Then, warily, he accepted it. He did not gaze into it at once. It was plain that he feared the thing. The missionary spoke reassurance.

The crowd tensed. Grandfather had to go through with what he had started or forfeit pride. He looked into the mirror. A cry of surprise escaped from his throat. He turned the handle, looking at the back, and saw his reflection disappear. When he turned it to the front side, there he was again! He spoke to his brother D'gba. . . .

D'gba reluctantly approached, his face contorted with scorn. An order from the chief was an order, brother or not. Every muscle in his body spoke of his aversion to the command but he dared not speak against it. Grandfather handed D'gba the mirror, pointed at the image. D'gba howled and fell to the ground, the mirror in his hand. He laid the fearful thing in the dust and smashed it with his fist. Perhaps he thought to liberate his trapped self from it, to get his face back. The glass broke, cutting his hand. Blood dripped from him as he stood up.

Blood has mystic significance to an African: Blood is life-stuff; life drips away with blood. . . .

While an excited murmur ran through the crowd and D'gba examined his red-dripping hand, the missionary spoke quickly and emphatically to Grandfather. Grandfather nodded and gave us the verdict. What had happened was due to D'gba's resentment of the white man's god. D'gba had been punished as we had all seen. The white man's god was capable of punishments far beyond this. What was the loss of a little blood compared to having to spend all of the time not yet come, rolling in the hot flames of hell? A black devil with horns kept the fires tended. . . .

The missionary followed up his initial triumph with a can opener. With great flourishes he opened the can of beans and tasted some of the contents to show they were not poisoned. He offered some to Grandfather who tasted a small portion and then larger portions, approving the flavor of this wonderful *ewa,* beans not cooked, yet ready to eat, coming all together from a shining "pod" which was hard like iron. The other articles were shown, demonstrated, explained. Grandfather was enchanted with the kaleidoscope, reluctant to put it down.

The missionary preached while the portions of whiskey were doled out, first to the chief and the elders, then to each villager in turn as they formed in line. Grandfather jerked his head at the first taste and coughed, but after the second attempt he was smacking his lips and requesting more.

A long time was required for the end section of the queue to come abreast of the keg. The young men had to defer to the elder ones in this as in all things, and many of the elders, after downing their allotments, would slip back into line with their age group for second helpings. . . . As many as drank and drew away and returned found themselves mellowed and ready to give themselves up to the new faith.

I noticed that Grandfather's eyes became blood-shot. When he stood up to walk he no longer moved with slow dignified royal steps. Uncertainty swayed him from side to side but he wavered toward the diminishing keg. His purpose was certain even if his feet were not. Grandfather was drunk! I did not know what drunkenness was so I attributed Grandfather's condition to his body's being possessed with the power of the new juju. I saw him waving the Bible in the air as he announced that we accepted the new religion for our own. It was true, then, I concluded, that the white juju was superior to our own. Its power had caught D'gba and drawn blood, its power had transformed Grandfather, its power produced the wonderful objects the missionary had brought, its power warmed the belly, so the men said who had swallowed the sacred elixir from the keg. . . .

Grandfather invited the white man to stay to dinner and for the night. The invitation was accepted. The women and children retreated to start the cooking and evening chores. Great fires were lighted in the compound and the warriors gathered around them. Good food was brought, steaming hot. I stayed as close to the missionary and his family as I dared. My eyes lingered on the little girl with the golden curls. I reasoned that she must be immensely wealthy to have gold-stuff for hair. It was because of her father's juju, of course, that this wealth had come to her and to her family.

. . . for the first time in my life I felt doubt about the desirability of a brown skin and kinky hair. Why did gold grow above the faces of little white girls, who according to the pictures sprouted shining wings as soon as they went to live in the glorious compound of worthy Deads, a compound glowing with gold under their pale little feet? How could they smile with what seemed a mother love delight as they peered down over the edge of the golden compound into a fiery pit . . . filled with black people who might have been So-Sos? Why did the horned demon who fueled the fires of hell have a black face like us? Why did he tooth his mouth with wild laughter while he seared the flesh of small boys who were as black as himself?

Perhaps the real reason why my limbs trembled and my hands shook was that a little of the pride and glory which I had felt in being a So-So youth had gone out with the light of this eventful day!

71   EUROPE'S IMPACT: POLITICAL

The economic and cultural changes in Africa described in the above two selections inevitably had far-reaching political repercussions. The traditional authority of tribal chieftains was undermined first by the new European administrators and then by the Western-educated Africans, resulting in the spread of new political ideas and aspirations which led up to the triumphant nationalist movement. The sources and the nature of this political revolution are reflected in the first of the following selections, a brief autobiographical sketch by Dr. Hastings Banda, leader of the Nyasaland nationalist party, who became prime minister of the new state of Malawi in 1964.* The second selection, by English writer Elspeth Huxley, analyzes the effect of the political revolution on Africa's traditional tribalism.†

Dr. Hastings Banda

I was born in Kasunga, Nyasaland, the son of an aristocratic family in my tribe. I was educated in a Church of Scotland mission. I left Nyasaland as a boy of 13

* Reprinted from H. K. Banda, "Return to Nyasaland," *Africa Today,* II (June 1960), 9, by permission of Africa Today.
† Reprinted from E. Huxley, "Two Revolutions That Are Changing Africa," *The New York Times Magazine* (May 19, 1957), pp. 9, 69–70, by permission of the publisher. Copyright © 1957 by The New York Times Company.

in standard three because I desired to get the kind of education I couldn't get in Nyasaland.

I walked to Johannesburg—a total of 1,000 miles—but not in a single stretch; I walked and walked and walked. Then I worked in the Rand mines, first underground, but then on the surface for the compound manager because I spoke English. I refused to go to the Dutch Reform Church and went to an African Methodist Episcopal Church. The Church helped me go to Wilberforce Academy in Ohio.

I received a diploma in 1929. I had talked to the Kiwanis Club in Marion, Indiana, and Dr. Herald—a white man—said that he wanted me to go to his alma mater, the University of Indiana. He helped me attend that university at Bloomington and from there I transferred to the University of Chicago. I received my Bachelor of Philosophy degree, studying political science and history, on December 22, 1931. Then I went to Meharry Medical School in Nashville, where I graduated in 1937. I continued my medical studies in Edinburgh and was an assistant medical officer in Liverpool, and then practiced in London.

When Federation of the Rhodesias and Nyasaland was suggested, I led the opposition in London. The Colonial Office said Federation was for economic, defense, and communications reasons, but the Southern Rhodesian whites demanded it to make sure that Nyasaland and Northern Rhodesia would not become independent states. Federation is not "partnership"—a word dangled as bait before British liberals—but it is domination by the racial policies of Southern Rhodesia which differ in degree but not in essence from those of South Africa. After independence, there can be genuine partnership, even Federation—but only of equals, entered into freely. Then Nyasaland might turn to Tanganyika, Northern Rhodesia, and Congo.

When Federation was imposed on my people in 1952, I decided to leave London. I went to Ghana and practiced medicine from 1953 to 1958. At the annual meeting of the African National Congress of Nyasaland in 1957 two resolutions were adopted, one calling for self-government, the other asking for secession from Federation. I was asked by my people to return to Nyasaland after 40 years to help them attain these objectives.

I returned on July 6, 1958. I toured the whole country and within less than four months I had all of Nyasaland on fire—politically. Because I refused to compromise, the government devised a story [of] . . . the so-called massacre plot. . . .

On March 3, 1959, more than 1,000 of us were arrested. I remained in prison for 13 months, without charges and without trial. What did I do in prison? I taught other prisoners. I studied the constitutional history of England and read biographies —of Washington, Jefferson, Lincoln, Franklin. I began my own autobiography. I was released on April 1, 1960. The British are the only colonial people who send a man to prison today only to invite him to Westminster [Parliament] if not Buckingham Palace tomorrow.

Elspeth Huxley

. . . Everywhere colonialism, in its old form, is on the way out. In places it has gone altogether. . . . In other countries it will linger on, but no one supposes that the winds of independence can be halted at this or that international boundary. . . .

The second revolution is the breakdown of tribalism, under which Africans have lived, not for a century or two, but for untold thousands of years. Tribalism is a pattern of living ingrained into their very bones and blood. . . .

Unquestioning loyalty to the chief or tribal council, and a reverence for ancestral spirits who remain active members of the family circle, are the twin pillars of tribalism. It is a system that binds people together, usually with bonds of ritual and secrecy, into close-knit units based on what anthropologists call the extended family —distant cousins and half-brothers-in-law as well as one's own parents and children—and for centuries it enabled them to survive and even prosper in the primitive conditions of pre-colonial society.

It is this system that is going, swept away by a great tide of Western education and political change. Nationalists like Nkrumah, and others less famous but as powerful in their own countries—Dr. Azikiwe and Chief Awolowo in Nigeria, Dr. Enderley in the Cameroons, Tom Mboya of Kenya, M. Houphouet-Boigny of the Ivory Coast, M. Senghor of Senegal, Julius Nyerere, the trade unionist of Tanganyika; Harry Nkumbula of Northern Rhodesia, Wellington Chirwa of Nyasaland— these and other educated, Westernized leaders ride the crest of the wave that is carrying to remote bush villages and roadless plains not simply Western customs and techniques, but a whole new social order.

Away with chiefs, welcome democracy; down with ritual, up with schools; out with peasantry, in with industry and trade unions; abolish the village council, set up the ballot box. These are the current demands, that is the revolution that is shaking to its foundations the oldest and most baffling continent of them all.

No revolution as profound as this can be made without destroying good as well as bad, without creating doubts as well as hopes. Votes, universal suffrage, Cabinets, Assemblies, Prime Ministers—these things are as foreign to Africa as refrigerators and telephones. The question is how many of them Africans will really want to keep. When the last palefaced civil servant has handed over his files to his native successor, will the set-up begin to drift back into something more native to the old Africa?

That is one doubt: that people only one generation removed from tribalism, still fearful of magic and ancestral spirits, still (in the main) illiterate and ignorant of the larger world, may find themselves unable to resist the blandishments of demagogues, and the temptation to barter their votes for impossible promises, or sell them to the highest bidder. Difficulties of keeping order may be such that leaders of the new central governments may take unto themselves the powers of dictators in order to prevent disintegration. There is, in short, the danger that the West is trying to sell the tribesmen of Africa something they will be unable to use, like television sets before there is any electricity.

Not long ago I asked an African politician, an Oxford graduate and now a Cabinet Minister, what, in his opinion, would happen after the Europeans withdrew. What about the talk of bribery, of rigged elections, of politicians lining their pockets with public money? (An independent tribunal, for instance, recently found the Prime Minister of Eastern Nigeria guilty of dipping into the treasury to prop up an insolvent bank, of which he and several members of his family were the directors.)

He replied indirectly. The spirit of the English Puritans, he said, acclimatized in North America, doesn't thrive in Africa. "It needs a cold winter," he smiled. "You never find it in the sunny countries—Spain, Italy, South America." He waved his cigar in an expansive gesture. "It may be," he added, "that we shall revert to more *human* standards."

And it may be that these things do not matter. The right to abuse freedom is, after all, inherent in the right to exercise it. And who are we to cast the first stone?

Chapter Thirty-two

The Americas
and the British Dominions

PEOPLING THE AMERICAS

72

Although Europe had a profound impact upon Africa and Asia during the nine-teenth century, even more far-reaching was the imprint left upon the Americas and the British dominions. The basic reason for this influence was the unprecedented mass emigration from Europe, which overwhelmed the native peoples in the overseas continents. This great emigration led to the Europeanization of the formerly under-populated portions of the globe. Such Europeanization could not occur in Africa or Asia, where the indigenous populations were too numerous and too advanced to be displaced by the Europeans. But the relatively underpopulated Americas (like Australia and Siberia) were inundated by a tidal wave of European immigrants. The first of the following selections describes the wild rush of 100,000 homesteaders into Oklahoma District on April 22, 1889, when President Benjamin Harrison declared this territory open for settlement. The second is an official report on the growing migration to the Canadian prairies; the report was submitted in 1904 by the Deputy Minister of Canada's Department of the Interior.* The third is an account by a pioneer English sheep raiser in Argentina of the influx of immigrants from various European countries.†

Oklahoma Rush

For several weeks before the opening, the country, then being ready for the re-ception of homesteaders, was cleared of all individuals except the soldiers stationed there to prevent the arrival of "sooners." The latter, however, ingeniously effaced

---

* Reprinted from H. C. Candee, "Social Conditions in our Newest Territory," *The Forum*, XXV (June 1898), 427–429; *Annual Report of the Department of the Interior for the Year 1903–1904* (Ottawa, 1905), x, xxix–xxx.
† Reprinted from W. Latham, *The States of the River Plate* (London, 1868), pp. 312–330.

309

themselves for the time only; for, when the signal gun was fired, they seemed to rise from the ground, as though Cadmus had been on earth again sowing the fabled dragon's teeth. Men who had herded cattle, and those who had traded with the Indians for years, were not to be outdone by the vigilance of soldiers ignorant of sheltering "draws," hidden "dug-outs," and obscuring fastnesses of scrub-oak and blue-stem. "A feller had to keep mighty quiet until the marshal's gun fired," said a successful "sooner," "every draw kept fillin' with men all night long; an' it was hard to keep from seein' and bein' seen."

With everything cleared for action, the crowd was lined up on the border of the new country awaiting the hour of noon, April 22, 1889. It was a crowd of determined almost desperate, men and women, many of whom, having failed in the fight for prosperity, had gathered here for a fresh trial. Every man's hand was against his fellow. His neighbor on the right placed there by accident, might be the one who would beat him in the race. The men who stood in line were composed of two classes: (1) those who had failed in every undertaking, and (2) others so young that this was their first bout with fortune. Some were mounted on ponies, which they had ridden from distant states; others were in farm-wagons in which they had journeyed from Kansas, Missouri, and even from Tennessee. The failure of Western Kansas after its period of booming was accountable for a large part of the enormous crowd that gathered at the Oklahoma border. The opportunity to try again so near home could not be neglected.

It was with difficulty that the crowd was restrained by the marshals; and, when finally the signal was given, a mad race began the results of which make interesting history. All men started as enemies. The reward was to the selfish and to the bully; and greed and strength were the winners. The number of homesteaders exceeded the number of claims; and more than one man pitched upon the same quarter section. In some cases as many as four or five insisted on the right of possession. Thus on the very first day began the contests which have ever since been a harvest to the lawyers, and have produced an unhappy condition of society unknown elsewhere. As an example, two families built their rude homes simultaneously on opposite corners of the same quarter-section; each family being positive of its own right. The help of the law was sought; decisions and reversed decisions resulted, harassing the contestants, until one, more unscrupulous and desperate than the other, shot his enemy through the window or among the outbuildings at twilight. This is not an exception, but a common condition of things.

Canadian Immigration

The steady increase in the flow of immigration that has been directed towards this country, the interest aroused amongst United States capitalists as to its possibilities, the attention which the wealth of is agricultural and other natural resources commands to-day in Great Britain, in Europe, and even in some of the most important British colonies, clearly show that Canada has at last emerged from a state of semi-stagnation in which it had remained for so many years, and its future advance, as judged by the remarkable progress of the past few years, must henceforth be by leaps and bounds.

That Canada, however, should be a nation of fifteen or twenty million inhabitants within a comparatively few years—and there are strong grounds for such belief from present indications—is a consummation to be sincerely wished for, but the question of number, desirable as it may be, is not the chief result aimed at by the department. The social character of the people that are being added to our population, and their adaptability to become loyal, prosperous and contented Canadians, is considered to be a matter of far greater moment. In this endeavor, I am glad to say, the department has been highly successful, as a careful analysis of the result of the work, both as regards the number of new arrivals and the desirable classes to which they belong will amply testify. . . .

From the returns submitted, it will be seen that the result of the work has been highly satisfactory. The total arrivals in Canada during the twelve months ending June 30 last, numbered 130,330, or, on an average, over two thousand five hundred settlers have located in the country every week during that period, and are now engaged in the development of its resources. . . .

It is the largest immigration in the history of Canada.

Immigrants in Argentina

After the War of Independence, many foreigners, chiefly British, found their way to these countries. After the notification of the treaty with Great Britain conceding to her subjects unrestricted trading rights, with protection for their lives, properties, stock, and merchandise, and exemption from military service, forced loans and all other exactions whatsoever, many British subjects settling in Buenos Ayres and the Banda Oriental purchased properties and live stock, entered into local trades and industries, or initiated new or improved systems of industry, mechanical trades, pastoral and agricultural pursuits, effecting great improvements in produce, and expanding the commerce between the two nations. . . .

Few natives ventured to make any improvement on their estates, and they were as slow to introduce the sheep industry on them as they were to improve their sheep stock when they had it. A universal feeling of mistrust pervaded all. They knew not when every peon on their establishments might be carried off for military service, or what contributions, exactions, or confiscations might be looked for. The protection which their treaties secured to foreigners, placed them under these circumstances at an advantage over the natives, inasmuch as the former were absolutely exempt from military service and from forced contributions, horses excepted, which were considered articles of war; and any injury to their properties, or the taking of their cattle to intestinal warfare, constituted claims for compensation under the existing treaties.

Induced by the low price of land and the greater security which they enjoyed, foreigners, more especially the British, purchased largely of the lands offered for sale, and devoted themselves to the sheep industry and the improvement of the almost valueless native or Creole sheep. Several large establishments were formed expressly for their improvement by crossing with Merino rams. . . .

Foremost among the actors in industrial undertakings were, as a matter of course, the foreign residents, and foreign capitalists cooperating from without. . . .

Moles and wharfs shot up, and a large extent of street surface was paved in the city of Buenos Ayres; the streets were lighted with gas; carriages, cabs, and omnibuses crowded them; houses—almost palaces—sprang up in every block; and the city increased rapidly in extent and population—the latter doubling itself in a single decade. Railways, canals, and telegraphs were projected, and are now in operation; steamers, in quick succession, coursed the rivers and connected every town of any importance with the commercial centres of Buenos Ayres and Montevideo; rural industries were prosecuted with eagerness, if with little skill, and men of all nationalities began to root themselves to the soil. . . .

Near the cities, the enclosure of lands for agricultural and horticultural purposes, scarcely before known, went on year by year to such an extent that today, around the city of Buenos Ayres, all the lands over a radius of 15 to 20 miles are subdivided and enclosed as farms or market-gardens, cultivated by Italians, Basques, French, British, and Germans. Mechanical trades kept pace with and contributed to, the general progress, these being, as a matter of course, almost monopolized by foreigners, as it was only from the immigrant ranks that the demand for skilled or other labour could be even partially supplied.

73   THE ENGLISH LANGUAGE OVERSEAS

The most striking example of the diffusion and adaptation of European culture is found in the field of language, such as French in Quebec, Portuguese in Brazil, Spanish in the rest of Latin America, and English in the United States and the British Dominions. The following selections show what has happened to the English language overseas, in Australia,* Canada,† and the United States.‡ The third selection emphasizes that the differences can be exaggerated and that the European languages have been less affected by adaptation than is commonly assumed.

Australia

"Ut's hard yacker, mate. I'm crook, and everything's up the spout."

In this manner, a particularly salty Australian bloke, a man who speaks some of the most vigorous and inventive slang on earth, might suggest that things could hardly be going worse.

The Australian peppers his speech with words that mean little to the uninformed: Yacker (work), crook (out of sorts), tucker (feed), sheila (girl), furphy (rumor), fair cow (anything that does not meet with one's unqualified approval), and 'owyergoin'mate orright? (hello).

But the great Australian adjective is bloody, a word that is avoided by polite company in England. On the continent down under, however, the word has become so commonplace that no one would hesitate to use it anywhere except the pulpit. In Aussie slang, it is just about the handiest little six-letter word available, and it would not be stretching things to give the time as, "One o'bloody clock, mate." . . .

Like the American, the Australian invented his slang out of time and circumstances in a raw, lusty country.

* Reprinted from *National Geographic News Bulletin* (Washington, D.C., May 12, 1961), by permission of the National Geographic Society.
† Reprinted from "A 'New' Language: Canadian English," *The New York Times* (November 29, 1959), by permission of the publisher. Copyright © 1959 by The New York Times Company.
‡ Reprinted from R. Quirk, "American English and English English," *The New York Times Magazine* (December 2, 1956), pp. 132 and 140, by permission of the publisher. Copyright © 1956 by The New York Times Company.

Going camping, an Australian might sleep in a wurley, gunyah, goondie, or humpy. All of these are aborigines' words for casual shelter.

He'd doubtless eat damper—bread baked in ashes. Things would certainly be fair cow if he couldn't find a billabong, or water hole. He'd boil water for tea in a tin that he'd call a billy.

If this particular Australian were traveling in the Outback, he might run across some provocatively named settlements—Hunchy Mama Creek, Venus Jump Up, Bust-My-Gall, or Broken Cart. However, the Aussie proved surprisingly sentimental in selecting place names, and the traveler would more likely encounter Anna Creek, Louisa Downs, or Alice Springs.

But you can bet your bottom dollar that the first thing a thirsty bloke would look for in Alice Springs would be a cruiser (very large glass of beer), schooner (next biggest), middy (10 ounces), or pony (the least).

In places where Australians come into contact with aborigines, they have developed a kind of pidgin patois. The result is not exactly the King's English or the Australian's English, but it does have stark, primitive dignity.

Consider this pidgin translation of the second verse of the 23rd Psalm: "Big Name makum camp alonga grass, takum blackfella walkabout longa, no fighten no more hurry watta." . . .

An indication of how far out Australian slang can go is the unofficial national song, "Waltzing Matilda." The expression's exact origin is obscure; it probably referred to a roaming man carrying his swag, or bundle. At any rate, the phrase had nothing to do with dancing or girls.

Canada

Canadians are becoming aware that they speak and write English in a distinctive way.

They are discovering what some go so far as to call the Canadian language—a unique conglomeration of spelling, pronunciation and vocabulary. . . .

The mainstreams are British and American, but there are colorful traces of Indian, Eskimo and French, plus words and phrases that are wholly Canadian.

The first big wave of American settlers that came north during and after the Revolution began a war of words with the entrenched British that is still going on today. Although many Anglicisms remain unshaken, modern communication facilities seem to be giving Americanisms the upper hand.

However, this tide has been somewhat offset by two factors: first, British immigration has far outstripped American, particularly in the post-war years; second, British English has traditionally enjoyed superior prestige.

The linguists report that the British pronunciation of schedule (shedule) is threatening to push the American (skedule) out of the dictionary.

However, the British newcomer soon finds that he gets blank stares when he talks of petrol, silencer, boot and demister so he switches to gas, muffler, trunk and windshield wiper.

There are other areas where a Briton will be quite at home, however. Most Canadians say blinds, tap and braces, rather than shades, faucet and suspenders.

In pronouncing "dance," most Canadians pronounce the "a" as in "dad"; the British pronounce it as in "father." Yet the Canadians pronounce lever like beaver and been like bean (not sever and bin, as do Americans). . . .

In spelling also the conflict between the main influences is evident. Many still prefer the British axe, catalogue, centre, colour, honour, jeweller, mediaeval, plough and programme. But the trend seems to favor American spelling, particularly where it is more compact.

Perhaps the most interesting field for the dictionary-makers is that of the true Canadianisms, some of which, like mountie, are widely used.

One of the best examples of distinctive pronunciation is the word khaki. In Canada it rhymes with car key, whereas in the States it rhymes with lackey and in Britain with hockey.

United States

British travelers in the New World since the eighteenth century have returned home with lurid tales of the "barbarous" English used there. This description was in fact used by an Englishman in the Seventeen Thirties of the word "bluff," which he had heard in the sense of "steep bank." A century later we find Dickens in "Martin Chuzzlewit" making sarcastic comments on words like "location" and pronunciations like "prod-ooce" and "terri-tory." During the same period American visitors to Britain returned with jeers about the Englishman's overfrequent use of "you know," his "wery" for "very," "anythink" for "anything" and his clipped words like "lib'ry" and "secret'ry." An early nineteenth-century American farce burlesqued British speech also with lines like "Halbert, did you 'ear 'im?" . . .

But, despite spirited American counterattacks of this kind, the undeniable historical priority of British English, as well as the still enduring prestige of the English Court, have left most Britons and many Americans with the belief that British English is somehow purer, more refined, less slangy than the New World variety. A typically nineteenth-century British attitude is illustrated in the story of a visit to England about 1850 by a young American lady of high social standing. At a party she got talking to a British officer who could not disguise his admiration for the way she was able to make herself understood. Unconscious of the implied insult, he took it upon himself to compliment her on her English; he even asked her if she were not remarkable among her compatriots. The girl answered, "Oh, yes, but then I had unusual advantages; there was an English missionary stationed near my tribe."

It is hard to imagine a similar exchange today. The growth of American prestige and other factors, such as the development of more sophisticated and tolerant attitudes to variations in speech (probably more prominently displayed today in Britain than in the United States), have contributed to a recognition of the right of American English (together with Australian English and other varieties) to be different from British English and yet be equally acceptable socially.

As for the extent of actual differences, there still remain serious misconceptions. These can be largely attributed to sensationalism and over-simplification on the part of most writers who offer commentaries on the regional variations within English. It is much easier to attract attention by concentrating on the differences that exist than on the broad area of agreement. It is engaging to read of what outlandish names others give to familiar objects; it is amusing to hear quips like "divided by a common language" and to read the largely invented stories of how Britons and Americans can misunderstand each other. . . .

There are popular lists of British and American variants arranged in double mutually exclusive columns which give a truly frightening impression of the degree of divergence between the major members of the English-speaking family. The British say "car," Americans, "automobile," we are told. What we are not told is that Americans use "car" too, and more frequently than "automobile" at that, and that "automobile" is readily understood in England, being found in the titles of the two motoring organizations, the Royal Automobile Club and the Automobile Association.

The British word "tap," we are told, corresponds to the American "faucet." Again there is truth in this so far as it goes; but it is dangerously incomplete—unless we know that many Americans use "spigot" instead; that both "spigot" and "faucet" have some currency in British dialects, and that having filled a glass from his faucet or tap, the American is likely to call it "tap-water." What Americans call "quotation marks" the British call "inverted commas." But there are many Britons who call them "quotation marks," too.

When the American says "sick," he means what the Englishman calls "ill," but throughout the British armed forces one "reports sick" at the "sick bay," and if lucky gets sent home on "sick leave," and needless to say, this is seldom on account of nausea. In fact there are parts of the United Kingdom where "sick" is the normal word and "ill" is regarded as highfalutin.

The American "mad" and British "angry" are another pair; people tend to ignore both the frequency of "mad" in this sense in Britain and also the substandard flavor attached to its usage in the United States. "Mail" and "post," "sidewalk" and "pavement" are not absolute divergences. "Pavement" is used in the sense of "sidewalk" not only in Britain but in Philadelphia and elsewhere. The "post" is often called "mail" in Britain and is carried in red mail vans, on mail trains, and on Royal Mail steamers; in America, mail is sorted at the post office, often takes the form of a postcard, bearing a stamp saying "United States Postage" and is delivered by a man who is often described as a postman.

And so one could go on. The long and imposing lists of so-called distinctively British and American words and usages are 75 per cent misleading: it turns out either that both the words so nearly separated are used in one or the other country, or that both are found in both countries but are used in slightly different contexts or in different proportions. At their best, such lists draw attention to differences in preferred usage in the two areas; they are certainly no index of mutual intelligibility. There is sufficient variety of speech on both sides of the Atlantic to familiarize us with most of the forms actually used by any native speaker of English.

Indeed, even in matters of pronunciation, it is difficult to find many absolute British and American distinctions. The broad "a" in the southern British "dance" is not unlike that heard in Boston. Nasalized vowels, so often regarded as solely American, are found in Liverpool and London; the Cockney, like the New Yorker, is apt to say "noo toon" for "new tune," and "lieutenant" is pronounced "lootenant" in the Royal Navy.

Noah Webster spent years trying, largely in vain, to create a linguistic gulf by encouraging Americans to say things like "ax" for "ask," "deef" and "heerd" for "deaf" and "heard." But in his maturity, he came to recognize that in all essentials Britons and Americans spoke the same language and that (as he said) it was highly "desirable to perpetuate the sameness." There is no reason to believe that history will prove false to his wish.

Chapter Thirty-three

Significance
of the period
for world history

74   Europe Dominates the World

The great outburst of imperialist activity in the latter part of the nineteenth century brought the entire globe under the rule of a handful of European powers. How crushing was this domination is reflected in the following observations of a well-known Hungarian Orientalist, Arminius Vambery, as he travelled through Central Asia at the turn of the century.* Europe's overwhelming mastery led to the doctrine of the "White Man's Burden," the classic expression of which is the poem by Rudyard Kipling, which follows.† Another expression was given by John Strachey, a British official in India who in 1888 stated bluntly that he and his fellow officials knew what was best for India, and that that country must remain under British rule for its own good.‡

Vambery

When, comfortably seated in our well-upholstered railway-carriage, we gaze upon the Hyrkanian Steppe, upon the terrible deserts of Karakum and Kisilkum, we can scarcely realise the terrors, the sufferings, and the privations, to which travellers formerly were exposed. . . . And great changes similar to those which have taken place in Central Asia may also be noticed in greater or less degree in other parts and regions of the Eastern world: Siberia, West and North China, Mon-

---

* Reprinted from A. Vambery, *Western Culture in Eastern Lands* (London: John Murray (Publishers) Ltd., 1906), pp. 1–4, by permission of the publisher.
† Reprinted from Rudyard Kipling, "The White Man's Burden," in *The Five Nations.* Reprinted by permission of Mrs. George Bambridge, Doubleday & Company, Inc., Methuen & Co. Ltd., and Macmillan Co. of Canada Ltd.
‡ Reprinted from J. Strachey, *India,* 3rd ed. (London: Macmillan & Co. Ltd., 1903), pp. 501–506.

golia, Manchuria, and Japan were in the first half of the nineteenth century scarcely known to us, and . . . we now find that the supreme power of the Western world is gradually making itself felt. The walls of seclusion are ruthlessly pulled down, and the resistance caused by the favoured superstitions, prejudices, and the ignorance of the sleepy and apathetic man in the East, is slowly being overcome . . . present-day Europe, in its restless, bustling activity will take good care not to let the East relapse again into its former indolence. We forcibly tear its eyes open; we push, jolt, toss, and shake it, and we compel it to exchange its world-worn, hereditary ideas and customs for our modern views of life; nay, we have even succeeded to some extent in convincing our Eastern neighbours that our civilisation, our faith, our customs, our philosophy, are the only means whereby the well-being, the progress, and the happiness, of the human race can be secured.

For well-nigh 300 years we have been carrying on this struggle with the Eastern world, and persist in our unsolicited interference, following in the wake of ancient Rome, which began the work with marked perseverance, but naturally never met with much success because of the inadequate means at its disposal. . . . We may admire the splendour, the might, and the glory of ancient Rome, we may allow that the glitter of its arms struck terror and alarm into the furthest corners of Asia; but in spite of all that, it would be difficult to admit that the civilising influence of Rome was ever more than an external varnish, a transitory glamour. Compared with the real earnest work done in our days by Western Powers, the efforts of Rome are as the flickering of an oil-lamp in comparison with the radiance of the sun in its full glory. It may be said without exaggeration that never in the world's history has one continent exercised such influence over another as has the Europe of our days over Asia.

From Kipling's *The White Man's Burden*

> Take up the White Man's burden—
> Send forth the best ye breed—
> Go bind your sons to exile
> To serve your captives' need;
> To wait in heavy harness,
> On fluttered folk and wild—
> Your new-caught, sullen peoples,
> Half-devil and half-child.
>
> Take up the White Man's burden—
> In patience to abide,
> To veil the threat of terror
> And check the show of pride;
> By open speech and simple,
> An hundred times made plain
> To seek another's profit,
> And work another's gain.
>
> Take up the White Man's burden—
> The savage wars of peace—
> Fill full the mouth of Famine
> And bid the sickness cease;

And when your goal is nearest
The end for other sought,
Watch sloth and heathen Folly
Bring all your hopes to nought.

Take up the White Man's burden—
No tawdry rule of kings,
But toil of serf and sweeper—
The tale of common things.
The ports ye shall not enter,
The roads ye shall not tread,
Go make them with your living,
And mark them with your dead.

John Strachey

. . . No reasonable man can doubt the answer that we must give to the question whether the 300,000,000 of people inhabiting the numerous countries of India have benefited by our government.

The first great and obvious fact, overshadowing all other facts in significance, in this, that in place of a condition of society given up, as it was immediately before our time, to anarchy and to the liability to every conceivable form of violence and oppression, we have now absolute peace. Let not this unspeakable blessing of the Pax Britannica be forgotten. There are not many European countries where protection to life and property is so complete. . . . Except when not unfrequently the fanaticism and intolerance of rival sects of Mohammedans and Hindus burst into violent conflict, and show what would instantly follow if the strong hand of our Government were withdrawn, unbroken tranquillity prevails. Justice is administered under laws of unequalled excellence and simplicity. There is hardly any country possessing a civilised administration where the public burdens are so light. . . .

Whether all this makes our Government really popular is another question. . . .

I never heard of a great measure of improvement that was popular in India, even among the classes that have received the largest share of education. No one who has lived, as I have done for the better part of my life, among the people can have towards them feelings other than those of sympathy and affection and respect. They have qualities which deserve all admiration, but they are intensely conservative and intensely ignorant, wedded, to an extent difficult for Europeans to understand, to every ancient custom, and between their customs and religion no line of distinction can be drawn. We often deceive ourselves in regard to the changes that are taking place. We believe that our Western knowledge, our railways, and our telegraphs must be breaking up the whole fabric of Hinduism, but these things, as I have said before, have touched only the merest fringe of the ideas and beliefs of the population of India. The vast masses of the people remain in a different world from ours. They dislike everything new, they dislike almost everything that we look upon as progress, and they live, for the most part, in blind ignorance of the aims and ideas of their rulers. . . .

It would thus be an error to suppose that the British Government is administered in a manner that altogether commends itself to the majority of the Indian population. This we cannot help. Considerations of political prudence compel us to tolerate much that we should wish to alter, and to abstain from much that we might desire to see accomplished, but, subject to this most essential condition, our duty is plain. It is to govern India with unflinching determination on the principles which our superior knowledge tells us are right, although they may be unpopular.

EUROPE'S IMPACT: ECONOMIC AND SOCIAL 75

Europe's domination of the globe was most evident in the economic sphere. Hundreds of millions of peasants in villages on all continents were forced to abandon their traditional self-sufficient manner of earning their living. Inexorably they were involved in the new money economy, producing for national or international markets. This basic change affected all aspects of peasant life, including family organization, social relationships, and religious practices. Clearly illustrated in the following selection are changes that occurred in the village of Nayon, in Ecuador, following the building of a railway in 1908.*

. . . Whether it be in Latin America, Asia, Africa, or elsewhere, village communities untouched by the industrial world tend to have common characteristics in contrast with the city. Most economic life is organized about the production of food. Specialization of labor tends to be by age and sex, and within each family is to be found knowledge of the basic techniques to produce the minimal necessities for food and shelter.

The members of the village community are known to one another. Social relationships tend to be on a face-to-face basis. Chiefs or headmen often are mediators rather than figures of authority. Although conflicts and methods of adjudicating them are always found, social controls tend to be indirect and informal. There is less need for a judge when everyone knows the rules. Social status and prestige are related to family size and standing and individual abilities. The social system tends to be limited to the village, even though integrated into some larger system governing relationships between villages. Religion or ritual affects most aspects of culture. Even if specialists are found, each family head is on occasion his own priest.

The village world tends to be stable in its social structure and adequate in fulfilling its cultural functions. It maintains its membership and satisfies in tolerable measure its basic physiological needs. Both birth rates and death rates are high, but the population tends to be in balance with resources and technology. Demands upon the individual for adjustment are limited to changes in age and status. Child-rearing practices tend to prepare individuals for adult life and to shape personalities to fit the existing social and cultural demands. The way of life appears to the individuals in it, and conditioned by it, to be rational, stable, satisfying; for them it is a proper way of life.

The urban way of life is very different, especially now that industrialism creates

* Reprinted from R. L. Beals, "The Village in an Industrial World," *The Scientific Monthly,* LXXVII (August 1953), 65–73, by permission of the American Association for the Advancement of Science.

even broader demands for markets and raw materials. Economic life involves far more than the production of food and raw materials. The family no longer is the economic unit, and shrinks toward the parents and dependent children. Labor grows increasingly more specialized and dependent on complex organization. No man can know or comprehend the sources of all the economic goods for which an industrialized society has created secondary needs; men grow increasingly interdependent.

Face-to-face social relationships of importance are no longer with relatives and neighbors, but with chance associates or in the many voluntary associations. Formality and impersonality mark social intercourse, just as formal controls, police, and judiciary replace the more informal machinery of village justice. When no man knows his neighbor, he tries to make him take an oath. . . .

I should like to describe an anthropologist's field trip to the exotically remote Ecuadorian village of Nayon. Here, scarcely six miles from the Equator, one can see in microcosm some of the problems that today face the industrial world and the yet uncounted millions of village dwellers.

THE VILLAGE OF NAYON. . . . The people of Nayon are Quechua-speaking Indians, as are their neighbors. Under missionary control after the Spanish conquest, Nayon was organized as a parish. . . .

Until about thirty years ago, the village seems to have been a self-sufficient agricultural community with a mixture of native and sixteenth century Spanish customs. Lands were abandoned when too badly eroded. The balance between population and resources provided a minimum subsistence. A few traders exchanged goods between Quito and the villages in the tropical barrancas, all within a radius of ten miles. Houses were dirt-floored, with thatched roofs, and pole walls, sometimes mud plastered. Guinea pigs ran freely about each house and were the main meat source. Most of the population spoke no Spanish. Men wore long hair and ponchos and concerned themselves chiefly with farming. Most formal controls and external relationships were managed by a resident parish priest, but informal leadership and familial controls governed social relationships. From the consolidation of the Spanish conquest until about 1920, no significant change occurred. In short, people lived within an integrated, internally consistent system of social relationships, habits, customs, values, and living techniques which were satisfactorily in balance with ecological conditions, and which supplied the necessary requirements for survival of the society. . . .

RECENT CHANGES IN NAYON. The completion of the Guayaquil-Quito railway in 1908 brought the first real contacts with industrial civilization to the high inter-Andean valley. From this event gradually flowed not only technological changes, but new ideas and social institutions. Feudal social relationships no longer seemed right and immutable; medicine and public health improved; elementary education became more common; urban Quito began to expand; and finally—and perhaps least important so far—modern industries began to appear, although even now upon a most modest scale.

In 1948–1949, the date of our visit, only two men wore long hair, and only two old-style houses remain. If guinea pigs are kept, they are penned; their flesh is now a luxury food, and beef is the most common meat. Houses are of adobe or fired brick, usually with tile roofs and often containing five or six rooms, some of which have plank or brick floors. Most of the population speaks Spanish. There is no resident priest, but an appointed government official who, with a policeman, represents authority. A six-teacher school provides education. Clothing is becoming city-like; for men it often includes overalls for work, and a tailored suit, white shirt, necktie, and felt hat for trips to Quito. Attendance at church is low and many festivals have been abandoned. Volley ball or soccer is played weekly in the plaza by young men who sometimes wear shorts, blazers, and berets. There are few shops, for most purchases are made in Quito, and from there comes most of the food, so that there is a far more varied diet than twenty-five years ago. There are piped water and sporadic health services; in addition, most families patronize Quito doctors in emergencies. Since 1949 the road has been paved, and bus service is more regular. There is one reputed millionaire (in sucres, the national currency, and the equivalent of about $150,000 U.S.), and several are classed as wealthy.

Thus, although to the casual observer Nayon still seems a timeless, sleepy farm village, in little more than a quarter of a century the changes in the direction of what North Americans call progress have been enormous. Let us examine the meaning of these changes in terms of the pattern of living. . . .

LOSS OF SELF-SUFFICIENCY.   The changes in housing and clothing mean greater dependence upon the outside world. Masons must be hired to lay adobe or brick or stone walls, and so a new kind of specialist has come into being, one who works for wages. For fine work, outside craftsmen are imported along with such materials as cement and tile. Sewing machines are now considered necessary, although much clothing is purchased.

Except for some new specializations, tools for the primary occupation of farming have undergone little change. The wooden beam plow drawn by oxen, and the dibble, hoe, shovel, mattock, and machete are the universal tools. But the crops and their use have undergone notable change. Maize or Indian corn is still the primary crop, but very little is harvested as grain. Almost all is sold in Quito as green corn to eat boiled on the cob, and a considerable amount of the corn eaten as grain in Nayon is imported. Beans, which do poorly here, are grown on a small scale for household consumption. Though some squash is eaten, most is exported. Sweet potatoes, tomatoes, cabbage, onions, capsicum peppers, and, at lower elevations, sweet yucca or arrowroot are grown extensively for export; indeed, so export-minded is the community that it is almost impossible to buy locally grown produce in the village. People cannot be bothered with retail sales. Although areas devoted to fruit are small, quantities in excess of household needs are sold in Quito. Oxen are kept for plowing, but there is no dairying; milk, if used, is brought from Quito. Donkeys, mules, and horses are kept by some as pack animals. A few people buy shoats and fatten them, but not many pigs are butchered locally; again they are sold in Quito. A few others do the same with cattle, buying in Otavalo to the north, fattening, and then selling in Quito.

Clearly, then, Nayon is no longer a self-sufficient village. It is now deeply enmeshed in the money economy of a larger region, and especially with the city of Quito. . . .

CHANGING SOCIAL RELATIONSHIPS.   A characteristic of the village is its homogeneity; there are few specialists and most people share the same skills and knowledge. Nayon, once primarily agricultural, is today a village of traders. . . . Some traders handle single transactions of $6,000 or more. Others travel from Peru to Colombia. In addition, we find scattered individuals who are oil-well riggers, construction workers of at least medium skills, and mechanics. There are also two school teachers. No Nayon youth has yet reached the University, but half a dozen are in advanced technical schools and one is in the Ecuadorian naval academy.

And, to keep the picture in some sort of balance, mention should be made of the persistence of older kinds of specialists such as blanket and belt weavers, and the development of a small, essentially landless class which survives as unskilled laborers, mainy on construction jobs in Quito.

The nature of Nayon religious life and participation has likewise changed. Nayon is still Catholic in the main, and the few who have become Protestants are disliked and distrusted. Indeed, despite the intelligent and wholehearted assistance of the parish priest, the greatest obstacle to securing cooperation for the Nayon study was the persistent suspicion that we were Protestant missionaries. Nevertheless, religious influence is declining in Nayon, especially among the younger people. The parish priest today must care for half a dozen parishes and no longer resides in Nayon. Few, indeed, wish him to. Although mass is held every Sunday, attendance is usually small. Young men rarely participate, although they do not start their Sunday games of volleyball, soccer, or pitching coins until mass is concluded. On occasion though, they have spoken rudely to the priest. Most religious festivals have been abandoned or reduced to celebration of the mass. Those still retained become increasingly secular, with emphasis upon social aspects, drinking, and dancing. Even the festival of the patron saint is a poor thing, shorn of most of its color and traditional folk dances. Religion in Nayon is essentially as formal and as restricted in its function and meaning as in any city.

PENALTIES OF SUCCESS.   So far, perhaps, this account sounds like a success story entitled, "Indian Village Adapts Rapidly to Modern Life." Many members of the group have accepted major shifts in the socio-cultural system with little difficulty and look forward to additional changes. Most people in Nayon are conscious of change and of its attendant difficulties, and believe they have met the situation well.

But a major finding of modern anthropology is that culturally established technologies, behavior patterns, value systems, and social structures tend to form closely integrated socio-cultural systems. If this be true, have Nayon people understood all the ramifications of change? Has all the population adapted equally well? Let us look for some entries on the debit side. What are the problems Nayon faces, and what are the forces released by its abandonment of a way of life that has been moderately successful for four hundred years? And what has impelled Nayon citizens to make this change? These are questions Nayon shares with the thousands of villages on every continent.

One characteristic of the village world is the existence of a balance between resources and population. Birth rates and death rates are in balance unless nearby cities absorb surplus population. Living standards tend to be relatively unchanging. In Nayon improved health conditions, erosion, and new living standards have between them destroyed this resources-population balance.

On the surface, it seems difficult to maintain that health conditions in Nayon have improved. Inadequate surveys of school children indicate that at least sixty to eighty per cent of the population is infested with one or more intestinal parasites. Goiter, avitaminoses, and other forms of malnutrition are prevalent. Measles, mumps, and chicken pox are considered normal for all children. Tuberculosis, malaria, and veneral disease are increasing. On the other hand, smallpox and whooping cough are fairly well controlled.

Unsatisfactory as the health situation may appear by our standards, the best test of it is the relationship between births and deaths. From the beginning of the registration of vital statistics in Nayon in 1936 through 1948, there were 287 more births than deaths. This is a population increase of nearly thirty per cent in thirteen years.

MAN AND THE LAND.   Natural resources have diminished as population has increased. Great gullies are destroying the most fertile land. Sheet erosion has removed all the top soil from large areas, exposing a hard and infertile clay subsoil. In areas under cultivation each torrential tropical rain removes top soil with frightening rapidity; streets are becoming gullies. Consequently, much land has been abandoned, and even the forested areas have been planted recently with the alien eucalyptus.

Diminishing resources and expanding population have caused excessive fragmentation of land holdings. . . .

Another measure of pressures on land is the changing price structure. Land prices increased from 3,000 to 11,700 per cent between 1918 and 1948.

These few data make it clear that the traditional balance with the environment has been destroyed at Nayon. Even if improved agricultural techniques and erosion control are introduced, approximately one-half of the Nayon children who reach adulthood must emigrate if the village is to maintain its present relatively low living standards on the basis of agriculture. Moreover, the Nayon standard of living is rising, and aspirations for a continued betterment are strong. Any further improvement of health conditions must mean an even greater emigration rate. Alternatively, other sources of livelihood must be found.

To some degree both of these solutions are already in operation. A few families have emigrated, mostly to the coastal lowland areas now being developed in Ecuador. Others have purchased land elsewhere and may soon emigrate. This trend probably will be accelerated. Many have resorted to more extensive trading and entrepreneurial activities. Others work for wages in the nearby city.

The economic problems created in Nayon by increasing population, diminishing land base, and demands for a rising living standard are world-wide in scope. Whether on Pacific islands, in Africa, or in Asia—wherever modern public health has begun to penetrate, or where outside agencies have put a stop to such population-limiting devices as war, famine, and infanticide—population is pressing hard upon resources and native technology. Everywhere, too, the solutions being tried are creating new social problems, for the fabric of any society and its culture is composed of functionally interrelated parts; alteration of any significant part must affect all the others.

EUROPE'S IMPACT: CULTURAL   76

Nineteenth-century Europe left its mark on the world in the cultural as well as the economic sphere. The Europeans, in their first period of expansion, did not particularly impress the peoples in the ancient centers of Asian civilization. In fact, the Moslems, Hindus, and Confucians tended to look down upon the Western sea captains and merchants as uncouth and crassly materialistic. By the beginning of the twentieth century, however, this attitude was for the most part reversed. More and more, Eastern spokesmen were conceding, albeit grudgingly, the superiority not only of Western technology but also of the European way of life in general. The first selection, from a Young Turk newspaper published in Cairo at the turn of the century, refers to "the light of civilization" emanating from the West.* The second selection,

* Reprinted from A. Vambery, *Western Culture in Eastern Lands* (London: John Murray (Publishers) Ltd., 1906), pp. 343, 344, by permission of the publisher.

written shortly after World War I by a distinguished Chinese scholar, states flatly that "real spirituality" is to be found not in the teachings of Eastern religions but in the labor-saving and life-saving inventions of Western science.*

Young Turk Newspaper

Five-and-twenty years ago, Sophia was full of crooked and dirty streets, such as we still see in Adrianople, Yanina, Monastir, etc., without any features to commend itself either for beauty or convenience, and with the exception of several places of worship, barracks, and prisons, there was nothing to denote any degree of culture. Since Sophia has been under Bulgarian government, one would scarcely recognize the place on account of the many improvements and changes which have been made. It now possesses straight wide streets, public squares, theatres, museums, zoological and botanical gardens, electric light, tramways, telephone, etc. And not only Sophia, but also Varna, Philippopolis, and other towns, have been Europeanized. Roumania, Servia, and Greece, as well as Bulgaria, have been illumined by the light of civilisation since they have become independent States. Crete will soon follow suit. When we look round in our own land and see how Adrianople, Brussa, Aleppo, Damascus, and Bagdad, all once centres of the empire, have failed to maintain their former glory and beauty, and have become desolate through utter neglect of the spirit of modernization, we pity them for the darkness and ignorance into which they have sunk. At Brussa and Adrianople, situated at very short distances from the capital, we still find the primitive waggons pulled by oxen, and omnibuses, even, are an unknown convenience. But why quote instances from provincial towns? Let us take Constantinople itself, with its million inhabitants, and in point of natural beauty excelling all other capitals. On the roughly paved streets dirt and filth lie deep, and dogs prowl about. Barracks abound, but the military are only there to suppress revolts; for personal safety little or no provision is made. Stamboul has no theatres, no botanical or zoological gardens—modern institutions which have found their way even into Australia and Siberia. . . . For God's sake, let us have done with this slowness, this negligence. Let us not turn our eyes away from the light of culture.

Chinese Scholar

In July, 1926, I arrived at Harbin, in Northern Manchuria, on my way to Europe. The modern city of Harbin was formerly a Russian Concession which grew up from a small trading centre into what is now called the "Shanghai of North China." With the development of the Russian Concession, there has grown up, a few miles away, the native city of Harbin which was once only a group of peasant villages. While I was touring through the city, I was struck by one interesting fact: whereas practically all the vehicles of locomotion in the native city were jinrickshas, or carriages pulled by human power, no 'ricksha was allowed to operate in the former Russian City which, though now under Chinese administration, still retained much of Russian influence and tradition. Transportation and travelling in the modern city of Harbin

* Reprinted from Hu Shih, "The Civilizations of the East and the West," in C. A. Beard, ed., *Whither Mankind* (New York: Longmans, 1928), pp. 28–31, by permission of David McKay Co., Inc.

were by tramways and taxicabs; 'rickshas carrying passengers from the native city must leave without a fare.

Here I made my great discovery in modern geography—I discovered the border-line between the Eastern and Western civilizations. The city of Harbin separates the East from the West by separating the jinricksha (man-power-carriage) civilization from the motor-car civilization!

Let all apologists for the spiritual civilization of the East reflect on this. What spirituality is there in a civilization which tolerates such a terrible form of human slavery as the 'ricksha coolie? Do we seriously believe that there can be any spiritual life left in those poor human beasts of burden who run and toil and sweat under that peculiar bondage of slavery which knows neither the minimum wage nor any limit of working hours? Do we really believe that the life of a 'ricksha coolie is more spiritual or more moral than that of the American workman who rides to and from his work in his own motor-car, who takes his whole family outing and picnicking on Sundays in distant parks and woods, who listens to the best music of the land on the radio almost for no cost, and whose children are educated in schools equipped with the most modern library and laboratory facilities?

It is only when one has fully realized what misery and acute suffering the life of 'ricksha-pulling entails and what effects it produces on the bodily health of those human beasts of burden—it is only then that one will be truly and religiously moved to bless the Hargreaveses, the Cartwrights, the Watts, the Fultons, the Stephensons, and the Fords who have devised machines to do the work for man and relieve him from much of the brutal suffering to which his Oriental neighbor is still subject.

Herein, therefore, lies the real spirituality of the material civilization, of mechanical progress *per se*. Mechanical progress means the use of human intelligence to devise tools and machines to multiply the working ability and productivity of man so that he may be relieved from the fate of toiling incessantly with his unaided hands, feet, and back without being able to earn a bare subsistence, and so that he may have enough time and energy left to seek and enjoy the higher values which civilization can offer him. Where man has to sweat blood in order to earn the lowest kind of livelihood, there is little *life* left, letting alone civilizaton. A civilization to be worthy of its name must be built upon the foundation of material progress. As one of China's statesmen said twenty-six centuries ago, "when food and clothing are sufficiently provided for, honor and disgrace can be distinguished; and when granaries are full, the people will know good manners." This is not to drag in the so-called economic interpretation of history: it is simple commonsense. Picture a civilization where boys and girls and old women with bamboo baskets tied to their backs and with pointed sticks in hand, flock to every dumping place of garbage and search every heap of refuse for a possible torn piece of rag or a half-burnt piece of coal. How can we expect a moral and spiritual civilization to grow up in such an atmosphere?

Then people may point to the religious life in those regions where the material civilization is low. I shall not discuss those Oriental religions whose highest deities appear on roadsides in the shape of human sex-organs. I shall only ask: "What spirituality is there, let us say, in the old beggar-woman who dies in the direst destitution, but who dies while still mumbling, *Nama Amita Buddha!* and in the clear conviction that she will surely enter that blissful paradise presided over by the Amita Buddha? Do we earnestly think it moral or spiritual to inculcate in that beggar-woman a false belief which shall so hypnotize her as to make her willingly live and die in such dire conditions where she ought not to have been had she been born in a different civilization?"

No! A thousand times No! All those hypnotic religions belong to an age when man had reached senility and felt himself impotent in coping with the forces of nature. Therefore he gave up the fight in despair and, like the disappointed fox in the ancient fable who declared the grapes sour because he could not reach them, began to console himself and teach the world that wealth and comfort are contemptible and that poverty and misery are something to be proud of. From this it was only a step to the idea that life itself was not worth living and that the only desirable thing was the blissful existence in the world beyond. And when wise men calmly taught these ideas, fanatics went further and practiced self-denial, self-torture, and even suicide. . . .

How is it that the outlook upon life has so radically changed? The change has come because in the last two centuries men have hit upon a few key-inventions out of which a vast number of tools and machines have been constructed for the control of the resources and powers in nature. By means of these machines men have been able to save labor and reduce distance, to fly in the air, tunnel the mountains and sail underneath the deep seas, to enslave lightning to pull our carriages and employ "ether" to deliver our messages throughout the world. Science and machinery seem to meet no resistance from nature. Life has become easier and happier, and man's confidence in his own powers has greatly increased. Man has become the master of himself and of his own destiny.

77 FIRST CHALLENGES TO EUROPE'S DOMINATION

Europe's domination of the globe seemed, in 1914, to be permanent and irresistible. Yet, it was beginning to be challenged in many parts of the colonial world. This was especially true after the 1904–1905 Russo-Japanese War, which excited colonial peoples everywhere with its spectacle of a small Asian kingdom defeating a great European power, and the contemporaneous Russian Revolution, equally inflammatory, which inspired corresponding revolutions against decrepit Oriental dynasties that had proven incapable of resisting European imperialism. Consequently, the decade after 1905 witnessed growing opposition to Europe's hegemony. Outright revolution upset the Manchu dynasty in China, the Kajar dynasty in Persia, and the Ottoman dynasty in Turkey; and agitation and disturbances were leveled against the British in India and the Russians in Central Asia. This pre-1914 awakening is significant as marking the beginning of the great colonial nationalist movements that were later to undermine and sweep away those European empires that were so impressive before World War I. The following selections describe this early awakening of peoples in several colonial areas.

Persia

*This nationalistic verse was written by a Persian reformer in 1896, shortly before suffering death in prison.**

* Cited in E. G. Browne, *The Persian Revolution of 1905–1909* (London: Cambridge University Press, 1910), p. xi, by permission of the publisher.

Ne'er may that evil-omened day befall
When Iran shall become the stranger's thrall!
Ne'er may I see that virgin fair and pure
Fall victim to some Russian gallant's lure!
And ne'er may Fate this angel-bride award
As serving-maiden to some English lord!

India

*In the following selection, Jawaharlal Nehru describes his reaction, as a boy of thirteen, to the news of Japan's victory over Russia.**

Japanese victories stirred up my enthusiasm, and I waited eagerly for the papers for fresh news daily. I invested in a large number of books on Japan and tried to read some of them. I felt rather lost in Japanese history, but I liked the knightly tales of old Japan and the pleasant prose of Lafcadio Hearn. Nationalistic ideas filled my mind. I mused of Indian freedom and Asiatic freedom from the thralldom of Europe. I dreamed of brave deeds, of how, sword in hand, I would fight for India and help in freeing her.

British Empire

A competent British observer, Maurice Baring, was in the Near East in 1909, and reported the impact of the Russo-Japanese War in these terms.†

The British Empire includes large dominions inhabited by Muslims, and ever since the Russo-Japanese War, in all the Moslim countries which are under British sway, there have been movements and agitations in favour of Western methods of government, constitutionalism, and self-government. There has been a cry of "Egypt for the Egyptians," and "India for the Indians," and in some cases this cry has been supported and punctuated by bombs and assassinations.

Indochina

Following the Russo-Japanese War, numerous Annamite students left Indochina for Japan in order to learn the secret of the success of the victorious nation. In the following letter written in December, 1905, one of these students calls on his fellow-countrymen to prepare themselves for the struggle against their French masters. ‡

---

* Reprinted from *Toward Freedom. The Autobiography of Jawaharlal Nehru* (New York: The John Day Company, Inc.; London: The Bodley Head Limited, 1941), pp. 29–30, by permission of The John Day Company and The Bodley Head Limited. Copyright 1941 by The John Day Company.
† Reprinted from M. Baring, *Letters from the Near East 1909 and 1912* (London, 1913), pp. 12–13.
‡ Cited in T. E. Ennis, *French Policy and Developments in Indochina* (Chicago: University of Chicago Press, 1936), p. 178.

. . . All powers, all profits are in the hands of the masters with the blue eyes, the red barbarians. And we, the yellow race, we are subjected by force to demoralization, to complete degradation. In order to obtain allies, it is necessary that we have recourse to representatives of our own race. I, your humble servant, an obscure student, having had occasion to study new books, and new doctrines, have discovered in a recent history of Japan how they have been able to conquer the impotent Europeans. This is the reason why we have formed an organization. . . . We have selected from among the young Annamites those most energetic, with great capacities for courage, and are sending them to Japan for study. . . . Several years have passed without the French being aware of this movement. This is why we have been able to increase our forces. At the present time there are about six hundred students from Indochina in Japan. Our only aim is to prepare the population for the future. . . . Have you created any organization for this purpose in your region?

Russian Central Asia

The stirring events of 1904–1905 contributed greatly to the political awakening of the subject Moslem peoples in Russian Central Asia, as described in the following analysis by an American scholar.*

The defeat of Russia in the Russo-Japanese War and the Revolution of 1905 called forth an unprecedented upsurge of activity among Russia's Muslims, especially among the Turco-Tatars. This political and national awakening resulted in the holding of three all Turkish congresses in Russia, 1905–06. The first, held in Nizhny-Novgorod in August 1905, proclaimed the need for Tatar or Muslim unity in order to deal effectively with social, cultural, and political problems. The second, convened in the Russian capital, St. Petersburg, January 13–23, 1906, prepared for Muslim participation in the first Russian Duma, and decided in favor of backing the Russian Constitutional Democrats (Kadets), headed by Paul Miliukov. The fact—an important one for the Muslims—that they won twenty-five seats in the first Duma led to a third All-Muslim Congress on August 16, 1906, at Makariev, near Nizhny-Novgorod, for the purpose of organizing a Muslim Party in Russia and inaugurating a Turkic cultural and social program with a strong Pan-Turkic bent. The organization of a Muslim faction in the Russian Duma also demonstrated the active role of the Turco-Tatars in the new Russian constitutional regime. The second Duma included thirty-five Muslim deputies, and even after the revision of the electoral law, there were ten in the Third Duma of 1907.

After the Revolution of 1905 and the October Manifesto, about forty Tatar periodicals came into existence, an important medium for the spread of Muslim political activity inside Russia and abroad. In Azerbaijan, the Revolution led to the organization of new schools, theaters, and newspapers. Two outstanding news organs, *Hayat* and *Irshad,* were established in 1905. Not only did they report news about Muslims inside Russia, but they also reprinted much about Young Turk revolutionary activity in the Ottoman Empire.

* Reprinted from I. Spector, *The First Russian Revolution. Its Impact on Asia* (Englewood Cliffs, N.J.: Prentice-Hall, Inc., 1962; A Spectrum Book), pp. 63–64.

All Asia

The Chinese nationalist leader, Dr. Sun Yat-sen, delivered a speech in Japan in 1924 in which he analyzed the effect of Japan's victory over Russia as follows: *

Thirty years ago . . . men thought and believed that European civilization was a progressive one—in science, industry, manufacture, and armament—and that Asia had nothing to compare with it. Consequently, they assumed that Asia could never resist Europe, that European oppression could never be shaken off. Such was the idea prevailing thirty years ago. It was a pessimistic idea. Even after Japan abolished the Unequal Treaties and attained the status of an independent country, Asia, with the exception of a few countries situated near Japan, was little influenced. Ten years later, however, the Russo-Japanese war broke out and Russia was defeated by Japan. For the first time in the history of the last several hundred years, an Asiatic country has defeated a European Power. The effect of this victory immediately spread over the whole Asia, and gave a new hope to all Asiatic peoples. In the year of the outbreak of the Russo-Japanese war I was in Europe. One day news came that Admiral Togo had defeated the Russian navy, annihilating in the Japan Sea the fleet newly despatched from Europe to Vladivostock. The population of the whole continent was taken aback. Britain was Japan's Ally, yet most of the British people were painfully surprised, for in their eyes Japan's victory over Russia was certainly not a blessing for the White peoples. "Blood," after all, "is thicker than water." Later on I sailed for Asia. When the steamer passed the Suez Canal a number of natives came to see me. All of them wore smiling faces, and asked me whether I was a Japanese. I replied that I was a Chinese, and inquired what was in their minds, and why they were so happy. They said they had just heard the news that Japan had completely destroyed the Russian fleet recently despatched from Europe, and were wondering how true the story was. Some of them, living on both banks of the Canal had witnessed Russian hospital ships, with wounded on board, passing through the Canal from time to time. That was surely a proof of the Russian defeat, they added.

In former days, the coloured races in Asia, suffering from the oppression of the Western peoples, thought that emancipation was impossible. We regarded that Russian defeat by Japan as the defeat of the West by the East. We regarded the Japanese victory as our own victory. It was indeed a happy event. Did not therefore this news of Russia's defeat by Japan affect the peoples of the whole of Asia? Was not its effect tremendous?

* Reprinted from Sun Yat-sen, *China and Japan* (Shanghai: China United Press, 1941), pp. 142–143.

WORLD OF
WESTERN DECLINE
AND TRIUMPH,
1914–

Chapter Thirty-four

World War I:
global repercussions

A Consensus on
the Origins of World War I

78

World War I represents a major turning point in world history because it began
Europe's decline as master of the globe. The question of responsibility for the war pro-
voked a prolonged controversy, particularly because the victorious Allies included a "war
guilt" clause in the Versailles Treaty on which they based their claims for reparation
payments. In 1935 French and German scholars attempted to reach an agreement on
this issue in order to reduce the polemics in their respective textbooks. The effort was
repeated in 1950 when a German group headed by Professor Ritter of the University of
Freiburg, and a French group headed by Professor Renouvin of the Sorbonne, reached
the following agreement on the origins of World War I.*

18) The documents do not permit attributing a premeditated desire for a
European war on the part of any government or people in 1914. Distrust was at
a peak and ruling circles were dominated by the idea that war was inevitable.
Each one accused the other of aggressive intentions; each accepted the risk of a
war and saw its only hope of security in the alliance system and the development
of armament.

19) Certain circles of the German General Staff thought the chances of success
for Germany were greater in 1914 than they would be in the succeeding years; but
one cannot deduce from this that the policy of the German government was determined by these considerations.
   b) The great majority of the French and German peoples did not want war,

* Reprinted from James A. Corbett, "France and Germany Agree—on the Past," *Historical*
Bulletin, XXXIII (March 1955), 158–62.

but in Germany, especially in military circles, there was a greater disposition than in France to accept the eventuality of a conflict.

This disposition stemmed from the place which the army held in German society; besides, Germany always felt threatened as a result of its geographic position in the center of Europe, particularly by the alliances between her possible adversaries.

c) The old opinion that Poincaré followed a policy leading to war is no longer accepted, even by German historians. However, the alliance system created in Europe a situation of such a character that Franco-Russian cooperation was felt by the Germans to be a direct danger.

20) The conflict of 1914 between Austria-Hungary and Serbia was the culmination of a long antagonism which had become manifest since the coming to power of Karageorgevitch in 1903. There was a conflict between the conception of the national state and the historic tradition of the multi-national Austro-Hungarian state. The latter felt threatened in its very existence while Serbia could not give up seeking its national ideal. As the problem of nationalities had not been solved by the government of Vienna within the framework of the Dual Monarchy it became a problem of European importance. Hence, the policy of localizing the war, followed at the beginning of the crisis in July by the governments of Vienna and Berlin, was destined to fail.

21) On the controversial question of the responsibility of the Serbian government in the preparation of the assassination at Sarajevo the Commission agrees that

a) there is no doubt of the link between the murderers and the Pan-Serbian movement;

b) direct complicity of the Serbian government in the preparation of the assassination has not been proved although it seems that certain members of this government had knowledge of it.

22) The Austro-Hungarian declaration of war on militarily ill-prepared Serbia was disastrous politically. The government of Vienna had no clear view as to the solution it would bring to the problem after crushing Serbia. The brutal rejection of the Serbian reply—a rejection which aroused astonishment even in Berlin—placed the Central Powers in the wrong before Europe. By resorting to arms the Austro-Hungarian government wished to forestall any diplomatic intervention on the part of the great powers and thus made a peaceful solution of the European crisis extremely difficult.

23a) Russia believed herself obliged in July, 1914, both by tradition and interest, to support Serbia against Austria-Hungary.

b) Although Sazonof personally feared war he wished to avoid a renewal of the failures Russian policy had suffered in the Balkans in 1909 and 1913, especially since her freedom of decision was limited by internal difficulties in Russia.

c) The Russian government considered the partial mobilization against Austria-Hungary an indispensable means of pressuring the government of Vienna into modifying its policy. If Russia changed from a partial mobilization to a general mobilization with all the political and military dangers this implied, she did so essentially for technical military reasons. These were invoked by the General Staff and carried greater weight than political considerations.

24a) In July, 1914, the British government sincerely desired the maintenance of peace and, with this in view, multiplied its attempts to mediate.

b) Under no circumstances, however, did it wish to permit Germany to defeat France. Satisfied with the results of the agreements made with Russia in 1907 it wished to avoid reviving Anglo-Russian antagonism on a world-wide scale.

c) Sir Edward Grey did not warn Germany clearly enough and in ample time that England would take the side of France and Russia in case of conflict because of hesitation in the British Cabinet and of its desire not to encourage, by taking prematurely an unequivocal position, an aggressive policy on the part of Russia.

d) Without the German violation of Belgian neutrality Sir Edward Grey would have found it difficult to persuade the British Cabinet and Parliament to intervene immediately in the war.

25) Although conversations on technical questions took place between the English and Belgian general staffs in connection with the first Moroccan crisis, it is beyond doubt that in the years before the war Belgium practiced a policy of strict neutrality.

26) French policy in 1914 was not determined by the desire for a war of revenge against Germany but by that of maintaining the Russian alliance which was considered an indispensable counterweight to German power. This pre-occupation led President Poincaré to promise, on July 23 during his visit to St. Petersburg, that the French government would invoke the treaty of alliance. This declaration meant, in the circumstances of the moment, that France would enter the war if Germany intervened with arms in an eventual Austro-Russian war.

b) The French government did not advise against Russia's partial mobilization against Austria-Hungary, but, on July 30, it recommended that Russia take no measure which might provoke a Germany reply. It is true that the Ambassador of France did not carry out completely the instructions of his government.

27) German policy did not aim to provoke a European war in 1914; it depended above all on obligations contracted with Austria-Hungary. To prevent the dissolution of Austria-Hungary which it considered dangerous, the Berlin government gave the government of Vienna assurances which amounted to a "blank check." The German government was dominated by the idea that it would be possible to localize a conflict with Serbia as in 1908–1909. However, it was prepared to run the risk of a European war in case of necessity. Consequently, it neglected to exercise in time a moderating influence on Austrian policy. It was only from July 28 on that Bethmann-Holweg took steps in this direction. But Moltke, convinced that a European war was inevitable, insisted, on July 30, as head of the German General Staff and for strictly military reasons, on hastening the order for general mobilization in Austria-Hungary.

The general mobilization of Russia, ordered July 30, necessarily obliged the German government to order mobilization. From July 31 on the attitude of Germany was determined, as was that of the other continental powers, by military considerations which gained the upper hand over political considerations. The decisions of the German government proceeded from the firm conviction that France could in no case remain neutral in the event of a Russo-German war and that a war on two fronts could only be won if it began with a campaign through Belgium in order to encircle and crush the French army quickly.

These military considerations inevitably led everywhere to the issuing of orders for mobilization and, in Germany, in addition to this, to the hastening of the sending of ultimatums and to the delivery of declarations of war.

79 The Significance of the Russian Revolution

The most significant by-product of World War I probably was the Russian revolution of 1917. This led to the establishment of the Union of Soviet Socialist Republics, thereby giving for the first time institutional reality to socialist theory. World history since 1917 has been profoundly influenced by this epochal event. Its significance is analyzed in the following comparative study by Isaac Deutscher, Marxist scholar and distinguished biographer of Stalin and Trotsky.*

An eminent French historian once wrote: "Consider the revolutions of the Renaissance: in them you will find all the passions, all the spirit, and all the language of the French Revolution." With some reservations, one might also say that if one considers the Great French Revolution, one can find in it the passions, the spirit, and the language of the Russian Revolution. This is true to such an extent that it is absolutely necessary for the student of recent Russian history to view it every now and then through the French prism. (The student of the French Revolution, too, may gain new insights if occasionally he analyzes his subject in the light of the Russian experience.) Historical analogy by itself is, of course, only one of the many angles from which he ought to approach his subject; and it may be downright misleading if he merely contents himself with assembling the points of formal resemblance between historical situations. "History is concrete"; and this means, among other things, that every event or situation is unique, regardless of its possible similarity to other events and situations. In drawing any analogy, it is therefore important to know where the analogy ends. I hope that I shall not offend badly against this rule; and I would like to acknowledge my great debt to the eminent French historians whose works on the French Revolution have helped me to gain new insights into the Russian Revolution.

It is well known that the controversy over the "Russian Thermidor" played in its time a great role in the struggles inside the Bolshevik party. Trotsky placed his thesis about the Russian Thermidor in the very center of his denunciation of the Stalinist regime. This issue was dealt with only indirectly in my political biography of Stalin. (In my view, the Russian counterparts to the Jacobin, Thermidorian, and Bonapartist phases of the revolution have in a curious way overlapped and merged in Stalinism.) A critical examination of this whole problem will be found in my *Life of Trotsky,* where it properly belongs. For the present I will concentrate on another perspective on recent Russian history, a perspective somewhat similar to that which was drawn by Albert Sorel in relation to the French Revolution in his monumental *L'Europe et la Révolution Française.* I have in mind the reassertion of national tradition in a revolutionary society.

The Bolshevik revolution of 1917 was in intention a radical break with Russia's

* Reprinted from I. Deutscher, "The French Revolution and the Russian Revolution: Some Suggestive Analogies," *World Politics,* 4 (April 1952), 369–81.

past, a break with her old social outlook, with her old methods of government, with her customs, habits, and traditions. It was a great and *pathetic* funeral of all the anachronisms inherited from centuries of backwardness, serfdom, and tyranny. The three post-revolutionary decades, however, saw a complex and contradictory development: on the one hand, Russia's advance, with gigantic stride, in industrialization and education, and a release of national energies such as only a great revolution can produce; on the other hand, an amazing resurrection of Russia's buried past, and the revenge of that past upon the present. It is as the embodiment of this contradictory development that I wish to consider Stalin. To an almost equal degree, Stalin represents the impetus given to Russia by the revolution and the triumph of the traditions of the *ancien régime* over the original spirit of the revolution. Yet, did not Napoleon I represent a similar phenomenon? Were not the revolutionary and the *Roi Soleil* blended in his personality as much as the Leninist and Ivan the Terrible (or Peter the Great) are blended in Stalin?

Those who are interested mainly in the individual psychology of historical personalities may be outraged by this comparison. Stalin, they may object, has none of the *élan,* the *esprit,* the charm, and nothing of the originality of mind and expression with which nature so richly endowed Bonaparte. This is willingly admitted. But we are concerned here with something else, with the respective functions of the two personalities in the history of their countries; and these ought to be viewed in the light of broader, impersonal factors, of the moving forces, the motives and objectives of the two revolutions, and in the light of their different social backgrounds and national traditions. Incidentally, even the contrast between the individual characteristics of the two men fits in with and can up to a point be explained by the contrast between their national backgrounds and traditions. Napoleon, the Emperor, descended indirectly from an absolute monarchy, the chief representative of which appears, in historical idealization, as the *Roi Soleil*. The Tsar who in a sense is Stalin's political ancestor could earn, even from his apologists, no brighter epithet than *Grozny*—the Awe-inspiring. Napoleon has the clear air, bright color, and elegance of Versailles and Fontainebleau as his background; while Stalin's figure harmonizes with the grim *ambiance* of the Kremlin. Thus, even the individual temper of the two men seems to reflect something impersonal.

Albert Sorel describes how heavily tradition weighed upon the revolution: "Events hurled them [the members of the Convention] abruptly into power: if they had had a taste for liberty, they would have had no spare time to serve an apprenticeship in it." The leaders of the Russian Soviets had just as little spare time in which to serve an apprenticeship in liberty as had the leaders of the Convention. "At the beginning of the Revolution, the minds of men rushed toward the ideal: everything was destroyed, everything was renewed; France was recreated, so to speak, after having been annihilated. . . . Disorder, anarchy, civil war ensued. Foreign war was added. The Revolution was threatened, France invaded. The Republicans had to defend at one and the same time the independence of the nation, the territory of the homeland, the principles of the Revolution, the supremacy of their party, even their own lives. . . . With pure reason confounded, they fell back brutally on empiricism: they turned from instinct to custom, to routine, to precedents: none were for liberty, countless numbers were for despotism. Thus all the processes of government of the *ancien régime* were seen to insinuate themselves, in the name of expedience, into the Revolution. Once having regained their place, they remained there as masters. All the theoreticians' art consisted of nothing more than masking and disguising them." How admirably these words suit the fortunes of the Russian Revolution as well!

Yet, while it is right to point to this reassertion of tradition, a reassertion that some may regard as natural and sound and others may view as a distortion of the revolution, it would be wrong to see in the post-revolutionary regime nothing but a prolongation of the *ancien régime*. Under the Empire, French history did not merely pick up the threads that had been violently snapped by the Convention; it wove the pattern of a new France and it worked the threads of tradition into that new pattern. The same may be said of Stalinist Russia. She may feel the revenge of the past on herself, but she does not revert to that past. The Bourbon monarchy could never have produced anything like the Napoleonic Code, that legal-philoso-phical mirror of a bourgeois society. Similarly, planned economy could never have come into existence within the framework of the old Russia. To make it possible, nothing less than the October Revolution was needed; and in it, in the principle and the practice of the planned economy, the October Revolution has survived and developed, despite the insinuation of "all the processes of government of the *ancien régime*."

In the case of the Russian Revolution, it would be even more unrealistic than in that of the French to deny or overlook what is essentially new and epoch-making in its achievement. There may have been some justification for Sorel's view that if the French Revolution had not taken place, the *ancien régime* would, in the course of time, have done some of the work that was accomplished only after its over-throw. The point is that within the shell of France's *ancien régime* the elements of a modern bourgeois society had achieved a relatively high degree of maturity; the revolution merely broke the shell and thereby facilitated and speeded up the organic growth and development of those elements. Even so, historians like Michelet, Jaurès, and others, who stressed the essentially new and creative work of the rev-olution, seem nearer the truth than Sorel, whose emphasis on historical continuity, so original and illuminating in many respects, appears in others to be exaggerated and essentially conservative. In the case of Russia, the limits within which the law of historical continuity operates are undoubtedly much narrower. The elements of the present collectivist society, with its planned economy—let us leave aside whether this society deserves to be called socialist or not—hardly existed under the surface of Russia's *ancien régime*. They are largely the conscious creation of the revolution and of the post-revolutionary government. As a builder of a new economy and a pioneer of new social techniques, Stalin, for all his limitations and vices—the limita-tions of an empiricist and the vices of a despot—is likely to leave deeper marks on history than any single French revolutionary leader. Here perhaps is the point at which the difference in the very nature of the two revolutions tends to make further comparisons misleading.

Let us now try to investigate how far the analogy holds good in a different field —in the French Revolution's foreign policy, in its impact on the world and the world's impact on it. Sorel, who surveyed this vast field with the greatest thorough-ness and understanding, tells us that "To come to terms with the French Revolu-tion, the old Europe abdicated its principles; to come to terms with old Europe, the French Revolution falsified its own. France had solemnly renounced conquests. . . . Victory made the Revolution bellicose. The war, begun for the defense of French territory, continued for the invasion of neighboring territories. After having conquered in order to liberate, France partitioned in order to retain." Reading this, one cannot help thinking of Yalta and Potsdam, where by acquiescing in the ex-pansion of Stalinist Russia, the statesmen of the capitalist West so clearly abdicated their principles, while Stalinist Russia, by insisting on strategic frontiers and on the absorption of most of the neighboring lands which had once been conquered by the

Tsars, so flagrantly falsified its own. Is it really true that history does not repeat itself? Or that in the repetition the original drama becomes a farce? Is it not rather that in its Russian repetition the French tragedy appears magnified and intensified, projected as it is from the European to the global scale and from an epoch preceding the steam engine to the age of atomic energy?

Let us once again compare the original with the repetition: "Not being able to destroy all the monarchies, she [the Revolution] was forced to come to terms with the monarchs. She vanquished her enemies, she pursued them on their own territory, she effected magnificent conquests; but to keep them at peace, it was necessary to treat; to treat, it was necessary to negotiate, and to negotiate was to return to custom. The *ancien régime* and the Revolution compromised not on principles which were irreconcilable, but on frontiers which were changeable. There existed only one idea in common on which the old Europe and Republican France could understand each other and come to an agreement: it was *raison d'état*. It ruled their treaties. The territories not having changed their places, and the ambitions of states remaining what they were, all the traditions of the old statecraft were reborn in the negotiations. These traditions accorded only too well with the designs of the revolutionaries . . . they placed at the service of the victorious Revolution the processes of the *ancien régime*." While from the angle of the internal development of the revolution it may be said that all the phases which correspond to Jacobinism, Thermidorianism, and Bonapartism have merged in Stalinism, in its foreign policy during World War II victorious Stalinism simply put to its service the processes of the *ancien régime*. I have described in my book how at Potsdam and Yalta Stalin's "conduct, aspirations, methods of action, even his gestures and caprices vividly resembled the behavior, the aspirations and gestures of Tsar Alexander I at the conclusion of the Napoleonic wars." And what was Stalin's conception of the preponderance of the Great Powers and of the division between them of spheres of influence if not that old *raison d'état*, the only idea which he held in common with Churchill and Roosevelt? That this *raison d'état* agreed, in a way, with a revolutionary design subsequent events were to reveal.

Russia, like France before her, has carried her revolution abroad. It was not, let us note, in the Jacobin and Republican period that Europe caught the revolutionary infection from France. And it was not in the heroic, Leninist period that the Bolshevik Revolution spread beyond Russian frontiers. The two revolutions were carried abroad by rulers who had first tamed those revolutions at home. "The Revolution was arrested in France and in a way congealed in military despotism; but, by the very action of that despotism, it continued to propagate itself in Europe. Conquest spread it among the peoples. Although greatly degenerated, it retained enough appeal to excite them. . . ." And again: "It was in that form that the Revolution appeared to have arrested itself and fixed itself in France; it was in that form that Europe understood it and imitated it." It is in its Stalinist, and not in its Leninist and Trotskyist form that the revolution has come to a halt and has fixed itself in Russia, and it is in this form that it has spread, to the amazement of disillusioned ex-Communists who have difficulty understanding how a revolution so greatly degenerated has been able to retain so much appeal.

Like Bonapartist France, Stalinist Russia has created a whole system of satellites. In this Stalin might find a grave warning to himself. It was the revolt of its own satellites that contributed so signally to the downfall of the Bonapartist empire. Two of these satellites, Prussia and Italy, inflicted on France some of its most severe setbacks. It was an Italian patriot who wrote in 1814 the following significant words: "It is painful for me to say it, for no one feels more than I the gratitude which we owe Napoleon; no one appreciates better than I the value of each drop of that generous French blood which watered the Italian soil and redeemed it; but I must be permitted to say it, for it is the truth: to see the French depart was an immense, an ineffable joy." We have heard Tito uttering similar words about the Russians, and who knows how many Eastern European Communists would be happy to utter them if they could? To Bonaparte, and many of his compatriots, the behavior of Italy and Prussia looked like the height of ingratitude. So does the behavior of Tito to Stalin. But what is it that gives rise to that "ingratitude"?

Neither of these systems of satellites has lacked redeeming features. "In the countries which France united with her territory or constituted in her image," says Sorel, "she proclaimed her principles, destroyed the feudal system and introduced her laws. After the inevitable disorders of war and the first excesses of conquest, this revolution constituted an immense benefit to the peoples. This is why the conquests of the Republic could not be confused with conquests of the *ancien régime*. They differed in the essential characteristic that, despite the abuse of principles and the deviations of ideas, the work of France was accomplished for the nations." Without repeating here my analysis of our contemporary counterpart to this phenomenon, I shall only say that I do not believe that the verdict of history on the Stalinist system of satellites will in this respect be more severe than it has been on the Bonapartist system. However, the French system of satellites was not saved by its redeeming features. It would be difficult to find a more brilliant and more convincing explanation of this fact than the one offered by Sorel:

"The French Republicans believed themselves to be cosmopolitans, they were that only in their speeches; they felt, they thought, they acted, they interpreted their universal ideas and their abstract principles in accordance with the traditions of a conquering monarchy. . . . They identified humanity with their homeland, their national cause with the cause of all the nations. Consequently and entirely naturally, they confused the propagation of new doctrines with the extension of French power, the emancipation of humanity with the grandeur of the Republic, the reign of reason with that of France, the liberation of peoples with the conquest of states, the European revolution with the domination of the French Revolution in Europe. . . . they established subservient and subordinate republics which they held in a sort of tutelage. . . . The Revolution degenerated into an armed propaganda, then into conquest. . . ." In the same way, the Russian Stalinists think of themselves as internationalists, but they feel, think, and act with the tradition of a conquering monarchy behind them; and so they, too, confuse the emancipation of mankind with the grandeur of their republic and the reign of reason with the rule of Russia. No wonder that the reaction of the satellite peoples tends to take a familiar form: "The peoples easily understood this language [of emancipation spoken by the revolution]. . . . What they did not understand at all was that, using this language, . . . she [France] aimed at enslaving them and exploited them. They made no distinction, moreover, between her and the man who governed her; they did not investigate the phases through which the French Revolution had passed, and how the Republic had transformed itself into an empire; they knew the Revolution only in the form of conquest. . . . and it was in that form that, even by virtue of its principles, they came to abhor it. They rose against its domination." We are not prophesying here a rising of the peoples against Stalinist domination. But there can be little doubt that the peoples of Eastern and Central Europe, who might have understood well the language of social emancipation spoken by Russia, cannot understand why they should become subordinate to Russia; that they, and others, make no distinction now between the Russian Revolution and "the man who governs"; that they are not interested in the stages by which the Republic of the Workers' and Peasants' Councils has become transformed into something like an empire; and that they know the Russian Revolution largely in the form of conquest.

Having indulged in these comparisons, I cannot but point out where and why this broad historical analogy ceases to apply. I shall not dwell on the obvious differences—in some respects important, in others irrelevant—between two revolutions, one of which was bourgeois in character and the other proletarian, at least in origin. Nor shall I expatiate on the major differences between the international scene as it looks now and as it looked a century and a half ago. But a few words ought perhaps to be said on one important development—the Chinese Revolution—which has come to light only very recently.

The lightning collapse of the Kuomintang and the absolute victory of the Communist armies have clearly altered the international balance of power. In the long run, the Chinese Revolution must also have its repercussions inside Russia. This revolution obviously deserves to be placed in a different category than the "revolutions from above" that took place in Eastern and Central Europe in the years 1945–1948. The latter were merely the by-products of Russia's military victory: "Although the local communist parties were its immediate agents and executors, the great party of the revolution, which remained in the background, was the Red Army." In contrast to this, even though it may have drawn moral inspiration from Russia, Chinese Communism can rightly claim that its revolution has been its own work and its own achievements. The very magnitude of the Chinese Revolution and its intrinsic momentum have been such that it is ludicrous to consider it as anybody's puppet creation. This is not a satellite of the Russian Revolution, but another great upheaval in its own right. For this phenomenon we find no parallel in the epoch of the French Revolution. To its very end the French Revolution stood alone. One can only think of an imaginary analogy: one may wonder what Europe would look like if, at the turn of the eighteenth and nineteenth centuries, Germany, then disunited and backward, had carried out more or less independently its own version of the French Revolution. A combination of a Jacobin or Bonapartist France with a unified, Jacobin Germany might have given history a direction different from that which France alone could impart to it. Perhaps there would have been no Waterloo. Or perhaps the anti-revolutionary forces of Europe would have joined hands much earlier and more resolutely than they did against France alone.

Both Stalinists and anti-Stalinists have recently begun to foster the legend that Stalin has been the actual inspirer of the Chinese Revolution. How is this to be reconciled with his role in the events in China in 1925–1927? How is this to be squared with Stalin's own statement at Potsdam that "the Kuomintang is the only political force capable of ruling China"? It may be argued that at Potsdam he was ostensibly disavowing the Chinese Communists only to trick his Western allies. But this was hardly the case. The version of events which seems much nearer to the truth is that until very late in the day Stalin had a low opinion of the ability of the Communist Party to bring China under its control, and that he went so far as to attempt, even in 1948, to dissuade Mao Tse-tung from launching the series of offensives which was to bring victory to Chinese Communism. A letter from Stalin to Mao to this effect was apparently read at the Conference of the Chinese Communist Party that took place shortly before the opening of the offensive; but the Conference rejected Stalin's advice.

In his untimely skepticism about the Chinese Revolution, Stalin appears true to character. He made a similar miscalculation in the middle 1920's, before Chiang Kai-shek started his great march to the north. In March 1926, the Russian Polit-buro discussed whether it should encourage Chiang (then still Moscow's ally and honorary member of the Executive of the Comintern) in his plans for the conquest of the whole of China. Stalin insisted that Chiang be advised to content himself with the area in the south, where he was in actual control, and to seek a *modus vivendi* with Chang Tso-lin's government which still controlled the north. Chiang disregarded this advice and shortly thereafter established his control over all of China. More than two decades later, Stalin again seems to have overrated the stability of an old and decaying regime and underrated the revolutionary forces opposed to it. With much more justification than Tito, Mao Tse-tung might there-fore say that not only did his regime owe little or nothing to Russian arms, but that he secured its triumph against Moscow's explicit advice.

Whatever the truth about Stalin's role in these events, the Chinese Revolution is likely to affect strongly the fortunes of Stalinism. In my book, Stalinism was shown to be primarily the product of the isolation of Russian Bolshevism in a capitalist world and of the mutual assimilation of the isolated revolution with the Russian tradition. The victory of Chinese Communism marks the end of that isola-tion; and does so much more decisively than did the spread of Stalinism in Eastern Europe. Thus, one major precondition for the emergence of Stalinism now belongs to the past. This should stimulate processes inside Russia, tending to overcome that strange ideology and frame of mind which formed themselves in the period of isolation. Yet we know how often in history effects do outlast causes; and for how long they do so!

While in one of its repercussions the Chinese Revolution tends to deprive Stalin-ism of its *raison d'être,* in another it tends to strengthen and consolidate it. Stalinism has not only been the product of isolated Bolshevism; it has also reflected the ascendancy of the oriental, semi-Asiatic and Asiatic, over the European element in Russia, and consequently in the revolution. Mao Tse-tung's victory enhances that element and imparts to it immense additional weight. How much more real must his own *Ex Oriente Lux* sound to Stalin himself now than it did in 1918, when he published it! So much indeed has the oriental element come to predominate in the whole international Communist movement that the struggle between Communism and anti-Communism is more and more becoming identified, not only geographi-cally, with the antagonism between East and West. The fact that Communism is in its origin a Western idea *par excellence* and that the West exported it to Russia is almost forgotten. Having conquered the East and absorbed its climate and tradi-tions, Communism in its Stalinist form not only fails to understand the West, but itself becomes more and more incomprehensible to the West. In Russia, the Greek Orthodox and Byzantine tradition has refracted itself in the revolution. Will the Confucian tradition now similarly refract itself through Chinese Communism?

The political history of Stalin is a tale not lacking in grimness and cruelty, but one ought perhaps to be cautioned against drawing from it a moral of disillusion-ment or despair, for the story is not yet finished. Nearly every great revolution has destroyed as many hopes as it has fulfilled; every revolution therefore has left be-hind it an aftermath of frustration and cynicism. As a rule, men have been able to do full justice to the whole experience only from a long perspective of time. "What do we know, after all?" Louis Blanc once wrote in a similar context. "In order that progress be realized, perhaps it is necessary that all evil alternatives be exhausted. The life of mankind is very long, and the number of possible solutions very limited. All revolution is useful, in this sense at least, that every revolution takes care of one dangerous alternative. Because from an unfortunate state of affairs societies sometimes tumble into a worse state, let us not hasten to conclude that progress is a chimera." Let us not hasten to do so.

WORLD WAR I IN WORLD HISTORY 80

From the viewpoint of world, rather than European, history, the significance of World War I is that it marks the beginning of the end of Europe's domination of the globe. Why this domination was now effectively challenged for the first time is made clear in the following analysis by K. M. Panikkar, an Indian historian and diplomat.*

The Great War of 1914–18 was from the Asian point of view a civil war within the European community of nations. The direct participation of Asian countries, during some stages of this conflict, was at the invitation and by the encouragement of one of the parties, the *entente* Powers, and was greatly resented by the Germans. It is necessary to emphasize this internal character of the European conflict to realize its full significance on the development of events in Asia.

We have already noticed that at the beginning of the twentieth century the European nations, in the enjoyment of unprecedented economic prosperity and political prestige, remained unshakably convinced that they had inherited the earth, and that their supremacy in Asia was permanent and was something in the nature of a predetermined Divine Order. It was the age of Kipling and the white man's burden, and it seemed the manifest destiny of the white race to hold the East in fee.

In 1914, when the German invaders had reached the Marne, divisions of the Indian Army under British officers had been rushed to France and had helped at the critical moment to stem the German tide. Later, they were extensively used in the defence of the Suez Canal and the Middle East and in campaigns elsewhere in Africa. In 1917, Siam declared war on Germany. An Indo-Chinese labour force had been recruited and was working in France. On August 14, 1917, China also joined the Allies. Thus all the nations of Asia were brought into the European civil war. However, opinion in India, China and even in Japan was at the time more pro-German than pro-Ally. In India, except among the ruling princes, there was no pro-British feeling, and public opinion rejoiced at every report of German victory and felt depressed when the Allies were winning. China declared war only with the greatest reluctance and for the express purpose of checkmating Japanese plans of aggression. In Japan itself, after the Shantung campaign, feeling against the Allies was most marked, and a Press campaign of great virulence was conducted against Britain at the end of 1916. Actually, though the Asian countries fought on the side of the Allies, public opinion in the East looked upon the conflict as a civil war in which neither party had a claim to the friendship of the peoples of Asia, and if any party could appeal to the sympathy of Asians it was the Germanic alliance which

* Reprinted from K. M. Panikkar, *Asia and Western Dominance* (London: George Allen & Unwin Ltd.; New York: The John Day Company, Inc., 1953), pp. 259–266, by permission of George Allen & Unwin Ltd.

had no tradition of Asian conquest and was allied with the chief Muslim Power, Turkey.

But the participation of Asian people in the war had far-reaching consequences. The Indian soldier who fought on the Marne came back to India with other ideas of the *Sahib* than those he was taught to believe by decades of official propaganda. Indo-Chinese Labour Corps in the South of France returned to Annam with notions of democracy and republicanism which they had not entertained before. Among the Chinese who went to France at the time was a young man named Chou En-lai, who stayed on to become a Communist and had to be expelled for activities among the members of the Chinese Labour Corps.

More important than these influences was the fact that the French and British administrations in Asia had to appeal to their subjects for moral support. To ask Indians and Indo-Chinese to subscribe to war loans for the defence of democracy and to prevent the world being overwhelmed by German *Kultur,* would have sounded as strange and callous irony unless accompanied by promises of democracy for themselves and freedom for their own cultures. When, besides subscriptions for war loans, Indians and Indo-Chinese were pressed to join up and fight to save democracy, the contradictions of the position became too obvious even for the colonial administrators. In India the demand was made openly by the nationalist leaders that prior agreement on political problems was necessary before support of the war could be considered a national programme.

Politically, a further weakening of the colonial and imperialist position came about as a result of President Wilson's declaration of fourteen points. In 1917, the doctrine of the "self-determination of peoples" had the ring of a new revelation. Whatever its effect was on the suppressed nationalities of Europe, in Asia it was acclaimed as a doctrine of liberation. As every Allied Power hastened to declare its faith in the new formula of Wilson (and it was soon raised to the position of an accepted "war aim" in the propaganda campaign against the Germans), the colonial Powers found it difficult to oppose openly or resist publicly the claims of Asian nations based on this formula. It became difficult to proclaim self-determination of peoples as a great ideal for the establishment of which Asian peoples should co-operate with Europeans and fight and lose their lives in distant battlefields, but which, however excellent, could not be applied to themselves. Self-government for colonial countries had thus to be accepted, and the claim to it could no longer be brushed aside as premature or stigmatized as sedition.

Apart from these political considerations economic forces generated by the war were also helping to undermine the supremacy of the West. Japan utilized the four years of war for a planned expansion of her trade in the East. German competition had been eliminated. Britain and France, engaged in a mortal struggle when their entire resources of production had to be directed towards victory, had also left the field fairly open. India gained her first major start on the industrial road and, with the strain on British economy, Indian national capital was placed in a position of some advantage. In fact the full results of the weakening of European capitalism became evident only after the war when the pre-eminence of London was challenged by America, and British capital, though still powerful, began to be on the defensive in India. The growth of capitalist enterprise in India, and the development of industries and participation by Indian capital in spheres so far monopolistically held by Britain, like jute, resulted directly from the weakening of the economic position of Britain.

Two other results of a general character may be indicated. The first, the growth of a powerful left-wing movement in the countries of Western Europe had a direct effect on shaping events in the Eastern Empire. The labour Party in England during the days of its growth had been closely associated with the nationalist movement in India. In fact, Ramsay MacDonald, the leader of the Socialist Party after the war, had been one of its champions from the earliest days. Similarly, Annamite nationalism had worked hand in hand with left-wing parties in France. In the period that immediately followed the war these parties had come to possess considerable influence in national affairs and, as we shall see, were instrumental in giving effect to policies which loosened the old bonds of political domination.

The second factor was, of course, the influence of the Russian Revolution. Imperialism meant something totally different after Lenin's definition of it as the last phase of capitalism and his insistence that the liberation of subject peoples from colonial domination was a part of the struggle against capitalism. Also, Russia's call for and practice of racial equality, abolition of the special privileges that Tsarist Russia had acquired in Persia and China, and her acceptance, in the first flush of revolutionary enthusiasm, of the independence of countries which had been previously annexed to Russia, made it difficult for Western nations which had so long claimed to stand for liberty and progress to deny the claims of Eastern nations.

Finally, the war had accelerated the pace of movements everywhere. For example, in India, the movement for independence which was confined to the intelligentsia in 1914 became a mass movement of immense proportions in 1919. Everywhere the case was similar. The *tempo* of events had acquired a momentum which few had foreseen and none had forecast in 1918. The war, on the world scale it was conducted in 1914–18, was in itself a great world revolution, and an impenetrable chasm has been created between the days preceding August 1914 and those following November 11, 1918.

One fact which stands out clear and illustrates this chasm in thought is the lack of faith in imperialist ideals in the period that followed the war. With the solitary exception of Churchill, there was not one major figure in any of the British parties who confessed to a faith in the white man's mission to rule. Successive Viceroys of India, Liberal, Conservative and non-party, professed publicly their adherence to the cause of Indian freedom. Secretaries of State from Edwin Montagu (1917–22) to Pethick Lawrence, including such stalwarts of Conservatism as Sir Samuel Hoare (Lord Templewood), claimed that they were working for the freedom of the Indian people and not for the maintenance of British rule. The French were no doubt more brave in their words, but the faith had gone out of them also.

Nowhere did this come out more clearly than in the treatment of China. Incidents which previously would have been dealt with sternly and for which territories and indemnities would have been exacted, were now only the subjects of a mild protest. Chiang Kai-shek's armies occupied the concessions at Hankow, and for months Hong Kong was subjected to an intensive trade boycott; these events would earlier have immediately led to a display of overwhelming naval strength. Britain in 1926 was prepared patiently to negotiate. Even the "old China hands," who had watched with regret the sudden eclipse of European prestige, though they acted the Blimps in their clubs, never seriously felt that Western authority could be re-established over China by the use of gunboats. There was no conviction left of the European's superiority or sense of vision.

Chapter Thirty-five

Nationalist uprisings
in the colonial world

81   Secularization of Turkey

The peace settlement arranged at the end of World War I ignored the nationalist aspirations of the colonial peoples, with the result that a wave of revolts broke out in the overseas lands. The most successful of these uprisings was that of the Turks. Under the inspired leadership of Mustapha Kemal they successfully repudiated the onerous Sèvres Treaty (August 10, 1920), replacing it with the Lausanne Treaty (July 24, 1923) which left Turkey free from foreign control. Kemal now proceeded with a comprehensive program of secularization, in accordance with his basic tenet that Westernization was essential to resist the West. His secularization drive is reflected in the two selections below: the first eliminating the Caliphate and the Ottoman dynasty,* and the second providing for a Western-type constitution.†

Abolition of the Caliphate,
March 3, 1924

Article 1: The Caliph is deposed. The office of the Caliphate is abolished, since the Caliphate is essentially comprised in the meaning and signification of [the words] Government and Republic.

Article 2: The deposed Caliph and all male and female members of the Imperial Family of the now extinguished Ottoman Sultanate, including the husbands of Im-

---

* Reprinted from A. J. Toynbee, *Survey of International Affairs, 1925* (Volume One): *The Islamic World Since the Peace Settlement* (London: Oxford University Press, under the auspices of the Royal Institute of International Affairs, 1927), p. 575, by permission of the publisher.
† Reprinted from E. M. Earle and H. Y. Hussein Bey, "The New Constitution of Turkey," *Political Science Quarterly,* 40, No. 1 (March 1925), 89, by permission of the Academy of Political Science.

perial princesses, are deprived in perpetuity of the right to reside within the boundaries of the territories of the Republic of Turkey. The issue of ladies related to this Imperial Family are subject to the terms of this article.

Article 3: The individuals mentioned in Article 2 are required to leave the dominions of the Republic of Turkey within a maximum period of ten days as from the date of proclamation of the present law.

Article 4: The individuals mentioned in Article 2 are deprived of the status and rights of Turkish nationality.

Article 5: From now onwards the individuals mentioned in Article 2 may not enjoy the disposal of real property within the boundaries of the Republic of Turkey. For the winding-up of their affairs they may have recourse, by proxy, to the public courts of law during a period of one year.

Constitution of the Turkish Republic, April 20 1924

Article 1: The Turkish State is a Republic.

Article 2: The religion of the Turkish State is Islam; the official language is Turkish; the seat of government is Angora.

Article 3: Sovereignty belongs without restriction to the nation.

Article 4: The Great National Assembly of Turkey is the sole lawful representative of the nation, and exercises sovereignty in the name of the nation.

Article 5: The legislative and executive powers are vested and centred in the Great National Assembly, which concentrates these two powers in itself.

Article 6: The Great National Assembly of Turkey exercises the legislative power directly.

Article 7: The Assembly exercises the executive power through the intermediary of the President of the Republic, whom it elects, and through a Cabinet chosen by him. The Assembly controls the acts of the Government and may at any time withdraw power from it.

Article 8: The judicial power is exercised in the name of the Assembly by independent tribunals constituted in accordance with the law.

SUN YAT-SEN TURNS TO THE SOVIET UNION 82

Turkey's success proved to be the exception. Elsewhere in the Middle East the Arabs passed under Western rule disguised by the mandate arrangement. Likewise India remained under Britain despite the efforts of Gandhi, while China continued to be torn between the warlords in the provinces and the Westerners in the ports. The Chinese nationalist leader, Dr. Sun Yat-sen sought foreign aid to unify the country, but, as described by the first selection,* only the Soviet Union responded. In the second selection, Sun emphasizes the importance of the contemporary colonial uprisings and of the

* Reprinted from George E. Sokolsky, in *China Year Book, 1928* (Tientsin, 1929), pp. 1320–1321.

347

support provided by the Soviet Union.* The final selection comprises Sun's deathbed message to the Central Executive Committee of the Soviet Union, in which he expressed hope for fraternal relations between China and Russia.†

Sun Yat-sen Seeks Foreign Aid

It is an error to assume that Dr. Sun Yat-sen was essentially anti-foreign. If his activities previous to 1924 are studied, the influences of the West, particularly Great Britain and the United States are always evident. The Government which he organized was based upon American models; his political party was made to resemble an American political party; his emphasis on a written constitution was American. The years of futile argumentation over constitutionalism, the lack of organization within the *Kuomintang* and in the Government, the inability to achieve success, the constant betrayals by military men, led Dr. Sun Yat-sen in 1923, to seek a reorganization of the entire mechanism. In 1923, he sent his A.D.C., Mr. Morris A. Cohen, to Canada and the United States to recruit World War veterans who would reorganize his army on a modern basis. He also utilized his then English secretary and soon, his Minister of Aviation, Mr. Eugene Chen, to confer with the British authorities at Hongkong and in London for assistance. Both missions failed. Dr. Sun then applied to the Germans, but they were unable to offer what he needed. He thereupon wrote to Mr. Karakhan in Peking requesting him to send a representative with whom he might discuss mutual relations. Michael Borodin was sent. With characteristic ability he saw that the basic problem was one of organization. He immediately promised to obtain from Soviet Russia arms and munitions on easy terms; he also agreed to provide a corps of military and civilian experts who would help to reorganize the party and the Government along Soviet lines. Borodin was appointed High Adviser to the *Kuomintang*. His first task then was to propose unity of principle, unity of party organization, and a strict party discipline.

Sun Yat-sen on the Colonial Revolts

Since the day of Japan's victory over Russia, the peoples of Asia have cherished the hope of shaking off the yoke of European oppression, a hope which has given rise to a series of independence movements—in Egypt, Persia, Turkey, Afghanistan, and finally in India. Therefore, Japan's defeat of Russia gave rise to a great hope for the independence of Asia. From the inception of this hope to the present day only 20 years have elapsed. The Egyptian, Turkish, Persian, Afghan, and Arabian independence movements have already materialized, and even the independence movement in India, has, with the passage of time, been gaining ground. . . . At present Asia has only two independent countries, Japan in the East and Turkey in the West. In other words, Japan and Turkey are the Eastern and Western barricades of Asia. Now Persia, Afghanistan, and Arabia are also following the European example in arming themselves, with the result that the Western peoples dare not look down on them. China at present also possesses considerable armaments, and when her unification is accomplished she too will become a great Power. We ad-

* Reprinted from T'ang Leang-li, *China and Japan: Natural Friends, Unnatural Enemies* (Shanghai: China United Press, 1941), pp. 145, 149, 150.
† Reprinted from "Reds Quote Sun Yat Sen in Far East," *The New York Times* (May 24, 1925), by permission of the publisher. Copyright 1925 by The New York Times Company.

vocate Pan-Asianism in order to restore the status of Asia. Only by the unification of all the peoples in Asia on the foundation of benevolence and virtue can they become strong and powerful.

But to rely on benevolence alone to influence the Europeans in Asia to relinquish the privileges they have acquired in China would be an impossible dream. If we want to regain our rights, we must resort to force. In the matter of armaments, Japan has already accomplished her aims, while Turkey has recently also completely armed herself. The other Asiatic races, such as the peoples of Persia, Afghanistan, and Arabia are all war-like peoples. China has a population of four hundred millions, and although she needs to modernize her armament and other equipment, and her people are a peace-loving people, yet when the destiny of their country is at stake the Chinese people will also fight with courage and determination. Should all Asiatic peoples thus unite together and present a united front against the Occidentals, they will win the final victory. Compare the populations of Europe and Asia: China has a population of four hundred millions, India three hundred and fifty millions, Japan several scores of millions, totalling, together with other peoples, no less than nine hundred millions. The population in Europe is somewhere around four hundred millions. For the four hundred millions to oppress the nine hundred millions is an intolerable injustice, and in the long run the latter will be defeated. . . .

At present there is a new country in Europe which has been looked down upon and expelled from the Family of Nations by the White races of the whole of Europe. Europeans consider it as a poisonous snake or some brutal animal, and dare not approach it. Such a view is also shared by some countries in Asia. This country is Russia. At present, Russia is attempting to separate from the White peoples in Europe. Why? Because she insists on the rule of Right and denounces the rule of Might. She advocates the principle of benevolence and justice, and refuses to accept the principles of utilitarianism and force. She maintains Right and opposes the oppression of the majority by the minority. From this point of view, recent Russian civilization is similar to that of our ancient civilization. Therefore, she joins with the Orient and separates from the West. The new principles of Russia were considered as intolerable by Europeans. They are afraid that these principles, when put into effect, would overthrow their rule of Might. Therefore they do not accept the Russian way, which is in accord with the principles of benevolence and justice, but denounce it as contrary to world principles.

*Sun Yat-sen's Message to the Soviet Union,
March 1925*

Dear Comrades:

While I lie here in a malady against which men are powerless, my thoughts are turned towards you and towards the fates of my Party and my country.

You are at the head of the union of free republics—that heritage left to the oppressed peoples of the world by the immortal Lenin. With the aid of that heritage the victims of imperialism will inevitably achieve emancipation from that international regime whose foundations have been rooted for ages in slavery, wars, and injustice.

I leave behind me a Party which, as I always hoped, will be bound up with you in the historic work of the final liberation of China and other exploited countries from the yoke of imperialism. By the will of fate I must leave my work unfinished, and hand it over to those who, remaining faithful to the principles and teachings of the Party, will thereby be my true followers.

Therefore I charge the Kuomintang to continue the work of the revolutionary nationalist movement, so that China, reduced by the imperialists to the position of a semi-colonial country, shall become free.

With this object I have instructed the Party to be in contact with you. I firmly believe in the continuance of the support which you have hitherto accorded to my country.

Taking my leave of you, dear comrades, I want to express the hope that the day will soon come when the U.S.S.R. will welcome a friend and ally in a mighty, free China, and that in the great struggle for the liberation of the oppressed peoples of the world both those allies will go forward to victory hand in hand.

With fraternal greetings,
SUN YAT-SEN

83   HERALD OF BLACK REVOLUTION

Africa also remained under Western rule after World War I, the only change being the replacing of Germany by Britain or France or Belgium. A pioneer leader against this foreign domination was the American Black, W. E. B. Dubois. He is the author of the following article which is exceptionally insightful since it was written in 1915, at the beginning of the war. Dubois called for a world-wide movement against White rule, and included the Blacks of the Americas in the movement. In his analysis and spirit, Dubois is a precursor of later Black revolutionaries such as Frantz Fanon who were to come into their own during the great revolutionary wave following World War II.*

Nearly every human empire that has arisen in the world, material and spiritual, has found some of its greatest crises on this continent of Africa, from Greece to Great Britain. As Mommsen says, "It was through Africa that Christianity became the religion of the world." In Africa the last flood of Germanic invasions spent itself within hearing of the last gasp of Byzantium, and it was again through Africa that Islam came to play its great rôle of conqueror and civilizer.

With the Renaissance and the widened world of modern thought, Africa came no less suddenly with her new old gift. Shakespeare's Ancient Pistol cries,

A foutre for the world, and worldlings base!
I speak of Africa, and golden joys.

He echoes a legend of gold from the days of Punt and Ophir to those of Ghana, the Gold Coast, and the Rand. This thought had sent the world's greed scurrying down the hot, mysterious coasts of Africa to the Good Hope of gain, until for the first time a real world-commerce was born, albeit it started as a commerce mainly in the bodies and souls of men.

* Reprinted from W. E. Burghardt Dubois, "The African Roots of War," *Atlantic Monthly*, 115 (May 1915), 707–14, by permission.

So much for the past; and now, today: the Berlin Conference to apportion the rising riches of Africa among the white peoples met on the fifteenth day of November, 1884. Eleven days earlier, three Germans left Zanzibar (whither they had gone secretly disguised as mechanics), and before the Berlin Conference had finished its deliberations they had annexed to Germany an area over half as large again as the whole German Empire in Europe. Only in its dramtic suddenness was this undisguised robbery of the land of seven million natives different from the methods by which Great Britain and France got four million square miles each, Portugal three quarters of a million, and Italy and Spain smaller but substantial areas.

The methods by which this continent has been stolen have been contemptible and dishonest beyond expression. Lying treaties, rivers of rum, murder, assassination, mutilation, rape, and torture have marked the progress of Englishman, German, Frenchman, and Belgian on the dark continent. The only way in which the world has been able to endure the horrible tale is by deliberately stopping its ears and changing the subject of conversation while the deviltry went on.

It all began, singularly enough, like the present war, with Belgium. Many of us remember Stanley's great solution of the puzzle of Central Africa when he traced the mighty Congo sixteen hundred miles from Nyangwe to the sea. Suddenly the world knew that here lay the key to the riches of Central Africa. It stirred uneasily, but Leopold of Belgium was first on his feet, and the result was the Congo Free State—God save the mark! But the Congo Free State, with all its magniloquent heralding of Peace, Christianity, and Commerce, degenerating into murder, mutilation and downright robbery, differed only in degree and concentration from the tale of all Africa in this rape of a continent already furiously mangled by the slave trade. That sinister traffic, on which the British Empire and the American Republic were largely built, cost black Africa no less than 100,000,000 souls, the wreckage of its political and social life, and left the continent in precisely that state of helplessness which invites aggression and exploitation. "Color" became in the world's thought synonymous with inferiority, "Negro" lost its capitalization, and Africa was another name for bestiality and barbarism.

Thus the world began to invest in color prejudice. The "Color Line" began to pay dividends. For indeed, while the exploration of the valley of the Congo was the occasion of the scramble for Africa, the cause lay deeper. The Franco-Prussian War turned the eyes of those who sought power and dominion away from Europe. Already England was in Africa, cleaning away the débris of the slave trade and half consciously groping toward the new Imperialism. France, humiliated and impoverished, looked toward a new northern African empire sweeping from the Atlantic to the Red Sea. More slowly Germany began to see the dawning of a new day, and, shut out from America by the Monroe Doctrine, looked to Asia and Africa for colonies. Portugal sought anew to make good her claim to her ancient African realm; and thus a continent where Europe claimed but a tenth of the land in 1875, was in twenty-five more years practically absorbed.

II

Why was this? . . .

The answer to this riddle we shall find in the economic changes in Europe. Remember what the nineteenth and twentieth centuries have meant to organized industry in European civilization. Slowly the divine right of the few to determine economic income and distribute the goods and services of the world has been questioned and curtailed. We called the process Revolution in the eighteenth century, advancing Democracy in the nineteenth, and Socialization of Wealth in the twentieth. But whatever we call it, the movement is the same: the dipping of more and grimier hands into the wealth-bag of the nation, until to-day only the ultra stubborn fail to see that democracy in determining income is the next inevitable step to Democracy in political power.

With the waning of the possibility of the Big Fortune, gathered by starvation wage and boundless exploitation of one's weaker and poorer fellows at home, arose more magnificently the dream of exploitation abroad. Always, of course, the individual merchant had at his own risk and in his own way tapped the riches of foreign lands. Later, special trading monopolies had entered the field and founded empires over-seas. Soon, however, the mass of merchants at home demanded a share in this golden stream; and finally, in the twentieth century, the laborer at home is demanding and beginning to receive a part of his share.

．　．　．

It is this paradox which has confounded philanthropists, curiously betrayed the Socialists, and reconciled the Imperialists and captains of industry to any amount of "Democracy." It is this paradox which allows in America the most rapid advance of democracy to go hand in hand in its very centres with increased aristocracy and hatred toward darker races, and which excuses and defends an inhumanity that does not shrink from the public burning of human beings.

Yet the paradox is easily explained: the white workingman has been asked to share the spoil of exploiting "chinks and niggers." It is no longer simply the merchant prince, or the aristocratic monopoly, or even the employing class, that is exploiting the world: it is the nation; a new democratic nation composed of united capital and labor. The laborers are not yet getting, to be sure, as large a share as they want or will get, and there are still at the bottom large and restless excluded classes. But the laborer's equity is recognized, and his just share is a matter of time, intelligence, and skillful negotiation.

Such nations it is that rule the modern world. Their national bond is no mere sentimental patriotism, loyalty, or ancestor-worship. It is increased wealth, power, and luxury for all classes on a scale the world never saw before. Never before was the average citizen of England, France, and Germany so rich, with such splendid prospects of greater riches.

Whence comes this new wealth and on what does its accumulation depend? It comes primarily from the darker nations of the world—Asia and Africa, South and Central America, the West Indies and the islands of the South Seas. There are still, we may well believe, many parts of white countries like Russia and North America, not to mention Europe itself, where the older exploitation still holds. But the knell has sounded faint and far, even there. In the lands of darker folk, however, no knell has sounded. Chinese, East Indians, Negroes, and South American Indians, are by common consent for governance by white folk and economic subjection to them. To the furtherance of this highly profitable economic dictum has been brought every available resource of science and religion. Thus arises the astonishing doctrine of the natural inferiority of most men to the few, and the interpretation of 'Christian brotherhood' as meaning anything that one of the 'brothers' may at any time want it to mean.

Like all world-schemes, however, this one is not quite complete. First of all, yellow Japan has apparently escaped the cordon of this color bar. This is disconcerting and dangerous to white hegemony. If, of course, Japan would join heart and soul with the whites against the rest of the yellows, browns, and blacks, well and good. There are even good-natured attempts to prove the Japanese "Aryan," provided they act "white." But blood is thick, and there are signs that Japan does not dream of a world governed mainly by white men. This is the "Yellow Peril," and it may be necessary, as the German Emperor and many white Americans think, to start a world-crusade against this presumptuous nation which demands "white" treatment.

Then, too, the Chinese have recently shown unexpected signs of independence and autonomy, which may possibly make it necessary to take them into account a few decades hence. As a result, the problem in Asia has resolved itself into a race for "spheres" of economic "influence," each provided with a more or less "open door" for business opportunity. . . .

. . .

III

Thus the white European mind has worked, and worked the more feverishly because Africa is the Land of the Twentieth Century. The world knows something of the gold and diamonds of South Africa, the cocoa of Angola and Nigeria, the rubber and ivory of the Congo, and the palm oil of the West Coast. But does the ordinary citizen realize the extraordinary economic advances of Africa and, too, of black Africa, in recent years? E. T. Morel, who knows his Africa better than most white men, has shown us how the export of palm oil from West Africa has grown from 283 tons in 1800, to 80,000 tons in 1913, which together with by-products is worth to-day $60,000,000 annually. He shows how native Gold Coast labor, unsupervised, has come to head the cocoa-producing countries of the world with an export of 89,000,000 pounds (weight *not* money) annually. He shows how the cotton crop of Uganda has risen from 3000 bales in 1909 to 50,000 bales in 1914; and he says that France and Belgium are no more remarkable in the cultivation of their land than the Negro province of Kano. The trade of Abyssinia amounts to only $10,000,000 a year, but it is its infinite possibility of growth that is making the nations crowd to Adis Abeba. All these things are but beginnings; "but tropical Africa and its peoples are being brought more irrevocably each year into the vortex of the economic influences that sway the western world." There can be no doubt of the economic possibilities of Africa in the near future. There are not only the well-known and traditional products, but boundless chances in a hundred different directions, and above all, there is a throng of human beings who, could they once be reduced to the docility and steadiness of Chinese coolies or of seventeenth and eighteenth century European laborers, would furnish to their masters a spoil exceeding the gold-haunted dreams of the most modern of Imperialists.

. . .

The present world war is, then, the result of jealousies engendered by the recent rise of armed national associations of labor and capital whose aim is the exploitation of the wealth of the world mainly outside the European circle of nations. These associations, grown jealous and suspicious at the division of the spoils of trade-empire, are fighting to enlarge their respective shares; they look for expansion, not in Europe but in Asia, and particularly in Africa. "We want no inch of French territory," said Germany to England, but Germany was "unable to give" similar assurances as to France in Africa.

The difficulties of this imperial movement are internal as well as external. Successful aggression in economic expansion calls for a close union between capital and labor at home. Now the rising demands of the white laborer, not simply for wages but for conditions of work and a voice in the conduct of industry, make industrial peace difficult. The workingmen have been appeased by all sorts of essays in state socialism, on the one hand, and on the other hand by public threats of competition by colored labor. By threatening to send English capital to China and Mexico, by threatening to hire Negro laborers in America, as well as by old-age pensions and accident insurance, we gain industrial peace at home at the mightier cost of war abroad.

.   .   .

IV

What, then, are we to do, who desire peace and the civilization of all men? Hitherto the peace movement has confined itself chiefly to figures about the cost of war and platitudes on humanity. What do nations care about the cost of war, if by spending a few hundred millions in steel and gunpowder they can gain a thousand millions in diamonds and cocoa? How can love of humanity appeal as a motive to nations whose love of luxury is built on the inhuman exploitation of human beings, and who, especially in recent years, have been taught to regard these human beings as inhuman? I appealed to the last meeting of peace societies in St. Louis, saying, "Should you not discuss racial prejudice as a prime cause of war?" The secretary was sorry but was unwilling to introduce controversial matters!

We, then, who want peace, must remove the real causes of war. We have extended gradually our conception of democracy beyond our social class to all social classes in our nation; we have gone further and extended our democratic ideals not simply to all classes of our own nation, but to those of other nations of our blood and lineage—to what we call "European" civilization. If we want real peace and lasting culture, however, we must go further. We must extend the democratic ideal to the yellow, brown, and black peoples.

To say this, is to evoke on the faces of modern men a look of blank hopelessness. Impossible! we are told, and for so many reasons,—scientific, social, and what not,—that argument is useless. But let us not conclude too quickly. Suppose we have to choose between this unspeakably inhuman outrage on decency and intelligence and religion which we call the World War and the attempt to treat black men as human, sentient, responsible beings? We have sold them as cattle. We are working them as beasts of burden. We shall not drive war from this world until we treat them as free and equal citizens in a world-democracy of all races and nations.

.   .   .

What the primitive peoples of Africa and the world need and must have if war is to be abolished is perfectly clear:

First: land.   To-day Africa is being enslaved by the theft of her land and natural resources. A century ago black men owned all but a morsel of South Africa. The Dutch and English came, and to-day 1,250,000 whites own 264,000,000 acres, leaving only 21,000,000 acres for 4,500,000 natives. Finally, to make assurance doubly sure, the Union of South Africa has refused natives even the right to *buy* land. This is a deliberate attempt to force the Negroes to work on farms and in mines and kitchens for low wages. All over Africa has gone this shameless monopolizing of land and natural resources to force poverty on the masses and reduce them to the "dumb-driven-cattle" stage of labor activity.

Secondly: We must train native races in modern civilization. This can be done. Modern methods of educating children, honestly and effectively applied, would make modern, civilized nations out of the vast majority of human beings on earth to-day. This we have seldom tried. For the most part Europe is straining every nerve to make over yellow, brown, and black men into docile beasts of burden, and only an irrepressible few are allowed to escape and seek (usually abroad) the education of modern men.

Lastly, the principle of home rule must extend to groups, nations, and races. The ruling of one people for another people's whim or gain must stop. This kind of despotism has been in later days more and more skillfully disguised. But the brute fact remains: the white man is ruling black Africa for the white man's gain, and just as far as possible he is doing the same to colored races elsewhere. Can such a situation bring peace? Will any amount of European concord or disarmament settle this injustice?

. . .

In this great work who can help us? In the Orient, the awakened Japanese and the awakening leaders of New China; in India and Egypt, the young men trained in Europe and European ideals, who now form the stuff that Revolution is born of. But in Africa? Who better than the twenty-five million grandchildren of the European slave trade, spread through the Americas and now writhing desperately for freedom and a place in the world? And of these millions first of all the ten million black folk of the United States, now a problem, then a world-salvation.

Chapter Thirty-six

Revolution
and settlement
in Europe to 1929

84   Roots of Bolshevik Victory in Russia

One of the critical turning points in European history between the two World Wars was the failure of the Allied intervention against the Bolshevik regime in Russia. This ensured the survival of the Soviet Union, with all its implications for world history to the present day. One reason for the ultimate Bolshevik victory was the role of the highly disciplined Communist Party, as described below in a firsthand account by the well-known English writer H. G. Wells.* Probably the principal reason was the attitude of the Russian peasants, the majority of whom were apolitical and wished above all to be left alone. But when forced to choose between the Whites and the Reds, they more frequently chose the latter simply because they believed this improved their chance of keeping the land they had seized during the revolution. This was the conclusion of C. R. Buxton, Secretary to the British Labor Delegation, which visited Russia in June 1920.†

H. G. Wells

From end to end of Russia, and in the Russian-speaking community through-out the world, there existed only one sort of people who had common general ideas upon which to work, a common faith and a common will, and that was the Communist Party. While all the rest of Russia was either apathetic like the peasantry, or garrulously at sixes and sevens, or given over to violence and fear, the Communists believed and were prepared to act. Numerically they were and are a very

---

* Reprinted from H. G. Wells, *Russia in the Shadows* (London: Hodder and Stoughton Ltd., 1920), pp. 61–64, by permission of the Executors of the Estate of the late H. G. Wells.
† Reprinted from C. R. Buxton, *In a Russian Village* (London: Labour Publishing Co., 1922), pp. 14–15, 19, 21, 26–27, 47–48, by permission of D. R. Buxton.

small part of the Russian population. . . . Nevertheless, because it was in those terrible days the only organisation which gave men a common idea of action, common formulas and mutual confidences, it was able to seize and retain control of the smashed Empire. It was and it is the only sort of administrative solidarity possible in Russia. These ambiguous adventurers who have been and are afflicting Russia, with the support of the Western Powers, Denikin, Kolchak, Wrangel and the like, stand for no guiding principle and offer no security of any sort upon which men's confidence can crystallize. . . . The Communist Party, however one may criticise it, does embody an idea, and can be relied on to stand by its idea. So far it is a thing morally higher than anything that has yet been brought against it. It at once secured the passive support of the peasant mass by permitting them to take land from the estates and by making peace with Germany. It restored order —after a frightful lot of shooting—in the great towns. For a time everybody found carrying arms without authority was shot. This action was clumsy and brutal but effective. To retain its power the Communist Government organised Extraordinary Commissions with practically unlimited powers, and crushed out all opposition by a Red Terror. Much that that Red Terror did was cruel and frightful, it was largely controlled by narrow-minded men, and many of its officials were inspired by social hatred and the fear of counter-revolution, but if it was fanatical it was honest. Apart from individual atrocities, it did on the whole kill for a reason and to an end.

C. R. Buxton

My host's name was Alexander Petrovich Emilianov. He was of the "middle" type of peasant, which formed the great majority of the village. About one-fifth of its people were considered "poor" peasants. Of "rich" peasants there were only four or five, I was told.

Tall, upstanding and vigorous, with short, brown beard, in a much-worn cloth suit and top-boots, Emilianov reminded me of a Scots gamekeeper in East Lothian, one of my earliest and best friends. I soon found that he was a man of shrewd intelligence. He could read with ease. At church, which I attended on the following Sunday, it was his function to read the Epistle; he stepped out from the standing crowd and read it in a loud and sonorous voice, facing the priest (who had just read the Gospel). He was evidently well versed in the Bible, and could hold his own in theological argument. . . .

Before the Revolution my host had had eight acres—about the average holding in that region. He had now no less than eighty-five. This was the tremendous fact that I had turned over and over in my mind as we bumped along. Tremendous, surely; for my host's case was a type, not only of thousands, but of millions of others. . . .

"Look there," said Emilianov, pointing out from the edge of the village field over the limitless rolling steppe. "All that was the land of the landlords (*barin*). You may drive forty *versts* in a straight line from here and see nothing else." I came to realise that, in effect, the villages and their "fields," large as they seemed, were but islands in an ocean of large properties. On all sides they had been hemmed in by the estates of the great landlords.

"Who owned all this land?" I asked.

"All sorts of landlords. One was a Cossack. Two were Samara merchants. One was a German, Schmidt, who bought his from the Crown. Some was held by the Monks. One was an estate of Maria Feodorovna, the Tsaritsa."

"What has happened to them?"

"They are mostly gone," he replied in a matter-of-fact tone. "Some are in Samara. Most of them have left Russia, I suppose." . . .

The landlords' land was seized in Ozero in the summer of 1917—that is, during the Kerenski *regime,* and before the Communists came into power. I was told afterwards that by October of that year there was not a single great estate left in the Samara "Government." But it appears that the formal allocation of the land did not take place until after the October (i.e., Communist) Revolution. With the land, the stock and implements were distributed also.

The Soviet of the *Uyezd,* Pugachev, allotted a certain quantity of land to each village in its area, Ozero among others. The Soviet of Ozero was specially elected for the purpose of dividing up the land, all the villagers having the right to vote. The Soviet then distributed the land according to an absolutely fixed principle, namely, five *desiatin* per "soul." No one was to have more than he and his family could work. Emilianov's family, including wife and children, amounted to seven, and that is why he had thirty-five *desiatin,* or approximately eighty acres. Appeals could be made to the Volost (or District) Soviet, and on one occasion I heard such an appeal being tried.

"And what do the peasants think of it all now?" I asked Emilianov.

"It's a fine thing, the Revolution. Every one is in favour of it. They don't like the Communist Party, but they like the Revolution."

"Why don't they like the Communist Party?"

"Because they are always worrying us. They are people from the towns and don't understand the country. Commissars—powerful persons—are continually coming. We don't know what to do with them. New orders (*prikazi*) are always coming out. People are puzzled. As soon as you understand one of them, a different one comes along."

"What party do most people belong to here?"

"None at all. They are non-party (*bezpartini*)." . . .

The general attitude of the peasants, so far as I could judge, was that they owed much to the Soviet Government in the matter of the land; they approved of the "principle of everybody being equal"; they often talked of the "true" Communist as being an ideal sort of person. But they complained bitterly of the absence of necessities, of the compulsory contributions, and the worry of perpetual orders and appeals, often hard to understand. They considered that the Government was responsible for all these evils alike, and that the peasant was somehow in a position of inferiority to the townsman.

And yet, in spite of all these complaints, when the opportunity was offered them to choose between Kolchak on the one side and the Soviet Government on the other, the peasants do not seem to have had much hesitation. . . .

They were for the Revolution; and for the moment the Soviet power was the embodiment of the Revolution. They grumbled and cursed at it; but when the opportunity was offered to overthrow it, they said "No."

The other great turning point in interwar European history was the failure of the Spartacists, the German equivalent of the Bolsheviks. Their faliure ensured that Bolshevism would not spread to Central or Western Europe, and that instead the new Soviet regime would itself be encircled and isolated until after World War II. One reason for the Spartacist defeat was that the German army was not as demoralized and mutinous as the Russian, so that it heeded to a considerable degree the following appeal for military discipline made by the moderate Socialist government that took office following the Kaiser's abdication.* Thus the regular army in Germany was used to crush Bolshevism rather than to further it, as in Russia. This is evident in the alliance concluded by Friedrich Ebert, Socialist Party leader and Chancellor of the Republic, with General Wilhelm Groener, Chief of the General Staff.†

Appeal for Military Discipline

The People's Government is inspired by the wish to see each of our soldiers return to his home as quickly as possible after his unspeakable sufferings and unheard-of deprivations. But this goal can only be reached if the demobilization is carried out according to an orderly plan. If single troops stream back at their own pleasure, they place themselves, their comrades, and their homes in the greatest danger. The consequences would necessarily be chaos, famine, and want. The People's Government expects of you the strictest self-discipline in order to avoid immeasurable calamity. We desire the High Command to inform the army in the field of this declaration of the People's Government, and to issue the following orders:

1. The relations between officer and rank and file are to be built up on mutual confidence. Prerequisites to this are willing submission of the ranks to the officer, and comradely treatment by the officer of the ranks.
2. The officer's superiority in rank remains. Unqualified obedience in service is of prime importance for the success of the return home to Germany. Military discipline and army order must, therefore, be maintained under all circumstances.
3. The Soldiers' Councils have an advisory voice in maintaining confidence between officer and rank and file in questions of food, leave, the infliction of disciplinary punishments. Their highest duty is to try to prevent disorder and mutiny.
4. The same food for officers, officials, and rank and file.
5. The same bonuses to be added to the pay, and the same allowances for service in the field for officers and rank and file.
6. Arms are to be used against members of our own people only in cases of self-defense and to prevent robberies.

* Reprinted from "The German Revolution," *International Conciliation,* No. 137 (April 1919), p. 548.
† Reprinted from R. G. L. Waite, *Vanguard of Nazism* (Cambridge: Harvard University Press, 1952), pp. 4–5, by permission of the publisher. Copyright 1952 by the President and Fellows of Harvard College.

The Ebert-Groener Alliance

On the evening of November 9, 1918, the harried Chancellor, his coat removed and his shirt stained with sweat, was pacing the offices of the Reichs-chancellery. The problem of the return of the field armies and a dozen others demanded immediate solution. He had put in a grueling day—a day that had seen him first fighting to preserve the monarchy and now trying desperately to save the Republic from extremism. Even his title of Chancellor rested on the legal fiction that Prince Max in conferring it was acting as Regent. He was exhausted and he was alarmed—not so much for himself but for the Germany his simple soul loved. The restless, milling crowds beneath his window did nothing to reassure him. In the gathering twilight, the signs that screamed "Down with the Traitors of the Revolution," "Down with Ebert-Scheidemann" were still plainly visible. He winced as the strident strains of the *Internationale* crowded up from the Wilhelmstrasse below. Suddenly the telephone rang. It was the secret line which connected the Chancellery with Army headquarters at Spa. Ebert's hand trembled as he lifted the receiver. Then he breathed more easily. It was all right after all! It was only his old friend General Groener. After exchanging nervous amenities, Ebert requested that the OHL [Supreme Command] supervise the withdrawal of the field armies. That was agreed to. The conversation continued:

EBERT. What do you expect from us?

GROENER. The Field Marshal expects that the government will support the Officers' Corps, maintain discipline, and preserve the punishment regulations of the Army. He expects that satisfactory provisions will be made for the complete maintenance of the Army.

EBERT. What else?

GROENER. The Officers' Corps expects that the government will fight against Bolshevism, and places itself at the disposal of the government for such a purpose.

EBERT. (after a slight pause) Convey the thanks of the government to the Field Marshal.

Chapter Thirty-seven

The five-year plans
and the Great Depression

FIVE-YEAR PLANS: GLOBAL REPERCUSSIONS   86

It is sometimes stated, with much justification, that Russia's Five-Year Plans are of greater historical significance than her Communist International. The International was singularly unproductive in its efforts to foment world revolution, whereas the Plans, by virtue of their overall success, have substantially influenced the course of world events. By the end of the first Plan in 1932, Russia jumped from the fifth to the second industrial power of the world. This spurt forward attracted much attention in the West, which was suffering during the 1930's from the Great Depression. The Soviet success was even more significant for the underdeveloped countries which aspired to rapid economic growth. The degree of significance is indicated in the following review by economist Robert L. Heilbroner of the book, The Soviet Model and Underdeveloped Countries, *by Charles K. Wilber.**

It is curious, after all these years, that to admit the success of the Soviet modernization effort should be a matter worthy of some note. Conservative economists still spend their time seeking to demonstrate that Russian growth rates are lower than their colleagues think they are; conservative economic historians take pleasure in demonstrating that Russian modernization would have taken place even without the Revolution, only perhaps faster. What Charles Wilber has done in his impressive *The Soviet Model and Underdeveloped Countries* is to set these criticisms into proper perspective simply by setting forth the best data we possess on the Russian experience in an admirably detached, objective and yet sympathetic way.

* Reprinted from Robert L. Heilbroner, "Underdevelopment," *The New Republic* (January 3, 1970), pp. 28–30, by permission of *The New Republic,* © 1969, Harrison-Blaine of New Jersey, Inc.

361

One irrefutable conclusion emerges. The Soviet effort was an incontrovertible success in terms of the development objectives now held by the backward nations —in terms, that is, of turning a poor, unproductive illiterate people into a modern industrial nation-state. Wilber makes his point most strikingly in regard to Central Asia, as the table . . . , adapted from his book, dramatically illustrates:

NONMONETARY INDICATORS OF ECONOMIC DEVELOPMENT FOR
SOVIET CENTRAL ASIA AND SELECTED UNDERDEVELOPED
COUNTRIES: BEFORE AND AFTER SOVIET DEVELOPMENT

Country	Percent of adults literate	Percent of population in cities over 20,000	Percent of population in secondary and higher education	Electricity generation, kwh per capita	Physicians per 100,000
Soviet Central Asia					
"before" (1926–28)	16	9.3	.16	4	17.4
"after" (1960–62)	87	27.8	5.46	820	139.1
Colombia					
(1960–62)	62	22.4	1.88	259	41.3
India					
(1960–62)	24	11.9	2.34	51	17.4
Turkey					
(1960–62)	30	14.5	2.00	99	34.4

The evidence (and I have reproduced only a portion of it) is overwhelming. Soviet Central Asia has made a leap that would be the envy of any of the backward nations—a leap that has effectively cleared the hurdle of peasant inertia and brought a hitherto backward area into the ambit of modern life.

Three questions remain to be asked: (1) how great was the cost (2) how typical of backwardness was the Central Asian milieu, and (3) what was the Soviet technique? Now, Mr. Wilber does not in any way minimize the cost, either in terms of the enormous wastefulness of some aspects of the Soviet program, especially its forced collectivization of livestock, or in terms of the brutality with which the transformation was made. In no sense whatsoever could he be called an "apologist" for Stalinist methods. Rather, he is interested in measuring these costs (which may have reached the horrible total of 5.5 million deaths) against the costs of non-development. And here the following table speaks for itself:

Countries grouped by per capita national income	Infant Mortality	Life Expectancy
	(average 1955–58)	
over $1,000	24.9	70.6
$575–$1,000	41.9	67.7
$350–$575	56.8	65.4
$200–$350	97.2	57.4
$100–$200	131.1	50.0
less than $100	180.0	41.7

To which a few additional comments on the ubiquitous costs of growth might be added: As Wilber points out, the impetus for early American growth derived in large part from exports of cotton, picked by slaves; English industrial acceleration owed no small part of its momentum to the merciless repression of its working classes and to its ruthless exploitation of India. None of this, of course, erases one iota of the human suffering caused by Soviet excesses (which Wilber feels were not a necessary part of the Soviet "model"), but it makes us view that suffering against its proper setting, which is the enormous anguish that is the silent and unrecorded reality of every day of life in the backward world.

But the cost would be to no avail if the Soviet Asian paradigm were inapplicable to those countries that now must find a rapid solution to their problems. Wilber is aware of this question and attempts to solve it by means of a cross-country comparison of nonmonetary indicators of development, some of which we have already seen. He concludes that "Soviet Central Asia was an underdeveloped area, with the characteristics of underdeveloped countries today." It should be pointed out, however, that Wilber does not take into explicit account the absence of high population pressure against land in Central Asia. In all honesty, we do not know to what degree this absence of population pressure facilitated the Soviet drive, or to what extent the disastrous man/land ratios of much of Asia or Africa would lessen the effectiveness of the Soviet model applied in these areas.

But last, what is the Soviet "model"? The basic ingredients are clear enough. They are, first, severance of all ties with foreign dominant economic powers, so that the resources of the developing nation can be used solely for its own benefit and not for that of an imperial homeland. Second, redistribution of economic and political power from the hands of indifferent or incapable regimes into the hands of a revolutionary government, one of whose main objectives must be modernization at all costs. Third, the collectivization of agriculture and the nationalization of heavy industry—steps that are the necessary precursors to the use of these sectors as parts of an over-all plan for forced investment and growth. Fourth, an all-out effort to develop "human capital" by intensive educational and training efforts.

Wilber is far from doctrinaire in asserting that a slavish repetition of these steps will result in modernization for all backward areas. "No model," he writes, "is transferable complete and in detail. Each country must take into account its own resource base, factor proportions, and historical and cultural traditions when evaluating development strategies." Moreover he believes that a "halfway democratic socialist regime" could probably supply whatever compulsion was needed, and that an absence of Communist dogma might improve the chances for a successful adaptation of the Soviet techniques. All these exceptions, however, only *increase* the basic relevance of the lessons that "The Soviet model" holds out for the backward world.

I am not certain that Wilber's moderately optimistic conclusions are quite as solid as he makes them out to be. That is, I am not sure that it is possible to follow the Soviet model without falling into totalitarianism and brutality—wars carry their own excesses, even wars against poverty. Nor am I sure that the Soviet model will yield successful results against the enormous obstacles of contemporary underdevelopment. . . . Yet, in the end, I would go even further than Professor Wilber. For with all the risks, I do not see any alternative to following the Soviet model, if famine and the catastrophic consequences are not to become the dominant realities of much of the underdeveloped world within another decade or two.

The Great Depression, like the Five-Year Plans, had a profound impact on the course of world affairs. It forced governments to adopt restrictive and exclusive economic measures which created friction between countries; it goaded governments to abandon disarmament for rearmament which provided jobs as well as imagined security; and it prompted certain national leaders to demand territorial expansion as the solution for their countries' ills. Indeed the Depression made possible, though not inevitable, the rise of aggressive regimes in Japan and Germany. Hitler himself was well aware of the effect of the Depression upon his political fortunes, as is evident in the following excerpts from two speeches: the first on January 27, 1932 (one year before he assumed office), when he emphasized the political dangers of unemployment; the second, on December 10, 1940, when he boasted of his success in eliminating unemployment. In the latter speech he also significantly interpreted World War II as a holy crusade of the have-not Germans and Italians to win a place in the sun from which they had been unjustly excluded.*

Hitler Speech, January 27, 1932

In my judgement, at the present moment the worst evil, an evil which I would characterize as not merely economic but in the highest sense of the word a national —"volkic"—evil, is unemployment. Always people see only six or seven million men who take no part in the process of production: they regard these men only from the economic standpoint and regret the decline in production which this unemployment causes. But, gentlemen, people fail to see the mental, moral, and psychological results of this fact. Do they really believe that such a percentage of the nation's strength can be idle if it be only for ten, twenty, or thirty years without exercising any mental effect; must it not have as its consequence a complete change of spirit?—and do people believe that that can remain without significance for the future?

Gentlemen, we know from our own experience that, through a mental aberration whose consequences you can in practice trace on every hand, Germany lost the War. Do you believe that when seven or eight million men have found themselves for ten or twenty years excluded from the national process of production, that for these masses Bolshevism could appear as anything else than the logical theoretical complement of their actual, practical, economic situation? . . .

To-day we stand at the turning-point of Germany's destiny. If the present development continues, Germany will one day of necessity land in Bolshevist chaos, but if this development is broken, then our people must be taken into a school of iron discipline.

Hitler Speech, December 10, 1940

My dear friends, if I had stated publicly eight or nine years ago: "In seven or eight years the problem of how to provide work for the unemployed will be solved,

---

* Reprinted from N. H. Baynes, ed., *The Speeches of Adolf Hitler* (London: Oxford University Press, under the auspices of the Royal Institute of International Affairs, 1942), I, 802–803, 824–825, by permission of the publisher.

and the problem then will be where to find workers," I should have harmed my cause. Every one would have declared: "The man is mad. It is useless to talk to him, much less to support him. Nobody should vote for him. He is a fantastic creature." Today, however, all this has come true. Today, the only question for us is where to find workers. That, my fellow countrymen, is the blessing which work brings. . . .

We have incorporated seven million unemployed into our economic system; we have transformed another six millions from part-time into full-time workers; we are even working over-time. And all this is paid for in cash in Reichsmarks which maintained their value in peacetime. In wartime we had to ration its purchasing capacity, not in order to devalue it, but simply to earmark a portion of our industry for war production to guide us to victory in the struggle for the future of Germany. . . .

I wish to put before you a few facts: The first is that in the capitalistic democratic world the most important principle of economy is that the people exist for trade and industry, and that these in turn exist for capital. We have reversed this principle by making capital exist for trade and industry, and trade and industry exist for the people. *In other words, the people come first.* Everything else is but a means to this end.

TWO APPRAISALS: TOYNBEE AND NEHRU   88

The combination of the Five-Year Plans and the Great Depression had a shattering impact on the Western world. The supreme self-confidence of the nineteenth century had been undermined by World War I, but had been partially restored during the late twenties. Now the disasters of the thirties led to a failure of nerve that was reminiscent of the last days of the Roman Empire, a point specifically made in the following selection by the distinguished British historian, Arnold J. Toynbee.* At the same time, some colonial leaders, impressed by the contrast between the Five-Year Plans and the Great Depression, were turning from the West and looking more toward the Soviet Union. This attitude is evident in the selection below by the Indian nationalist and democratic socialist, Jawaharlal Nehru.†

Arnold J. Toynbee

The year 1931 was distinguished from previous years—in the "post-war" and in the "pre-war" age alike—by one outstanding feature. In 1931, men and women all over the world were seriously contemplating and frankly discussing the possibility that the Western system of Society might break down and cease to work. By the time when this possibility thus presented itself, Western Society had come to

* Reprinted from A. J. Toynbee, *Survey of International Affairs, 1931* (London: Oxford University Press, under the auspices of the Royal Institute of International Affairs, 1932), pp. 1-6, by permission of the publisher.
† Reprinted from *Toward Freedom: The Autobiography of Jawaharlal Nehru* (New York: The John Day Company, Inc.; London: The Bodley Head Limited, 1941), pp. 229-232, by permission of The John Day Company and The Bodley Head Limited. Copyright 1941 by The John Day Company.

embrace all the habitable lands and navigable seas on the face of the planet and the entire living generation of Mankind; and, within narrower geographical limits, it had been in existence as "a going concern," without any breach of continuity, for some twelve or thirteen centuries. Western Civilization had been living and growing continuously, with only occasional and never more than temporary checks and set-backs, ever since the end of the interregnum which had followed the break-down of the antecedent "Classical" Civilization and the break-up of the "Classical" super-state, the Roman Empire. In the West, that interregnum had closed, at the turn of the seventh and eighth centuries of the Christian Era, with the emergence of a new order of society embodied in Western Christendom; and this small and rudimentary society—the world of Bede and the world of Charlemagne—was the geographical nucleus and the historical embryo of "the Great Society" of 1931. During the intervening centuries, Western Civilization had gone from strength to strength; and, while it had never been dispensed from the struggle for existence, or been deprived of the perpetual stimulus of repeated challenges, it had always responded victoriously, and the Gates of Hell had not prevailed against it. In 1931, the members of this great and ancient and hitherto triumphant society were asking themselves whether the secular process of Western life and growth might conceivably be coming to an end in their day. . . .

Among the generation living in 1931, every man and woman of forty years of age and upwards had grown to maturity, before the outbreak of the General War of 1914–18, in a mental atmosphere in which the prospect of Western Society breaking down was virtually inconceivable. In this "pre-war" age, the sense of power and security in Western minds was actually enhanced and not diminished by the disinterment of the material remains of ancient civilizations which were so utterly extinct that even their names had been forgotten. When the discovery of the buried civilizations of Egypt and Mesopotamia was followed by similar discoveries in Crete and Asia Minor and the Indus Valley and Central America, the pictures of these "finds" in the illustrated papers evoked a feeling of pride in the enterprise and acumen and technical skill of Western archaeologists (akin to the pride in the conquest of the ether or the air) and a sense of satisfaction in the inference that the children of Western Civilization in these latter days were not as other men had been. So far from serving as a *memento mori,* like the mummy which was carried round with the last course at an Egyptian banquet, these disinterred corpses of extinct civilizations encouraged the "pre-war" generation of modern Western Society to "acquiesce," with the historian of the decline and fall of the Roman Empire, "in the pleasing conclusion that every age of the world has increased, and still increases, the real wealth, the happiness, the knowledge, and perhaps the virtue, of the human race."

This dogmatic belief in an automatic, invincible and interminable progress had been inherited intact, by the "pre-war" generation, from Gibbon and his contemporaries; and the potency of eighteenth-century optimism is demonstrated by the robust declaration of faith in the dogma of his age which Gibbon made—in the celebrated phrases just quoted—at the crisis of the American Revolutionary War and in spite of the historian's own sceptical temperament and affectation. In Gibbon's day, the dogma of progress had already been fortified by a hundred-years' currency in which the new faith had not been contradicted by experience. In 1781, Western Society had not been threatened with destruction by attack from a human enemy since the Osmanlis had raised their second and last siege of Vienna in A.D. 1683.

.   .   .

The catastrophe, however, which Western minds were contemplating in 1931 was not the destructive impact of any external force but a spontaneous disintegration of society from within; and this prospect was much more formidable than the other.

In the face of an external menace, the human spirit can find relief in either endurance or action. The onslaught of an overwhelmingly stronger human enemy can be resisted to the death; an act of God can be accepted with resignation; but when we feel that "we are betrayed by what is false within," we are apt to find ourselves spiritually paralysed in face of the most deadly peril with which humanity is ever confronted. "Do not ye understand that whatsoever entereth in at the mouth goeth into the belly and is cast out into the draught? But those things which proceed out of the mouth come forth from the heart, and they defile the man." Like human beings, human societies are apt to perish—when they do perish—from internal ills. A historian surveying the past in 1931 might doubt whether any of the civilizations which were known to have become extinct by that date had been done to death by external blows; and Western Civilization, at any rate, was still alive to testify that it had suceeded in surviving all the external menaces—human or divine, actual or imaginary—with which it had been confronted so far during the twelve or thirteen centuries that had elapsed since its birth. To find an historical precedent for the threat of spontaneous internal distintegration—the incipient failure of will and wisdom and vitality—with which Western Society felt itself threatened in 1931 for the first time in its history, the historian would have to cast his mind back behind the birth of Western Society to the death of the Society which had preceded it. In the breakdown of the "Classical" Civilization and break-up of the Roman Empire which occurred after the death of Marcus Aurelius, and in the fatal and final relapse, after the death of Theodosius, from a temporary rally, we have the appalling spectacle of a society which did disintegrate spontaneously from within through self-betrayal and self-defilement. In the third century and in the fifth century of the Christian Era, men and women must have been confronted in full view, as their inexorable doom, with that outlook of which other men and women were catching a terrifying glimpse in 1931.

. . . .

Jawaharlal Nehru

With all her blunders, Soviet Russia had triumphed over enormous difficulties and taken great strides. . . . While the rest of the world was in the grip of the depression and going backward in some ways, in the Soviet country a great new world was being built up before our eyes. Russia, following the great Lenin, looked into the future and thought only of what was to be, while other countries lay numbed under the dead hand of the past and spent their energy in preserving the useless relics of a bygone age. In particular, I was impressed by the reports of the great progress made by the backward regions of Central Asia under the Soviet regime. In the balance, therefore, I was all in favor of Russia, and the presence and example of the Soviets was a bright and heartening phenomenon in a dark and dismal world. . . .

Russia apart, the theory and philosophy of Marxism lightened up many a dark corner of my mind. History came to have a new meaning for me. The Marxist interpretation threw a flood of light on it, and it became an unfolding drama with some order and purpose, howsoever unconscious, behind it. In spite of the appalling waste and misery of the past and the present, the future was bright with hope, though many dangers intervened. It was the essential freedom from dogma and the scientific outlook of Marxism that appealed to me. It was true that there was plenty of dogma in official communism in Russia and elsewhere, and frequently heresy hunts were organized. That seemed to be deplorable, though it was not difficult to understand in view of the tremendous changes taking place rapidly in the Soviet countries when effective opposition might have resulted in catastrophic failure.

The great world crisis and slump seemed to justify the Marxist analysis. While all other systems and theories were groping about in the dark, Marxism alone explained it more or less satisfactorily and offered a real solution. . . .

Vague communistic and socialistic ideas had spread among the intelligentsia, even among intelligent Government officials. The younger men and women of the Congress, who used to read Bryce on democracies and Morley and Keith and Mazzini, were now reading, when they could get them, books on socialism and communism and Russia. . . . Everywhere there was in evidence a new spirit of inquiry, a questioning and a challenge to existing institutions.

Chapter Thirty-eight

Drift to war, 1929–1939

THE ORIGINS OF THE SECOND WORLD WAR   89

Whereas the late 1920's were years of stabilization and settlement, the 1930's, by contrast, were years of recurring crises, and eventually of war. The settlement of the twenties was challenged in the following decade by aggressive revisionist powers: Germany and Italy in Europe, and Japan in the Far East. For a variety of reasons, this challenge was not met by the status quo powers, with the result that aggression followed aggression until the showdown in 1939. In the following selection, an American authority on diplomatic history analyzes the combination of factors culminating in the outbreak of World War II.*

Scholarly histories of the origins of the First World War began to appear within a few years of the close of hostilities. A dozen years later, the magisterial studies by Sidney B. Fay and Bernadotte E. Schmitt had appeared in this country, and comparable works had been completed by European scholars. It is now eighteen years since V-E Day, but no studies comparable to Fay or Schmitt have appeared. In part this contrast is explained by the slowness with which the diplomatic papers concerning the years from 1919 to 1939 are being made available. Far more important, however, is the fact that scholars do not believe that a history of the origins of the Second World War can be written with substantial completeness from diplomatic records. In their studies of the years before 1914, Fay and Schmitt did consider subjects like nationalism and imperialism, but the thread that holds their story together is the history of negotiations between governments, and in particular the history of the European alliance system.

No such single thread suffices to give unity to European diplomatic history be-

* Reprinted from Raymond J. Sontag, "The Origins of the Second World War," *Review of Politics*, XXV (1963), 497–508, by permission of the publisher.

tween the wars. For understanding of the events which culminated in the catastrophe of the Second World War, the historian must leave the foreign offices and explore the totality of the tumultuous history of those years. The magnitude of the task explains the fact that no even moderately satisfactory telling of the whole story has been attempted. However, excellent studies have been made of parts of the story, and every student working in the field has in his mind a working sketch of the story as a whole. Here, not even such a sketch will be attempted, but merely a statement of those aspects of the interwar period which, to one observer, are central to an understanding of the origins of the Second World War.

I

Before the Treaty of Versailles came into force on January 20, 1920, conditions had been created which made the prevention of a second war difficult. On the continent of Europe, the still not completely drawn new frontiers were made possible only by the collapse of three great empires—Germany, Russia, and Austria-Hungary. The Habsburg Monarchy was dead, although fear of its revival continued to haunt central Europe. Germany and Russia, however, were only temporarily weakened. When the giants revived, what would happen to the new map, particularly to the smaller states of central and southeastern Europe? These states had a total population equal to that of the United States but a population divided among a dozen weak and often antagonistic states. Unaided they could not hope to survive when Germany and Russia revived.

The peacemakers had sought to protect the new map by the Anglo-American treaty of guarantee to France, by providing for a continuation of the Supreme Council of the victors to stand guard over the treaties, and by the guarantees against aggression contained in the Covenant of the League of Nations. In January 1920, however, it was evident that the United States, the power which had determined the outcome of the war, would accept no responsibility for the protection of the treaty settlement. During the years that followed, our counry was more often an obstacle than an asset to efforts to achieve stability in Europe. As for the British, they could not withdraw completely from participation in European affairs, but what support they did give was wavering, and they flatly refused to promise any support for the map of central and southeastern Europe.

Our defection, and the partial withdrawal of the British, left France to defend the Treaty of Versailles. The result was disastrous. Acutely conscious that their primacy rested on the artificial weakness of Germany, the French set out to keep Germany weak by enforcing every provision of the Treaty of Versailles. Even Briand was obliged to retreat when he attempted a reconciliation with Germany at Thoiry, and as late as 1931 the French compelled the abandonment of the Austro-German customs union, even though the cost was the financial collapse of Europe. Throughout, the policy of France was dominated by fear of what would follow German resurgence.

Conversely, the defection of the United States and Britain inevitably encouraged the Germans to believe that they need not accept the treaty. German resistance might rise to actual revolt, as during the Ruhr invasion, or it might wane, as during the Stresemann years. But the resistance never ceased, and Germans never lost the belief that the territorial settlement in central Europe was temporary, to be changed when German power revived.

No one, of course, can demonstrate that, if there had been effective force behind the Treaty of Versailles, the map would have become stabilized, and the peoples of Europe would have settled down to the tasks of peacetime existence. The lack of effective force behind the treaty, however, did make certain French intransigence, German resistance, and the fearful, precarious, Kafka-like history of Central Europe in the interwar years.

II

The second circumstance which made difficult the prevention of war was economic dislocation, chronic dislocation throughout, threatening complete disintegration in the catastrophe of the great depression. Even economists found the theory in which they had been trained before 1914 of little use in solving the problems of the interwar years; it is not strange, therefore, that statesmen were baffled to understand abstruse matters like terms of trade, balance of payments, productivity of labor, and the relation of production to consumption. The consequences of economic dislocation were momentous. Without the financial chaos in Italy after 1918, the triumph of fascism would have been unlikely. The German social structure cracked under the strain of inflation, rationalization, and depression, and social disintegration provided the opportunity for Hitler to attain power. The memory of the inflation of the twenties paralyzed successive French ministries in the thirties. Desire to cut loose from economic storms sweeping over the world after 1931 in part explains the triumph of isolationism in this country and the reluctance of Britain in the Baldwin era to assume the leadership of Europe. Everywhere, the feeling of being in the grip of problems for which the wisdom of the past offered no solution prepared men to accept new and desperate remedies.

Finally, the surge of Soviet industrial production, in exactly the years when industrial indices elsewhere were plummeting, helps to explain the growing conviction among the younger generation in western Europe that Russia was the land of youth and promise, the hope for the future. Actually, of course, Marxism in these years did not provide the key to unlock the secrets of history; it is an easy game to list the wrong guesses of Soviet theorists and statesmen. The experience of these years did not vindicate Marxism as a science, but that experience certainly did discredit orthodox classical economic theory. Probably of greater importance than any contribution of John Maynard Keynes to economic theory was the confidence which he imparted to young intellectuals, and to some statesmen in Britain and America, that there was a way out of the depression without the sacrifice of human freedom, without accepting either fascist or communist totalitarianism.

III

Intimately connected with economic dislocation were two other disturbing characteristics of the interwar years, the pressure of the lower classes for social change, and the pressure of subject peoples for freedom from imperial rule.

The pressure for social change reaches far back, of course, in European history, and that pressure had produced substantial results by 1914. After 1918, resistance to social change, already growing in the early years of the century, became much stronger as the vast formless lower middle classes, and the peasants also, found themselves being pressed down by economic changes which few understood. From these classes came the mass support for Mussolini's Black Shirts and Hitler's Brown Shirts, and for the other fascist movements. In France, the middle-class Radical

Socialists shifted unhappily between alliance with the left and alliance with the right, and by these shifts contributed greatly to the instability of French political life. In central and southeastern Europe where the middle classes were weak, it was the Green International of the peasants which expressed a type of radicalism hostile both to the old ruling classes and the city workers. Because, after 1933, Hitler turned away from the socialism promised in his earlier program, it is likely to be forgotten that he was brought to power by a mass desire, not just for nationalism, but also by passionate and widespread desire for a socialism which was non-Marxian and representative of the lower middle class, but still revolutionary.

The demand of the city workers for social change was, therefore, weakened by the increasing difficulty, or the impossibility, of continuing the old alliance with large segments of the middle class. The strength of the city workers was even more seriously impaired by the split on the left, the split between socialists and communists. The fatal consequences of that split in Germany were shown in the first weeks of the revolution in 1918 when, to ward off communist efforts to force a second revolution, the leaders of the Weimar Republic entered into alliance with the old military, industrial, and administrative leaders of Germany. In the last years of the Weimar Republic, the communists tacitly cooperated with the Nazis, confident that "in order to grasp the bourgeoisie by the throat, it is necessary to step across the corpse of social democracy." The decisive importance of the split on the left is not as obvious in other countries, but it had its effects everywhere, and everywhere the effects were evident in foreign as well as domestic policy. When there was alliance between the parties of the left, as during the Popular Front in France in 1936, another weakness appeared. Because the Communist Party of France was a partner in the Popular Front, and because the obedience of the Communist Party to orders from Moscow had been repeatedly demonstrated, it was easy for the parties of the right to attack the Popular Front as a tool of the Soviet Union, and to denounce the French alliance with Russia as support for international communism. The split on the left, therefore, not only slowed, or even reversed, the movement towards social change; that split, together with Soviet control over communist parties in other countries, is of great importance in international affairs.

Between 1914 and 1939 the history of every great power of Europe, and most of the lesser powers, was decisively influenced by the struggle for social change— except Britain. In Britain there was social change, change of almost revolutionary proportions, but (unlike Russia, Italy, and Germany) Britain had no revolution, and (unlike France) British policy was not paralyzed by social strife. Rather, as a Scottish labor leader pointed out, Britain entered the Second World War more united than in 1914. Many circumstances of British history and British social life enter into any explanation of this singular good fortune. In part, however, and again as the Scottish labor leader maintained, some of the credit must go to Stanley Baldwin. Baldwin's fumbling foreign policy is partly responsible for the fact that there was a second world war. But Baldwin's ability both to win the support of labor, and to force the Conservative Party into the path of social reform, must form part of any explanation of British strength and unity when the war came.

IV

The revolt of dependent peoples against their masters played a less obvious role in the origins of the Second World War than it had in precipitating the first: the murders at Sarajevo on June 28, 1914, like the Young Turk revolution, the Bosnian crisis, and the Balkan wars, were all related to this revolt. Between the wars, the revolt was global in extent, and the rise of Chinese nationalism provided at least the occasion for the explosion of Japanese imperialism which did materially affect international politics from the Manchurian adventure in 1931 to Pearl Harbor a decade later. But Japanese expansion, like the conquest of Ethiopia by Italy, represented the effort of a second-class power to take advantage of the preoccupation of the stronger powers with more pressing problems. Similarly, no major results flowed from the efforts of the Soviet Union to execute a flank attack on the capitalist powers by allying with colonial nationalist movements. So far as the origins of the Second World War are concerned, these efforts had their greatest importance as one element in the reluctance of Britain and France to ally with the Soviet Union. Popular sympathy in Britain for the revolt of the colonial peoples did, however, in part explain the inability of the British government to make the concessions necessary to hold Italy and Japan away from alliance with Germany. It is also true that the preoccupation of Britain with the task of meeting the demands of the subject peoples of the Empire was one of the ingredients of the appeasement policy. In these ways the revolt of the colonial peoples did contribute indirectly to the coming of war in 1939.

V

The condemnation of imperialism, dominant in the United States, strong in Britain, and a force to be reckoned with in France, is part of the intangible but vitally important moral temper prevailing in the West. It is, I suppose, universally accepted that the moral consequences of the First World War were much greater than those of the Second World War. In part the contrast is explained by the fact that the First World War shattered the dominant illusion that man was progressing towards the solution of differences through discussion between reasonable men, while by 1939 few cherished illusions [remained] about the reasonableness, much less the gentleness, of man. Much more important was the cumulative effect over the years from 1914 to 1918 of all that is concealed in the words "war of attrition." In the trenches and on the barbed wire, spirit as well as flesh rotted. The result was summed up in the title of a British book on the war, C. E. Montague's *Disenchantment,* disenchantment with many things, but disenchantment above all with war itself.

At the end of 1918, the disenchantment was probably as general and as complete in Germany as in England. A change came in Germany with the announcement of the terms of the Treaty of Versailles, and especially as Germans pondered the indictment implied in Article 231, the so-called war guilt clause. Whatever those who drafted that article intended, it could be interpreted as an accusation that the German people were responsible for all the horror inflicted on the world by the war. To the Germans this meant that their sons, nearly two millions of them, had died in an ignoble, a base cause. Against that charge, the German people revolted. Revulsion against war did persist. Some of the most effective antiwar tracts, books like *All Quiet on the Western Front,* appeared much later. But from the spring of 1919 the German mind was becoming prepared to believe myths like the charge of the stab in the back.

Under the stress of the years that followed, Germans came to hate each other, and to fight each other over most things, but they were united in a nationalism which included determination to overthrow the Treaty of Versailles. By 1932, walking among the trees of the Hofgarten in Munich, one might have come suddenly on a sunken stone court. On the walls were inscribed the names of the thirteen thousand men of Munich who had been killed in the First World War. Standing there in the silence, looking up from this hole in the ground to the encircling trees, one could think that this was the Germany left by the war and the years since the war, a hole in the ground, a stone foundation of frustrated, outraged nationalism. In the next six years, on that foundation Hitler was to build, with the aid of the German people, aid given gladly for the most part, a prison house for Germans, for every German. On that foundation he also built the fortress from which the German people moved in perfectly disciplined formation to attempt the subjugation of Europe and the extermination of the "inferior" peoples who occupied ground needed as living space for the master German race.

In the years after 1919, the German people convinced themselves that their young men, fighting in a noble cause, had almost achieved victory when traitors at home stabbed them in the back. In Britain and France, and also in the United States, the conviction grew that their young men had died in an unnecessary war which had shaken the foundations of European civilization, and that another war would complete the ruin of European civilization. In December, 1918, the Allied governments could confidently assert that "the responsibility of Germany for the war has been incontestably proved." Two years later Lloyd George was saying that all governments, including the German government, "staggered and stumbled" into war, and the more scholars studied the origins of the war, the more mixed was the verdict they returned. The war itself, which had seemed so noble an effort while it was being fought, became in Keynes' phrase "a nightmare interlude" even when described with the enthusiasm of Winston Churchill. The attack on the Treaty of Versailles began immediately. Keynes' *Economic Consequences of the Peace,* certainly one of the most influential books of this century, appeared at the end of 1919. With the fervor of an Old Testament prophet, Keynes attacked the moral foundation of the treaty; much of the argument of those in Britain who supported Hitler's demand for "justice" in the thirties is a paraphrase of Keynes.

By 1926, Stanley Baldwin was asking, "who in Europe does not know that one more war in the West, and the civilization of the ages will fall with as great a shock as that of Rome?" Three years later, Winston Churchill, at the end of *The Aftermath,* warned that the advance of military technology was so rapid that in another war mankind itself might be exterminated. By 1937, Aldous Huxley's *Encyclopedia of Pacifism* stated as a demonstrated fact that, after aerial bombardment with new weapons, "the chief use of the army will be, not to fight an enemy, but to try to keep order among the panic-stricken population at home." In that year, Bertrand Russell said the obvious conclusion was that if Hitler invaded England, the Nazis should be welcomed like tourists: "Whatever damage the Germans could do us would not be worse than the damage done in fighting them, even if we won." He believed the damage would not, in fact, be great: "The Nazis would find some interest in our way of living, I think, and the starch would be taken out of them." [1]

Statesmen responsible for the security of their country could not, of course, accept the possibility of invasion as lightheartedly as Bertrand Russell. However, determination not to repeat the mass slaughter of 1914–18, and dread of the consequences of another world war, entered the thought and the action of French and British statesmen. Back of French military doctrine, which, proceeding from the axiom that "fire kills," ended with faith that the fixed fortifications of the Maginot

[1] *The New York Times,* April 2, 1937, p. 9.

374

Line would permit successful defense with a minimum sacrifice of life, there was the memory of Verdun and the other battles of the war of attrition. When the British ceaselessly repeated Liddell Hart's dictum, "defense is paramount," and when they chilled their French allies by repeated declarations that Britain would never again send a mass army to the continent, their thinking was undoubtedly overshadowed by the fear "taking grisly shape in the twilight," as Stanley Baldwin put it, "that the Great War, by the destruction of our best lives in such numbers, has not left enough of the breed to carry on the work of Empire." [2]

Baffling economic shifts, social strife, the problems of empire, the realization that Germany had been beaten by force in 1918 and held down by the threat of use of force from 1918 to 1933 without breaking the German will to resist, and above all the dread of another holocaust like that of 1914–18—all these paralyzed the will of French leaders by 1936. After that, France followed passively in the tow of Britain.

VI

Those who supported Neville Chamberlain in his policy of appeasement, and most Englishmen did support that policy until March, 1939, were influenced but not dominated by these same problems and fears. The difference lay partly in the more real British confidence in the superiority of the defense over the offense in modern warfare. The difference lay partly also in confidence resulting from lack of acquaintance with defeat. Chiefly, however, Chamberlain and his followers were sustained by the entirely erroneous conviction that Germans and Italians would, if their grievances were removed, appreciate the ruinous folly of war. In his more pessimistic moods, Chamberlain feared Hitler was insane, and therefore might not recognize that resort to war was madness. Until the end, however, Chamberlain seemed to hold firmly to the belief that only a madman could fail to see what he saw so clearly, that by peace men could attain all those things which made life desirable, while by war men would be engulfed in a common ruin. One of the greatest forces making for war was the British conviction, implicit through the interwar years, explicit after Chamberlain became Prime Minister in April, 1937, that human nature was everywhere the same, that under modern conditions no sane man could hope for real victory in war, and that bellicose sentiments such as those evident in Germany and Italy resulted from grievances which must be removed so that the necessity for peace would be evident, even to Germans and Italians.

There was one other related element which helps to an understanding of British and French reluctance to use force: fear of what would follow the defeat of Fascist Italy or Nazi Germany. Now, clearly, now obscurely, the fear obtrudes that if Mussolini or Hitler suffered military defeat, he would be overthrown and replaced by a communist regime. Here again the Soviet Union enters as a negative force in the drift towards war. The weight of the evidence is very much against those who argue that Chamberlain was working to promote war between Nazi Germany and the Soviet Union. The evidence is strong, however, that he, and French statesmen, dreaded a clash with Mussolini or Hitler partly because of fear that communism would fill the vacuum left by the collapse of the Fascist or Nazi regime.

Appeasement had precisely the opposite effect from that intended by Chamberlain. Hitler was borne to power by a popular movement which demanded both

[2] Stanley Baldwin, *On England,* Penguin ed. (London 1938), p. 113.

social change at home and freedom from the restraints of the Treaty of Versailles. From his first days in power, Hitler showed clearly that he had no intention of bringing about revolutionary social change within Germany; his regime would stand, or fall, on his ability to achieve success abroad. At least through his militarization of the Rhineland in March, 1936, he would undoubtedly have been forced to retreat without a serious fight if confronted with military force. Whether, once he embarked on territorial expansion two years later, he would have retreated without full-scale war is doubtful. However, unless one is prepared to distort or disregard clear and conclusive evidence, there can be no escape from the conclusion that appeasement had exactly the opposite effect from the one intended. Appeasement convinced Hitler, and Mussolini also, that they could move ahead with less risk and more speed. Appeasement did not induce them to be "reasonable"; appeasement convinced them only that their opponents were cowards, afraid to fight. Whatever stress one places in the nobility of Chamberlain's aspiration, and his policy did embody some of mankind's most noble aspirations, the consequences of his policy, and of French policy, were disastrous.

VII

At the same time, the direct and overwhelming responsibility of the Nazi regime for the coming of the war is clear and incontestable—unless again one is prepared to distort or ignore the evidence. By 1937 the British and French governments were willing, indeed eager, to give Germany not only freedom from the restraints of the Treaty of Versailles; they were willing to give Germany preponderance in central and southeastern Europe. In his conscious thought, Hitler would have been temporarily content if the countries of central Europe accepted a dependent status: even after his stormy interview with Schuschnigg in February, 1938, Hitler spoke of the necessity for an "evolutionary" solution of the Austrian problem. In practice, however, the kind of dependence he was willing to accept was unobtainable without actual conquest. The government of what was left of Czechoslovakia after Munich showed a desperate eagerness to make concessions which would anticipate Hitler's every whim, yet he was driven by his impatience for total control to the fatal step of annexing Bohemia and Moravia. If he had displayed, even after the annexation of Austria, the extraordinary ability to wait which he had shown in the decade before 1933, or even the patience he had shown in foreign affairs before 1938, it is probable that Germany could have won a position of leadership in Europe far higher than that achieved by Bismarck. Unlike Bismarck, however, in success Hitler had no consciousness of the limits of the possible. By driving beyond those limits, be brought his country, and Europe, to ruin. And the German people, after making all allowance for the difficulty not only of dissent but even of clear vision under a totalitarian regime, share the responsibility of the Nazi regime for the tragedy of the Second World War.

At this point the task of the historian ends, and the task of the citizen begins. In his great speech after V-E Day, Winston Churchill admonished his countrymen to study the past because "it is only from the past that one can judge the future." Just because the history of the interwar years is so important a part of the human experience upon which citizen and statesman alike must build their understanding of the present age, it is the duty of the historian to make certain that the record of those years is examined with scholarly detachment and presented without distortion.

Chapter Thirty-nine

World War II:
global repercussions

ATOM BOMBS ON JAPAN: TWO VIEWPOINTS

90

The most momentous event of World War II doubtless was the dropping of atomic bombs on Hiroshima and Nagasaki in August 1945. This heralding of the new atomic age in the form of nuclear holocausts is of obvious significance for the future course of world history. This is apparent in the following two selections, representing the viewpoints of the American policy-makers and of the victims in Hiroshima. The first is by Secretary of War Henry L. Stimson, who relates how and why his government decided to use the bombs.* The second selection comprises the reflections of American scientist J. Bronowski while reviewing the book, Death in Life: Survivors of Hiroshima, *by Robert Jay Lifton, Professor of Psychiatry at Yale University.†*

Henry L. Stimson

U.S. POLICY TOWARD JAPAN IN JULY 1945. The principal political, social, and military objective of the United States in the summer of 1945 was the prompt and complete surrender of Japan. Only the complete destruction of her military power could open the way to lasting peace.

Japan, in July 1945, had been seriously weakened by our increasingly violent attacks. It was known to us that she had gone so far as to make tentative proposals

---

* Reprinted from Henry L. Stimson, "The Decision to Use the Atomic Bomb," as it appeared in *Harper's Magazine,* CXCIV (February 1947), 97–107, by permission of Harper & Row, Publishers, Inc. and Hutchinson & Co. Ltd.; later incorporated in the chapter "The Atomic Bomb and the Surrender of Japan," from *On Active Service in Peace and War* by Henry L. Stimson and McGeorge Bundy. Copyright 1947 by Henry L. Stimson.

† Reprinted from J. Bronowski, "The Psychological Wreckage of Hiroshima and Nagasaki," *Scientific American* (June 1968), pp. 131–135, by permission of W. H. Freeman and Company. Copyright © 1968 by Scientific American, Inc. All rights reserved.

to the Soviet government, hoping to use the Russians as mediators in a negotiated peace. These vague proposals contemplated the retention by Japan of important conquered areas and were therefore not considered seriously. There was as yet no indication of any weakening in the Japanese determination to fight rather than accept unconditional surrender. If she should persist in her fight to the end, she had still a great military force.

In the middle of July 1945, the intelligence section of the War Department General Staff estimated Japanese military strength as follows: in the home islands, slightly under 2,000,000; in Korea, Manchuria, China proper, and Formosa, slightly over 2,000,000; in French Indo-China, Thailand, and Burma, over 200,000; in the East Indies area, including the Philippines, over 500,000; in the by-passed Pacific islands, over 100,000. The total strength of the Japanese Army was estimated at about 5,000,000 men. These estimates later proved to be in very close agreement with official Japanese figures.

The Japanese Army was in much better condition than the Japanese Navy and Air Force. The Navy had practically ceased to exist except as a harrying force against an invasion fleet. The Air Force had been reduced mainly to reliance upon Kamikaze, or suicide, attacks. These latter, however, had already inflicted serious damage on our seagoing forces, and their possible effectiveness in a last-ditch fight was a matter of real concern to our naval leaders.

As we understood it in July, there was a very strong possibility that the Japanese government might determine upon resistance to the end, in all the areas of the Far East under its control. In such an event, the Allies would be faced with the enormous task of destroying an armed force of five million men and five thousand suicide aircraft, belonging to a race which had already amply demonstrated its ability to fight literally to the death.

The strategic plans of our armed forces for the defeat of Japan, as they stood in July, had been prepared without reliance upon the atomic bomb, which had not yet been tested in New Mexico. We were planning an intensified sea and air blockade, and greatly intensified strategic air bombing, through the summer and early fall, to be followed on November 1 by an invasion of the southern island of Kyushu. This would be followed in turn by an invasion of the main island of Honshu in the spring of 1946. The total U.S. military and naval force involved in this grand design was of the order of 5,000,000 men; if all those indirectly concerned are included, it was larger still.

We estimated that if we should be forced to carry this plan to its conclusion, the major fighting would not end until the latter part of 1946, at the earliest. I was informed that such operations might be expected to cost over a million casualties to American forces alone. Additional large losses might be expected among our Allies, and, of course, if our campaign were successful and if we could judge by previous experience, enemy casualties would be much larger than our own.

It was already clear in July that even before the invasion we should be able to inflict enormously severe damage on the Japanese homeland by the combined application of "conventional" sea and air power. The critical question was whether this kind of action would induce surrender. It therefore became necessary to consider very carefully the probable state of mind of the enemy, and to assess with accuracy the line of conduct which might end his will to resist.

With these considerations in mind, I wrote a memorandum for the President, on July 2, which I believe fairly represents the thinking of the American government as it finally took shape in action. This memorandum was prepared after discussion and general agreement with Joseph C. Grew, Acting Secretary of State, and Secretary of the Navy Forrestal, and when I discussed it with the President, he expressed his general approval.

July 2, 1945

Memorandum for the President.

PROPOSED PROGRAM FOR JAPAN

1. The plans of operation up to and including the first landing have been authorized and the preparations for the operation are now actually going on. This situation was accepted by all members of your conference on Monday, June 18.

2. There is reason to believe that the operation for the occupation of Japan following the landing may be a very long, costly, and arduous struggle on our part. The terrain, much of which I have visited several times, has left the impression on my memory of being one which would be susceptible to a last-ditch defense such as has been made on Iwo Jima and Okinawa and which of course is very much larger than either of those two areas. According to my recollection it will be much more unfavorable with regard to tank maneuvering than either the Philippines or Germany.

3. If we once land on one of the main islands and begin a forceful occupation of Japan, we shall probably have cast the die of last-ditch resistance. The Japanese are highly patriotic and certainly susceptible to calls for fanatical resistance to repel an invasion. Once started in actual invasion, we shall in my opinion have to go through with an even more bitter finish fight than in Germany. We shall incur the losses incident to such a war and we shall have to leave the Japanese islands even more thoroughly destroyed than was the case with Germany. This would be due both to the difference in the Japanese and German personal character and the differences in the size and character of the terrain through which the operations will take place.

4. A question then comes: Is there any alternative to such a forceful occupation of Japan which will secure for us the equivalent of an unconditional surrender of her forces and a permanent destructon of her power again to strike an aggressive blow at the "peace of the Pacific"? I am inclined to think that there is enough such chance to make it well worthwhile our giving them a warning of what is to come and a definite opportunity to capitulate. As above suggested, it should be tried before the actual forceful occupation of the homeland islands is begun and furthermore the warning should be given in ample time to permit a national reaction to set in.

We have the following enormously favorable factors on our side—factors much weightier than those we had against Germany:

Japan has no allies.

Her navy is nearly destroyed and she is vulnerable to a surface and underwater blockade which can deprive her of sufficient food and supplies for her population.

She is terribly vulnerable to our concentrated air attack upon her crowded cities, industrial and food resources.

She has against her not only the Anglo-American forces but the rising forces of China and the ominous threat of Russia.

We have inexhaustible and untouched industrial resources to bring to bear against her diminishing potential.

We have great moral superiority through being the victim of her first sneak attack.

The problem is to translate these advantages into prompt and economical achievement of our objectives. I believe Japan is susceptible to reason in such a crisis to a much greater extent than is indicated by our current press and other current comment. Japan is not a nation composed wholly of mad fanatics of an entirely different mentality from ours. On the contrary, she has within the past century shown herself to possess extremely intelligent people capable in an unprecedentedly short time of adopting not only the complicated technique of Occidental civilization but to a substantial extent its culture and its political and social ideas. Her advance in all these respects during the short period of sixty or seventy years has been one of the most astounding feats of national progress in history—a leap from the isolated feudalism of centuries into the position of one of the six or seven great powers of the world. She has not only built up powerful armies and navies. She has maintained an honest and effective national finance and respected position in many of the sciences in which we pride ourselves. Prior to the forcible seizure of power over her government by the fanatical military group in 1931, she had for ten years lived a reasonably responsible and respectable international life.

My own opinion is in her favor on the two points involved in this question:

a. I think the Japanese nation has the mental intelligence and versatile capacity in such a crisis to recognize the folly of a fight to the finish and to accept the proffer of what will amount to an unconditional surrender; and

b. I think she has within her population enough liberal leaders (although now submerged by the terrorists) to be depended upon for her reconstruction as a responsible member of the family of nations. I think she is better in this last respect than Germany was. Her liberals yielded only at the point of the pistol and, so far as I am aware, their liberal attitude has not been personally subverted in the way which was so general in Germany.

On the other hand, I think that the attempt to exterminate her armies and her population by gunfire or other means will tend to produce a fusion of race solidity and antipathy which has no analogy in the case of Germany. We have a national interest in creating, if possible, a condition wherein the Japanese nation may live as a peaceful and useful member of the future Pacific community.

5. It is therefore my conclusion that a carefully timed warning be given to Japan by the chief representatives of the United States, Great Britain, China, and, if then a belligerent, Russia by calling upon Japan to surrender and permit the occupation of her country in order to insure its complete demilitarization for the sake of the future peace.

This warning should contain the following elements:

The varied and overwhelming character of the force we are about to bring to bear on the islands.

The inevitability and completeness of the destruction which the full application of this force will entail.

The determination of the Allies to destroy permanently all authority and influence of those who have deceived and misled the country into embarking on world conquest.

The determination of the Allies to limit Japanese sovereignty to her main islands and to render them powerless to mount and support another war.

The disavowal of any attempt to extirpate the Japanese as a race or to destroy them as a nation.

A statement of our readiness, once her economy is purged of its militaristic influence, to permit the Japanese to maintain such industries, particularly of a light consumer character, as offer no threat of aggression against their neighbors, but which can produce a sustaining economy, and provide a reasonable standard of living. The statement should indicate our willingness, for this purpose, to give Japan trade access to external raw materials, but no longer any control over the sources of supply outside her main islands. It should also indicate our willingness, in accordance with our now established foreign trade policy, in due course to enter into mutually advantageous trade relations with her.

The withdrawal from their country as soon as the above objectives of the Allies are accomplished, and as soon as there has been established a peacefully inclined government, of a character representative of the masses of the Japanese people. I personally think that if in saying this we should add that we do not exclude a constitutional monarchy under her present dynasty, it would substantially add to the chances of acceptance.

6. Success of course will depend on the potency of the warning which we give her. She has an extremely sensitive national pride and, as we are now seeing every day, when actually locked with the enemy will fight to the very death. For that reason the warning must be tendered before the actual invasion has occurred and while the impending destruction, though clear beyond peradventure, has not yet reduced her to fanatical despair. If Russia is a part of the threat, the Russian attack, if actual, must not have progressed too far. Our own bombing should be confined to military objectives as far as possible.

It is important to emphasize the double character of the suggested warning. It was designed to promise destruction if Japan resisted, and hope, if she surrendered.

It will be noted that the atomic bomb is not mentioned in this memorandum. On grounds of secrecy the bomb was never mentioned except when absolutely necessary, and furthermore, it had not yet been tested. It was, of course, well forward in our minds, as the memorandum was written and discussed, that the bomb would be the best possible sanction if our warning were rejected.

THE USE OF THE BOMB.   The adoption of the policy outlined in the memorandum of July 2 was a decision of high politics; once it was accepted by the President, the position of the atomic bomb in our planning became quite clear. I find that I stated in my diary, as early as June 19, that "the last chance warning . . . must be given before an actual landing of the ground forces in Japan, and fortunately the plans provide for enough time to bring in the sanctions to our warning in the shape of heavy ordinary bombing attack and an attack of S-1." S-1 was a code name for the atomic bomb.

There was much discussion in Washington about the timing of the warning to Japan. The controlling factor in the end was the date already set for the Potsdam meeting of the Big Three. It was President Truman's decision that such a warning should be solemnly issued by the U.S. and the U.K. from this meeting, with the concurrence of the head of the Chinese government, so that it would be plain that *all* of Japan's principal enemies were in entire unity. This was done in the Potsdam ultimatum of July 26, which very closely followed the above memorandum of July 2, with the exception that it made no mention of the Japanese Emperor.

On July 28, the Premier of Japan, Suzuki, rejected the Potsdam ultimatum by announcing that it was "unworthy of public notice." In the face of this rejection we could only proceed to demonstrate that the ultimatum had meant exactly what it said when it stated that if the Japanese continued the war, "the full application of our military power, backed by our resolve, will mean the inevitable and complete destruction of the Japanese armed forces and just as inevitably the utter devastation of the Japanese homeland."

For such a purpose, the atomic bomb was an eminently suitable weapon. The New Mexico test occurred while we were at Potsdam, on July 16. It was immediately clear that the power of the bomb measured up to our highest estimates. We had developed a weapon of such a revolutionary character that its use against the enemy might well be expected to produce exactly the kind of shock on the Japanese ruling oligarchy which we desired, strengthening the position of those who wished peace, and weakening that of the military party.

Because of the importance of the atomic mission against Japan, the detailed plans were brought to me by the military staff for approval. With President Truman's warm support, I struck off the list of suggested targets the city of Kyoto. Although it was a target of considerable military importance, it had been the ancient capital of Japan and was a shrine of Japanese art and culture. We determined that it should be spared. I approved four other targets, including the cities of Hiroshima and Nagasaki.

Hiroshima was bombed on August 6 and Nagasaki on August 9. These two cities were active working parts of the Japanese war effort. One was an army center, the other was naval and industrial. Hiroshima was the headquarters of the Japanese Army defending southern Japan and was a major military storage and assembly point. Nagasaki was a major seaport, and it contained several large industrial plants of great wartime importance. We believed that our attacks had struck cities which must certainly be important to the Japanese military leaders, both Army and Navy, and we waited for a result. We waited one day.

Many accounts have been written about the Japanese surrender. After a prolonged Japanese cabinet session in which the deadlock was broken by the Emperor himself, the offer to surrender was made on August 10. It was based on the Potsdam terms, with a reservation concerning the sovereignty of the Emperor. While the Allied reply made no promises other than those already given, it implicitly recognized the Emperor's position by prescribing that his power must be subject to the orders of the Allied Supreme Commander. These terms were accepted on August 14 by the Japanese, and the instrument of surrender was formally signed on September 2, in Tokyo Bay. Our great objective was thus achieved, and all the evidence I have seen indicates that the controlling factor in the final Japanese decision to accept our terms of surrender was the atomic bomb.

The two atomic bombs which we had dropped were the only ones we had ready, and our rate of production at the time was very small. Had the war continued until the projected invasion on November 1, additional fire raids of B-29's would have been more destructive of life and property than the very limited number of atomic raids which we could have executed in the same period. But the atomic bomb was more than a weapon of terrible destruction; it was a psychological weapon. In March 1945, our Air Force had launched its first great incendiary raid on the Tokyo area. In this raid more damage was done and more casualties were inflicted than was the case at Hiroshima. Hundreds of bombers took part and hundreds of tons of incendiaries were dropped. Similar successive raids burned out a great part of the urban area of Japan, but the Japanese fought on. On August 6, one B-29 dropped a single atomic bomb on Hiroshima. Three days later a second bomb was dropped on Nagasaki, and the war was over. So far as the Japanese could know, our ability to execute atomic attacks, if necessary by many planes at a time, was unlimited. As Dr. Karl Compton has said, "It was not one atomic bomb, or two, which brought surrender; it was the experience of what an atomic bomb will actually do to a community, *plus the dread of many more,* that was effective."

The bomb thus served exactly the purpose we intended. The peace party was able to take the path of surrender, and the whole weight of the Emperor's prestige was exerted in favor of peace. When the Emperor ordered surrender, and the small but

382

dangerous group of fanatics who opposed him were brought under control, the Japanese became so subdued that the great undertaking of occupation and disarmament was completed with unprecedented ease.

A PERSONAL SUMMARY.   In the foregoing pages I have tried to give an accurate account of my own personal observations of the circumstances which led up to the use of the atomic bomb and the reasons which underlay our use of it. To me they have always seemed compelling and clear, and I cannot see how any person vested with such responsibilities as mine could have taken any other course or given any other advice to his chiefs.

Two great nations were approaching contact in a fight to a finish which would begin on November 1, 1945. Our enemy, Japan, commanded forces of somewhat over 5,000,000 armed men. Men of these armies had already inflicted upon us, in our breakthrough of the outer perimeter of their defenses, over 300,000 battle casualties. Enemy armies still unbeaten had the strength to cost us a million more. *As long as the Japanese government refused to surrender,* we should be forced to take and hold the ground, and smash the Japanese ground armies, by close-in fighting of the same desperate and costly kind that we had faced in the Pacific islands for nearly four years.

In the light of the formidable problem which thus confronted us, I felt that every possible step should be taken to compel a surrender of the homelands, and a withdrawal of all Japanese troops from the Asiatic mainland and from other positions, before we had commenced an invasion. We held two cards to assist us in such an effort. One was the traditional veneration in which the Japanese Emperor was held by his subjects and the power which was thus vested in him over his loyal troops. It was for this reason that I suggested in my memorandum of July 2 that his dynasty should be continued. The second card was the use of the atomic bomb in the manner best calculated to persuade that Emperor and the counselors about him to submit to our demand for what was essentially unconditional surrender, placing his immense power over his people and his troops subject to our orders.

In order to end the war in the shortest possible time and to avoid the enormous losses of human life which otherwise confronted us, I felt that we must use the Emperor as our instrument to command and compel his people to cease fighting and subject themselves to our authority through him, and that to accomplish this we must give him and his controlling advisers a compelling reason to accede to our demands. This reason furthermore must be of such a nature that his people could understand his decision. The bomb seemed to me to furnish a unique instrument for that purpose.

My chief purpose was to end the war in victory with the least possible cost in the lives of the men in the armies which I had helped to raise. In the light of the alternatives which, on a fair estimate, were open to us, I believe that no man, in our position and subject to our responsibilities, holding in his hands a weapon of such possibilities for accomplishing this purpose and saving those lives, could have failed to use it and afterwards looked his countrymen in the face.

As I read over what I have written, I am aware that much of it, in this year of peace, may have a harsh and unfeeling sound. It would perhaps be possible to say the same things and say them more gently. But I do not think it would be wise. As I look back over the five years of my service as Secretary of War, I see too many stern and heartrending decisions to be willing to pretend that war is anything else than what it is. The face of war is the face of death; death is an inevitable part of every order that a wartime leader gives. The decision to use the atomic bomb was a decision that brought death to over a hundred thousand Japanese. No explanation can change that fact and I do not wish to gloss it over. But this deliberate, premeditated destruction was our least abhorrent choice. The destruction of Hiroshima and Nagasaki put an end to the Japanese war. It stopped the fire raids, and the strangling blockade; it ended the ghastly specter of a clash of great land armies.

In this last great action of the Second World War, we were given final proof that war is death. War in the twentieth century has grown steadily more barbarous, more destructive, more debased in all its aspects. Now, with the release of atomic energy, man's ability to destroy himself is very nearly complete. The bombs dropped on Hiroshima and Nagasaki ended a war. They also made it wholly clear that we must never have another war. This is the lesson men and leaders everywhere must learn, and I believe that when they learn it they will find a way to lasting peace. There is no other choice.

J. Bronowski

The second world war began in the summer of 1939 with a pact between Hitler and Stalin and ended six years later with the dropping of two atomic bombs on Japan. To almost everyone at the time the second of these events was as unexpected and shocking as the first had been. Evidently the huge enterprise of inventing, building and mounting the atomic bomb had been the best-kept secret of the war. And for most people, scientists and nonscientists alike, it also turned out to be the most grisly secret. After the first days of trumphant wonder a kind of shudder went through the world, a swell of fear and revulsion together, which 20-odd years have now smoothed out of our memories. Everyone at the time had a sense of guilt about the atomic bomb, and although most people naturally shifted the blame to science, that desperate disclaimer was also a sign of penitence.

Twenty years is too long for sorrow, which time does not so much heal as blunt. The bombs that wiped out Hiroshima and Nagasaki have been allowed to become modest weapons in the tactical armory, and people read with resigned indifference that hydrogen bombs more than a hundred times as powerful are carried overhead in clusters 24 hours of the day. In that ebb time of conscience, in which we let governments argue *about* disarming, the moral impulse of 1945 has been eroded. We might have supposed that the sense of guilt had been washed away without a trace, had not Professor Lifton discovered it still haunting (of all people) the survivors of Hiroshima. The discovery gives his quiet and penetrating book a kind of cosmic irony that, more than any burst of righteousness, ought to shake us all out of our somnambulism.

Professor Lifton had spent four years in Japan, off and on since the war, before he paid a visit to Hiroshima. For the last two of those years he had worked on a psychological and historical study of Japanese youth. There he found (among other things) what we all know and resolutely forget:

"The great majority had either no memory of the war at all or only the most meager recollections of it. But what became clear when I explored with them their sense of themselves and their world was the enormous significance for them, however indirectly expressed, of the fact that Japan alone had been exposed to atomic bombs."

So he decided early in 1962 to stay on for another six months and to spend them in Hiroshima, with a few days in Nagasaki added.

His method of study was to interview 75 people, usually for two periods of two hours each. The interviews were carried out in Japanese through a research assistant, although Professor Lifton does speak some Japanese. Forty-two of those interviewed were chosen for their known and articulate prominence in atomic bomb matters, and the other 33 were taken at random from the official list. All were *hibakusha,* which means that either they were within the city limits when the bomb fell, or entered the inner city in the next 14 days, or came into close contact with bomb victims, or that their mother was in one of these groups and was pregnant with them at the time.

Several different estimates have been made of the number of people killed by the bombs in Hiroshima and Nagasaki. I shall stick to the figures that my colleagues and I in the British Mission to Japan worked out in November, 1945, there. We computed that in Hiroshima when the bomb fell on August 6 there were 320,000 people, of whom 80,000 were killed, and that in Nagasaki on August 9 there were 260,000 people, of whom 40,000 were killed. Large numbers of people have died since then from the aftereffects of radiation from the atomic bombs. Allowing for these and for normal deaths over 20 years, the figures are in fair agreement with the official number of *hibakusha* now, namely 160,000 from Hiroshima and 130,000 from Nagasaki.

The scenes after the bombs fell have been described in eerie detail by John Hersey from the testimony of survivors in Hiroshima and by Dr. Takashi Nagai at first hand in Nagasaki. Every victim believed the bomb had exploded directly above him. Those in the open were badly burned by the flash, so that often their own families could not recognize them. (This happened to two of Professor Lifton's survivors.) Those indoors were buried and when they struggled out, almost naked, they found themselves surrounded by fires. Everyone who could move filed in numb silence to the rivers; the injured were abandoned and could be heard in the still heat crying for water. Professor Lifton quotes one of his survivors who was a schoolgirl at the time:

"I felt my body to be so hot that I thought I would jump into the river. . . . The teacher from another class, a man whose shirt was burning, jumped in. And when I was about to jump, our own class teacher came down and she suddenly jumped into the river. . . . Since we had always looked up to our teachers, we wanted to ask them for help. But the teachers themselves had been wounded and were suffering the same pain we were."

Another of Professor Lifton's survivors, a professor of history, saw the destruction from a hill overlooking the city:

"That experience, looking down and finding nothing left of Hiroshima—was so shocking that I simply can't express what I felt. . . . Hiroshima didn't exist—that was mainly what I saw—Hiroshima just didn't exist."

But those inside the city saw a greater destruction in the breakdown of human consciousness, so that the refugees seemed to them to be "a people who walked in the realm of dreams":

"Those who were able walked silently toward the suburbs in the distant hills, their spirits broken, their initiative gone. When asked whence they had come, they pointed to the city and said, 'That way,' and when asked where they were going, pointed away from the city and said, 'This way.' They were so broken and confused that they moved and behaved like automatons."

So much for what we knew and have been diligently burying in the backs of our minds. What have 20 years done to those 290,000 people who were there and who cannot so easily tidy away the memory of what they saw and how they behaved? Is there indeed a single theme in their lives? Are they still dominated by the atomic bombs?

Certainly Hiroshima has become the atomic bomb city. It has a Peace Park, of course, a memorial hall, a children's monument and a Peace Museum. There is a cenotaph with the inscription: "Rest in peace. The mistake shall not be repeated." The word "mistake" is ambiguous enough to make many citizens feel that they are being blamed for the bomb. (This is a common complaint among *hibakusha*, which they express in the ironic sentence "I apologize for having been exposed to the atomic bomb.") A reinforced concrete building almost under the bomb that stood up to the blast pretty well has been preserved as a permanent Dome of Peace, even though some survivors are still distressed by the sight of it.

But these sober *memento mori* are put in the shade by the other showplace of the peace industry, which is the Hiroshima entertainment district. Nowhere else in Japan is there such a splendor of bars, cafés, restaurants, geisha houses, dance halls and what Professor Lifton politely calls "transient quarters for various kinds of illicit sex." Those who saw the film *Hiroshima, Mon Amour* will remember the contrast between the two aspects of the new Hiroshima, and the strange implication that nevertheless ran behind it that they are inseparable. And so they are: the bomb is entwined in the lives of those who survived it, whether they lead a children's march or show their keloid scars in a Hiroshima brothel. The *hibakusha* leaders may rage at those who "sell the bomb," but their anger is also a form of self-accusation; they cannot help themselves, they must exploit the bomb like any crippled postcard-seller.

The *hibakusha* have not been able to escape the ambivalence that always dogs the victim of misfortune. They would like other people to treat them as though they were normal, and at the same time they are hurt if they are not given special sympathy. The effect of these contradictory demands is to frighten those who were not exposed to the bomb, so that survivors find it hard to get jobs, to marry and even to mix with others. Twenty years ago their neighbors were afraid because the *hibakusha* were still psychologically numb, were often ill and (who knows?) might beget monsters. But now the alienation is different in temper, and simply puts the *hibakusha* aside as people who *have something else on their minds*.

The clear August day in 1945 possesses the mind of the survivor as an experience unlike any other, which totally overthrew his inner ordering of the world. He had woken that morning with the confidence, built so carefully through the years of growing up, that things go like this and not otherwise—that teachers help you, that the city is a solid home and that people act together by choice. By nightfall that framework of unwritten laws that had seemed to be laws of nature had fallen apart into meaningless pieces—the teacher had jumped into the river, Hiroshima didn't exist and its people behaved like automatons. Just as sometimes a great man has the order in the world revealed to him in a vision (René Descartes on November 10, 1619, for example, and Blaise Pascal on November 23, 1654), so ordinary men and women in Hiroshima that day had a direct vision of a counterrevelation: the failure of the human order in the world. Professor Lifton calls this "the replacement of the natural order of living and dying with an unnatural order of death-dominated life." Thus his stress is on "the indelible imprint of death immersion," when I would stress the fatal immersion in the collapse of human values. But in principle Professor Lifton and I are at one, and what he finds is the same withdrawal of confidence, a cutting of the roots of conduct, that I felt there three months after the bomb was dropped.

Somehow the roots have to heal, of course; the delinquents disappear from Hiroshima's station, the widows move into the entertainment district and the men whose assurance has been sapped ask their firms without fuss to let them work at lesser jobs. But a psychological wound that is healed is still a wound, a kind of bomb scar or keloid of the personality, which expresses in another form the ambiguity of the *hibakusha*. They have been the victims of a disaster that was manufactured by others, yet their sense of failure is more anguished than we expect, and we see that there is another wound under the scar. The victim has not only been a victim; he has also witnessed and (by his inaction) has condoned the action of turning one's back on other victims. Every survivor has memories of those he did not help:

"I heard many voices calling for help, voices calling their fathers, voices of women and children. . . . I felt it was a wrong thing not to help them, but we were so much occupied by running away ourselves that we left them."

"His head was covered with blood, and when he saw us he called to us. . . . 'Yano [he said to my daughter], please take my child with you. Please take him to the hospital over there.' . . . I heard later that he survived . . . but that the child died. . . . And when I think of not helping him despite his begging me to help, I can only say that it is a very pitiful thing."

Because family ties are strong in Japan the memories are particularly painful in those who feel they neglected their parents. For example, a girl who was 14 at the time is full of remorse for her father's death, although she only complained that his wounds smelled.

The keloid on the personality of the survivor at Hiroshima and Nagasaki is the sense of guilt. "I apologize for having been exposed to the atomic bomb" is not altogether a joke after all, if we read it to mean "I apologize for having *survived* the atomic bomb." Even when the victim was helpless at the time and could have done nothing to help, he is disrupted by doubt and a feeling of inadequacy. All around him people died; why did he deserve to live? Will that act of *hubris* be visited on his children? "Those who died are dead," a survivor from Nagasaki said to Professor Lifton, "but the living must live with this dark feeling." There is no shaking off the divided feeling between one's own fate and the fate of others, between suffering and fear, between pity and revulsion. It is symbolized by the memory that comes to one *hibakusha* at a Japanese feast:

"The color of my brother's keloid—the color of his burns—mixes together with my feeling . . . what I saw directly—that is, the manner in which he died—that's what I remember. . . . The color was similar to that of a dried squid when broiled —so that I think of it whenever I see dried squid. . . . I have . . . a very lonely feeling."

The *hibakusha* resents his own feeling of guilt, yet he cannot resolve it; he is equally unhappy as victim and as survivor. The inner struggle between the roles of victim and survivor is displayed particularly plainly by the Japanese, for two reasons. First, they are brought up in a rigid code of family and social propriety, so that the breakdown of conduct at Hiroshima and Nagasaki was very stark for them. And second, the Japanese pay much attention to symbolic meanings, so that the division in the *hibakusha*'s feelings is constantly reinforced by the ambivalence in the symbols that express them. (For example, the citizens of Hiroshima are wild supporters of their baseball team, but it usually comes in last.)

It was therefore natural for Professor Lifton to think of applying his theme also to some other body of survivors who are not Japanese. In his last chapter, "The Survivor," he makes some comparisons with the men who went through the Nazi concentration camps and lived. What he says here is worth reading, and is evidently consistent with his findings in Japan. But since he has had to take his evidence at second hand from other people's writings we now miss the force of direct speech that makes the rest of the book so convincing. We can see that those who survived the camps are troubled by guilt memories as the *hibakusha* are, but the analysis has become more formal, and there is just a hint of a classroom thesis in the argument.

For the rest, I am convinced by Professor Lifton's powerful book, and I am at variance with his analysis at only one point. As his choice of title shows, he is preoccupied with death as the visible cause and symbol of the survivor's guilt, and in fact he commonly uses the single phrase "death guilt" for it. He says early on, "I shall use the term 'death guilt' throughout the book to encompass all forms of self-condemnation associated with literal or symbolic exposure to death and dying."

Now, it is true that the victims of the man-made disasters at which we have stood by were much exposed to death and dying. I have quoted the casualty figures at Hiroshima and Nagasaki—and as for the concentration camps, "a person who fully adhered to all the ethical and moral standards of conduct of civilian life on entering the camp in the morning would have been dead by nightfall." Nevertheless, I think that the distress of the survivors was caused, more profoundly than by the encounter with death, by the dissolution of "the ethical and moral standards of conduct of civilian life" that robbed them of their bearings.

Certainly the fear of death (and of the unpredictable way death would strike in Hiroshima and Auschwitz) is the infecting virus that begins the social dissolution. Yet the girl in Hiroshima filled with remorse for her father's death had not killed him; what she blamed herself for was disrespect. Or think of one of the men I wrote about in *The Face of Violence,* say Joseph Wiener, once professor of international law at the University of Vienna, whom the Nazis drove mad and put in charge of the camp pigs. He informed against prisoners who stole food from the pig swill; yet it was not the presence of death that deranged him but (as he knew in his sane moments) the debasement in his person of human dignity. Such examples seem to me to make plain that what unhinges the victim's self and leaves it rudderless is not an inner split between life and death but a split between himself and the social order. From childhood he has been taught to submit his own demands to those of society (this is my theme in *The Face of Violence*) and suddenly not life but society dies; he sees walk into the open the anarchy he once dreamed of in secret.

I have left to last the question that must be uppermost for many readers: What did the Japanese think of the Americans, who, after all, had dropped the atomic bombs? I found this the most puzzling issue to get to grips with 20-odd years ago, and it seems to be so still. The Japanese seldom spoke out in plain resentment; perhaps they were either too stunned or too polite. They seemed mostly to be aware that we knew as little about the effects of the bomb in advance as they did; one or two professors spoke to me ironically about the "experiment," and the deepest anger Professor Lifton finds is at having been treated like guinea pigs.

Many Japanese feel they were singled out as no white enemy would have been, as something less than human; some of them may have seen the pictures of Japanese looking like vermin (like the Nazi pictures of the Jews) that were current in America during the war. There was a rumor in Nagasaki when I was there that the atomic bomb burned only dark-skinned people; it was not true, but it put the right pinch of scientific fact in the racial stew.

But the dominant feeling was and is that Americans are simply insensitive.

Professor Lifton gives many examples to justify that: the early censorship, the display of power and wealth, the clinical examinations and the policy of studying the victims without treating them. . . .

.   .   .

There is nothing to say about the prospect that has not been said already. As Professor Lifton's book demonstrates, we have to get it into our heads that the atomic weapons do not create casualties but chaos—a lasting chaos of the human values. The *hibakusha* are haunted and lamed by a shame that is not their own, and that is 20 years old—and so are we. Like them we have an ambivalence between self and society, nation and humanity, that prevents us from forming any policy of right conduct. And the guilt that comes from facing two ways bites deeper, because it prevents us from crystallizing any *principle* of right conduct. Professor Lifton's last message is that we should learn what he calls survivor wisdom, and no one can now doubt that survivor wisdom says that only men of principle survive whole.

Chapter Forty

End of empires

91   Mao Tse-tung on World Revolution

The second world war, unlike the first, was followed by successful colonial revolutions that culminated in the dissolution of most of the European empires except for the Portuguese. But economic independence did not accompany the political; indeed the gap between rich and poor countries tended to widen rather than to narrow. Thus charges of "neo-colonialism" were made by new revolutionaries who demanded social revolution to supplement the political. These revolutionaries frequently looked to Peking rather than to Moscow for inspiration. The fact that Russia was now an affluent as well as a "white" society caused it to be regarded as a part of the global "establishment." Hence the significance of the following exposition of Mao's views by Marshal Lin Piao.* Although Mao confidently expects that China's revolutionary experience will be repeated on a global scale, he stresses that China can provide only a model, and that foreign revolutions must be genuinely indigenous if they are to be successful.

The Chinese Revolution is a continuation of the great October Revolution. The road of the October Revolution is the common road for all people's revolutions. The Chinese Revolution and the October Revolution have in common the following basic characteristics: (1) Both were led by the working class with a Marxist-Leninist party as its nucleus. (2) Both were based on the worker-peasant alliance. (3) In both cases state power was seized through violent revolution and the dictatorship of the proletariat was established. (4) In both cases the socialist system was built after victory in the Revolution. (5) Both were component parts of the proletarian world revolution.

* Reprinted from Lin Piao, *The International Significance of Comrade Mao Tse-tung's Theory of People's War* (Peking: Foreign Languages Press, 1965), pp. 42–59.

Naturally, the Chinese Revolution had its own peculiar characteristics. The October Revolution took place in imperialist Russia, but the Chinese Revolution broke out in a semi-colonial and semi-feudal country. The former was a proletarian socialist revolution, while the latter developed into a socialist revolution after the complete victory of the new democratic revolution. The October Revolution began with armed uprisings in the cities and then spread to the countryside, while the Chinese Revolution won nationwide victory through the encirclement of the cities from the rural areas and the final capture of the cities.

Comrade Mao Tse-tung's great merit lies in the fact that he has succeeded in integrating the universal truth of Marxism-Leninism with the concrete practice of the Chinese Revolution and has enriched and developed Marxism-Leninism by his masterly generalization and summation of the experience gained during the Chinese people's protracted revolutionary struggle.

Comrade Mao Tse-tung's theory of people's war has been proved by the long practice of the Chinese Revolution to be in accord with the objective laws of such wars and to be invincible. It has not only been valid for China, it is a great contribution to the revolutionary struggles of the oppressed nations and peoples throughout the world.

The people's war led by the Chinese Communist Party, comprising the War of Resistance and the Revolutionary Civil Wars, lasted for twenty-two years. It constitutes the most drawn-out and most complex people's war led by the proletariat in modern history, and it has been the richest in experience.

In the last analysis, the Marxist-Leninist theory of proletarian revolution is the theory of the seizure of state power by revolutionary violence, the theory of countering war against the people by people's war. As Marx so aptly put it, "Force is the midwife of every old society pregnant with a new one."

It was on the basis of the lessons derived from the people's wars in China that Comrade Mao Tse-tung, using the simplest and the most vivid language, advanced the famous thesis that "political power grows out of the barrel of a gun."

. . .

In view of the fact that some people were afflicted with the fear of the imperialists and reactionaries, Comrade Mao Tse-tung put forward his famous thesis that "the imperialists and all reactionaries are paper tigers." He said:

> All reactionaries are paper tigers. In appearance, the reactionaries are terrifying, but in reality they are not so powerful. From a long-term point of view, it is not the reactionaries but the people who are really powerful.

The history of people's war in China and other countries provides conclusive evidence that the growth of the people's revolutionary forces from weak and small beginnings into strong and large forces is a universal law of development of class struggle, a universal law of development of people's war. A people's war inevitably meets with many difficulties, with ups and downs and setbacks in the course of its development, but no force can alter its general trend toward inevitable triumph.

. . .

Many countries and peoples in Asia, Africa, and Latin America are now being subjected to aggression and enslavement on a serious scale by the imperialists headed by the United States and their lackeys. The basic political and economic conditions in many of these countries have many similarities to those that prevailed in old China. As in China, the peasant question is extremely important in these regions. The peasants constitute the main force of the national-democratic revolution against the imperialists and their lackeys. In committing aggression against these countries, the imperialists usually begin by seizing the big cities and the main lines of communication, but they are unable to bring the vast countryside completely under their control. The countryside, and the countryside alone, can provide the broad areas in which the revolutionaries can maneuver freely. The countryside, and the countryside alone, can provide the revolutionary bases from which the revolutionaries can go forward to final victory. Precisely for this reason, Comrade Mao Tse-tung's theory of establishing revolutionary base areas in their rural districts and encircling the cities from the countryside is attracting more and more attention among the people in these regions.

Taking the entire globe, if North America and Western Europe can be called "the cities of the world," then Asia, Africa, and Latin America constitute "the rural areas of the world." Since World War II, the proletarian revolutionary movement has for various reasons been temporarily held back in the North American and West European capitalist countries, while the people's revolutionary movement in Asia, Africa, and Latin America has been growing vigorously. In a sense, the contemporary world revolution also presents a picture of the encirclement of cities by the rural areas. In the final analysis, the whole cause of world revolution hinges on the revolutionary struggles of the Asian, African, and Latin American peoples who make up the overwhelming majority of the world's population. The socialist countries should regard it as their internationalist duty to support the people's revolutionary struggles in Asia, Africa, and Latin America.

.   .   .

Comrade Mao Tse-tung made a correct distinction between the two revolutionary stages, *i.e.,* the national-democratic and the socialist revolutions; at the same time he correctly and closely linked the two. The national-democratic revolution is the necessary preparation for the socialist revolution, and the socialist revolution is the inevitable sequel to the national-democratic revolution. There is no Great Wall between the two revolutionary stages. But the socialist revolution is only possible after the completion of the national-democratic revolution. The more thorough the national-democratic revolution, the better the conditions for the socialist revolution.

.   .   .

The Chinese Revolution provides a successful lesson for making a thoroughgoing national-democratic revolution under the leadership of the proletariat; it likewise provides a successful lesson for the timely transition from the national-democratic revolution to the socialist revolution under the leadership of the proletariat.

.   .   .

Just as the Japanese imperialists' policy of subjugating China made it possible for the Chinese people to form the broadest possible united front against them, so the U.S. imperialists' policy of seeking world domination makes it possible for the people throughout the world to unite all the forces that can be united and form the broadest possible united front for a converging attack on U.S. imperialism.

. . . After World War I, the imperialists lacked the power to destroy the new-born socialist Soviet state, but they were still able to suppress the people's revolutionary movements in some countries in the parts of the world under their own rule and so maintain a short period of comparative stability. Since World War II, however, not only have they been unable to stop a number of countries from taking the socialist road, but they are no longer capable of holding back the surging tide of the people's revolutionary movements in the areas under their own rule.

U.S. imperialism is stronger, but also more vulnerable, than any imperialism of the past. It sets itself against the people of the whole world, including the people of the United States. Its human, military, material, and financial resources are far from sufficient for the realization of its ambition of dominating the whole world. U.S. imperialism has further weakened itself by occupying so many places in the world, overreaching itself, stretching its fingers out wide and dispersing its strength, with its rear so far away and its supply lines so long. As Comrade Mao Tse-tung has said, "Wherever it commits aggression, it puts a new noose around its neck. It is besieged ring upon ring by the people of the whole world."

.   .   .

Everything is divisible. And so is this colossus of U.S. imperialism. It can be split up and defeated. The peoples of Asia, Africa, Latin America, and other regions can destroy it piece by piece, some striking at its head and others at its feet. That is why the great fear of U.S. imperialism is that people's wars will be launched in different parts of the world, and particularly in Asia, Africa, and Latin America, and why it regards people's war as a mortal danger.

U.S. imperialism relies solely on its nuclear weapons to intimidate people. But these weapons cannot save U.S. imperialism from its doom. Nuclear weapons cannot be used lightly. U.S. imperialism has been condemned by the people of the whole world for its towering crime of dropping two atom bombs on Japan. If it uses nuclear weapons again, it will become isolated in the extreme. Moreover, the U.S. monopoly of nuclear weapons has long been broken; U.S. imperialism has these weapons, but others have them too. If it threatens other countries with nuclear weapons, U.S. imperialism will expose its own country to the same threat. For this reason, it will meet with strong opposition not only from the people elsewhere but also inevitably from the people in its own country. Even if U.S. imperialism brazenly uses nuclear weapons, it cannot conquer the people, who are indomitable.

Vietnam is the most convincing current example of a victim of aggression defeating U.S. imperialism by a people's war. The United States has made South Vietnam a testing ground for the suppression of people's war. It has carried on this experiment for many years, and everybody can now see that the U.S. aggressors are unable to find a way of coping with people's war. On the other hand, the Vietnamese people have brought the power of people's war into full play in their struggle against the U.S. aggressors. The U.S. aggressors are in danger of being swamped in the people's war in Vietnam. They are deeply worried that their defeat in Vietnam will lead to a chain reaction. They are expanding the war in an attempt to save themselves from defeat. But the more they expand the war, the greater will be the chain reaction. The more they escalate the war, the heavier will be their fall and the more disastrous their defeat. The people in other parts of the world will see still more clearly that U.S. imperialism can be defeated, and that what the Vietnamese people can do, they can do too.

History has proved and will go on proving that people's war is the most effective weapon against U.S. imperialism and its lackeys. All revolutionary people will learn to wage people's war against U.S. imperialism and its lackeys. They will take up arms, learn to fight battles, and become skilled in waging people's war, though they have not done so before. U.S. imperialism like a mad bull dashing from place to place, will finally be burned to ashes in the blazing fires of the people's wars it has provoked by its own actions.

Chapter Forty-one

End of bipolarism

92   THE ORIGINS OF THE COLD WAR

As World War II neared its end, the latent differences between Russia and her Western allies came to the fore. The root causes of the resulting Cold War have become the subject of debate amongst historians in recent years. When the Cold War was at its height, official explanations as to its genesis prevailed with relatively few challenges. But with the waning of the Cold War, the intellectual climate became more suitable for objective analysis, so that a new revisionist historiography appeared. In the following selection a distinguished American historian analyzes the views of some of the major revisionist writers.*

More than a year has passed since Arthur Schlesinger, Jr. announced that the time had come "to blow the whistle before the current outburst of revisionism regarding the origins of the cold war goes much further." Yet the outburst of revisionism shows no signs of subsiding. On the contrary, a growing number of historians and political critics, judging from such recent books as Ronald Steel's "Pax Americana" and Carl Oglesby's and Richard Shaull's "Containment and Change," are challenging the view, once so widely accepted, that the cold war was an American response to Soviet expansionism, a distasteful burden reluctantly shouldered in the face of a ruthless enemy bent on our destruction, and that Russia, not the United States, must therefore bear the blame for shattering the world's hope that two world wars in the 20th century would finally give way to an era of peace.

"Revisionist" historians are arguing instead that the United States did as

* Christopher Lasch, "The Cold War, Revisited and Re-Visioned," *The New York Times Magazine* (January 14, 1968), pp. 26, 27, 44, 46, 51, 54, 59, by permission of the author and publisher. Copyright © 1968 by The New York Times Company.

much as the Soviet Union to bring about the collapse of the wartime coalition. Without attempting to shift the blame exclusively to the United States, they are trying to show, as Gar Alperovitz puts it, that "the cold war cannot be understood simply as an American response to a Soviet challenge, but rather as the insidious interaction of mutual suspicions, blame for which must be shared by all."

Not only have historians continued to re-examine the immediate origins of the cold war—in spite of attempts to "blow the whistle" on their efforts—but the scope of revisionism has been steadily widening. Some scholars are beginning to argue that the whole course of American diplomacy since 1898 shows that the United States has become a counterrevolutionary power committed to the defense of a global status quo. Arno Mayer's monumental study of the Conference of Versailles, "Politics and Diplomacy of Peacemaking," which has recently been published by Knopf and which promises to become the definitive work on the subject, announces in its subtitle what a growing number of historians have come to see as the main theme of American diplomacy: "Containment and Counterrevolution."

Even Schlesinger has now admitted, in a recent article in Foreign Affairs, that he was "somewhat intemperate," a year ago, in deploring the rise of cold-war revisionism. Even though revisionist interpretations of earlier wars "have failed to stick," he says, "revisionism is an essential part of the process by which history . . . enlarges its perspectives and enriches its insights." Since he goes on to argue that "postwar collaboration between Russia and America [was] . . . inherently impossible" and that "the most rational of American policies could hardly have averted the cold war," it is not clear what Schlesinger thinks revisionism has done to enlarge our perspective and enrich our insights; but it is good to know, nevertheless, that revisionists may now presumably continue their work (inconsequential as it may eventually prove to be) without fear of being whistled to a stop by the referee.

The orthodox interpretation of the cold war, as it has come to be regarded, grew up in the late forties and early fifties—years of acute international tension, during which the rivalry between the United States and the Soviet Union repeatedly threatened to erupt in a renewal of global war. Soviet-American relations had deteriorated with alarming speed following the defeat of Hilter. At Yalta, in February, 1945, Winston Churchill had expressed the hope that world peace was nearer the grasp of the assembled statesmen of the great powers "than at any time in history." It would be "a great tragedy," he said, "if they, through inertia or carelessness, let it slip from their grasp. History would never forgive them if they did."

Yet the Yalta agreements themselves, which seemed at the time to lay the basis of postwar cooperation, shortly provided the focus of bitter dissension, in which each side accused the other of having broken its solemn promises. In Western eyes, Yalta meant free elections and parliamentary democracies in Eastern Europe, while the Russians construed the agreements as recognition of their demand for governments friendly to the Soviet Union.

The resulting dispute led to mutual mistrust and to a hardening of positions on both sides. By the spring of 1946 Churchill himself, declaring that "an iron curtain has descended" across Europe, admitted, in effect, that the "tragedy" he had feared had come to pass. Europe split into hostile fragments, the eastern half dominated by the Soviet Union, the western part sheltering nervously under the protection of American arms. NATO, founded in 1949 and countered by the Russian-sponsored Warsaw Pact, merely ratified the existing division of Europe.

From 1946 on, every threat to the stability of this uneasy balance produced an immediate political crisis—Greece in 1947, Czechoslovakia and the Berlin blockade in 1948—each of which, added to existing tensions, deepened hostility on both sides and increased the chance of war. When Bernard Baruch announced in April, 1947, that "we are in the midst of a cold war," no one felt inclined to contradict him. The phrase stuck, as an accurate description of postwar political realities.

Many Americans concluded, moreover, that the United States was losing the cold war. Two events in particular contributed to this sense of alarm—the collapse of Nationalist China in 1949, followed by Chiang Kai-shek's flight to Taiwan, and the explosion of an atomic bomb by the Russians in the same year. These events led to the charge that American leaders had deliberately or unwittingly betrayed the country's interests. The Alger Hiss case was taken by some people as proof that the Roosevelt Administration had been riddled by subversion.

Looking back to the wartime alliance with the Soviet Union, the American Right began to argue that Roosevelt, by trusting the Russians, had sold out the cause of freedom. Thus Nixon and McCarthy, aided by historians like Stefan J. Possony, C. C. Tansill and others, accused Roosevelt of handing Eastern Europe to the Russians and of giving them a preponderant interest in China which later enabled the Communists to absorb the entire country.

The liberal interpretation of the cold war—what I have called the orthodox interpretation—developed partly as a response to these charges. In liberal eyes, the right-wingers made the crucial mistake of assuming that American actions had been decisive in shaping the postwar world. Attempting to rebut this devil theory of postwar politics, liberals relied heavily on the argument that the shape of postwar politics had already been dictated by the war itself, in which the Western democracies had been obliged to call on Soviet help in defeating Hitler. These events, they maintained, had left the Soviet Union militarily dominant in Eastern Europe and generally occupying a position of much greater power, relative to the West, than the position she had enjoyed before the war.

In the face of these facts, the United States had very little leeway to influence events in what were destined to become Soviet spheres of influence, particularly since Stalin was apparently determined to expand even if it meant ruthlessly breaking his agreements—and after all it was Stalin, the liberals emphasized, and not Roosevelt or Truman, who broke the Yalta agreement on Poland, thereby precipitating the cold war.

These were the arguments presented with enormous charm, wit, logic and power in George F. Kennan's "American Diplomacy" (1951), which more than any other book set the tone of cold-war historiography. For innumerable historians, but especially for those who were beginning their studies in the fifties, Kennan served as the model of what a scholar should be—committed yet detached—and it was through the perspective of his works that a whole generation of scholars came to see not only the origins of the cold war, but the entire history of 20th century diplomacy.

It is important to recognize that Kennan's was by no means an uncritical perspective—indeed, for those unacquainted with Marxism it seemed the only critical perspective that was available in the fifties. While Kennan insisted that the Russians were primarily to blame for the cold war, he seldom missed an opportunity to criticize the excessive moralism, the messianic vision of a world made safe for democracy, which he argued ran "like a red skein" through American diplomacy.

As late as 1960, a radical like Staughton Lynd could still accept the general framework of Kennan's critique of American idealism while noting merely that Kennan had failed to apply it to the specific events of the cold war and to the policy of containment which he had helped to articulate. "Whereas in general he counseled America to 'admit the validity and legitimacy of power realities and aspirations . . . and to seek their point of maximum equilibrium rather than their reform or their repression'—'reform or repression' of the Soviet system were the very goals which Kennan's influential writings of those years urged."

Even in 1960, however, a few writers had begun to attack not the specific applications of the principles of *Realpolitik* but the principles themselves, on the grounds that on many occasions they served simply as rationalizations for American (not Soviet) expansionism. And whereas Lynd in 1960 could still write that the American demand for freedom in Eastern Europe, however misguided, "expressed a sincere and idealistic concern," some historians had already begun to take a decidedly more sinister view of the matter—asking, for instance, whether a country which demanded concessions in Eastern Europe that it was not prepared to grant to the Russians in Western Europe could really be accused, as the "realist" writers had maintained, of an excess of good-natured but occasionally incompetent altruism.

Meanwhile the "realist" interpretation of the cold war inspired a whole series of books—most notably, Herbert Feis's series ("Churchill-Roosevelt-Stalin"; "Between War and Peace"; "The Atomic Bomb and the End of World War II"); William McNeill's "America, Britain and Russia: Their Cooperation and Conflict"; Norman Graebner's "Cold War Diplomacy"; Louis J. Halle's "Dream and Reality" and "The Cold War as History"; and M. F. Herz's "Beginnings of the Cold War."

Like Kennan, all of these writers saw containment as a necessary response to Soviet expansionism and to the deterioration of Western power in Eastern Europe. At the same time, they were critical, in varying degrees, of the legalistic-moralistic tradition which kept American statesmen from looking at foreign relations in the light of balance-of-power considerations.

Some of them tended to play off Churchillian realism against the idealism of Roosevelt and Cordell Hull, arguing, for instance, that the Americans should have accepted the bargain made between Churchill and Stalin in 1944, whereby Greece was assigned to the Western sphere of influence and Rumania, Bulgaria and Hungary to the Soviet sphere, with both liberal and Communist parties sharing in the control of Yugoslavia.

These criticisms of American policy, however, did not challenge the basic premise of American policy, that the Soviet Union was a ruthlessly aggressive power bent on world domination. They assumed, moreover, that the Russians were in a position to realize large parts of this program, and that only counterpressure exerted by the West, in the form of containment and the Marshall Plan, prevented the Communists from absorbing all of Europe and much of the rest of the world as well.

It is their criticism of these assumptions that defines the revisionist historians and distinguishes them from the "realists." What impresses revisionists is not Russia's strength but her military weakness following the devastating war with Hitler, in which the Russians suffered much heavier losses than any other member of the alliance.

Beginning with Carl Marzani's "We Can Be Friends: Origins of the Cold War" (1952), revisionists have argued that Russia's weakness dictated, for the moment at least, a policy of postwar cooperation with the West. Western leaders' implacable hostility to Communism, they contend, prevented them from seeing this fact, a proper understanding of which might have prevented the cold war.

This argument is spelled out in D. F. Fleming's two-volume study, "The Cold

War and Its Origins" (1961); in David Horowitz's "The Free World Colossus" (1965), which summarizes and synthesizes a great deal of revisionist writing; in Gar Alperovitz's "Atomic Diplomacy: Hiroshima and Potsdam" (1965); and in the previously mentioned "Containment and Change."

But the historian who has done most to promote a revisionist interpretation of the cold war, and of American diplomacy in general, is William Appleman Williams of the University of Wisconsin, to whom most of the writers just mentioned owe a considerable debt. Williams's works, particularly "The Tragedy of American Diplomacy" (1959), not only challenge the orthodox interpretation of the cold war, they set against it an elaborate counterinterpretation which, if valid, forces one to see American policy in the early years of the cold war as part of a larger pattern of American globalism reaching as far back as 1898.

According to Williams, American diplomacy has consistently adhered to the policy of the "open door"—that is, to a policy of commercial, political and cultural expansion which seeks to extend American influence into every corner of the earth. This policy was consciously and deliberately embarked upon, Williams argues, because American statesmen believed that American capitalism needed ever-expanding foreign markets in order to survive, the closing of the frontier having put an end to its expansion on the continent of North America. Throughout the 20th century, the makers of American foreign policy, he says, have interpreted the national interest in this light.

The cold war, in Williams's view, therefore has to be seen as the latest phase of a continuing effort to make the world safe for democracy—read liberal capitalism. American-style—in which the United States finds itself increasingly cast as the leader of a world-wide counterrevolution.

After World War II, Williams maintains, the United States had "a vast proportion of actual as well as potential power vis-à-vis the Soviet Union." The United States "cannot with any real warrant or meaning claim that it has been *forced* to follow a certain approach or policy." (Compare this with a statement by Arthur Schlesinger: "The cold war could have been avoided only if the Soviet Union had not been possessed by convictions both of the infallibility of the Communist word and of the inevitability of a Communist world.")

The Russians, by contrast, Williams writes, "viewed their position in the nineteen-forties as one of weakness, not offensive strength." One measure of Stalin's sense of weakness, as he faced the enormous task of rebuilding the shattered Soviet economy was his eagerness to get a large loan from the United States. Failing to get such a loan—instead, the United States drastically cut back lend-lease payments to Russia in May, 1945—Stalin was faced with three choices, according to Williams:

He could give way and accept the American peace program at every point—which meant, among other things, accepting governments in Eastern Europe hostile to the Soviet Union.

He could follow the advice of the doctrinaire revolutionaries in his own country who argued that Russia's best hope lay in fomenting world-wide revolution.

Or he could exact large-scale economic reparations from Germany while attempting to reach an understanding with Churchill and Roosevelt on the need for governments in Eastern Europe not necessarily Communist but friendly to the Soviet Union.

His negotiations with Churchill in 1944, according to Williams, showed that Stalin had already committed himself, by the end of the war, to the third of these policies—a policy, incidentally, which required him to withdraw support from

Communist revolutions in Greece and in other countries which under the terms of the Churchill-Stalin agreement had been conceded to the Western sphere of influence.

But American statesmen, the argument continues, unlike the British, were in no mood to compromise. They were confident of America's strength and Russia's weakness (although later they and their apologists found it convenient to argue that the contrary had been the case). Furthermore, they believed that "we cannot have full employment and prosperity in the United States without the foreign markets," as Dean Acheson told a special Congressional committee on postwar economic policy and planning in November, 1944. These considerations led to the conclusion, as President Truman put it in April, 1945, that the United States should "take the lead in running the world in the way that the world ought to be run"; or more specifically, in the words of Foreign Economic Administrator Leo Crowley, that "if you create good governments in foreign countries, automatically you will have better markets for ourselves." Accordingly, the United States pressed for the "open door" in Eastern Europe and elsewhere.

In addition to these considerations, there was the further matter of the atomic bomb, which first became a calculation in American diplomacy in July, 1945. The successful explosion of an atomic bomb in the New Mexican desert, Williams argues, added to the American sense of omnipotence and led the United States "to overplay its hand"—for in spite of American efforts to keep the Russians out of Eastern Europe, the Russians refused to back down.

Nor did American pressure have the effect, as George Kennan hoped, of promoting tendencies in the Soviet Union "which must eventually find their outlet in either the break-up or the gradual mellowing of Soviet power." Far from causing Soviet policy to mellow, American actions, according to Williams, stiffened the Russians in their resistance to Western pressure and strengthened the hand of those groups in the Soviet Union which had been arguing all along that capitalist powers could not be trusted.

Not only did the Russians successfully resist American demands in Eastern Europe, they launched a vigorous counterattack in the form of the Czechoslovakian coup of 1948 and the Berlin blockade. Both East and West thus found themselves committed to the policy of cold war, and for the next 15 years, until the Cuban missile crisis led to a partial detente, Soviet-American hostility was the determining fact of international politics.

Quite apart from his obvious influence on other revisionist historians of the cold war and on his own students in other areas of diplomatic history, Williams has had a measurable influence on the political radicals of the sixties, most of whom now consider it axiomatic that American diplomacy has been counterrevolutionary and that this fact reflects, not a series of blunders and mistakes as some critics have argued, but the basically reactionary character of American capitalism.

Some radicals now construe these facts to mean that American foreign policy therefore cannot be changed unless American society itself undergoes a revolutionary change. Carl Oglesby, for instance, argues along these lines in "Containment and Change." From Oglesby's point of view, appeals to conscience or even to enlightened self-interest are useless; the cold war cannot end until the "system" is destroyed.

Williams thought otherwise. At the end of the 1962 edition of "The Tragedy of American Diplomacy," he noted that "there is at the present time no radicalism in the United States strong enough to win power, or even a very significant influence, through the processes of representative government"—and he took it for granted that genuinely democratic change could come about only through representative processes. This meant, he thought, that "the well-being of the United States depends—*in the short-run but only in the short-run*—upon the extent to which calm and confident and enlightened conservatives can see and bring themselves to act upon the validity of a radical analysis."

In an essay in Ramparts last March, he makes substantially the same point in commenting on the new radicals' impatience with conservative critics of American diplomacy like Senator Fulbright. Fulbright, Williams says, attracted more support for the position of more radical critics than these critics had attracted through their own efforts. "He hangs tough over the long haul, and that is precisely what American radicalism has never done in the 20th century."

As the New Left becomes more and more beguiled by the illusion of its own revolutionary potential, and more and more intolerant of radicals who refuse to postulate a revolution as the only feasible means of social change, men like Williams will probably become increasingly uncomfortable in the presence of a movement they helped to create. At the same time, Williams's radicalism, articulated in the fifties before radicalism came back into fashion, has alienated the academic establishment and prevented his works from winning the widespread recognition and respect they deserve. In scholarly journals, many reviews of Williams's work —notably a review by Oscar Handlin of "The Contours of American History" in the Mississippi Valley Historical Review a few years ago—have been contemptuous and abusive in the extreme. The result is that Williams's books on diplomatic history are only beginning to pass into the mainstream of scholarly discourse, years after their initial publication.

Next to Williams's "Tragedy of American Diplomacy," the most important attack on the orthodox interpretation of the cold war is Alperovitz's "Atomic Diplomacy." A young historian trained at Wisconsin, Berkeley and King's College, Cambridge, and currently a research fellow at Harvard, Alperovitz adds very little to the interpretation formulated by Williams, but he provides Williams's insights with a mass of additional documentation. By doing so, he has made it difficult for conscientious scholars any longer to avoid the challenge of revisionist interpretations. Unconventional in its conclusions, "Atomic Diplomacy" is thoroughly conventional in its methods. That adds to the book's persuasiveness. Using the traditional sources of diplomatic history—official records, memoirs of participants, and all the unpublished material to which scholars have access—Alperovitz painstakingly reconstructs the evolution of American policy during the six-month period March to August, 1945. He proceeds with a thoroughness and caution which, in the case of a less controversial work, would command the unanimous respect of the scholarly profession. His book is no polemic. It is a work in the best—and most conservative—traditions of historical scholarship. Yet the evidence which Alperovitz has gathered together challenges the official explanation of the beginnings of the cold war at every point.

What the evidence seems to show is that as early as April, 1945, American officials from President Truman on down had decided to force a "symbolic showdown" with the Soviet Union over the future of Eastern Europe. Truman believed that a unified Europe was the key to European recovery and economic stability, since the agricultural southeast and the industrial northwest depended on each other. Soviet designs on Eastern Europe, Truman reasoned, threatened to disrupt the economic unity of Europe and therefore had to be resisted. The only question was whether the showdown should take place immediately or whether it should be delayed until the bargaining position of the United States had improved.

At first it appeared to practically everybody that delay would only weaken the position of the United States. Both of its major bargaining counters, its armies in Europe and its lend-lease credits to Russia, could be more effectively employed at once, it seemed, than at any future time. Accordingly, Truman tried to "lay it on the line" with the Russians. He demanded that they "carry out their [Yalta] agreements" by giving the pro-Western elements in Poland an equal voice in the Polish Government (although Roosevelt, who made the Yalta agreements, believed that "we placed, as clearly shown in the agreement, somewhat more emphasis" on the Warsaw [pro-Communist] Government than on the pro-Western leaders). When Stalin objected that Poland was "a country in which the U.S.S.R. is interested first of all and most of all," the United States tried to force him to give in by cutting back lend-lease payments to Russia.

At this point, however—in April, 1945—Secretary of War Henry L. Stimson convinced Truman that "we shall probably hold more cards in our hands later than now." He referred to the atomic bomb, and if Truman decided to postpone the showdown with Russia, it was because Stimson and other advisers persuaded him that the new weapon would "put us in a position," as Secretary of State James F. Byrnes argued, "to dictate our own terms at the end of the war."

To the amazement of those not privy to the secret, Truman proceeded to take a more conciliatory attitude toward Russia, an attitude symbolized by Harry Hopkins's mission to Moscow in June, 1945. Meanwhile, Truman twice postponed the meeting with Churchill and Stalin at Potsdam. Churchill complained, "Anyone can see that in a very short space of time our armed power on the Continent will have vanished."

But when Truman told Churchill that an atomic bomb had been successfully exploded at Alamogordo, exceeding all expectations, Churchill immediately understood and endorsed the strategy of delay. "We were in the presence of a new factor in human affairs," he said, "and possessed of powers which were irresistible." Not only Germany but even the Balkans, which Churchill and Roosevelt had formerly conceded to the Russian sphere, now seemed amenable to Western influence. That assumption, of course, had guided American policy (though not British policy) since April, but it could not be acted upon until the bombing of Japan provided the world with an unmistakable demonstration of American military supremacy.

Early in September, the foreign ministers of the Big Three met in London. Byrnes—armed, as Stimson noted, with "the presence of the bomb in his pocket, so to speak, as a great weapon to get through" the conference—tried to press the American advantage. He demanded that the Governments of Bulgaria and Rumania reorganize themselves along lines favorable to the West. In Bulgaria, firmness won a few concessions; in Rumania, the Russians stood firm. The American strategy had achieved no noteworthy success. Instead—as Stimson, one of the architects of that strategy, rather belatedly observed—it had "irretrievably embittered" Soviet-American relations.

The revisionist view of the origins of the cold war, as it emerges from the works of Williams, Alperovitz, Marzani, Fleming, Horowitz, and others, can be summarized as follows. The object of American policy at the end of World War II was not to defend Western or even Central Europe but to force the Soviet Union out of Eastern Europe. The Soviet menace to the "free world," so often cited as the justification of the containment policy, simply did not exist in the minds of American planners. They believed themselves to be negotiating not from weakness but from almost unassailable superiority.

Nor can it be said that the cold war began because the Russians "broke their agreements." The general sense of the Yalta agreements—which were in any case very vague—was to assign to the Soviet Union a controlling influence in Eastern Europe. Armed with the atomic bomb, American diplomats tried to take back what they had implicitly conceded at Yalta.

The assumption of American moral superiority, in short, does not stand up under analysis.

The opponents of this view have yet to make a very convincing reply. Schlesinger's recent article in Foreign Affairs, referred to at the outset of this article, can serve as an example of the kind of arguments which historians are likely to develop in opposition to the revisionist interpretation. Schlesinger argues that the cold war came about through a combination of Soviet intransigence and misunderstanding. There were certain "problems of communication" with the Soviet Union, as a result of which "the Russians might conceivably have misread our signals." Thus the American demand for self-determination in Poland and other East European countries "very probably" appeared to the Russians "as a systematic and deliberate pressure on Russia's western frontiers."

Similarly, the Russians "could well have interpreted" the American refusal of a loan to the Soviet Union, combined with cancellation of lend-lease, "as deliberate sabotage" of Russia's postwar reconstruction or as "blackmail." In both cases, of course, there would have been no basis for these suspicions; but "we have thought a great deal more in recent years," Schlesinger says, ". . . about the problems of communication in diplomacy," and we know how easy it is for one side to misinterpret what the other is saying.

This argument about difficulties of "communications" at no point engages the evidence uncovered by Alperovitz and others—evidence which seems to show that Soviet officials had good reason to interpret American actions exactly as they did: as attempts to dictate American terms.

In reply to the assertion that the refusal of a reconstruction loan was part of such an attempt, Schlesinger can only argue weakly that the Soviet request for a loan was "inexplicably mislaid" by Washington during the transfer of records from the Foreign Economic Administration to the State Department! "Of course," he adds, "this was impossible for the Russians to believe." It is impossible for some Americans to believe. As William Appelman Williams notes, Schlesinger's explanation of the "inexplicable" loss of the Soviet request "does not speak to the point of how the leaders could forget the request even if they lost the document."

When pressed on the matter of "communications," Schlesinger retreats to a second line of argument, namely that none of these misunderstandings "made much essential difference," because Stalin suffered from "paranoia" and was "possessed by convictions both of the infallibility of the Communist word and of the inevitability of a Communist world."

The trouble is that there is very little evidence which connects either Stalin's paranoia or Marxist-Leninist ideology or what Schlesinger calls "the sinister dynamics of a totalitarian society" with the actual course of Soviet diplomacy during the formative months of the cold war. The only piece of evidence that Schlesinger has been able to find is an article by the Communist theoretician Jacques Duclos in the April, 1945, issue of Cahiers du communisme, the journal of the French Communist party, which proves, he argues, that Stalin had already abandoned the wartime policy of collaboration with the West and had returned to the traditional Communist policy of world revolution.

Even this evidence, however, can be turned to the advantage of the revisionists.

Alperovitz points out that Duclos did not attack electoral politics or even collaboration with bourgeois governments. What he denounced was precisely the American Communists' decision, in 1944, to withdraw from electoral politics. Thus the article, far from being a call to world revolution, "was one of many confirmations that European Communists had decided to abandon violent revolutionary struggle in favor of the more modest aim of electoral success." And while this decision did not guarantee world peace, neither did it guarantee 20 years of cold war.

Schlesinger first used the Duclos article as a trump card in a letter to The New York Review of Books, Oct. 20, 1966, which called forth Alperovitz's rejoinder. It is symptomatic of the general failure of orthodox historiography to engage the revisionist argument that Duclos's article crops up again in Schlesinger's more recent essay in Foreign Affairs, where it is once again cited as evidence of a "new Moscow line," without any reference to the intervening objections raised by Alperovitz.

Sooner or later, however, historians will have to come to grips with the revisionist interpretation of the cold war. They cannot ignore it indefinitely. When serious debate begins, many historians, hitherto disposed to accept without much question the conventional account of the cold war, will find themselves compelled to admit its many inadequacies. On the other hand, some of the ambiguities of the revisionist view, presently submerged in the revisionists' common quarrel with official explanations, will begin to force themselves to the surface. Is the revisionist history of the cold war essentially an attack on "the doctrine of historical inevitability," as Alperovitz contends? Or does it contain an implicit determinism of its own?

Two quite different conclusions can be drawn from the body of revisionist scholarship. One is that American policy-makers had it in their power to choose different policies from the ones they chose. That is, they could have adopted a more conciliatory attitude toward the Soviet Union, just as they now have the choice of adopting a more conciliatory attitude toward Communist China and toward nationalist revolutions elsewhere in the Third World.

The other is that they have no such choice, because the inner requirements of American capitalism *force* them to pursue a consistent policy of economic and political expansion. "For matters to stand otherwise," writes Carl Oglesby, "the Yankee free-enterpriser would . . . have to . . . take sides against himself. . . . He would have to change entirely his style of thought and action. In a word, he would have to become a revolutionary Socialist whose aim was the destruction of the present American hegemony."

Pushed to what some writers clearly regard as its logical conclusion, the revisionist critique of American foreign policy thus becomes the obverse of the cold-war liberals' defense of that policy, which assumes that nothing could have modified the character of Soviet policy short of the transformation of the Soviet Union into a liberal democracy—which is exactly the goal the containment policy sought to promote. According to a certain type of revisionism, American policy has all the rigidity the orthodox historians attribute to the U.S.S.R., and this inflexibility made the cold war inevitable.

Moreover, Communism really did threaten American interests, in this view. Oglesby argues that, in spite of its obvious excesses, the "theory of the International Communist Conspiracy is not the hysterical old maid that many leftists seem to think it is." If there is no conspiracy, there is a world revolution and it *"does* aim itself at America"—the America of expansive corporate capitalism.

Revisionism, carried to these conclusions, curiously restores cold-war anti-Communism to a kind of intellectual respectability, even while insisting on its immorality. After all, it concludes, the cold warriors were following the American national interest. The national interest may have been itself corrupt, but the policy-makers were more rational than their critics may have supposed.

In my view, this concedes far too much good sense to Truman, Dulles and the rest. Even Oglesby concedes that the war in Vietnam has now become irrational in its own terms. I submit that much of the cold war has been irrational in its own terms—as witness the failure, the enormously costly failure, of American efforts to dominate Eastern Europe at the end of World War II. This is not to deny the fact of American imperialism, only to suggest that imperialism itself, as J. A. Hobson and Joseph Schumpeter argued in another context long ago, is irrational—that even in its liberal form it may represent an archaic social phenomenon having little relation to the realities of the modern world.

At the present stage of historical scholarship, it is of course impossible to speak with certainty about such matters. That very lack of certainty serves to indicate the direction which future study of American foreign policy might profitably take.

The question to which historians must now address themselves is whether American capitalism really depends, for its continuing growth and survival, on the foreign policy its leaders have been following throughout most of the 20th century. To what extent are its interests really threatened by Communist revolutions in the Third World? To what extent can it accommodate itself to those revolutions, reconciling itself to a greatly diminished role in the rest of the world, without undergoing a fundamental reformation—that is, without giving way (after a tremendous upheaval) to some form of Socialism?

Needless to say, these are not questions for scholars alone. The political positions one takes depend on the way one answers them. It is terribly important, therefore, that we begin to answer them with greater care and precision than we can answer them today.

93   President de Gaulle's Independent Course

Europe's global hegemony gave way during the immediate postwar years to an American–Russian predominance. Western Europe was economically dependent on the United States, while the Cold War forced the various European countries to look to one or the other of the superpowers for protection. This bipolarism, however, gradually disintegrated as Europe became increasingly prosperous and economically independent, and as the Cold War waned after the mid-50's. A striking example of the new international balance was President de Gaulle's recognition of Communist China in the face of strong American disapproval. In a news conference held on January 31, 1964, President de Gaulle gave the reasons for his policy of recognition.*

We are going to speak of China. China—a great people, the most numerous on earth. . . .

This country's entry into contact with the modern nations has been very hard and very costly. The many European, American, Japanese demands, interventions,

* Reprinted from *The New York Times* (February 1, 1964), by permission of the publisher and Reuters Limited. Copyright © 1964 by The New York Times Company.

expeditions, invasions, were for it so many humiliations and mutilations. Then many national upheavals, and also the will of the elite to transform the country at all costs so that it might reach the condition and the power of the people that oppressed it, led China to the revolution.

Certainly, Marshal Chiang Kai-shek, to whose valor, patriotism, spiritual elevation, I am duty bound to render homage, feeling certain that history and the Chinese people will one day do the same, Marshal Chiang Kai-shek, after leading China to the Allied victory that in the Pacific put the seal on the Second World War, tried to channel the torrent.

Since then an enormous effort, which was imperative anyway, concerning the development of natural riches, industrial development, agricultural production, education against the scourges inherent in this country, famine, epidemics, soil erosion, the overflowing of the rivers, etc., has been undertaken throughout the territory.

As always in a Communist system, what was achieved entailed terrible human suffering, an implacable constraint of the masses, immense losses and wasting of goods, the crushing and decimation of innumerable human values. However, results were achieved that are due in part to the action of the totalitarian machine and also to the ardor of a proud people who want to better themselves in all fields and who are capable of deploying treasures of courage and ingenuity whatever the circumstances.

It is true that Soviet Russia first of all provided China with quite considerable assistance: the opening of credits for the purchase of machinery and supplies, mining and industrial equipment, the installation of whole factories, the direct training of students and specialists, the sending of engineers, technicians and qualified workers, etc.

This was the time when the Kremlin planned to keep China under its control and thereby dominate Asia. But the illusions have been dissipated. Doubtless there remains between Moscow and Peking a certain doctrinal solidarity which can express itself in the world ideological competition. But under this mantle, more and more torn, there appears a difference of national policies.

The least one can say on this subject is that in Asia, where the frontier separating the two states, from the Hindu Kush to Vladivostok, is the longest in the world, the interest of Russia, which is one of conserving and maintaining, and that of China, which needs to grow and to take, cannot be confused.

Considering that for 15 years almost the whole of China has been gathered under a Government that rules it and that she shows herself abroad as an independent, sovereign power, France was disposed in principle, and for years now, to establish regular relations with Peking.

Moreover, certain economic and cultural exchanges were already taking place and, with America, Britain, the Soviet Union, India and other states, we were led in 1954, at the Geneva conference, when the fate of Indochina was settled, to negotiate with the Chinese representatives.

And it was the same in 1962, in the same form and in the same town, when the Laos situation was more or less defined.

But with the weight of evidence and reason making itself felt more and more every day, the French Republic decided to place its relations with the People's Republic of China on a normal, in other words diplomatic, basis.

We met in Peking an identical intention. It was then that the two countries agreed to accomplish the necessary. I spoke of the weight of evidence and reason and in fact in Asia there is no political reality concerning Cambodia, Laos, Vietnam, or India, Pakistan, Afghanistan, Burma, Korea, or Soviet Russia or Japan, etc., that does not interest or concern China.

On this Continent, there is no imaginable peace or war without her being implicated and it is inconceivable to suppose that it is possible ever to conclude a neutrality treaty concerning the states of Southeast Asia, to which we French show a very special and cordial attention, without China's being a party to it.

But also China's mass, its value and its present needs and the dimension of its future all lead her to manifest herself more and more in the interest and the concerns of the whole universe. Indeed it is clear that France must be able to hear China directly and also to make herself heard by China.

What is already being done, economically speaking, with regard to China, what is being done by us, and which can be improved, will no doubt for a long time be limited, and it is the same with regard to investments we are already making in Chinese industrial development.

In the case of technique, the situation is no doubt very different, as the sources of technique in France are more and more valuable and China represents for French technique an almost infinite field.

Then who knows whether the affinities that exist between the two nations regarding everything concerning spiritual matters, and taking also into account the fact that deep down they have always felt for each other sympathy and consideration, will not lead them to a growing cultural cooperation? In any case this is sincerely desired here.

So Peking and Paris have agreed to exchange ambassadors. Obviously on our part there is nothing in that implying any kind of approval of the regime that at present dominates China.

By establishing with this country, with this state, official relations as many other free nations have done before and as we have done with other countries which suffer similar regimes, France only recognizes the world as it is.

94   POLYCENTRISM VERSUS THE BREZHNEV DOCTRINE

Just as de Gaulle pursued a policy independent from that of the United States, Rumania asserted herself in relations with the Soviet Union. The trend began in Eastern Europe with Tito's heresy in 1948, burst forth again with the Polish and Hungarian outbreaks in 1956, and thereafter gained strength quietly but steadily. By April 1964 it had developed to the point where the Rumanian Communist Party issued the following statement in support of "polycentrism" or equality and independence in the relations between Communist states and parties.* In August 1968 "polycentrism" was rudely set back with the invasion of an increasingly liberal Czechoslovakia by the Soviet army with East German, Hungarian, Polish, and Bulgarian units. In justification of the invasion, a Pravda *article of September 25, 1968, enunciated what might be termed the "Brezhnev doctrine" claiming the right to invade any socialist neighbor considered to be abandoning the socialist camp.†*

* Reprinted from *Statement on the Stand of the Rumanian Workers' Party Concerning the Problems of the World Communist and Working Class Movement . . . April 1964* (Agerpress: Rumanian News Agency, n.d.), pp. 28–33, 46, 49–51.
† Reprinted from *Pravda,* September 25, 1968 (transl. by Novosti, Soviet press agency).

The economic and technical-scientific progress of the socialist countries relies on the relations of co-operation and mutual assistance established between them. These fruitful relations have seen a steady development; they have proved their efficiency, making a particularly important contribution to the successes scored by the socialist countries.

With a view to the complete utilization of the advantages of these relations, the Council of Mutual Economic Assistance was set up. According to its Rules, its aim is to contribute, through the uniting and co-ordination of efforts, to the development of the national economy, to speeding up economic and technical progress, to raising the level of industrialization of the less developed countries, to the steady increase in labour productivity and to the ceaseless improvement in the welfare of the peoples in the member countries.

Co-operation within CMEA is achieved on the basis of the principles of fully equal rights, of observance of national sovereignty and interests, of mutual advantage and comradely assistance.

As concerns the method of economic co-operation, the socialist countries which are members of CMEA have established that the main means of achieving the international socialist division of labour, the main form of co-operation between their national economies is to co-ordinate plans on the basis of bilateral and multilateral agreements.

During the development of the relations of co-operation between the socialist countries which are members of CMEA, forms and measures have been suggested, such as a joint plan and a single planning body for all member countries, interstate technical-productive branch unions, enterprises jointly owned by several countries, inter-state economic complexes, etc.

Our Party has very clearly expressed its point of view, declaring that, since the essence of the suggested measures lies in shifting some functions of economic management from the competence of the respective state to the attribution of superstate bodies or organisms, these measures are not in keeping with the principles which underlie the relations between the socialist countries.

The idea of a single planning body for all CMEA countries has the most serious economic and political implications. The planned management of the national economy is one of the fundamental, essential and inalienable attributes of the sovereignty of the socialist state—the state plan being the chief means through which the socialist state achieves its political and socio-economic objectives, establishes the directions and rates of development of the national economy, its fundamental proportions, the accumulations, the measures for raising the people's living standard and cultural level. The sovereignty of the socialist state requires that it effectively and fully avails itself of the means for the practical implementation of these attributions, holding in its hands all the levers of managing economic and social life. Transmitting such levers to the competence of super-state or extra-state bodies would turn sovereignty into a notion without any contents.

All these are also fully valid as concerns inter-state technical-productive branch unions, as well as enterprises commonly owned by two or several states. The State Plan is one and indivisible, no parts or sections can be separated from it in order to be transferred outside the state. The management of the national economy as a whole is not possible if the questions of managing some branches or enterprises are taken away from the competence of the Party and government of the respective country and transferred to extra-state bodies. . . .

Such is the viewpoint of the Rumanian Workers' Party as concerns the nature of the relations of economic co-operation between the socialist countries in the present stage of history.

Undoubtedly if some socialist countries deem it fit to adopt in the direct relations between them forms of co-operation different from those unanimously agreed upon within CMEA, that is a question which exclusively concerns those countries, and can be decided by them alone in a sovereign way. . . .

At the same time, the socialist international division of labour cannot mean isolation of the socialist countries from the general framework of world economic relations. Standing consistently for normal, mutually advantageous economic relations, without political strings and without restrictions or discriminations, the Rumanian People's Republic, like the other socialist states, develops its economic links with all states irrespective of their social system. . . .

The transformation of socialism into a world system, the winning of power by the working people in a number of states, has faced the communist and workers' parties with the task of radically changing not only social relations on a national level, in their own country, but also of organizing mutual relations between these countries, of working out the norms of co-operation in the framework of a great world community of states. This has arisen as an entirely new problem, for which there was no previous practical experience—and which was all the more complex as it concerned countries differing in size, might, degree of economic, political and social development, in addition to their national distinctions and historical peculiarities.

By promoting in the international arena a qualitatively new system of relations, unprecedented in history, the communist and workers' parties in the socialist countries have placed at the foundation of these relations the principles of national independence and sovereignty, equal rights, mutual advantage, comradely assistance, non-interference in internal affairs, observance of territorial integrity, the principles of socialist internationalism. . . .

Of late, the divergencies in the international communist and working-class movement have deepened, and the public polemic has assumed particular sharpness. Instead of a debate imbued with the endeavour to bring standpoints closer to each other and to find solutions based on Marxist-Leninist ideology, forms and methods have been adopted in the course of the public polemic which considerably envenom relations between parties, and offensive judgements, as well as accusations and the ascribing of certain intentions are being resorted to.

Strict observance of the principle that all Marxist-Leninist parties enjoy equal rights, of the principle of non-interference in other parties' domestic affairs, of each Party's exclusive right to solve its own political and organizational problems, of appointing its leaders, of orienting its members in problems of internal and international politics—is an essential condition for the correct settlement of issues in which there are divergencies, as well as of all problems raised by their common struggle.

. . . .

There does not and cannot exist a "parent" party and a "son-party," parties that are "superior" and parties that are "subordinate," but there exists the great family of communist and workers' parties, which have equal rights. No party has or can have a privileged place, or can impose its line and opinions on other parties. Each party makes its own contribution to the development of the common treasure store of Marxist-Leninist teaching, to enriching the forms and practical methods of revolutionary struggle for winning power and building the socialist society.

In discussing and confronting different points of view on problems concerning the revolutionary struggle or socialist construction, no party must label as anti-Marxist, anti-Leninist the fraternal party whose opinions it does not share. . . .

It is inconceivable that in relations between communist parties reciprocal and deeply offensive accusations be levelled against the leaders of a fraternal party as being "the biggest revisionists of our time," who are in "collusion with U.S. imperialism," and "throw wide open the gates for the restoration of capitalism," or that they are "trotzkyites" who "furiously attack world socialism," "partners on the right-flank of the American 'wild men.' "

Brezhnev Doctrine

In connection with the events in Czechoslovakia, the question of the correlation and interdependence of the national interests of the socialist countries and their international duties acquire particular topical and acute importance.

The measures taken by the Soviet Union, jointly with other socialist countries, in defending the socialist gains of the Czechoslovak people are of great significance for strengthening the socialist community, which is the main achievement of the international working class.

We cannot ignore the assertions, held in some places, that the actions of the five socialist countries run counter to the Marxist-Leninist principle of sovereignty and the rights of nations to self-determination.

The groundlessness of such reasoning consists primarily in that it is based on an abstract, nonclass approach to the question of sovereignty and the rights of nations to self-determination.

The peoples of the socialist countries and Communist parties certainly do have and should have freedom for determining the ways of advance of their respective countries.

However, none of their decisions should damage either socialism in their country or the fundamental interests of other socialist countries, and the whole working class movement, which is working for socialism.

This means that each Communist party is responsible not only to its own people, but also to all the socialist countries, to the entire Communist movement. Whoever forget this, in stressing only the independence of the Communist party, becomes one-sided. He deviates from his international duty.

Marxist dialectics are opposed to one-sidedness. They demand that each phenomenon be examined concretely, in general connection with other phenomena, with other processes.

Just as, in Lenin's words, a man living in a society cannot be free from the society, one or another socialist state, staying in a system of other states composing the socialist community, cannot be free from the common interests of that community.

The sovereignty of each socialist country cannot be opposed to the interests of the world of socialism, of the world revolutionary movement. Lenin demanded that all Communists fight against small-nation narrow-mindedness, seclusion and isolation, consider the whole and the general, subordinate the particular to the general interest.

The socialist states respect the democratic norms of international law. They have proved this more than once in practice, by coming out resolutely against the attempts of imperialism to violate the sovereignty and independence of nations.

It is from these same positions that they reject the leftist, adventurist conception of "exporting revolution," of "bringing happiness" to other peoples.

However, from a Marxist point of view, the norms of law, including the norms of mutual relations of the socialist countries, cannot be interpreted narrowly, formally, and in isolation from the general context of class struggle in the modern world. The socialist countries resolutely come out against the exporting and importing of counterrevolution.

Each Communist party is free to apply the basic principles of Marxism-Leninism and of socialism in its country, but it cannot depart from these principles (assuming, naturally, that it remains a Communist party).

Concretely, this means, first of all, that, in its activity, each Communist party cannot but take into account such a decisive fact of our time as the struggle between two opposing social systems—capitalism and socialism.

This is an objective struggle, a fact not depending on the will of the people, and stipulated by the world's being split into two opposite social systems. Lenin said: "Each man must choose between joining our side or the other side. Any attempt to avoid taking sides in this issue must end in fiasco."

It has got to be emphasized that when a socialist country seems to adopt a "non-affiliated" stand, it retains its national independence, in effect, precisely because of the might of the socialist community, and above all the Soviet Union as a central force, which also includes the might of its armed forces. The weakening of any of the links in the world system of socialism directly affects all the socialist countries, which cannot look indifferently upon this.

NATO THREAT SEEN. The antisocialist elements in Czechoslovakia actually covered up the demand for so-called neutrality and Czechoslovakia's withdrawal from the socialist community with talking about the right of nations to self-determination.

However, the implementation of such "self-determination," in other words, Czechoslovakia's detachment from the socialist community, would have come into conflict with its own vital interests and would have been detrimental to the other socialist states.

Such "self-determination," as a result of which NATO troops would have been able to come up to the Soviet border, while the community of European socialist countries would have been split, in effect encroaches upon the vital interests of the peoples of these countries and conflicts, as the very root of it, with the right of these people to socialist self-determination.

Discharging their internationalist duty toward the fraternal peoples of Czechoslovakia and defending their own socialist gains, the U.S.S.R. and the other socialist states had to act decisively and they did act against the antisocialist forces in Czechoslovakia.

The most dramatic, and perhaps the most significant, manifestation of the new pluralism in world affairs has been the conflict between the two Communist giants, the Soviet Union and China. In marked contrast to the thirty-year treaty of "friendship, alliance and mutual assistance" which they signed in 1950, the two powers have drifted apart to the point of engaging in unrestrained name-calling, ideological vituperation, and open rivalry all over the globe. The bitterness is reflected in the following selections from an article in the Peking* People's Daily *(January 1, 1963) entitled "The Difference between Communist Togliatti and Us," and a point-by-point rebuttal carried in* Pravda *(January 6, 1963), official organ of the Communist party of the Soviet Union. Later exchanges have been much more virulent, but the basic issues remain those debated below.*

Peking People's Daily

. . . What are the real differences between them [the Italian Communists] and us? They are manifested mainly in the following three questions:

1. The CCP [Communist Party of China] holds that the source of modern war is imperialism. The chief force of war and aggression is U.S. imperialism, the most vicious enemy of all the peoples of the world. In order to defend world peace, it is necessary to expose the imperialist policies of aggression and war unceasingly and thoroughly, and call on the people of the world to maintain a high degree of vigilance.

·   ·   ·

It will be recalled that three years ago, following the "Camp David talks," some persons in the international Communist movement made propaganda in a big way about Eisenhower's sincere desire for peace, saying that this ringleader of U.S. imperialism was just as concerned about peace as we.

Now we hear some people saying that Kennedy is even more concerned about world peace than Eisenhower was and that Kennedy showed his concern for the maintenance of peace during the Caribbean crisis. One would like to ask: Is this way of embellishing U.S. imperialism the correct policy for defending world peace?

The intrusion into the Soviet Union of spy planes sent by the Eisenhower administration, the aggression against Cuba by the Kennedy administration, and a hundred and one other acts of aggression around the world by U.S. imperialism, and its threats to world peace—have these not repeatedly confirmed the truth and shown that the ringleaders of U.S. imperialism are no angels of peace but monsters of war? And are not those people who try time and time again to prettify imperialism deliberately deceiving the peoples of the world?

2. The CCP holds that world peace can only be securely safeguarded in the resolute struggle against imperialism, headed by the U.S. by constantly strengthening the Socialist camp, and by constantly strengthening the national and democratic

---

* Reprinted from "The Tiger vs. the Bear," *The Chicago Sun-Times* (January 20, 1963), by permission of the publisher.

movements in Asia, Africa, and Latin America, the people's revolutionary struggles in various countries and the movement to defend world peace.

To achieve world peace it is necessary to rely mainly on the strength of the masses of the people of the world and on their struggles. In the course of the struggle to defend world peace, it is necessary to enter into negotiations on one issue or another with the governments of the imperialist countries, including the government of the U.S., for the purpose of easing international tension, reaching some kind of compromise and arriving at certain agreements subject to the principle that such compromises and agreements must not damage the fundamental interests of the people.

However, world peace can never be achieved by negotiations alone, and in no circumstances must we pin our hopes on imperialism and divorce ourselves from the struggles of the masses.

3. The CCP holds that the struggle for the defense of world peace supports, is supported by, and indeed is inseparable from the national liberation movements and the people's revolutionary struggles in various countries. The national liberation movements and the peoples' revolutionary struggles are a powerful force weakening the imperialist forces of war and defending world peace.

.   .   .

It would simply result in a phony peace or bring about an actual war for the people of the whole world if you pin your hopes of peace on imperialism, and take a passive or negative attitude towards the national liberation movements, as advocated by those who attack the CCP. This policy is wrong and all Marxist-Leninists, all revolutionary people, all peace-loving people must resolutely oppose it.

On the question of war and peace, the differences with Togliatti find striking expressions in our respective attitudes to nuclear weapons and nuclear war. . . .

Togliatti and certain others talk volubly about "the suicide of mankind" and the "total destruction" of mankind. They believe that "it is in vain even to discuss what could be the orientation of these fragments of survivals regarding social order."

We are firmly opposed to such pessimistic and despairing tunes. We believe that it is possible to attain a complete ban on nuclear weapons in the following circumstances: the Socialist camp has a great nuclear superiority; the peoples' struggles in various countries against nuclear weapons become broader and deeper; having further forfeited their nuclear superiority, the imperialists are compelled to realize that their policy of nuclear blackmail is no longer effective and that their launching of a nuclear war would only accelerate their own extinction.

If, after we have done everything possible to prevent a nuclear war, imperialism should nevertheless unleash nuclear war, without regard to any of the consequences, it would result in the extinction of imperialism and definitely not in the extinction of mankind.

Comrade Togliatti and certain other comrades have strongly opposed the Marxist-Leninist proposition of the CCP that "imperialism and all reactionaries are paper tigers."

Comrade Togliatti said that it "was wrong to state that imperialism is simply a paper tiger which can be overthrown by a mere push of the shoulder." Then there are other persons who assert that today imperialism has nuclear teeth, so how can it be called a paper tiger?

Prejudice is farther from the truth than ignorance. In the case of Comrade Togliatti and certain other comrades, if they are not ignorant, then they are deliberately distorting the proposition of the CCP. In comparing imperialism and all reactionaries with paper tigers, Comrade Mao Tze-tung and the Chinese Communists are looking at the problem as a whole and from a long-term point of view and are looking at the essence of the problem. What is meant is that, in the final analysis, it is the people who are really powerful, not imperialism and the reactionaries.

Comrade Mao Tze-tung first put forward this proposition in August, 1946. With great lucidity he said:

"All reactionaries are paper tigers. In appearance, the reactionaries are terrifying, but in reality they are not so powerful. From a long-term point of view, it is not the reactionaries but the people who are really powerful. . . ."

Comrade Mao Tze-tung's analysis of imperialism and all reactionaries is completely in accord with Lenin's analysis. In 1919 Lenin compared the "universally mighty" Anglo-French imperialism to a "Colossus with feet of clay."

We ask, what is wrong with Lenin's position? Is this proposition of Lenin's "outmoded"?

. . .

On peaceful coexistence we have another difference with those who are attacking us. We hold that the question of peaceful coexistence between countries with different social systems and the question of revolution by oppressed nations or by oppressed classes are two different kinds of questions, and not questions of the same kind.

The principle of peaceful coexistence can apply only to relations between countries with different social systems, not to relations between oppressed and oppressor nations, nor to relations between oppressed and oppressing classes. For an oppressed nation of people the question is one of waging a revolutionary struggle to overthrow the rule of imperialism and the reactionaries; it is not, and cannot be, a question of peaceful coexistence with imperialism and the reactionaries.

. . .

Some people have repeatedly charged China with creating difficulties in the Caribbean situation and with wanting to plunge the world into a thermonuclear war. This slander against China is most malicious and most despicable.

How can one possibly interpret the resolute support which the Chinese people gave to the Cuban people in their struggle against international inspection and in defense of their sovereignty as meaning that China was opposed to peaceful coexistence or wanted to plunge others into a thermonuclear war?

Does this mean that China also should have applied pressure on Cuba to force her to accept international inspection, and that only by so doing would China have conformed to this so-called "peaceful coexistence"?

We neither called for the establishment of missile bases in Cuba nor obstructed the withdrawal of the so-called "offensive weapons" from Cuba. We have never considered that it was a Marxist-Leninist attitude to brandish nuclear weapons as a way of settling international disputes. Nor have we ever considered that the avoidance of the thermonuclear war in the Caribbean crisis was a "Munich."

What we did strongly oppose, still strongly oppose, and will strongly oppose in the future, is the sacrifice of another country's sovereignty as a means of reaching a compromise with imperialism. A compromise of this sort can only be regarded as 100 per cent appeasement, a "Munich" pure and simple.

Hitherto, history has not witnessed a single example of peaceful transition from capitalism to socialism. Communists should not pin all their hopes for the victory of the revolution on peaceful transition. The *bourgeoisie* will never step down from the stage of history of its own accord. This is a universal law of class struggle.

Communists must not in the slightest degree relax their preparedness for revolution.

Moscow Pravda

. . . The most important, the most vital problem of our time is the problem of war and peace. In real life the choice is: either peaceful coexistence between states with different social systems or a devastating war. There is no other alternative.

The question arises: What position should the Communists take? Only one—the position of peaceful coexistence.

The Socialist countries do not need war. They are successfully developing in peaceful conditions and will be victorious in the peaceful economic competition with capitalism, which fact will be of exceptional importance for making the peoples choose the socialist way as the only correct one.

The Albanian leaders—Enver Hoxha for instance—boast that they do not agree with those who "regard peaceful coexistence as the general line of the foreign policy of the Socialist countries."

But what then is the general line? War? If so, where is then the difference between such an approach to the solution of the question about the victory of communism or capitalism and the viewpoint of the adventurist circles of imperialism?

In point of fact, the only difference is that the frenzied imperialists have lost faith in the ability of capitalism to stand its own in the competition with socialism, while the dogmatists do not believe in the possibility of the victory of communism in the conditions of peaceful competition of states with different social systems.

But which Marxist-Leninist would agree that the way to the victory of communism lies through a thermonuclear war?

The most important thing in the struggle for peace is to curb the aggressors in time, to avert war, to prevent it from flaring up. This is particularly necessary in view of the unprecedented destructive force of modern weapons.

In contrast to these propositions, the dogmatists emphasize that nuclear war is not to be feared, that modern weapons are monstrous only "in the opinions of the imperialists and reactionaries," that "the atom bomb is a paper tiger." This is nothing but renunciation of the main goal in the struggle for peace indicated in the statement of the policy of peaceful coexistence.

The dogmatists present peaceful coexistence as "renunciation of the struggle for the exposure of imperialism," as "discontinuation of the struggle against imperialism."

They do not understand that competition in peaceful conditions is one of the most important battlegrounds between socialism and capitalism. As regards the struggle against imperialism proclaimed by the dogmatists, it boils down to mere high-sounding invective phrases and foul language.

Historically, it fell to the lot of the Soviet people to bear the brunt of the struggle against imperialist warmongers. It is not an easy task to bear such a burden. The Soviet people even not infrequently have to deny themselves things they need.

Who was it that extinguished the raging flames of war in the Suez Canal Zone in 1956 by compelling the British-French-Israel aggressors to beat a retreat? Who was it that in 1957 prevented the invasion of Syria prepared by the imperialists?

Who was it that in 1958 prevented war in the Near East and in the area of Taiwan Strait from flaring up?

It was the Soviet Union, all countries of the Socialist camp, the peace forces. They, and above all the might and the vigorous actions of the U.S.S.R., compelled the imperialist warmongers to retreat. . . .

The postwar years have not witnessed a more acute international crisis, fraught with the danger of a world-wide thermonuclear conflagration, than the recent crisis created by American imperialism in the Caribbean area. . . .

Now that the crest of the crisis is behind, representatives of the "leftist phrase-mongers" are striving slanderously to present the case as if the Soviet Union had capitulated to imperialism and even agreed to a "second Munich."

But everyone who unbiasedly analyzes the results of the liquidation of the crisis in the Caribbean area sees that there is not a grain of truth in the accusations of the dogmatists, that the phrases they utter are actually calculated to provoke war.

The crisis was settled on the basis of mutual concessions and sensible compromise. The solution of disputed questions between states without wars, by peaceful means—this is precisely the policy of peaceful coexistence in action. . . .

The beacon of freedom in the Western Hemisphere is burning still brighter. Is this a "Munich"? Is this a retreat? The authors of the term "second Munich" are obviously at odds with elementary history and know not what they are speaking about. . . .

A modern war cannot be approached with old yardsticks. A world war, if we fail to prevent it, will immediately become a thermonuclear conflict, will lead to the death of millions upon millions of people, to the destruction of tremendous material values, to the devastation of whole countries.

In their cynical gamble with human lives, certain people dare to scoff at those who defend the lives of hundreds of millions of people, accusing these fighters of "cowardice" and "spinelessness." But Communists, the more so Communist statesmen and political leaders, cannot act like these irresponsible penhacks. . . .

To impose on the Communist movement their definition of modern imperialism and to ignore its atomic fangs, some people claim that the "paper tiger" thesis is tantamount to Lenin's definition of imperialism as a "colossus on clay feet."

It is common knowledge, however, that the figurative expression does not cover or substitute all the substance of V. I. Lenin's all-round definition of imperialism. Moreover, this expression stresses that imperialism is still strong (colossus), but it stands (on clay feet) on an unstable basis and is rent by internal contradictions.

The "paper tiger" definition of imperialism speaks only of its weakness. The main point, however, is that what we need are not paper definitions, stubbornly thrust upon us, but a genuine analysis of contemporary imperialism: disclosure of its vices, weaknesses and laws, leading to its ruin; and at the same time a sober assessment of its forces, including the huge atomic and other military potential.

.   .   .

To believe that a recipe for a Socialist revolution can be invented to suit all times and all countries, and to thrust it upon the fraternal parties operating in the specific conditions of their countries, is to do a harmful thing, to display haughtiness alien to Communists, to set oneself as a teacher of all Communist parties, and a teacher divorced from life, at that, and therefore incapable of offering anything but dogmatic formulas. . . .

Communists cannot but feel gravely concerned over the thesis launched recently that there is a "temporary majority" in the international Communist movement which "persists in its mistakes," and a "temporary minority" which "boldly and resolutely upholds the truth."

This thesis only serves to justify a split of the Communist movement and renunciation of the common positions of the Marxist-Leninist parties.

This contention is especially harmful in that it is associated with an incredible pretension to proclaim one party the true heir of Lenin, and all other parties to be apostates from Marxism-Leninism. . . .

What the Communists need is not division into "majority" and "minority," but unity, unity, and once more unity.

Chapter Forty-two

Decline and triumph of the West

TRIUMPH OF EUROPE: ECONOMIC 96

An obvious and basic feature of the present age is the decline of the West, as evidenced by the end of the European empires and by the economic-military primacy of the United States and the Soviet Union. But, paradoxically, this is also the age of the triumph of the West because of the accelerating diffusion of Europe's three great revolutions: economic, scientific, and political. This diffusion is at the basis of the current process of modernization that is transforming the entire globe. It should be noted that today the stimuli toward modernization may come not only from Europe but also from the United States or the Soviet Union or even China. Yet the roots go back to Western Europe, where the economic, scientific, and political revolutions originated. Consequently, the modernization of the globe—now proceeding at an accelerated pace—represents, directly and indirectly, the triumph of Europe.

This is particularly noticeable in the economic field, for the primary objective of the underdeveloped states, after attaining political independence, is to develop their economies as rapidly as possible. This objective is illustrated by the following two selections: the first is from the official Nigerian publication, News from Nigeria, *December 14, 1970,* which sets forth the new five-year plan designed to counter the destruction wrought by the civil war which ended in January 1970 and to continue Nigeria's pre-war economic development and expansion. The second is a description by an American correspondent of the effect of Western wealth on Masai tribesmen of Kenya.†*

* Reprinted from *News from Nigeria*, Vol. 2, No. 3 (December 14, 1970), 4, 6–8, by permission of the Nigerian Consulate-General.
† Reprinted from Anthony Lewis, "Romance and Reality in Africa," *The New York Times* (January 10, 1970), by permission of the publisher. Copyright © 1970 by The New York Times Company.

. . .

TOTAL EXPENDITURE. The total planned expenditure over the plan period is expected to amount to £1,596 million of which the net public capital expenditure programme is £780 million. The Federal Government programme is about £420 million, while the programmes of all the states amount to £359 million.

. . .

The following are the major programmes and projects in the Plan, sector by sector:

(a) *Rehabilitation:* Rehabilitation of power, transport, communications systems in the war-affected areas where these physical assets have been damaged during the war, and in the other parts of the country where these assets have been left in a state of disrepair due to lack of use and maintenance.

(b) *Agriculture, Livestock, Forestry and Fishery:* Planned capital expenditure by all the Governments is £132.7 million for a National Agricultural Bank, improvement in land use, irrigation and conservation schemes, agricultural education and research programmes and improvement in livestock, fisheries and forestry production.

(c) *Industry:* Total planned public investment expenditure in this sector is £86.1 million.

. . .

Major Projects Include:
   (i) loans to rehabilitate industries in the war-affected areas;
  (ii) iron and steel mill;
 (iii) fertilizer plants;
  (iv) second petroleum refinery;
   (v) liquefied petroleum and gas;
  (vi) pulp and paper mill;
 (vii) chemical complex;
(viii) palm kernel crushing plants;

(d) *Fuel and Power:* Total planned expenditure is £45.3 million. Emphasis is on capacity utilization and replacement. Major projects include:
   (i) rehabilitation of power in the war-affected areas.
  (ii) rural electrification;
 (iii) expansion of the grid system to utilize installed capacity at Kainji;
  (iv) expansion and improvement of power supplies in existing load centres, and
   (v) extension of power supply to Niger.

. . .

(e) *Transport:* Total planned public investment is £242.6 million, of which road transport alone takes £169.2 million for the expansion and improvement of road-network system in the country. . . .

. . .

(f) *Communications:* Total planned capital expenditure on the communications sector is £42.6 million. . . .

. . .

(g) *Education:* Total planned capital expenditure is £138.9 million. Projects are designed to increase the general level of education, to reduce the educational gap between the different states in the country and between the urban and rural areas and to increase the supply of high-level and intermediate-level personnel in the country. . . .

.   .   .

(h) *Health:* Total planned capital expenditure is £53.8 million. Programmes and projects in this sector are designed to restore facilities and services destroyed or damaged during the war, expand schemes for the maintenance of environment sanitation, provide schemes for the control of epidemic diseases, develop trained medical manpower through the provision of appropriate training facilities and programmes, re-organise hospital services, and develop research facilities and activities.

Masai

One of the great experiences for the visitor in East Africa is seeing the Masai, the warrior herdsmen who inhabit the dry plains of southern Kenya and northern Tanzania. Of all tribes they match the dream of the exotic and the noble in primitive life.

Cattle are the center of Masai life, the measure of capital and power. In the language there is just one word for cows and people. The diet consists primarily of cow's blood, drained a little at a time, mixed with milk. Wherever the Masai are, there are great herds, moved here and there for pasture by the boys of the family.

The Masai have not been bound by place. They build their little villages of round, straw-roofed houses, then in time burn them down and move on. They wander back and forth through this border town [Namanga, Kenya], regarding the political boundary as an irrelevance.

The cultural facts are less striking than the appearance of the Masai. They are a tall people, sinewy and much given to ornament.

The visitor driving south from Nairobi suddenly sees a Masai man against the sky, wrapped in a red cloak, his hair and face smeared with red dye, great earrings in his ears and always a long spear in his hand. To be a man he must be able to kill a lion with that spear.

That warrior figure seems to have what Western man so misses: solitude, independence, the ability to take care of himself and live his own life. We see him free of the restraints of life in a developed society.

SYMBOL AND MYTH. A visitor of any sensitivity finds himself hoping that the Masai—and really all the remote people of the earth, whom they symbolize—will not seek the comforts of civilization. For he knows that with physical prosperity there comes no spiritual peace. He measures his own tensions against the poetic vision of Masai life and would say: Do not change.

Alas, the hope is an empty one, impossible of fulfillment. It is built on a romantic fallacy, the myth of the contented savage.

The life of the Masai is not so poetic as it appears. There are insects and drought and disease. Hunger is a recurrent reality.

It is not surprising, therefore, that as the Masai come into contact with a way of life that offers greater material benefits and more security, they want it. Students of undeveloped societies say that when a subsistence group meets the cash economy, it quite quickly and inevitably wants a share. The Masai are not immune from that process.

Five years ago some of the tribe learned that cattle bred from superior bulls would produce better offspring; instead of drying up or even dying during droughts, as many Masai cows did, they would continue to give milk. Today in Kenya half the Masai cows are artificially inseminated. Even more remarkably, many families have got over the idea of wealth in sheer numbers of cattle and are slaughtering bull calves for meat.

Other Masai, especially in northern Tanzania, have settled down and become farmers, growing cash crops. They ride bicycles, which is less romantic but possibly more pleasant than walking endless miles on dusty tracks.

If the outsider purges himself of romanticism and admits the inevitability of change, he can still rightly hope that the corrupting effects will be limited. For in Africa as in Tahiti, the sudden descent of Western wealth into the simple society can destroy a culture without providing a substitute, turning people to degrading envy and servility.

TOURIST ATTRACTION. Any country dependent on tourism risks that kind of corruption. Build a giant hotel in the bush, with a bar in the middle of its swimming pool, and imagine the effect on the tribesmen trying to live on a few goats or cows or roots.

The floor of Ngorongoro Crater in Tanzania is covered with wild animals—one of the spectacular tourist attractions of Africa. There is also a Masai village.

The other day a group of Europeans on safari stopped for lunch in a thicket of thorn trees. After a few minutes half a dozen small Masai boys approached through the forest, saying nothing but obviously hoping for the remains of the picnic. The African ranger guiding the safari looked at the boys and said over and over:

"It is not a good character. It is not a good character."

97   TRIUMPH OF EUROPE: SCIENTIFIC

Scientific development, recognized as a prerequisite for both military and economic strength, is as much sought after as economic growth. The motives and objectives of this pursuit of science are evident in the following resolution adopted by the Parliament of India on March 12, 1958.*

The key to national prosperity, apart from the spirit of the people, lies in the modern age in the effective combination of three factors, technology, raw materials and capital, of which the first is perhaps the most important, since the creation and adoption of new scientific techniques, in fact, make up for a deficiency in natural resources and reduce the demands on capital. But technology can only grow out of the study of science and its applications.

The dominating feature of the contemporary world is the intense cultivation of

---

* Reprinted from A. Ranganathan, "Science in Modern India," *Impact of Science on Society,* IX, No. 4 (1959), 222–223, by permission of UNESCO.

science on a large scale and its application to meet a country's requirements. It is this which, for the first time in man's history, has given to the common man in countries advanced in science a standard of living and social and cultural amenities which were once confined to a very small privileged minority of the population. Science has led to the growth and diffusion of culture to an extent never possible before. It has not only radically altered man's material environment but, what is of still deeper significance, it has provided new tools of thought and has extended man's mental horizon. It has thus influenced even the basic values of life and given to civilization a new vitality and a new dynamism.

It is only through the scientific approach and method and the use of scientific knowledge that reasonable material and cultural amenities and services can be provided for every member of the community, and it is out of a recognition of this possibility that the idea of a Welfare State has grown. It is characteristic of the present world that the progress towards the practical realization of a Welfare State differs widely from country to country in direct relation to the extent of industrialization and the effort and resources applied in the pursuit of science.

The wealth and prosperity of a nation depend on the effective utilization of its human and material resources through industrialization. The use of human material for industrialization demands its education in science and training in technical skills. Industry opens up possibilities of greater fulfilment for the individual. India's enormous resources of man-power can only become an asset in the modern world when trained and educated.

Science and technology can make up for deficiencies in raw materials by providing substitutes, or, indeed, by providing skills which can be exported in return for raw materials. In industrializing a country, a heavy price has to be paid in importing science and technology in the form of plant and machinery, highly paid personnel and technical consultants. An early large-scale development of science and technology in the country could therefore greatly reduce the drain on capital during the early and critical stages of industrialization.

Science has developed at an ever-increasing pace since the beginning of the century, so that the gap between the advanced and backward countries has widened more and more. It is only by adopting the most vigorous measures and by putting our utmost effort into the development of science that we can bridge the gap. It is an inherent obligation of a great country like India, with its traditions of scholarship and original thinking and its great cultural heritage, to participate fully in the march of science, which is probably mankind's greatest enterprise today.

The Government of India has accordingly decided that the aims of their scientific policy will be:

1. To foster, promote and sustain, by all appropriate means, the cultivation of science, and scientific research in all its aspects—pure, applied and educational.
2. To ensure an adequate supply, within the country, of research scientists of the highest quality and to recognize their work as an important component of the strength of the nation.
3. To encourage and initiate, with all the possible speed, programmes for the training of scientific and technical personnel, on a scale adequate to fulfil the country's needs in science and education, agriculture and industry and defence.

4. To ensure that the creative talent of men and women is encouraged and finds full scope in scientific activity.
5. To encourage individual initiative for the acquisition and dissemination of knowledge and for the discovery of new knowledge in an atmosphere of academic freedom.
6. In general, to secure for the people of the country all benefits that can accrue from the acquisition and application of scientific knowledge. The Government of India has decided to pursue and accomplish these aims by offering good conditions of service to scientists and according them an honoured position, by associating scientists with the formulation of policies, and by taking such other measures as may be deemed necessary from time to time.

98   TRIUMPH OF EUROPE: POLITICAL

The contemporary diffusion of Europe's political revolution is tangibly and dramatically manifested in more than fifty countries that have won their independence within two decades after World War II. Prime Minister Harold Macmillan of Great Britain recognized the force of this movement in a speech given before the Parliament of South Africa on February 3, 1960.* After pointing out the European origins of the "wind of change" sweeping the colonial world, he warned his audience that they were failing to take it into account and that the consequences were likely to be felt throughout the globe.

As I have traveled through the Union, I have found everywhere, as I expected, a deep preoccupation with what is happening in the rest of the African continent. I understand and sympathize with your interest in these events, and your anxiety about them.

Ever since the break-up of the Roman Empire, one of the constant facts of political life in Europe has been the emergence of independent nations.

They have come into existence over the centuries in different shapes with different forms of government. But all have been inspired with a keen feeling of nationalism, which has grown as nations have grown.

In the twentieth century, and especially since the end of the war [World War II], the processes which gave birth to the nation-states of Europe have been repeated all over the world. We have seen the awakening of national consciousness in peoples who have for centuries lived in dependence on some other power.

Fifteen years ago this movement spread through Asia. Many countries there, of different races and civilizations, pressed their claim to an independent national life.

Today the same thing is happening in Africa. The most striking of all the impressions I have formed since I left London a month ago is of the strength of African national consciousness.

In different places it may take different forms. But it is happening everywhere. The wind of change is blowing through the continent.

Whether we like it or not, this growth of national consciousness is a political fact. We must all accept it as a fact. Our national policies must take account of it.

Of course, you understand this as well as anyone. You are sprung from Europe, the home of nationalism.

And here, in Africa, you have yourselves created a full nation—a new nation. Indeed, in the history of our times, yours will be recorded as the first of the African nationalisms.

And this tide of national consciousness which is now rising in Africa is a fact for which you and we and the other nations of the Western world are ultimately responsible.

For its causes are to be found in the achievements of Western civilization in pushing forward the frontiers of knowledge, applying science in the service of human needs, expanding food production, speeding and multiplying means of communication, and, above all, spreading education.

As I have said, the growth of national consciousness in Africa is a political fact and we must accept it as such. I sincerely believe that if we cannot do so, we may imperil the precarious balance of East and West on which the peace of the world depends.

The world today is divided into three great groups.

First, there are what we call the Western powers. You in South Africa and we in Britain belong to this group, together with our friends and allies in other parts of the Commonwealth, in the United States of America, and in Europe.

Secondly, there are the Communists—Russia and her satellites in Europe and China, whose population will rise by 1970 to the staggering total of 800,000,000.

Thirdly, there are those parts of the world whose people are at present uncommitted either to communism or to our Western ideas. In this context, we think first of Asia and of Africa.

As I see it, the great issue in this second half of the twentieth century is whether the uncommitted peoples of Asia and Africa will swing to the East or the West.

Will they be drawn into the Communist camp? Or will the great experiments in self-government that are now being made in Asia and Africa, especially within the Commonwealth, prove so successful and by their example so compelling, that the balance will come down in favor of freedom and order and justice?

The struggle is joined and it is a struggle for the minds of men. What is now on trial is much more than our military strength or our diplomatic and administrative skill. It is our way of life.

The uncommitted nations want to see before they choose. What can we show them to help them choose right? Each of the independent members of the Commonwealth must answer that question for itself.

It is the basic principle for our modern Commonwealth that we respect each other's sovereignty in matters of internal policy. At the same time, we must recognize that in this shrinking world in which we live today, the internal policies of one nation may have effects outside it.

We may sometimes be tempted to say to each other, "Mind your own business." But in these days I would myself expand the old saying so that it runs: "Mind your own business, but mind how it affects my business, too."

Let me be very frank with you, my friends. What governments and parliaments in the United Kingdom have done since the war in according independence to India, Pakistan, Ceylon, Malaya and Ghana, and what they will do for Nigeria and the other countries now nearing independence—all this, though we take full and sole responsibility for it, we do in the belief that it is the only way to establish the future of the Commonwealth and of the free world on sound foundations.

All this, of course, is also of deep and close concern to you. For nothing we do in this small world can be done in a corner or remain hidden. . . .

It may well be that in trying to do our duty as we see it, we shall sometimes make difficulties for you. If this proves to be so, we shall regret it.

But I know that even so you would not ask us to flinch from doing our duty. You, too, will do your duty as you see it.

I am well aware of the peculiar nature of all the problems with which you are faced here in the Union of South Africa. I know the differences between your situation and that of most of the other states in Africa.

You have here some 3,000,000 people of European origin. This country is their home. It has been their home for many generations. They have no other. The same is true of the Europeans in Central and East Africa.

As a fellow member of the Commonwealth, it is our earnest desire to give South Africa our support and encouragement, but I hope you won't mind my saying frankly that there are some aspects of your policies which make it impossible for us to do this without being false to our own deep convictions about the political destinies of free men, to which in our own territories we are trying to give effect.

99   GLOBAL HOMOGENIZATION

The diffusion of Europe's three revolutions is creating a world that is becoming more and more homogenized, despite the growing pluralism in power relationships. This process of global homogenization is evident in the following reports by American correspondents in various parts of the globe. The final report shows that homogenization is taking place within the United States itself, and for essentially the same reasons that it is occurring abroad. This selection should be compared with the preceding one, describing the same process occurring in Japan in a very similar manner.

New Guinea

A message in pidgin English is being carried through steaming rain forests, across snow-crested mountains and up crocodile-filled rivers throughout this territory. It says:

"Ol pipol belong Papua-New Guinea vote long bigfella No. 1 Council liklik time."

It means that all residents of the territory will vote for a new House of Assembly beginning Feb. 15.

Getting this message, and its implications, to the people has been a staggering task for the Australian administration. For months, hundreds of political-education teams have trekked to the remote corners of the land to tell the Papuans what the "elekson" is all about. [*The New York Times,* February 8, 1964.]

Mongolia

Outer Mongolia still lives by the social pattern carved across her terrain by the ruthless hand of Genghis Khan. But after nearly 700 years this remote Asian country stands on the brink of change. . . . What is happening in Outer Mongolia is simply this: the nation's Communist rulers have embarked on a program designed to catapult the country from the thirteenth to the twentieth century within not more than ten years. . . . The essence of the program is: full speed ahead in a plan to change a nation of nomads into a nation based on the agriculture of the plow and the industry of the production line. [*The New York Times,* August 3, 1959.]

Southern Rhodesia

African brides-to-be in Southern Rhodesia are rebelling against Lobola—the traditional marriage price that has been paid in cattle to parents for centuries.

Middle-class African girls who are abandoning in the cities and towns their beads and skins for European-style dresses, chic hats, and high-heeled shoes are protesting that the Lobola system has become "a humiliating, masculine racket."

Their outcry, "We are no longer mere goods and chattels," is symptomatic of the urge in modern Africa to snap the shackles of slavish tribal custom and to gain equality with the male in a country where the law of the kraal (village) is still deep-rooted and dies hard. [*The New York Times,* September 25, 1960.]

Borneo

A great awakening is taking place among the Dyaks, the former headhunters of the vast and primitive island of Borneo.

These people, a bit weary of being described as charming savages, are increasingly discarding their loincloths and leaving their skull-decorated long houses, putting on sport shirts and long pants and migrating down river to the big cities.

"Teach us how to read and write, to be doctors, engineers, business men; give us typewriters, transistor radios, outboard motors for our dugouts"—these are the new battle cries of the Dyaks, who once told an inquisitive European, "You like books, we like heads." [*The New York Times,* November 26, 1960.]

Vietnam

The ao dai, traditional long-flowing Vietnamese costume worn by women over ankle-length silk pants, is on its way out for many teenage girls in Saigon.

The girls are switching to Western-style miniskirts, many of them in garish psychedelic colors, and all the other trappings of youngsters in big Western cities.

With their natural grace, long hair and dark beauty, Vietnamese girls are well suited to the brightly colored creations that have become the rage here.

With giant sunglasses, patent-leather snub-nosed shoes and enormous bows in their hair, the Saigon girls look much like Westerners. [*The New York Times,* March 31, 1969.]

Pakistan

The women of Pakistan are on the verge of achieving the legal right to choose their husbands and to divorce them. . . .

Under old laws, a woman has virtually no rights. As a girl she may be sold or given away. Once wed, she is the servant of her husband. He may take a second wife or any number of wives.

The proposed code would bar marriage of girls under 16 years old and boys under 18. The presence and consent of both parties would be required. Divorce would be permitted only upon presentation of grounds in court. Furthermore, a husband seeking another wife would have to prove in court his ability to support all his wives and children in the manner to which they had been accustomed. [*The New York Times,* March 27, 1960.]

Bolivia

The Prado La Paz, a central boulevard (in La Paz, Bolivia) looks almost like the main street of a southwestern United States city when school lets out, except for Indian women in brown bowler hats and babies slung over their backs in colored ponchos. Bolivian girls wear their hair in pony-tails, dress in toreador pants or skirts, bobbysox or saddle shoes. Boys by preference wear blue jeans and black leather jackets. In an Indian market place an Aymara girl tending her mother's stand solemnly chews what turns out with a pink pop to be not the traditional coca leaves but bubble gum. [*The New York Times,* March 20, 1959.]

Japan

The impact of television programs, now received on an estimated 20 million sets, or almost one set for each of Japan's 24.1 million families, extends to clothing and speech patterns as well. Tadashi Okuyama, who publishes TV Guide, notes that "clothing fashions in the big cities and the countryside are now almost the same."

"We used to be able to tell whether people were Tokyoites or hicks," he says, "but this is no longer possible."

Similarly, according to Donald Ritchie, a critic of many aspects of Japanese culture, regional dialects are disappearing under the influence of "Tokyo Standards," the language that is spoken on television, Slang words, such as "saiko" ("the very best") and "saitei" ("the very worst") have become common through television usage. [*The New York Times,* February 17, 1967.]

United States

The approach to every American city seems the same. The road widens and divides, traffic thickens, an intersection light appears—an outdoor movie, motels, a wrecked car dump with its most unbelievably flattened specimens next to the high-road. . . . Then, where through-route cement jolts into municipal maintenance macadam, spreads the new subdivision—cellar excavations going on at one end, baby carriages and ranch houses standing at the other. Then comes a city avenue in violent transition—gas stations, used car lots, down-at-heel mansions, the banker's home of 80 years ago now the Aleppo Temple, the stately house where the cast-iron deer once stood now labeled "Tourists." Here are the older, maple-tree suburbs, a white church with many-paned windows, the new high school. . . . At the center of town they have cut down the elms to widen Main Street. Here is the row of chains: Woolworth, Sears, A&P; the familiar drugstore; the local hotel (run from Chicago); the corner diner by the depot; the high office buildings; the green square and the war monument.

Here are the inevitable groups of teenagers, all in blue jeans, slouching around the entrance to the drugstore or the movie house, their poses, their gestures stylized like figures from a ballet. Boys and girls in jeans, chewing gum, smoking, hanging around the drugstore in a terrible effort to be casual until one of them gets his first car and it's zoom-zoom-zoom with everybody else.

Across town you reach the river, the factories, the poorer homes, the slums. . . .

You can walk down the streets at night in the new suburban subdivisions and see six families to a block looking at the same picture after supper. How they ever passed the time before TV nobody can guess. Now they have everything, prize fights, religion, Westerns, breathless cash prizes. They have a tidal-wave of advertising, new desires and discontents—above all a feeling of identification, of belonging, and a common denominator of accent, clothes and viewpoint. [T.R.B. in *The New Republic,* September 19, 1955. Copyright © 1955 Harrison-Blaine of New Jersey, Inc.]

Index